THE CHANGING POSITION OF WOMEN IN FAMILY AND SOCIETY

A Cross-National Comparison

INTERNATIONAL STUDIES IN SOCIOLOGY AND SOCIAL ANTHROPOLOGY

General Editor
K. ISHWARAN

VOLUME XXXIV

EUGEN LUPRI (ED.)

THE CHANGING POSITION OF WOMEN IN FAMILY AND SOCIETY

A Cross-National Comparison

LEIDEN — E. J. BRILL — 1983

THE CHANGING POSITION OF WOMEN IN FAMILY AND SOCIETY

A Cross-National Comparison

EDITED WITH AN INTRODUCTION BY

EUGEN LUPRI

LEIDEN — E. J. BRILL — 1983

ISBN 90 04 06845 7

Copyright 1983 by E. J. Brill, Leiden, The Netherlands

All rights reserved. No part of this book may be reproduced or translated in any form, by print, photoprint, microfilm, microfiche or any other means without written permission from the publisher

PRINTED IN HUNGARY

For Anne

TABLE OF CONTENTS

ACKNOWLEDGMENT IX
PREFACE XI

I. INTRODUCTION

1. The Changing Positions of Women and Men in Comparative Perspective
   EUGEN LUPRI 3

II. WOMEN IN CAPITALIST COUNTRIES

A. NORTH AMERICA

2. The Changing Roles of Canadian Women in Family and Work: An Overview 43
   EUGEN LUPRI and DONALD L. MILLS
3. A Comparative View on the Changing Position of Women in the United States 78
   AIDA K. TOMEH

B. EUROPE

4. The Position of Women in the Netherlands: Marginal Change 120
   H. M. IN 'T VELD-LANGEVELD, I. J. SCHOONENBOOM and L. IN 'T VELD
5. Female Marital Behaviour in French Society 136
   ANDRÉE MICHEL
6. The Position of Austrian Women in the Family: Some Data, Many Questions, and a Few Interpretations 148
   EVA KÖCKEIS-STANGL
7. The Changing Role of Women: The Case of Italy 179
   ALESSANDRO CAVALLI
8. Changing Sex Roles in the Greek Family and Society 190
   CONSTANTINA SAFILIOS-ROTHSCHILD and MARCELLINUS DIJKERS

C. ASIA

9. The Changing Status and Role of Women in Japan 207
   YORIKO MEGURO and KIYOMI MORIOKA

TABLE OF CONTENTS

III. WOMEN IN SCANDINAVIAN AND SOCIALIST COUNTRIES
A. SCANDINAVIA

10. The Changing Role of Swedish Women in Family and Society 225
    JAN TROST
11. Economic and Family Roles of Men and Women in Northern Europe: A Historical and Cross-National Comparison 243
    ELINA HAAVIO-MANNILA

B. EASTERN AND SOUTHERN EUROPE

12. Soviet Women in Family and Society 261
    G. A. SLESAREV and Z. A. YANKOVA
13. Women and the Family in Poland 276
    RENATA SIEMIEŃSKA
14. Women in Czechoslovakia 296
    ALENA K. WAGNEROVÁ
15. Change in the System of Social Power: Conditions for the Social Equality of Women in Yugoslavia 311
    OLIVERA BURIĆ

IV. WOMEN IN AFRICA

16. Women's Roles and Conjugal Family Systems in Ghana 331
    CHRISTINE OPPONG
17. The Changing Position of Black Women in South Africa 344
    ANNA F. STEYN and J. M. UYS

V. EMPIRICAL STUDIES OF SEX ROLE BEHAVIOUR

18. Economic Recession and Swiss Women's Attitudes Towards Marital Role Segregation 373
    THOMAS HELD and RENÉ LEVY
19. Egalitarianism in Marriage? Graduate Education and the Sexual Division of Labour in the Canadian Family 396
    GLADYS L. SYMONS
20. Wife and/or Worker: Sex Role Concepts of Canadian Female Students ... 418
    ANN B. DENIS
21. The Industrialization of Housework 430
    MARGRIT EICHLER

Contributors 444
Index 449

ACKNOWLEDGMENT

M Y STUBBORN INSISTENCE that we rely exclusively on original papers from native experts of the particular countries involved resulted in this volume being five years in the making. Without the patience and full cooperation of the contributors, it could not have appeared in its present form. To them I shall always be grateful. Any merit it may have is to their credit; the weaknesses and inadequacies are entirely mine.

Dr. K. Ishwaran, editor of the series, has been most helpful in publishing this volume. Dr. Donald L. Mills—colleague, collaborator, friend—also deserves deep thanks for continuous encouragement and assistance. Dr. Lowell Brandner provided invaluable editorial help. The final editing was completed while I was a Resident Killam Fellow at the University of Calgary. I should like to acknowledge my sincere gratitude to the Board of Governors of the University of Calgary for this award. It is conceivable that the manuscript would have reached print without the talents and skills of my secretary, Mrs. Phyllis McCarthy, but I do not see how.

Finally, I would like to thank Jean Kent for assistance in preparing the final typescript and for her able proofreading services.

EUGEN LUPRI

The University of Calgary
Calgary, Alberta, Canada

PREFACE

In RECENT YEARS, professionals and the lay public alike have been preoccupied with the position of women in family and society. The proclamation of 1975 as *Women's Year* attested that the "woman's question" had been recognized as a universal one. Feminists, particularly, have called our attention to numerous inequities that women face in the midst of riches that characterize almost all advanced societies.

Are women of today *on a par* with men on the job? Are incomes of women equal to men's in comparable positions? Are women equally distributed throughout the professions? Are they equally represented in institutions of higher learning? Do women have an equal say in political and economic decision-making? Has women's dramatic increase in work activity outside the home been paralled by an equally dramatic shift in the sex composition of the occupational structure? Is the modern family really egalitarian? Do mothers who work for pay receive a significant share of help from their husbands in child care and household chores? In short, has gender equality been achieved at home, on the job, and in society at large? The answer to those and other similar questions that this volume addresses is NO.

The volume's purpose is to provide comprehensive information and source materials on why gender inequality persists and to suggest current research issues on the changing roles of women and men. The phenomenon of gender relations is viewed here through the eyes of an international team of social scientists. The idea for this volume came from the editor's interest in cross-national research and the conviction that human behaviour to be more fully understood must be examined across time and space. By presenting current information on positions of women and men in 18 countries, the comparative framework provides the student of society an opportunity to study similar trends in different cultural and national settings.

The cross-national information will enable interested readers to determine in most instances whether certain structural barriers to gender equality exist independently of their varied social settings or whether they occur only in a certain societal setting. By broadening the range of societal variation, comparative data on women's and men's changing positions will greatly enhance our understanding of both the nature and the direction of those changes as well as their barriers. If this volume has any merit, it is its attempt to document comparatively the structural and institutional contexts where gender equality has been achieved and where resistance persists. While the extent of change in the position of women varies from one country to another, some patterns in the persistence of women's inequality emerge in all 18 countries.

Preparing this volume has been a painful experience for the editor and the contributors. The editor's principle objective to accept only *original* contributions that were *current* and by *native* experts delayed the publications several years. In an age and setting where university professors are held accountable for their scholarly productivity on an annual basis, such a deferment of gratification must strain the best of any international colleagueships, as it did the editor's conscience. That English is *not* the first language of the large majority of the contributors compounded the problem and contributed to the delay. Editing, rewriting, and the necessary correspondence across oceans were tremendously time consuming. Because of the stringent requirements and varied circumstances, some countries initially selected had to be discarded. Those that survived the editor's scrutiny, the contributor's endurance, and the test of time constitute the "sample" of this volume.

While it would have been desirable to select a sample of countries with more systematic rigour to examine the changing roles of women and men in varied national settings, this volume is no exception to the difficulties facing a comparative study. To ensure as much comparability as possible, all potential contributors were invited to report on their own country and to submit a fairly self-contained chapter in which they would attempt to:

1. trace historically the changing position of women in as many institutional sectors as possible, including the family and the economy;
2. discuss the division of labour in the family and to detail how family variables may impede or promote gender equality;
3. isolate other structural variables that may operate as barriers to full gender equality;
4. document whether the position of women has been improving more, about the same, or less than the position of men; and finally
5. support all generalizations by such empirical evidence as census and survey materials.

The contributors who could not follow those suggestions were encouraged to submit topics of their own choosing. Many did but only a few of their contributions could be included in the last section of this volume. All other contributors more or less followed the suggested format. Since the availability and nature of census and survey materials vary greatly from one country to another, data base lines often differ. And it remained for the native experts to select what they considered appropriate data and to interpret them as they saw fit. The resulting lack of comparability and coherence must be taken into account.

Another major problem was language. Contributors were requested to submit their chapters in English and, as already mentioned, nearly all went through several versions of preliminary editing, rewriting, and final editing. It is one of the most profound truths about human languages that each colours the whole mode of apprehension. Because language and thought are closely related, great care was taken to preserve the originally intended meaning, which often meant sacrificing style and fluency for substance. The editor resisted many temptations to "edit out" jargon, ideological or otherwise.

Students interested in the sociology of knowledge will find in this volume different but bountiful streams of evidence showing that the social scientists' perceptions of the "woman's problem" and the manner in which they attempt to conceptualize it are highly related to the ideological, linguistic, and intellectual milieu in which social scientists work. The evidence supports the view of those, including the editor, who maintain that a value-free social science is a contradiction in terms.

The editor made no attempt to integrate into a coherent text the wide range of cross-national data here presented. That may be a basic shortcoming of this volume, but at least three interrelated reasons spoke against such an attempt from the outset. First, one of the purposes of the volume is to make available to English-speaking social scientists current comparative materials not readily accessible on the changing roles of men and women. Self-contained chapters on specific countries best achieve that purpose. Second, a meaningful integration of cross-national data presupposes some sort of an overarching theoretical framework. However, current sociological theory is noninclusive and divergent in its epistemological assumptions about the nature of social phenomena. Sociological theory of gender relations is incomplete, inconsistent, and highly contradictory. Moreover, it is highly culturebound and its basic concepts are value-laden. Theoretical integration should follow, not precede, comparative analysis. Third, a comprehensive theoretical integration of such a wide range of cross-national data as presented is simply beyond the confines of an anthology of this nature. While a modest first step in that direction was attempted in the INTRODUCTION, a detailed theoretical synthesis of all of the comparative materials must await future labours. The editor, however, thinks that this volume contains the data base for the much needed theoretical effort.

The volume is organized into five parts. In PART ONE, The Changing Positions of Women and Men in Comparative Perspective, the editor sketches the recent historical origin of gender inequity, discusses three basic theoretical approaches that underlie the study of changing roles of women and men in contemporary society, and in an overview delineates several universal patterns of females' role changes and shows how structural barriers in the workplace and at home combine to impede women's full equality in society at large around the world.

PART TWO is divided into three geographical sections on North America, Europe, and Asia that deal with the changing positions of women and men in several capitalist nations. In the first section Eugen Lupri and Donald L. Mills present an overview on the changing roles of Canadian women in family and work, and Aida K. Tomeh discusses in some breadth and depth the position of women in the United States. In the second section, rich data are presented about the situations of men and women in five European countries: in France by Andrée Michel; The Netherlands by H. M. in't Veld-Langeveld, I. J. Schoonenboom and L. in't Veld; Austria by Eva Köckeis-Stangl; Italy by Alessandro Cavalli, and in Greece by Safilios-Rothschild and Marcellinus Dijkers. In the third section, Yoriko Meguro and Kiyomi Morioka detail the evolution of women's roles in Japan.

In PART THREE, comparative materials on the changing positions of men and women in Scandinavian and socialist countries are presented. In the first section, Jan Trost discusses recent changes in Sweden, and Elina Haavio-Mannila of Finland does a comprehensive historical and cross-national analysis of the intersecting of work and family roles in Finland, Sweden, Norway, Poland, and the Soviet Union. The second section provides informative evidence on the changing positions of women in several socialist countries. G. A. Slesarev and Z. A. Yankova highlight women's situations in family and society in the U.S.S.R. showing improvements in, as well as barriers to, Soviet women's sexual equality. Renata Siemieńska discusses the position of women in Poland; Alena K. Wagnerová traces the changing roles of Czech women in several sectors and argues forcefully for making the world of work a more humane place for both men and women; and Olivera Burić details several characteristic phases in women's struggle for emancipation arguing cogently for changes in the systems of social power–to bring about greater equality in Yugoslavia and everywhere.

In PART FOUR, the changing status of African women is selectively represented by a study of Christine Oppong on women's family roles in Ghana and by Anna F. Steyn and J. M. Uys' detailed description of the changing positions of black women in South Africa.

Finally, PART FIVE consists of several empirical studies of sex role behaviours and attitudes. Thomas Held and René Levy document connections between economic recessions and Swiss women's attitudes toward sex role segregation. Two Canadian sociologists analyze gender relations among Canadian students. Gladys L. Symons tackles the thorny problem of egalitarianism among married students, and Ann B. Denis examines data on sex role concepts among female undergraduates. Part Five, and for that matter the volume, closes with a perceptive discussion by Margrit Eichler on the importance of understanding *housework* to comprehend better the positions of both women and men in modern society.

The Appendix lists this volume's contributors, with information on their educational backgrounds, a few selective examples of their previously published works, their main research interests, and their current institutional affiliations.

PART ONE

INTRODUCTION

The Changing Positions of Women and Men in Comparative Perspective

EUGEN LUPRI

The University of Calgary, Calgary, Canada

Introduction

The Separation of Home and Work

OF THE MANIFOLD CHANGES brought about by the Industrial Revolution, none is more ubiquitous than the separation of home and work. It is also central to this volume because its effects still have profound implications for the positions of both women and men in modern society. In preindustrial society, familial and work activities overlapped and the family formed the basic economic unit of production. Even though women had lower status than men, the husband depended on his wife's and children's contributions to the family enterprise. As Zaretsky (1976: 22) documented, before the Industrial Revolution the "prevalent form of family life in England... was that of an economically independent commodity-producing unit." No clear-cut division of familial and work roles existed. Contrary to much current ahistorical thinking in North American family sociology, the wife in preindustrial society held considerable labour and bargaining power due to her productive role in the family economy. In fact both spouses depended heavily on one another's economic and affectional support. In the early stages of the Industrial Revolution, the family remained the productive unit, either through the "putting out" system or by bringing the whole family into the early manufacturing institution. By the 19th century the factory system had eliminated most of the productive functions of the nonfarm family (Zaretsky, 1976). In Marx's terms, it prepared the stage for the ensuing oppression of women and the family's subordination to class relations. It separated men from women and gave way to the ideology of separate "spheres" for men and women.

The separation of home and work not only destroyed the economic union of husband and wife but also reorganized dramatically child, female, and male labour (Abbott, 1910). The locus of economic production shifting from the family to the factory established the basis for developing a new division of labour both at home and factory. Even so early forms of factory organization tended to preserve the economic and social unity of the family because the whole family worked as a unit with complete separation of home and work coming gradually. In time child labour was eliminated and women were transformed into a marginal labour force. The concept of the housewife emerged, setting the stage for the development of a distinctive division of labour according to sex. The husband's responsibility came to be understood as one of a wage earner, while the wife's domain centred around what Zaretsky calls "human values", or the preservation of familial unity in terms of love, personal happiness, and domestic felicity. As Zaretsky (1976: 47) observes, "the split in society between 'personal feelings' and 'economic production' was integrated with the sexual division of labour". The separation of home and work thus fostered the creation of an ideology of separate spheres for women and men.[1]

One important consequence of the shift of economic production to the factory system was an alteration in family structure–affecting both spouses and children, but most notably women.[2] The family not only ceased to be the basic unit of economic production and social participation but became a *supportive* system for the newly established industrial economy. Correspondingly, the wife's former productive role in the family economy changed to a subservient and subordinate role. To be sure, she had considerable control over all household activities such as child-rearing, cooking, washing, cleaning, mending, food production and processing, and so on, which required great skills and gave her status in the family. However, the myriads of household labours were not directly income producing, so she depended almost entirely on her husband's wages. Even though women and children comprised a large segment of the industrial labour force whose brutalized working conditions, long hours, and low wages Friederich Engels so vividly describes in his *Die Lage der arbeitenden Klasse in England* (1845: 252–506), employed women's wages became supplementary to their husbands, and their position gradually became one of financial and economic dependency. Moreover, men and women became estranged from one another. As Engels (1845: 435) wrote in his description of the working class in England:

> Family life for the worker is almost impossible under the existing social system...the various members of the family only see each other in the mornings and evenings, because the husband is away at work for the whole day. His wife and children are perhaps at work as well and they may be working in different factories. Under these circumstances how can family life exist?

1 How this ideological development found expression and support through religion, especially Puritanism, is aptly discussed by Christopher Hill in his *Society and Puritanism in Pre-Revolutionary England* (New York, 1967).
2 As is well known, men's status suffered greatly in the market place because industrialization also helped divorce the concept of work from the concept of life itself, created the concept of workers as reasonably standardized and interchangeable cogs in any overall system, brought with it the reduction of craftsmanship to a fragment of a process and thereby alienated the workers from their work and made their skills superfluous.

Such a description stands in sharp contrast to the one given by Thompson (1963: 307) about the family life of weavers in pre-revolutionary England. He says:

> The young children winding bobbins, older children watching for faults, picking over the cloth, or helping to throw the shuttle in the broadloom; adolescents working a second or third loom; the wife taking a turn at weaving, in and among her domestic employments. The family was together, and however poor meals were, at least they could sit down at chosen times. A whole pattern of community life had grown up around the loom-shop; work did not prevent conversation or singing.

Family relations and economic production formed a community bond in preindustrial society. Perhaps that is why working-class fathers defended child labour for a long time (Smelser, 1959). Economic production in the loom-shop tended to preserve ties between the parents and their children. The separation of home and work brought an end to the family economy, an end to prevailing family bonds.

Women's changing position must be seen not only against this historical background but also in relation to men's changing positions at home and at the work place. And even more important, alterations in men's and women's positions must be related to changes in the larger economic context in which they occur.

In an attempt to apply functional analysis to social history, Smelser (1959) examined the impact of changes in the British cottontextile industry on the family division of labour between 1770 and 1840. While such an approach to an important period of the Industrial Revolution tends to concentrate on abstract processes such as invention, innovation, reorganization, capitalization, and production at the expense of exploitation, oppression, subordination, domination, conflict, misery, and human sufferings, Smelser isolated a process of the Industrial Revolution, *structural differentiation,* which has relevance for the present volume. Because the industrial structure of labour changed in the late 18th and early 19th centuries, pressures exerted on the division of labour in the working-class families led to drastic alterations of the family economy. Several sequences led to the emergence of a new form of family structure, the most important of which was differentiation of new work roles for men and women in the traditional family economy. Smelser (1959: 180) aptly distinguishes two processes of differentiation:

1. The differentiation of the family economy as a whole from textile production as a whole, by which the family unit was segregated from its traditional productive roles; and
2. The differentiation of occupational roles *within* the family unit.

It is precisely those two similar, but analytically distinct, processes of structural differentiation that changed dramatically the positions of both men and women in the family and the economy. It is my contention that the changes benefitted men more than women and that present sexual inequities are deeply rooted in the process of structural differentiation in family and society. Various attempts to explain the sexual division of labour and the valuations of women's and men's roles lack theoretical closure. While physiological and biological explanations simply cannot completely account for gender roles and their valuations, sociological explanations are also incomplete.

Structural-functional Explanations of Gender Roles

Functional explanations of gender roles centre around the *origin* of the sexual division of labour (see, for example, Parsons and Bales, 1955; Zelditch, 1955; Smelser, 1959; Goode, 1961), but fail to deal conceptually or empirically with gender *inequity*. Zelditch (1955) was most explicit in this respect. He stated:

> 1. If the nuclear family constitutes a social system stable over time, it will differentiate roles such that instrumental leadership and expressive leadership of the system are discriminated.
> 2. If the nuclear family consists in a defined "normal" complement of the male adult, female adult, and their immediate children, the male adult will play the role of the instrumental leader and the female adult will play the role of the expressive leader (314–315).

The cross-cultural data Zelditch draws upon to support his contention of the universal existence of the instrumental-expressive role dimension according to sex recently have been challenged on the grounds of their questionable reliability, comparability, and categories used (Aronoff and Crano, 1975). Traits considered feminine and masculine show so much cultural variation and diversity that it is questionable that these behavioural patterns can be regarded as sex-linked. While Zelditch at least is prepared to doubt the logical necessity about the connection between the instrumental-expressive dimension and male-female role structures, Parsons's functional explanation is even more metaphysical and normative. He appears to take "what *is* as an indication of what, almost certainly, must *be*" (Morgan, 1975: 46). Parsons is quite specific as to the origin of this sex-linked role differentiation. He states:

> In our opinion the fundamental explanation of the allocation of the roles between the biological sexes lies in the fact that the bearing and early nursing of children establish a strong presumptive primacy of the relation of mother to the small child and this in turn establishes a presumption that the man, who is exempted from these biological functions, should specialize in the alternative instrumental direction (Parsons and Bales, 1960: 23).

To Parsons the distinction is by no means a pattern of the past but most signicfiantly an essential feature of modern North America, particularly middle class U.S. society, so it seems. Recent changes in U.S. family and society are seen far from implying an "erasure of the differentiation of sex roles". In fact, recent social change in many respects "reinforces and clarifies it" (Parsons, 1955: 23). It is the articulation between the family and the occupational system that focuses the instrumental responsibility sharply on one adult *male* member. Parsons is again quite clear about the basis of this sex-linked structure when he says "...it is fundamentally by virtue of the importance of his occupational role as a component of his familial role that in our society we can unequivocally designate the husband-father as the 'instrumental leader' of the family as a system" (1960: 13). Thus, while the role of the adult male is primarily anchored in the occupational world, the female role is anchored primarily in the internal affairs of the family. In interpreting the rise in participation of women in the labour force Parsons argues that:

> ...even if, as seems possible, it should come about that the average married women had some kind of a job, it seems most unlikely that this relative balance would be upset; that either the roles would be reversed, or their qualitative differentiation in these respects completely erased (1960: 15).

As documented in this volume, Parsons is correct in saying that the balance of the sex roles will not change significantly with an increase of women, single or married, in the labour force. Where women have gained entry into the higher levels, they remain very much restricted to the areas of teaching, nursing, social work, and clerical jobs, that is, to occupational roles that tend to have either a prominent built-in expressive component or are highly supportive of male roles, or both.

Nevertheless, Parsons's image of the family and the roles husband and wife have is so tied to the functional perspective that "whatever is, must be," that the image masks what may have been initially an accurate observation by theoretically denying any alternative developments or any possibility of countertrends. It ignores *a priori* that it is possible, theoretically and empirically, that either husband *or* wife can perform *both* roles, and that significant role changes can occur over the family life cycle. And finally, functional explanations notoriously do not address themselves to the inequality that has developed in association with the sexual division of labour.

A Conflict View of Gender Roles

Functional theory says nothing about the strains and stresses that the traditional roles place on women who want to play the "instrumental" role in society or on men who want to play an "expressive" role. It is also silent about the dysfunctions to society preventing half of the population from participating fully in economic life. The functionalists' preoccupation with the question of how sex role inequalities arose has tended to ignore the important question as to why inequities *persist*. It comes as no surprise, then, that feminist scholars have been able to document a strong sexist bias in much of past and current sociological writings, particularly in family sociology (Huber, 1973). Many of the feminists' criticisms and arguments are informed by Marxian theory, often applying the concept of class to the woman's question and women's liberation. Use of the term *class* implies inequality and exploitation (Morgan, 1975) and, therefore, comes close to the present status and position of women in family and society. However, not all feminist writers take a stratification approach to sexual inequality. One may argue with some justification that women as a group do not constitute a class, as Winston (1971) has aptly done. Women are members of families, families of the upper class, the working class, the *Lumpenproletariat*.

In arguing the notion that women as a group represent a social class, the radical feminist Marlene Dixon (1971: 154) has succinctly summarized the issue:

> ...sisterhood temporarily disguised the fact that all women do not have the same interests, needs, and desires. Working-class women and middle-class women...have more *conflicting* interests than could ever be overcome by their common experience based on sex discrimination.

Thus, sexism is becoming less important to women than "class oppression," as women are increasingly subject to economic exploitation outside the home. In fact, as the ensuing chapters and data strikingly demonstrate, gender inequities in the economic realm are quite pronounced. Moreover, U.S. (Tomeh) and Canadian (Lupri and Mills) data on income differentials between women and men reveal that the gap is widening. Perhaps Szymanski's (1976: 50) provocative thesis that "...the lot of working-class women, although sexism persists, is becoming more and more like that of working-class men" is tenable and one that we cannot afford to ignore.

Along the same line, although from a much more fundamental Marxian perspective, Smith (1973) has cogently argued for a framework that views the role of women and family relations within the context of political economy. She sees the modern family as maintaining and upholding a system of class inequality with both women and men exploited. This view makes explicit the point that Marxian theory does not see the family as such as an oppressive institution. As Winston (1971) has pointed out, abolishing the family as we know it today would not change women's relation to production, household status, male supremacy, material inequality, child care, etc.

Hacker (1951) argued that women can be regarded as a minority group in society, in much the same way as are racial, ethnic, religious, or other minorities who suffer from discrimination. Parallels between sexism, ageism, and racism can easily be drawn and ascribed status differences empirically substantiated. The parallel is imprecise because women, unlike most other minorities, are found in equal proportion to the dominant group in every class. As Lupri and Mills, in their contribution on Canada, point out early in their analysis, women's status is derived from their husbands or fathers. Moreover, women in advanced societies generally outnumber men. The stratification of women and men, therefore, takes an unusual and different form. Women are found at every position in the class hierarchy, but at any position they have an inferior status to men in similar positions.

Collins (1971) argues persuasively that sexual inequalities are *structural* and, like any other structural inequality, are based on conflict of interests between dominant and subordinate groups. Sexual inequalities prevent the lower-status group from making the best use of its talents and skills and thereby provide greater opportunities for the upper-status groups. Men can enjoy superior status only if women have an inferior status, so the existing sex role patterns allow men to maintain political, social, psychological and economic privileges. Men, the dominant group, benefit from the existing arrangements and have little inclination or wish to change them, which led Lupri and Mills to conclude their analysis of the changing roles of Canadian women with the prediction that "since men profit most from present structural inequities at home and at work and they also hold the power to alter inequities, any changes directed at achieving full gender equality will evolve slowly, if at all." In other words, the *status quo* is rewarding to men; conversely any change or innovation is perceived as threatening to those who hold the power to determine and enforce policy. Because sexual inequalities have become institutionalized and present cultural norms reflect the interest of the dominant group, gender roles continue to reinforce the patterns of male dominance.

As Marx maintained, both the dominant and the subordinate groups in any structured social inequality tend to accept the ideology that legitimizes the social structure. It is hardly surprising then, that many women see the existing arrangements as "given," if not "natural." The Marxian notion of *false consciousness* is most appropriate in this context, a subjective perception of one's situation that is not congruent with the objective facts. To be sure, the women's liberation movement has questioned and challenged the inequities that are built into existing sex roles. And, undoubtedly, the movement has made a number of important inroads. It is also clear that in many areas progress toward producing gender equality has been extremely slow. In some instances–for example, income and occupational segregation–retrogressive trends are apparent.

The persistence of gender-specific job segregation and the increase in wage differentials between women and men are but two of several symptoms that the vicious circle of sexual inequities appears to be almost irreversible in the social structure of modern industrial society. Radical feminists (for example, Firestone, 1978; Smith, 1973) view the inequities as inherent in the structure of capitalist society and, therefore, argue that drastic revolutionary change of the total system is inevitable if full sexual equality in all spheres is to be achieved. Radical feminism attempts to solve the problem of analyzing the discrimination (oppression) of women by making it *the* problem. Mitchell (1978: 42) wants to see *why* women always have been oppressed, and *how* they are oppressed now. To her these are truly feminist questions and she pleads pointedly that we should "...try to come up with some Marxian answers."

The "exploitation perspective," by and large, has not appealed to most North American sociologists who are apt to view Marxian perspectives as alien and inappropriate for the analysis of North American society. Pleck (1978: 485) recently put it succinctly in a critical summary: "The exploitation perspective may provide an adequate basis for indicting men, but by itself it does not provide a basis for helping them change." He then argues for a third approach that has emerged over the past decade or so: The Changing-roles Perspective.

An Emerging Framework: The Changing-roles Perspective

The underlying basis for the third approach to studying sexual equality is a macrosocial and historical view of the evolution of family and work roles for both women and men. Pleck (1978: 485) termed it the "changing roles perspective," thereby making explicit that the contemporary scene reflects simply a "transitional problem of adjustment."[3] This perspective utilizes the "dual-approach" to the problem of sexual inequality advanced by the influential work of Myrdal and Klein (1956) in the mid-1950's. They introduced the notion of "women's two roles," calling attention to the fact that while men continue to specialize primarily in occupational roles outside the home, married women are forced to increasingly combine work outside the home with the traditional family roles. In their painstaking analysis, Myrdal and Klein made explicit that it is *wives* who added a *second* role, that of paid employment. Those authors' observations prompted Rapoport and Rapoport (1972) to conceptualize the slower rate of change in men's roles in the family compared with the rapid rate in women's roles in work outside the home as a "psychological lag." Their thesis was highly influenced by Myrdal's (1967) earlier contention that men desperately need to have two roles as well–adding household tasks and child care to their occupational role.

In the field of family sociology Young and Willmot's (1975) historical analysis of family changes has recently gained international attention. Their prediction culminates in what they term the "symmetrical family." They say the family has moved through three stages of development the past 150 years: from preindustrial to industrial to symmetrical. Of particular interest here is their view of the contemporary conjugal family, which is decidedly "symmetrical" in function and structure. Marriage roles have progressively become less segregated. While wives are more likely to be in the work force, husbands are more likely than in the past to be involved in doing work traditionally defined as woman's work–housekeeping, child care, cooking, and so on.

Along with other family sociologists Young and Willmot also argue that family life has become more "privatized." The modern nuclear family emphasizes self-realization, intimacy, companionship, and joint decisionmaking–perhaps more an utopian ideal than a realistic assessment of the family in modern industrial society. It ignores the great class variation and family diversity in non-English speaking industrial countries. However, Young and Willmot call to our attention, as Pleck (1978: 485) observed, that the "single most important manifestation of change in the male role in contemporary society is an increased family role, just as increased labour force participation is the most important change in the female role," which provides some support for their assertion that the contemporary family is gradually becoming

---

3 I am heavily indebted to Joseph E. Pleck (1978), from whose recent synthesis of the "Changing-roles Perspective" I borrowed freely.

"symmetrical." Examining this thesis against cross-national data may prove useful because it focuses on presumed changes that have special significance not only for the situations of women and men in the family but also for their positions in the society at large.

Gender Relations in Comparative Perspective

The Data Base

Comparative studies provide a powerful means for broadening generalizations developed in single societies by letting one examine propositions in a cross-national setting. The need for cross-national analyses is particularly great in studying gender relations, a field where concepts, assumptions, theoretical approaches, and data interpretation are both highly culture-bound and ideologically based. The comparative approach provides researchers with an opportunity to study similar trends in different cultural and social settings and thereby maximizes variation. Durkheim (1895) likened the comparative method to that of the classical experimental design; since social phenomena escape the context of the experimenter, he thought the comparative method is the only one suited to sociology. He distinguished three applications of the comparative approach or, in his words, of co-variations: (1) comparison of societies generally alike but differing in certain aspects, (2) analysis of variations in one society at one point, i.e., intrasocietal comparisons, and (3) comparisons of societies generally dissimilar that share some common features.

The comparative approach used in this volume entails aspects of all three applications. As Table 1 shows, the 18 nations included in this comparative study of the changing roles of women in family and society share several *similar characteristics* such as the differentiation of roles on the basis of sex, the prevalence of nuclear family structures, an industrial base in most instances, and at least the implicit political mandate of equality of sexes. They are *dissimilar* with respect to their geography, ecology, religion, size, population density, language, tradition, history, democratic heritage, and culture. Perhaps they differ most strikingly in political *ideology* and *economic development*. The political diversity is characterized by the capitalist, socialist, and communist nations included. Economic development varies through high, medium, and low. And finally, a few contributors used intrasocietal comparisons, that is comparisons that trace the changing roles of both women and men over time as well as between different occupational, familial, and other institutional structures.

The Index of Differentiation in Table 1 provides a crude measure of societal differentiation. The scores range from 21.1 (Ghana) to 109.4 (USA), indicating marked differences in the 18 nations' degree of complexity and structural differentiation of

Table 1

Population Base and Degree of Societal Differentiation of this Volume's Eighteen Countries, 1977/78

Country	Population[1] (thousands)	Index of Differentiation Score[2]
AFRICA		
Ghana	10,475	21.1
South Africa (1970)	21,794	45.3
AMERICA, NORTH		
Canada	23,499	89.9
United States	218,059	109.4
ASIA		
Japan	114,155	41.5
EUROPE		
Austria	7,512	51.3
Czechoslovakia	15,164	65.5
Finland	4,755	47.5
France	53,241	57.5
Greece	9,284	31.0
Italy	56,696	42.3
Norway	4,042	55.2
Poland	35,096	54.8
Sweden	8,284	62.7
Switzerland	6,327	51.6
The Netherlands	13,936	58.0
Yugoslavia	22,014	26.2
U.S.S.R.	258,932	51.3

1 Source: Population Index (1979), Vol. 45, No. 1, 162 170.
2 Source: Marsh (1967), Appendix 1. Societal differentiation, defined as the number of structurally distant and functionally specialized units, like roles and collectivities, was measured in terms of the percentage of males in nonagricultural occupations and the gross energy consumption in megawatt-hours per capita for one year. To construct a single index, Marsh (1967: 334) converted the raw scores of measurement to standardized scores.

basic institutional units. I deliberately refrained from developing a more sophisticated comparison by constructing an index with which to compare all countries directly. Such a rank ordering appears to me to be arbitrary and theoretically premature at this juncture.

To test empirically hypotheses deduced from theory, it would have been desirable to use more scientific rigour in selecting nations, but this volume is no exception to the difficulties such a comparative analysis faces. Not the least of its shortcomings is its incomplete and unsystematic cross-national coverage. Another shortcoming is the lack of comparability of the data from the 18 nations included. While the editor broadly delineated the institutional processes and structures within which the changing roles of women and men may be assessed, it remained for the native expert(s) of each country to select the appropriate data and to interpret them. The availability and nature of the survey and census materials vary considerably from country to country. The resulting lack of comparability is a genuine problem. The present state of theorizing in gender relations is divergent, highly eclectic, and tends to be concerned mainly with providing definitions and sometimes also to be oriented towards miniature theories, such as the structural-functional and conflict models. These two theories and others are competing with one another in their underlying assumptions, as the earlier discussion of the three "theoretical" frameworks makes abundantly evident. At best they serve as sensitizing models, each carving out and emphasizing different aspects of reality. An *inclusive* theory of gender relations defined as a system of interrelated definitions and propositions that is both empirically verifiable and universally valid does not yet exist. Research, and particularly comparative research, in family and gender relations suffers from this lack of theory.

Despite the shortcomings in theory, comparative methodology, and data base, the societies included in this volume represent a wide variation in the national *settings* in which institutional processes and structures may or may not operate as barriers to gender equality in family and society at large. The settings are national societies with clearly demarcated political boundaries. We can thus determine in most instances whether certain structural barriers to gender equity hold true independently of their varied societal settings, or whether they occur in certain societies only. By broadening the range of variation, comparative data on both men's and women's roles will enhance our understanding of the direction of, and the barriers to, changes in the social structure.

Emerging Themes in Women's Changing Roles

Even though contributors to this volume approached the analysis and description of the changing roles of men and women in their respective countries from different perspectives, deal with different issues, and in so doing rely on different sources, the resulting wide range of comparative data lend themselves to generating several common themes. One of the best substantiated is that in almost all advanced industrialized nations women's participation in the economy has changed dramatically in both volume and composition. Particularly pervasive is the increase in the number of *married* women entering or re-entering the labour force during the past decade.

A second theme that emerges concomitantly with women entering the labour market is that both structural and interpersonal barriers to women's full economic and social equality persist. While the resistance varies from country to country, it is evident that complete gender equality has not been achieved by any nation represented here, perhaps by none in the world. However, the comparisons show that the nature and direction of women's role changes are highly related to the extent that solving the "woman's question" is a necessary pre-condition for economic development and expansion of a given nation and the extent that the solution is embraced by a political ideology.

A third theme that emerges clearly is that the very structure of the nuclear family, of which the vast majority of both women and men are an integral part, operates as an effective constraint to women's full equality in this cross-section of societies.

A corollary pattern of a different kind also emerges. It is related to the vulnerability of women's position to reversals, crises, recessions, and even minor set-backs in the economy at specific times. A brief discussion of emerging cross-national patterns on women's work force activity, on barriers to women's full equality in the occupational system, and on the changing family roles is now in order.

1. *Women's Labour Force Participation.* Whether one examines rates that women participate in the labour force in the less developed nations represented here, such as South Africa and Ghana, in highly developed nations like the United States, the Soviet Union, Canada, Sweden, and other Scandinavian countries, or in those nations that lie somewhere between the extremes such as Greece, Yugoslavia, and France, for example, the major trend in labour force participation appears to be clear-cut. All contributors, except those from Austria and Italy, report, explicitly or implicitly, a marked and steady increase in the proportion of women who work for pay. Slesarev and Yankova document that in 1970 nearly 90 percent of all Soviet women of working age were either employed (80%) or studying (7.5%). In pre-revolutionary Russia, only 19 percent of the women were in "special and individual occupations." They state with pride: "At present the Soviet Union leads the world with its high level of women's vocational and professional activities." Indeed, Soviet women's labour force rates equal 94 percent of that of men. Similar but somewhat less marked increases are observed by Siemieńska for Poland; Wagnerová for Czechoslovakia, and particularly Trost, for Sweden. A more recent international comparison for crude activity rates of both men and women of all ages is presented in Table 2. Data in Table 2 show that women in most socialist and Scandinavian countries have spearheaded *mass* female employment in the world. Haavio-Mannila details historically and comparatively the varied developments of both women's and men's employment in the primary, secondary, and tertiary sectors for Scandinavian countries, Poland, and the Soviet Union.

The North American continent is lagging but recent data indicate the gap is narrowing. In 1975, for example, 46 percent of all U.S. women of working age were employed in the labour force compared with 36 percent ten years earlier. The Canadian situation corresponds closely as Lupri and Mills reported. The 30 percent of all Canadian women working for pay in 1961 had increased to 45 percent in 1976, up 50 percent in only 15 years.

European data reflect similar trends, although increases there are less marked and with wider variations among countries. The Netherlands, as reported by in't Veld-Langeveld, Schoonenboom and in't Veld, has a relatively low participation rate for women but increases over time are shown, especially for married women. Michel

Table 2

Labour Force Participation Rates[1] and Female Share of Labour Force in Eighteen Countries, 1975 and 1960's

	1975			1960		
	Male Participation Rate	Female Participation Rate	Female Share of Labour Force	Male Participation Rate	Female Participation Rate	Female Share of Labour Force
Soviet Union	82.1	71.4	42.5	91.3	75.7	38.0
Poland	88.7	73.2	37.2	93.1	65.5	34.7
Czechoslovakia	85.9	69.2	34.9	88.7	59.2	30.2
Ghana	90.2	62.1	31.6	94.7	59.9	29.7
Japan	93.7	59.2	30.2	90.1	54.9	28.1
Finland	83.2	58.8	29.8	92.2	55.5	28.8
Austria	88.6	53.8	28.0	93.4	55.2	29.5
United States	86.8	51.3	26.1	90.5	41.1	20.9
Yugoslavia	90.5	49.8	25.3	95.8	49.1	25.4
Sweden	86.3	51.2	25.3	88.0	45.4	22.5
Switzerland	96.0	51.6	25.1	98.6	41.6	21.0
France	86.6	48.2	23.8	84.9	45.7	22.8
South Africa*	89.9	45.1	22.8	—	—	—
Greece	91.2	42.3	21.7	92.5	42.4	21.9
Canada	86.7	42.8	21.3	87.9	33.7	16.7
Norway	86.6	34.4	17.0	95.7	28.4	14.2
Italy	84.9	31.9	16.2	92.3	29.6	15.1
Netherlands	87.8	30.8	15.2	94.2	26.4	13.3

1 Labour Force of all ages divided by the population aged 15 to 64.
* No comparable data available.
Source: International Labour Office, Yearbook of Labour Statistics, 1978, Special Table; 1970, Table 1; the 1960's data for the Soviet Union are taken from the Special Table of the 1970 edition of the above source.

documents that between 1968 and 1976 the employment rate of French women increased in all age groups. Women's employment in Austria differed by being much earlier, then declining. Even before World War I, labour force participation for Austrian women was relatively high (Köckeis-Stangl reports 41% for 1910; 37% for 1934; 36% for 1961; and 30% for 1971). The early high rates stemmed from a high proportion of women working on farms, then as the agricultural sector declined overall labour force participation declined. However, Köckeis-Stangl states that an increase is emerging for women employed in the *nonagricultural sector*.

Italy is another interesting "deviant" case. It has, at present, one of the lowest female labour force participation rates of all West European countries. Cavalli reports a steady decline of female employment over the past two decades and speaks of women being expelled from the labour market because of Italy's economic development. Women's expulsion from the primary sector (where the rate of female employment in traditional domestic farming was high) has not been paralleled by adequate development in industry and the service sectors. Peculiar demographic factors, lack of child care facilities, an almost identical wage structure for men and women, and a unique positive relation between supply and demand in the female labour market all combine to keep Italian women out of the labour force.

Now however, a modern adaptation of the preindustrial "putting-out system" has emerged and, as Cavalli documents, almost two million Italian women carry on heavy and highly diversified industrial production of goods in their living rooms, where women and children busily work around the "machine." Not surprisingly, such working women do not become a statistic of the official labour force rate.

The Italian case, as detailed by Cavalli, offers an excellent example of the inadequacy of the modernization thesis, which has educational and occupational opportunities accruing to women as societies develop economically.

Japan, too, shows a somewhat unique development in that traditional sex role patterns persist in a highly segregated work structure. Meguro and Morioka trace the historical and cultural factors that operate as barriers; however, they also document a slow but steady increase in female labour force participation over time. Roughly speaking, one of every three Japanese adult women was gainfully employed in 1975.

Even though black women in South Africa are still to a large extent employed in the agricultural sector, they are gradually entering a structurally differentiated labour market, so Steyn and Uys report. South African black women's participation in this broader labour market is considerably less than that of men, but gradual alterations in this respect led to women comprising almost 34 percent of the total Black labour force in 1970, compared with only about 19 percent in 1946. Oppong, implicitly, reports similar trends for Ghana.

In summary, these limited, selective and varied data document in a comparative setting a pattern of rising women's employment in the labour market that Pleck (1978: 485) stated "manifests the most important change in the female role." The finding is consistent with the research reported in other national and cross-national studies. But a more significant pattern observed is that in all countries the increase in overall female labour force participation stems primarily from entry and reentry of *married* women into the economy. Indeed, data presented by Tomeh for the United States, Michel for France, as well as by Lupri and Mills for Canada show that the proportion of married women entering the labour force has increased twice as fast as for all women. No wonder, then, that these authors consider the increase in the proportion of married women who work for pay the single most dramatic and pervasive change in the status of women since World War II. Similar trends are documented by other contributors.

A second noteworthy and equally significant emerging pattern is that perhaps the largest increase in labour force activity in more *recent* years has been by the group generally viewed as least likely to work outside the home, *young mothers*. While the North American and the French materials document this pattern most conclusively, statistical data from other countries support this new rising trend as well. These two patterns–the increase among *married* women and among *young mothers*–manifest a change in the female role of great significance and consequence. The change clearly reflects the ever increasing *intersecting* of women's roles in family and work.

These and other data document that women's participation in the economy has gone through two major changes the past few decades. First was the increased numbers of middle-aged women in the labour force–the proportion of married women workers aged 45 to 64, in Canada, for example, increased five-fold from 1951 to 1977. In more recent years it is the increased numbers of young mothers who *remain* in the work force. The new life course pattern that is emerging for women is one in which family and work roles are coordinated throughout adult life. Today work force participation for women in most industrialized nations forms a M-shaped graph; however, if the trend continues, the graph will approximate an inverted U-shaped curve for labour force participation, which is characteristic of men's labour force participation in developed nations. Many of the socialist countries, particularly the Soviet Union with a female labour force participation rate of 80 percent and the Scandinavian countries, especially Finland and Sweden, where male participation rates are declining, have already achieved an approximate inverted U-shaped curve. A strong indication in the comparative data is that the rest of the world is not far behind. But other evidence suggests caution in generalizing and predicting from the data. Haavio-Mannila in this volume observes that the economically based curvilinear hypothesis explains but a part of the differences in women's economic activity in Scandinavian countries and argues that one must take into account the complex interrelationship of economic, cultural, and demographic factors in determining women's involvement in the economy. Yet sexual symmetry of work participation in the labour market appears to be in the making. As Burić appropriately states in this volume, it is an historical fact that women have joined the general work army and it seems an historical inevitability that they will remain in it.

The increase in the sheer numbers of women entering the work structure is by no means theoretically irrelevant. As a single woman is joined by other women in the work place, she becomes less visible as a prototype. Universalistic criteria are more likely to be applied and her success or failure on the job will increasingly be based on her performance as an individual rather than on particularistic criteria such as age and sex. Having more women in the work place is *one* of the necessary conditions to reversing the traditional stereotyping of the "two separate spheres for men and women," to which we alluded earlier. Numbers do matter in any social group, particularly in work groups. Structural-functional explanations of gender roles, often based on research in small groups (Parsons and Bales, 1955), have failed to take into account the ever increasing involvement of wives in the work structure. As Kanter (1977) demonstrated recently, one's position in the work setting has more influence on productivity, self-esteem, and competence than early socialization experience.

As discussed previously, the central thesis of the "changing roles perspective" is the evolution of family and work roles for both women and men. The cross-national data on female labour force activity fully support this thesis of participation *rates*, that is, the *number* of women entering the work force, are used as a data base. All countries, particularly socialist countries, show dramatic increases in work activity outside the home for *married* women, and more recently, for *young* mothers. A symmetry of work roles for husbands and wives is being approximated in the Soviet Union and Sweden and is emerging clearly among other socialist and capitalist nations. Whether this dramatic shift in *women's work* roles is paralleled by an equally dramatic shift in *men's family* role remains to be seen.

2. *Barriers to Women's Equality*. The interplay of changes in the population structure increased the supply of employable women (a period of high birth and marriage rates followed by low ones, a decrease in family size, changes in the age structure, high divorce rates, a general decrease in age at marriage, etc.). And the market's demand for cheap labour made it easy for masses of women to enter and reenter the labour force. Oppenheimer (1973) provides some pertinent insights into these demographic changes for the United States. Her basic argument is that the demand for female labour grew with economic expansion. By and large, that holds true for many economically developed countries whether economic expansion is driven by the profit motive or by any other ideological factor.

Numbers matter but what matters more is the effect they have had on the sex structure of the occupational force. In other words, has the dramatic increase in volume led to an equally dramatic change in the *sexual segregation* of the labour force? Before tackling that question, let us examine formal education as an avenue to occupational success and mobility.

2.1. Women's Level of Education

The ideological push toward sexual equality in all areas of social life has been strongest in socialist countries, particularly the Soviet Union, followed closely by Scandinavian countries, particularly Sweden. The goal of achieving complete equality between the sexes is an integral part of the political and economic ideology of socialist countries, notably the Soviet Union. Article 35 of the Constitution of the USSR, cited by Slesarev and Yankova in their chapter, ensures and promotes equal *educational* opportunity for women, a most important avenue to effect sexual equality. The Soviet authors state that now women are *on a par* with men in educational attainment, although figures in their Table 2 show that the proportion of men with "Higher Education" exceeds that of women, while the proportion of women with "Secondary Education" exceeds that of men. But the differences are minimal in both categories and the Soviet authors document that in *growth* rates of education, women are ahead of men.

Educational data for Czechoslovakia, presented by Wagnerová, show a similar trend. While the average educational level for women is still lower than for men, it nearly equals that of men who are less than 40 years old and exceeds that of men below 25. Poland introduced a quota plan in 1967 to upgrade education of women. As Siemieńska details sexual differences at university levels diminish over time. Educational developments in Sweden are similar: by and large gender equality has been achieved. Burić reports that Yugoslav women gain secondary, college, and university education at a faster rate than men.

The other contributions also reveal that great strides have been made in other countries to ensure equal educational opportunities for boys and girls. Even though gender equality has by no means been achieved, the gap in higher education between men and women is narrowing everywhere, although somewhat slower than in socialist countries. European countries show wider variation in the extent to which both sexes obtain an university education, reflecting some sexism and elitism in their educational systems. Although recent governmental educational policies reintroduced sex-based curricula in Japan's high schools, Meguro and Morioka mention rising education for Japanese women.

In North America the most effective means of social mobility is formal education, and in recent decades educational opportunities have widened for both sexes in the United States and Canada. Mass education is essentially an American ideal, notably for citizens of the United States. Furthermore, a much larger proportion of 20-year olds attend university in the United States than in Canada. However, sex differences exist in both countries. In the United States, 15 percent of white males aged 25 and over have four or more years of college, compared with 8.6 percent of white females. There is little difference between the sexes of blacks, among whom both sexes have a university-completion range of about half that of white females. Similarly, in Canada for those 15 years and older the proportions with four or more years of college were 6.5 for males and 2.9 for females in 1975. Canadian women had a higher percentage with secondary education than men (56.7% to 49.1%).

To summarize, except in the Soviet Union, educational achievement still is correlated with sex, especially in higher education. In all countries males were more likely to attain higher education than females. The discrepancy between the sexes is narrowing at speeds that vary from one country to another.

Women in socialist countries have achieved greater equality in education than women in capitalist countries. Soviet women are currently ahead of men. Other cross-national studies have documented that educational attainment also depends on social class origins. For example, North American high school students from lower socio-economic classes are less likely to attend university than those from middle and upper classes. While class origin affects both sexes, it affects women more than men. In socialist countries class distinctions are less sharply drawn than in capitalist countries so class origin is a greater barrier to women's educational equality in capitalist countries.

Educational inequalities between the sexes also are reflected in the *type* of study pursued, once women enter institutions of higher learning. In all countries, it appears women are more likely to pursue studies high in "expressive components" such as the humanities, teaching, nursing, and social work, while men are more likely to study fields high in "instrumental components" like law, science, engineering, and medicine. The Soviet Union is an exception: there women rather than men are notoriously overrepresented in science, engineering, and medicine.

What is the effect of the sexual differences in educational qualification on the occupational status of women? Do traditional sexlinked occupations become desegregated as more women attain education? Does occupational disadvantage translate into income disadvantage? What are some cross-national patterns?

2.2. Women in the Occupational Structure

With an increasing number of women entering the work force, earning university degrees and further professional training, then the logical question is, what effect have these trends had on the traditional unbalanced distribution of women and men in the occupation system? Occupation is the most important component of status for most people in all societies, and it is through work outside the home that women's status in the larger society *may* improve. Additionally, it is through work that both women and men find self-expression and self-realization.

A distinctive feature of the Soviet Union is not only that women number almost half of the labour force, but also, as Slesarev and Yankova point out, a substantial proportion of women work in the "privileged trades and professions." In the public health field, for example, 81 percent of all workers are women. Three of four (74%) of the medical doctors are women, and women constitute approximately the same high proportion (72%) of all teachers and college instructors. Those changes in women's work lead Slesarev and Yankova to conclude that "for the first time in history, socialism has made professions which require maximum creative effort mass women's professions." While many of the professions are characterized by unbalanced sexual segregation in favour of women, areas of occupational inequality also persist and a "key problem is the problem of rational employment of women." Soviet women are underrepresented among scientific and scholarly researchers, judges, those receiving awards for meritorious work, those receiving the title of Hero of Socialist Labour, and those whose jobs require high levels of technical skill and creative ability. As the Soviet authors state, "...the inadequate solution of this problem inhibits... the removal of the leftovers of actual inequality." Even though they surpass men in level of education, women frequently lag behind them in industrial skill-categories to say nothing of the lag in the many vocations that require the physical strength and endurance that men possess (Slesarev and Yankova).

The Soviet Union represents an interesting and perhaps trendsetting case for studying changing gender norms in the occupational sectors. On the one hand, the professions there experienced a process of desegregation to the extent that the pendulum has swung the other way: now women predominate in public health, college teaching, medicine, and engineering. On the other hand, gender-specific occupational segregation and income differences persist in many sectors of the economy. The Soviet authors view this inequality between the sexes as a key problem in their planned economy.

An overall persistence of occupational inequality is echoed, implicitly as well as explicitly, by all authors who address the issue. While improvements have been made in all nations, particularly socialist ones, none has achieved full sexual equality in the occupational sectors. In Poland, for example, the number of women entering traditionally male dominated professions is increasing so slowly that in "reality occupational segregation by sex exists." Similarly in Czechoslovakia women's penetration into male dominated professions has been much slower than the proportional increase of women into such traditional female professions as teaching, health, and communication. Trend data from other European countries reveal similar patterns except that in Yugoslavia a reversal to conventional occupational norms is emerging with greater sexual segregation. Yugoslavian data from 1962 to 1972 indicate that women's involvement in leadership positions in seven sectors is declining, even though those sectors traditionally had enjoyed a high concentration of females (Burić, Table 8).

Tomeh, for the United States, reports that "despite the steady increase in women's employment, there has been little change in the direction of greater similarity in the occupational distribution of men and women." Only 2 in 100 women are in administration or managerial jobs; fewer than 5 women in 100 are found in the professions; and among the 2500 presidents, vice-presidents, and board chairpersons, only 15 women direct a company's major operations.

The tenacity of occupational segregation by sex also is revealed clearly by Canadian data (Lupri and Mills, Table 11). Whether they are female or male occupations, they have desegregated very slowly over four decades. While the overall growth in the professional work force of Canada has been quite notable, women's share of the increase has been negligible. The substantial number of Canadian women entering the labour market have, by and large, been absorbed by the service sector.

Women's disproportionate share in certain professions, their absence from the highest occupational levels, and their remaining clustered primarily in service and clerical jobs account at least in part for reported lower salaries paid to women around the world. Women's transitional work status and high job turnover also contribute to lower earnings than men, but full-time women workers also are paid less than men (Tomeh, U.S.A.). When women are better educated than men, women's

Table 3

Divorce Rates in this Volume's Eighteen Countries for 1975, 1965, and 1955

Country	Number per 100,000 Population		
	1975	1965	1955
The Soviet Union	335	134	60
Poland	127	77	49
Czechoslovakia	218	132	105
Finland	214	99	85
Sweden	264	124	121
Ghana[1]	—	—	—
United States	482	254	230
Canada	222	46	38
Japan	108	97	85
Austria	149	116	129
France	127	74	72
Yugoslavia	118	111	110
Switzerland	151	84	89
South Africa[2]	53	30	29
Greece	41	41	30
Norway	145	69	58
The Netherlands	152	55	51
Italy[3]	19	—	—

Source: United Nations Demographic Year Book, 1977, Table 25; 1968, Table 34.
[1] No data available.
[2] Coloured population.
[3] No legal provision for divorce in 1965 and 1955.

wages are lower than men's even when both hold the same positions (Siemieńska, Poland). With few exceptions, Canadian women earn less than men for work of equal value, even when their education, training, and experience are comparable (Lupri and Mills.)

To summarize, the cross-national evidence shows clearly that gender roles are unevenly distributed in the economy and it is predominantly men who occupy the functionally significant positions in the power and reward structure. The trend of occupational segregation according to sex is so pervasive that we call it a universal pattern. Undoubtedly changes have occurred over the past three decades, but while the number of women entering the economy is highly impressive and still rising, upward mobility for women is, by and large, minimal and restricted to fields and roles with expressive components. Oftener than not women's work roles are supportive of men's roles. Clearly, then, quantity has not brought a qualitative change in the sex structure of the economy. Notwithstanding the gain women have achieved in the Soviet Union, sex discrimination in the occupational structure prevails in all nations.

3. *The Nuclear Family: Help or Hindrance to Women's Equality?* The dramatic increase observed earlier in labour force activity by married women and young mothers is strikingly paralleled by an equally pervasive trend in family life: *a marked increase in the divorce rate*. The comparative data on crude divorce rates presented in Table 3 document the pervasiveness of this trend for almost all countries.

We must reject at the outset any causal connection between increased employment of wives and increases in divorce rates. Only carefully designed "before-and-after" studies will show whether family conflict is associated with and a consequence of the wife's occupying a provider role. However, we may assume with some certainty that the dramatic and consistent increase in the divorce rates reflects strains in existing marital relations.

Other trends such as the disinclination of young people to marry, the growing tendency to live together in a free partnership or as singles, the falling birth rate, the finding that wives are more likely than husbands to initiate divorce proceedings, the lower remarriage rate for women compared with men, and the observation that women wait longer than men to remarry, all combine to point toward women's general dissatisfaction with marriage. These demographic trends as well as data from other studies document convincingly that it is women rather than men who feel estranged in and from marriage.

Considerable cross-national evidence shows that: more wives than husbands report marital frustration and dissatisfaction; more wives than husbands report marital problems; more wives than husband consider their marriages unhappy; more wives than husbands report negative feelings, have considered divorce or separation, have regretted their marriages; and fewer report positive companionship (Bernard, 1972, 1975; Pross, 1973; Platt, 1972).

These studies and data suggest that there are *two* realities in marriage, "HIS" and "HERS" (Bernard, 1972). How do family roles differ by sex? How have they evolved over time? How is the evolution of family roles affected by work roles and how do family roles structure work roles? Does the evolution of family and work roles affect wives and husbands differently? The cross-national data presented shed considerable light on these questions, although the answer depends at times on the countries involved. Role prescriptions and their changes must be interpreted in the social and cultural contexts in which they evolve. However, some universal patterns emerge and it is those that interest us here. The social structure of the family consists of the positions that family members occupy in relation to each other. Sociologists around the world tend to agree that the two most important family dimensions are division of labour and division of power. We need to examine the evolution of family roles within these two limited but significant structures for both husbands and wives. What are the cross-national findings?

3.1. The Familial Power Structure

Decline of paternal authority in the twentieth century is one of the most frequently recorded family changes. Cross-cultural evidence to support a change from the traditional patriarchal to a more egalitarian conjugal power structure is overwhelming (Rodman, 1967, 1972, 1976; Michel, 1967; Lupri, 1965, 1969, 1976; Safilios-Rothschild, 1967, 1970; Oppong, 1970). Despite methodological and conceptual limitations of almost all of the international studies, a number of consistent findings emerged.[4] One distinct pattern is that wives' work for pay significantly increases their power vis-a-vis their husbands.[5] While the effects of the wives' employment vary by social class position and family size and are influenced by existing normative and cultural conditions, the available comparative data suggest that the *economic* role determines the wives' increased power in the family. Employed wives have more power than nonemployed wives. Economic independence, or parts thereof, translates into greater egalitarianism at home. The importance of the *economic* factor in the power distribution between the sexes is further substantiated by another cross-national pattern. Depending on the cultural context (Rodman, 1972), traditional patriarchalism survives more likely in the upper class where economic power is concentrated in the hands of men. But more important for this argument is noting that wives of lower classes gain substantially more power by working outside the home than do wives of middle and upper classes (Lupri, 1969, 1976). The difference between the power of the employed and nonemployed wives decreases as the husband's occupation and income increase. Clearly economic power translates into family power.

Many contributors to this volume have reported similar findings elsewhere: for example, Michel (1967) for France, Burić (1967) for Yugoslavia, Safilios-Rothschild (1967) for Greece, Haavio-Mannila (1968) for Finland, Trost (1969) for Sweden, Lupri (1969) for West Germany, Oppong (1970) for Ghana, and Lupri (1965) for Italy, Great Britain, the United States, and West Germany have all observed that structural differentiation, women's changing economic roles, and equalitarian family patterns are highly correlated and appear to implicate each other. Corroborative evidence is provided in this volume by Slesarev and Yankova for the Soviet Union, by Wagnerová for Czechoslovakia, Siemieńska for Poland, Köckeis-Stangl for Austria, Tomeh for the United States, and Lupri and Mills for Canada.

Yet, family patriarchalism persists, even in highly industrialized nations. A cross-national comparison of family authority patterns in five nations showed that in

---

4 Literature dealing with theoretical, conceptual, and measurement problems of the process of family power dynamics is voluminous. For recent critiques see, for example, Brinkerhoff and Lupri, 1978; Lupri, 1976; Hill, 1975; Cromwell and Olson, 1975; Turk, 1975; Bell and Turk, 1972; Sprey, 1972; Gillespie, 1971; Safilios-Rothschild, 1969, 1970.

5 Safilios-Rothschild (1969, 1970) has seriously challenged the support for this generalization as well as many of the underlying assumptions of the "resource theory of marital power" that most international scholars have used in interpreting their findings.

Mexico and Italy two of five families were husband-dominant, in West Germany one of four, and in England and the United States slightly less than one of five (Baumert and Lupri, 1963; Lupri, 1965). The authors document that the extent of paternal authority is structurally differentiated. Within societies husband-dominance is more prevalent in rural than in urban areas and the extent of rural-urban differences varies inversely with the degree of structural differentiation (Lupri, 1976). Thus, while considerable cross-cultural evidence shows that paternal authority is declining in favour of a more egalitarian family system, husband-dominance is by no means absent. Discussing the Canadian setting, Lupri and Mills concluded: "...according to decisionmaking scales wives appear to be equal...but in reality, wives only make decisions in areas in which they are expected to–areas of lesser importance." Slesarev and Yankova speak of the evolution of a new Soviet family system based on an actual equality and cooperative effort, but also conclude that "...nevertheless, there remains the underlying contradiction which calls for immediate solution."

Undoubtedly, some form of sexual inequality in the conjugal power structure tends to persist. The lack of economic resources reinforces the wife's dependency vis-a-vis her husband because her power is derived largely from her family roles which, traditionally, have been accorded low esteen. These traditional barriers impede the evolution of equalitarian family norms and cannot be fully compensated for by the wife's employment because her income is often *supplementary* to her husband's. Thus, while male supremacy in the family is declining, wives have not yet achieved equality with their husbands.

3.2. The Division of Labour in the Family

The research literature contains a great wealth of comparative data on the division of labour in the family. Since the publication of *The Use of Time* by Alexander Szalai et al. (1972), time-budget data from twelve nations have become available and shed considerable light on work and family roles of *both* husbands and wives. Now a comparative data base substantiates strikingly the existence of a clear-cut *marital* division of labour in modern society. Comparative studies by anthropologists, ethnologists, sociologists, and historians had long estbalished, of course, such a division of labour according to sex in traditional societies. The merit of the time-budget study is that we now have a comparative and contemporary data base that permits us to quantify male-female *differences* in work and family roles by holding certain crucial variables constant. It is precisely such quantifiable comparative data that are needed to show the untenability of certain theoretical assumptions about the changing roles of women and men at home and at work. Let us look at some basic family patterns that emerge in this volume and then examine them in relation to the findings from the international time-budget study.

Socialist nations above all have been preoccupied with the position of women in the family because of those nations' ideological concern for developing socialist economies. A socialist economy is a planned economy with women's labour constituting an essential and integral component of national production. If family roles interfere with women's economic roles, the state institutes mechanisms to help *women* carry out their family roles.

The Soviet authors addressing this issue, state that these problems are "...due to drawbacks in the organization of every-day services and due sometimes to the stand taken by the husband." Their own budget analyses support the general observation in other societies that Soviet wives, too, are overburdened with household chores. Slesarev's and Yankova's figures show that the wives do six times more cooking than their husbands, about twelve times more washing and laundry; and twice as much grocery shopping. Almost apologetically they report that other activities, for example, child care, are more evenly divided between the sexes. The international time-budget study shows that in the Soviet Union, on average, employed women spend 26 minutes per day on child care compared with 12 minutes for employed men, i.e., Soviet women spend more than twice as much time on child care as their husbands do (Szalai et al., 1972: 693, Table 4–2.13, USSR).

The marital division of labour is best documented when gainful employment *and* housework are seen as total work environments and time spent in each are shown separately for employed women and employed men. Table 4 presents such data as minutes spent per day on total work, total housework, total household care, total child care, and available free time.[6] To facilitate comparison, women's time spent on tasks in both work domains is used as a base when the differences between men and women are computed. A glance at Table 4 makes evident that, despite the wide range of cultural diversity across the six nations, patterns in sex role differences in all work-related activities as well as in free time emerge in very marked form. In all six countries women spent less time in total gainful employment than men. Women in the socialist countries, except Yugoslavia, tend to spend more time on the job than do women in France or the United States. The greater cross-national variation among women than among men is noteworthy. The two extreme settings, the U.S.S.R. and the United States, show that Soviet women, on average, spent 6.6 hours at work outside the home compared with 5.6 hours for U.S. women, reflecting, no doubt, U.S. women's greater share in part-time employment. However, total time in the job for *men* in the two countries is identical (7.6 hours per day). This pattern is somewhat reflected in the computed total worktime difference between women and men. Women in the socialist countries of the Soviet Union, Poland, and Czechoslovakia devote a greater share of their total day to work outside the home than wo-

---

6 These four areas of total work-related activities include 13 primary activities. They are for Total Work: main job, second job, other work, and travel to job; for Total Housework: cooking, home chores, laundry, and marketing; for Total Household Care: gardening, taking care of pets, shopping, other household care; for Total Child Care: basic child care and other child care.

Table 4

Time spent in Average Minutes per Day by Employed Women and Men in Indicated Primary Activities and Free Time, Six Countries, mid-1960

Primary Activity	Soviet Union	Czecho-slovakia	Poland	Yugoslavia	France	United States
TOTAL WORK[1]						
Women	393	367	385	334	356	321
Men	431	445	457	428	436	432
Difference	−38	−78	−72	−94	−80	−111
TOTAL HOUSEWORK[1]						
Women	185	206	195	209	186	157
Men	33	52	38	25	33	28
Difference	+152	+154	+157	+174	+153	+129
OTHER HOUSEHOLD CHORES[1]						
Women	31	32	20	22	22	43
Men	46	46	34	40	49	37
Difference	−15	−14	−14	−18	−27	+6
TOTAL CHILD CARE[1]						
Women	38	32	34	30	29	23
Men	30	20	23	12	11	12
Difference	+8	+12	+11	+18	+18	+11
TOTAL FREE TIME						
Women	196	178	211	235	181	247
Men	293	270	290	307	244	289
Difference	−97	−92	−79	−72	−63	−42

Source: Adapted from Szalai et al. (1972: 681–695; Table 4-2.1-4-2.15).

[1] The four main areas of Total Work, Total Housework, Other Household Chores, and Total Child Care comprise 13 primary activites. This table excludes 24 primary activities such as total personal needs, total nonwork-travel, study and participation, total mass media, and total leisure. The difference in time spent and free time between men and women was calculated to facilitate comparison.

men do in the two capitalist countries, France and the United States. But men, on the whole, do not. This cross-national pattern of sex differences in the labour market emerges most dramatically between the United States and the Soviet Union.

Marital division of labour in the home presents another illuminating pattern. Irrespective of the cross-national variation in women's total work outside the home, employed women in *all* countries, spent, on average, 2½ to 3 hours per day more on housework than employed men. Such uniformity in the pattern is noteworthy, notwithstanding the range between women in the United States (2.1 hrs. per day) and women in Yugoslavia (3.1 hrs.). The universal plight of the *employed* woman is strikingly revealed by these data.

Compared with the time spent in work and in housework, time devoted to "other household care" and "child care" is relatively minimal. Except in the United States, men predominate in other "household chores" and women, as expected, predominate in "child care." The rather small amount of time devoted to child care is an artifact of the aggregate data analysis and needs a brief explanation. As seen in Table 4, women's time devoted to child care averaged about 30 minutes per day as a primary activity across all six nations when calculated on a per capita basis for all respondents. However, when the data are limited to those with children, the average is about 65 minutes, with 30 minutes being spent by employed men and 72 minutes by employed women. Unfortunately, such breakdowns are not given for each country surveyed.

The marked difference between the sexes in the availability of free time reinforces earlier observations that the dual role creates extreme time pressure for employed women. After their day's obligations are done, each has an hour or two less free time than an employed man. Sex *differences* in free time increase as we move from France and the United States to the socialist countries. Employed women in the Soviet Union have 1.6 hours less free time than their male colleagues, while in the United States the sex difference is only .7 hours.

Similar patterns emerge when time spent on the four areas are summed and presented separately for employed women and employed men (Table 5). Women devote from 1 to 1 ½ hours daily more to work and housework than men do. The earlier observed sex differences appear again. They are significantly greater in the socialist countries.

Table 5

Total Work Load in Hours per Day for Employed Women and Employed Men in Six Countries

Country	Employed Women	Employed Men	Difference
Soviet Union	10.7	9.0	1.7
Czechoslovakia	10.6	9.3	1.3
Poland	10.6	9.2	1.4
Yugoslavia	9.9	8.4	1.5
France	9.8	8.8	1.0
United States	9.1	8.4	.7

Source: Computed from data in Table 4.

To sum up, employed women are a lot busier than their male counterparts in all countries, but particularly in socialist countries. Thus the sex difference in time devoted to the *two* work domains is greater in the four socialist countries than in the two capitalist countries. Notwithstanding the differences by country, the plight of the employed woman pervades the time-budget data from all six nations.

It may be reasonable to generalize the findings from a sub-sample of six nations to the total sample of eighteen nations represented in this volume for at least four reasons. First, the time-budget data presented consistently point in the same direction; second, the same data from the other six nations of the international time-budget study[7] reveal similar patterns; third, many contributors to this volume implicitly substantiate inequities in the division of labour by sex. And finally, other studies in the literature come to the same conclusion. In other words, no deviant case appears to exist.

All told, then, the time-budget data from the international study together with information presented in this volume form a rather compelling stream of evidence strongly suggesting that employed women, unlike employed men, are grossly overburdened in all countries, and that substantial inequities in the marital division of labour persist. And most important, the present social organization of the nuclear family system remains as one of the greatest barriers to women's equality.

The Persistence of Structural Barriers to Women's Equality

Structured Inequality

By way of an overall summary, then, it seems reasonable to say that we have almost come full circle. Before the Industrial Revolution, the family constituted an economical unit of production. Both husband and wife as well as their children were economically productive with work activity in the home.

Industrialization brought with it not only a differentiation of productive tasks but also separation of home and work. Paid work by men in the factory came to be distinguished from women's unpaid work at home, housework. This process of differentiation created the role of the housewife and, in turn, fostered the creation of an ideology of separate spheres for women and men. The distinctive division of labour according to sex that developed came to be seen as natural: for men to specialize in market activities and women in home activities.

To be sure, in the earlier phases of the factory system, women and children were forced by economic necessity into factories and thus separated from their households; and men were able to supervise their own wives and children and thus maintain their authority as household heads. In the later phases, however, child labour was eliminated and women were transformed into a marginal labour force. Women's "proper" place came to be centred around *Kirche, Küche,* and *Kinder,* i.e., the home, —notwithstanding the historical fact that women always worked in the fields.

Today women again form an integral part of the modern economy. However, it was not until World War II and its immediate aftermath that demographic forces and economic expansion, together with ideological and value changes, combined to

---

7 The other six countries are: Bulgaria, German Democratic Republic, Federal Republic of Germany, Belgium, Hungary, and Peru.

draw masses of women into the market place. Now women everywhere are joining an ever-growing reserve army of workers and they are there to stay. And it is with the more recent dramatic increase in married women's share in paid work that we have almost come full circle since the preindustrial era.

The pervasive work participation among wives, young and old, manifests the most important change in women's roles. The new life course pattern that is emerging for women is one in which family and work roles are intertwined throughout adult life. On the basis of the sheer number of jobs, a symmetry of work roles for men and women is in the making, clearly reflecting the ever increasing intersecting of women's roles in family and work. And it is in the context of married *women's* increased share in paid work that the comparative materials provide support for the changing-roles perspective.

However, this impressive change in the volume of female employment has not led to an equally impressive change in occupational segregation by sex. Instead, the persistance of sexual segregation in the occupational structure remains one of the most pervasive patterns of resistance to women's equality everywhere. Women's transient work status forces them to accept low-skilled, low-prestige, and low-paying jobs. While women are highly represented in certain professions like nursing, social work, teaching, and library work, men are overrepresented in the higher positions within these fields. Even in the sectors in which women predominate men are more likely to hold supervisory positions. Working-age women's level of education has improved everywhere, when compared with men, however, this avenue of social mobility has made only little impact on women's occupational status, prestige, or income, with the possible exception of the Soviet Union. Even there, the proportion of women in the higher professional echelons tends to decrease as the rank advances.

In many instances it was shown that the gap between pay for women and men doing similar work actually widened rather than narrowing during the last decade. Moreover, in capitalist countries class origin has a more devastating effect on women's social mobility than it has on men's. Thus, women's transient position in the work force, job discrimination, and class origin are persistent structural barriers that impede women's equality in the occupational system. Clearly, then, because occupational sex segregation persists across all nations, quantity has not brought about a qualitative change in the economy. A quarter of a century ago, Parsons said about the balance of sex roles in the American work force:

> ...on higher levels of typically feminine occupations are those of teacher, social worker, nurse, private secretary and entertainer. Such roles tend to have a prominent expressive component, and often to be supportive of masculine roles. Within the occupational organization they are analogous to the wife-mother role in the family (1955: 15).

Parsons also anticipated an increase in the proportion of married women entering the labour force but he made it quite explicit that even if it

> ...should come about that the average married woman had some kind of a job, it seems most unlikely that this relative balance would be upset; that either the roles would be reversed, or their *qualitative* differentiation in these respects completely erased (1955: 15).

As this volume's comparative materials document, Parsons rather accurately predicted the trend in changing sex roles. At work, as we observed, men are more likely to carry on *instrumental* activities and women, *affective (expressive)* activities, notwithstanding Soviet women's penetration and predominance in certain professional fields with prominent instrumental components.

But, on the whole, the comparative data on occupational segregation make abundantly evident that in capitalist and socialist countries nothing is more impressive than the sexual disparity in the economy, always highly associated with a variation in power according to sex. It is predominantly men who occupy high positions in the reward and power structures. So pervasive and persistent is this universal pattern that we must seriously question one major assumption of the changing-roles perspective which holds that "men can and will change if appropriate educational and social policies are implemented" (Pleck, 1978: 485).

This volume's comparative materials show convincingly that men hold the power in at least three strategically significant key sectors for bringing about change in the social structure: the economy, the polity, and the educational system. If men *desire* to bring about gender equity in society, they certainly can because they wield the power in appropriate decision-making bodies. But it appears that change is forthcoming only slowly, if at all.

Structural-functional theory does not tell us why the traditional imbalance of power is upheld, i.e., why male supremacy survives so persistently.[8] What are the institutional barriers that impede gender equities in the economy, the polity, and the family? Conflict theorists (Simmel, 1904, 1955; Dahrendorf, 1956, 1958, 1961, 1963, 1968; Smith, 1973; Gouldner, 1970; Coser, 1956, 1967, 1968; Collins, 1971; Schmidt-Relenberg et al., 1976) argue that all inequalities are structural inequalities based on conflicts of interests between the dominant and the subordinate groups. And, as we have seen, sexual inequalities are structural inequalities.

Men can enjoy a superior status only if women have an inferior one, and the existing sex role patterns allow men to maintain their political, social, psychological, and economic privileges. It is the dominant men who profit most from existing arrangements, so they have little inclination to change the *status quo*. Marx cogently argued that both the dominant and the subordinate groups in any structured social inequality tend to accept the ideology that legitimizes the social structure.

---

8 Parsons, however, states that the segregation of work and family roles according to sex protects the family against destructive competition between husband and wife and internal rivalry (1949: 193).

The thesis that sexual inequalitites are structural and grounded in conflicts of interests between the dominant and the subordinate groups was further strengthened when we examined the sphere that is least amenable to public influence and governmental legislation: the privatized nuclear family. In fact, the patterns of sexual inequality found in work organization are strikingly paralleled in family organization. At work *and* at home, men carry on *instrumental* roles and women carry on *expressive* roles. Moreover, among dual-working couples substantial sexual inequalities exist in the marital division of labour. Everywhere, persisting traditional norms prescribe sex-segregated, unequal division of household work, child care, and the availability of free time. Typically these norms have been reinforced by the efforts of organized education and religion, along with mass communication media.

Problems faced by working mothers or working wives have not been solved anywhere and their plight pervades every known time-budget study. It is in this context that we contend that the major obstacle to further change is the nuclear family itself. More pointedly, the sex-structure of family organization remains one of the most powerful barriers to women's equality. Men's greater power at home and at work, so it seems, accrues from the very inequality women experience in both domains. This vicious circle impedes gender equality in the whole society everywhere.

An equitable solution to the double burden of employed women can be achieved only if marital roles are restructured. While the problem of sexual inequality is fundamentally structural, it is also personal. Thus, reciprocal role changes require that both women *and* men are willing to redefine their marital and work roles. The work organization must become flexible enough to accommodate a sex-free division of labour so that family responsibilities can be dealt with more fully and equitably. Similarly there must be fuller sharing by males of household and family tasks. The comparative evidence makes abundantly clear that women everywhere have begun to redefine their traditional role obligations by engaging in paid work; men must now redefine their roles at home as well as in the political and economic institutions where they hold the power.

A Final Theoretical Note

The comparative study of gender relations is a field that lacks universal concepts, methods, and investigators. Indeed, the existing literature is mainly produced by social scientists in North America and Europe. Where investigators have considered the "woman's question," they have–in line with their theoretical interests–treated sex role research within the confines of an eclectic set of theoretical assumptions. Future comparative work needs to consolidate data in a more unitary, holistic, theoretical manner. The conceptual distinction between housework and work for pay must be clarified because it now tends to reify the *sexual* division of labour and thereby unduly emphasizes the separation of family and work. It perpetuates the notion of different spheres for men and women as well as the double standard, so pervasive in the social structure of all societies. It has led to well-meant, but nevertheless ill-conceived, legislation and reforms designed to remedy women's problems.[9] As in theory so in practice, fitting together work and family life has long been seen as a "problem" for women, but not for men. However, the "woman's problem" is a general social problem, reflecting the human condition as a whole, and this is just as much a "man's problem." It can only be solved by restructuring the complete system, by redefining women's and men's roles, and finally, by treating housework and paid work as *family work* (Pleck, 1978).

Theoretically, then, the family must be conceptualized as a unit with a set of task requirements inside and outside the household (Eriksen, Yancey, and Eriksen, 1979). Such a perspective entails examining family role sets that evolve to perform necessary tasks. Then what has previously been "... thought of as men's work (employment outside the home) and as women's work (the performance of household tasks) can be viewed as one set of task requirements for which a particular solution has evolved" (Eriksen, Yancey, and Eriksen, 1979: 301).

Structural-functional theory fails to come to grips with either the unitary character of family work or existing gender inequality in the social structure. Instead, it posits that the major social structures, like the family, economy, and polity, contribute to the *integration* and *adaptation* of the system in which they operate, so the emphasis is mainly on sub-system analysis, and only secondarily on systematic interchanges. Often the sub-systems are treated as independent and almost autonomous units. If functionalists focus on the intersecting of family and economic roles, they give primacy and undue weight to tracing the role of the adult *male* as undisputably the "instrumental leader."

Overconcern with consensus renders functional analysis insensitive to such conflict-generating variables as structural inequality. Moreover, the *persistence* of a given structure is seen as beneficial and necessary for the maintenance of society as a whole. Sexual inequality, as one form of structural inequality, therefore persists

9   In Canada, grounds for establishing more child care facilities, for example, often are couched in words that reflect what supposedly constitutes "women's work." Expressions such as "to remedy women's overload," or "to lighten the burden of working mothers," or "to aid married women in caring for their children" appear daily in Canada's newspapers and speeches made by politicians at all levels.

   Academic institutions are no exceptions. Harris (1970: 294) reports that a "concession has recently been made by Princeton University, where nontenured *women* faculty may, at their option, delay their tenure decision if they find that *family* responsibilities make it difficult for *them* to complete the necessary publications within the normal seven-year limit (my emphasis)."

   Clearly the emphasis has been and still is to the present day on the difficulties *women* encounter in reconciling the incompatibility of occupational and family roles. Again, one is forced to ask why women and not men should encounter greater incompatibility in reconciling marital and occupational roles. Inherent in all such measures is a strong bias in favour of the *status quo* in the family and work place.

because it is functional for the system as a whole. Change is the exception, not the rule. When functionalists deal with change, they tend to see it as a relatively slow process occuring within each sub-system. Radical sociologists, for example, Szymanski (1976), maintain that the structural functional approach to gender relations is a theoretical tool for the maintenance of the status quo. Hence it is ill-equipped to deal with the "woman's problem."

Undoubtedly the changing-roles perspective is an improvement over functional analysis. It focuses specifically on the evolution and interplay of men's and women's economic and family roles and thus treats present gender inequities as transitional. According to Pleck (1978), the contemporary scene reflects simply a "transitional problem of adjustment." Along the same line, Rapoport and Rapoport (1972) argue that men's slower rate of role changes constitute a "psychological lag." It is implied that *in time* a sexual symmetry of work and family roles will evolve. In the light of the pervasive persistence of sexual inequality at home and in the work place as well as "reversals" (the wage gap between men and women widening rather than narrowing and certain professions and occupations not de-segregating at all) observed in capitalist and socialist countries, this assumption is an overly optimistic one, at best. More basically, the changing-roles perspective underestimates the structural grounding of gender inequality in society as a whole.

The conflict assumption is most sensitive to the repeatedly made observation that the "woman's problem" is a structural one and that its solution requires fundamental and comprehensive changes. Conflict theory also conceptualizes work as an integral part of all social relations. Economic activity conditions all other social processes and it is, therefore, untenable to separate family life from the economic institutions of society. Existing gender inequities allow men, as a dominant group, to maintain political and economic privileges over women, the subordinate group. Changes will evolve slowly, if at all, because men hold the power in key positions of the family, economy, and the polity. Exploitation will persist until the social structure is changed at its very basis.

BIBLIOGRAPHY

Abbott, Edith
    1910 *Women in Industry*. New York: Appleton.
Acker, Joan
    1973 "Women and social stratification: a case of intellectual sexism." *American Journal o Sociology* 78, 4:936-45.
Aronoff, J., and W. D. Crano
    1975 "A re-examination of the cross-cultural principles of task segregation and sex role differentiation in the family." *American Sociological Review* 40 (February) : 12-20.
Baumert, G., and Eugen Lupri
    1963 "New aspects of rural-urban differentials in family values and family authority structure." *Current Sociology* 12:46-54.
Beauvoir, Simone de
    1949 *Le Deuxième Sexe* (2 vol.). Paris: Librairie Gallimard.

Bernard, Jessie
- 1972 *The Future of Marriage.* New York: Bantam Books.
- 1975 *Women, Wives, Mothers.* Chicago: Aldine.

Blood, R. O. Jr., and D. M. Wolfe
- 1960 *Husbands and Wives: The Dynamics of Married Living.* Glencoe, Illinois: Free Press.

Blood, R. O. Jr., Reuben Hill, Andrée Michel and Constantina Safilios-Rothschild
- 1970 "Comparative analysis of family power structure: problems of measurement and interpretation." Pp. 525–535 in Reuben Hill and René Konig (eds.), *Families in East and West: Socialization Process and Kinship Ties.* The Hague: Mouton.

Brinkerhoff, M. B., and E. Lupri
- 1978 "Theoretical and methodological issues in the use of decisionmaking as an indicator of conjugal power: some Canadian observations." *Canadian Journal of Sociology* 3, 1: 1–20.

Brown, B. W.
- 1978 "Wife-employment and the emergence of egalitarian marital role prescriptions, 1900–1974." *Journal of Comparative Family Studies* IX, 1: 5–17.

Burić, O., and A. Zecevič
- 1967 "Family authority, marital satisfaction, and the social network in Yugoslavia." *Journal of Marriage and the Family* 29: 325–336.

Collins, Randal
- 1971 "A conflict theory of sexual stratification." *Social Problems* 19 (Summer 1971): 3–20.

Coser, Lewis A.
- 1956 *The function of Social Conflict.* London: Routledge and Kegan Paul.
- 1967 *Continuities in the Study of Social Conflict.* New York: Free Press.
- 1968 "Conflict: social aspects." pp. 232–236 in *International Encyclopedia of the Social Sciences* III. New York: Macmillan.

Cromwell, R., and D. Olson
- 1975 "Multidisciplinary perspectives of power." pp. 15–37 in R. Cromwell and D. Olson (eds.), *Power in Families.* New York: John Wiley.

Daheim, Hansjürgen
- 1973 *Der Beruf in der Modern Gesellschaft.* Köln: Westdeutscher Verlag.

Dahlström, Edmund (ed.)
- 1967 *The Changing Roles of Men and Women.* London: Gerald Duckworth & Co.

Dahrendorf, Ralph
- 1956 *Soziale Klassen und Klassenkonflikt.* Stuttgart: Enke Verlag.
- 1958 "Toward a theory of social conflict." *Journal of Conflict Resolution* II (June): 170–183.
- 1961 *Über den Ursprung der Ungleichheit unter den Menschen.* Tübingen: Mohr.
- 1963 *Die Angewandte Aufklärung.* München: Piper.
- 1968 *Pfade aus Utopia.* München: Piper.
- 1968 *Die Funktionen Sozialer Konflikte.* München: Piper.

Dixon, Marlene
- 1971 "Why women's liberation?" *Divided we Stand,* by the editors of Ramparts. San Francisco: Canfield Press.

Dodge, Norton T.
- 1966 *Women in the Soviet Economy.* Baltimore: The Johns Hopkins Press.

Durkheim, Emile
- 1895 *Les Règles de la Méthode Sociologique.* Paris: Alcan.

Engels, Friedrich
- 1845 *Die Lage der Arbeitenden Klasse in England.* Leipzig.
- 1884 *Der Ursprung der Famile, der Privateigentums, und des Staates.* Berlin.

Epstein, Cynthia F.
- 1970 "Encountering the male establishment: sex-status limits on women's careers in the professions." *American Journal of Sociology* 75: 965–982.

Ericksen, J. A., W. L. Yancey and E. P. Ericksen
    1949 "The division of family roles." *Journal of Marriage and the Family* 41 (No. 2, May): 301–313
Firestone, Shulamith
    1978 "The dialectic of sex." Pp. 130–135 in Alison M. Jaggar and Paula Rothenberg Struhl (eds.), *Feminist Frameworks*. New York: McGraw Hill.
Forgarty, Michael P., Rhona Rapoport, and Robert N. Rapoport
    1971 *Sex, Career and Family*. London: George Allen & Unwin.
Gillespie, D.
    1971 "Who has the power?: the marital struggle." *Journal of Marriage and the Family* 33: 445–458.
Goode, W.
    1961 *Struktur und Funktion der Familie*. Köln-Opladen: Westdeutscher Verlag.
    1963 *World Revolution and Family Patterns*. Glencoe: The Free Press.
Gouldner, Alvin W.
    1970 *The Coming Crisis of Western Sociology*. New York: Basic Books.
Grønseth, Erik
    1971 "The husband provider role: a critical appraisal," in Andrée Michel (ed.), *Family Issues of Employed Women in Europe and America*. Leiden: E. J. Brill.
Habermas, Jürgen
    1963 *Theorie und Praxis: Sozialphilosophische Studien*. Neuwied: Luchterhand.
    1969 "Analytische wissenschaftstheorie und dialectik," in T. W. Adorno et al. (eds.), *Der Positivismusstreit in der Deutschen Soziologie*. Neuwied: Luchterhand.
Hacker, Helen
    1951 "Women as a minority group." *Social Forces* 30 (No. 1): 60–69.
Hartman, Heidi
    1976 "Capitalism, patriarchy, and job segregation by sex." *Signs* 1 (3 Pt. 2): 137–170.
Hill, R.
    1975 "Foreword." Pp. vii xiii in R. Cromwell and D. Olson (eds.), *Power in Families*. New York: John Wiley.
Holmstrome, Lynda L.
    1972 *The Two-Career Family*. Cambridge, Mass.: Schenkman Publishing Company.
Horkheimer, Max
    1970 *Traditionelle und Kritische Theorie*. Frankfurt A. M.: Fischer.
Horna, J.
    1977 "Women in East European socialist countries." Pp. 137–151 in M. P. Marchak (ed.), *The Working Sexes*. Vancouver: Institute of Industrial Relations, University of British Columbia.
Huber, Joan
    1973 *Changing Women in a Changing World*. Chicago: The University of Chicago Press.
Kandel, D., and G. Lesser
    1972 "Marital decision-making in American and Danish urban families." *Journal of Marriage and the Family* 34 (February): 134–138.
Kanter, R.
    1977 *Men and Women of the Corporation*. New York: Basic Books.
Knudsen, Dean
    1969 "The declining status of women: popular myths and the failure of functionalist thought." *Social Forces* 48 (December): 183–193.
Lamousé, Annette
    1969 "Family roles of women: a German example." *Journal of Marriage and the Family* 31: 145–152.
Lashuk, Maureen Wilson and George Kurian
    1977 "Employment status, feminism and symptoms of stress: the case of a Canadian Prairie city." *The Canadian Journal of Sociology* 2: 195–204.

Lopata, Helen
1971 *Occupation Housewife.* New York: Oxford University Press.
Lupri, E.
1965 "Industrialisierung und strukturwandlungen in der familie: ein interkultureller vergleich." *European Journal of Sociology* 5: 57–76.
1969 "Contemporary authority patterns in the West German family: a study in cross-national validation." *Journal of Marriage and the Family* 31: 134–144.
1969a "Theoretical and methodological problems in cross-national research." *Zeitschrift der Europäischen Gesellschaft für Ländliche Soziologie,* Vol. IX, 2: 99–113.
1976 "Gesellschaftliche differenzierung und familiale autorität." Pp. 323–352 in Eugen Lupri and Günther Lüschen (eds.), *Soziologie der Famile.* Zweite Auflage. Köln: Westdeutscher Verlag.
Marsh, Robert
1967 *Comparative Sociology.* New York: Harcourt, Brace & World.
Marx. Karl
1960 *Karl-Marx-Studienasugabe:* Bp. I: *Frühe Schriften;* Bd. II: *Thesen über Feuerbach;* Bd. III: *Die Deutsche Ideologie;* Bd. IV: *Politische Ökonomie.* Hersg. H. J. Lieber. Stuttgart: Enke.
1962 *Das Kapital. Marx Engels-Werke,* 23, 24 und 25. Berlin: Dietz
1964 Verlag.
Marx, Karl, and Frederick Engels
1963 *The German Ideology.* New York: International Publishers.
Meissner, M., Elizabeth W. Humphreys, Scott M. Meiss and William J. Scheu
1975 "No exit for wives: sexual division of labour and the cumulation of household demands." *The Canadian Review of Sociology and Anthropology* 12 (Pt. 1): 424–439.
Michel, A.
1967 "Comparative data concerning the interaction in French and American families." *Journal of Marriage and the Family* 29 (May): 337–344.
Mitchell, Juliet
1978 "Woman's estate." Pp. 142–154 in Alison M. Jaggar and Paula Rothenberg Struhl (eds.), *Feminist Frameworks.* New York: McGraw Hill.
Morgan, D. H. J.
1975 *Social Theory and the Family.* London: Routledge & Kegan Paul.
Myrdal, Alva
1967 "Foreword," in E. Dahlström (ed.), *The Changing Roles of Women and Men.* London: Duckworth & Co.
Myrdal, Alva, and V. Klein
1956 *Women's Two Roles: Home and Work.* London: Routledge & Kegan Paul.
Nye, F. I.
1976 "Husband-wife relationship." Pp. 262–281 in F. I. Nye and L. W. Hoffman (eds.), *Working Mothers.* San Francisco: Jossey-Bass Publishers.
Oakley, Ann
1972 *Sex, Gender, and Society.* London: Temple Smith.
1974 *The Sociology of Housework.* Bath, England: Pitman Press.
Olson, D., and R. Cromwell
1975 "Methodological issues in family power." Pp. 131–150 in R. Cromwell and D. Olson (eds.), *Power in Families.* New York: John Wiley.
O'Neil, William (ed.)
1972 *Women at Work.* Chicago: Quadrangle Books, Inc., and Toronto: Burns and MacEachern Ltd.
Oppenheimer, Valerie K.
1973 "Demographic influence on female employment and the status of women." *American Journal of Sociology,* Vo. 78 (January): 946–961.
1974 "The life-cycle squeeze." *Demography* 11: 237–245.

Oppong, C.
   1970 "Conjugal power and resources: an urban African example." *Journal of Marriage and the Family* 32: 676-680.

Parsons, Talcott
   1949 "The social structure of the family." Pp. 173-201 in Ruth Anshen (ed.), *The Family: Its Function and Destiny*. New York: Harper and Brothers.
   1955 "The American family: its relations to personality and the social structure," in Talcott Parsons and Robert F. Bales, *Family, Socialization and Interaction Process*. Glencoe: The Free Press.

Parsons, Talcott, and R. Bales
   1955 *Family, Socialization and Interaction Processes*. Glencoe, Illinois: The Free Press.

Platt, Wolfgang
   1972 *Die Familie in der DDR*. Frankfurt: Fischer Verlag.

Pleck, Joseph E.
   1977 "The work-family role system." *Social Problems* 24: 417-427.
   1978 "Men's Family Work: Three Perspectives and New Data". *The Family Coordinator* 28 (4): 481-488.

Pross, Helge
   1973 *Gleichberechtigung im Beruf? Eine Untersuchung mit 7000 Arbeitnehmerinnen in der EWG*. Frankfurt: Athenaum Verlag.

Rapoport, Robert and Rhona Rapoport
   1965 "Work and family in contemporary society." *American Sociological Review* 30 (June): 381-394.

Rapoport, R. and R. Rapoport
   1972 "Working women and the enabling role of the husband." Paper presented at the 12th Family Research Seminar, International Sociological Association, Moscow, (June).

Rodman, Hyman
   1967 "Marital power in France, Greece, Yugoslavia, and the United States: a cross-national discussion." *Journal of Marriage and the Family*, XXIX, 2 (May): 320-324.
   1972 "Marital power and the theory of resources in cultural context." Pp. 50-69 in Eugen Lupri and Günther Lüschen (eds.), *Comparative Perspectives on Marriage and the Family*. Special issue of the Journal of Comparative Family Studies III, 1 (Spring).
   1976 "Eheliche Macht und der Austausch von Ressourcen im Kulturellen Kontext." Pp. 121-142 in Eugen Lupri and Günter Lüschen (eds.), *Soziologie der Familie*. Köln-Opladent: Westdeutseher Verlag (2nd ed.).

Rossi, Alice
   1964 "The equality of women: an immodest proposal." *Daedalus* 93 (Spring): 607-652.

Safilios-Rothschild, C.
   1967 "A comparison of power structure and marital satisfaction in urban Greek and French families." *Journal of Marriage and the Family* 29: 345-352.
   1969 "Dual linkages between the occupational and family systems: a macrosociological analysis." *Signs* 1, 3, Pt. 2 (Spring): 51-60.
   1969 "Family sociology or wives' family sociology: a cross-cultural examination of decision-making." *Journal of Marriage and the Family* 31: 290-301.
   1970 "The study of family power structure: a review, 1960-1969." *Journal of Marriage and the Family* 32: 539-552.

Schmidt-Relenberg, N., et al.
   1976 *Familiensoziologie-Eine Kritik*. Stuttgart: Enke.

Simmel, Georg
   1904 "The sociology of conflict." *American Journal of Sociology* IX, (January): 490-525.
   1955 *Conflict and the Web of Group Affiliations*. Translation by Kurt H. Wolff and Reinhard Bendix. Chicago: The Free Press.

Smelser, Neil
   1959 *Social Change in the Industrial Revolution*. Chicago: The Univresity of Chicago Press.

Smith, Dorothy E.
- 1973 "Women, the family and corporate capitalism." Pp. 5–35 in M. Stephenson (ed.), *Women in Canada*. Toronto: New Press.
- 1975 "An analysis of ideological structures and how women are excluded: considerations for academic women." *Canadian Review of Sociology and Anthropology* 12: 353 369.

Sprey, J.
- 1972 "Family power structures: a critical comment." *Journal of Marriage and the Family* 34: 235–238.

Szalai, A. et al. (eds.)
- 1972 *The Use of Time*. The Hague: Mouton.

Szymanski, A.
- 1976 "The socialization of women's oppression." *Insurgent Sociologist*, Vol. 6, (Winter): 31–58.

Theodore, Anthena
- 1971 *The Professional Woman*. Cambridge, Mass.: Schenckman Publishing Co.

Thompson, E. P.
- 1963 *The Making of the English Working Class*. New York: Praeger.

Turk, J.
- 1975 "Uses and abuses of family power." Pp. 81–94 in R. Cromwell and D. Olson (eds.), *Power in Families*. New York: John Wiley.

Turk, J., and N. Bell
- 1972 "Measuring power in families." *Journal of Marriage and the Family* 34: 215–222.

Wilkening, E. A., and E. Lupri
- 1965 "Decision-making in German and American farm families: a crosscultural comparison." *Sociologia Ruralis* 5: 366–385.

Winston, Henry
- 1971 "Women's liberation: a class approach." *Political Affairs* 50 (July): 1–10.

Winston, Fern
- 1971 "The family: is it obsolete?" *Political Affairs* 50 (August): 56–69.

Young, Michael, and Peter Willmott
- 1975 *The Symmetrical Family*. Middlessex: Penguin Books.

Zaretsky, Eli
- 1976 *Capitalism, The Family, and Personal Life. A Canadian Dimension Pamphlet*. No publisher shown.

Zelditch, Morris
- 1955 "Role differentiation in the nuclear family: a comparative study." Pp. 307–342 in Talcott Parsons and Robert F. Bales (eds.), *Family, Socialization and Interaction Process*. New York: The Free Press.

PART TWO

WOMEN IN CAPITALIST COUNTRIES

A. NORTH AMERICA

The Changing Roles of Canadian Women in Family and Work: An Overview*

EUGEN LUPRI and DONALD L. MILLS

The University of Calgary, Calgary, Canada

> Women have always done society's dirty work, at first mainly in the home, now increasingly outside it.
> (W. L. O'Neill, 1972: 42)

Introduction

GIVEN THE PRIMACY assigned to economic variables in any advanced industrial society, the research attention sociologists have devoted to women's economic contribution has been relatively modest. This research deficit is a clear reflection of both the relatively low status women have experienced and still encounter in the productive sector of the economy and their ambivalent position in family and society at large. The reason for this neglect is quite obvious: The status of women is derived largely from men (Blake, 1974).

Even though several analyses assist greatly in furthering our understanding, the fact remains that systematic study of the interplay of family and work life has suffered from the lack of data from longitudinal studies that trace the changing nature of women's work and family roles[1]. This chapter examines some of the sociological

---

* We are grateful to Professors Merlin Brinkerhoff, Harry Hiller, Jarmila Horna, Carolyn Larsen, Marlene Mackie and Gladys Symons for their comments on previous drafts ot this chapter. Adelle Karmas provided able research assistance. Any errors are, of course, solely our responsibility. The data collection was partly supported by a grant from the University of Calgary Research Grants Committee.

1 Some notable exceptions are Ostry, 1968; the Royal Commission on the Status of Women in Canada, 1970; Spencer and Featherstone, 1970; Spencer, 1973; Skoulas, 1974; Boyd and Eichler, 1975; Meissner, 1975; Ambert, 1976; Cook, 1976; Gunderson, 1976; Schmid, 1976; Marchak, 1977; Stephenson, 1977; Armstrong and Armstrong, 1978; and Boyd, 1978; and it is the recent studies that are also concerned with the nature the change and the lack of implementation of recommended policies designed to correct gender-specific inequalities. For a detailed and updated annotated bibliography, see M. Eichler, et al. (1977).

The book by Pat Armstrong and Hugh Armstrong, *The Double Ghetto: Canadian Women*

information available and attempts to identify key issues associated with the changing role of Canadian women in family and work.

As already noted, this matter has not wholly escaped the attention of our social researchers. Two decades ago the Canada, Department of Labour (1959: 7) undertook a large-scale, one-time sample survey of urban married women working for pay "to see how their employment pattern is affected through the years by personal circumstances that arise from their married status." This is a recognition of the interdependence of family and employment. And a decade later to set an example for the nation by redressing the unequal job treatment of women, the federal government studied among its own employees the relevance of such things as marital and socieconomic statuses, family responsibilities, maternity leave policies, community child care facilities, and nursery schools (Judek, 1968).

In 1970 the resourceful and prestigious Royal Commission on the Status of Women in Canada predicted labour force participation rates for women from 1970 to 1980. First and foremost, predictions made for the younger age groups underestimated significantly the increase in the participation rates since 1970. In fact, the projections were already outdated within five years, for by 1975 the participation rates had already surpassed by a sizable margin the rates the experts predicted for 1980. Secondly, the Commission overestimated considerably the change for the older age groups. On the basis of the most recent data it is highly unlikely that the projections for the older age groups will become reality.

These two errors in prediction do serve, however, to highlight truly consequential social trends in Canadian life. Indeed, the single most dramatic and pervasive trend in the status of Canadian women since World War II has been the increase in the proportion of married women who work for pay.[2] The five-fold increase in the proportion of married women entering the labour force has been almost twice the increase for all women. But more important, the largest increase in labour force activity has been by the group generally viewed as least likely to work—mothers of preschool-age children. It is perhaps here that the Royal Commission, along with other experts, erred with respect to the increasingly significant role young married women were to play in the Canadian economy. Interestingly, the experts' error reflects traditional beliefs held by the vast majority of Canadians, that the mother's first and

---

    and Their Segregated Work (Toronto: McClelland and Stewart, 1978) is a recent study and one that shares many of the objectives of this overview. Unfortunately, it became available to us too late to have its promising materials integrated into this chapter.

2 In the ensuing text we use the terms "working" and "employed" as well as "nonworking" and "nonemployed" interchangeably to avoid repetitions: obviously, full-time housewives produce useful goods and services, but technically they are nonemployed according to official statistics. All statistics pertaining to labour force participation are based on official definitions of Statistics Canada (see Statistics Canada (1976), 1971 Census of Canada, Occupations, Vol. III, Part 2. Ottawa, Trade and Commerce (November): 16).

foremost obligation is to her home and children. It represents a most illustrative case of how normative expectations run counter to actual behaviour, i.e., young mothers entering the labour force at an ever-increasing rate despite apparent societal disapproval of such action.

Another pervasive trend in Canadian marriage relations during the past decade has been the marked increase in divorce rates reflecting, perhaps, strain in the marital relationship. Indeed, we find a systematic and steady increase in the divorce rates from World War II to the present, with dramatic increases in the past decade. From 1968, when the new Divorce Law went into effect, to 1977, the crude divorce rate made a five-fold increase, so almost one in three new marriages ended in formal dissolvement. A legitimate question raised by laymen and experts alike is: Does employment of married women outside the home increase the divorce rate? While there is widespread consensus among both professionals and laypersons that understanding the relationship between doing paid work and increase in the divorce rate is important, there seems to be little agreement about the nature of the relationship. Does marital strain lead women to seek employment outside the home, or does such work lead to marital strain? Is this a spurious relationship? Or are we, perhaps, trapped by what has become known as the ecological fallacy? These questions can only be answered adequately by longitudinal data which are not available in Canada.

For a better understanding of what is involved here, however, it may be useful to explore several potentially important contextual variables. Canada has seen a moderate level of industrialization in the twentieth century, but it has a unique pattern of growth because of its primary extractive economy. Moreover, to a greater extent than any other advanced industrialized nation in the world, Canada is owned and controlled financially by other nations, principally the U.S.A. (In more recent years both West Germany and Japan increasingly participate in foreign ownership and control.) Furthermore, Canada has been experiencing rapid urbanization, particularly during the most recent decades.

Even though Canada's vast area of land stretching from the Arctic to the 49th Parallel and the Great Lakes-St. Lawrence River Seaway, and from the Atlantic to the Pacific Oceans comprises nearly 10 million square kilometres, the population of around 24 million inhabitants is not large. About nine of ten Canadians live in a relatively small strip of territory that extends 150 kilometres north of the U.S. border. Put another way, 76 percent of the total population live in urban centers, and 56 percent in 23 metropolitan areas, most of which have experienced an impressive growth rate during the last decades.

In short, Canadian society possesses the characteristics of an urbanized society. Yet the lack of a fully-developed secondary industrial sector poses economic problems that are, perhaps, found in no other western industrialized nation. It is for this reason that Canada may also, in some respects, be compared to a developing nation. In fact, while cultural inundation from the U.S.A. through exposure to mass media, educational models, and similar life-styles undoubtedly has had its influence, the consequences for Canadian society often result in different social patterns.³

Preliminary to an adequate understanding of the changing role of women in family and work relations in modern industrial society is a need to account for the persistence of structural and interpersonal barriers to full gender equality; to demonstrate where these barriers are more likely to persist; and to explore social structures and processes that sustain them.

Specifically, the major aim of this analysis is to present an overview by examining empirically possible interrelationships between women's occupational and marital roles. Questions thereby raised bear directly on the problem of causality and concern how the institutions of marriage and work are interrelated, the limits of integration, and what areas of autonomy exist. In pursuing these questions we are forced to rely, by and large, on previously published data, primarily Canadian census materials. In addition, some survey and poll data also are incorporated in our analysis. The inherent pitfalls of drawing causal inferences from aggregate and trend data are manifold. Although the danger of the ecological fallacy looms, it is possible nevertheless to gain some general inferences about what appears to be occurring as well as what may lie ahead.

The following discussion is divided into two major parts. Part I deals with the changing role of Canadian women in family life and labour force participation. Trend data, broken down by a number of relevant variables, are presented and critically examined. Part II examines strains and stresses related to the intersection of occupational and familial roles. While the complexity of the problem and the unavailability of longitudinal data require caution and restraint in our interpretation, some apparent patterns, indicating strains and stresses in women's roles, clearly emerge.

Part I: Family Composition and Labour Force Activity

In attempting to trace the changing nature of women's social roles in Canadian society, special significance must be given to family and work roles. Attention first focuses on highlighting some of the changes in the marital composition of the total population. Such an analysis must be seen against the background of broader changes in the social structure.

---

3 The underlying assumption of many American and Canadian sociologists is that, by and large, Canadian social patterns can be equated with American social patterns. To us this is a questionable assumption. In fact, we find it much more useful in our research endeavours to assume the opposite. That is, analytically, we treat the existence of American-Canadian similarities as highly problematic.

Marital Status in the Demographic Context

Data in Tables 1 through 6 provide background information for Canada and place ascribed statuses such as age and sex and achieved statuses such as marital status in a demographic context over time. It should be noted that Canada, like many

Table 1

Percent Distribution of the Population 15 Years and Over by Selected Characteristics and Years, Canada

Year	Population (000s)		Single (%)		Married (%)		Widowed (%)		Divorced (%)	
	Male	Female	Male	Female	Male	Female	Male	Female	Male	Female
1901	1,816	1,708	44.8	38.2	51.1	52.9	4.1	8.8	—	—
1931	3,715	3,379	41.0	34.0	54.9	57.3	4.0	8.5	0.1	0.1
1951	4,920	4,837	32.1	25.7	63.8	64.5	3.8	9.4	0.3	0.4
1971	7,531	7,655	31.6	25.0	64.9	63.9	2.5	9.8	1.0	1.3
1976	8,429	8,666	31.3	24.6	64.9	63.4	2.2	9.8	1.4	2.1

Sources: Compiled from Statistics Canada, Vital Statistics, Vol. 11, Tables 1, 2, 11; 1976 Census of Canada, Bulletins 4.2, 4.3, 4.4, Tables 2, 6, 12; 1966 Census of Canada, Vol. 11, Table 78.

other industrialized nations, has experienced rapid expansion of both population and economic activity since the turn of the last century. It doubled its total population from 5,371,315 in 1901 to 10,376,786 in 1931, and more than doubled it again to 23,800,100 in 1978. Against this background of economic and demographic expansion, the data presented reflect several basic changes in the social structure that merit brief mention.

As may be seen in Table 1, the proportion of married, widowed, and divorced has increased for both males and females, while the proportion of singles decreased during the 75 years. Noteworthy are both the decline in the proportion of married females since the mid-1960's and the increase in widowed and divorced women. Canadian women's greater reluctance to remarry, their tendency to wait longer when they do, their greater life expectancy, together with the normative expectation to marry older men, may account for these female-male differences.

While the number of families has continued to increase over the years reflecting the continuous growth of Canada's population, the marriage rate has been declining the past two decades and is expected to decline further (Table 2). In sharp contrast, the divorce rate has seen a consistent and, in recent years, a very rapid increase. The decline in age at first marriage is undoubtedly related to both of these trends.

Age at first marriage has been declining consistently for both brides and grooms and the age difference between them is also gradually diminishing (Table 3). However, more recent and as yet unpublished data for 1977 corroborate what may already be

Table 2

Marriages and Divorces per 100,000 Population, 1921–1977, Canada

Year	Number of Marriages	Marriage Rate	Number of Divorces	Divorce Rate
1921	71,254	790	558	6
1931	68,239	640	700	7
1941	124,644	1,060	2,462	21
1951	128,408	920	5,270	38
1961	128,475	700	6,563	51
1971	191,324	890	29,685	138
1975	197,585	870	50,611	222
1976	193,343	840	54,207	236
1977	186,787	800	55,370	238

Sources: Compiled from Statistics Canada, Vital Statistics, Vol. 11, Tables 1, 2, 11; 1976 Census of Canada, Bulletins 4.2, 4.3, 4.4, Tables 2, 6, 12; 1966 Census of Canada, Vol. 11, Table 78.

Table 3

Average Age and Age Differences at First Marriage for Brides and Grooms, 1941–1976, Canada

Year	Bride	Groom	Differences in Age
1941	24.4	27.6	3.2
1951	23.8	26.6	2.8
1961	22.9	25.8	2.9
1971	22.6	24.9	2.3
1976	22.7	25.0	2.3

Sources: Compiled from Statistics Canada, Vital Statistics, Vol. 11, Tables 1, 2, 11; 1976 Census of Canada Bulletins 4.2, 4.3, 4.4, Tables 2, 6, 12; 1966 Census of Canada, Vol. 11, Table 78.

indicated in the 1976 figures, namely, that the decline appears to have reached its lowest level and that reversals may be expected in the future. Both the recent decline in fertility rates (Table 4) and the decrease in the number of children per family (Table 5) are indications of further contraction of the nuclear family in twentieth century Canadian society as is the yet relatively small but growing proportion of one-parent families.

Also, the number of childless couples has increased markedly the past decade along with a growing proportion of one-parent families headed by women (Table 6). These trends all reflec tbasic changes in the social structure and the expectation of greater variability in family patterns and values. They indicate also an increasing willingness of Canadians to accept a variety of alternatives to traditional family structures.

Table 4
General Fertility Rate, 1921-1977, Canada

Year	Number of Live Births	Fertility Rate
1921-30	249,017	3.30
1931-40	235,989	2.82
1941-50	324,811	3.20
1951-60	442,945	3.80
1961-65	456,534	3.60
1966-70	372,910	2.51
1971	362,187	2.19
1972	347,319	2.02
1973	343,373	1.93
1976	359,987	1.57
1977	360,733	1.55

Sources: Compiled from Statistics Canada, Vital Statistics, Vol. 11, Tables 1, 2, 11; 1976 Census of Canada, Bulletins 4.2, 4.3, 4.4, Tables 2, 6, 12; 1966 Census of Canada, Vol. 11, Table 78.

Table 5
Number of Families and Number of Persons per Family, 1966-1976, Canada

Year	No. of Families (000's)	Persons per Family	Children per Family
1966	4,518	3.9	1.9
1971	5,070	3.7	1.7
1974	5,359	3.6	1.6
1976	5,727	3.5	1.6

Sources: Compiled from Statistics Canada, Vital Statistics, Vol. 11, Tables 1, 2, 11; 1976 Census of Canada, Bulletins 4.2, 4.3, 4.4, Tables 2, 6, 12; 1966 Census of Canada, Vol. 11, Table 78.

Table 6
Families by Size and Type, 1961-1976, Canada

Year	Number of Families		One-parent with Female-Head (000's)	Number of Children of One-parent Families
	Two-parent (000's)	One-parent (000's)		
1961	3,800 (91.6%)	347 (8.4%)	272 (78.4%)	n.a.
1966	4,154 (91.8%)	371 (8.2%)	300 (80.8%)	2.2
1971	4,605 (90.5%)	477 (9.9%)	377 (79.0%)	1.8
1976	5,168 (90.2%)	559 (9.8%)	464 (83.0%)	n.a.

Legend: n. a. = not available
Sources: Compiled from Statistics Canada, Vital Statistics, Vol. 11, Tables 1, 2, 11; 1976 Census of Canada, Bulletins 4.2, 4.3, 4.4, Tables 2, 6, 12; 1966 Census of Canada, Vol. 11, Table 78.

Work Patterns

The proportion of Canadian women of working age in the work force, which was fewer than one in five in 1931, more than doubled during the 45-year reporting period. As seen in Table 7, the proportion increased two and one-half times by 1976,

Table 7

Female Labour Force Participation Rates by Marital Status, 1931–1976, Canada

Year	Participation Rate*				Married Women to Total Women in Labour Force
	Married %	Single %	Other %	Total Female %	%
1931	4	47	21	20	10
1941	4	80	20	21	10
1951	11	58	19	24	30
1961	22	54	23	30	50
1971	33	48	28	37	57
1976	43	56	31	45	61

Sources: Dominion Bureau of Statistics, 1931 Census, Vol. VII, Table 26; 1941 Census, Vol. II. Table 7, and Vol. VII, Table 5; 1951 Census, Vol. II, Tables 1 and 2, and Vol. IV, Table 19; and 1961 Census, Vol. III, Part 2, Table 9, and Vol. I, Part 3, Table 78; and Table 11, 1976 edition, *Women in the Labour Force*.

* Defined as the percentage of all persons aged 15 years and over who are in the labour force. The participation rate for married women is that percentage of all married women in the population who are in the labour force.

with the most rapid increase the past 15 years. Obviously, the marked rise in women's labour force participation rates not only has had a notable effect on the size and composition of the work force but, more important, has had significant impact on the life-styles of both men and women and the roles they play within the family context. Among the many factors promoting or discouraging labour force entry, those bearing upon changes in family roles are of immediate interest here.

Marital Status and Children

Single women have much higher rates of labour force activity than do married women. The singles' rate rose slightly more than one-fifth from 1931 to 1976. However, the participation rate of married women rose much more sharply, twelve-fold, over the same period. Correspondingly married females' share of the labour force in less than two decades went from 13% to 20% between 1961 and 1975, while their male counterparts decreased from 54% to 46%. Both single males and females showed essentially no change from 17.8% to 17.6%, and 11.3% to 11.5%, respectively during the same period (Statistics Canada, 1977).

The pattern of change is quite clear and significant. The participation rate for married women increased much faster than the rate for any other group. In 1976 the rates for married women and all women were almost identical. While marriage per se still reduces the labour force activity of women, participation rates for married women are expected to continue to rise and marital status per se will become a less significant factor in determining work force activity.

Children are one of the main factors deterring married women from seeking employment outside the home. They still have significantly lower participation rates. Although the presence of small children remains a significant factor in reducing the participation rates of married women, their participation in the work force has shown considerable growth (Table 8). In fact, married women with preschool-age children

Table 8

Labour Force Participation Rate of Mothers by School Attendance, Married Women and All Women, Canada, 1967 and 1973.

	1967	*1973*	*Growth Rate*
All Women	34%	37%*	10%
Married Women	28	34*	17
Total Women with Children	21	35	67
Women with only full-time School Children	28	42	50
Women with School and Preschool Children	15	26	73

Sources: Labour Canada. "Data on All Women and Married Women," *Women in the Labour Force* (1973 edition). Ottawa: Information Canada. Boyd, M., M. Eichler, and J. R. Hofley, "Women with Children," in Gail C. A. Cook (ed.), *Opportunity for Choice*. Ottawa: Statistics Canada, 1976, p. 29.

* 1972 data.

had the greatest growth rate between 1967 and 1973, an overall increase of 73 percent in those few years, compared with only 17 percent for all married women. This trend is also congruent with recent survey findings (Bruce, 1978) that show that children as a structural barrier to young mothers' employment is gradually breaking down. In sum, a second distinctive pattern of change is clearly emerging: young mothers with small children are re-entering and remaining in the work force, which largely explains the recent rise in the participation rate of married women.

The Age Factor

Important changes have occurred in the participation rates of women of all ages (Table 9). The comparison by age shows that even at the highest level of participation, Canadian married women's work activity differs dramatically over the course of their life cycle. Men's rates—not shown in Table 9—do not vary by stage in the life cycle, except for those in the very young age group, 14/15–19, and those in the very old age group, 65 years and older. Except for them, participation rates for men remain fairly constant at 87 to 93 percent across ages. Interestingly, the data in Table 9 viewed over time show that while increasing age diminishes married women's

Table 9

Age and Marital Status of Females, Showing Their Labour Force Participation Rate in Canada 1951–1977

Year	Total Participation Rate All Females	Age and Marital Status of Females											
		14/15–19		20–24		25–34		35–44		45–54		55–64	
		S*	M*	S	M	S	M	S	M	S	M	S	M
1951	24%	38%	16%	76%	17%	76%	11%	71%	11%	64%	9%	59%	4%
1961	30	33	23	80	26	77	19	74	21	69	21	56	12
1971	37	31	34	78	47	85	36	80	37	79	36	64	23
1977	46	46	54	79	61	86	50	81	53	75	46	59	28
Rate of Increase	92%	24%	238%	4%	259%	12%	355%	14%	382%	21%	411%	20%	600%
"Stouffer Index of Change"**	29	13	45	13	53	42	44	34	47	31	40	20	25

Source: Census of Canada, 1951, Vol. X, Table 17, and 1961, Vol. XXX, Tables 3 and 15; *Women in the Labour Force*, Labour Canada, 1971 Facts and Figures, Table 11; *Women in the Labour Force* (1976 ed.), Labour Canada, Table 37; *Women in the Labour Force* (1977 ed.), Labour Canada, Table 8.

* "S" = single; "M" = married.
** A measure that accounts for the fact that an increase from one level of percentage to some maximum percentage (such as 100 percent) will be affected by the size of the base percentage. It is a more sensitive and more relevant measure than the "rate of increase" used above that takes the percentage at one time and uses the absolute percentage points between that one and the succeeding one as a proportion of the original percentage. Using the Stouffer approach, for example, an increase from 75 to 85 percent is twice as great as an increase from, say, 50 to 60 percent. The formula is:

$$\frac{\text{Difference in percentage points from Time A to Time B} \times 100}{\text{Difference between 100\% and Time A percentage}}$$

Stouffer, Samuel A., et al., *Studies in Social Psychology in World War*, II Vols. I–IV (Princeton: Princeton University Press:, 1949/50); see, especially, Vol. IV: *Measurement and Prediction*.

probability of being in the work force, the change percentage increases in a very regular pattern with increasing age. Over the quarter of a century from 1951 to 1975/76, the greatest increase in rate of labour force participation was by married women 55–64 years old, followed by married women in the next youngest age groups, 45–54, 33–44, and so on. However, Table 9 also shows that participation rates for the older age groups are still relatively low compared with rates for younger ones. Because the measure of change by proportionate increase in the initial level is inadequate for comparisons whose baselines vary for the two time periods compared, we also use a more sensitive and relevant measure of change ("Stouffer Index of Change"). On the basis of this measure, the greatest change in work activity was among married women 20–24 years old, followed by the age group, 35–44 (Table 9). This finding corroborates our earlier observation of a new pattern of rising labour force participation among youthful mothers. The high rate of increase among married women in the 35–44 age group reflects the "labour force re-entry phenomenon" observed also in many other industrialized countries.

Education

The striking relationship between educational attainment and female employment in Canada has been well established in the research of Ostry (1968), Allingham and Spencer (1968), Spencer and Featherstone (1970), and Skoulas (1974), with a direct relationship found between educational level of females and the likelihood of their holding or seeking paid work. For females, noteworthy increases occurred from 1961 to 1976 whereas, for males, the participation rates have not altered appreciably. The highest rate of change was among women with university education–an increase in participation from 48 percent in 1961 to 67 percent in 1976. The corresponding rates for males remained constant at around 91–92 percent. This pattern also holds for both men and women with high school education. Yet it is not just those appropriately trained who are more likely to be hired.

Sangster (1973: 55) and Symons (1978: 17) have shown that important attitudes are shaped in the primary, secondary and tertiary educational institutions with the result that females do not develop interests or pre-occupational skills in a full array of work activities. Instead females ultimately become concentrated in humanities, business and commercial, personal service, medical and community services programs in high school, community colleges, and universities; thus, they avoid sciences and applied sciences courses.

Despite this self-imposed and "guided" channelling, an increasing proportion of women is becoming more highly educated (Zsigmond and Rechnitzer, undated)– inducing what Motuz (1974: 3) has termed "a direct and indirect effect on participation in the labour force." The indirect effect influences attitudes toward marriage age (e.g., later or not at all), child-bearing (e.g., deferred and fewer), and occupation (e.g., potentially high reward career). The direct effect is most noticeable with married women–as observed in the sophisticated econometric study by Skoulas (1974: 88):

> ... even when education was used as a proxy for the nonpecuniary aspects of a job, supplementing the wife's market wage variable, the findings indicate a positive relationship between wife's education and her propensity to be in the labour force.

Beyond the secondary level, Canadian women are not so well educated as men, and accordingly, are placed in jeopardy as far as a wide range of job opportunities is concerned. And it is a double jeopardy for married women; they are less likely to work outside the home, and when they do, they are the most vulnerable and, thus, more likely to be unemployed–just one of several structural barriers to full gender equality in the world of work.

Occupation

Canada's labour force is characterized by gross discrepancies between females' and males' occupations (Table 10). Equally significant is that distributions over time show but limited erosion of these sex-linked patterns. This persistence of sex role segregation has been supported by recent survey data.

Brinkerhoff (1977), who surveyed a sample of high school students in a large Western Canadian city, identified several objective and subjectively perceived barriers that, together with occupational sex-typing, all operate "to funnel girls' choices into traditional occupations" (301). Women's work has been stereotyped to reflect socially "desirable" attributes of female roles as sexual partners (compliance and non-competitiveness), homemakers (tolerance of routine and uncomplaining tirelessness), and mothers (nurturance and forbearance). No doubt the alleged distinction of "instrumental" versus "expressive" as linked to male and female role activities (Parsons and Bales, 1955) has gained widespread attention and, in part, has provided these stereotypes with a theoretical legitimation. Furthermore, it is not uncommon for employers to characterize women as "temperamentally unsuited" for managerial work. And although females have proportionately a greater involvement in professional and technical occupations, the occupations are overwhelmingly teaching and nursing. It is worth noting that this participation pattern has not altered over the decades, whereas men have markedly increased their professional and technical work, particularly in the high status (remuneration, prestige) occupations in this category.

In contrast, the bureaucratization of clerical activities has absorbed the largest share of women seeking paid work; and clerical occupations have been thought ideally suited to the circumstance of married women—unconcerned with careers as they are often thought to be because they deliberately seek part-time and part-life employment.

Also of interest (Table 10) is the decreased share taken up by service (particularly domestic personal service) occupations in the female labour force as this type of work has become mechanized in the home. Analogously, the decreasing involvement of women in factory-production, process work is a consequence of mechanization and unionization which have been inhospitable to females sharing the enhanced reward systems of assembly-line work, while males have benefitted more and more from this reorganization of industrial activity.

Table 10

Labour Force 15 Years and Over, By Sex, Showing Percentage Distribution by Occupation Divisions*, Canada, 1931–1971

Census Year	Manager[1] F%[10] M[10]	Prof. Tech.[2] F% M	Clerical[3] F% M	Sales F% M	Service Recr.[4] F% M	Transp. Commo.[5] F% M	Farmers[6] F% M	Other Extract.[7] F% M	Craft. Produc.[8] F% M	Labour[9] F% M
1931	1.6 6.5	17.8 3.9	18.0 4.7	7.0 5.0	33.8 4.2	2.4 5.8	3.6 33.7	— 4.4	14.0 18.6	1.7 13.4
1941	2.0 6.6	15.7 4.7	18.6 4.8	7.1 4.4	34.2 4.5	1.7 6.0	2.3 31.6	— 6.0	17.0 23.8	1.4 7.6
1951	3.3 9.4	14.5 5.4	28.1 6.3	8.7 4.6	21.4 6.6	2.9 7.3	2.8 19.5	— 5.3	16.5 27.4	1.8 8.1
1961	3.3 10.5	15.8 7.8	29.6 7.1	8.6 5.8	23.0 8.7	2.2 7.7	4.4 12.5	— 3.9	11.9 28.9	1.2 7.1
1971	3.3 11.4	18.2 11.6	34.5 7.1	7.9 6.1	19.7 9.3	1.5 7.5	3.8 7.7	— 2.7	9.6 29.5	1.3 7.2
Rate of Increase	106 75	2 197	92 51	13 22	−42 121	−38 29	6 −77	— −39	−31 59	−24 −46
"Stouffer Index of Change"	17 52	5 80	201 25	10 12	−213 53	−9 18	2 −392	— −18	−51 131	−4 −72

Source: Statistics Canada, 1971 Census of Canada, "Occupations-Historical, for Canada and Provinces," Vol. III, Part 2, Table 1. June 1978.

a The total female labour force in 1931 was 663,493 and male 3,244,988; counterparts in 1971 were: female 2,960,098 and male 5,648,606, including those whose occupation was "not stated."
b Rate of Increase = comparison of 1931 and 1976 proportions of labour force by means of percentage increase or decrease.
c Stouffer Index of Change (see description in Table 9).
d Numbers are too small to warrant calculation of percentage of change in distribution or Stouffer Index of Change.
1 Manager = managerial occupations.
2 Prof. Tech. = professional and technical occupations.
3 Clerical = clerical occupations.
4 Service Recr. = service and recreation occupations.
5 Transp. Commo. = transport and communication occupations.
6 Farmers = farmers and farm workers.
7 Other Extract. = other extractive, including loggers and related workers; fishermen, trappers and hunters; miners, quarrymen and relate workers.
8 Craft. Produc. = craftsmen, production process and related workers.
9 Labour = labourers.
10 F% = percentage of female labour force; M% = percentage of male labour force.
* Occupations for 1931, 1941, 1951 and 1971 were rearranged or recoded on the basis of the 1961 Canada Classification.

The tenacity of occupational segregation according to sex may be seen clearly in Table 11, which shows illustrative professional occupations over four decades. Whether they are "female" or "male" occupations, they desegregate quite slowly.

Table 11
Percentage Distribution of Working Females and Males By Leading Occupational Groups in Canada for Selected Years

	OCCUPATIONAL GROUP AND SEX			
Year	Professional		Clerical	
	F^1 %	M^1 %	F %	M %
1931[a]	18	3	18	4
1941[a]	15	4	19	5
1951[a]	14	4	27	6
1961[c]	15[b]	8[b]	29	7
1971[c]	16	11	31	7
1976[d]	19[e]	12[e]	35	7

[1] F=Female; M=Male.
[a] 1931–1951 data from Statistics Canada. "Labour Force", 1951, Vol. IV, Table 2.
[b] Includes professional and technical occupations.
[c] Statistics Canada, 1971 Census of Canada, "Occupations-Historical for Canada and Provinces," Vol. III, Part 2, Table 1 (June 1978).
[d] Statistics Canada, The Labour Force. December 1976, Table 4d.
[e] Includes: Natural Sciences, Engineering and Mathematics; Social Sciences; Religion; Teaching; Medicine and Health; Artistic, Literary and Recreational Occupations.

Moreover, males move into "female" professions usually only when the extrinsic reward system becomes substantially better, while women are more likely to enter "male" professions for their intrinsic satisfactions. In fact, from 1931 to 1976, for example, the proportion of the female labour force doing professional work remained relatively constant (18% to 19%), whereas the male labour force share increased fourfold (3% to 12%). Thus, the enormous growth in female clerical work has provided the major portion of employment for the burgeoning Canadian female labour force.

Education and Occupation

Consider the interplay of education and occupation for the two sexes (Table 12), for example, in elite managerial and administrative occupations. Women possessing a university degree and the obvious impact of education on occupational attainment cannot offset or counteract the overriding salience of sex status — an advantage which holds in all instances save for those least educated. Indeed, a substantial proportion of university-educated women find themselves relegated to clerical work. The lowly "services" together with clerical work, teaching, and nursing are the preponderant paid activities for females in Canada, and education fails to liberate women (and men) from persistent patterns of segregation according to sex.

Table 12

*Percentage Distribution of the Labour Force by Selected Occupations,
For Selected Levels of Schooling and Sex, Canada, 1971*[a]

Occupation	Less than Grade 9		Grades 12 and 13		Completed Vocational[b]		University Degree		All Educ. Levels	
	F[d] %	M[d]	F %	M	F %	M	F %	M	F %	M
Managerial and Administrative[c]	1	1	3	8	3	6	6	19	4	14
Teaching	—	—	7	1	7	2	41	20	10	7
Health & Medicine	3	—	12	1	20	2	12	10	15	27
Clerical	9	4	47	12	38	6	15	4	43	16
Services	28	10	8	9	12	10	3	2	20	21
Product Fabricating[e]	14	10	1	8	2	15	—	1	7	16

[a] Labour Canada. "Women in the Labour Force, Facts and Figures. Part 3-Miscellaneous,' 1976. Table 10, pp. 27–38.
[b] Completed vocational course.
[c] All educational levels.
[d] F=Female; M=Male.
[e] Product fabricating, assembling and repairing.
— Less than .5%.

Part II: Strains and Stresses

In this part we analyze some data from both census and survey materials—data that reflect strains and stresses among working wives, housewives, and divorced as well as unemployed women. As the previous trend analysis has shown, married women's entry into the labour force accounts for the sharp increase in the overall female labour force participation rate over the past decades, with a noteworthy increase over the past five years. These trend data also clearly reflect a new pattern of rising work participation among youthful mothers as well as the labour force "re-entry phenomenon" among middle-aged married women.

It also should be recalled that since 1960 the increased tendency of married women to work more than offsets the greater proclivity to marry and to marry at a lower age. Middle-aged married women, perhaps more than any other group, provide an excellent setting for the study of the interrelationship of work and family activities and the stresses and strains inherent in the roles of working married women. It is our contention that these age groups also represent stages in the family life cycle that affect married men and women differently. Furthermore, the life cycle "squeeze" (Oppenheimer, 1974) provides a most powerful motive for middle-aged women to enter or re-enter the labour force.

Associated strains and stresses outside the work place are examined in the following dimensions: societal attitudes, role overload, dissatisfaction in marriage and work, divorce, underemployment and unemployment, and egalitarianism.

Attitude of Society

While the trends sketched above will undoubtedly continue, still the vast majority of all Canadian working women participate in economic activity only as an adjunct to their primary role inside the home, notwithstanding the recent rapid increase in the number of widowed, divorced, and separated women and the growing proportion of households headed by women. Moreover, Armstrong and Armstrong (1975) contend that the majority of Canadian women work out of financial necessity. Similarly, Connelly forcefully argues that "married women are 'freed' to work because of the creation of 'necessities' which in fact determine their need to work"; thus she believes "Canadian women are used as a reserve army" in the labour force which also explains their state of "oppression" (Connelly, 1977: 26).

In addition whether one looks at the increase in the proportion of married women in the labour force, the age distribution of those working, the types of jobs and occupations married women hold, or the comparative earnings of women and men, full equality has not yet been achieved and likely will not be achieved for a long time. McDonald (1975: 4) shows that "... women in Canada who work full-time earn on the average about 60 percent as much as male full-time workers ... and (more important) the gap is increasing."

Both Canadian men and women assume that the primary obligation of a woman is to her home and family. In response to the question, "Do you feel that mothers with preschool-age children should stay home and spend full-time with their children?" three out of four (75%) Canadians believe that mothers should stay home with their children (Women in Canada, 1976: 50). Suprisingly, a breakdown by age and sex showed no significant difference in attitudes toward mothers working. The same survey, done at the end of International Women's Year (December, 1975), found that one out of every four (26%) Canadians held firmly to the traditional male attitude, which perceives women as having relatively limited abilities and few roles outside the home. Women were just as convinced of this stereotype as were men. Yet only about one in seven (15%) of the 1,117 Canadians interviewed in this national sample strongly disagreed with the statement that "Work of equal value should get equal pay regardless of sex." Men and older people of both sexes are somewhat more likely to hold this sexist attitude. Almost four in ten (39%) Canadians agreed with the statement "It is justifiable to pay women less than men because they are a greater risk and are more likely to change employment or quit because of home circumstances." And more than one-fifth (22%) agreed that men should be given preference in all kinds of jobs and positions–an attitude more widely held among men and more widely accepted by older than by younger people.

Gibbins, Ponting and Symons (1978) provided corroborative data in an attempt to assess to what extent feminist perspectives have affected the Canadian consciousness. They presented the following statement to a cross-section of 1,832 Canadians in 1976: "When children are young, a mother's place is in the home"; not surprisingly, more than four out of five Canadians agreed with the statement, and the researchers found no significant differences between females and males. Along the same line they found that only one out of five Canadians disagreed with the statement "Although a wife's career may be important, she should give priority to helping her husband advance his career." Schreiber (1975: 72) comes to the same conclusion and puts it more pointedly by saying "...Canadian women (in 1971) were not so eager to partake of the benefits of 'liberation' as otherwise might have been supposed from a casual perusal of women's liberation literature." Boyd (1974: 17), in an analysis of Canadian public opinion data, sums up well our contention, when he says that "... negative attitudes towards married women who have young children and who work were still very strong throughout the 1960's and 1970's."

As these survey materials document, it is clearly normative for women to give primacy to their home and children. Because this general attitude is a social reality rather than individually determined, employed wives are under the constant pressures and contraints that arise from the discrepancies between personal and group norms. Canadian society's negative attitude toward the working wife affects particularly the self-esteem of young mothers in the labour force.

Role Overload

On weekends when many housewives reduce their household tasks, employed women typically double the time they spend on housework in an effort to catch up (Szalai, et al., 1972). Working wives are thus very dependent on the "help" of their husbands which, surveys have shown, is more likely forthcoming when the wife is employed (Lupri, 1976; Brinkerhoff and Lupri, 1978), but is usually quite insufficient in amount. As a result, working women with families tend to be very hard pressed. This and more has been most convincingly demonstrated for the Canadian setting by Meissner, et al. (1975).

While Szalai and his collaborators had to rely on aggregate data from independent samples of men and women, Meissner and colleagues interviewed, separately, married couples from metropolitan Vancouver and were thus able to compare the time records of both husband and wife. By and large, their results support those of international surveys and clearly confirm that the stage of the life cycle affects working husbands and wives differently.

According to Meissner and his colleagues "...these data indicate that most married women do the regular, necessary, and most time-consuming work in the household every day. In view of the small and selective contribution of their husbands, the women can anticipate doing it for the rest of their lives." In terms of the tremendous differences between husbands and wives, "... the detailed time budgets tell a story of the dependent labour of married women whose entire days are affected, activity by activity, while their husbands keep the day of 'their' work and leisure intact in its overall composition and its component activities" (p. 433). According to their data, the husbands' contribution to housework, measured in actual hours spent, remains essentially the same for older or younger and more or less educated husbands, whether or not their wives work for pay or have a child under ten years of age. Meissner's group argue convincingly that the rising demand for the employment of married women contains an inherent contradiction and they sum up their analysis by saying that "... paid work offers to married women the potential of at least some financial independence from their husbands but, at the same time, confirms their domestic dependency in the menial and subordinate character of much of their paid work" (p. 437/38). Hence, as appropriately put in the title of their report, "No Exit for Wives."

Mackie (1976), analyzing data on the attitudes of working wives towards their combined housewife-paid worker roles in an urban centre in Western Canada, found that working wives recognize and resent the stress placed upon them by excessive demands on their time and energy. More than one-half (53%) of the 198 working women interviewed agreed with the statement, "A lot of times I feel so tired," as compared with about one-third (35%) of those wives (229) who were not in the labour force. And more than two-fifths (43%) agreed with the statement, "It makes me mad to see my husband relax while I do housework."

Cook (1975: 28) in a recent and comprehensive study of working mothers concluded: "Whether married women work or not, they get little assistance with housework from their husbands. When they work, they must still carry the major responsibility for care of home and children."

There is no doubt, role overload and role conflict exist. Attempts to integrate work with home life are associated with an intensification of worries and concerns (Burke and Weir, 1976: 284). Although one would expect that the increase of stress might be reflected in the health and attitudes of working wives, this was not found by Burke and Weir (1976), who assessed the state of physical and mental health among working women and housewives. "Working women appeared to be in better physical and emotional health than housewives, held more positive attitudes towards life in general, and towards marriage in particular" (284/85).[4]

---

4 Cumming, Lazer, and Chisholm (1975) come to the same conclusion. They used suicide as an index of role strain and found no support for a role-conflict, role-overload model. Working wives have lower suicide rates than nonworking wives.

It appears that work outside the home opens up avenues for the construction of a new reality (Berger and Luckman, 1966) for married women and constitutes a powerful liberating release from the monotony and drudgery of housekeeping. Indeed, some recent studies in the United States have shown that employed wives are not so vulnerable to depression as are full-time housewives (Mostow and Newberry, 1975).

Outside work itself, unlike housework, is more likely to contribute to both self-concept and self-esteem. Yet the social reality of traditional marital roles prevents the housewife from exploring these alternative constructions. She is physically isolated and socially insulated from women whose occupations or jobs are a component of their identity. Thus, the social reality of traditional housework may indeed constitute a powerful depressant for the homemaker. An alternative social construction which includes a redefinition of the traditional male role–one which is shared equally by both husbands and wives–is not yet widely accepted.

Perhaps the requirements that presently govern work relations on the job and those that govern marital relations in the nuclear family are incompatible and do not permit complete integration of egalitarian norms and gender equality in the home. In a seminal analysis of the relationship between the division of labour and sexual inequality, Meissner (1977) maintains that the hierarchical, competitive, and instrumental nature of the work place makes it difficult for men to fulfill co-operative and open-ended requirements so characteristic of family, marriage and household relations in the nuclear setting. And yet full gender equality will not occur without more changes in household responsibilities (Gunderson, 1976), that is, changes that reflect more household activity on the part of husbands.

Dissatisfaction in Marriage and Work

Disenchantment in marriage has been a popular topic for discussion among both Canadian laypersons and professionals. Despite its intriguing nature, marital satisfaction among Canadian couples has been a neglected area of investigation. Our assessment relies entirely on a report by Lupri and Frideres (1976, 1981) who based their findings on a cross-section of 464 couples, with spouses interviewed separately, in an urban center of Western Canada. The data included here document once more the existence of what Safilios-Rothschild (1969) perceptively called two "realities" in the marital relationship–the husband's subjective reality and the wife's subjective reality–two perspectives that often do not coincide.

Lupri and Frideres (1981) found that marital satisfaction among these Canadian couples follows two patterns–once the data are broken down by family life cycle. They found, most important, that the emerging pattern is a curvilinear one for both husbands and wives. Particularly for wives, there is a substantial decrease in general satisfaction associated with a high level of negative feelings in marital interaction during the child-bearing and child-rearing phases. The lowest stage of marital satisfaction for both husband and wife is reached in middle age (about 45–54); after that a substantial increase in marital satisfaction is experienced by both spouses, particularly by the wives.

A second pattern emerges: It appears that husbands and wives are differentially affected by family life cycle experiences. In general, family life experiences are associated with marital satisfaction more for wives than for husbands. Wives' marital satisfaction starts higher, falls lower, and ends up higher than their husbands' marital satisfaction.

A breakdown by socioeconomic class revealed an interesting pattern as well. While the curvilinear relationship was maintained, wives of the upper classes were consistently less satisfied than middle-class wives and the latter, in turn, showed consistently lower marital satisfaction than did lower-class wives.

The literature on marital satisfaction and work status tends to suggest that working wives should be more satisfied with their marriages than wives not in the labour force. Lupri and Frideres' data do not support such a claim and, in fact, provide data that tend to point in the opposite direction.

While both groups of women follow the same curvilinear pattern, nonworking wives (except in the age group 35–44) show more marital satisfaction than do working wives. These Canadian findings lend modest support to the role accumulation hypothesis (Nye, 1976), which posits that outside employment of the wife generates additional stress which decreases marital satisfaction. However, the small sample (464 couples) did not permit finer distinctions, e.g., whether working wives sought employment for intrinsic or extrinsic rewards, whether their husbands were supportive of their working, or whether the wives were working part-time of full-time. Because of these limitations, further longitudinal data are needed to show that the wife's outside employment leads to decreased marital satisfaction.[5]

Nevertheless, the interdependence of familial roles and employment may be further explored on the basis of available data. In the work sphere, it is only since the late 1960's that Canadian men's and women's contrasting work attitudes have been measured periodically, systematically, and nation-wide. There is some evidence, according to the Canadian Gallup Poll, that women were less inclined than men in recent years "to agree that they fit their job" and according to Burstein, et al. (1975: 55), "female displeasure with the qualitative aspects of work is increasing." Yet in the nationwide Labour Canada survey of 1974, Burstein and his colleagues found that women appear to be more satisfied than men with their supervisors at work, and slightly more satisfied with their job's personal relations and its comfort and convenience. Men and women were equally dissatisfied with the job challenge affor-

---

[5] This is only one of the major objectives of the longitudinal research being undertaken by Professors Jarmila Horna, Eugen Lupri and Donald L. Mills of the University of Calgary, Calgary, Alberta, Canada, aimed at tracing the relationships of family and work roles for both men and women over time.

ded, but the men were somewhat more satisfied with their promotional opportunities and financial returns. This suggests that women have quite different pay expectations and that they tolerate other employment conditions that men would find objectionable. "The average female is far more likely than her male counterpart to be engaged in part-time work, and to be receiving a lower salary at a lower level job that is probably in the service sector" (Burstein, et al., 1975: 56). It is little wonder, then, that women are less psychologically committed to their work.

Divorce Trends

Projecting present trends shows a continuing increase in the proportion of married women entering the labour force and in the number of couples seeking a divorce. Thus, while the exact causal nexus that may link these two phenomena has yet to be established, interesting parallel trends in Canadian divorce patterns merit closer scrutiny.

First, the rates (Table 2) show a sharp and consistent increase since 1968 when the new Divorce Act, which liberalized divorce laws in Canada, went into effect. (Estimated for 1980 is one divorce for every three new marriages.[6]) Secondly, and perhaps more important, when the rates are broken down by province, those that enjoy the highest female labour force participation rates like Alberta, British Columbia and Ontario, also experience the highest divorce rates. Thirdly, Canada's divorce rates do not follow the patterns of divorce in other comparable industrialized nations. The history of the divorce laws, the ethnic mosaic, the religious diversity and the variation in population density, all tend to mitigate against uniform patterns (Peters, 1976).

Does employment of married women increase the divorce rate? General reviews of the research on divorce and female labour force participation usually agree that marital satisfaction and work outside the home are related. There is no agreement, however, on the direction of the causal influence. As in so many other instances, "before-and-after" studies that examine women's and men's roles before and after employment of women are lacking. In the absence of longitudinal data, a cursory inspection of some aggregate data must suffice.

The age distribution of spouses at time of divorce, the duration of their marriage, and a breakdown by age cohorts all indicate some interesting, uniquely Canadian patterns. All reflect the rather high average age at divorce for both husbands and wives: 40 and 37 years, respectively, in 1973. Exactly one-half of all divorced Canadian couples had been married 13 years or longer; one in four, 20 years or longer. The finding that Canadian wives who married under age 20 are highly vulnerable is

---

6 Because of the decline in the marriage rate (800 in 1977), these ratios tend to be inflated somewhat.

consistent with American data. While only one-fourth of all brides were under 20, nearly one-half of all divorced wives had married before they were 20 years old.

The question is: Do these patterns reflect a backlog of unhappy marriages or a long-term trend? Working outside the home may be conducive to the development of nonfamilial interests and activities. The fact that the trend toward wider participation of married women in the labour force in Canada and elsewhere parallels the marked increase in divorce rates suggests that research in this area may be especially fruitful for understanding alternative family and work patterns of the future.

The steady increase in the divorce rate over the past decade has made a large segment of the Canadian population available for remarriage. While most divorced people eventually remarry, Canadian women are less likely to do so than Canadian men. Yet, the remarriage rates are high for both sexes: about 90 percent of divorced men and 75 percent of divorced women eventually remarry. Not only are Canadian women less likely to remarry, they also wait much longer than men to remarry, particularly longer than the younger men (Kuzel and Krishnan, 1973). In addition the normative expection that women marry older men and that divorced men marry single women, as well as women's greater longevity, mitigate against an equal proportion of divorced men and women. Thus, in Canada, as in most Western societies, divorced women outnumber divorced men, more than three to two in 1976 (Statistics Canada, 1978a: Table 17).

Boyd (1977) has recently documented the plight of divorced and separated women in Canada. By all the measures considered, divorced women display more extreme employment patterns than any other group examined. For example, the overall labour force participation rate of 67 percent for divorced women is about 11 percent higher than the one for single women. The rate for divorced women with children under six year of age is striking: their participation rate is 52 percent, almost twice the rate for a comparable married group with children under six and husband present, only four percent less than the rate for single women (56%), and more than 20 percent higher than the rate for working wives with no children (40%). Not surprisingly, the female age group 35–44 has the highest paid work participation rate (73%) of all age groups, compared with 55 percent for the same age group with the husband absent and about 40 percent for those with husbands present.

When income is considered, sexual discrimination surfaces very distinctly. In fact, the average family headed by a divorced women had an income ($ 4,237) in 1972, only half that of a household headed by a divorced male ($ 8,622) (Boyd, 1977: 59). From the evidence, then, divorced women appear to be the ones that experience the greatest persistence of labour force inequalities.

Underemployment and Unemployment

It is no suprise to find that currently nearly all (98%) Canadian married men work "full-time", while their female counterparts (78%) work less than 30 hours per week (Statistics Canada, 1978b: 38). More married woman would like to work full-time, but family obligations, childcare responsibilities, and a severe shortage of adequate childcare facilities are barriers to full-time employment. Furthermore, certain employment practices deliberately dictate the hiring of females on a part-time, "casual labour" basis to avoid paying regular wages and providing attendant "fringe benefits." These barriers and practices create a pattern of female underemployment—a powerful structural barrier making it hard for women to achieve sexual equality in the all-important area of work (Marsden, 1977).

Although the crude unemployment rate remained less for women than for men during the three decades preceding the mid-1970's (e.g., 2.5% and 3.6% in 1946), in recent years (e.g., 1977) women have experienced higher rates (9.5%) than men (7.3%) (Gunderson, 1976: 106). Moreover, the sophisticated multivariate analysis by McIlveen and Sims (1978: 33) of the frequency that individuals experience unemployment and the length of time they are unemployed—called "unemployment flow"—show that between 1964 and 1975 Canadian rates increased for women of all ages such that "higher frequency and longer duration combined to produce often dramatic increases in unemployment rates."

Marriage contributes to unemployment as it is associated with a "higher unemployment rate for females and a lower unemployment rate for males, other things being equal" (Gunderson, 1976: 127). Besides, when other factors are held constant, marriage per se actually raises female unemployment about two-thirds of a percentage point and lowers male unemployment slightly more than five percentage points (111). That marital status affects married women in the labour force more negatively than it does married men is clearly demonstrated in Table 13 which presents data on employment flows for July, 1978. Among both job losers and job leavers, married women are the ones highly overrepresented and most vulnerable to unemployment.

Gunderson's data also show that "having a university degree as opposed to an elementary school education or less did not significantly reduce female unemployment, but did reduce male unemployment" (1976: 111). In addition, certain anomalies in data collection together with the propensity of women to become discouraged and "drop out" of the labour force during an economic recession all conspire to underestimate "real" female unemployment (Gunderson, 1976: 103–104)—a hidden unemployment, which in effect compounds the unemployment patterns described here.

A mixture of female ambivalence about doing paid work (particularly found among wives) together with reluctant employers who think that women are not sufficiently committed to doing paid work, reinforces employer resistance to training

Table 13

Flows of Unemployment* by Sex and Marital Status, July, 1978, Canada

Marital Status and Sex	Share in Labour Force %	Job Losers %	Job Leavers %
Single Men	29.3	45.5	50.5
Single Women	33.3	29.8	29.3
Married Men	67.2	49.6	44.4
Married Women	57.2	60.9	60.6
Other Men	3.5	5.0	5.1
Other Women	9.6	9.8	9.6
ALL MEN	62.7	64.5	48.8
ALL WOMEN	37.3	35.5	51.2

Source: Statistics Canada, *The Labour Force*. Ottawa. Table 4, p. 17, and Table 41, p. 55.
* The seasonally adjusted unemployed level was 927,000 persons in July, 1978, or 8.4%.

and promotion programmes—a policy Gunderson describes as "last to be hired, first to be fired" (1976: 104–105).

Egalitarianism

Familial Equality. It is generally inferred that an increase in the wife's outside employment will lead to greater egalitarianism in family and society (Brown, 1978; Pool, 1978). Such an interpretation is often based on the personal resource theory, which ignores class and power dimensions of the larger social structure, which men control. It is for these reasons that Eichler (1975) argues that only when equality of access by men and women to the labour market exists will equalitarian marriages be possible in Canada. However, Boyd (1974), in analyzing public opinion data, concludes that changes in the direction of greater sexual equality have indeed taken place over the past two decades. This is expressed in a trend toward marital equality as reported by many studies in the United States, Europe, and Africa. These investigations found support for Blood and Wolfe's (1960) proposition that when the wife works, her power within the family increases and egalitarianism in marriage is more likely to prevail.[7]

Yet Brinkerhoff and Lupri (1978) found that their sample of wives who work outside the home were slightly less powerful than nonworking wives. Although, overall they discovered a high degree of egalitarianism among these Canadian couples, a careful examination of the decision-making items revealed unexpected differences. These researchers interviewed husbands and wives separately and thus were able to

---

[7] It should be noted that some studies have found no relationship between the wife's work status and marital egalitarianism; see, for example, Hoffman, 1960; Safilios-Rothschild, 1967; Centers, Raven and Rodrigues, 1971.

explore the problem of intra-familial congruence between husband's and wife's responses. More important, however, they had the couples rate items as to their attributed degree of importance and frequency. Brinkerhoff and Lupri (1978: 17) concluded their analysis with the following statement: "... according to decision-making scales wives generally appear to be equal or even more powerful than husbands. But, in reality, wives only make decisions in areas in which they are expected to—areas of less importance."

This finding not only raises methodological questions about the adequacy of decision-making items as a measurement of conjugal power and the generalizations subsequently reported in the literature, but it also throws considerable doubt on the imputed nexus between the increase in married women's work participation and the trend toward egalitarianism in family and society in Canada and elsewhere. These doubts are strengthened when occupational segregation patterns are traced over time.

Occupational Segregation Patterns

The persistence of sexual inequality in the occupational sector is reflected in the data summarized in Table 14. This same pattern is made patently evident by Armstrong and Armstrong (1975: 372–76) for "leading female occupations" during 1941–1971, both in terms of female percentages of a given occupation, for example, stenographers and typists, and as a percentage of all women workers ("concentration").

Another fact for reflection: while the female share of "craftsmen, production process and related workers" in 1931 was nearly equivalent to their overall share of the labour force, the labour force proportion was essentially the same 40 years later, so exclusion of females from this occupational category increased at a time when it enjoyed both greatly extended unionization and expanded occupational rewards. Similarly, the relatively low-paying clerical occupations became increasingly segregated according to sex.

In contrast, although managerial occupations became somewhat less segregated, they were, and are still, overwhelmingly male dominated, with females relegated typically to low-level management. In addition, even though "professional and technical" occupations became slightly less segregated during 1931 to 1971, women have been and continue to be concentrated in lower-status teaching and nursing jobs. And it should be noted that these trends persist to the present (Statistics Canada, 1978b: 25). Indeed, even though Canadian women have been more widely distributed in the total number of different specific occupations in this century it is in reality a limited dispersion with only token numbers in many occupations (Armstrong and Armstrong, 1975: 383).

Table 14

Labour Force 15 Years and Over, Showing Percentage of Each Sex
in Each Occupation Division as of 1961, for Canada, 1931–71

	Year and Sex					
	1931		1951		1971	
Occupation	F	M	F	M	F	M
All Occupations	17.0	83.0	22.0	78.0	34.4	65.6
Farmers, etc.	2.1	97.9	3.9	96.1	20.0	80.0
Other Extractive	0.3	99.7	0.1	99.9	—	100.0
Craftsmen, Production Process and Related	13.4	86.6	14.5	85.5	14.2	85.8
Labourers	2.6	97.4	5.9	94.1	8.6	91.4
Clerical	43.8	56.2	55.8	44.2	71.1	28.9
Managerial	4.8	95.2	9.1	90.9	12.7	87.3
Sales	22.4	77.6	35.0	65.0	39.4	60.6
Transport and Commo.	7.9	92.1	10.0	90.0	9.2	90.8
Professional and Technical	48.5	51.5	43.3	56.7	44.1	55.9
Service and Recreation	62.2	37.8	47.7	52.3	51.6	48.4

Source: Computed from "Table 1. Labour Force 15 Years and Over, by Sex, Showing Numerical and Percentage Distributions by Occupation Divisions, as of 1961, Canada (1) and Provinces, 1931–71." Occupations-Historical, for Canada and Provinces. Vol. III—Part 2, Bulletin 3.2–2 (June, 1978). Statistics Canada.

Earnings Differentials

One of the paramount indicator of status in our society is earnings, and it is precisely here that some of the most notable sex discrepancies exist. With few exceptions, Canadian women earn less than men for work of equal value and even when their education, training and experience are comparable (McDonald, 1977). Although some of the discrepancy may be attributed to so-called "productivity-related factors" such as education, experience, training, and turnover, there is a very obvious residual of discrimination on the part of consumers, co-workers and employers whose motives may include anxiety about job security, custom, misinformation and prejudice (Gunderson, 1976: 120). According to Gunderson's calculations, between 1961 and 1971 there was little if any improvement in the ratio of female earnings to male earnings in "all occupations." (This parallels the more limited finding of Ostry (1968) for an earlier period.) Armstrong and Armstrong (1975: 378) undertook parallel calculations of 1971 census data on the 22 "largest female occupations" (e.g., "elementary and kindergarten teachers" and "nurses, except supervisors") and found that in no instance was the average income of women as much as four-fifths that of men in the same specific occupation.

Gunderson (1976: 122) observed that "overall it appears that the wage gap increased slightly during the 1960's, remained constant for full year, full-time workers but increased slightly for all wage earners ... (as) proportionately more females worked part-time or part of the year." Moreover, it is the married women living with their husbands, along with the middle-aged who are most out-of-step with men in terms of their earnings. "This may reflect the fact that many older females have their labour market employment interrupted for household activities; hence their earnings peak earlier than those for males, who accumulate (greater) labour market experience" (123). In addition, Gunderson's regression analysis shows that while married men can anticipate earning several thousand dollars more per year than single men, the difference between married and single women is negligible. And even the implementation of equal pay legislation in some political jurisdictions appears to have had little effect (Gunderson, 1975). Armstrong and Armstrong (1975: 378) conclude that

> ... the relationship between pay and segregation in the leading female occupations is clear. More women entered those occupations with the lowest pay and the highest pay differentials while more men entered the occupation with the highest pay and the lowest pay differential.

Furthermore, although education goes some way toward equalizing the differentials, it apparently does not compensate wholly.

The Promise of Education

The likely effect of education on women's entry into the labour force is noted by Armstrong and Armstrong (1975: 380) but they caution that

> ... although education appears to exert a more powerful influence on the labour force participation of women than most other factors, we should not assume that educational achievement is the major force for most women in determining whether they will seek employment ...And the influence of educational achievement on a wife's labour force participation may be modified, even countered by an unambiguously economic factor: her husband's income.

To support this plausible argument, these two researchers cite the work of Ostry (1968), Skoulas (1974), and Spencer and Featherstone (1970), much of which seems to point to the conclusion that women work out of economic need.

Is this an overly-pessimistic assessment, or are educational trends ultimately going to produce a situation in which certain stresses experienced by Canadian women will be reduced? The data are not encouraging. The female enrollment rate in advanced education is increasingly less than that of men; and without advanced education "credentials", it becomes ever more difficult for women, particularly married women, to enter high reward managerial and professional occupations (Robb and Spencer, 1976).

At the same time, however, perhaps some future change in segregation and earnings patterns is foreshadowed in the 1962/63—1975/76 full-time university undergraduate enrollment statistics. For certain fields of specialization the females per 100 males have increased: five-fold in commerce and business administration (to 20%) and law (to 27%); and two-fold in medicine (to 28%), yet only half again as much in science (to 30%) (Robb and Spencer, 1976: 60; Symons, 1978: 16). As Robb and Spencer (1976: 57) have shown, although the age-specific educational retention rate of females of age 17 was the same as for males in 1951–52 (at 32%) and has improved in the intervening two decades, the rate has increased more for males (to 65%) than females (at 59%) in full-time education; and by the time people reach the 22–24 age group, the enrollment rate is three and one-half times greater for males.

Other trend data for 1962/63 to 1972/73 show that ratios for part-time students per 100 full-time students have remained widely different for both men and women, with undergraduate women about two times as likely as their male counterparts to be attending university part-time, although at the graduate level women and men have come to be about equally likely to attend part-time. In one sense the crucial indicator is the number of degrees granted to Canada's women and men. Statistics Canada indicates that while from 1920/21 to 1974/75 the percentage of bachelor and first professional degrees earned by women increased from 25 percent to 44 percent, at the master's level the proportion increased only slightly (from 21 percent to 28 percent), and for doctorates earned, the percentage has remained almost constant at 15 percent in 1920/21 and 16 percent in 1974/75. Marsden (1977: 42) charges that the Canadian educational system still suffers from "sex bias," that it denies access to a full array of training programmes, and that women continue to be exploited as a "secondary labour force."

Does the evidence, then, support the claim of a general trend toward egalitarianism in Canadian society? While there is apparent improvement in some specific areas, it seems that the gap in sexual equality persists and that fundamental structural changes are wanting.

Conclusion

In this overview the main emphasis has been placed on tracing the changing role of women in family and work. As we have documented, Canadian women since World War II have entered the labour force in increasing numbers and we predict that this trend will continue. In more recent years young mothers have shown a most dramatic increase in paid work—a new pattern also observed in other industrialized nations. Although the presence of children remains a deterrent to young mothers entering the labour force, both recent census and survey data strongly indicate that this structural barrier is gradually breaking down. Clearly, then, young wives and young mothers are increasingly sharing the economic burdens of new households, and they are doing so at younger and younger ages. Thus, the age of economic maturity has been deferred for men, but not for women.

acceptable for men to reverse the traditional sequence of
turity to precede rather than follow economic maturity.
ge women still spend less time in the labour force than
is to remain on the job longer than heretofore: women
iter the work force; they work more years than before,
iarried and whether or not they have children; and they
And, as we have documented, married women contribute
t of time to household chores than men do, even though
ivolved in work outside the home.
rs of women entering the labour force have, by and large,
ice sector. Overall growth in the professional work force
the share in this work increase taken by Canadian women
lition, we found gender-specific occupational segregation
with the income gap widening—reflected in greater job
age differentials between men and women. Besides not
ire to do, women—especially married women—have less paid employment than desired, and they are more vulnerable to unemployment.

Sex-linked occupations tend to remain segregated. Education, the supposedly historic avenue to success in North American society, appears not to serve as a corrective for work and family life imbalances, but instead strongly favours men. Thus, the influx of large masses of women into the labour force has not produced an appreciable change in women's status but instead has perpetuated many of the traditional patterns of gender-role segregation and inequality in the occupational system.

Although the proportion of women who work for pay and the number of years they work are still rising and will continue to rise in the future, Canadian society appears to afford only token provision for this as reflected in insufficient maternity leave and the lack of crèches, kindergartens, child care facilities, and flexible working arrangements. If housewives are expected to work outside the home, such services and facilities must be provided and be made widely available. Not providing such services may have very serious effects on women's physical and mental health, on conjugal life, and on the quality of the work done by women outside their homes (Bruntz, 1962: 429).

As we have documented, Canadian society's attitude toward young working mothers is highly negative. It is normative for Canadian women to give primacy to their husbands, home, and children. Consequently, this new pattern of rising participation among all married women, young and old, must be seen against the background of a contradiction in Canadian family roles and work roles.

Of course, in reality, there is nothing inherently contradictory in these roles per se: it is more a situation of female role overload and male role underload. (Canadian husbands, like their fellow husbands around the world, contribute relatively little time to household tasks compared with their working wives.) Rising expectations together with "engineered needs" are such that a majority of the wives claim to work out of financial "necessity." It appears that these working wives value greatly their gain of financial independence, even at the price of being overburdened at home. One would suspect that these multiple roles must generate frustration, anxiety, and ambiguity. However, Canadian survey data do not tend to support such a suspicion. On the contrary, the majority of employed wives appear to be content. When housewives are compared with employed women, the latter group was reported to be in better physical and mental health, actually communicating better with their husbands, and maintaining more positive attutudes toward life in general (Burke and Weir, 1976). It appears, then, that the potential pressures and tensions associated with the "double role" taken by employed wives, may be offset, at least in part, by perceived independence, satisfaction, and increased self-esteem derived from working outside the home.Additional data from in-depth interviews that shed light on these dimensions are needed.

Strains and stresses are clearly revealed by the tremendous increase in the Canadian divorce rate. The plight of Canadian divorced and separated women is a manifestation of the manifold inequalities that exist in Canadian society. Reported higher rates of mental illness among women, particularly married women, perhaps reflect greater distress in their role changes. These data are consistent with data on marital satisfaction as they document quite clearly the existence of strains and stresses inherent in role transitions at specific stages in the life cycle. Married women are affected much more than are married men, especially at mid-life.

In summary, full egalitarianism in family and society has not yet been achieved. While public opinion tends to favour it, empirical examinations of the existing power structure and division of labour in the Canadian family, of job segregation and of income differentials do not support such egalitarian sentiments. Not unexpectedly, while marriage per se has a positive effect on occupational mobility, on work status, on employment, and on income for men, the opposite is true for women. Clearly the domestic, institutional and social customs that keep women in the home are far less susceptible to change than are formal legal and regulatory barriers to women's emancipation.

Problems associated with aspects of family structure and functions are often "solved" by insisting on and reinforcing the traditional family norm, rather than seeking new and alternative arrangements that might be more effective. More important, the inequities experienced by many employed wives are a direct result of the transient status they hold in the labour force, which, in turn, is brought about by the role they have to perform in the home. In other words, the structural inequality wives experience in the home, and which may motivate them to seek employment, is translated into structural inequality on the job. Thus, while married women increasingly enter and re-enter the labour force and seemingly achieve equality with men by so doing, in reality they exchange one state of dependence for another, which, indeed, is a vicious circle for employed wives. Hence structural and interpersonal barriers tend to persist, preventing a complete institutionalization of gender equality in family and work.

Considering that men profit most from present structural inequities at home and at work and that they also hold the power to alter the inequities, any changes directed at producing gender equality in both spheres will probably evolve slowly, if at all. In the meantime, recall O'Neill's fitting statement: "Women have always done society's dirty work, at first mainly in the home, now increasingly outside it."

BIBLIOGRAPHY

Allingham, John D.
    1967 *Women Who Work:* Part 1. *The Relative Importance of Age, Education and Marital Status for Participation in the Labour Force.* Special Labour Force Studies No. 5. Ottawa: Dominion Bureau of Statistics (Cat. No. 71–509).

Allinghham, John D., and B. G. Spencer
    1968 *Women Who Work:* Part 2. *Married Women in the Labour Force: The Influence of Age, Education, Child-bearing Status and Residence.* Special Labour Force Studies, Series B, No. 2. Ottawa: Dominion Bureau of Statistics (Cat. No. 71–514).

Ambert, A. M.
    1976 *Sex Structure,* 2nd edition. Don Mills, Ontario: Longman Canada Ltd.

Armstrong, H., and P. Armstrong
    1975 "The segregated participation of women in the Canadian labour force, 1941–1971." *Canadian Review of Sociology and Anthropology* 12, 4 (November): 370–384.
    1978 *The Double Ghetto.* Toronto: McClelland and Stewart.

Berger, P., and T. Luckmann
    1966 *The Social Construction of Reality.* Garden City, N. Y.: Doubleday.

Bernard, Jessie
    1972 *The Future of Marriage.* New York: Bantam.
    1975 *Women, Wives, Mothers.* Chicago: Aldine.

Blake, Judith
    1974 "The changing status of women in developed countries." *Scientific American* 231 (September): 136–47.

Blood, Robert O., and D. M. Wolfe
    1960 *Husbands and Wives: The Dynamics of Married Living.* Glencoe Illinois: Free Press.

Boyd, M.
    1974 "Equality between the sexes: the results of Canadian Gallup polls, 1953–1973." Paper presented at the Annual Meetings of the Canadian Sociology and Anthropology Association (August).
    1975 "English Canadian and French Canadian attitudes toward women: results of the Canadian Gallup polls." *Journal of Comparative Family Studies* 6: 153 169.
    1977 "The forgotten minority: the socio-economic status of divorced and separated women." Pp. 46–71 in P. Marchak (ed.), *The Working Sexes.* Vancouver, B. C.: Institute of Industrial Relations.

Boyd, M., Margrit Eichler, and John Hofley
    1976 "Family: functions, formation and fertility." Pp. 13–52 in Gail C. A. Cook (ed.), *Opportunity for Choice.* Ottawa: Information Canada.

Brinkerhoff, M. B.
    1977 "Women who want to work in a man's world: a study of the influence of structural factors on role innovativeness." *Canadian Journal of Sociology* 2, 3: 283–303.

Brinkerhoff, M. B., and E. Lupri
   1978   "Theoretical and methodological issues in the use of decisionmaking as an indicator of conjugal power: some Canadian observations," *Canadian Journal of Sociology* 3, 1: 1–20.
Brown, B. W.
   1978   "Wife-employment and the emergence of egalitarian marital role prescriptions, 1900–1974." *Journal of Comparative Family Studies* IX, 1: 5–17.
Bruce, Christopher J.
   1978   "The effect of young children on female labour force participation rates: an exploratory study." *Canadian Journal of Sociology* 3, 4 (Fall): 431–439.
Bruntz, Francois
   1962   "The part-time employment of women in industrial countries." *International Labour Review* 86, (November): 425–442.
Burke, Ronald J., and Tamara Weir
   1976   "Relationship of wives' employment status to husband, wife and pair satisfaction and performance." *Journal of Marriage and the Family* 38, (May): 279–287.
Burstein, M., N. Tienhaara, P. Hewson, B. Warrander
   1975   *Canadian Work Values Findings of a Work Ethic Survey and A Job Satisfaction Survey*. Ottawa: Information Canada.
Butler, P. M.
   1976   "Single and dual wage earning and family involvement in the work world." Pp. 310–323 in K. Ishwaran (ed.), *The Canadian Family Revisited*. Toronto: Holt, Rinehart and Winston.
Canada, Department of Labour
   1958   *Married Women Working for Pay in Eight Canadian Cities*. Ottawa: Queen's Printer.
Canada, Department of Labour
   1959   *Occupational Histories of Married Women Working for Pay in Eight Canadian Cities*, Ottawa: Queen's Printer.
Canada, Department of Labour, Women's Bureau
   1975   *Women in the Labour Force: Facts and Figures*. Ottawa: Information Canada.
Centers, R., B. H. Raven, and A. Rodrigues
   1971   "Conjugal power structure: a reexamination." *American Sociological Review* 36: 263–278.
Connelly, P. M.
   1977   "The economic context of women's labour force participation in Canada." Pp. 10–27 in P. Marchak (ed.), *The Working Sexes*. Vancouver, B. C.: Institute of Industrial Relations.
Cook, A.
   1975   *The Working Mother*. Cornell University: New York State School of Industrial Relations.
Cook, Gail C. A. (ed.)
   1976   *Opportunity for Choice: A Goal for Women in Canada*. Ottawa, Information Canada.
Cook, Ramsay, and Wendy Mitchinsin (eds.)
   1976   *The Proper Sphere*. Toronto: Oxford University Press.
Cumming, Elaine, Charles Lazer, and Lynne Chisholm
   1975   "Suicide as an index of role strain among employed and not employed women in British Columbia." *The Canadian Review of Sociology and Anthropology* 12 (Pt. 1): 462–470.
Decision-Marketing Research Ltd.
   1976   *Women in Canada*. Toronto: Mimeographed, Released by Office of the Coordinator, Status of Women, Ottawa.
Eichler, Margrit
   1975   "Sociological research on women in Canada." *The Canadian Review of Sociology and Anthropology* 12 (Pt. 1): 474–481.
   1977a "The prestige of occupation housewife." Pp. 151–175 in P. Marchak (ed.).

1977b "Sociology of feminist research in Canada." *Signs: Journal of Women in Culture and Society* 3, 2: 409–442.
Eichler, Margrit, J. Newton, and L. Primrose
1977 "A bibliography of social science materials on Canadian women, published between 1950–1975." Pp. 276–360 in M. Stephenson (ed.).
Fogarty, Michael P., Rhona Rapoport, and Robert N. Rapoport
1971 *Sex, Career and Family*. London: George Allen and Unwin.
Gibbins, R., R. Ponting, and G. L. Symons
1978 "Attitudes and ideology: correlates of liberal attitudes towards the role of women." *Journal of Comparative Family Studies*, Special Issue: *Women in the Family and Employment: A Cross-cultural View* IX, 1: 19 40.
Gunderson, M.
1976 "Work patterns." Pp. 93–142 in Gail C. A. Cook (ed.).
Hoffman, L. W.
1960 "Parental power relations and the division of household tasks." Pp. 215–230 in F. I. Nye and L. W. Hoffman (eds.), *The Employed Mothers in America*. Chicago: Rand McNally.
Ishwaran, K. (ed.)
1976 *The Canadian Family Revisited*. Toronto: Holt, Rinehart and Winston.
Judek, Stanislaw
1968 *Women in the Public Service*. Ottawa: Queen's Printer.
Kirkaldy, Anne
1975 *Determinants of Labour Force Participation of Married Women in Canada*. Unpublished M. A. Thesis. Calgary: The University of Calgary.
Kubat, D., and D. Thornton
1974 *A Statistical Profile of Canadian Society*. Toronto: McGraw-Hill Ryerson Ltd.
Kuzel, P., and P. Krishnan
1973 "Changing patterns of remarriage in Canada, 1961–1966." *Journal of Comparative Family Studies* 4: 215–224.
Larson, Lyle E.
1976 *The Canadian Family in Comparative Perspective*. Scarborough, Ontario: Prentice-Hall.
Lashuk, Maureen Wilson, and George Kurian
1977 "Employment status, feminism and symptoms of stress: the case of a Canadian prairie city." *The Canadian Journal of Sociology* 2: 195 204.
Lupri, E.
1976 "Gesellschaftliche Differenzierung und familiale Autorität." Pp. 323–352 in Lugen Lupri and Günther Lüschen (eds.), *Soziologie der Familie*. Zweite Auflage. Köln: Westdeutscher Verlag.
Lupri, E., and J. Frideres
1976 "Marital satisfaction and the family life cycle: the Canadian case." Paper presented at the 1976 Annual Meetings of the Canadian Sociology and Anthropology Association, Quebec City, (May).
1981 "The quality of marriage and the passage of time." *Canadian Journal of Sociology* 6(3):283–305.
Mackie, Marlene
1976 "Role constraints and married women." Paper presented at the Symposium on the Working Sexes, University of British Columbia, (October).
Marchak, M. P.
1977 "The Canadian labour farce: jobs for women." Pp. 148–159 in M. Stephenson (ed.), *Women in Canada*, revised edition. Don Mills, Ontario: General Publishing Co. Ltd.
Marchak, M. P. (ed.)
1977 *The Working Sexes*. Vancouver, B. C.: Institute of Industrial Relations.

Marsden, L. R.
    1977 "Unemployment among Canadian women: some sociological problems raised by its increase." Pp. 28–45 in P. Marchak (ed.).

McDonald, L.
    1975 "Wages of work: a widening gap between women and men." *Canadian Forum*, April-May: 4–7.
    1977 "Wages of work: a widening gap between women and men." Pp. 181–193 in M. Stephenson (ed.).

McIlveen, N., and H. Sims
    1978 *The Flow Components of Unemployment in Canada*. Special Labour Force Studies, Series A, No. 11. Ottawa: Statistics Canada.

Meissner, M.
    1977 "Sexual division of labour and inequality: labour and leisure." Pp. 160–180 in. M. Stephenson (ed.).

Meissner, M., Elizabeth W. Humphreys, Scott M. Meis, and William J. Scheu
    1975 "No exit for wives: sexual division of labour and the cumulation of household demands." *The Canadian Review of Sociology and Anthropology* 12 (Pt. 1): 424–439.

Mostow, E. and P. Newberry
    1975 "Work and depression in women: a comparison of workers and housewives in treatment." *American Journal of Orthopsychiatry* 45: 538–548.

Motuz, C.
    1974 *Sociological Factors Influencing Labour Force Participation Rates-An Overview*. Ottawa: Department of Manpower and Immigration. Mimeographed.

Nye, F. I.
    1976 "Husband-wife relationship." Pp. 263–281 in F. I. Nye and L. W. Hoffman (eds.), *Working Mothers*. San Francisco: Jossey-Bass Publishers.

O'Neill, W. L. (ed.)
    1972 *Women at Work*. Chicago: Quadrangle Books, Inc., and Toronto: Burns and MacEachern Ltd.

Oppenheimer, V. K.
    1974 "The life-cycle squeeze." *Demography* 11: 237–247.

Ostry, Sylvia
    1968 *The Female Worker in Canada. 1961 Census Monograph*. Ottawa: Dominion Bureau of Statistics.

Ostry, Sylvia, and Mahmood A. Zaidi
    1972 *Labour Economics in Canada*, 2nd edition. Toronto: Macmillan.

Parsons, T., and R. Bales
    1955 *Family: Socialization and Interaction Processes*. Glencoe, Illinois: Free Press.

Peters, J. F.
    1976 "Divorce in Canada: a demographic profile." *Journal of Comparative Family Studies* VII: 335–349.

Pike, Robert
    1975 "Legal access and the incidence of divorce in Canada." *The Canadian Review of Sociology and Anthropology* 12: 115–133.

Pool, Ian D.
    1978 "Changes in Canadian female labour force participation, and some possible implications for conjugal power." *Journal of Comparative Family Studies* IX, 1: 41–52.

Robb, L. A., and B. Spencer
    1976 "Education: enrolment and attainment." Chapter 3 in Gail C. A. Cook (ed.).

Royal Commission on the Status of Women in Canada
    1970 *Report*. Ottawa: Information Canada.

Safilios-Rothschild, C.
    1967 "A comparison of power structure and marital satisfaction in urban Greek and French families." *Journal of Marriage and Family* 29: 345–352.

1969 "Family sociology or wives' family sociology: a crosscultural examination of decision-making." *Journal of Marriage and the Family* 31: 290–301.
1970 "The study of family power structure: a review, 1960–1969." *Journal of Marriage and the Family* 32: 539–552.
1976 "Dual linkages between the occupational and family systems: a macro-sociological analysis." *Signs* 1: 51–60.

Sangster, D.
1973 *The Role of Women in the Economy.* Ottawa: Department of Manpower and Immigration (mimeographed).

Schmid, Carol
1976 "The changing status of women in the United States and Canada: an overview." *Sociological Symposium* 15 (Spring): 1–27.

Schreiber, E. M.
1975 "The social bases of opinions on woman's role in Canada." *The Canadian Journal of Sociology* 1, 1: 61–74.

Skoulas, N.
1974 *Determinants of the Participation Rate of Married Women in the Canadian Labour Force: An Econometric Analysis.* Ottawa: Statistics Canada.

Smith, Dorothy E.
1975 "An analysis of ideological structures and how women are excluded: considerations for academic women." *Canadian Review of Sociology and Anthropology* 12: 353–369.

Smith, Dorothy E., and S. J. David (eds.)
1975 *Women Look at Psychiatry.* Vancouver, B. C.: Press Gang Publishers.

Spencer, B. G.
1973 "Determinants of the labour force participation of married women: a micro-study of Toronto households." *Canadian Journal of Economics* VI, 2 (May): 222–238.

Spencer, B. G., and D. C. Featherstone
1970 *Married Female Labour Force Participation: A Micro Study.* Special Labour Force Studies, Series B, No. 4. Ottawa: Dominion Bureau of Statistics.

Statistics Canada
1971 *Census.* Ottawa: Information Canada.
1976 *Vital Statistics, 1974,* Volume II: *Marriages and Divorces.* Ottawa: Information Canada.
1977 "Table 6.5. Labour Force by Sex, Age and Marital Status." Ottawa: Minister of Industry, Trade and Commerce.
1978a *Population Demographic Characteristics—Marital Status.* Catalogue No. 92–8324, Bul. 2.5, Table 17. Ottawa: Minister of Industry, Trade and Commerce.
1978b *The Labour Force.* Catalogue No. 71–001 (August). Ottawa: Minister of Industry, Trade and Commerce.

Stephenson, Marylee (ed.)
1977 *Women in Canada,* revised edition. Don Mills, Ontario: General Publishing Co. Ltd.

Stouffer, S. A. et al.
1949/ *Studies in Social Psychology in World War* II, Vols. I–IV. Princeton: Princeton University Press.
1950

Symons, Gladys
1978 "Can women translate education into occupational mobility?" *University Affairs* 19, 6 (July): 16–17.

Szalai, A., et al. (eds.)
1972 *The Use of Time: Daily Activities of Urban and Suburban Populations in Twelve Countries.* The Hague: Mouton.

Zsigmond, Z. E., and E. Rechnitzer
(n. d.) *Projected Potential Labour Force Entrants from the Canadian Educational Systems 1971 to 1985.* Ottawa: Statistics Canada (photocopy).

A Comparative View on the Changing Position of Women in the United States

AIDA K. TOMEH

Bowling Green State University,
Bowling Green, Ohio, U.S.A.

THE FOCUS OF THIS PAPER is on the changing position of American women in various social institutions—the economy, polity, education and the family with special emphasis on the structural correlates of sex role orientation in a modern industrial society. The data for this study draws on available literature in the field as well as on a recent study conducted in Spring, 1976, based on a random sample of college students of a middle-sized university in Ohio.[1]

An Overview of the Changing Status of Women

Striking changes in the position of women are taking place in the American society today. The new work roles of women and the changing definitions of their roles in the family are, in part, a reflection of discontent with the traditional view of sex roles and of concern with major issues of equality and participation in the larger society. Women have become increasingly conscious of the weak position in decision-making and lack of freedom to exercise personal choice in careers and family life. Traditional feminine attributes as appropriate and expected role sets are being challenged by many women. The emerging qualities of feminine assertiveness, independence, and self-esteem that would have been dampened by the conventions of the past

---

1 The data were collected from a questionnaire based on a random sample of classes. All classes were included except laboratory or recitation sessions, field, intern or practicum experience, independent readings, performance of the arts, thesis or dissertation research. A 20 percent random sample of classes was drawn and the permission of the instructor to administer the questionnaire during a regularly-scheduled class period was sought. Thirty classes were selected via the sampling procedure and 27 participated. All data were collected during a two-week peiod and 642 completed questionnaire schedules were obtained. The questionnaire consisted of several questions on a variety of issues related to sex roles such as attitudes toward the employment of women, personality role behavior, role conflict and a variety of other male/female values and attitudes as well as familial and demographic variables. All questions were close-ended with the exception of occupation.

are beginning to flourish in the socialization process of females (Marmor, 1972). Traits like passiveness, obedience, and submission are no longer seen as desirable characteristics to encourage in developing the female's personality or as satisfaction—producing attributes of the female role (Whitley and Poulsen, 1975). Findings of the present study support this trend as shown in Table 1.

The present research examines different dimensions of sex role orientation—personality sex role behavior, self-actualization of women, attitudes towards the employment of women, sex role conflict and institutionalized equality. A special feature of these attitudinal scales used in this analysis is the reconstruction of items in a nontraditional sense based on a conceptualization of a sex role continuum as one which involves lesser or greater degrees of nontraditional traits placed along the same axis for men and women. This approach emphasizes the role-sharing model where husbands or fathers have no necessary monopoly on instrumental and adaptive behavior and wives or mothers are not confined to expressive roles. Instead, sharing of such roles can occur within the family as well as in other social units.[2]

Table 1 examines personality sex role behavior defined as representing an emphasis in which women's and men's personality traits are of equal potential (reconstructed items of a scale on feminine role behavior originally used by Kammeyer, 1964). Greater egalitarianism is indicated by stronger preferences for men and women having a similar personality disposition (low mean scores). Traditionalism is indicated by endorsing a stereotypical personality differential where women are characterized as expressive and men as instrumental (high mean scores).

The data distribution in Table 1 shows that women are significantly more willing to accept personality similarities in men and women than are men. Although the male responses are not extremely traditional, men are not as accepting as women in perceiving a similar personality disposition—one of the areas that appears to invite little concensus between the sexes.

Another aspect of the changing status of women is their preference for individualistic utilities. Accordingly, Table 2 analyzes self-actualization as part of the new position of women which represents an emphasis on the wife's interests *equal* to

[2] The response pattern to items in each of the scales on sex role orientation uses a fourpoint format: strongly agree, agree, disagree, strongly disagree ranked from "1" to "4" respectively; "1" designates a nontraditional response and "4" designates a traditional response. For all respondents a mean score was obtained for each item in each scale. Low mean scores indicate a nontraditional attitude, while high means represent traditional responses. The reliability of the sex role orientation measures tested by correlating each item to the total score of a given scale (Pearson r) is significant at the .001 level. The correlation coefficients between the different scales are moderate and statistically significant at the .001 level. The largest obtained correlation is between nontraditional personality sex role behavior and institutionalized equality ($r = .60$, $N = 624$), and the lowest correlation is between attitudes toward the employment of women and sex role conflict ($r = .22$, $N = 608$). These results suggest that while it is feasible to consider the scales as part of the same general concept there appears to be some independence among the different scales to warrant treating them as separate variables. (Not ascertained cases have been deleted from statistical analysis),

those of husbands and children (revised items originally used by Scanzoni, 1975, 1976). Nontraditionalism is indicated by stronger preferences for the wife's individualistic benefits where the concerns for the husband and children come first (low means).

An examination of the data in Table 1 clearly shows that females are significantly more likely than males to indicate a preference for the wife's individualistic interests. This suggests that men are more interested in having wives pursue familistic concerns instead of individualistic benefits. However, in only one instance do both men and women disagree with the view that a woman may have to sacrifice her social life if it interferes with her career. To the extent that leisure activities represent expressive pursuits, males and females tend to assign social duties to women in addition to

Table 1

Mean Personality Sex Role Behavior Scores by Sex

Items	Sex	
	Females (N=388)	Males (N=230)
Women can be as good leaders as men.*	1.47	2.11
Women are becoming as aggressive as men.*	1.76	2.07
Men can be as sympathetic as women.**	1.72	1.87
Men and women can be emotional.*	1.43	1.61
Both men and women are able to reason logically.*	1.44	1.66
Women can be as intellectual as men.*	1.32	1.68
Both men and women are artistically inclined.*	1.50	1.78
Chemistry as a major for a college woman is as acceptable as home economics.*	1.60	1.81
Social work as a major for a college man is as acceptable as engineering.*	1.62	1.92

T-test for significance of differences between the sexes significant at:
$p < .0001 = *$
$p < .01 \ \ = **$

their career involvement. It is in the context of self-actualization roles that females and males differ significantly in most of their responses. At the same time, it seems that both sexes have had some exposure to the new changes in sex roles, that is, although women are endorsing an egalitarian viewpoint, men are not totally rejecting role modernity for women to any extreme extent.

Evidence based on the changing status of women is not limited to college students. A national sample of women questioned by Roper organization in 1973 showed that 57 percent of the women favored efforts to strengthen their new rising status as compared to the figures reported in 1971 and 1972 by Harris poll in which 40 percent and 48 percent expressed such support.

A group of active feminists in the National Organization for Women (NOW) have already begun efforts to reassess the direction of the movement to combine women's liberation with more options and alternatives for men. This attempt may have the effect of having men endorse women's greater role modernity.

Although appropriate targets for changes in sex role inequalities on a societal basis have emerged to provide equal opportunities (i.e., ideological challenges of the women's movement, participation of women in the labor force, ability to control fertility, political debates on equality, etc.), the commitments of both men and women to equality remain somewhat ambiguous. This may be due to the traditional views about sex role differentiation and the costs and consequences of equality for the family and other institutions.

The Economy

One of the most important events which has profoundly affected the organization of the family is the movement of women into the labor force. Some of the factors that converged to give impetus to this movement are increased production, technological convenience, availability of birth control devices, the rise of egalitarian ideologies, women's rights and other related conditions.

Table 2

Mean Self-Actualization Scores by Sex

Items	Sex	
	Females (N=387)	Males (N=231)
A woman may want to get a higher education and utilize her talents and skills to achieve self-satisfaction.*	1.48	1.73
A woman may want to forego children if they interfere with her career.*	1.92	2.15
A wife's career is of equal importance to her husband's.*	1.86	2.24
A woman may have to forego social and leisurely activities if they interfere with her career.	2.28	2.37
A wife should be able to make long range plans for her occupation in the same way a husband does for his.**	1.86	2.03
If a wife is not satisfied enough she should take a job.*	1.93	2.24
There should be more good day-care centers and nursery schools so that more young mothers could work.*	1.90	2.27

T-test for significance of differences between the sexes significant at:
$p < .0001 = *$
$p < .003\ \ = **$

However, the single most dramatic trend in the status of women since 1940 has been the increase in the proportion of married women who work for pay. All age groups of married women had substantially higher rates of labor force participation in 1960 than in 1940 or 1950. In 1972, 41 percent of all married women were employed compared to 31 percent in 1960 (U.S. Department of Labor, Bureau of Labor Statistics, 1971). The largest recent increase in labor force activity has occurred for the group least likely to work—mothers of preschool children. By 1970, one-third of all mothers with a child under six years old were employed (U.S. Department of Labor, Bureau of Labor, Statistics, 1971). Among wives with children under the age of three, 29 percent were in the labor force in March, 1973, an increase of 10 percent in a decade.

Recent analysis (Waite and Stolzenberg, 1976) shows that the forces which kept the wife out of the labor force in the past (i.e., age of the wife and the presence of young children) have tended to decrease from 1940 to 1960 while forces which encourage participation have tended to increase or remain constant (i.e., wife's wage potential, previous work experience). This trend is likely to continue through the 1970's.

Although women make up about two-fifths of the labor force, in no western society is paid work outside the home considered desirable for married women and mothers; only in some eastern European countries, in Chinese and African societies are women expected to work and contribute to the economy equally with men (Boserup, 1970). Survey data suggest that a substantial minority of American men oppose their wives working. They cite conflicts with women's home responsibilities and the fear that women will deprive men of jobs (Hudis, 1976: 269).

Similar results are echoed among college students. Table 3 shows attitudes towards the employment of married women by sex (reconstructed items originally used by Hewer and Neubeck, 1964). A nontraditional response represents a positive endorsement for the employment of married women (low means), whereas traditionalism indicates a preference to keep married women out of the labor force (high means).

It is observed, for example, that in most instances, females have a significantly more favorable outlook towards the employment of married women as compared to men (Table 3). However, in the presence of preschool children, or in getting financial returns for money spent on education or in meeting an obligation to society, men and women are equally inclined not to favor the employment of married women, though the differentials are significant in favoring a more traditional attitude on the part of men. In any event, the above results indicate that women's vulnerability compounded by the responsibility of young children tends to pose a barrier to their employment. Only in one instance do women appear to be significantly more traditional than men. This is when latent benefits do not accrue to the husband as a result of the wife's participation in the labor force.

It is also worth noting that where the employment of married women is of an economic value, that is in supporting the family or meeting basic financial responsibilities or providing material things for the family, men tend to favor their employment. The point to be emphasized is that men reach consensus with women on the employment of married women when economic necessity is the issue.

American culture has always emphasized that a man should define himself in terms of his work and is expected to earn money regardless of need—as he gains from his work a sense of autonomy and self-esteem. For women work had a different meaning and they were not encouraged to define themselves in terms of the work they did but rather in terms of their husband's or father's work. Although economic considerations may be the most frequent reasons for work cited by women, there are those who are working not because of economic need, but as a way to acquire independence, prestige, friendship (Booth and Hess, 1974), and identity.

Table 3

Mean Attitudinal Scores towards the Employment of Married Women by Sex

Items	Sex	
	Females (N=382)	Males (N=222)
Women hold jobs after they are married because they are needed outside the home even when there are preschool children.**	2.53	2.70
...to get financial return for money they spent on their own education.**	2.15	2.34
...to meet an obligation to society instead of becoming a wasted resource.**	2.40	2.54
...because housework provides inadequate opportunity for the expression of intellectual interests.**	1.82	2.03
...because staying at home does not allow sufficient challenge to talents (acting, broadcasting, writing, etc.).**	1.75	1.98
...because they owe it to themselves to make use of their abilities.**	1.68	2.08
...to enjoy working in their field of specialization.*	1.49	1.83
...to provide an opportunity to work with others who have similar interests and objectives.**	1.66	2.06
...because they want to try out what they have been specially trained for.**	1.76	2.04
...so they can have a life of their own.**	2.05	2.27
...to earn money to support their family	1.90	1.89
...even when their husbands have completed their education.**	1.77	1.91
...to meet basic financial responsibilities.	1.83	1.89
...to provide important things for home and family, like a car, school costs, etc.	1.93	1.96
...to provide their children with advanced educational training.*	1.95	2.17
...because men are not the only ones responsible for the financial care of their children.**	1.83	1.99
...because it would give their husbands more status.**	3.10	2.98
...because they are equal to men in ability.*	1.92	2.31

T-test for significance of differences between the sexes significant at:
    $p < .0001 = *$
    $p < .002$ to $.05 = **$

Recent analysis of women's status (Treiman and Terrill, 1975a) suggests it is no longer reasonable to assume that the social status of husbands determines that of their wives. They cite the high proportion of married women in the labor force (U.S. Bureau of the Census, 1970; U.S. Department of Labor, 1974: 24; Ferriss, 1971: 85–87) as a rationale for the individual assessment of women's status. Empirical evidence further shows (Ritter and Hargens, 1975) that married women do not evaluate their status on the basis of their husband's occupation (Felson and Knoke, 1974 for contrary conclusions) and that educational and occupational characteristics of wives make an important contribution to household social standing (Rossi, et al., 1974: 178; Hudis, 1976).

Labor force participation and survey results aside, there is a more general criticism of the husband's status representing the entire unit of the family which stems from the fact that in 1973, 27 percent of women between ages 20 to 64 currently were not married and living with a spouse (U.S. Department of Labor, 1974: 13). Husband's status for this segment of the population is inapplicable for assessing the status of these women.

Moreover, at present in the U.S., in about one-half of the families, the wife works and in a much larger percent of families the wife has worked during some stages of the life cycle. There is also evidence indicating that the existence of equal status between spouses or a wife's higher status is not a rare phenomenon and that such a situation does not cause competition or marital instability (Day, 1961; Martin and Jacobsen, 1975). On this basis, it cannot be assumed that only men can achieve status while women have only access to derived status through their husbands.

Increasingly, the family models that prevail in the American society during most of the family life cycle stages suggest that working wives have two statuses: one individually achieved and the other derived through their husbands. Although a certain percentage of women have jobs and qualifications that often entitle them to a status equal or to higher than that of their husbands, it is questionable whether such husbands are accorded prestige through the derived status of their wives as noted previously (Table 3). In any event, these arguments suggest the importance of assessing women's economic status in their own right. It is on this basis that a stratification model based on a traditionally sex differentiated family may no longer be applicable in the assessment of the status position of the majority of American families.

Occupational Distribution of Women: Despite the steady increase in women's employment there has been little change in the direction of greater similarity in the occupational distribution of men and women (Gross, 1968; Knudsen, 1969). This contradiction can be explained, in part, in terms of the women's frequent decisions to combine homemaking and careers. The usual incompatible demands of the family and the labor market may lead to criteria for job selection which differ from those of men. These occupational choices are economically possible because women can generally rely on the financial contribution of their husbands and are culturally expected to give priority to familial over occupational responsibilities. This is borne out by the fact that even at the present time women continue to fill many jobs that seem to be extensions of their expressive familial roles. The jobs usually have an unskilled, uncreative, and service orientation (Mitchell, 1972: 50).

In the last 30 years women have entered occupations which have been unattractive for men and jobs in which women have a traditional dominance—clerical work, secretaries, typists, telephone operators, and the like (Treiman and Terrill, 1975b). In more specific terms, women comprise 57 percent of all service workers and 97 percent of all domestic servants (Cook, 1975: 11). In contrast, only 2 in 100 women are in administration or managerial jobs; less than 5 women in 100 are found in the professions (Mitchell, 1972: 50); and only 15 women among the 2500 presidents, vice-presidents, and board chairpersons direct the country's major corporations.

During the 1960's, women's representation in the professions increased, but in the same small percentage that it had in the preceding decades. According to census figures, 2.4 percent of American laywers in 1940 were women, 3.5 percent in 1960, and 4.9 percent in 1970. In medicine, women constituted 6.5 percent of the profession in 1969 and 9.3 percent in 1970. The small size of the increase is accounted for by the time required for entry into the legal and medical professions. The 1970 census reflects decisions made by professional schools and applicants during the mid-sixties. In the fall of 1974, first-year law school classes were 23.7 percent female compared to 15.7 percent in 1971. In medicine 22.2 percent of the 1974 entering class were women, twice the proportion reported in 1970. The increase in applications and admission in these areas indicated, in part, women's new preferences.

The representation of women in labor unions is no exception. The percentage of U. S. women workers who are union members is 10.4; the corresponding figure for male workers is 28. Women are also a disproportionate minority in union decision-making bodies. Only recently have union women become active and begun to demand representation in union decision-making. In 1974, a national coalition of women for the AFLCIO and independent unions was formed in the U.S. Although the activity of women in unions, as elsewhere, is constrained by their lack of training and by the demands of home and children, there is a growing feeling that women should participate more in union affairs to get a hearing for their demands regarding wages, promotion, child care, and sex integration.

In terms of occupational stratification, a high proportion of female jobs are subordinate to male-labeled jobs. However, when male jobs are subordinate, they are rarely under the jurisdiction of a female-labeled job. Recent research (Osmond and Martin, 1975) based on college students suggests that males are least willing to accept women in supervisory, decision-making, and leadership roles outside the family, and the females appear equally as insistent not only that women should occupy male positions but that they can perform in them as well as men.

Results of Table 4 on sex role conflict (i.e., situations where men and women have reversed roles) partially support the above position in that men are significantly less likely than women to accept a woman supervisor. The data also show that, as compared to women, it is a significantly uncomfortable situation for men to have wives earn a higher salary than their husbands. In this same area of response, women perceive doll play to be equally acceptable for boys and girls, while men significantly object to this kind of role sharing. On the other hand, relationships between men and women are not greatly affected when wives have a higher educational level or when they are married to younger men. At the same time, men and women are in agreement that men who are passive and obedient and women who are assertive and aggressive in work situations are not rewarded on the job. It is apparent that the interactive patterns between males and females may be seriously affected when economic considerations are in question and when men take on feminine characteristics.

Table 4

Mean Role Conflict Scores by Sex

Items	Sex	
	Females (N=387)	Males (N=230)
If a wife/girlfriend has a higher educational level than her husband/boyfriend, it would not make a difference in their relationship to each other.	2.29	2.38
If a man is married to an older women, it would not upset their relationship to each other.	2.01	2.06
If my immediate supervisor at work was a woman, it would make no difference in the way I feel about my work.*	1.65	2.09
Men who are passive and obedient in work situations are not rewarded on the job. (reversed scoring)	2.45	2.52
Women who are assertive and aggressive in work situations are not rewarded on the job. (reversed scoring)	2.22	2.28
A husband should not feel uncomfortable if his wife earns a higher salary than he does.*	1.93	2.12
It is certainly as acceptable for boys as for girls to play with dolls.*	2.01	2.55
More women than men feel guilty about breaking up their families when they have young children.* (reversed scoring)	2.76	2.46

T-test for significance of differences between the sexes significant at: $p < .0001 = *$

It must be noted, however, that the frequently documented discrepancy between attitudes and behaviors might suggest that while males in subordinate positions (with females as superordinates) might not particularly like their status, they will go along with it. The issue is still whether male attitudes will prevent women from attaining high positions. This point is critical in view of the recent feminist charges that it is males who have in the past excluded women from top level decision-making positions in areas such as industry, business, politics, and the like (Kemper, 1974, on the relationship between ascribed status and differential amounts of power). In view of the increasingly high rates of women in the labor force and the high likelihood of exrafamilial interaction taking place in large scale organizations, future research must address itself to the study of the relationship between organizational behavior and sex bias which may exclude females from positions of influence. Whether women ultimately will be assimilated into the leadership of business, industry and the profession in sizable numbers remains to be seen.

It has been claimed, however, that women lack the stamina and temperament for high level work, that their home obligations are too demanding, and that their commitment to work and ambition to succeed are at a low level. As a result, women have been discouraged from managerial jobs and other professional positions. Excluding women from these fields compounds the consequences of inequality because they cannot compete with men who have the credentials for important positions in politics, business or other related areas.

Women have become aware that a belief that they possess special traits as a group is used to prevent them from a wide variety of jobs. Women are beginning to compete for jobs that require aggressive skills and assertive personality traits (Dulury, 1973). These assertive traits have long been recognized as part of the standard equipment necessary for males to succeed in the competitive American market place (Scott, 1958; Tiger, 1969), while, traditionally, assertiveness in women has not been considered a necessary or even desirable personality trait for entering the job market. The idea that men should work to the limits of their endurance and that women should handle child care, meals and home maintenance is now challenged by both sexes.

Men and women are questioning constraints on either ascribed or achieved status that are not germane to the work performed but serve to restrict favored jobs to individuals and groups who now control them. There are strong objections to stereotyping because of the new consciousness that when either sex is expected to choose a certain type of activity because of their sex, their freedom to pursue individual interests is diminished. A man, for example, who becomes a nurse or kindergarten teacher is stereotyped as a person who lacks ambition or is neurotic because his work day involves women and children, rather than other men. Likewise, a woman who becomes a policewoman may be considered "too strong" or not strong enough for the job. Stereotypical labels have, therefore, inhibited the equal representation of men and women in various occupations.

For all types of work, women tend to be paid less than men (Cook, 1975; Tomeh, 1975) even for equivalent work and effort (Suter and Miller, 1973). The discrepancy is attributed to discontinuous work patterns and high job turnover among women. But when full-time workers are compared, women still are paid less. Some attribute the outcome to the low militancy and lack of organization of women in unions

(Suter and Miller, 1973). Yet the Civil Rights Act of 1964 which provides the legal foundation for women's rights along with the efforts of women's organizations have proved successful in reducing sex discrimination. It was the Equal Employment Opportunities Commission and women lawyers, for example, who sued the American Telephone and Telegraph (AT and T) Company, the largest employer of women in the world, and won the case forcing the AT and T to provide goals and time-tables for hiring and promotion of both women and minority employees as well as back and immediate pay to persons who had been denied promotion or who were underpaid in their job classification. This is evidence that women can use power to support their position. And the legislation giving middle-class women an opportunity to be hired as lawyers, meant that working-class women had the opportunity to be promoted as supervisors in factories and business.

Other research based on working women supports the thesis that, currently, married women experience lower earnings and returns in relation to their occupational status and schooling as a result of reduced labor force seniority and occupational decision-making which stresses the importance of job characteristics other than earnings (Hudis, 1976). For example, women living with a spouse may tend to optimize the attraction of job characteristics such as working hours or the commuting distance to work, factors which may require them to accept lower earnings.

Much of the literature on the career aspirations of adolescents indicates that few girls aspire to life-time career characteristics of continued labor force participation. This proposition gains support based on the findings of the present study which show that about 50 percent of the college women intend to drop out of the labor force intermittently as their children are growing up. Sweet's study (1973) on female labor force participation includes an examination of labor force commitment and earnings for American wives in 1960. His analysis shows that, among wives, greater labor force commitment and fewer family responsibilities are associated with higher earnings.

The above research suggests that among women who are labor force participants, familial responsibilities often are of central importance when occupational decisions are made. Married working women who simultaneously occupy two statuses are faced with competing demands i.e., home and childcare obligations and the responsibilities of an occupational role. Although it has been shown that husbands of working women are more likely to contribute to household management and childcare than are husbands of nonemployed women, the burden still falls unequally on the wife (Hoffman, 1963; U.S. Department of Labor, Women's Bureau, 1971). When conflicts between the demands of these two roles occur, the requirements of the family take precedence (Coser and Rokoff, 1971: 538). This resolution is likely to reduce strain within the family, though it may have negative consequences for women's occupational attainment and earnings. In order to compete with the economic rewards of employment the roles of worker and mother must become compatible (Fong, 1976).

This can be achieved partly by promoting childcare facilities, granting maternal and paternal leaves, having fewer children, permitting flexible work shedules and other institutional changes.

Recent trends in the U.S. suggest that the traditional benefits to women have, indeed, declined. Female and male wage levels have dramatically risen since World War II. Intercohorts shifts in mean educational and occupational status and earnings for married persons in the experienced civilian labor force of 1962 and 1973 represent socio-economic improvements for both men and women. The educational and occupational achievements of women have kept pace with men's and the ratio of female to male earnings has declined for husbands and wives (Featherman and Hauser, 1976). Economists have argued that these changes create an increased opportunity cost to staying home full-time, thus, making strict adherence to the traditional allocation of women's and men's time less attractive to women (Santos, 1975). The noted decline in family size, the choice on the part of some couples to remain childless (U.S. Bureau of the Census, 1975) in addition to the rising divorce rates and the increase in the proportion of families headed by women (Ross and MacIntosh, 1973) imply increased costs associated with the traditional wife-mother career.

Female mobility and status attainment: Although the proportion of women in the labor force is increasing, little is known about female mobility and status attainment. The first comparison of male and female mobility patterns conducted by DeJong and others (1971), concludes that male and female mobility patterns are basically similar. Tyree and Treas (1974) re-analysis which utilizes more appropriate analytic techniques, shows that DeJong and his colleagues have exaggerated the similarity of male and female mobility patterns.

In contrast to the findings on occupational mobility, Treiman and Terrill (1975a) find the status attainment processes of males and females to be quite similar. The latter findings are also supported by McGlendon's (1976) study based on NORC General Social Survey of 1972–1974 where education is found to be the most important factor for allocating both white males and females to positions in the status hierarchies. However, the similarities in the status hierarchies are built on quite dissimilar occupational structures where two-thirds of the working women are concentrated in white-collar jobs (mostly clerical) as compared to less than one-half of the men in the same job classification. The concentration of women in white-collar jobs is responsible for the female status attainment with men, though the same status between the sexes does not result in income equality (Suter and Miller, 1973; Treiman and Terrill, 1975a).

Although American women are getting higher level jobs, their jobs are still being labeled female and women are not on the same path to the top as are men (Epstein, 1975a, 1975b). Women who are corporate assistant vice-presidents, for example, are in charge of affirmative action plans and personnel programs instead of production and sales. Only the latter jobs lead to higher managerial positions. When women occupy jobs that entail personal relationships, their rewards usually do not correspond to the occupational rewards men on the way to success expect, such as raises and promotion (Epstein, 1976); their pay is more likely to be in the form of a bonus or a gratis attitude. As a result, such informal rewards become highly valued and women tend to alter their expectations to what they can get rather than to what the rewards in the work situation ought to be.

There are still other subtle dimensions in the upward mobility of females especially in professional fields. In these areas, ability is usually cultivated through experience. Lawyers, for example, learn to acquire skill in handling a variety of cases in courts and administrative assistants learn leadership techniques from their superiors, whereas women to a large extent have been excluded from this training even when their jobs are appropriate for serving such apprenticeships. Perhaps in specific dual-career marriages, the development of female career patterns is apt to be more affected by the informal structure of the occupation. Results of a five-year longitudinal study (Martin and Jacobsen, 1975) of dual-career marriages of professional sociologists suggest that the marital pair share views, clues and opinions relevant to occupational success more than do single professionals. Although the analysis is limited to a specific profession there is an indication that professional advantages tend to accrue to the wife of a professional husband. However, whether professional benefits tend to accrue to the husband of a professional wife is questionable.

Although some research findings seem to document the structural similarity in the status attainment of men and women, the role the informal network system plays in the upward mobility of the sexes is dissimilar. Informal structures and supports are necessary to growth and development. Hence, excluding women from these opportunities prevents them from receiving the stimulation they need to develop.

The Polity

For the most part politics has been viewed traditionally as a male activity. Formal laws and informal norms have kept women from assuming positions of political leadership and decision-making in most societies, with a few historical exceptions.

Cultural definitions of women's roles in society have restrained their political interest and participation. As with work roles, political roles conflict with the roles of wife and mother in that family responsibilities and children make political activity extremely hard to pursue and may even suppress an interest in it. Thus, campaigning, running for office or simply being involved in politics is secondary to home activities. A recent study (MacPherson, 1975), shows that male campaigners seldom face questioning as to the quality or extent of the care they give their children or the affection they give their wives. Wives who campaign are apt to be considered neglectful of family responsibilities. On the other hand, if they are attentive mothers their ability to run for public office may be questioned. Paradoxically, when women campaign for their husbands, they tend to be glorified. While family responsibilities comprise only part of the problem in the political activity of women, they are not viewed as winners and they rarely have the contacts to tap the financial resources that men have or the informal contacts to mobilize these resources in the political arena.

Despite these difficulties, American women are not completely stifled. Although a smaller proportion of women than men vote in national elections, the proportion is changing. (Lansing, 1974: 22). Since employment and the level of education are both rising for women, there will be more women voters in the future. It is also reported that female political activists (women in pressure groups, party workers, legislators, bureaucrats) show marked differences in levels of participation when compared to their male counterparts (Lansing, 1974: 22). These findings suggest that changes are taking place in the political life of women. Although their numbers remained small in 1974, women were elected to several important posts in their own right as governors of states, lieutenant governors and congresswomen. (No women elected to the Senate.) In January of 1975 women constituted 8 percent of state legislators (Citizens Advisory Council on the Status of Women: 22). Thus, the political activity of women gives evidence of a steady increase over past decades.

Another change is noticeable in the demographic composition of women who are in politics. A recent study (Kirkpatrick, 1974) shows that women who held state political office in the past typically came from backgrounds in voluntary service and had been active in church and school affairs. They were older on the average than male legislators, running for office over the age of 40, while 90 percent of their male counterparts had made their first political attempt before that age. Presently, women are running for public office at a younger age and those seeking higher office are almost all lawyers. Since more women are now entering law schools, it seems likely that more of them will seek political office and will have the training and experience in debate and negotiations.

To improve the political status of women, the National Women's Political Caucus (NWPC) was formed in 1971 to seek the development of the political potential of women. NWPC was responsible for raising campaign funds, seating more women delegates at political conventions and for seeking caucus endorsement favourable to its positions on issues of women's equality. The organization has been also important as a symbol of women's growing political concerns and frustrations together with other groups such as NOW, the Women's Campaign Fund, the Women's Lobby and other established women's groups all of whom are adopting a more active political stand. In a comparative sense, the NWPC represents a new form of political activity.

It is extremely doubtful that sex status will cease to be a criterion for work assignments in political activities. Since political life represents the highest rank system of power in society, it is closely guarded. Hence, for women to enter the networks of political activity, they have to progress in political careers by all the routes men take or they have to associate with other women to form powerful pressure groups. In other words, achieving a high socioeconomic position in society is necessary but not sufficient—women have to learn how to make political gains. Unless they are in a position of power and influence, American women will continue to have a weak position in society.

Education

Education has been one of the important channels of upward mobility in the United States. Yet women were barred from higher education, including professional schools, until the middle of the 19th century. Those schools that admitted women prior to the 1970's usually imposed informal quotas on their admission, keeping women students about 5 percent of the total. Until the 1960's women were dropping out of college to get married. Cultural attitudes that regarded women as having less need for education than men continued to discourage them from education in many areas especially at high levels. Even privileged women with credentials identical to those of men have been prevented from progressing in a status hierarchy appropriate to their training.

In the late 1960's and 1970's the women's movement won actions to prevent exclusionary quotas on the basis of sex. Since 1971 with the enactment of the comprehensive Health Manpower Training Bill, schools of medicine, dentistry, pharmacy and veterinary science can no longer qualify for federal funds if they discriminate in admissions on the basis of sex. Institutions have also been forced to adopt affirmative action programs by seeking recruits among minority groups and women. Separate sex colleges were desegregated on the grounds that separate education is unequal education. New regulations have been proposed by the Department of Health, Education and Welfare to end all forms of sex discrimination remaining in education and to broaden the participation of women in education at all levels.

The changes in the status of women have encouraged more young women to complete college and go to graduate school. Women have moved into higher education in greater numbers. For the young mother with small children and for older women, returning to school has brought some problems. The need for child care centres, the demands of family commitments, inflexible work schedules and the pressures of their new roles are some of the difficulties that women have had to confront. The educational structure in its present form is poorly suited to women returning to school after their children have grown up and to young married women who wish to complete their education before starting a family (Feldman and Feldman,

1973; Tomeh, 1975: 41). However, some of the activities of women returning to school include pressuring for guidelines under the new Title IX of the Education Act Amendment of 1972 to bar discrimination against women who because of family responsibilities attend school part-time and/or at a later age.

Once in school, women find that their self-images are inadequately represented in books and the media. A number of studies document the stereotyped images of men and women in children's picture books and textbooks (U'ren, 1971; Nilsen, 1971; Ehrlich, 1971; Weitzman et al., 1972; Tomeh, 1975: 35). School books have tended to present children and adults playing stereotyped roles idealized by the culture. They show girls engaged in dressing dolls while boys are playing ball; mothers baking cookies and fathers carrying a brief case. Even in college textbooks, women as an object of study are largely ignored; only in the field of marriage and family are they seen to exist.

In an attempt to examine the extent to which college students adhere to stereotypical images in play situations, respondents in the present study were asked to indicate the degree of their agreement or disagreement with the statement that "it is certainly as acceptable for boys as for girls to play with dolls" (Table 4). The females were significantly less traditional than their male partners ($T=8.41$, $p<0001$). In other words, males objected to boys playing with dolls while females thought it was acceptable. This suggests that role exchange is not quite acceptable to males at the level studied. Perhaps a change in the way males and females are portrayed in the mass media and in other educational materials will begin to show women in leading roles. Attempts in this direction are taking place. Feminist presses established in the 1970's began to publish books showing boys cooking and playing with dolls while girls were playing with trucks, mothers working and fathers caring for children. In addition, NOW, State departments and the American Association of School Administrators took action to amend textbooks that depicted women and girls in stereotypical ways. The basic concern here is not with reversed roles, but with an honest attempt to show that men and women can exchange roles.

Another mechanism of sex role reinforcement found in the American educational system is found in the authority structure (Tomeh, 1975). In elementary schools, the large majority of all teachers are women while most of the principals are men. In secondary schools, there is an equal balance between male and female teachers but 92 percent of high school principals are male. At the college level, female models are under-represented. It has been suggested that at each educational level, students of the opposite sex have disadvantages in their educational experience. Sexton (1969) shows that working-class boys were discriminated against by women teachers who tend to reward boys according to feminine attributes—compliance, passivity, etc. At the college level, the hearings on discrimination at various institutions in the 1970's heard women report on their biased treatment by male professionals who believe women are not worth an academic investment because they will leave to have a family.

Although the above practices are changing as positions in the labor force and in politics are changing, women still report subtle resistance to their academic participation.

The Family

Social changes rarely occur without affecting the structure and function of the family. Conversely, family roles that individuals play have major implications for the role they play in other social institutions. Traditionally, most family systems have limited the participation of women outside the family while men were expected to participate in external activities. Some sociologists maintain that this division of labor provides stability and continuity in the family. Others argue that stability is achieved at the cost of repressing the needs and interests of both men and women.

To some extent, the integration of traditional roles with changes in the economic and political roles has become problematic. Proponents of the new view insist on freedom to reject family roles assigned on the basis of sex. The women's movement, for example, has led women to question the inequality implicit in family relations and the law by which husbands are defined as "head of household." This pressure had brought about changes in family relations. Domestic responsibilities, once considered the role of women alone, have become a norm among a growing proportion of young husbands whose young wives work and refuse to bear the exclusive burden of household responsibilities. But not many men are willing to be involved in domestic tasks and child care to the same degree that women by tradition have been involved. To men the issue of the connection between role norms and children is not as relevant as it is for women who consider it of central importance so long as they continue to find themselves in a subordinate position to men (Gillespie, 1971). The family as the central interest to women is also borne out in the present study. In response to the statement: "More women than men feel guilty about breaking up their families when they have young children" (Table 4), a significant proportion of women report guilt feelings about this situation as compared with men ($T = -4.61$, $p < .0001$).

A recent study by Osmond and Martin, (1975) based on a sample of college students shows that the great amount of sex differentiation and sex typing occurs in the familial role. They find that members of both sexes accept a fairly sharp division of labor by sex within the family, with the female continuing to have primary responsibility for home and child care. These results suggest that little sex role change has occurred in the family. This position is not strongly substantiated in the present study (Table 5), though the differential by sex continues to be significant in the area of institutionalized husband-wife equality (reconstructed scale items originally used by Scanzoni, 1975, 1976). Here the emphasis is on permanent institutional behavior performed by the husband in response to his wife's occupational interests which are not in

Table 5

Mean Institutionalized Husband-Wife Equality Scores by Sex

Items	Sex	
	Females (N=382)	Males (N=229)
Earnings of working wives are as important as those of the husband.*	1.83	2.10
When the wife works, the husband should share equally in the responsibilities of children.*	1.57	1.91
When the wife works, the husband should share equally in household chores such as cooking, cleaning, and shopping.*	1.68	2.03
A father and mother should spend an equal amount of time with their young children.*	1.43	1.69
A father could care for young children in the same way as a mother could care for them.*	1.79	2.16

T-test for significance of differences between the sexes significant at: $p < .0001 = *$

accordance with traditional male expectations. The husband's and the working wife's interests are of equal importance. Nontraditionalism is indicated by a stronger acceptance of egalitarianism (low means), while role traditionalism is indicated by lesser preference for the kinds of individual gratifications for wives (high means).

An examination of the data in Table 5 shows that in each instance of family responsibility, women are significantly more egalitarian than men in family role sharing. Women are also significantly more likely than men to consider the earnings of working wives as important as those of the husband. Thus, institutionalized equality between husband and wife within the context of the family is not readily accepted by men. It is important to note that since these results reflect an educated sample of young adults, one might expect even more traditional responses of a less educated sample. If the attitudes of a college group can be taken as indicator of sex role change, findings of the present study suggest some moderate changes in the traditional sex distribution of familial roles in the future. These will be led for the most part by women.

Structural and Normative Constraints on the Family: In industrial societies such as the United States where more women have chosen to work, men and women live with role strain that comes from conflict between the duties attached to different roles (Rapoport and Rapoport, 1969, 1971; Bebbington, 1973; Burke and Weir, 1976). Some of these stresses arise from the reorganization of roles within the marriage itself while others arise from the conflict of dual-career family patterns with society at large.

Early studies, as well as more recent ones (Feld, 1963) find that working wives experience wide-spread guilt and anxiety about adequately fulfilling maternal and housewife roles in addition to their work roles. Nye (1974) suggests that any adverse effects of working may be mitigated by whatever psychological, sociological or economic benefits the wife perceives as accruing to herself and the family by virtue of her employment.

Yet those who combine household and employee roles tend to be more satisfied with their work, communities, family income, children and home (Nye and Hoffman, 1963) than traditional housewives. Working wives have a higher sense of self-esteem, more confidence and a greater sense of personal competence and autonomy (Feldman and Feldman, 1973; Burke and Weir, 1976) than nonworking wives. The positive attitudes and psychological disposition of working wives may tend to compensate for the conflicts that arise from playing multiple roles. At the same time, by entering the realm of work, women are moving into an area highly regarded by society. In taking this step, women feel that they are improving their status in relation to the existing cultural values as well as lessening the intensity of worries and concerns they appear to have as a result of integrating work with home.

As for the effect of the wife's employment on the husband-wife relationship, most of the early studies (Gianapoulous and Mitchell, 1957; Feld, 1963; Gover, 1963; Powell, 1963; Nye and Hoffman, 1963) found small differences favoring unemployed wives over employed wives on measures of marital status, satisfaction and adjustment. These differences were more evident between wives of lower-class families than between wives of middle-class families. Recent research data (Orden and Bradburn, 1969; Feldman and Feldman, 1973) suggest that these differences no longer persist between working and nonworking middle-class wives, though they continue to appear between lower-class wives. Axelson (1970) finds that husbands of housewives are more likely to evaluate marriage positively than are husbands of working wives. Orden and Bradburn (1969) report that husbands and wives indicate higher marital happiness when the wife is in the labor market out of choice than when she is employed out of economic necessity or when she is a housewife. Burke and Weir's (1976) study based on 189 married husband-wife pairs shows that husbands of working wives are *less* content with marriage as compared to husbands of housewives.

Thus, the benefits which accrue to the wife and family from her participation in the labor force do not appear to mitigate the strains husbands experience in this situation. Other studies (Bebbington, 1973) suggest that husbands accept wives working out of a sense of equality, and because they want to see the wife happy (Poloma and Garland, 1971).

Komarovsky (1973) in a study of college men found that many conceded the case for equality but were disturbed to think of its effect on their personal lives and hoped that their wives would conform to a traditional pattern and assume home responsibilities until the children were of shool age. Holstrom (1972) suggests that men who are helping at home are assimilating functions which are regarded in the hierarchy of socio-cultural values as less skillful especially since a man's prestige and success are linked to his ability to function in the business world. While the working wife's sense of self-esteem is being enhanced, the husband is experiencing a discrepancy between selfimage and actual roles as well as experiencing other difficulties related to the partial loss of the active support system that a wife provides.

Industrialization and the rise of bureaucracy with its emphasis on universal criteria created the dominance of economic roles over family roles for men. For men and women who work outside the home, no institutional mechanisms are available to alleviate the pressures they experience from role conflict. Even men feel constrained by the institution in which they work. Husbands who wish to help with the children find it difficult to take time off from work. Likewise, since women are expected to make the family their first priority and work as secondary, once they are in the job market, the bureaucratic structure becomes insensitive to their family obligations. A common adaptation to this pressure has been the segregation of women to occupations that complement family activities or the tendency to allocate to a majority of women roles outside the regular labor force.

While it is legitimate to consider the roles of wife and mother as economic, i.e. standing in some economic relationship with the labor market and having some income, our conventions lead us to ignore those roles as part of the stratification system. Nevertheless, the institution of childbearing and homemaking as the domain of women is one of the major bases of sexual inequality of socio-eocnomic opportunity. Moreover, the emphasis on monetary values leads work at home to be thought of as nonproductive, without prestige and power irrespective of the socio-economic background of those women who work in the home. Thus, the transition to modern society with its structure of role priorities and its inflexibility has created some problems for both the American family and the larger society.

Recently, the women's movement has focused attention on the consequences of the prevalent belief that work done in the home by women or men is nonproductive. Efforts are being made to have the government correct the problem that derives from this view. Economists are also being urged to identify the economic value of housework and to find ways to extend benefits to reward unpaid workers in the home (James, 1975; Johnson, 1975; Bergmann, 1973). National income accounting excludes unpaid household labor from the measure of society's product (Lekachman, 1975: 95).

If the household can be conceived in economic terms as an enterprise unit in which husbands and wives invest cash and services (food, clothes, transportation, cleaning, shopping, etc.), then some social and legal guarantees need to be outlined. The fact that such a system is not available anywhere in the world, from the most industrial to the least developed country, does not mean a conceptualization of the family as an economic unit is not possible.[3]

---

3 A group of economic researchers in the Social Security Administration in the United States has established the value of housework performed by the average American housewife by

Interestingly, recent research (Aronoff and Crano, 1975) applying a newly developed data base (Murdock's Ethnographic Atlas, 1967), investigated the degree to which males assumed the role of task specialist in the subsistence economy of 862 societies over five critical subsistence variables. It revealed that women contributed an average of 44 percent of subsistence production. This new study provides no support for Parsons and Bales' proposition that a universal feature of the social structure of the family is sex role specialization of tasks.

Since the likehood of altering the view of the institution of childbearing and homemaking to an economic enterprise is not forseeable in the near future, women need to search for ways to gain extrafamilial benefits. Consequently, not only are women having fewer children[4] (Scanzoni, 1976), they are deferring slightly the age at which they are having first children. Young people are now believed to express more approval for childless marriages but only very few actually want to be childless. The present birth rate is continuing to decrease and if the American woman continues to bear children at the 1971 rate, i.e., 1.8 children (U.S. Department of Commerce, Social and Economic Statistical Bureau and U.S. Bureau of Census, 1972: 54), by the time she is 32 years of age, she will have 42 years of life left to fill after her children have entered school.

Empirically, results of the present study substantiate some national trends. The data show, for example, that 42 percent ideally prefer to have 2 children, 32 percent indicate three or four children as the ideal number of children, with only 7 percent preference for no children. About two-thirds of the respondents prefer to have the ideal combination of an equal number of boys and girls. However, the second preferred ideal is either all boys or an excess of boys over girls while the opposite combination is least popular. These findings basically suggest an equality in family size by sex with preference for boys over girls as the second best ideal. The latter is a reflection of marital standards of sex role behavior. To the question of the ideal age for women to marry, 59 percent of the women say the ideal age for women to marry is between 22 and 24 years, while 45 percent of men choose the same age category. Results remain basically the same when sex is controlled. Although the pressure

---

calculating the market cost of each of the tasks carried out. The estimate ranges from $ 5,389 per year for housewives aged 15—29, to a peak of $ 6,417 for those aged 25—29 to $ 2,942 for those aged 60—64 (the New York Times, January 13, 1976).

4 Census data show that in June, 1971, white married women aged 14—24 with 1—3 years of college expected 2.34 children. Women with 4 years or more of college expected 2.16 children (U. S. Bureau of the Census, 1974, No. 236). By 1973, white wives, as a whole, aged 18—24 expected 2.3 children (U.S. Bureau of the Census, 1974, No. 48). There has been a general society-wide move toward expecting a two child family, as evidenced by 1973 census data showing that among all 18-24-year-old childless wives, 61.4 percent expect only two children (U.S. Bureau ot the Census, 1974, No. 265).

to get married for this age is greater for women than men, which in a sense is a traditional pattern, age at marriage has increased.

The above changes in company with the increase in women's age at birth of the first child (i.e., the age at which she attains the status of mother) mean that women, as a group, can fulfill the obligation of other status commitments for a longer period. They can enter the labor force as a means of productively expanding their post-childbearing lives, obtain more job training and involve themselves more fully in their careers.

Studies based on large national samples of women in their mid-twenties (Waite and Stolzenberg, 1976; Bumpass and Westoff, 1970: 95), show that women tend to limit their fertility plans so as to accomodate their plans to participate in the labor force, and women's fertility expectations do seem to affect their plans for labor force participation. However, the effect of the latter relationship is rather small whereas the effect of the former relationship (i.e., the effect of labor force participation plans on fertility expectations) is rather substantial.

In the meantime, changes in the husband's role behavior are not substantial. Men will continue with what they have always had, namely, access to instrumental benefits even under the most egalitarian situations prescribed by role dimensions. Women who seek individualistic rewards may feel compelled to reduce costs; and it may be that in marital relationships men who are more egalitarian would agree with their wives, limited birth plans rather than take an active role in determining them.

The changing work roles of women in American society are forcing other institutions to become more sensitive to the needs of the family. For example, if women are to have well-paid jobs and work satisfaction, bureaucracies will find it more difficult to transfer husbands to another company—a requirement for executive advancement when the family was regarded as subjected to the occupational needs of the husband and father. Yet the other needs of the family—if they were evaluated as highly—would impose a constraint on the behavior thought necessary for the husbands' success in the business world.

A study based on a national sample of white women college graduates and their spouses (Duncan and Perrucci, 1976) shows that the relative "fullness" of the wife's labor force participation, as measured by the prestige of her occupation or contribution to the total family income, is inconsequential to familial migration. In contrast, the nature of the husband's occupation significantly affects the couple's migration probability. When the couple moves in partial response to the husband's occupational situation, the move is unfavorable to the wife's continued participation in the labor force (Long, 1974, for similar findings).

Another study less analytic than the above, (Holmstrom, 1970; 1972) concluded on the basis of 20 dual-career families in the United States, that a woman's decision as to where she might live is very much influenced by the career of her husband which is in accordance with social expectations. In most of these same couples, the husband's decision about where to live was significantly influenced at least once by the career of his wife (Holmstrom, 1970: 518).

The above results suggest that, if mobility is related to career success, it would be to each spouse's advantage to choose a location independent of the other's interest. Career opportunities may force the husband and wife to move in opposite directions while they may wish to remain together as a family. However, at least attitudinally and based on results of the present sample, there appears to be a growing realization that a man should not arbitrarily expect his family to adjust to the demands of his profession (45 percent). And a large majority of respondents (78 percent) feel that a married man should realize that his wife's career may very well interfere with his job. In either case, however, females have a significantly more favorable attitude than males ($T=2.17$, $p<.03$; $T=3.82$, $0<.0001$, respectively). In response to such hypothetical situations as who should be most willing to move if his/her spouse is transferred to a better job, 58 percent report that either spouse is willing but 37 percent prefer the wife to move with the husband. In another instance, where husband and wife work in jobs which require commuting between 25–35 miles, living half-way is the most chosen alternative (62 percent) while the second preference is for the husband to commute (23 percent). Although these results suggest the emergence of an egalitarian pattern, the second best choice is within the confines of a traditional pattern.

Now that women are working in increasing numbers, organizations may have to take account of the family as a unit where husband and wife both work and bureaucratic structures need to adjust to changing patterns. The norms surrounding sexual division of labor and stratification especially in the occupational sector of society have come under strong attack. Pressure will also come from individuals who need flexible work schedules to meet family demands.

Women's growing activity in the labor force has repercussions on family life as well. In most instances, competing in the world of work involves full-time and sometimes overtime work. Consequently, one's position as a family member receives no support and it becomes increasingly difficult to function as a parent. In part, this may explain why many people are less willing to assume the responsibility of parenthood and this in turn may be related to a declining birthrate and an increasing rate of divorce and separation. Thus, it may be questionable whether the parental role is diminishing or it is the matter of switching roles.

In American society, the rewards for marriage and parenthood are not high. The penalties and stresses are on the increase even in economic terms since the tax laws now make it more profitable for a working couple to live together rather than marry. This living-together pattern, while more and more accepted, is not an emerging family model. There appears to be a need to order priorities and rearrange the style of living so that people who want to function as parents can do so without strain. Special efforts need to be made to change the world of work so as to recognize that for a family to function, parents and adults need an opportunity to be with children.[5] Strict work schedules are likely to alienate family members unless alternative systems of child-raising are developed. Since the latter is a costly proposition, a reorganization of the occupational system to free parents (men and women) to be with family members is a better answer.

Through the efforts of a few leaders like Farrell (1975) some men have formed liberation groups with the intention of de-emphasizing the demands made upon men by the market place. Some change is occurring in the courts and men are beginning to win child custody in divorce cases. In other cases, men are demanding paternity leaves from school and teaching, and equal rights to the social security survivors benefits as widowers.

Given the present structure of social institutions, it is a heavy responsibility for both women and men to perform well in all the areas of life in which they are now supposed to have competence. Today the American nuclear family is overburdened with the need to be providers, workers, partners, companions, ideal parents, etc. The demands of these roles have resulted in a high percentage of marriages ending in divorce yet some of the tensions are outside the marriage and are created by the inability of other institutions to adjust to changes taking place within the family. Even with today's economic pressures, young people seem to want to live by more realistic values and to have a family life based on family sharing. The "new family" has individual needs that will aggregate and become problems for society if other social institutions do not come to the rescue.

Structural Correlates of Sex Role Orientation

It is evident from the above discussion on the institutional position of American women that some advances, though not major ones, have been made in law, education, the polity, the economy and in certain other spheres of society. Changes in the social structure and adjustments in social institutions cannot go far without changes in ideology or in the social definition of the sexes. This section will examine changes in sex role orientation and identify the structural characteristics of those who endorse nontraditional attitudes and behaviors.

Some studies report that sex role stereotypes are still subscribed to by a substantial proportion of young American adults (Bayer, 1975; Broverman, et al., 1972). These young adults include a large number of college students, health professionals, educators and business people who will interact with children and act as role models. Nonetheless, there appears to be evidence of change in sex role attitudes. Parelius

---

5 Parenthetically, Sweden recently passed a law to say that when a child is ill, parents can take leave from their jobs with the father required to take half of the leave and the mother half. The mother cannot take it all. This represents a legal recognition that children need both parents.

(1975: 151) compared representative samples of students from an Eastern woman's college in 1969 and again in 1973 and found sizeable shifts toward feminism during this time interval. The greatest changes in the direction of egalitarianism were in their attitudes toward work, financial responsibilities and division of labor in the home. The study also reported that women respondents perceived themselves changing more than men, a conclusion which other studies also verify (Scanzoni, 1976; Bayer, 1975). Data presented previously also show that while both sexes generally take an egalitarian position, the ratio of increase is significantly greater for females than males.

Similarly, Scanzoni (1976) compared college students in 1971 and 1974 on sex role dimensions and reported greater support for female modernity among 1974 respondents. The 1974 women also indicated an intention to work more frequently than 1971 women. Men in 1974 were more willing for females to work than were 1971 men. The expectation of men and women working at high status jobs did not change much in three years. This latter finding is supported by the results of the present investigation which shows that 51 percent of the respondents have intentions to be in professional jobs, 21 percent in semi-professional positions, 13 percent in clerical occupations and the rest are not sure. The expectation of holding high white-collar jobs is a function of the sample which represents an articulate segment of the population—the college group. However, it is unlikely that college men and women will have the same expectation regarding equal pay for the same type of occupation. It may well be that men expect higher paying jobs than women.

It appears then from the above findings that increases in sex role egalitarianism —over time—may be related to the high intentions of females working as well as to the males' intentions to support females working, though the latter may be contingent on economic need as noted earlier. Nonetheless, women consistently expect to work more frequently than men expect their wives to work. These findings support the notion that the subordinate group is the one most concerned about structural change.

While studies mentioned above seem to document a change in sex role standards over the last few years, it is important to identify the structural characteristics of those who support this change. This identification will provide some insight into where the significant areas of change in sex equality exist and will allow a description of the target groups which may be playing an important role in women's place in society.

Socio-economic status: It has been claimed that the potential for change toward a nontraditional sex orientation lies largely within higher education. This is partly because much of the current feminist leadership can be found in academic circles (Rossi and Calderwood, 1973) and partly, because the leaders of the second generation are the students presently enrolled in higher education (Epstein and Bronzaft,

1972 for a similar view). Holter (1970) notes that preferences for greater rights and benefits for women have occurred most forcefully among the better educated. This view receives support empirically where studies have been shown that college women give less support to traditional roles than other women at all points in time; they do not however, appear, to have adopted egalitarian view-points more quickly than other women (Mason, Czajka and Arber, 1976).

With greater numbers of women attaining higher levels of education (U.S. Bureau of the Census, 1973) younger women may begin to scale down preferences for familistic rewards and seek greater levels of individualistic gratification, as shown in the previous tables. This does not imply that modern American women will reject the core female role of wife and mother. They may, however, postpone marriage, have fewer children, pursue careers or adopt other alternative life styles. In this respect, research shows (Mason, Czajka and Arber, 1976) a stronger association between women's attitude toward their roles in the family and labor force in 1973 and 1974 than in 1970. This seems to be consistent with the emphasis of the women's movement on the interrelatedness between these two roles. Thus, both education and the "movement" have contributed to wider dissemination of social science research—research that has found little evidence to support such traditional sex role-related misconceptions as the idea that maternal employment harms children or that women are naturally less suited than men for responsible professions. However, when a comparison is made between the effect of exposure to feminist ideas or other familistic variables on sex role attitudes, research indicates (Mason, Czajka and Arber, 1976) that educational attainment and employment experience are most indicative of traditional norms and beliefs. In other words, those with the most recent employment experience and those who have completed college are least traditional in outlook.

A number of other studies, based for the most part on college students, also show a positive relationship between a female's own level of education and her sex role outlook (Mason and Bumpass, 1975; Brogan and Kutner, 1976; Bayer, 1975; Scanzoni, 1975; Duberman and Azumi, 1975). Some of these studies further show that, among undergraduate female students, the educational level of the mother is related to the sex role orientation of the daughter. The argument is that more highly-educated mothers are likely to be more nontraditional in sex role outlook and tend to transmit, this orientation to their daughters (Brogan and Kutner, 1976; Mason and Bumpass 1975; Meier, 1972 for similar results on males and females).

Similarly, the mother's involvement in occupational roles outside the home during the daughter's school years is positively related to the sex role orientation of the daughters (Meier, 1972; Brogan and Kutner, 1976). This is consistent with the view that daughters of mothers who work outside the home tend to be less traditional in sex role outlook than are daughters whose mothers do not work (Nye and Hoffman, 1963: 301).

In this research multiple classification analysis (MCA) is used to examine the contribution of various structural characteristics to variation in each of the sex role orientation dimensions discussed earlier.[6] Accordingly, Table 6 shows the relative contribution of socio-economic variables to variation in each of the sex role orientation dimensions both before and after controlling all independent variables.[7]

It is observed that the socio-economic status of parents taken together accounts for only a small portion (i.e., from two to sixteen percent) of the variation in most of the dimensions of sex role orientation of daughters and sons. For the female group, either the mother's occupation or her work experience is related to most aspects of sex role orientation, though the coefficients are rather low. Father's occupation is equally important in the personality sex role behavior and sex role conflict of his daughter. For each of the predictor variables, after controlling for the remaining ones, the beta does not vary much from eta which suggests that mother's occupation, her work experience, or the father's occupation are somewhat important in accounting for certain phases of sex role orientation.[8] An examination of the sub-categories of each of these variables indicates that nontraditional sex role attitudes are associated with the mother's and father's higher occupational level, as well as the mother's greater work experience.

---

[6] Multiple classification analysis (Andrews, et al., 1967) is used to examine the remaining differences in each of the dimensions of sex role orientation among male and female college students after statistically controlling for all other independent variables. This procedure treats each category of each independent variable as a dummy variable. Using additive multiple least-squares regression, it adjusts the mean of the dependent variable for each category of the independent variables by the amount of deviation from the total sample (grand) mean that is due to intercorrelation with other independent variables in the analysis. In other words, the MCA relates a number of predictor variables to a dependent variable, in the context of an additive model. Eta represents the ability of each predictor to explain variation in the dependent variable; as a measure of correlation, it can be compared with other etas from the same or different MCAs. Beta is the ability of the predictor to explain variation after adjusting for the effects of all other predictors; as such, it can only be used to compare the relative importance of predictors within one MCA. The multiple r is adjusted for degrees of freedom and the adjusted multiple r^2 may be thought of as the amount of intercorrelation the analysis corrected for.

[7] The dependent variables, i.e., aspects of sex role orientation, represent a total score for all the items in each scale for every respondent. The subcategories for the independent variables are as follows: education of father and mother—high school or less, more than high school; occupation of father and mother — professional and semi-professional, clerical and skilled, unskilled and kindred workers; mother's work experience — mother does not work, mother works or has worked while children are growing up; college status — freshman, sophomore, upperclassmen and women or graduate; age — 18-19, 20-21, 22 or over; religious preference — Protestant, Catholic, other; size of hometown — 14,999 or less, 15,000-49,999, 50,000 or more; birth order — oldest, in between, youngest; size of family and ideal number of children — three or less, four or more; sex of siblings—same sex, equal number of boys and girls, more boys than girls, more girls than boys.

[8] Andrews, et al. (1967: 117-119), point out that the square of beta is not exactly interpretable as the percent of explained variation in the dependent variable. This is why beta-squared is an estimate. The important point for the present study is that this coefficient provides a measure of the *relative* importance of the various predictors.

Table 6

Relative Contribution to Variation in Sex Role Orientation Scores by Socio-Economic Status before and after Covariance Adjustment* for each Sex (MCA)

Predictors	Females (N=310)		Males (N=166)	
Personality				
sex role behavior	Eta	Beta	Eta	Beta
Socio-economic status				
Mother's education	.03	.02	.14	.02
Mother's occupation	.04	.04	.15	.20
Mother's work experience	.12	.14	.17**	.26
Father's education	.08	0.2	.17	.05
Father's occupation	.14	.14	.19	.14
	multiple $r^2 = .038$		multiple $r^2 = .107$	
Self-actualization of women	Eta	Beta	Eta	Beta
Socio-economic status				
Mother's education	.05	.11	.02	.04
Mother's occupation	.07	.10	.05	.12
Mother's work experience	.10	.12	.18	.22
Father's education	.01	.05	.10	.00
Father's occupation	.07	.09	.22	.22
	multiple $r^2 = .031$		multiple $r^2 = .088$	
Attitudes towards the employment of women	Eta	Beta	Eta	Beta
Socio-economic status				
Mother's education	.07	.03	.08	.04
Mother's occupation	.14	.14	.10	.21
Mother's work experience	.05	.04	.24**	.33
Father's education	.05	.01	.19	.05
Father's occupation	.07	.05	.25**	.24
	multiple $r^2 = .026$		multiple $r^2 = .159$	
Sex role conflict	Eta	Beta	Eta	Beta
Socio-economic status				
Mother's education	.00	.00	.05	.07
Mother's occupation	.04	.06	.12	.15
Mother's work experience	.07	.07	.08	.13
Father's education	.01	.08	.02	.04
Father's occupation	.10	.15	.15	.14
	multiple $r^2 = .021$		multiple $r^2 = .052$	
Institutionalized equality	Eta	Beta	Eta	Beta
Socio-economic status				
Mother's education	.01	.08	.12	.02
Mother's occupation	.12	.14	.09	.13
Mother's work experience	.10	.10	.19**	.23
Father's education	.02	.00	.17	.02
Father's occupation	.01	.02	.24	.22
	multiple $r^2 = .027$		multiple $r^2 = .108$	

* Covariance adjustment refers to controlling for all of the other variables listed in each heading.
** Significance of F $p < .05$ level.

For the male group, most of the predictor variable coefficients show an increase. However, it may be of interest to note that the mother's socio-economic background is not unrelated to the sex role orientation of her son especially in maintaining the son's nontraditional personality sex role behavior. On all the other socio-economic factors, mother's work experience continues to play a part in the son's attitudes toward the employment of married women (Eta=.24), in the self-actualization of women (Eta=.18), and in institutionalized equality (Eta=.19). Even when other factors are controlled, the beta values for most of the above etas are not reduced which indicates that some of the socio-economic variables cannot be completely ignored in the study of sex role orientation. Father's occupation has a noticeable effect on all aspects of the son's sex role orientation (Eta=.15–.24). However, the education of father is less important and is not in itself a sufficient predictor of the sex role orientation measures.

It is clear, however, that, for females, socio-economic status, especially the mother's, does not emerge to be a strong predictor of sex role attitudes as seems to be suggested in previous studies. On the other hand, for males, socio-economic status including mother's work experience, is a relevant predictor in this respect.

Lipman-Blumen (1972) using a sample perhaps even more homogeneous than undergraduate college students (i.e., Boston area graduate student wives) found no relationship between socio-economic status, including mother's employment, and sex role orientation (see Scanzoni, 1975 for lack of association between social status background and role modernity). It is possible that persons from higher status backgrounds may have internalized fairly comparable sets of sex role structures. Variations in degree of role egalitarianism may be sharper in heterogenous class backgrounds than in a homogenous group such as graduate college students.

At least in population groups where socio-economic status makes a difference in the level of nontraditional sex role orientation, it may well be that, as power becomes more evenly distributed in society, traditional sexual norms promoting sexual division of labor and sexual stratification will recede in the face of those norms which favor achieved statuses.

In the future, trends in women's schooling and employment may be more important for predicting attitudinal changes than are trends in other variables (i.e., family formation/dissolution, or other related factors). The educational distribution of American women and their roles in the labor force have shifted upward during the past decade; for this reason alone, the proportion of women giving support to the traditional roles of the sexes may decline.

Demographic Variables: A number of other demographic variables have also been analyzed with respect to sex role outlook. The general tendency of age, for example, is to be associated with conservatism and thus it is expected that older persons will be more sexist than younger persons (Duberman and Azumi, 1975);

Bayer, 1975). Results contrary to this view are reported by Mason, Czajka and Arber, (1976) showing that older women are no less egalitarian in outlook than those marrying at a younger age.

Table 7 takes into consideration the relative contribution of selected demographic characteristics to the variation in each aspect of sex role orientation. College status, age, religious preference, and size of hometown taken together account for between two to seven percent of the variation in sex role modernity. Demographic variables explain a smaller proportion of the variation in sex role outlook than does socio-economic status. For the female group, age at best explains 5 percent (Eta=.23) of the variation in the self-actualization of women. Although age does not have a strong effect on this aspect of sex role orientation, women who are over 20 years of age seem to be the supporters of this viewpoint. The same is true for the male group (Eta=.18) except that those who support the self-actualization of women are at least over 22 years of age. For both sex groups, the explanatory power of age, when other demographic characteristics are controlled, is reduced (Beta=.12 and .10 respectively) which indicates that age alone is not a sufficient estimate of the individualistic interests of women. It is further observed that for the male group only, age contributes to the variation in institutionalized equality (Eta=.18) which is supported mostly by men over 22 years of age.

Overall, the lack of a strong association between age and sex role orientation may be related to the homogeneity of the college group where the large majority are between 18 and 24 years of age (86%). Heterogeneous samples may produce greater variation in role modernity. The absence of large attitudinal differences according to age may also suggest that attitudinal change has occurred for most cohorts of women and men.

Further analysis of the data distribution in Table 7 shows that college status for both sexes plays a role in the self-actualization of women (Eta=.24 for females and .22 for males) and to a lesser extent in institutionalized equality even when other factors are held constant. Proponents of such egalitarianism are upperclassmen and women as well as graduate students (Bayer, 1975 for similar results). These results are consistent with the view that educational attainment is conducive to sex role equality, though this may not be true of all aspects of sex role equality.

When religion is considered, it appears that Catholics are consistently, though to a modest degree, opponents of the egalitarian sex role position (Scanzoni, 1976). Non-Catholics and especially those with no religious preference endorse nontraditional sex role ideologies (Brogan and Kutner, 1976; Bernard, 1975). The present study indicates that religious identification is hardly a predictor of the sex role dimensions under consideration. It may well be that the effects of religion are diminishing, or, it is possible that among samples which included both college and non-college youth, religion might exhibit stronger correlations with sex roles than it does in this sample.

Research results on urban-rural experiences and sex role orientation are somewhat inconsistent. Some studies report (Duberman and Azumi, 1975; Bayer, 1975) that urban background is less likely than rural background to produce sexist attitudes. Other research (Mason, Czajka and Arber, 1976) shows no significant relationship between region of residence and sex role attitudes. In the present study, size of home-

Table 7

Relative Contribution to Variation in Sex Role Orientation Scores by Demographic Characteristics before and after Covariance Adjustment for Each Sex (MCA)

Predictors	Females (N=356)		Males (N=209)	
Personality sex role behavior	Eta	Beta	Eta	Beta
Demographic characteristics				
Age	.09	.03	.09	.12
College status	.10	.08	.06	.06
Religious preference	.05	.04	.08	.09
Size of hometown	.07	.06	.10	.10
	multiple $r^2 = .017$		multiple $r^2 = .028$	
Self-actualization of women	Eta	Beta	Eta	Beta
Demographic characteristics				
Age	.23	.12	.18	.10
College status	.24	.17	.22	.19
Religious preference	.07	.03	.09	.09
Size of hometown	.09	.06	.04	.03
	multipre $r^2 = .075$		multipre $r^2 = .066$	
Attitudes towards the employment of women	Eta	Beta	Eta	Beta
Demographic characteristics				
Age	.08	.08	.12	.15
College status	.05	.07	.08	.12
Religious preference	.07	.08	.10	.10
Size of hometown	.09	.09	.03	.05
	multiple $r^2 = .023$		multiple $r^2 = .034$	
Sex role conflict	Eta	Beta	Eta	Beta
Demographic characteristics				
Age	.07	.08	.09	.06
College status	.03	.01	.08	.03
Religious preference	.07	.07	.09	.09
Size of hometown	.04	.05	.07	.08
	multiple $r^2 = .013$		multiple $r^2 = .021$	
Institutionalized equality	Eta	Beta	Eta	Bet
Demographic characteristics				
Age	.09	.04	.18*	.18
College status	.10	.08	.12	.10
Religious preference	.06	.04	.10	.11
Size of hometown	.09	.09	.12	.13
	multiple $r^2 = .021$		multiple $r^2 = .068$	

* Significance of F $p < .05$ level.

town, like most of the other demographic variables, does not produce strong effects. For men, however, size of hometown is slightly related to institutionalized equality (Eta=.12) and non-traditional personality sex role behavior (Eta=.10). Although no appreciable effects are observed, it is interesting to note that in these two areas of modernity, men who are residents of small and medium-size cities seem to endorse these views. At least some phases of modern sex role ideologies are reaching male students who come from different-sized cities. In sum, however, demographic variables, such as the ones studied here, seem to be weak predictors of sex role orientation.

Family Variables: In terms of family size, it has been shown (Mason, Czajka and Arber, 1976) that women with large families tend to be less egalitarian in outlook than those with smaller ones and women with no children are often the least egalitarian of all. Other familistic variables (e.g., marriage duration, number of children, women's involvement in marriage and childbearing, age at first marriage, marital status, husband's age to wife) are not shown to predict attitudinal changes towards the roles of the sexes. At the same time, a study based on a nationally representative survey of college students (Bayer, 1975) describes the students who endorse traditional women's roles as more likely to subscribe to marrying soon and to raising a family as a primary life objective. They are also less likely than students in general to support equal opportunity relative to women's employment, are more conservative in their politics, and are more authoritative in most of their attitudes and opinions.

Table 8 considers selected family structural variables in relation to sex role orientation. Altogether, familial variables account for between one to fifteen percent of the variation in sex role orientation compared to the previous predictors. The explanatory power of familial variables is almost similar to socio-economic status. An examination of the data distribution shows that family variables play more of a role in the sex orientation of males than of females.

For example, it is clear that for women the best predictor of sex role orientation based on self-actualization, attitudes towards the employment of women and institutionalized equality is the desired number of children (Eta=.21, .13 and .12 respectively). Those who aspire to a small family size are in favor of women's individualistic benefits and their employment. They support to some extent institutionalized equality even when other factors are controlled. Other familistic factors do not show appreciable contribution to variation in the different aspects of sex role orientation. At least for women, role egalitarianism is not dependent upon the structural characteristics of their families. In contrast, most of the familial variables appear to affect the sex orientation of men. It can be seen, for example, that birth order, sex of siblings and ideal number of children are associated with nontraditional personality sex role behavior, individualistic interests of women and institutionalized equality even when other variables are held constant. Again, it can be seen, that birth order is consistently related to all aspects of sex role orientation except sex role conflict even

Table 8

Relative Contribution to Variation in Orientation Scores by Family Structural Variables before and after Covariance Adjustment for Each Sex (MCA)

Predictors	Females (N=353)		Males (N=205)	
Personality sex role behavior	*Eta*	*Beta*	*Eta*	*Beta*
Family structural variables				
Size of family	.05	.05	.06	.06
Birth order	.05	.05	.17	.18
Sex of siblings	.07	.06	.10	.09
Ideal number of children	.07	.07	.19*	.18
	multiple $r^2 = .014$		multipre $r^2 = .072$	
Self-actualization of women	*Eta*	*Beta*	*Eta*	*Beta*
Family structural variables				
Size of family	.01	.01	.14	.08
Birth order	.05	.07	.21	.17
Sex of siblings	.05	.07	.16	.11
Ideal number of children	.21*	.22	.29*	.29
	multiple $r^2 = .052$		multiple $r^2 = .145$	
Attitudes towards the employment of women	*Eta*	*Beta*	*Eta*	*Beta*
Family structural variables				
Size of family	.05	.09	.09	.09
Birth order	.04	.07	.21*	.21
Sex of siblings	.06	.07	.08	.06
Ideal number of children	.13*	.15	.16	.16
	multiple $r^2 = .030$		multiple $r^2 = .083$	
Sex role conflict	*Eta*	*Beta*	*Eta*	*Beta*
Family structural variables				
Size of family	.02	.01	.06	.09
Birth order	.10	.10	.07	.08
Sex of siblings	.05	.07	.14	.14
Ideal number of children	.05	.05	.12	.12
	multiple $r^2 = .016$		multiple $r^2 = .041$	
Institutionalized equality	*Eta*	*Beta*	*Eta*	*Beta*
Family structural variables				
Size of family	.03	.18	.15	.11
Birth order	.10	.13	.18	.15
Sex of siblings	.06	.05	.13	.08
Ideal number of children	.12	.12	.08	.09
	multiple $r^2 = .034$		multiple $r^2 = .060$	

* Significance of F $p < 0.5$ level.

when other variables are controlled (Eta=.17–.21). Ideal number of children is an equally relevant predictor except in the case of institutionalized equality (Eta=.16–.29). Size of family and sex of siblings are best predictors of the self-actualization of women and institutionalized equality. Sex of siblings is also slightly predictive of sex role conflict. A detailed examination of the subcategories of these variables shows that youngest children, small ideal number of children, small family size and the presence of equal cross-sex siblings in the family are most conducive to a nontraditional outlook among men. Furthermore, the fact that the structural composition of the family is related to their sex ideology and their predictive power cannot go completely unnoticed. To a certain extent, the same is true of socio-economic status and other demographic variables.

The above findings suggest that women, as compared to men, may not only have overcome the inhibiting effect of their background characteristics but as well have either been influenced by the ideology of the women's liberation movement or have identified with supportive models who have motivated and encouraged them to adopt modern sex role views. Women also may be developing strong self-initiative to help them overcome the pressure of sex role traditions. In fact, further analysis of data not reported here shows that for women the predictive power of attitudes towards the women's movement as well as other nontraditional family-related attitudes are far greater in importance than any background characteristic in accounting for the variation in all aspects of sex role orientation presented here (28–50 percent). The pervasive influence of the women's movement has also affected men and their opinion of the women's movement in addition to other nontraditional attitudes is predictive of their sex role outlook as evidenced by further analysis of the data (26–46 percent explained variance).

In all, the contribution of background characteristics to the sex ideology of women college students is relatively weak, whereas for college men it is more consistent and stronger. Nonetheless, an understanding of the structural correlates of sex role orientation is important for understanding some of the processes by which attitudinal change may or may not have been effected.

Conclusion

This paper has examined the changing position of American women in different social institutions with special attention to the empirical study of the structural correlates of sex role orientation. The former concern is based on an analytic review of the literature while the latter attempt utilizes an innovative methodological approach in the study of sex roles directed toward a role-sharing model rather than a function paradigm based on a dichotomy between the sexes. Thus, the different items of the sex role orientation scales were reconstructed with the view of a sex role continuum conceptualized as one which involves lesser or greater degrees of nontraditional traits placed along the same axis for men and women. This procedure is sensitive to present social needs and captures the newly-rising status of women and the changing role of men.

From an institutional perspective, the role of women in the United States, as elsewhere, has become a controversial issue because the roles typically assigned to women in the family—work, politics and education—are structured to keep women subordinate to men and so excluded from the sphere of decision-making and from prestigious positions. Changes in expectations regarding the place of both men and women in society have created considerable discussion and debate in the American society, culminating in the women's movement.

A dramatic change in the position of women has resulted from their growing participation in the labor force, even women with young children. Until recently, women have been drawn into the work force to take sex segregated jobs that are low in rank, pay and prestige and that have few advancement opportunities. The jobs most frequently characterized as female are clerical jobs while professional occupations command a very small minority of women. The sextyping of occupations has resulted, in part, from quotas restricting the percentage of women in professional schools, from discrimination in hiring, from invidious distinctions between men's and women's jobs and from formal and informal practices which tend to perpetuate the status quo. Although legislative changes have abolished discriminatory acts, women are still kept out of male circles by being excluded from the personal network system of contacts which is an important channel in providing information about occupational opportunities and the politics of work. However, as the representation of women in graduate and professional schools continues to increase, women may learn about the clues to advancement through the work of their own collegiate networks.

Real barriers continue to exist for women in extra-familial roles because society still assigns them the primary responsibility for child care and offers few available alternatives. Some families are designing their own adaptations by adopting marriage styles where husband and wife share home responsibilities and attempt a flexible approach to their occupational activities. However, translating egalitarian attitudes into behavior poses a strain on the family in view of the stringent demands of the occupational sphere. Strain has also arisen from the ambiguity created in men and women who are in the process of exchanging role expectations related to their own and others' roles. Last but not least there is the problem of sorting out intimate and personal relationships that fit in with other obligations.

On empirical grounds, the general profile of American society seems to be tending toward a role-sharing model for women where the privileges, opportunities and responsibilities of the sexes are divided about equally. Men, however, seem to favor a certain degree of sex role differentiation. In this respect, the functional approach, based on a dichotomy between the sexes, cannot be applied equally to both sexes as a way to meet present social needs. Results of the present study show that in all aspects of sex role orientation, both males and females take a moderate nontraditional position. Yet within this moderate stance the large majority of the items elicited a significantly more modern response from females, a finding supported by previous research (Parelius, 1975; Scanzoni, 1976; Bayer, 1975).

When the personality sex role behavior dimension is considered, women perceive that men and women have the same personality disposition on such traits as leadership ability, aggression, sympathy, emotion, logic, intellectualism, artistic inclination, and academic pursuits. For each of these personality traits men, however, show significant resistance to conceding this equality especially in the areas of leadership ability and aggressive behavior.

When the question of the self-actualization of women is considered, men generally refuse to accept the wife's interests as equal to those of her husband and children while women insist on the right to their individualistic concerns. These findings suggest that men continue to perceive women primarily in terms of family and children, while their work is secondary. Similarly, when the emphasis is on permanent institutionalized behavior performed by the husband in response to his wife's occupational endeavors, women concurred with this egalitarian posture whereas men showed some reservations in accepting institutionalized equality especially in earnings, household chores, and ability to care for young children. These results are in line with traditional male expectations where the husband's interests are considered more significant than the interests of his working wife.

Similarly, attitudes toward the employment of women elicit, for the most part, significant positive responses from females. However, the differential disappears when the work of women is of an economic necessity. Under this circumstance, men are more willing to accept the employment status of females. However, both men and women do not favor the employment of women in the presence of young children, or in order to get financial return for money spent on their eduaction or to meet an obligation to society. Though the difference by sex is significant, men's objection is greater than that of women.

Given the above sex differentials, the potential for role conflict cannot be underestimated especially for men since they are less likely to endorse an egalitarian position. In this sense some problems in the relationships between men and women may arise when traditional sex roles are reversed. For men, the problem becomes acute when their supervisors are women or when wives earn a higher salary or when women are better educated, or are older than their husbands. Perhaps the important issue here is the extent to which such resistant attitudes on the part of men can hinder the advancement of women. Thus, change in sex role orientation towards a more modern, nontraditional attitude may be needed in situations where males appear to hold to very traditional beliefs.

In addition to measuring sex role orientation by sex, this paper has explored the structural correlates of sex role attitudes in an attempt to shed some light on the processes through which attitudinal change may have occurred. Results show that structural positions represented by socio-economic status are slightly related to women's sexual attitudes. Though the coefficients are low, they show either the mother's occupation or her work experience to be associated with less traditional outlooks. For males—in addition to occupation—mother's socio-economic status is of some consequence to her son's sex role orientation. Other demographic or family composition variables explain only a very small amount of the variation in the sex role ideology of women.

Background characteristics, however, have a greater effect on the sex ideology of men than on women. This suggests that men are still under the influence of differential socialization while the sex role attitudes observed for women appear to be ideological, that is, not simply a product of women's structural circumstances and position within society. Further analysis of the data suggests that the nontraditional characteristic of women is, in part, caused by exposure to the women's movement and other nontraditional norms. As the theory of cognitive dissonance suggests, the very fact that more women tend to be nontraditional in their attitudes may mean that it has become increasingly difficult for them to believe that this orientation can be inhibited by their background characteristics. Since structural correlates do not differentiate to any appreciable extent, women's support for nontraditional sex roles, predicting support for those roles lies in the attitudes of women within all population subgroups or in some of them. This may be another way of assessing the possibility that the movement has influenced women's attitudes.

It must be recalled that college samples represent a fairly homogeneous population with respect to sex role norms. Sampling in the larger society that includes persons with a heterogeneous background may reveal greater variation in degree of sex role egalitarianism and structural characteristics. Although some of the results of other research based on college students and similar to those reported here were discovered, additional research is needed at various levels in society and with both men and women to determine any continuing patterns in sex role relationships and to understand the dynamics of sex role attitude change in the American population.

REFERENCES

Andrews, Frank, James Morgan, and John Sonquist
    1967 *Multiple Classification Analysis: A report on a Computer Program for Multiple Regression using Categorical Predictors.* Ann Arbor, Michigan: Institute for Social Research, The University of Michigan

Aronoff, Joel and William D. Crano
    1975 "A re-examination of the cross-cultural principles of task segregation and sex role differentiation in the family." *American Sociological Review* 40 (February): 12–20.

Axelson, L.
    1970 "The working wife: Difference in perception among negro and white males." *Journal of Marriage and the Family* 32 (August): 457–464.

Bayer, Alan E.
    1975 "Sexist students in American colleges: A descriptive note." *Journal of Marriage and the Family* 37 (May): 391–399.

Bebbington, A. C.
    1973   "The function of stress in the establishment ot the dual-career family." *Journal of Marriage and the Family* 35 (August): 530–537.

Bergmann, Barbara R.
    1973   "The economics of women's liberation." In Ruth B. Knudsin, Annals of the *New York Academy of Sciences*, Vol. 208 (March 15): 154–160.

Bernard, Jessie
    1975   Sex Role Transcendence and Sex Role Transcenders. Pp. 43–68 in *Women, Wives, Mothers: Values and Options*. Chicago; Aldine Publishing Co.

Booth, Alan and Elaine Hess
    1974   "Cross-sex friendship." *Journal of Marriage and the Family* (February): 38–47.

Boserup, Ester
    1970   *Woman's Role in Economic Development* (New York: St. Martin's Press).

Brogan, Donna and Nancy Kutner
    1976   "Measuring sex role orientation: A normative approach." *Journal of Marriage and the Family* 38 (February): 31–40.

Broverman, Inge, et al.,
    1972   "Sex Role Stereotypes: A Current Appraisal." *Journal of Social Issues.* 28 (February): 59–78.

Bumpass, Larry and Charles Westoff
    1970   *The Later Years of Childbearing*. Princeton University Press.

Burke, Ronald J. and Tamara Weir
    1976   "Relationship of wives' employment status to husband, wife, and pair satisfaction and performance." *Journal of Marriage and the Family* 38 (May): 279–287.

Citizens Advisory Council on the Status of Women
    1975   *Women in 1974*. Washington, D.C., U.S. Government Printing Office: 7–8.

Cook, Alice
    1975   *The working mother:* A survey of problems and programs in nine countries (Ithaca: New York State School of Industrial and Labor Relations, Cornell University).

Coser, Rose Laub and Gerald Rokoff
    1971   "Women in the occupational world: Social disruption and conflict." *Social Problems* 18 (Spring): 535–554.

Day, Lincoln
    1961   "Status implications of the employment of married women in the U.S." *American Journal of Economic Sociology* 20 (4): 390–398.

DeJong, et al.
    1971   "Patterns of female intergenerational occupational mobility: A comparison with male patterns of intergenerational occupational mobility." *American Sociological Review* 36 (December): 1033–1042.

Duberman, Lucile and Koya Azumi
    1975   "Sexism in Nepal." *Journal of Marriage and the Family* 37 (November): 1013–1021.

Dulury, George (ed.)
    1973   *1973 World Almanac and Book of Facts*. New York: Doubleday and Co.

Duncan, R. Paul and Carolyn Cumings Perrucci
    1976   "Dual occupation families and migration." *American Sociological Review* 41 (April): 252–261.

Ehrlich, C.,
    1971   "The Male Sociologists' Burden: The Place of Women in Marriage and The Family Texts," *Juornal of Marriage and the Family.* 33 (August): 421–430.

Epstein, F. C., Gilda F. and Arline L. Bronzaft
    1972   "Female freshmen view their roles as women." *Journal of Marriage and the Family* 34: (November) 671–672.

Epstein, Cynthia Fuchs
    1975a   "Tracking and careers: The case of women in American society." Pp. 26–34 in Eleanor

L. Zuckerman (ed.), *Women and Men: Roles, Attitudes, and Power Relationships*. New York: The Radcliffe Club.
   1975b "Institutional barriers: What keeps women out of the executive suite?" In Francine E. Gordon and Myra H. Strober (eds.), *Bringing Women into Management*. New York: McGraw-Hill.
   1976 "Sex role stereotyping, occupations, and social exchange." *Women Studies* 3: 185–194.

Farrell, Warren
   1975 *The Liberated Man* (New York: Bantam).

Featherman, David L. and Robert M. Hauser
   1976 "Sexual inequalities and socio-economic achievement in the U.S. 1962–1973." *American Sociological Review* 41 (June): 462–483.

Feld, Sheila
   1963 "Feelings of adjustment." Pp. 331–352 in F. I. Nye and Lois W. Hoffman (eds.), *The Employed Mother in America*. Chicago: Rand McNally.

Feldman, H. and M. Feldman
   1973 *The Relationship Between The Family and Occupational Functioning in a Sample of Rural Women*. Ithaca, New York: Cornell University.

Felson, Marcus and David Knoke
   1974 "Social status and the married woman." *Journal of Marriage and the Family* 36 (May): 516–521

Ferriss, Abbott L.
   1971 *Indicators of Trends in the Status of American Women*. New York: Russell Sage.

Fong, M. S.
   1976 "The early rhetoric of women's liberation: Implications for zero population growth." *Journal of Marriage and the Family* 38 (February): 127–140.

Gianapoulous, A. and H. W. Mitchell
   1957 "Marital disagreement in working wife marriages as a function ot husband's attitudes towards wife's employment." *Journal of Marriage and the Family* 19 (November): 373–378.

Gillespie, Dair L.
   1971 "Who has the power? The marital struggle." *Journal of Marriage and the Family* 33 (August): 445–458.

Gover, D. O.
   1963 "Socio-economic differential in the relationship between marital adjustment and wife's employment status." *Journal of Marriage and the Family* 25 (November): 453–458.

Gross, Edward
   1968 "Plus ca change...? The sexual structure of occupations over time." *Social Problems* 16 (Fall): 198–208.

Hewer, V. H., and G. Neubeck
   1964 "Attitudes of College Students toward Employment Among Married Women." *Journal of Personnel and Guidance,* 43 (February): 487–592.

Hoffman, Lois W.
   1963 "The decision to work." In F. I. Nye and C. W. Hoffman (eds.), *The Employed Mother in America*. Chicago: Rand McNally.

Holmstrom, Linda L.
   1970 "Career patterns of married couples." Pp. 516–524 in Athena Theodore (ed.), *The Professional Woman*. Cambridge: Schenkman.
   1972 *The Two Career Family*. Cambridge: Schenkman.

Holter, Harriet
   1970 Sex Roles and Social Structure. Oslo: Universitet Forlaget.

Hudis, Paula M.
   1976 "Commitment to work and to family: Marital-status differences in women's earnings." *Journal of Marriage and the Family* 38 (May): 267–278.

James, Estille
　1975　"Income and employment effects of women's liberation." Pp. 379–400 in Cynthia B. Lloyd (ed.), *Sex Discrimination and The Division of Labor*. New York: Columbia University Press.
Johnson, Shirley
　1975　"The impact of women's liberation on marriage, divorce, and family life-style." Pp 401–426 in Cynthia B. Lloyd (ed.), *Sex Discrimination and The Division of Labor*. New York: Columbia University Press.
Kammeyer, Kenneth
　1964　"The Feminine Role: An Analysis ot Attitude Consistency." *Journal of Marriage and the Family* 36 (August): 295–305.
Kemper, Theodore D.
　1974　"On the nature and purpose of ascription." *American Sociological Review* 39 (December): 844–853.
Kirkpatrick, Jeanne J.
　1974　*Political Woman*. New York: Basic Books.
Knudsen, Dean
　1969　"The declining status of women." *Social Forces* 48. (December): 183–193.
Komarovsky, Mirra
　1973　"Cultural Contradictions and sex roles: The Masculine Case." *American Journal of Sociology* 78 (January): 873–884.
Lansing, Marjorie
　1974　"The American women: Voter and activist." Pp. 5–24 in Jane S. Jacquette (ed.), *Women In Politics*. New York: Wiley.
Lekachman, Robert
　1975　"On economic equality." *Signs: Journal of Women in Culture and Society* 1 (Autumn): 93–102.
Lipman-Blumen, Jean
　1972　"How ideology shapes women's lives." *Scientific American* 226 (January): 32–42.
Long, Larry H.
　1974　"Woman's labor force participation and the residential mobility ot families." *Social Forces* 52: (March) 342–348.
MacPherson, Myra
　1975　*The Power Lovers: An Intimate Look at Politicians and Their Marriages*. New York: G. P. Putman's and Sons.
Marmor, Judd
　1972　"Changing patterns of femininity and masculinity." Pp. 68–73 in Nona Glazer-Malvin and Helen Youngelson Waehrer (eds.), *Women in a Man-Made World*. Chicago, Illinois: Rand McNally and Co.
Martin, Thomas W. and R. Brooke Jacobsen
　1975　"The impact of dual-career marriage on female professional careers: An empirical test of a parsonian hypothesis." *Journal of Marriage and the Family* 37 (November): 734–742.
Mason, Karen Oppenheim and Larry L. Bumpass
　1975　"U.S. women's sex role ideology, 1970." *American Journal of Sociology* 80 (March): 1212–1219.
Mason, Karen Oppenheim, John L. Czajka and Sara Arber
　1976　"Change in U.S. women's sex-role attitudes, 1964–1974." *American Sociological Review* 41 (August): 573–596.
McGlendon, McKee J.
　1976　"The occupational status attainment process of males and females." *American Sociological Review*. 41 (February): 52–64.
Meier, Harold C.
　1972　"Mother-centeredness and college youths' attitudes toward social equality for women: Some empirical findings." *Journal of Marriage and the Family* 34 (February): 115–121.

Mitchell, Judith
    1972   "Women: The longest revolution." Pp. 45–52 in Nona Glazer-Malvin and Helen Youngelson Waehrer (eds.). *Women In a Man-Made World*. Chicago, Illinois: Rand McNally Co.
Murdock, A. P.
    1967   "Ethnographic atlas: A summary." *Ethnology* 6 (April): 109–236.
Nilsen, Aileen Pace
    1971   "Women in children's literature." *College English* 32 (May): 918–926.
Nye, F. I.
    1974   "Effects on mother." Pp. 207–225 in L. W. Hoffman and F. Ivan Nye (eds.), *Working Mothers*. San Francisco: Jossey-Bass.
Nye, F. I. and L. W. Hoffman
    1963   *The Employed Mother in America*. Chicago: Rand McNally.
Orden, S. R. and N. M. Bradburn
    1969   "Working wives and marital happiness." *American Journal of Sociology* 74 (January): 392–407.
Osmond, Marie Withers and Patricia Yancey Martin
    1975   "Sex and sexism: A comparison of male and female sex-role attitudes." *J. of Marriage and the Family* 37 (November): 744–758.
Parelius, Ann P.
    1975   "Emerging sex role attitudes, expectations, and strains among college women." *Journal of Marriage and the Family* 37 (February): 146–154.
Poloma, Margaret and Neal Garland
    1971   "The Married Professional Woman: A study in the tolerance of domestication." *Journal of Marriage and the Family* 33 (August): 531–540.
Powell, K. S.
    1963   "Family Variables," Pp. 231–240 in F. I. Nye and L. W. Hoffman (eds.), *The Employed Mother in America*. Chicago: Rand McNally.
Rapoport, R. and R. N. Rapoport
    1969   "The dual career family." *Human Relations* 22 (February): 3–30.
    1971   *Dual Career Families*. Baltimore: Penguin Books.
Ritter, Kathleen V. and Lowell L. Hargens
    1975   "Occupational positions and class identification of married working women: A test of the asymetry hypothesis." *American Journal of Sociology* 80 (January): 934–948.
Ross, Heather L. and Anita MacIntosh
    1973   "The emergence of households headed by women." Washington, D. C.: *The Urban Institute*, Working Paper 776-01.
Rossi, Alice S. and Ann Calderwood (eds.)
    1973   *Academic Women on the Move*. New York: Russell Sage.
Rossi, Peter H., et al.
    1974   "Measuring household social standing." *Social Science Research* 3 (September): 169–190.
Santos, Fredricka Pickford
    1975   "The economics of marital status." Pp. 244–268 in Cynthia B. Lloyd (ed.), *Sex, Discrimination, and the Division of Labor*. New York: Columbia University Press.
Scanzoni, John
    1975   *Sex roles, life styles and childbearing: changing patterns In Marriage and Family*. New York: The Free press.
    1976   "Sex role change and influences on birth intentions," *Journal of Marriage and the Family* 38 (February): 43–58.
Scott, John Paul
    1958   *Aggression*. Chicago, Illinois: The University of Chicago Press.
Sexton, Patricia
    1969   *The Feminized Male*. New York: Random House.

Suter, Larry E. and Herman Miller
 1973 "Components of Income differences between men and career women." *American Journal of Sociology* 78: 962–974.
Sweet, James A.
 1973 *Women in the Labor Force,* New York: Similar Press.
Tiger, Lionel
 1969 *Men in Groups.* New York: Random House.
Tomeh, Aida K.
 1975 *The Family and Sex Roles.* Toronto: Holt, Rinehart and Winston, Canada/New York
Treiman, Donald J. and Kermit Terrill
 1975a "Sex and the process of status attainment: A comparison of working men and women." *American Sociological Review* 40 (April): 174–200.
 1975b "Women, work, and wages Trends in the female occupational structure." Pp. 157–191. in K. Land and S. Spilerman (eds.). *Social Indicator Models.* New York: Russell Sage
Tyree, Andrew and Judith Treas
 1974 "The occupational and marital mobility of women." *American Sociological Review* 39: (June) 294–302.
U.S. Bureau of the Census
 1970 *Statistical Abstract of the United States:* 1970. Washington, D.C.: U.S. Government Printing Office.
 1973 *Current Population Reports.* Series Pp. 23, No. 44 Washington, D.C.: United States Government Printing Office.
 1975 "Fertility expectations of American women: June 1974." *Current Population Reports,* Series P-20, No. 277. Washington D.C.: U.S. Government Printing Office.
U.S. Department of Commerce. Social and Economic Statistics Bureau and U.S. Bureau of Census
 1972 *Statistical Abstract of the U.S. 93rd Annual Edition.* Wm. Lerner (ed.), Washington, D.C.: Government Printing Office.
U.S. Department of Labor, Bureau of Labor Statistics
 1971 "Children of women in the labor force." *Special Labor Force Report,* No. 134. Washington, D.C.: U.S. Government Printing Office.
U.S. Department of Labor, Women's Bureau
 1971 "Working women and their family responsibilities: United States experience." Washington, D.C.: U.S. Government Printing Office.
U.S. Department of Labor
 1974 "Marital and family characteristics of the labor force in March, 1973." *Bureau of Labor Statistics.* Special Labor Force Report, No. 164. Washington, D.C.: U.S. Government Printing Office.
U'ren, Marjorie B.
 1971 "The image of women in textbooks." In Vivian Gornick and Barbaara K. Moran (eds.), *Women in Sexist Society.* New York: Basic Books.
Waite, Linda J. and Ross M. Stolzenberg
 1976 "Intended childbearing and labor force participation of young women: Insights from non-recursive models." *American Sociological Review* 41 (April): 235–252.
Weitzman Lenore et al.
 1972 "Sex Role Socialization in Picture Books for Pre-School Children." *American Journal of Sociology* 77 (May): 1125–1150.
Whitley, Marilyn Peddicard and Susan B. Poulsen
 1975 "Assertiveness and sexual satisfaction in employed professional women." *Journal of Marriage and the Family* 37 (August): 573–581.

B. EUROPE

The Position of Women in The Netherlands: Marginal Change*

H. M. IN'T VELD-LANGEVELD, I. J. SCHOONENBOOM,
and L. IN'T VELD

Scientific Council for Government Policy in the Netherlands
The Hague, The Netherlands

Situation after World War II

IN THE NETHERLANDS, the first wave of feminism died about 1920 when the feminists had realised an important goal: the right to vote. During the next three decades we see a consolidation and step by step diffusion of the rights and obligations women had acquired: the right to formal education, the right—as well as the duty—of unmarried women to do paid work. In the family, the wife gradually acquired a position which was no longer inferior to the husband's. This egalitarian relationship found expression in the free choice of a marriage partner, a (nearly) equal say in family matters and social disapproval of extramarital relations of the man. Subsequently, marriage and family laws were changed as well. What remained unaltered were the role division, in the family as well as in society, and the social and financial dependence of the wife on her husband.

After World War II, the Netherlands was a country with a high birth rate and a low divorce rate, and an unquestioned role division between man and woman, husband and wife. (For example, only 2% of all married women did paid work.) The sharp lines of demarcation between the different religious denominations shielded them from outside influences and thus contributed to the *status quo*.

The Fifties

The expansion of economic activity was a first impulse towards change in the status of women. Economic growth and improvement of social conditions were

---

* To a large extent the article is based on a report by the authors that has been published in the series "Voorstudies en Achtergronden" of the Scientific Council for Government Policy, The Hague (*De emancipatie van de vrouw*, 1976). The article was presented to the editor in 1977, and at the time of publishing in 1981 part of the quantitative material was brought up to date.

given a high priority in the fifties and sixties. A general expansion of employment resulted including those areas where women were traditionally employed. Women worked in the traditional "feminine" sectors: nursing, teaching (especially young children), clerical work, hostess functions, the retail trade, domestic work and selected industrial sectors (e.g., the textile industry). The scale effects associated with economic expansion entailed an enormous growth in administration and thus extra office work. The economic expansion went hand in hand with the emergence of the welfare state. The extension of health services and education (also caused by the rising birth rate) increased the demand for female nurses and teachers. The growth of the government machinery, in general, also caused increased labour demand, especially for clerical staff.

At the same time, social progress resulted in more schooling for girls as well as for boys (although girls lagged and continue to lag behind). Increased prosperity and social security made it possible for couples to marry earlier. Economic expansion caused geographic mobility which in turn led to increased social mobility and decreased social control. The marriage market grew and economic and social independence were gained at an earlier age. These developments caused a decrease in the supply of single women in the labour market. Marriage, after all, implied withdrawal from the labour market according to the dominant values of the time.

In the fifties this situation did not result in significant numbers of married women engaging in paid work, although there was an increase. (In 1960, 4% of married women were employed against 2% in 1947.) It is interesting to note, however, that already a change in attitudes was evident among several important groups. Although this change was carefully formulated and did not assault major values, it implied a reorientation of the pattern of values towards acceptance of working married women. It was especially apparent among those groups which placed a strong emphasis on the promotion of the affluent society and the welfare states—groups such as the Liberal Party, the Labour Party and the (socialist) federation of trade unions. The great social importance attached to the family prevented explicit approval of women developing their talents outside the home, which in any case was still a rarity. Instead the change was made legitimate by appealing to an accepted higher value: the personal responsibility of the married couple, which alone was to determine whether the family situation allowed the mother to work.[1]

---

[1] The same phenomenon is noticeable in the motivations of working women judging by the results of English and German research from the fifties. Employed women found impetus for going out to work in their desire to give financial support to their families, not from any personal need. They said that they would stop working as soon as the family had no further need of support. This moment, however, was constantly postponed.

The Sixties

In the sixties these developments gained in strength and led to an increase in the numbers of working wives. (The statistics show 11% in 1973, still considerably less than in other countries of Western Europe.) The great emphasis on achievement and consumption caused a weakening of the remaining resistance among both men and women. At the same time other factors were contributing to the emergence of new claims concerning a change in the position of women.

One factor was the growing secularization of society. Not only did the percentage of nonchurch members increase, but the involvement of members of the different denominations declined as well. In a way the churches, too, were secularized from within: social issues, the problems of "here and now" received more attention. Concepts such as worldly "liberation" and "justice" grew in importance in their deliberations. (The new concepts also applied to women as, for example, the 1974 World Council of Churches Conference on "sexism.") In the late sixties and the seventies the churches became less of a force for preserving traditional values than they had been in the fifties.

The protest movements were another factor. Of those which arose in several countries, the Dutch Provo Movement was one of the most vigorous. It questioned facts and circumstances which up until that time had been largely taken for granted. Through this and other (student) protest movements several groups became conscious of their minority position, among them women. The growing interest in sensitivity training, encounter groups, mystical groups etc. suggests that emotional values were gaining in significance at the cost of "rational" values such as achievement, efficiency, and competitiveness. The latter were questioned in relation to the growing importance of protection of the environment, consumption of energy and international differences in prosperity. In short, more emphasis was laid on values up till then considered "feminine."

One change worth mentioning separately was the disappearance of the taboo on sexuality. Women became conscious of the fact that increased sexual freedom was not the same as sexual equality. Of the changes within the family the most marked was the change in the birth rate. After 1964, the birth rate—which had been slowly decreasing, with the exception of the baby boom after World War II—declined rapidly. In 1965 oral contraceptives came on the market and in 1971 they were included in the national health insurance package. This meant an official, positive sanctioning of what was earlier considered to be an objectionable practice.

There were other changes related to fertility. The first interval (period between marriage and birth of first child) increased from 1.9 years in 1965 to 3.3 years in 1979. Changes in the second interval have been less. Employment, however, influences fertility, in combination with the amount of education. Married women are more inclined to work as their level of schooling climbs higher. Working wives of all educational levels have a longer first interval than nonemployed wives. (There is no difference in the second interval.) There is a negative correlation between participation in the labour force and marriage fertility for all levels of schooling, but the effect is stronger as the amount of education increases (Nimwegen and De Vries, 1974: 60).

Even before feminism manifested itself, some change was noticeable in the views on children's upbringing. In relation to the employment of the mother the question was raised (although not conclusively answered) which is more important, the quantity or the quality of attention the mother gives the child? The decreasing birth rate

Table 1

Birth rate (number of births per 1000 persons in the 15–49 years age group)

1945/1949	25.9
1950/1954	22.1
1955/1959	21.3
1960	20.8
1961	21.3
1962	20.9
1963	20.9
1964	20.7
1965	19.9
1966	19.2
1967	18.9
1968	18.6
1969	19.2
1970	18.3
1971	17.2
1972	16.1
1973	14.5
1974	13.7
1975	13.0
1976	12.9
1977	12.5
1978	12.6
1979	12.5

Source: Central Bureau of Statistics

and the life in apartment buildings, instead of one-family-houses, resulted in loss of opportunities for the young child to make contacts with other children. Playrooms for two and three-year-olds were set up, where the children could play on two or three mornings a week. This lightened the task of the mother a little, although it did not allow her much of an increase in personal freedom.

The Rise of Feminism

As a result of these changes a climate was created favourable to the rise of feminism as a social movement, the importance of which lies in a reformulation of values concerning the positions of women and men and in a rearrangement of value-priorities. Until this time, justification for the new behaviour of women had been sought as something apart from society so as not to impair current interpretations and priorities in values. This, however, could contribute little to genuine structural social change. Women's "deviant" behaviour was merely tolerated, certainly not stimulated. Yet a married woman has to pay the full price for working outside the home. She has a double task: she has to organize day-care for her children, she has to manage a job where she may have to accept discrimination, work not up to her ability, unequal pay, limited career opportunities. This double task is ignored by the economy as there exist insufficient possibilities for part-time work and no provisions for leave of absence when children are ill. According to Dahlström (1967: 170-172) four value-patterns existed in the 19th century concerning the position of women: the traditional Christian, the liberal, the romantic and the Marxist pattern. By 1968 the "traditional" values had lost their force. The legal rights claimed by the "liberal" value-pattern had been acquired. "Romantic" values had prevailed for several decades: man and woman complement each other and therefore are destined for the fulfillment of different roles, both of which are valuable. The new feminism opposes these ideas, but contains in itself different lines of thought. There is a Marxist trend. There are also a number of new patterns:

1) Although the family role is the prerogative of the woman in the first pattern (Christian) she should, as far as family duties will allow, have equal opportunities for playing a full part in society, and especially in work. Breadwinning remains the duty of the husband. Provisions must be enacted to implement this equality between men and women, both to alleviate (especially through part-time childcare) family duties, and to maximize opportunities for work such as part-time work, flexible working hours, and special leave when children are ill, etc. This pattern may be defined as a "liberal" one, adapted to changed conditions.

2) The second pattern assumes absolute equality of men and women, both inside and outside the family. Only in this way can a married woman organize her own life, and only then is she economically and socially independent. The desired role for women and men should combine the general characteristics of the current roles of both men and women. Recently many supporters of this pattern have become convinced that in order to realize this value-pattern, society has to move in a socialist direction. This pattern can be called "the absolute equality pattern."

3) The third pattern, supported mainly by women, presupposes a society determined by those values which are currently subordinate and labelled as "feminine" —values such as sensitivity, cooperation and creativity. This would involve a complete

restructuring since society is currently dominated by such "masculine" values as "coolness", rationality, competition, authoritarianism, etc.[2]

It is not correct to reduce the function of the feminist movement exclusively to the formulation of new value-patterns although these are very important. Certainly several feminist groups have, each in their various ways, aroused public and government opinion and still do. But their independent influence on structural change is not easily discernible, largely because their groups are small, consisting mainly of women with a high level of education. In fact, their "elitist" character may have given rise to as much resistance as to positive response.

Actual Position of Women

Here is an overview of recent changes in the position of women under the influence of the forces mentioned above and a comparison with the new value-patterns which suggest goals for further change.

Education

There are differences between the sexes:
a) in participation, measured in age-specific attendance rates;
b) in level of schooling;
c) in output, measured in percentages that leave school holding a certificate;
d) in choice of types of school;
e) in choice of subjects within the school.[3]

---

2   We leave out those who accept the utopian belief of a free choice of role-behaviour for everybody. This seems to be a phrase used by politicians when they need to avoid making a choice rather than a value-pattern which directs judgment or behaviour.
3   So that the educational data is comparable to that of other nations a few explanatory notes are in order:
   a) Compulsory school attendance ends at the age of 16.
   b) In the Netherlands, after primary schooling, there are two possibilities for futher education: secondary schooling and vocational training. There is a growing preference for secondary schooling, viz. 4, 5 and 6 years. Among girls with four years secondary schooling (in 1971-72) 56% pursued no further day-time education compared with 33% among boys. The corresponding figures for 1977-78 were 28% and 16%. Among boys and girls with five and six years secondary schooling there was no difference in further participation. Educational possibilities after secondary schooling (5 resp. 6 years) are higher vocational education (HBO) and university. Participation in HBO increased during the period 1968-1974; for men by 8% and for women by 15%; participation in university education by 5% and 21%. Differences, however, are still considerable: in 1979/1980, 59% of HBO students were male and 41% were female; for university students the percentages were 70% and 30%, respectively.
   c) A much greater proportion of women than of men do not finish university education. In secondary education there is not much difference in output. In vocational training the output is higher for boys than for girls.

Table 2 gives the percentages of men and women of three age groups attending day-school. Although in the course of time more women go to school until a later age, differences between the sexes still exist.

Employment

There is an increase in married women working in all age groups, although the increase is more marked among younger women (Table 3). The increase is nearly as strong among women with children as among women without children. The increase is highest among women whose husbands are under 30. The participation

Table 2

Age-specific school attendance rates of men and women, for 1958, 1971 and 1980

Age	1958		1971		1980	
	Men	Women	Men	Women	Men	Women
16	68%	34%	88%	65%	89%	87%
17	55%	22%	77%	42%	70%	64%
18	40%	14%	62%	27%	51%	39%

Source: Central Bureau of Statistics.

in the labour force of women with children under 5 years, however, did not change between 1960 and 1973. The family cycle has a substantial influence on labour force participation: paid work as a principal activity is done mainly by women under 25 without children; occupational activity, part-time as well as full-time, decreases sharply for women with children under 6; both part-time and full-time work increase again when the child is between 6 and 15. In 1960 32% of employed women were part-time workers, in 1971 50%. In 1975 61% of the married working women worked part-time.

Although the average level of education of the female population is considerably lower than that of the male population, the average level of education of employed women is higher. The data of 1973 lead to the conclusion that labour force participation of married women increases with level of education, especially when paid work is the principal activity. In 1973 women are strongly over-represented in the following

---

d) Technical, agricultural and nautical schools are 96% filled by boys; schools for home economics, 99% by girls. Commercial, economic and clerical schools have as many boys as girls on the lower level; on the middle level boys outnumber girls as well as on the highest level. Participation of men and women in the different types and on the different levels of vocational education reflects the difference in occupational roles for men and women.

e) In the choice of subjects on different educational levels the traditional preference of women for arts and literature and of men for the sciences is confirmed.

occupations: physicians, nurses and kindred occupations; secretaries and typists; shop assistants and other sales people; domestic and service personnel; caretakers and cleaning women; washers and hairdressers; tailors; seamstresses, and such. In all other occupations they are under-represented. It also appears that they are mainly employed in those occupations in which they are over-represented. Note that they too work in a smaller number of industry groups than men do. Nearly half of the

Table 3

Age-specific labour force participation rates of men, single and married women above 15 years of age, for 1960 and 1973

Age	Men		Women					
			single		married		total	
	1960	1973	1960	1973	1960	1973	1960	1973
15–19	63	40	61	47	13	31	59	46
20–24	91	84	80	82	11	32	52	54
25–29	97	96	77	78	6	15	21	24
30–34	99	98	72	68	4	11	13	16
35–39	99	98	68	66	4	10	13	15
40–44	99	98	63	61	5	10	13	16
45–49	98	95	57	52	4	9	14	15
50–54	97	92	49	45	4	7	14	14
55–59	93	84	38	33	3	6	12	12
60–64	81	68	22	19	2	3	8	8
65 and more	20	3	4	1	0	1	2	1
Total	83	74	50	41	4	11	21	22

Source: Central Bureau of Statistics, Sociale Maandstatistiek, April 1975

working women (only 18% of the men) are employed in noncommercial services. The labour market for women becomes still more limited as their level of education increases: 85% of women with middle and higher education work in noncommercial services against 27% of men.

Women find part-time work in the foodstuff industry, footwear industry, retail trade and in the public and commercial services (mainly teaching, medical and social services, hotels and restaurants). A study of businesses with more than 100 employees produced the following results:

— "part-timers" are employed only when "full-timers" are not available;
— except in teaching, medical and other social services, "part-timers" do the most simple work;
— mostly older women who are "out of children" are recruited for part-time work;

— businesses do not intend to stimulate part-time work for other than the lowest job levels (with the exception of the fore-mentioned services);
— part-time workers (especially married women) have a higher level of education than full-time workers in the same job (Jong et al., 1974).

Political participation

Participation of women in representational public bodies at the national, provincial and local level is still minimal, although the increase is noticeable (Table 4). This is not due to too few women members in political parties—in 1971 the percentage of female members of seven political parties varied between 12% and 33%. It is due instead to the fact that being a woman is an obstacle to being nominated and the view that female candidates are not popular with the electorate (Bandt, 1972).

Table 4

Percentages of women in representational public bodies

	Second Chamber	Provincial States	Town Councils
1966	8.7%	6.5%	4.8%
1970	9.3%	7.3%	7.2%
1974	14.0%	8.9%	9.9%
1979	14.0%	16.5%	12.5%

Source: A. Hoogerwerf, ed., Gelijkheid en ongelijkheid in Nederland, 1975, and Nederlandse Vrouwenraad.

Participation in voluntary organizations

Little data is available except from the membership lists of trade unions and this shows the percentage is small but increasing. In 1975 15% of all working women were organized in trade unions. According to an investigation a few more working women than nonworking women with children participate in voluntary social activities (Instituut voor Psychologisch Marktonderzoek, 1974).

Legal position

Many of the remaining differences between the legal status of women and men have disappeared or will shortly disappear from legislation. There are, however, laws that still reflect the traditional role division. The most important ones are the social security laws (old age pension, unemployment insurance, etc.), all of which assume the husband to be breadwinner and the wife to be homemaker.

Position in the family

Changes that have taken place in the birth rate and in the birth pattern have already been referred to. Recently a new phenomenon—voluntary childlessness—has emerged. In recent years there has been a rather strong increase in couples who prefer to remain childless. In 8% of the marriages contracted in the period 1968–1972 couples chose not to have children of their own according to estimates of the Nederlands Interuniversitair Demografisch Instituut, 1975. Feminism made the legislation on *abortus provocatus* a political issue and although the abortion law of 1980 is a compromise, *de facto* the struggle has been won because many abortion clinics are functioning now.

The significance of all this lies in the evidence it offers for the lessening importance of the traditional mother role for women. This is not to say that women do not have the principal responsibility for the upbringing and care of the children, even though the need for fathers to give the children attention is accentuated nowadays. But marriage has increasingly become an institution which is no longer chiefly devoted to reproduction and to the socialization of offspring.

Opinions and Values Concerning the Position of Women and Men

Opinions on the occupational activity of married women with children of school age changed considerably in the period 1965–1970. After 1970 we see by and large a consolidation (Table 5). According to data from 1965 and 1974 opinions about voluntary childlessness have changed remarkably too. In 1965, 66% judge voluntary childlessness, unless for medical reasons, unacceptable; in 1974 only 16% hold this opinion. The part of the population that approves of a conscious choice for childlessness rose from 22% to 65%.

In 1968, 38% think there are no circumstances which justify abortion, in 1974 only 15%. In 1970 44.6% do not agree with the statement: "A woman must be able to have an abortion if she wishes"; in 1975, 35.3% and in 1979, 41.7% do not agree.

Table 5

Opinion on paid work by married women, distribution in percentages

Paid work by women with children of school age	1965	1970	1975	1979
Recommendable	1.7	16.1	13.6	11.4
Not objectionable	14.6	40.3	44.1	54.7
Objectionable	83.7	43.6	42.3	33.9
	100	100	100	100

Source: Social and Cultural Planning Bureau, 1980.

Other significant changes between 1970 and 1979 are these: to a lesser extent (30% vs. 15%) it is thought unnatural for women in a leadership position to supervise men; to a lesser extent (70% vs. 59%) women are thought better fitted for the upbringing of children; to a lesser extent (22% vs. 12%) people think that a good education is less important for girls than for boys (Social and Cultural Planning Bureau, 1980).

An important question arising from these findings is whether the change in opinions and attitudes has implications for the division of male and female responsibilities. Several studies show that on this point hardly any change is noticeable. Activities outside the home are tolerated, even considered important, but according to the majority of respondents, they should not go on at the cost of the upbringing of children or the carrying out of household tasks or if they affect the position of the man. There is hardly any difference in opinion between men and women on these matters.

More working than nonworking women have ideas fitting into the previously-mentioned "absolute equality pattern," but they form a minority. It is impossible to derive, from recent research, the exact distribution of the different value-patterns. A rough interpretation of data leads to the conclusion that the "adapted liberal pattern" now has the dominant position but on a verbal level only, as it has not been factually realized yet. Values of the "absolute equality pattern" receive perceptible support. The studies give no indication as to the prevalence of the third pattern previously labelled as "feminine," nor as to the Marxist pattern, which would require a complete restructuring of existing economic realities.

Expectations

Are these changes a step in an ongoing process which are likely to end in either equality between the sexes or in the dominance of "feminine" values? Unfortunately, such hopeful prospects seem unlikely. While women are allowed more latitude in the form of social (occupational or other) participation, this is only within the limits of the existing role division. The margin between old and new has been widened by divesting motherhood of its central importance and by reducing the claims of the mother role. There has been hardly any change in the role of the wife.

And even the participation in society is mainly a matter of rhetoric. Actual possibilities are very limited, especially for part-time work. The number of women in the labour market will probably grow from 1,603,800 in 1980 to 2,049,900 in 2000 (Bron, 1980). Only a few years ago it seemed that the number of women in the labour market could not grow fast enough to meet the demand. Now, however, it is evident that these numbers cannot be absorbed. The participation of women in society is not yet a norm generally accepted and self-evident, with the result that women get the worst of it, if they happen to become rivals of men. Even if we assume a resumption of economic growth, although at a lower level than in the sixties, even with this growth the labour market position of (married) women is very uncertain. Working women are confined to a very small number of industry groups and occupations. The higher the level of education the more limited the number. In the past, women were in a strong position simply because of the separate job markets for women and men. However, this position is made vulnerable by the limited size of the female labour market, particularly if women enter the market *en masse*. Current choice patterns for boys and girls at school do not suggest that there will be an essential change with respect to the separation of roles in the future. As girls opt for more and more education they will eventually narrow their range of possible jobs.

The following considerations may promise a gloomy outlook for women's position in the labour market in general, and for part-time women workers in particular:

1) the slowing down of economic growth unfavourably affects job opportunities, particularly in those areas on which women depend (taking into consideration women's improved level of education), i.e. the services sector and specifically the non-commercial services sector;

2) the lesser rate of economic growth may lead to an over-qualified working population. If highly qualified men are forced to seek employment below their capacity, men and women may find themselves in competition. In such a situation preference will be given to the male, especially where "nonfeminine" jobs are concerned;

3) the considerable increase in the number of women without young children who can engage in full-time employment will limit the opportunities for women who can work only part-time;

4) long term prospects in the labour market appear to be most favourable at a lower job level, e. g., in retail trade and clerical work.

As already noted above, the existence of separate job markets for women and men is an obstacle in the way of a change in women's position. In itself, however, it is a manifestation of a role division which remains unaltered, because any change would affect the man's position. The educational system, however, has a certain autonomy. It can try to influence the occupational choices of girls and boys so as to make small penetrations on the other sexes' job market.

The positive influence of economic development—a factor in the sixties strongly conducive to change in women's position—is not so certain anymore. Of the other factors which contributed in the sixties some have a continuing influence, viz. the increase in educational level of women and the low birth rate. Feminism is dubious as a factor; the movement is still very limited in numbers. Some feminist groups have turned to more "introvert" activities (encounter groups for women or pursuing science in a feminine way, etc.). Other factors are nonrecurrent. Changes in values concerning sexuality, authority, use of energy, etc. may slowly diffuse, but there is no reason to expect them to spread faster than values concerning equality of the sexes. New positive factors may come up, but are not yet perceptive. All in all, it seems unlikely that changes in the position of women will continue *linea recta* in the direction of absolute equality. A gradual spread of the "adapted liberal pattern" and a step-by-step realization of new gains accompanied by much struggle and conflict seem more probable.

A functionalist explanation may throw another light on this conclusion. Allowing latitude for more social participation by women was functional for the economic system which needed manpower. At the same time it was—and still is—functional for the continued existence of the prevailing family type. All during the last 50 years, textbooks on family sociology have described modern marriage as a relationship meant mainly for the giving and receiving of affection, dedicated to fostering supportiveness and, as a consequence, extremely fragile. In the Netherlands this type of marriage has become generally accepted as a norm after World War II. More and more people married and marriage was contracted at an ever younger age, but after 1965 a spectacular increase in the divorce rate occurred. Recent predictions are that in the near future one out of five (Nederlands Interuniversitaiv Demografisch Instituut, 1976), even one out of three (Scientific Council, 1976) new marriages will end in divorce. Undoubtedly, secularization has contributed to the fact that unhappy marriages are dissolved now. But the increase in divorce is not an expression of less emotional investment in marriage. On the contrary, Veenhoven (1949, 1966, 1969 and 1974) showed from four studies that there is an absolute increase in association between marital satisfaction and happiness during the last twenty years. Additionally, marital satisfaction compared to job satisfaction and health satisfaction became a stronger predictor of happiness in the last decades. There are other data which both show how much people make of marriage and, at the same time, reveal the problematic aspects (Kooy, 1969; Social and Cultural Planning Bureau, 1976).

It is the woman who is the most dependent on marriage and on whom is made the strongest demand to make marriage a success. After all, it is her main task in life. The emotional overburdening of marriage appears to have more consequences for women than for men. More women than men seek help with counseling agencies; more women than men call upon their family doctor with vague complaints. But for women today some latitude has resulted from the weakened demands of the mother role and from the increased opportunities for participation in society. The increased toleration of incidental extra-marital relationships is another mechanism for easing tensions in marriage (Social and Cultural Planning Bureau, 1976). Marriage in its actual form has been saved, at least for the time being, but its inherent problems remain unchanged.

The image of women is changing. Their ambiguous position, however, does not exclude the possibility of opposite developments, perhaps back to "Kirche, Küche Kinder", *or* a very gradual change towards more equality. The latter depends on the question of the changing image of the male. Feminists have put into words a new image, but the old image still holds its own and is solidly anchored in the structural separation of private and public spheres of life, and in the organization of production. To become socially accepted the realization of a new image has to be rewarding (Parsons and Bales, 1956: Chapter 2). For men the immediate rewards of giving up their traditional role are insufficient, maybe even nonexistant. Men will not readily accept household duties that women themselves are not satisfied with anymore, no more than they will accept reduced career possibilities, loss of status, or even more strain on marriage due to the additional tensions rising from occupational competition between husband and wife.

Whatever changes the family may undergo, under pressure of emotional overloading, will not necessarily lead to more equality of husband and wife. If a new family form emerges with greater role similarity, this will be a consequence of the more equal position women will have acquired in society. Such a position, however, is dependent on the social acceptance of a new image of man. Society must provide adequate rewards in order to induce men to live up to this new image. This implies a society where mankind, and more specifically the human male, does not derive recognition, status, income, development of capacities, and satisfactions mainly from occupational work but (also) from other sources, such as efforts on behalf of general or group interests, personal development in one way or another, cooperation and giving and receiving of affection. The fundamental social and economic changes this requires make the outlook for attaining equality between the sexes rather sombre.

Further change in the position of women seems to be possible only in the context of broader societal change and there are still few signs of change in this direction. In some groups of well-paid younger intellectuals a certain saturation with material goods is noticeable and a tendency to be less career-oriented. These are people who, for instance, reduce their weekly working time to four-fifths of the normal load. But, as has been noted, such signs are rare.

In the years to come, the labour market may suffer more or less permanent employment shortages and this may lead to a compulsory redistribution of work. The result may be conditions under which a new system of values concerning work can come into being. Speculations of this kind while captivating, do little more than show the radical changes that will be required.

Summary

Immediately after World War II the position of women relative to men was characterised by egalitarianism in marriage within the limits of the traditional role division, and inequality outside marriage. Very few married women worked. The birth rate was high, divorce rate low.

During the fifties and sixties economic expansion was, in several ways, a powerful force for changes in the behaviour of women. The necessary legitimation of this changed behaviour left current interpretations and priorities in values unimpaired, which impeded structural changes.

In the sixties other factors helped to create a climate in which feminists could give voice to new conceptions of the relative positions of women and men.

Data on education, employment, political participation, participation in voluntary associations, legal position, position in the family, show that in several ways women are catching up. At every point, however, where the traditional role division is threatened, they meet opposition—in the family as well as outside of it. Women are allowed more latitude in the form of social participation but only within the limits of the existing role division. The margin, however, has been widened by divesting motherhood of its central importance and by reducing the claims of the mother role.

A functionalist explanation sees the recent changes in women's position as induced by needs of the economic system and the demands of the nuclear family system.

For further change man will have to give up his traditional role, a step which requires fundamental economic and social restructuring.

REFERENCES

Bandt, M. L. den
    1972 *De rol van de vrouw in de Nederlandse politiek*.
Bron, J. A. H.
    1980 *Arbeidsaanbod—projecties 1980–2000*. (Scientific Council for Government Policy, The Hague)
Central Bureau of Statistics.
    1974 *Huwelijksvruchtbaarheid, een cohortanalyse 1937–1971*.
Dahlström, E. (ed.)
    1967 *The changing roles of men and women*. London
Deggeler, L.
    1972 *De werkende vrouw in Nederland*. Haarlem.
Instituut voor Psychologisch Marktonderzoek
    1974 *Maatschappelijke participatie van vrouwen met gezinsverantwoordelijkheid*. Schiedam.
Jong, J. R. de, C. J. H. Intven and P. Visser,
    1974 *Beter ten halve gewerkt?* Leiden.
Kooy, G. A.
    1969 *Het huwelijk in Nederland*. Utrecht.
Nederlands Interuniversitair Demografisch Instituut, The Hague
    1975 *Demografie*, nr 12.
    1976 *Demografie*, nr 17.
Nimwegen, N. van, and H. de Vries,
    1974 *De gehuwde werkende vrouw en haar kindertal*. Sociologisch Instituut, University of Utrecht
Parsons, T. and R. F. Bales
    1956 *Family, Socialization and Interaction Process*. London.
Scientific Council for Government Policy
    1978 *The next twenty-five years*. The Hague

Social and Cultural Planning Bureau
  1976   *Social and Cultural Report.*
  1980   *Social and Cultural Report.*
Veenhoven, R.
  1978   *The growing impact of marriage* (unpublished paper Erasmus University Rotterdam).
Veld-Langeveld, H. M. in't, and I. J. Schoonenboom
  1976   *De emancipatie van de vrouw.* (Scientific Council for Government Policy, The Hague).

Female Marital Behaviour in French Society

ANDRÉE MICHEL

National Center of Scientific Research, Paris, France

Introduction

DURING RECENT YEARS, French families have tended to approximate the behaviour patterns observed in American families for the past ten years: decreased marriage and birth rates, increase in the number of divorces, unprecedented augmentation in the percentage of women with young children exercising a professional activity, etc. This behaviour has led the author firstly, to discuss the lessened popularity of marriage and the family among contemporary French women and secondly, to follow this with a presentation of data providing evidence of the resistance of the French men to women's autonomy which may explain these changes.

Decreased Motivation of French Women for Marriage and Family

Indications of decreased motivation for marriage among French women may be seen in the following factors: decrease in the marriage rate for women; increase in age at first marriage; negative correlation between the educational level of the woman on the one hand and the marriage rate and age at first marriage on the other; increase in the number of single persons and in the divorce rate. These changes in France reflect similar changes in the United States.

Decrease in the marriage rate

In the United States, Paul Glick (1975: 15–26) notes that "since 1965, the annual number of first marriages has not been keeping pace with the rapid growth in the number of persons in the prime years for first marriage—those who were born soon after World War II."

In France, the Institute of Statistics (1975) similarly indicates that since 1965 the increase in the number of marriages is below what it would have been if the rate of marriages had remained the same as that recorded between 1961 and 1964. This reduction is especially evident in the case of women, for whom the marriage rate decreased for all ages between 1964 and 1968. From 1968 to 1972, this rate continued to drop for women over thirty, but marriage increased among younger women. According to the Institute (INSEE), 1973 witnessed an important drop in both the male and female marriage rates, even among individuals of less than 20 years of age. The greatest drop was recorded in the 20–24 age bracket. In 1978, there were 62,000 marriages less than in 1972.

This decrease in the marriage rate is accompanied, in France as in the United States, by an increase in the age at first marriage. In the United States, Glick (1975: 17–18) points out that "the average woman at first marriage today is 21 years old. During the approximately 15 years of the post-World War II baby boom, the average woman had been 20 years at marriage—one year younger." According to the author, this information reveals that "young women are now postponing marriage longer than their mothers did in the late 1940's and early 1950's."

In France, this same tendency has become apparent to various researchers (Roussel, 1975: 89). According to a report published in *Population* (1976), the average age at first marriage was 22.40 for women and 24.41 for men in 1973. The average age at first marriage is approximately $1\frac{1}{2}$ years higher than in the United States, and the difference of age between the two sexes at first marriage equals two years.

Educational level and professional qualifications as related to motivation for marriage among French women

The negative relationship between educational level and the marriage rate of women is evident in both France and the United States. Glick (1975: 18) notes that the 1970 census (U.S.A.) revealed that 8% of women aged 35 to 44 with a university degree and 19% of those who attended graduate school were single. Although Glick points out that this last percentage has greatly decreased in comparison with the figure for 1960, the fact remains that educated women in the United States marry less frequently than those having less education.

The same tendency may be observed in France. According to Roussel (1975: 92), educational level is an important discriminating factor even among individuals comprising the same socio-professional category. One observes differences averaging one or two years in the marriage age of wives when age is associated with their level of education. Thus, French women without university degrees married to professional men or those in high administrative positions have an average age at first marriage of 23.9; whereas, this is increased to 25.5 years for those women married to men at the same socio-professional level where the women themselves have obtained a university degree.

In general, the higher the educational level of a woman, the greater her age at first marriage. Even women who have received some technical training tend to marry later than those who have completed only primary school (Calot and Deville, 1971: 3–42).

Table 1 presents a summary of these data.

A certain incompatibility appears in the statistics on marriage in France when one compares the number of married persons in the age group from 40 to 49 as well as the early age of first marriage with the level of professional qualification attained by French women. According to Roussel (1975: 78) the number of married persons from 40 to 49 is positively related to the level of professional qualification of the men; however, an inverse relationship is found for women. In addition, with the exception of women comprising the agricultural category, marriage is indirectly related to their lack of qualification. No such relationship is apparent for men.

Thus the average age at first marriage is 24 for French women pursuing a profession or holding an important administrative position; 23.7 years for those in less important administrative posts; 23.2 years among women employed in other white collar positions; and 23 years for women holding blue-collar jobs.

Roussel (1975) presents the following statistics concerning single women: the proportion is 27% among women in executive positions; 23% among those in middle management posts; 17% in the lower level of the white collar category; 16% in qualified women factory workers; and 11% among those holding semi and unskilled jobs.

Table 1

Age at First Marriage for French Women by Level of Education, 1971

Educational Level	Age at First Marriage
No diploma	23.0 years
Primary school diploma	23.0 years
Technical training	23.9 years
High school diploma	24.5 years
University degree	25.6 years
All levels combined	23.1 years

Finally, there are four times more unmarried women than unmarried men, aged 45 to 49, teaching liberal arts subjects in the public school system (30% to 7%) and six times more single women than single men teaching mathematics (29% to 5%). Since the constraints encountered by women in public school teaching are generally less severe than those encountered in other professions, i.e., women teachers generally regard their work favorably since mothers have their vacations at the same time as their children, we should expect a lower percentage of single women in this profession. The fact that the percentage is raised provides another criterion of the incompatibility between education and marriage for a woman.

Table 2 summarizes the relationship between marriage and the number of single women between 40 and 49 years of age by professional qualification.

Refusal of married women to relinquish their professional identity

Another indication of a changing attitude concerning marriage among French women is their refusal to relinquish their own identity by abandoning their professional role following marriage. Statistics in both the United States and France reveal that during the past ten years the most important increase in employment was among married women with small children. In 1961, 17% of American women with children less than three years of age were employed outside the home; by 1973, this number had increased to 32% (Bernard, 1975: 582:593).

Table 2

Age at First Marriage and Percentage of Unmarried French Women (40–49 Years of Age), by Level of Professional Qualification, 1970

Professional	Age at First marriage	Percentage unmarried (40–49 yrs.)
Executive positions	24.0	27%
Lower administration posts	23.7	23%
Other white collar jobs	23.2	17%
Skilled positions	22.9	16%
Nonskilled positions	23.0	11%
All categories combined (housewives and workers)	23.0	3.6%

Data in Table 3 show the increase in labour force participation for women of different age groups and by number and age of children.

These data reveal that between 1968 and 1975:
— the employment rate of women increased in all age groups;
— the increase is higher among women with young children than among women without children (9% vs. 1%);
— the highest increase occurred among mothers less than 25 years of age and among mothers, aged 25 to 29, with one child of less than two years of age (13% and 16%, respectively);
— the same trend is visible among married women, aged 25 to 29, with two children less than two years of age.

The data indicate quite clearly that the greatest change in labour force participation took place among women who are in their reproductive age, between 20 and 29. This is indicative of an attitudinal change towards motherhood among young French mothers who no longer feel obliged to stay home after their first child. It is after their second child, however, that they feel compelled to stay home because of lack of child-care facilities or because the price of such services, when they exist, tend to exceed their income. The obstacle to employment is no longer caused by the mother's traditional role but rather by external constraints of economic pressures and the environment.

Table 3

Labour Force Participation Rate of Married Women by Age groups and Number and Age of Children, 1962, 1968 and 1975, France

Age and Years		No Children	One Child less than 2 years	Two Children less than 2
Women less than 25 years old	1962	64	41	16
	1968	73	43	17
	1975	80	56	24
Percent Increase		+7%	+13%	+7%
Women aged	1962	68	42	21
25 and 29	1968	76	51	27
	1975	84	67	39
Percent Increase		+8%	+16%	+12%
Women of all	1962	36	39	26
Age Groups	1968	36	44	29
	1975	37	53	37
Percent Increase		+1%	+9%	+8%

Source: I. N. S. E. E., 1962, 1968, 1975.

Table 4 reveals that the level of professional activity of French women increases in direct relationship to their level of education.

Note that there are approximately twice as many employed women among those having completed some sort of training beyond high school as among those having completed only primary school. The statistics also reveal that a woman who has completed technical school has many more possibilities of finding employment than one having a high school diploma in general education (Michal, 1973).

Table 5 indicates that the professional activity of a married woman is more likely to be maintained following the birth of children when she has a higher level of education (Michal, 1973).

Two women out of three without children or with one child and holding a diploma superior to the high school level are listed as employed; whereas, this proportion is only 27% among married women without children and who lack a diploma of any type and 35% among married women with one child and no diploma. The employment rate for women with several children varies considerably according to the educational level of the mother.

Divorce

As is well-known, the divorce rate is rising at an accelerated pace in the United States: "The divorce rate had soared to the high level it had reached soon after the end of World War II, and an estimated one out of every three marriages of women 30 years old had been, or would eventually be, dissolved by divorce" (Glick, 1975: 16).

Table 4

Employment Rate of French Women by Level of Education, 1968

No diploma	Grade school diploma	High school diploma	Superior to High school
26.4%	34%	46%	59%

In France, the same tendency can be observed. After the peak which followed War II, the annual number of divorces remained around 31,000 between 1954 and 1963. Since then it has increased rapidly, especially after 1969. In 1979, the number of divorces reached 90,000. The number of marriages being dissolved rose from 10% in 1964 to 16% in 1971 (INSEE, 1975). Yet it must be added that France is still at that intermediary stage where the underprivileged classes encounter difficulty in obtaining a divorce (Vallot, 1971).

Table 5

Employment Rate of French Women by Level of Education and Number of Children, 1968

	No Children	1 Child	2 Children	3 Children	Total
No Diploma	27	35	23	14	27
Primary school diploma	37	42	27	19	34
Superior to high school diploma	62	67	57	43	59

In the United States, the improvement in the level of education and in the professional qualifications of women was accompanied by an increase in the divorce rate. Glick points out that while the divorce rate is less for men aged 35 to 44 with a higher socio-economic level than for men of a lower socio-economic level, the reverse is true for American women of the same age group: "Those who have the most education and the most income being generally less likely to enter marriage or to maintain continuing marriage, on the average, than those with lesser achievement in their education background and their work experience" (Glick, 1975: 23).

In France, the analysis of data relating to divorce and separation reveals that working women request a divorce more often than housewives because their employment assures them a degree of independence which the latter do not have. Among the total number of divorces granted in 1968, 60% of the proceedings were initiated by women as opposed to 40% by men (Jaulerry, 1971: 167). However, among divorced employed women the proportion who take the initiative in obtaining a divorce is even higher. In 1970 this figure rose to 70.5% as compared with 58% for divorced housewives (Roussel, 1975: 28).

In general, the statistics concerning the divorce rate in France confirm those collected throughout Western Europe: "The opportunity for women to become economically independent is perhaps the most decisive factor here. Thus, countries with a smaller proportion of women in the labour force have lower divorce rates than those where a higher percentage of women go out to work. Countries where over 50% of working women are married have higher divorce rates than those where the greater number of working women are single" (Kunzel, 1974: 379 388).

The rise of the divorce rate in France indicates that the younger the husband, the higher the divorce rate. Also the percentage of divorces for men of less than 25 was 3%, 4% and 6% in 1962, 1965 and 1968, respectively (Jaulerry, 1971: 163). For women aged less than 23, these respective proportions for the same years were 4%, 5% and 7%. Thus we see that young couples are increasingly unwilling to remain in an unhappy marriage. This seems especially evident on the part of young women who at less than 23 years of age had a higher divorce rate than young men of less than 25 during the years 1962, 1965, and 1968. The two-year difference in age is analogous to the two-year difference between conjoints in average age at marriage for the younger generation in France.

Resistance of the French Society to Women's Autonomy in Marriage and Society

The preceding statistics indicate that among young women it is those who are employed, who are better qualified or have a higher level of education who, in contrast to the housewives, marry less frequently and somewhat later, remain less often in an unhappy marriage and renounce their professional activity less frequently after the birth of their children.

Although inequality in marriage is not recognized as a cause of divorce in French courts, the reciprocity of exchange within the couple has become one of the principal demands of young women in contemporary industrial societies. (This is a thesis which the author (Michel, 1972) supported several years ago.) This equality includes the equality related to functions of authority, participation in professional life, child-training, and the performance of domestic duties. It does not, of course, refer to a mechanical equality where each decision or each domestic task must be equally shared by the spouses but is concerned instead with a flexibility of roles in both the home and the professional life so that both partners share equally in the duties and responsibilities. Such sharing does not presuppose that the wife will sacrifice her professional life to the life of the family nor that the husband has the right to make decisions without taking account of his wife's opinions. It does presume, however, that child-training and domestic tasks will be equally shared. These conditions are far from being realized in French families, although a law passed in 1970 decreased the authority of the husband and increased that of the wife. Research carried out in 1964 revealed that for women with equal education, twice as many of those employed outside the home received their husbands' help with housework as did housewives (Michel, 1974).

The same research indicated that the dissatisfaction of the wife increases in proportion to the increase in the husband's authority, the inequality of decision-making power between the couple ($y=.15$) and with the absence of a sharing of domestic responsibilities ($y=.09$) (Michel, 1970). The correlation in the third case could not be perfect as it was not the exact amount of assistance provided by the husband which was the determining factor but rather the correspondence between the expectations of the wife and the amount of aid provided. It was noted, for example, that women with high school education received their husbands's help more often than those with only grade school education. However, the level of expectation of the former predisposed them to consider this help as insufficient more often than did the expectations of the latter group of women. Thus, the group which received more help was often the one to be less satisfied since their higher level of education had led them to expect more assistance from their husbands (Michel and Picard, 1971).

Taking into account that the level of aspiration of women is higher among those with a higher education, we find support for the hypothesis that a woman's satisfaction in marriage is a function of the equality of exchange between the spouses or, conversely, that her dissatisfaction is a function of the inequality of exchange between them.

We must now examine the evidence of resistance among French men to the idea of an equality of spousal exchange. Several studies attest to this resistance. In her study of French youth, Agnes Pitrou (1972) found that only 42% of the young men favoured the employment of their future wives outside the home, whereas 68% of the young women of the same age indicated that they planned work following marriage. These differences may be attributed to a dissimilar socialization of the two sexes resulting either from identification with the parent of the same sex (the mother being generally responsible for housework), or from constant evidence of different parental expectations for the two sexes. For example, research conducted among the youth in a town on the outskirts of Marseille indicated that 80% of the young girls helped with the housework as opposed to only 42% of the boys (Sabran, 1973).

A survey carried out in 1972 by the National Institute of Demographic Studies on 2,142 subjects representing a national sample of the population revealed that the concern for equality within the couple and for autonomy for the wife was much more frequently expressed by women than by men. Thus approximately one out of two (45%) declared that employment represented an advantage for a woman as working women enjoy greater equality and independence; while only about a third of the male subjects expressed this view (34%). The same study revealed that while more than two-thirds of French women felt that it was not wise to make a decision concerning the couple without the consent of the other spouse, only 58% of the men expressed the same sentiment (Biogeol et al., 1975: 141–5).

Another study carried out by Nicole Tabard, in 1971, on 762 families receiving Social Security payments (family allowances) and representing a national cross-section of this population had previously indicated that men are much more opposed than their wives to employment for married women. The same results were obtained from blue and white collar workers as well as those in administrative positions, in spite of the fact that working conditions are completely altered by level of qualification. Whether the wife was in the work force or remained at home, whether she had few or many children, seemed not to affect these results (Tabard et al., 1974: 179). In addition, the author observed that in case of conflict concerning whether or not the wife should work, it was generally the opinion of the husband which prevailed—often in an authoritarian manner. We are thus still far away from the realization of an equality of exchange between husbands and wives.

In 1975, the Commission of the European Communities conducted a survey among the nine members of the community to determine the attitudes of both sexes toward the emancipation of women. Approximately 9,500 subjects, aged 15 and above representing a cross-section of the national populations, responded to a questionnaire containing fifty questions. The results revealed that scarcely more than half of French males less than 25 years of age (55%) would prefer that their wives have a career; whereas, approximately three-fourths (72%) of the young women of that age group indicated that they preferred to work outside the home. In the age group 25 to 54 years, the differences are still significant: less than one out of two males (45%) would prefer that his wife work as opposed to two out of three (67%) among women of the same age group. However, among all of the nine countries of the European Community, France has the highest percentage of men preferring that their wives pursue a career. Belgium (52%) and France (56%) are the only two countries where a majority of males under 25 years of age expressed this preference. Everywhere else, the percentage for males was less than 50%: Italy, 45%; West Germany, 42%; Ireland, 38%; Great Britain, 35%; Holland, 35%; Denmark, 19%; and Luxemburg, 35% (Commission of European Communities, 1975).

In their attitudes regarding the political role of women the difference between male and female responses are smaller but demonstrate the same tendencies as in the sample above. A bare majority (55%) of French males, less than 25 years of age, agree that politics should be as much the concern of women as of men, as opposed to 62% of French women. In addition, 54% of French males in the same age group compared to 58% of the females would place as much confidence in a woman as in a man to represent them in Parliament, this revealing the lack of confidence of a strong minority of youth of both sexes concerning representation in Parliament. Of the nine Common Market countries, only Denmark and Holland have a higher percentage than France of males less than 25 years of age who would place as much confidence in a female as in a male representative in Parliament: Denmark, 70%; Holland, 56% (Commission of European Communities, 1975).

Conclusion

The preceding data reveal that, even if some young French women still entertain prejudices which limit their political life, those who are well-educated and hold a position requiring certain qualifications no longer readily accept the restrictions and constraints which marriage and family impose both legally and by custom in the daily life of women. They also tend to obtain a divorce more quickly when the marriage is a failure. The relationship between the couple is more egalitarian if the wife is employed, has more education, and a higher degree of job qualification.

Among the legal constraints that married women encounter, in spite of recent changes in the laws relative to marriage, is the fact that the husband still possesses certain privileges regarding the administration of property held in common by the couple. For example, the authorization of the wife is not necessary for the sale of stocks and shares.

The restrictions which a woman encounters in marriage concern the double responsibility represented by attempting to manage home and family in addition to a career, for it is still unusual for French fathers to participate *equally* in the domestic and child-training tasks. The result is that women with children have much less time to devote to their professional life, to other activities outside the home, and to leisure than do those who have no children. A publication concerning timebudgets of French women interviewed in 1971 revealed that women without children dedicate an hour per day more to their professional life than the mother with one or two children: 8.4 hours as opposed to 7.8 hours per day (Riandey, 1976). At the same time, it was pointed out that employed women with children devote an hour less per day to physiological activities (sleeping, eating and personal care) than housewives. Thus, the woman who works outside the home is penalized in comparison with the housewife since inadequate community facilities do not provide sufficient assistance with housework and child care. In addition, she cannot depend on her husband for help as social customs still free him from an equal responsibility for domestic tasks and child-training. Only 43% of the male subjects of this study assisted their wives with housework during the week—even when the latter were employed and the couple had children. This figure decreased to 29% when women were not in the work force. The respective percentages for the husband's assistance on Sundays were 41% and 37%. With regard to child care, the percentage of French fathers who help to bathe and dress the children, assist them with their homework or accompany them to school during the week is calculated at 29% for families where the mother is employed as opposed to 6% in homes where she is not employed. Thus we see that the employment of women has a definite influence on the restructuring of masculine and feminine roles among couple. However, the preceding statistics indicate that this restructuring affects at present only a minority of couples—unquestionably those in the youngest age group.

French social legislation as well as social customs still distinguish between masculine and feminine roles in marriage and the family. The result is that French women fulfill a double role, a professional and domestic one, while men are excused from the latter. This situation—regarded as unjust by many young French women—has undoubtedly contributed to a decrease in the marriage and birth rates, an increase in the divorce rate and the emergence of a Women's Liberation Movement in France which advises young women to avoid marriages where inequality exists and where the wife may be forced to assume a double responsibility.

REFERENCES

Bernard, Jessie
    1975 "Notes on changing life styles." *Journal of Marriage and the Family* 57 (August): 582–593.
Boigeol, Anne et al.
    1975 *Le Divorce et les Français,* tome I. Enquête d'Opinion, Vol. 69. Paris: Presses Universitaires de France.
Calot, Gerard and Deville, Jean-Claude
    1971 "Nuptialité et fécondité selon le milieu socio-culturel." *Economie et Statistique* 27 (October): 3–42.
Commission of the European Communities
    1975 "Femmes et Hommes d'Europe." Bruxelles: Commission des Communautés Européennes.
Glick, Paul
    1975 "A demographer looks at American families." *Journal of Marriage and the Family* 37 (February): 15–26.
INSEE
    1975 Données Statistiques sur les Famillles, serie M. 48 (November). Paris: Institut National de la Statistique.
Jaulerry, Eliane
    1971 "Les dissolutions d'union en France étudiées à partir des minutes de jugement." *Population,* numéro special 26 (June): 167.
Kunzel, Renate
    1974 "The connection between the family cycle and divorce rates: analysis based on European data." *Journal of Marriage and the Family* 36 (May): 379–388.
Michal, Marie G.
    1973 *L'Emploi Feminin en 1968,* serie D. 25 (November). Paris: Collection INSEE.
Michel, Andrée
    1970 "Wife's satisfaction with husband's understanding in Parisian urban families." *Journal of Marriage and the Family* (August): 351–359.
    1974 *Activité professionnelle de la femme et Vie Conjugale.* Paris: Centre National de la Recherche Scientifique
    1978 *Sociologie de la Famille et du Mariage.* Paris: Presses Universitaires de France. (2nd. ed.).
Michel, A. and F. Picard
    1971 "Some differentials of the marital satisfaction of French working wives in the Paris area." *International Journal of Sociology of the Family* 1 (March): 1–17.
Pitrou, Agnes
    1972 *La Famille dans la Vie de tous les Jours.* Toulouse: Privat
    1976 "Rapport sur la situation démographique de la France en 1974." *Population* 31 (January-February): 15–26.

Riandey, Benoît
  1976 *Le Budget-Temps des Mères de Famille (Besoins et Aspirations des Familles et des Jeunes: Analyses Complémentaires)*, tome III. Paris: Caisse Nationale des Allocations Familiales et Centre de Recherches et de Documentation sur la Consommation.
Roussel, Louis
  1975 *Le Mariage dans la Société Française*. Paris: Presses Universitaires de France.
Roussel, Louis et al.
  1975 *Le Divorce et les Français*, tome II. Paris: Presses Universitaires de France.
Sabran, Jacques
  1973 *La Petite Patrie Retrouvée: Etude Sociologique d'Adolescents du Bassin Minier de Provence*. Paris: Presses Universitaires de Grenoble.
Tabard, Nicole et al.
  1974 *Besoins et Aspirations des Familles et des Jeunes*. Paris: Caisse Nationale des Allocations Familiales et Centre de Recherches et de Documentation sur la Consommation.
Vallot, Francoise
  1971 "Mariages et divorces à Paris: analyse des actes de mariage de quatre cohortes." *Population,* numero spécial 26 (June): 67–100.

The Position of Austrian Women in the Family

Some Data, Many Queries, and a Few Interpretations

EVA KÖCKEIS-STANGL

The University of Innsbruck, Innsbruck, Austria

THE EDITOR OF THIS VOLUME has asked me to report on how structural changes in Austria have affected the position of women in family and society. When agreeing to undertake this task I though it was a fairly easy one because results from quite a number of studies on Austrian females are available (Gaudart and Schulz, 1971; Haller, 1973; Hausa, 1968 and 1969; Kreutz, 1973; Kreutz and Fürnschuss, 1971; Rosenmayr *et al.*, 1969a and 1973; Schulz, 1976; Stock, 1974; Szinovácz, 1975; etc.) as well as a six-volume government-sponsored report on the situation of Austrian women published on the occasion of Women's Year (Karl, 1975).

Upon closer consideration, however, I found I could not meet all of the demands of this task and would have to offer something much more modest. On the one hand, there is very little exact information on how and to what extent the position of women in the family really has been altered. And on the other hand the perplexing question of how to decide which structural changes have brought about these merely vaguely-perceived alterations. Causal attributions of this kind appear to me particularly difficult to establish when no one spectacular structural change has occurred but rather, as seems to be the case in Austria, many simple and modest developments have taken place in the economic and demographic structure, on the political scene, in legal provisions and social norms, in the educational system, etc. These developments are certainly interconnected in some way, although they are occasionally also contradictory. Definite evidence (or at least cogent arguments) are required to show that a particular structural change may actually be viewed as causative. Reciprocal effects must also be considered; recent changes in laws on abortion, on marriage and divorce are probably in part the result of previous changes in actual family living but may concomitantly be viewed as factors for further familial changes.

Since the literature on female roles has, at least in German-speaking countries, developed a strong tendency for sweeping statements, my way out of the dilemma will be a series of attempts to pinpoint some very concrete issues. I shall first try to present evidence for changes in the family position of Austrian women and will then deal at some length with the oft-heard tenet that labour force participation is the most important prerequisite for enhancing this family position. I shall do this by analyzing past developments of female labour force participation in Austria and then trying to gauge, mainly from a study on young Austrian working wives, the actual effects of being gainfully employed. The latter offers a good opportunity to analyze the woman's share in familial decision-making and to discuss why women do not want to be the main decision-makers. This, together with some results on anticipatory socialization for marriage will be the basis for my claim that, at present, the main obstacle for achieving a truly equitable marital partnership is the perception held by women of what constitutes an ideal marriage rather than their non-participation in the labour force or their husbands' opposition to such participation.

Evidence of changes in the family position

I must confess at the outset that my fairly painstaking search for data that would indicate how much change and what kind of change in woman's position in the family has actually occurred, has not unearthed anything very substantial. Except for demographic data, I can offer no time-series whatever and I shall have to resort to comparing replies given by respondents of different age groups at *one* point instead of several points in time.

A few such age-cohort comparisons are available from recent attitude surveys on marital norms (Karl, 1975: vol. 1). Among both males and females, the younger respondents are more likely to give "progressive" and "up-to-date" replies. Younger respondents are somewhat more likely to deny that women marry mainly to obtain male protection and that a husband's capabilities should outstrip his wife's (17). They are also less likely to view creativity and productivity as male prerogatives (11) and a little more willing to concede that a wife's educational superiority need not be detrimental to marriage (18). On all such items there are consistent sex-differences such that males in the 16–24 age bracket approximately concur with females aged 60 and over. Among the younger respondents, as well as among those who have received more formal education, the gap between normative attitudes held by men and women seems to be widening, which may indicate that younger and better educated women are somewhat more prepared to "defend their rights."

Taken altogether, however, the survey data certainly do not point to dramatic changes in normative attitudes. The age group differences might be due merely to the respondents' different position in the lifecycle or to some other similar intervening variable. An attitude survey recently undertaken among women and girls who are office-holders in, or who are active members of some women's and youth organizations, yields no age-differences concerning normative attitudes on feminist issues (Schulz, 1976a: 27). Among the women and girls with more liberal organizational attachments, those belonging to youth organizations appear to hold somewhat less progressive views than those belonging to women's organizations and committees (1976a: 30).

Some additional information is available from a report of interviews with a sample of sixteen-year-old girls and their mothers living in Vienna (Gaudart and Schulz, 1971). Surprisingly the intergenerational differences are by no means all in favour of the daughters. On the very general normative questions, the girls display a somewhat more emancipative stance than their mothers (e.g., more opposition to items such as "women are to stay at the hearth"). More concrete items, however, seem to reveal that the daughters will probably be at least as much family-oriented, once they are married, as the older generation. There is little indication that the girls will be more oriented towards outside employment which they rate as even less central to a married woman's life than their mothers do. If the girls hold to their views and practice in marriage what they now preach, the main intergenerational difference will be a stronger accent on the husband-wife relationship as compared to the accent on child-raising and household duties (Gaudart and Schulz, 1971: 28).

There seems to be a general sentiment in Austria in favour of taking from husbands the right to make their wives obey. Legal norms have just been altered to comply with this conviction and the definition of the husband as head of the family has been omitted. Jurists now view marriage as a contract giving the contracting parties almost full autonomy in the forming, as well as in the termination, of their relationship (Schwind, 1976). Nevertheless, the marriage relationship has by no means become fully equal. Most men, as well as most women, still think that *the husband should be "der Überlegenere"* (the superior). However, superiority is no longer automatically *ascribed* to the husband simply because he fills this role; instead, it is felt that his superiority has to be *achieved* through being more capable, more intelligent and more mature than his wife. It is, therefore, considered as definitely detrimental to a harmonious relationship if the wife in any way surpasses her husband, i.e., makes more money, is better educated, or is older than he is. Instead, the wife should be somewhat inferior to him in all these matters. That is the ideal.

An analysis of the respective ages of brides and bridegrooms of marriages taking place in different years offers an opportunity to see whether any change has occurred concerning this aspect of marital asymmetry.[1] As can be seen in Table 1 absolutely no overall change has taken place in this respect since 1965. Of all the women marrying before they turn thirty, a full third still marry a man at least five years their senior while about half choose a bridegroom of approximately equal age (i.e., at the most two years older than they are themselves). Girls marrying before they reach twenty are particularly likely to be at least five years younger than their bridegrooms. This is the only group where the data show some tendency towards a reduction of the age-

[1] Pfeil (1968: 64) has directly established from her respondents that the main reason for desiring an age-difference between husband and wife is so that he can be the leading partner; biological reasons were mentioned much less frequently, and economic ones hardly at all.

Table 1

*Maintainance of the Age-Gap between Husband and Wife
(Austrian marriages concluded in 1965, 1970, and 1974)*

a) *Percentage of brides marrying a groom at least three years older than they are*

Year of marriage	Age of bride			
	Below 20	20–24	25–29	All aged below 30
1965	77	50	39	55
1970	73	51	40	55
1974	71	51	42	56

b) *Age distribution of brides, by year of marriage*

Year of marriage	Age of bride						
	Below 20	20–24	25–29	30–39	40–49	50 and more	All marriages
1965	22.9	44.3	16.5	8.7	4.6	3.1	100% (56.738)
1970	24.3	44.2	16.0	8.7	4.2	2.6	100% (52.773)
1974	27.4	42.0	14.6	9.7	3.5	2.6	100% (49.296)

Source: Calculated from "Statistisches Jahrbuch der Republik Österreich" 1966, 1971, 1975.

difference but this is offset by the female trend towards earlier marriage and thus there is no overall change. The average age-difference between husband and wife has remained as wide for couples marrying in the 70's (3.1 years) as it was before World War II [1928, 2.8; 1937, 3.1 (Karl, 1975 (4): 95)].

Over the long period, drastic changes have occurred in the probability of marrying as well as in the marriage-age (Table 2). In 1971, three-quarters of the female population had married before they were 26, while in 1951 this proportion was not reached until they had turned thirty. (In 1934, 75% were married by age 35; in 1880, 75% by age 46.)

As existing norms were by no means in favour of women postponing their marriage up to their late twenties or even beyond, these figures obviously imply that finding a marriageable man was not an easy feat at least up to World War II. (The uncertainties and anxieties thus aroused figure prominently in many novels of that time.) At the turn of the century fully 20 percent of all females remained single throughout their lives; before World War II, this figure was reduced to 14 percent, and presently less than 10 percent never marry.

It may be that family sociologists have as yet paid too little attention to these developments. There is little evidence that the family position of unmarried adult women has been considered except by gerontologists. To be the odd single daughter, sister, or aunt in a family household is not a pleasant existence and very rarely a role chosen intentionally. Her affiliative and sexual needs are probably more wont to be exploited than the married woman's; and in all likelihood this holds even for those unmarried women who set up households of their own. The likelihood of having to play these roles has evidently greatly decreased, perhaps more than is shown in

Table 2

Changes in Female Marriage Patterns

Percent single (never married)

	1880	1910	1934	1951	1961	1971
Of total population aged 15 and over	47	42	36	28	25	22
Of age group 20–24	86	81	81	66	58	45
Of age group 40–44	27	21	20	14	12	10
Of age group 60–64	24	19	15	15	14	12

Source: Census figures quoted in Karl (1975, vol. 4: 89).

census data because it makes sense to treat as if married those women who live permanently with a man even though they are not legally married. Those who subscribe to feminist slogans that recommend avoiding or escaping marriage cannot, so far, be identified demographically.

In sum, then, it has become considerably easier for a woman to get married and this also holds for subsequent marriages. After a first marriage has been dissolved due to divorce (which is just slightly more frequent than before the war), women now have a much greater chance to remarry (Karl 1975 (4): 99 and 94). Even in this area, however, definite evidence of sexual asymmetry remains. After both widowhood and divorce, men have still a much greater likelihood of remarriage than women have. By age forty, women (single, widowed, or divorced) have only half the men's probability of finding a marriage partner (19 and 98). Furthermore, it is only women whose marriage chances are reduced by increased formal education. Of the women in the 40 to 44 age bracket, only 65 percent of those with a university degree are married, compared to 76 percent of the women with higher secondary education and even 82 percent of those with less (Karl, 1975 (3): 119). Although there may well be some highly educated women who prefer to stay single, it seems fair to assume that this situation is mainly due to their reduced marital eligiblity which results from the preference to maintain educational asymmetry among married couples.

From all of this we can conclude that developments described in this section have enhanced the family position of the Austrian woman to some moderate extent: she is able to be somewhat less fearful of not finding a husband, or of divorcing one she is not happy with; and she is definitely less obliged to obey her husband. Nevertheless, truly symmetrical relationships are as yet hardly coveted. *The social norm of male superiority in marriage is still present, although justified by new arguments.* It is kept up by—among other things—a strong tendency to maintain a considerable age-difference, as well as an educational difference between husband and wife.

Changes in female labour force participation

In contrast to the United States and Canada, for example, overall female employment rates in Austria were high even before World War I. They have slightly decreased since then as the following table shows:

Percentage of total female population in the labour force

	1910	1934	1951	1961	1971
Austria	41	37	35	36	30
U.S.			22	26	30

Thus, if we follow the tenet that female labour force participation has the direct and immediate effect of enhancing woman's position in the family, we should be led to expect that Austrian females have had a much more favourable position at the beginning of this century than in the United States and that since then this position has somewhat deteriorated. Even without reliable comparative data, it seems likely that neither of these assumptions is borne out by the facts.

Obviously, something is wrong here; either the basic tenet that increased labour force participation enhances woman's position, or the data. Let us see what could be wrong with the data.[2]

A first and important objection may be raised over the fact that the trend-data presented above use the total female population of the respective census years as a percentage basis and thus take account of neither the changes in the age-structure of the population (fewer children and more aged persons) nor of the normative and factual changes concerning the age-span considered as "working-age." Age-specific rates of labour force participation would solve this problem but they are not available for the earlier censuses. A feasible substitute—so it seems to me—can be gained by using the male labour force participation rates as a percentage base for calculating standardized rates for females. But as Table 3 shows, no matter whether this or any other method of calculation is used, female work-rates decrease rather than increase.

Let us see whether we can tackle this perplexing result from yet another point of view. We might well assume that labour force participation has emancipative effects

[2] It ought to be mentioned right away that the decrease in female labour force participation in 1971 cannot be accounted for by less overall demand for labour; the situation on the labour market was at least as favourable in 1971 as in the previous census years.

only if it consists of employment outside one's own family. It is rather obvious that work within the family business will hardly give a woman added independence because it usually means that her husband or father is concomitantly her work-boss. Women holding this workstatus are classified as "helpers" ("Mithelfende") in Austria; for others who are employed in the regular sense, I shall have to use the term "employees" for want of a better English expression.

Table 3

Labour Force Participation Rates, by Sex, Austria

	1910	1934	1951	1961	1971[a]
(1) Of total female population	41	37	35	36	30
(2) Of total male population	63	65	64	61	54
(3) Of female population aged 15 to 60	[b]	[b]	51[c]	57	53
(4) Female rates relative to male rates	65	57	55	60	56

[a] Up to 1961, all farmers' wives were automatically classified as "helpers" ("Mithelfende"). In 1971, about one-third of farmers' wives classified themselves instead as housewives. The 1971 figures quoted in this table have thus to be raised by just over one percent in order to be comparable with the former censuses.
[b] Not available; rough estimate for 1910 at least 58%
[c] Estimated from incomplete data, rather over- than underestimated

Source: Firnberg and Rutschka (1967: 22, 16) and current census data; own estimates and calculations.

"Helpers" are particularly common in agriculture and, because of the relative shrinkage of this economic sector, the number of women working as "employees" has probably increased despite the decrease in overall labour force participation noted above.[3] The respective data shown in Table 4, however, confirm even this expectation only to a very modest extent. The proportion working as employees (manual or nonmanual) has remained very nearly stable. (The figure for 1971 is the same as for 1961, and has risen by no more than 3.5 percentage points compared to 1951, and even a mere 2.3 compared to 1910.)

A drastic change has occurred only in the number of women working (preponderantly as helpers) on the family farm or in some other kind of family business. (This has dropped from 21 percent in 1910 to a mere 7 percent in 1971.) It is clear from this that it would be definitely worthwhile to investigate how withdrawal of women from participation on the family farm into the narrower precincts of the household has affected their standing in the family, especially since a similar development seems

---

3 The percentage of the female labour force that worked in the agricultural sector has decreased from 53% in 1919 to 17% in 1971. A small part of this decrease is due to the fact that up to 1961 all farmers' wives were automatically classified as "helpers," whereas in 1971 this was left to their own discretion.

Table 4

Women's Labour Force participation as "Employees", and as "Helpers" (or Self-employed) expressed as a percentage of the total female population

	1910	1934	1951	1961	1971
Working as "helpers" in family-business (or self-employed)	20.6	15.8	16.6	13.1	7.4
Working as "employees" (manual or nonmanual)	20.6	20.9	19.4	22.9	22.9

Source: calculated from data in Firnberg and Rutschka (1967) and the 1971 census figures; figures for 1910 are based on estimates.

to have taken place on an even larger scale in some other European countries such as Italy.

It is not impossible that in this particular case relinquishment of labour force participation has had the overall effect of improving woman's family position. Here are some reasons:

1. Farm families are likely to adhere more strongly than any other part of the population to an ideal of male dominance and virility, with the husband/father as nearly unchallenged boss of both the family and the farm. In spite of their extremely high labour force participation (as "helpers"), farm women are more willing than others to leave final decisions to their husbands. Farm girls strongly prefer to marry anybody but a farmer (Rosenmayr et al. 1969b: 312), which probably indicates not only their reservations against doing farm work but also their desire to elude the patriarchal family pattern still prevalent on farms.

2. The relinquishing of the wife's work-status as "helper" usually coincides with her husband's move from agriculture to some other sector of the economy, for example, into a factory. Even if this shift is not accompanied by a geographical move to a more urban community, it probably opens the family to somewhat more liberal influences and in any case removes the near-dictatorship of the farm-owner (often the woman's father or father-in-law rather than her husband) over all the family members working on "his" farm.

Among female "employees," two important shifts have occurred: (1) an increase in the amount of nonmanual, white-collar work and (2) an increase in the number of married women. Let us look more closely at the second of these developments. It seems fairly certain that up to World War I, seeking outside employment and being married were hardly compatible. Some women chose to work rather than marry and very many more worked because they had not yet been able to marry. And a considerable proportion never had the chance to marry at all, because pre-industrial norms and even legal provisions (up to 1880) barred couples from marrying as long as the husband did not have a secure means for maintaining a family. In 1910, 42 percent of all females aged fifteen and over were still single (in 1880: 47 percent).

Although no appropriate cross-tabulation is available from the 1910 census, a rough estimate makes it abundantly clear that nearly all female employees must have been unmarried. The situation in which outside employment was combined with marriage became possible only very gradually (Table 5). By 1951, 12 percent of all married women were "employees" while a further 20 percent were engaged in the family business. In 1971, the percentage of wives going out to work had risen to 25 percent and sample surveys carried out since show that this percentage is still rising. (The percentage working in the family enterprise has dropped to 12 percent.)

Table 5

Changes in the Participation Rates of Married Women
(Percent in labour force of all married women)

	1951	1961	1971
Working as "helpers" in family-business (or self-employed)	20	20	13
Working as "employees" (manual or nonmanual)	12	20	25
Total in labour force	32	40	38
Married women as a percentage of all female "employees"	27	36	47
Married women as a percentage of all females in the labour force	39	47	53

Source: Calculated from data in Firnberg and Rutschka (1967) and current census data.

Here, then, we have a fairly dramatic change: *More than twice as many Austrian women presently combine the roles of wife and "employee" than was the case two or three decades ago.* (We have still to establish how increased labour force participation produces an improved status for wives within the family.) It must be added that this change has only partly been brought about by alterations in the economic system *per se*. It is at least as much due to changes in the family system, i.e. the trend toward more and earlier marriages as we indicated previously.

This trend toward earlier marriage with the young wife remaining in the work force in order to help buy and equip a new home is also noted elsewhere (e.g., Blood and Wolfe, 1960: 105). What may be a peculiarly Austrian pattern is that at *least half the wives who have worked during the honeymoon period do not completely stop work when the first baby arrives.* Many just avail themselves of the "Karenzurlaub," i.e., the right to maternity leave for a full year after childbirth with a kind of unemployment benefit as well as the guarantee to be reinstated in their former position, or to resume work when the child turns three and is accepted into kindergarten.

On the other hand, the so-called three-phase pattern —work until the birth of the first child; stay home till the children reach adolescence; then return to work—

is as yet very rare in Austria. It is difficult to obtain a job after such a long break. Employers are sceptical and the women themselves are afraid that their occupational skill has declined during the long absence. In addition, the family's financial needs are usually not as pressing as they were in the initial stages of the marriage. The result is that these middle-aged women usually remain at home and, after a few years, take to looking after their first grandchildren, thus enabling the daughter or daughter-in-law to remain at work.

Table 6

Participation Rates of Women Married to "Employees"

a) *By number of children below age 15*

	Children				
	None	One	Two	Three	Four and more
Husband is blue-collar worker	51	42	28	25	22
Husband is white-collar worker	44	36	22	15	16

b) *By women's age*

	Below 21	21–30	31–40	41–50	51–60
Husband is blue-collar worker	58	41	37	42	34
Husband is white-collar worker	51	44	33	37	23

Source: Sample-survey results from the "Mikrozensus" in 1969, see: Lebens- und Erwerbsverhältnisse der weiblichen Bevölkerung in Österreich; Vienna 1972, Bundesministerium für Soziale Verwaltung.

It is somewhat difficult to establish how many wives follow each of the patterns just outlined because available age-specific work rates (e.g., Karl, 1975: 116) usually include those working as "helpers". However, the figures shown in Table 6 include only the wives of "employees" who are unlikely to work as "helpers". So it is reasonably certain that of the wives of blue-collar "employees" with one child as many as 40 percent are in outside employment. The lower part of Table 6 suggests that no more than 5 percent of employees' wives return to work after age forty.

Normative censuring of employed mothers

The prevalent norms concerning female employment do not at all mirror the actual situation. Norms and facts do correspond in respect to unmarried women; normative prescriptions for wives, however, are decidely discrepant from what actually happens.

In parallel with popular convictions in other industrial countries, Austrians are nearly unanimous that unmarried females without children should go to work (Table 7) and concede that unmarried mothers ought to seek employment. But, what about wives? An increasing majority of the population accepts the fact that young wives might remain at work until the birth of the first child—which, in fact, most women do. However, returning to work only after the children have grown is definitely more frequently "preached" than practiced. On the other hand, going to work when there are children to be looked after—and a husband/provider available—is heavily censured by all but a small minority—although it is practised fairly often as we have seen. On this issue the dissonance between norms and actions is so dramatic that it is useful to look into the matter more closely.

Table 7

Opinion-Survey Data on Work-Norms for Women
(Percent agreeing to female employment)

	Males	*Females*
If woman is not married	89	94
If woman is married but childless	84	88
If woman is married mother, and		
— children are older than 15	59	71
— children are of school-age	16	18
— children are of Kindergarten-age	20	22
— children are below age three	2	5

Source: Results obtained by "IFES" from representative population sample in 1974; quoted in Karl, 1975: vol. 5, p. 77.

The most striking aspect of the normative censuring against the outside employment of young mothers is that it is almost equally shared by those who themselves act (or have acted) against this norm. For instance, in an interview-study of 16-year-old girls and their mothers in Vienna, the mothers who did work were as adamant on the question as were those who did not go to work. (In both groups a mere 11 percent answered in the affirmative to the question, "Should a mother go out to work when there are small children to look after?") (Gaudart and Schulz, 1971: 99). This result is further corroborated by a large-scale investigation. The respondents in this study were married women aged 20 to 30, all working as blue-collar or white-collar employees. Table 8 summarizes the results from this study and line (b) makes it clear that those who do have small children still share the general norm against the employment of mothers almost as unanimously as those working wives who do not (as yet) have children.

The main cause of this strange situation is evidently economic pressures. The great majority of these young mothers—particularly the blue-collar workers—continue employment because the family budget needs their contribution, and only a very few consider interest in their job as their main work-motive (Table 8, (c)). The majority wants to and expects to quit work as soon as the home is fully equipped

Table 8

*General Norms and Personal Attitudes towards Employment Held by Young Working Wives
(Study of the Vienna Institute of Sociology)*

	Factory-workers		Sales-women		Office-workers	
	no child	with children	no child	with children	no child	with children
	(N=235)	(N=507)	(N=132)	(N=78)	(N=188)	(N=144)
a) In favour of married women without children going to work	74	76	76	81	79	90
b) In favour of married women with children going to work	5	9	3	12	6	13
c) Main personal motive for going to work:						
economic pressure (financial grounds)	76		72		69	
relief from household, relation to works-mates	10		11		17	
interest in her job	5		12		13	
d) Would continue to work even if no financial necessity	41	32	62	36	55	79
e) *Wants* to continue working for the next ten years	23	28	22	34	26	46
f) *Expects* to continue working for the next ten years	23	29	41	45	37	64
g) Would prefer part-time work	28	23	26	30	28	19
h) Considers her job as very gratifying	13	14	27	26	17	21
i) Considers her household-work as very gratifying	42	37	25	30	16	10
k) Husband helps with household chores		34		43		45
l) Husband helps with child-care	—	33	—	40	—	39
m) Husband *not* opposed to wife's employment		67		72		73
n) Plans to or would like to work after age forty		24		22		25
o) In favour of her daughter going to work after marriage		62		73		81
p) In favour of her daughter going to work when a mother		14		7		9

Sources: Haller (1973); Szinovácz (1975) Rosenmayr, Haller, Szinovácz (1973).

(lines e and f). It may thus be said that most of these women—especially the working-class wives—view their work-role as a sort of temporary extension of their family-role.[4] Szinovácz, one of the main authors of this study, therefore concludes (Karl, 1975 (1): 30):

[4] According to their husbands' educational and occupational status, half of the saleswomen of this study and about a quarter of the wives working in offices may be considered to belong

These women 'interpret' their own situation, their behavioral deviation from the general social norm as exceptional. They view it as being justified by their specific personal and familial circumstances but do not consider it acceptable as a general value-orientation and therefore deny its legitimacy for other women.

Szinovácz stresses that "changes in the actual situation—such as continuous employment of women—do not necessarily lead to corresponding changes in the respective value-orientations and role-expectations."[5]

This seems a fair enough explanation for the hiatus between norms and actions. Further information and deliberation are required, however, in order to establish how outside employment under such circumstances might affect the woman's standing in the family and her general capacity for emancipation. A clear-cut answer appears very difficult, especially in view of the fact that no extended Austrian study, embracing both working wives and housewives, is available. Nevertheless it is possible to reach some tentative conclusions, by making an analysis of the Viennese studies of young working wives undertaken by Haller (1973) and Szinovácz (1975).

Types of work-commitment and their consequences

From Haller's analysis of the wives' work-commitment, four major types of commitment seem to be present:

1. Wives who work but want to quit as soon as possible; who hold strong anti-employment norms; who rarely see any positive aspects in their jobs (except their earnings) and who consider their home-duties as much more gratifying than their job.

2. Wives with somewhat stronger work-commitment, the result of dissatisfaction with their husbands' earning power and occupational status, and with having to accept a permanent provider-role rather against their will; have frequently married beneath their station.

3. Wives who rather enjoy their work, take an interest in it, want and expect to continue their employment; usually earn somewhat but not very much less than their husbands; are upwardly mobile, relative to their family of origin and with respect to formal education and their own occupational status as well as their husbands'. All this combines to give these wives a sense of personal achievement independent

---

to working-class families. (On the other hand, about a quarter of the wives doing factory work have husbands in white-collar occupations.) Upper middle-class families are hardly included in this study. See also Table 12.

5 However, females presently in their teens who have not yet reached the stage of being themselves working wives hold definitely more liberal normative attitudes on the employment of mothers (Mittenecker, 1974: 21; Mechler et al., 1975). It remains to be seen whether this is an age-specific attitude (i.e. whether the cohort will change its mind after marriage); quite possibly, this signals a durable generational change of attitudes.

of their efforts within the household which they tend to consider as rather boring and unsatisfactory. These women are at least as likely as the other respondents to already have one or two children; rarely plan to have any more.

4. Wives rather similar to Type 3 as far as their own attitudes and inclinations are concerned but seemingly barred from realizing their hopes of continued employment by some circumstantial hindrance (possibly their husbands' opposition and/or no chance that their children could be properly looked after while they remain at work).

The respondents have not actually been typed and probably a good number could not be typed due to inconsistencies in their replies (Köckeis-Stangl, 1976a) and/or factual inconsistencies between their feelings, plans and attitudes.

A rough estimate of the respective sizes of these types can nevertheless be gained by a cross-tabulation of just two items, namely (a) the desire to remain and (b) the expectation of remaining at work during the next ten years (Table 9). Wives who neither want to nor expect to continue their employment (Type 1) definitely constitute the majority. They are particularly numerous among the blue-collar workers and even among the office-workers, they are more numerous than any of the other types.

Table 9

Desire for, and Expectation to Remain at Work as a rough guide to work commitment among young working wives

	Factory workers %	Sales-women %	Office-workers %
Neither wants to nor expects to remain at work (type 1)	56	49	41
Does not want to, but expects to remain at work (approximates type 2)	17	25	26
Wants to and expects to remain at work (type 3)	11	17	24
Wants to, but does not expect to remain at work (type 4)	16	9	9
	100% (568)	100% (169)	100% (309f
Not ascertained (no reply etc.)	30% (808)	25% (225)	11% (346)

Source: Haller, 1973: 210.

The wives doing manual work are least likely both to desire continued employment and to feel confident that they can realize this intention; a mere tenth of them appear to belong to Type 3.

Among the office-workers, wives who both want to and expect to continue their work are considerably more numerous; however, they still constitute but one-quarter of this group.

Work commitment is thus obviously related to the woman's occupational status and it is fairly certain that we would find even more adherents of Type 3 among the Austrian semi-professional and professional women who were not represented in this study. (This has been ascertained for Germany by Pfeil, 1961: 181.)

The lives of women belonging to Type 3 are rather obviously being enriched by the fact that they go to work. They seem to manage their dual role obligations sufficiently well and derive considerable satisfaction from their jobs which tend to be more interesting and more autonomous than those held by most other women. *For Type 3 the tenet of female employment as a pathway to emancipation certainly holds* and it is probably also applicable to the women of Type 4, if whatever barriers they envisage for their continued employment turn out to be surmountable. The tenet might eventually hold for the wives of Type 2 who start out feeling they have to stay at work—much against their inclination—in order to make up for their husbands' deficiencies. It might well turn out that their work status will serve to bolster a personal identity which has been damaged by not having been able to marry a sufficiently successful husband. It is possible that their work status may serve some of these women as a means of emancipation either *within* their rather unhappy marriage or else *from* their present marriage, i.e., it may facilitate their divorce.

It is the conviction of the author, however, that this tenet of the emancipative effects of being employed is untenable for the majority of working-class wives, i.e., the completely home-oriented women of Type 1. The way in which these working wives interpret their situation all but precludes the possibility that employment could serve them as a means for attaining greater self-reliance and autonomy. A person who views her job as but a brief interlude before she can truly settle down in what she considers her splendid new home is neither likely to get involved with the concerns of her firm (that might lead to a more responsible position) nor with the concerns of her work-mates that might lead to collective action, trade-unionist or political activities. A mother who goes to work and at the same time maintains the general view that a mother ought *not* to be employed, can probably allay her feelings of guilt only by overstressing her familial duties. She is thus likely to strive constantly to keep her husband and her children as well taken care of as if she were not employed and probably rarely demands their cooperation in managing the household.

The data which will be referred to below strengthen this conviction that these wifely conceptions of role-obligations are only partly to be blamed on husbands. Through processes spelled out somewhat more explicitly elsewhere (Köckeis, 1970a: 177-181 and 1970c), growing up in working-class families has instilled in both wives and husbands a rigid value-orientation favouring conformity and obedience. This orientation will remain more pervasive the less schooling and occupational skills these wives have been able to obtain. The humdrum and/or closely-supervised jobs the women with little training usually have obtained after school, are ceratinly not apt to stengthen their feelings of personal efficacy and self-reliance. No wonder that the women do not enjoy this kind of work; it leaves them even less leeway for autonomy and creativity than caring for their household and children.

(No researcher has as yet asked *males* doing similar work whether they desire to keep their jobs if there were no financial necessity to do so. I wonder whether males would give more affirmative replies than the females, if a researcher were prepared to skip the ethnocentric barrier which has hitherto precluded the asking of such a question.)[6]

In sum, then, it is valid to conclude that the type of work done and the subjective interpretation of a wife's role-obligations—both closely connected to previous socialization experiences—are decisive determinants of the way in which she will be affected by her employment. It seems possible that labour force participation is more of a corollary and consequence than an independent determinant of emancipation. The writer maintains that changes in women's role-conceptions and their standing in the family emerge from changes and developments other than their increased employment. It is difficult to marshal any direct evidence from Austrian studies for this supposition; several related ones, will, however, be discussed below.

Employed wives and the control of family decisions

One piece of evidence for the positive effects of being employed has often been thought to come from the fact that working wives appear to have more say in family decisions. Research undertaken in the United States, the German Federal Republic, France, Greece, Yugoslavia, Japan and Puerto Rico has established that husbands of employed wives tend to get lower scores than males married to nonworking wives on indices of husband's decision power (Lupri, 1970: 342; Rodman, 1970: 126). Such indices, sometimes referred to as "male authority index," are usually constructed from answers to questions on how decisions in a particular family are customarily arrived at in a range of areas. Lupri has been able to show, from data he collected in Germany, that the above mentioned relationship holds as well when the husband's social status or income is controlled and that the lower the husband's social status, the more the employment of the wife will reduce his power score (Lupri, 1970: 343).

Similar questions asking whether the wife, the husband, or both jointly decide

---

6 An Austrian comparative study of male apprentices and higher secondary school students does show that the occupational sphere is much less central for teenage working-class boys than for their student counterparts when they consider what they will achieve by age 25 (Danneberg, 1963: 14).
Furthermore, when Pfeil (1968: 95) asked a representative sample of twens at Hamburg what it was that made their lives worthwhile, not so many more men (36%) than women (24%) mentioned their occupations.

were asked for eight different decision areas[7] in the study on young Austrian working wives already referred to. Szinovácz (1975) has extensively analyzed these data without, however, calculating any scores across the eight areas. If this is done, it becomes particularly clear that most of these couples decide jointly in most areas. The mean results are: 1.10 areas are decided by the wife, 1.30 are decided by the husband and 5.60 out of the total of eight areas are decided jointly.

Table 10

Familial Decision Control and Marital Happiness of Young Working Wives
Measures of decision control within the family by wife's evaluation of how happy her marriage is

Blue-collar workers

Marital happiness:	High (N=135)	Medium (N=354)	Low (N=206)	All (N=277)
"Index of male decision power"	8.46	8.18	7.71	8.03
Average number of areas decided by:				
husband	1.44	1.25	1.33	1.32
wife	0.98	1.07	1.62	1.27
both jointly	5.58	5.68	5.05	5.39

Saleswomen

Marital happiness:	High (N=64)	Medium (N=109)	Low (N=41)	All (N=217)
"Index of male decision power"	8.22	8.42	8.41	8.31
Average number of areas decided by:				
husband	1.22	1.39	1.76	1.40
wife	1.00	0.97	1.25	1.08
both jointly	5.78	5.64	4.99	5.51

Office-workers

Marital happiness:	High (N=96)	Medium (N=173)	Low (N=66)	All (N=342)
"Index of male decision power"	8.69	8.36	8.46	8.39
Average number of areas decided by:				
husband	1.08	1.13	1.46	1.15
wife	0.38	0.74	1.00	0.74
both jointly	6.53	6.13	5.54	6.09

Source: calculated from Szinovácz (1975: 123 and 316).

7 These decision areas were: family budgeting; changes concerning furnishing and decoration of the home; invitation of guests; visiting; where to spend the holidays; final say when making important purchases; which newspaper to buy or subscribe to; decisions about the family car.

The high frequency of joint decisions produces a queer consequence for scores calculated in analogy to the "index of male decision power" outlined above (wife decides=0, both decide=1, husband decides=2). It turns out that a subgroup which by this means gets the highest score does not necessarily contain more couples where the husband really decides on his own than do the contrasting subgroups. Table 10 demonstrates that *high scores on this index can just as well result from a higher-than-average frequency of joint decisions.* Thus, the index would lead one to misjudge the office-workers' husbands as being more authoritarian than the husbands of the factory-workers and saleswomen. Actually, however, just those couples where the wife works in an office seem to be the most egalitarian ones in this study, i. e., reporting the greatest number of joint decisions. Joint decisions appear to be rarest in the factory-workers' families where, however, nearly as many decisions are made solely by the women themselves as by their husbands.

The pitfalls of the "index of male decision power" become even more obvious, if further results in Table 10 are considered. The index would mislead us into believing that wives consider their marriage to be happier the more authoritarian their husband. If this were so, it would be a devastating blow to all those concerned with female emancipation. Luckily, this is just an artifact due to this index; matters are not really as they appear. It is evident for all three categories of working wives that it is not increased male decision power but rather the *high frequency of joint decisions that contributes to their feelings of being happily married.* Both saleswomen and office-workers indicate clearly that their marriages are happier when their husbands make fewer decisions on their own. For the factory-workers it appears particularly important that they, themselves, do not have to make decisions on their own. Similar relationships between decision control and the wife's personal happiness are substantiated by Szinovácz (1975: 334).

Women thus seem to like an increase in their decision-making power only up to the point of taking part in joint decisions. Having to decide on their own is not entirely appreciated. This is probably due to the high premium women put on "togetherness" in marriage, plus the fact that—at least for a woman—having complete decision control over one area also seems to imply that she cannot count on her husband taking any part in the *duties* of that particular area. This important corollary of female decision control has been well documented by Szinovácz (1975: 740). For instance, from amongst the very few wives who decide on their own which type of car is to be bought, nearly all also have to *wash* the car, one of the few chores carried out by the husbands in the majority of other families (745). Similarly, husbands are least likely to carry out daily shopping duties if the wife alone is in control of the family budget (714).

Further data confirm this relationship. For all six comparisons set out in Table 11, joint-decision areas are most frequent and solely female-decision areas are least frequent when the husband (rather than the mother, mother-in-law or no-one) is

Table 11

Decision Control and Familial Help Pattern

a) *Decision control by main source of assistance for household-work**

	Factory-workers			Sales-women			Office-workers		
Assistance from:	Mother (N=229)	None (N=215)	Husband (N=254)	Mother (N=49)	None (N=56)	Husband (N=98)	Mother (N=78)	None (N=69)	Husband (N=148)
Average number of areas decided by:									
husband	1.37	1.33	1.18	1.67	1.40	1.31	1.50	1.26	1.02
wife	1.60	1.29	0.88	1.15	1.09	0.85	1.04	1.05	0.49
both	5.03	5.38	5.94	5.18	5.51	5.84	5.46	5.69	6.49

b) *Decision control by main source of assistance for childcare***

	Factory-workers		Sales-woman		Office-workers	
Assistance from:	Mother (N=225)	Husband (N=152)	Mother (N=34)	Husband (N=31)	Mother (N=51)	Husband (N=57)
Average number of areas decided by:						
husband	1.41	1.28	1.81	1.10	1.10	1.28
wife	1.49	1.17	1.55	0.85	1.49	0.74
both	5.10	5.55	4.64	6.05	5.41	5.98

Source: Calculated from Szinovácz (1975: 734 736).

* Assistance with household-work by persons other than the wife's mother, mother-in-law or husband is very rare in this sample according to Szinovácz. The column "assistance from mother" includes the wives mainly helped by their mother-in-law.
* Concerns childcare outside of the wife's work-hours. Practically all respondents with child (ren) get such assistance, again almost exclusively extended by their mother (or mother-in-law) or their husband.

the wife's main assistant for householdwork and child care. Furthermore, in all but one of the six comparisons, the husband's participation in home-duties leads also to a reduction of the number of decision areas handled by him alone. Thus, if a husband shares in what are traditionally considered to be female tasks, there is a strong tendency for him to share all decisions with his wife, both those in traditionally female and in traditionally male areas. Both these aspects of marital partnership—joint decision-making as well as the husband's willingness to help in the home—contribute significantly to making the wives feel more happily married and considering themselves more successful as wives and mothers (Szinovácz, 1975: 330, 772, 750, 757).

Thus, the prospect of gaining or maintaining increased familial decision power through continued employment (an effect suggested by the results obtained by Lupri and others) might not be considered an asset by women like the ones included in the Austrian study, if it implies that they would have to make more decisions on their own. It would, therefore, be most interesting to know whether the lower scores on the "index of male decision power" reported for couples with working, as against nonworking, wives are actually the result of fewer singlehanded male decisions. Only if it turns out that female employment reduces the husband's decision power by increasing the number of joint decisions, is there merit in the argument that employment should be advocated *because* it increases female decision power within marriage. From a subjective point of view there seems to be no point in aiming to tip the balance of power within a marriage beyond the point of equilibrium.

Social class and changes in decision control

As in most other countries (see Rodman, 1970: 124) the calculations of an "index of male decision power" from the Austrian study of young working wives yield higher scores the higher the husband's social class (Table 12, a). Tabulations by occupational status, income, and education also show highly positive correlations. The relationship thus seems to correspond exactly to the prediction of the "resource-theory."[8] However, upon closer examination, some of the drawbacks of this index become apparent. Actually the extent of solely male-decision areas remains remarkably constant over all social class categories included in this sample, whereas joint decisions steadily increase and solely female decisions decline, the higher the husband's social status.

These results, then, are much better interpreted by assuming different subcultural norms than by resource-theory, particularly if one takes into consideration the fact that the same tendency (increase of joint decisions and decrease of solely female decisions) is also evident the higher the wife's social status (Table 12, b). Szinovácz (1975: 169) seeks to explain the empirical relationship between social status and joint decision-making by assuming that norms of partnership between husband and wife are more common in the middle-class than in the lower social classes. This notion is well supported by many socialization studies all of which point towards less authoritarian structures at present in urban middle-class families, both between

---

8 Although there exist several, somewhat discrepant, formulations of resource-theory, it ought to suffice here to quote Blood's (1963) revised version as formulated by Lupri (1970: 337): "Insofar as marital power is being measured by decisions pertaining to transactions between the family and the external system, the relative participation of husband and wife in the external system will determine the intra-familial power relationship. Decision power is mainly derived from individual resources (such as income, social status, education) usable for fulfilling the spouse's needs."

husbands and wives and between parents and children (Kohn, 1969; Köckeis, 1970a: 181 and 1970c: 98–106); Newson, 1970: 583; Brandis and Henderson, 1970: 149).

This by no means obscures the fact that middle-class families formerly were characterized by predominantly husband-dominance. One assumes that this was true for all propertied classes and that it still holds for most farm families, perhaps too for older middle-class and upper-class couples and/or those with nonemployed

Table 12

Decision Control and Social Class

	a) *By husband's social class*			b) *By wife's social class*		
Class*:	1 (N=371)	2 (=571)	3+4 (N=308)	1 (N=668)	2 (N=212)	3+4 (N=383)
"Index of male decisionpower"**	7.86	8.27	8.55	8.05	8.31	8.36
Average number of areas decided by:						
husband	1.30	1.28	1.33	1.32	1.41	1.20
wife	1.44	1.09	0.78	1.27	1.10	0.84
both jointly	5.26	5.71	5.89	5.41	5.49	5.96

	c) *By relative social status of husband and wife*					
	Wife in social class 1+2			Wife in social class 3+4		
Husband:	Lower (N=54)	Same (N=379)	Higher (N=409)	Lower (N=198)	Same (N=130)	Higher (N=28)
"Index of male decisionpower"**	7.68	8.04	8.36	8.16	8.49	8.81
Average number of areas decided by:						
husband	1.25	1.35	1.37	1.08	1.34	1.26
wife	1.57	1.31	1.01	0.92	0.87	0.45
both jointly	5.18	5.34	5.62	6.00	5.81	6.29

Source: Calculated from Szinovácz (1975: 178 and 209).
* Social class was defined by both occupational status and education:
   class 1 = unskilled and semiskilled manual workers with but statutory education
   class 2 = skilled manual and lower nonmanual workers having attended trade school
   class 3 = skilled manual and nonmanual workers with some higher secondary schooling
   class 4 = persons with a higher-secondary-degree (Matura); they are all nonmanual workers
** For explanation, see text on p. 95–96.

wives. This assumption is supported by Kreutz (1973: 202) for Austrian families at a somewhat later stage in the family-life-cycle as well as, indirectly, by the fact that the middle-class women included in the study of young working wives feel most unhappy if their husbands follow the old pattern and assume too much decision control (Table 10). Two-generation comparisons made by Lupri (1970: 329) for several countries make it abundantly clear that global changes lead from sex-segregated to increasingly joint familial decision-making.[9]

The writer submits, however, *that this global change takes on quite a different form in working-class families*. Whereas middle-class families change from predominantly male to joint decisions, the change that seems presently to be occurring in the working-class families of the developed countries is rather *from predominantly female decision control to joint decisions*. This change appears to be taking place more slowly and/or occurring with a timelag as compared to the change in the middle class.

The evidence from novels, personal accounts and a few precise historical documents, leads to the assumption that at least up to the first part of this century British as well as Austrian working-class husbands tended to leave almost all concrete decisions concerning their home and family to the wife. The husband seems to have remained rather aloof from family matters, probably owing mainly to his long and arduous work-hours at the factory or mine, and the tendency to spend most of his scanty leisure-hours away from home and with male peers. This pattern does not necessarily imply a total abdication of patriarchal rights; it might instead have been merely a delegation of cumbersome tasks to the wife, coupled with a strict maintenance of role segregation. Whereas decision-making under conditions of comparative plenty may be a rather pleasurable and power-enhancing task, all decisions, when the family budget is tight under poverty or near-poverty conditions, take on a different quality. In most cases they turn into a dire and never-ending struggle "to make ends meet" with hardly any chance of personal sideprofit for the decision-maker.

It may be that this perspective offers a better explanation than resource-theory for the present-day structure of decision-making in working-class families as well as for the wive's attitude towards it. As was noted in Table 12, the number of decision-areas controlled by the wife alone is greater the lower the family's social status. It is also greater for the factory-workers living in the (presumably more conservative) small industrial communities than for those living in Vienna.

Furthermore, the longer these women have already been married and the more children they have, the more decision areas they have to deal with by themselves. (The average is 0.99 for childless factory workers and rises to 1.60 for those with two or more children.) Joint decision-making is therefore most in vogue during the honeymoon period while later on many working-class husbands tend to revert to

---

[9] A closer look at Lupri's (1970: 329) comparisons between the decision structure of the parent generation and that of the "present" generation supports my view insofar as, for these socially heterogeneous samples, the intergenerational relative decrease of families with predominantly *female* decision control is at least as great as the relative decrease of families with predominantly male decision control. That is, these change data agree well with my notion that propertied classes have changed from male dominance towards more joint decisions, whereas the industrial working-class is changing from female decision dominance towards joint decisions.

the traditional subcultural pattern and leave an increasing number of decisions to their wives.

That decision-making on their own is more a burden than an asset for these women (although now hardly any of them live below the povertyline) is also borne out by the fact that among the factory-workers the percentage of wives who "can use at least a quarter of their own income for personal expenses" is lowest when they themselves (rather than their husbands, or the two together)[10] control decision areas such as the family budgeting and major purchases. All this helps to explain why these working-class women, as has already been noted in Table 10, feel happier the fewer decisions they have to make on their own.

It is to be hoped, however, that the above-mentioned material aspects are not the crux of the matter. The directly emotional aspects of maintaining a marital relationship in accord with their ideal of romantic love, companionship, and mutual understanding are probably even more important for most of the working-class wives. As will be pointed out in the next section, working-class females appear at least as much attached to this ideal as do those with higher social status. It is, however, much more difficult for them to realize their ideal because of the still evident working-class male's tendency towards aloofness from his wife and children (Komarovsky, 1962; Kohn and Carroll, 1960: 390; Kreutz, 1973: 222). Almost any compromise and adjustment, therefore, seem worthwhile for many of these wives if they feel that this helps avoid the resurgence of this tendency in their husbands.

In a few informal interviews with (nonworking) middle-aged wives of blue-collar workers, almost all started discussing their husband in terms of how seldom he went out on his own, how little pocket-money he kept for himself and how much he participated in home-life (playing with the children, doing repairs—or, at the least, just "being home"). These, together with his occupational success were, almost invariably, the wives' main criteria for affirming how good a husband they had. Keeping the husband at home was very much considered to be a main wifely task, accomplished by good housekeeping, good cooking, and above all, by never openly contradicting the husband and always putting his needs before her own.

What appear to middle-class researchers as "obvious" signs of female inequality is thus frequently considered by the women themselves as their most fruitful tactics for achieving what they presently view as a true marital partnership.

---

10 Szinovácz (1975: 765) therefore assumes that the decision control wielded by these women frequently is merely a *delegated* control occasioned by subcultural norms rather than an outcome of their resource-potential or their relative power vis-á-vis their husbands. Under such circumstances it appears rather doubtful whether a mere count of who controls how many of the family decision areas provides an adequate base for the analysis of marital power structures. Possibly more fruitful might be studies of how decisions are actually arrived at in joint decision areas, e. g. what happens if husband and wife do not agree in some matter and whose opinion is finally agreed to.

Anticipatory socialization for marriage

Although it is frequently being maintained that girls are trained right from infancy for their subservient adult role, there is evidence that nowadays girls are no longer at a disadvantage during childhood and early adolescent socialization. The main changes in attitude and personality—changes leading towards the acceptance of an inferior role—seem to occur only after the girls have turned 15 or 16 and with the prospect of marriage drawing closer. As yet unpublished results from two studies of boys and girls of school age provide the main basis for this assumption. Both these investigations included large samples of children aged 13 to 14 as well as their parents.[11]

Particularly in the south-Tyrolean study undertaken in 1973, it turns out that girls of 13 are, on the whole, no more restrictively treated by their parents than are the boys. Except for evenings out, girls are even rather less strictly controlled by the parents and are given more personal freedom. (For similar German results see Freese, 1976: 86 96). Parents are also somewhat more willing to tolerate the girls' participation in adult discussions. All this, as well as the girls' better educational achievement, can perhaps be attributed to their better adjustment and stronger internalization of parental and school norms.

However, further responses obtained directly from the children point in a different direction (Table 13). Among both the German-speaking and the Italian-speaking students of South-Tyrol, girls obtained significantly higher scores than boys on indices of "need for autonomy," "nonconformity to pressure," and "acceptance of innovations." According to the survey, at age 13 boys are more inclined than girls to be "yea-sayers" (Köckeis, 1976a) and to subscribe to a more traditional-conformist student-strategy at school (involving emphasis on orderliness and obedience rather than on independent attitudes and criticism of their teachers). The inferiority syndrome of adult females does, nevertheless, cast its shadow ahead in the area of self-esteem. In South-Tyrol as well as in Voitsberg (Köckeis, 1974: 13), girls scored consistently lower on an index of achievement-oriented self-esteem (cf. also Hausa, 1968 and 1969).

In spite of this and a still visible tendency on the level of general norms to accord more schooling to boys (Rosenmayr et al., 1973: 38), parents were actually more likely to send girls on to higher secondary schools because they performed considerably better than boys in primary and lower secondary schools.[12]

11 The "Voitsberg" study of 1968 included all the several hundred children in grades 4 and 8 in a rural, semi-industrialized region of Southeastern Austria (see Köckeis and Fischer, 1967; Köckeis, 1970a and 1970c). The "Südtirol" study investigated a birth-cohort sample of South-Tyrol (Alto Adige), a partly German-speaking province of Northern Italy; it was conducted in 1973 (see Köckeis-Stangl et al., 1974; Wieser, 1975; Köckeis-Stangl, 1976b).
12 Both in Voitsberg and in the German-speaking sample from Südtirol, girls not only received better marks at school, they also scored higher than the boys on intelligence and school

Austrian educational statistics confirm the latter results and show that girls will presently soon catch up with boys in matters of formal education. Among the students of higher secondary schools qualifying for university entrance[13], the per-

Table 13

Sex Differences on some Personality and Attitude Dimensions at Age 13–14
Mean scores obtained in the "Südtirol"-study*

	German-speaking sample			Italian-speaking sample		
	Boys (N=473)	Girls (N=428)	t-test	Boys (N=189)	Girls (N=144)	t-test
Anxiety at school	3.53	3.52	—	3.51	3.99	—
Achievement-oriented self-esteem	4.50	4.26	p. 05	4.97	4.42	p .01
Need for achievement	5.45	5.37	—	4.98	5.08	—
Need for affiliation	7.97	8.34	p .01	7.87	7.40	p .05
Need for autonomy	12.02	12.63	p .01	11.99	12.95	p .01
Nonconformity to pressure	7.00	7.37	p .05	7.34	8.17	p .01
Acceptance of innovations	4.84	5.07	p. 05	4.33	4.67	p .05
Progressive-critical (vs. traditional-conformist) strategy at school	14.67	15.25	p .05	14.58	15.43	p .05
Yea-saying-tendency (response-set)	3.69	3.26	p .01	3.41	3.09	p .01

* All indices are scaled such that higher scores signify more of the quality expressed by the name of the index than lower scores.
For details of the "Südtirol"-study see footnote (11).

centage of girls has risen from 36 percent in 1955 to 46 percent in 1973 (Karl, 1975, Vol. 3: 109). Over the same period, the female quota among university entrants has risen from .25 to .41 (Höllinger, 1975: 71).

Thus, equality between the sexes seems to have been achieved to a considerable extent up to adolescence. After that, however, the female strengths mentioned above are seemingly lost—or perhaps purposely hidden—as the prospect of marriage

---

achievement tests. Among the predominantly urban Italian students of Südtirol, however, there were no such outstanding differences between the sexes, and the boys' further educational aspirations were definitely higher than the girls'.
Provisionally, I would interpret this to mean that definite cognitive advantages of girls over boys may be restricted to rural populations where masculinity is still closely associated with physical strength and prowess; doing school-work, reading, and even thinking may thus still be considered somewhat inappropriate for boys.

13 That is, schools that lead to the "Matura"-examen. In the somewhat less demanding higher secondary schools ("Berufsbildende mittlere Schulen"), girls have already for several years constituted the majority; some of these latter schools, however, concentrate heavily on home economics and seem to accentuate the traditional female role image (Gaudart and Schulz, 1971: 131).

draws nearer. A study of fifteen-year-old girls from all the major school-types, undertaken by Kreutz (1973) provides valuable information on this stage. It is supplemented by unpublished data from another Austrian study including both male and female higher secondary school students aged 15 to 17 (Mechler et al., 1975).

As many as 95 percent of the girls are determined to marry (Mechler et al., 1975) but most of them feel by no means completely certain of being able to achieve this status (Kreutz, 1973: 248). Nevertheless, the strategy girls envisage for obtaining a husband seems to be passive rather than active and to consist mainly of making themselves optimally eligible for the man who will somehow turn up and intuitively be judged to be the one and only true marriage partner. Indeed, over two-thirds of the girls from all social classes believe that "for every women there exists but one true partner whom she ought to marry" (Kreutz, 1973: 274). This strong belief in the principle of romantic love is coupled with the girls' conviction that their parents would hardly interfere with their choice of marriage partner; furthermore, the majority of them are determined to suffer parental sanctions rather than refrain from marrying a beloved man their parents dislike (Kreutz, 1973: 254–63).

These teenagers have thus obviously achieved considerable autonomy from their parents; this is, however, coupled with a strange lack of autonomy, vis-à-vis their future husbands. For instance, although nearly all adolescent girls desire to have children, about 40 percent are willing to marry a man they love even if he doesn't want to have children (Kreutz, 1973: 272). Surprisingly, this percentage is the greater the more autonomy girls have in matters of partner-choice (1973: 273).

This willingness to subscribe to whatever attitudes the prospective husband may hold seems to be a direct outcome of the girls' version of romantic love. The answer given by a girl of 16 when asked whether she intended to continue in her profession once she was married, is most revealing: "I really can't say," she replied, "after all, how am I to know presently whether the man I fall in love with will be in favour of his wife going to work." She, herself, wanted to keep on working but nevertheless had no intention of basing her choice of spouse on his concurrence with her wishes. "I shall choose the man I love," she continued, "and love means, above all, that we understand each other; so I must adjust to what he wants. After all, a marriage where each partner follows his/her own course wouldn't be the thing." This girl was evidently willing to forsake her self-determination for the envisaged glories of a loving marital relationship. (Let us hope that she is but one extreme case.)

However, the preponderance of love as the motive for marriage is also very evident from the large-scale study by Mechler et al. (1975) involving students of higher secondary schools. Out of a long check-list offering answers to the question, "Why do you want to marry?" as many as 91 percent of the girls (and 78 percent of the boys) ticked "out of love," while the next-frequent reason—"to ensure constancy of the relationship" — was merely checked by one-third. Most surprisingly, a mere 4 percent of the girls ticked "in order to be provided for" as a reason for marrying, whereas the corresponding male item, "in order to have somebody to look after my household," still drew checks from 27 percent of the boys.

At least for girls who are receiving some form of further education, the aspect of marriage offering them economic security and relieving them from the necessity to go to work is, apparently, no longer uppermost in their minds. For young women such as these, then, the willingness to adapt themselves so much to a future husband can hardly be based on immediate economic reasons. Nevertheless, a German study of girls attending the *Gymnasium* (the most demanding of higher secondary schools) revealed that half of these teenagers still maintain that the husband ought to be "the superior spouse" and that "a woman ought to marry a man who is more intelligent and more educated than she is," although the same respondents hold very progressive attitudes on almost all other aspects of family life and female roles (Reitz, 1974: 129).

It is definitely risky to collate results from different studies in such a way, yet it seems fairly certain that the model of marriage based wholly on love and mutual understanding is interpreted by the majority of young women as making it necessary for them to prepare for an inferior role within their future family.

Extended reading of marriage advertisements confirms the view that a presentation of self as "truly female" is still thought to be very much required for increasing one's chances of finding a husband. The display of virtues such as adaptability, empathy and emotionality seems to be at least as important as mentioning good looks and housekeeping capability. On the other hand, although I have found that explicit rejections of "homeliness" ("kein Hausmütterchentyp") occur practically only in ads placed by (apparently rather left-wing) intellectuals, e.g., in the German weekly "Die Zeit," would-be brides in almost all types of newspaper ads seem to have little reserve in mentioning their occupational qualification and/or status. Allusions to female earning-power appear to be nearly as attractive to male candidates as a mention of property. Even in marriage ads, female role conflicts are visible.

Girls are increasingly expected to become fairly seriously involved in their training and occupation and they themselves concur with these norms. Yet the model of marriage they strive for demands of them to develop, or at least display, quite opposite qualities.

Supplementary remarks and conclusions

Despite its length, this contribution has by no means dealt with all aspects of Austrian women's position in the family, and other studies are available dealing for instance with premarital and marital sexual standards (Mechler, 1976), as well as reproductive behaviour and family planning (Grafinger, 1973). For lack of both space and pertinent information, I have not sufficiently elaborated on the men's contribution to the definition, as well as the burdens, of female family roles.

Thus, the analysis may appear to have laid too much blame on the women themselves. Marriage, after all, is at least a two-person-game, and any interpretation that considers only the wife's point of view is necessarily lopsided. Our very concern for the position of women ought to motivate us to extend our information-gathering to married men as well as prospective husbands. The barriers, for instance, against extending the (as yet) so very limited male participation in tasks of household and child care, probably do lie mainly with men. We know, however, far too little about how they come into being. Possibly, male teenagers' and twens' perceptions of what their prospective female partners require of them cause the young men to overstress and display traditional male qualities as much as seems to be the case with the girls concerning "truly female" characteristics. Maybe, household tasks are subsequently abhorred by husbands just because undertaking them is felt to be incompatible with, or even threatening danger to, the laboriously acquired "truly male" image.

The interplay between normative orientations and psychological processes stressed in this article certainly provides but a limited view. Yet it may offer a useful perspective for understanding why developments toward equalitarian and symmetrical marital relationships are so slow and full of detours. Just because marriage has remained so important to women and because the personal, individualized relationship has acquired even additional significance for the husband, are both still so ill-equipped for equal partnership.

Neither the achievement of near-equality between girls and boys in childhood and early adolescent socialization, nor married women's increasing employment outside the family is sufficient for changing the woman's marital role. As long as a would-be bride is so much afraid that she may be "left behind" and so convinced that there exists but one ideal partner destined for her, she can hardly bargain for a partner willing to respect her need for personal autonomy. As long as a girl believes that hers can only be a happy marriage if she defines her partner as being superior to herself in almost all respects, just so long will she be inclined to bury her need for autonomy and to forget about her own intellectual abilities. As long as a wife assumes that she can secure her husband's full participation in family life only by letting him have the final say on most issues and by not expecting him to do any housework, even the independence gained from work outside the home cannot really alter her familial role. The normative belief that a harmonious relationship requires the wife to act as an inferior partner provides a formidable barrier to emancipation within marriage.

I agree with Haller (1973: 104) and others that the institution of marriage may presently be viewed as the main impediment to women's emancipation in the occupational sphere and other areas outside the family. Yet I do not think that avoidance of marriage (or similar forms of fairly permanent heterosexual relationships) offer a suitable solution for many women. Without guarantee of some permanency, women may be even more likely to focus all their attention on the fate of an ongoing or prospective relationship.

I would rather set my hopes on the further modification of the institution of marriage. After all, marriage as an institution—i.e., the complex of social and legal norms associated with it—depends on what the actors concerned believe in and re-enact.

Perhaps a new opportunity for change will be provided when the young women involved in the present educational boom reach adulthood. Women with more formal education already hold somewhat less subordinate notions of their family role. In addition, the entrance upon the marriage market of this new cohort of girls with nearly as many educational degrees as their male counterparts may well bring on a fairly quick relinquishment of the present and still valid norm that the wife must on no account be better educated than her husband. Otherwise, an increasing number of men and women would not be able to marry at all. Of course, on the pessimistic side, the educational advancement of women and the disappearance of this norm could mean that a wife with superior education might become even more intent on hiding her knowledge and intellectual capacity in order to maintain the marriage model of the compliant wife.

Effects of a structural change can hardly ever be safely predicted. Results depend on how the change is interpreted by the actors; social scientists can but venture an educated guess.

REFERENCES

Blood, Robert O., Jr. and Donald M. Wolfe
    1960 *Husbands and Wives. The Dynamics of Married Life.* New York: Free Press.
Brandis, Walter and Henderson, Dorothy
    1970 *Social Class, Language and Communication.* London: Routledge & Kegal Paul.
Danneberg, Erika
    1963 *Lebensziele in der Pubertät.* Vienna: Österr. Institut für Jugendkunde.
Firnberg, Hertha and Rutschka, Ludwig S.
    1967 *Die Frau in Österreich.* Vienna: Österreichischer Gewerkschaftsbund.
Freese, Hans-Ludwig
    1976 *Schulleistungsrelevante Merkmale der häuslichen Erziehungsumwelt.* Ergebnisse einer Untersuchung über Jungen und Mädchen der 7. Klasse Gymnasium. Berlin: Max-Planck-Institut für Bildungsforschung.
Gaudart, Dorothea and Schulz, Wolfgang
    1971 *Mädchenbildung, wozu?* Vienna: Österr. Bundesverlag.
Grafinger, Josef
    1973 *Soziologische Aspekte der Familienplanung.* Vienna: mimeogr. dissertation.
Haller, Max
    1973 *Die Frau in der Gesellschaft; eine soziologische Studie junger Frauen in Beruf und Familie.* Vienna; mimeogr. dissertation, 2 vols.
Hausa, Horst
    1968 *Selbstbild und soziale Anpassung jugendlicher Mädchen.* Vienna: dissertation.

1969 "Selbstbild und soziale Anpassung von Mädchen; theoretische Anlage und Ergebnisse einer empirischen Studie," pp. 473–510, in: Rosenmayr, L. and Höllinger, S., *Soziologie Forschung in Österreich.* Vienna: Böhlau.
Heizer-Winter, Martha
1976 *Doppelmoral bei österreichischen Jugendlichen.* Innsbruck: dissertation.
Höllinger, Sigurd
1975 "Die wissenschaftlichen Hochschulen," pp. 21–194, in: *Die Hochschulen in Österreich,* OECD-Bericht 1975, vol. 1. Vienna: Bundesministerium f. Wissenschaft. v. Forschung.
Karl, Elfriede (ed.)
1975 *Bericht über die Situation des Frau in Österreich.*
vol. 1: Das Rollenbild der Frau in der Gesellschaft.
vol. 2: Die Frau im österreichischen Recht.
vol. 3: Die Bildungssituation u. Bildungschancen der Frau.
vol. 4: Die persönliche Situation der Frau.
vol. 5: Die Frau im Beruf.
vol. 6: Die gesundheitliche Situation der Frau.
vol. 7: Die Frau im öffentlichen Leben.
Vienna: Bundeskanzleramt.
Klein, Kurt, Bartunek, Ewald and Janik, Wilhelm
1974 *Berufslaufbahnen von Frauen; Ergebnisse des Mikrozensus.* Vienna: Bundesministerium für Soziale Verwaltung.
Köckeis-Stangl, Eva
1970a "The Value Clash between Working Class Subcultures and the School," pp. 165–183, in: *Social Science Information,* vol. 9.
1970b "Familienbeziehungen alter Menschen," pp. 508–527, in: Lüschen, G., and Lupri, E., *Soziologie der Familie.* Opladen: Westdeutscher Verlag.
1970c "Sozialschicht, Wertorientierung und Schulerfolg," pp. 86–107 in: Bodzenta, E. and Kaufmann, A., *Österreichisches Jahrbuch für Soziologie 1970.* Vienna: Springer.
1974 *Der Stellenwert von Selbsteinschätzungen im schulischen Sozialisationsprozess.* Report to the 29th Congress of the German Psychological Society; Innsbruck; mimeogr.
1976a *Zustimmungstendenz: Handlungsstrategie unterprivilegierter Gruppen in Befragungssituationen.* Report to the Bochum Conference on Developmental Psychology; Innsbruck: mimeogr.
1976b "Bildungsforschung in Südtirol," pp. 49–51, in: *ÖZS–Österreichische Zeitschrift für Soziologie, Vol. 1*
Köckeis-Stangl, Eva, and Marina Fischer
1967 *Determinanten für den Besuch weiterführender Schulen.* Vienna: mimeogr.
Köckeis-Stangl, Eva, and Gstettner, Peter, Seidl, Hadwig and Seidl, Peter
1974 *Bildungsprobleme unter der Lupe: Konzeption und Durchführung der Untersuchungen an Südtiroler Mittelschulen.* Bozen: Assessorat für Unterricht und Kultur.
Kohn, Melvin
1969 *Class and Conformity.* Homewood (Ill.): The Free Press.
Kohn, Melvin, and Caroll, Eleanor E.
1960 "Social Class and the Allocation of Parental Responsibility," p. 372–392, in: *Sociometry,* vol. 23.
Komarovsky, Mira
1962 *Blue-Collar-Marriage.* New York: Random House.
Kreutz, Henrik
1973 "Jugend und Zukunft; eine empirische Untersuchung der sozialen Situation, der Ziele und Pläne von 15 jährigen Mädchen in Österreich," pp. 21–312, in: Rosenmayr, L., and Kreutz, H., *Rollenerwartungen der weiblichen Jugend.* Vienna: Österr. Bundesverlag.
Kreutz, Henrik and Fürnschuss, Grete
1971 *Chancen der Weiterbildung; soziologische Untersuchungen zur Mädchenbildung in Österreich.* Vienna: Österr. Bundesverlag.

Lupri, Eugen
- 1970 "Gesellschaftliche Differenzierung und familiale Autorität," pp. 323–352, in: Lüschen, G., and Lupri, E., *Soziologie der Familie*. Opladen: Westdeutscher Verlag.

Mechler, Hans-Jürgen
- 1976 "Schülersexualität und Doppelmoral; ein erster Bericht über eine Repräsentativerhebung in Österreich," pp. 25–36 in: *ÖZS*–Österr. Zeitschrift für Soziologie, vol. 1.

Mechler, Hans-Jürgen, and Kroath, Franz and Plössnig, Franz (with others)
- 1975 *Sexualverhalten österreichischer Jugendlicher;* Tabulation of basic results. Innsbruck manuscript.

Mittenecker, Erich
- 1974 *Bildungsreserven bei jungen Industriearbeitern*. Vienna: Bundesministerium für Soziale Verwaltung.

Newsom, John and Newsom, Elizabeth
- 1970 *Four Years Old in an Urban Community*. Harmondswort: Penguin Books.

Pfeil, Elisabeth
- 1961 *Die Berufstätigkeit von Müttern*. Tübingen: Mohr.
- 1968 *Die 23 jährigen; eine Generationenuntersuchung am Geburtenjahrgang 1941*. Tübingen: Mohr.

Reitz, Gertraud
- 1974 *Die Rolle der Frau und die Lebensplanung von Mädchen*. München: Juventa.

Rodman, Hyman
- 1970 "Eheliche Macht und der Austausch von Ressourcen im kulturellen Kontext," pp. 121–143 in: Lüschen, G., and Lupri, E., *Soziologie der Familie*. Opladen: Westdeutscher Verlag.

Rosenmayr, Leopold and Amann, A., Grafinger, J., Haller, M., Handl., J., Holzinger, W., Strolz, M. K., Szinovácz, M.
- 1969a *Die junge Frau und ihre berufliche Zukunft*. Vienna: mimeogr.

Rosenmayr, Leopold, and Kaufmann, Albert and Knollmayer, Eva
- 1969b "Belastungen der Frau in der Landwirtschaft," pp. 299–318 in: Rosenmayr, L. and Hollinger, S., *Soziologie; Forschung in Österreich*. Vienna: Böhlau.

Rosenmayr, Leopold, and Haller, Max and Szinovácz, Maximiliane
- 1973 *Barrieren im beruflichen Aufstieg; Studien über die junge Arbeitnehmerin im Spannungsfeld von Beruf, Haushalt und Familie*. Vienna: Bundesministerium für Soziale Verwaltung.

Schulz, Wolfgang
- 1976a *Werthaltungen und Einstellungen von Frauen-, Familien- und Jugendorganisationen zum Wandel in der Situation der Frau*. Vienna: Bundesministerium für Soziale Verwaltung.
- 1976b "Theoretische und empirische Analyse der Frauenrolle–Orientierungshilfe für Pädagogen," pp. 16–30, in: Holl, A. and Saipt, O. W., *Österreichisches Jahrbuch für Soziologie 1975*. Vienna: Böhlau.

Schwind, Fritz
- 1976 "Verliebt, verlobt, verheiratet, geschieden? Die Reform des Scheidungsrechts will zwischen Soll- und Istzustand vermitteln," p. 6, in: *Die Presse*, of December 11, 1976.

Stock, Franz-Michael
- 1974 *Zum Beispiel: Mädchenbildung; Aspekte sozialökonomisch bedingten Ausbildungsverhaltens*. Innsbruck: mimeogr. dissertation.

Szinovácz, Maximiliane
- 1975 *Entscheidungsstruktur und Aufgabenverteilung in jungen Familien*. Ergebnisse einer Untersuchung an berufstätigen Frauen und Müttern in Wien, Niederösterreich und dem Burgenland. Vienna: mimeogr. dissertation, 3 vols.

Wieser, Ilsedore
- 1975 *Jugendliche Laufbahnziele als Orientierungswerte der Bildungsplanung*. Bozen: Assessorat für Unterricht und Kultur.

The Changing Role of Women: The Case of Italy

ALESSANDRO CAVALLI

The University of Pavia, Italy

HAVE THERE BEEN RADICAL CHANGES in the role of women in Italian society over, say, the last twenty years? If one puts this question to a certain number of people, both male and female, one is likely to receive three different answers. Some, perhaps a majority, will say: yes, in its transition from a traditional agricultural to a modern industrial society, Italy has witnessed, among other things, a significant redefinition of the role of women. (This answer is, of course, correct, but the opinion it expresses is superficial and not particularly illuminating.) A second group will warn: do not be blinded by what appears on the surface and on the front pages of newspapers for the very large majority of Italian women are as they have always been and as they naturally should be, i.e., good mothers and housewives. A third group, finally, will answer: little has changed in they way Italian women act and experience their roles and they still have a long way to go before becoming modern, emancipated, autonomous persons.

As in the case of other social developments, similarly regarding the role of women —processes of change are often better explained by those who maintain that there has been no change at all, either because they resist change, or, conversely, because they want to promote it more vigorously.

In the absence of data from public opinion surveys, the impression is that these last two groups are growing in numbers and becoming increasingly vociferous. A good test was provided by the 1976 general elections, for here, for the first time, every political party felt the need, in its campaign, to address itself specifically to the female electorate; to include many women in its lists of candidates to Parliament; and, finally, to manage to have them elected with an unprecedented number of votes.

Women are no longer merely a demographic entity in census data; they are becoming social actors and, probably, a social force in their own right.

As a matter of fact, in recent years problems concerning the status and the rights of women have been, and still are, at the centre of political controversy. To take some examples: first, the debate over the new family legislation, which regulates in a more egalitarian manner economic and patrimonial relationships within married couples;

second, the controversy over divorce, culminating in the referendum which rejected by a large majority the attempt to render divorce unconstitutional; and, finally the dispute over the new liberal legislation on abortion and the referendum of 1980 where almost two-thirds of the citizenship voted in favour of the new law.

It is probably difficult for an external observer to understand the degree to which these problems have aroused public attention and emotional involvement and the crucial role they have played in defining new political cleavages in a country where collective action and political participation have traditionally been at very high levels. All of this testifies that changes have occurred, indeed, and at a dramatic pace in the condition of women in Italy. But to try to explain what caused these changes and in what direction they are likely to evolve in the future, raises a set of quite difficult questions.

We have for some time now been nurtured in the very naive and optimistically-biased belief that economic development, however defined, induces a larger process of social change, known as modernization, which, along with other desirable results, produces greater educational and occupational opportunities for women and therefore tends to reduce the differences between the status of men and women.

The Italian case offers a good example of the inadequacy of this thesis, and of the much more problematic nature of the relationship between social change and changes in sex roles.

Italy, as is well known, is a peculiar mix of development and underdevelopment, of tradition and modernity. The country attained its political unity late (1861), and since then regional differences, marked as they were at the beginning, have become even more marked, adding new disequilibria to the old ones. In terms of economic development, the absolute distance between the industrialized North and the still predominantly rural South has never before been so great. But, despite this marked economic dualism, a process of cultural unification has somehow taken place, due largely to the spread of the national educational system, the diffusion of mass media and the intense internal and international migrations.

At the beginning of the century, in the South and in the rural areas of the North and the Centre, the rural extended family was the prevailing feature of the social structure. As in other countries, this pattern did not involve a sharp division between the sphere of production and that of domestic life; women, in other words, took a very active role in productive activity. But with industrialization and with the introduction of the factory system the division of labour between sexes becomes more sharply defined. As many authors have pointed out, male roles tend to be defined in terms of the occupational system and female roles in terms of the family system. At the same time, however, the process of industrialization and of modernization stimulates strong aspirations for greater equality between the sexes and strengthens the belief that modern society should provide equal educational and occupational opportunities for both men and women.

It must be judged to be a serious contradiction of modern industrial societies that what is offered to women with one hand is then denied them with the other. This contradiction is particularily acute in societies, such as the Italian one, in which the process of industrialization has been rapid, uneven and ridden with social conflicts. One way to attack this problem is to look at the data showing the increase in the level of education of men and women over the last twenty years.

Table 1

Percentage distribution of population by educational level and sex

	Male			Female		
	1951	1961	1971	1951	1961	1971
High school or university degree	5.4	6.9	10.2	3.2	4.3	7.3
Lower middle-school	7.1	11.2	16.6	4.9	8.0	12.8
Less than lower middle school	77.0	75.4	69.2	76.7	77.7	73.6
Illiterates	10.5	6.5	4.0	15.2	10.0	6.3
Index from the above data (1951 = 100)						
High school or university degree	100	127	189	100	137	230
Lower middle-school	100	120	237	100	163	260
Less than lower middle school	100	98	90	100	101	96
Illiterates	100	61	38	100	65	41

Source: Census data.

The rate of change in the diffusion of educational opportunities has been much more intense for women than for men and more so for women in the underdeveloped regions (South and North-East) than in the advanced areas of the North and Centre. These data also give us a glimpse into a very peculiar characteristic of Italian development—the growing gap between the output of the school system and the labour market, between the supply and demand for highly-trained people. The level of education increases more in the regions where occupational opportunities are lower, a phenomenon that has caused the school to be dubbed "a parking space for the unemployed". Since this situation affects educated women more than others, it will receive further attention shortly.

The data reported also show that, even if women now have much more access to higher education than before, the distance (measured in percentage points of people having attained a university degree) between men and women has still increased and tends to become greater in the advanced regions than in the backward ones. This again illustrates that economic development does not automatically produce greater equality between the sexes.

In any case, even in the age groups where education is compulsory (at present under 14, but initiatives are under way to push the limit to 15 or even 16), the number of girls not attending school is larger than the number of boys. (Apparently, for

Table 2

Percentage distribution of population with university degree by sex and geographical region

	Male			Female		
	1951	1961	1971	1951	1961	1971
North-West	1.7	2.1	2.5	0.4	0.7	1.1
North-East	1.2	1.6	2.1	0.2	0.4	0.8
Centre	2.2	2.7	3.5	0.5	0.8	1.5
South	1.5	1.8	2.3	0.3	0.6	1.0
Index from above data (1951=100)						
North-West	100	125	148	100	159	256
North-East	100	134	170	100	175	317
Centre	100	124	156	100	161	286
South	100	122	156	100	181	322

Source: Census data.

poor parents a girl is still more useful at home than at school.) This difference increases with age; girls account for 48.5% of the total enrolment in elementary schools, 46.9% in lower middle schools, 42% in high schools and 39% in universities (1973–74), whereas women total 51.3% of the population over six years of age.

As most studies show, girls are very selective in the choice of the type of school they attend. Their number is greater than that of boys in professional schools leading to elementary school teaching (girls are 90% of total enrolment in these schools), in art schools (64%), in technical schools preparing for clerical occupations (53%), and even in those schools for children of the upper and upper-middle classes. Girls are more numerous in the "liceo classico", centred around literature and philosophy (53%), than in the "liceo scientifico", based on mathematics and natural sciences (38%).

The same situation can be found at the university level where girls account for one-fourth of the enrolment in medicine, economics and law, one-fifth in physics and chemistry, less than 10% in engineering, but 60% in biology and 75% in literature and philosophy.

The gap between the school system and the labour market, which has been noted before (and which accounts for the country's very high rate of intellectual unemployment), appears to exercise its most striking effects on the female population. In fact the participation of women in the labour force is decreasing steadily, so much so that it has been possible to speak of a process of expulsion of women from the labour market. This process is a peculiar consequence of the particular type of economic development of the country, in which expulsion from the primary sector (where the rate of employment of women in traditional domestic farming was high) has not been paralleled by adequate development in industry and in the service sectors.

Italy has, in fact, one of the lowest labour force participation rates for the female population of all of the West European countries. Whereas in the United Kingdom (U.K.) (1971) and in France (1968) the work activity rate for women (which measures, as is known, those officially employed, plus the officially unemployed plus those in search of first employment) averages, respectively, 33 and 28%, the rate in Italy (1973) is slightly less than 19%. Only Spain (1970) has an even lower rate (13%).)

The situation has changed rapidly in the last 15–20 years. In the late fifties, more than one woman out of four was considered active, but since then the number of women working in agriculture has decreased to less than half (2,345,000 in 1959, 1,024,000 in 1972). In the same period, those working in industry lost something like 240,000 working places, and the only increase is shown in the service sector with the creation of 220,000 new jobs for women.

One can speak of a real exodus from the land (more than five million people left agriculture in two decades) to the urban areas, but this process has been, particularly in the central and southern regions, more one of urbanization than of actual industrialization. While young males migrating North could find more opportunities in the slowly expanding industries, the young spouses who eventually accompanied them had, to a very large extent, to abandon work outside the home.

The decrease in industrial employment for women, particularly in the more advanced regions of the North, is, however, a complex phenomenon. Not only did migrant women find difficulty getting jobs in the urban areas where they had come to live, many native female workers in the same areas lost their jobs because they were replaced by male migrant workers. In the face of a large supply of labour, employers found it more profitable to use male instead of female workers. This is, of course, due to a large extent to the fact that labour productivity is higher for males than for females.

There are many reasons why women are not competitive with men in the labour market:

1) in Italy there has never been a condition of full employment for men searching for a job and, in Italian society, male unemployment is considered a greater evil than female unemployment;
2) wage differentials between men and women are less marked in Italy than in other Western countries, and employers have therefore little incentive to hire women as their work is not significantly cheaper;
3) labour legislation for the protection of women workers during pregnancy and in the period following each child birth is very progressive in Italy, but this very fact produces serious obstacles to the employment of married women. Employers tend to avoid hiring workers who are likely to be absent from work for prolonged periods of time and who show a high rate of absenteeism yet cannot be fired due to the legal protection accorded to motherhood.

Given this situation on the demand-side for female labour, one would expect a high rate of female unemployment. But this is not the case. Female unemployment was higher when employment itself was higher, which suggests that the decreasing demand for female labour discourages women from offering their services on the labour market. There is, therefore, a close link between supply and demand and the correlation between the two factors is positive rather than negative. Moreover, female employment was traditionally higher in those industrial sectors which are historically declining (textiles, clothing, etc.).

The data on labour force participation rates of the female population by age-groups give us some new and important hints on the supply structure of female labour in Italy compared with other West European countries.

Table 3

Labour Force Participation (Activity)

Rates of Female Population By Age-groups in Italy, France and the United Kingdom (U.K.)

Age-groups	Italy (1973)	France (1968)	U.K. (1971)
14–19	26	31	53
20–24	44	62	60
25–29	36	51	43
30–34	32	42	45
35–39	31	41	55
40–44	31	43	60
45–49	30	45	62
50–54	26	45	59
55–59	16	42	51
60–64	9	32	28
65+	2	8	19

Source: G. Fua, *Occupazione e capacita produttiva: la realta italiana,* Bologna, Il Mulino, 1976.

These figures tell us three important things: 1) compared with France and the U.K., the number of women in the labour force in Italy is exceptionally low, even in those age groups whose activity rate is highest; 2) as in the other countries, the number of active women decreases after marriage and child-birth; 3) there is no return to work outside the home when children reach school age.

These patterns are also connected to demographic factors which show a high rigidity in time. Girls marry quite late in Italy: the average age at marriage now is 24 years and 3 months compared with 25, twenty years ago. The birth of children is quite spaced out in time. On the average, the first child is born when the mother is 25, the second when the mother is 28 and the third when she is 31 years old. If we consider the case of a mother with three children (a not-infrequent case even though family size is sharply declining), our data show that when the last child reaches school age the mother is in her late thirties, too late in most cases to resume work even if employment opportunities were available.

Moreover, the lack of public facilities for child care (kindergartens, nursery schools, etc.) and the fact that full-time schooling is practically non-existent, at least as regards to public schools, make it extremely difficult for a mother to have a full-time occupation outside her home. Part-time work, on the other hand, is almost exclusively limited to the teaching professions, and, in fact, it is here that we find the highest proportion of working women.

All these factors help to explain the strikingly low participation of women in the labour force. Nonetheless, there is a widespread impression, supported by several research findings, that the official data do not tell the whole story about female work. There is, in other words, a hidden face which escapes surveillance by the national statistical offices. In fact, the peculiar distortions of industrial development in Italy have produced the diffusion of several and at times extravagant forms of "black labour", i.e., of work not officially registered as such and for which employers evade paying fees for social security and medical care, and for which they overlook the rules regulating working hours, hiring and firing practices, and so on.

One of the most widespread form of "black labour" is the so-called "lavoro a domicilio" (work at home), a modern version of the "putting out" system, typical of the spinning and weaving industry in the very early stages of the Industrial Revolution. When they subscribe to this system, manufacturing firms split the work process into single operations to be executed outside the factory. The variety of forms assumed by this practice is immeasurable. It is known to be widespread in many industries, ranging from knitting and clothing to fine mechanics and even electronic components. It is not uncommon—in many workers' homes—to have a section of the living space reserved for the "machine", around which women, and older children, are busy working.

Recent estimates indicate that the number of women working "at home" total no less than 1.5 million, and probably total as high as 2 million. The activity rate for women is therefore likely higher than the official figures. (It should be between 24 and 26%, which is still low but not too far removed from West European standards.)

Again, this phenomenon has attained astonishing proportions because supply and demand for this kind of labour combine in a particular way. Employers pay lower wages, avoid concentration of the labour force and, particularly, the problems of unionization; women workers can stay at home and look after their children, and, at the same time contribute to the family income. Of course, the burden of both jobs (domestic and for the outside "boss") is very heavy indeed, but women can bear this situation because everything is done for the family's well-being and for this type of sacrifice women have been reared from their early childhood.

From what has been said to this point, it should be clear that class differences matter a great deal in the analysis of women's changing roles in Italy. It now seems useful to summarize what has already been said and, in so doing, to draw a synthetic picture of the social status of women within the different social classes.

(I) *Rural classes.* As we have seen, rural classes have been largely depleted by both internal and external migrations, but, while internal migrations are permanent and to a large extent involve new families, external migrations (for example, towards North European countries) are more frequently temporary and almost exclusively involve men between 20 and 40 years of age.

On the other hand, those types of cultivation (e.g., rice) which, in the past, have used large numbers of female day-labourers, have by now been almost completely mechanized. The remaining women working on the land tend, therefore, to be older and confined to the noncapitalistic sector of agriculture. For them living conditions and everyday activity have not changed much and, if anything, have turned to the worse after the departure of the young and the males. It is here, in any case, that the familistic values of the traditional culture continue to display their more resistant foothold (Banfield, 1958).

(II) *Working classes and lower-middle classes.* For reasons that need not be explained here in detail, it is important to draw a distinction between unstable and stable working classes (Balbo, 1976). We consider as belonging to the unstable working class a family in which the husband-father has no full-time occupation or no occupation at all and in which the earnings of other family members are determinant in assuring minimal conditions of survival. All sorts of extra-domestic occupational roles for women are found with great frequency at this level: full-time jobs for the mother-wife and for unmarried daughters; precarious part-time occupations; "domicile" work; etc. Resources to meet the family needs very often tend to be insufficient because the possibility of using the benefits of public services depends upon the existence of stable working conditions, a circumstance at variance with the defining characteristic of this class. The woman then becomes the agent mediating between the lack of adequate resources and family needs and her role appears in these cases to be particularly "over-burdened".

The stable working class, on the contrary, is characterized by the dominance of the occupational role of the father outside the family and by the domestic role of the mother inside it. The division of labour between the sexes is here more pronounced and, in this aspect at least, there is a high homogeneity among both manual and white-collar working families. When these conditions are met, full-time work for women is present only for unmarried girls; married women at this level work only if they can adjust extra-domestic work to the dominant family role (therefore, marginal and/or part-time and/or "domicile" work) and their earnings are simply additional to the more substantial source of family income provided by the husband's occupation. Here the satisfaction of family needs is assured by the full access to existing public services (even if Italy cannot be considered a welfare state given the extension and the "quality" of services offered) on the one side, and by the availability of women in their role as housewives on the other. The well-being of the family in this category rests heavily on the fact that there is little competition between the domestic-private role and extra-domestic public role of the mother-wife, since the first definitely transcends the latter.

(III) *Upper-middle and upper classes.* The upper-middle and upper classes show a larger heterogeneity in women's roles than the two above. There is here no economic constraint for women to assume working roles outside of the family. The occupational position of the husband is sufficient to permit access to private services offered by the market (private schools, private medical care, housemaids, etc.) which lighten the burden of the mother-wife's domestic duties. Moreover, the need for additional income sources is not felt as a family problem. The woman in this position is able to choose between the traditional role of housewife and the opportunity to work outside of the family, and she also has a larger autonomy in deciding how to spend what she has earned if she has decided to work. The choice is, of course, not entirely free, since the opportunities offered by the labour market are fairly limited even for educated women, but this is in any case the sector where demand, though limited, has been expanding in recent decades. The school system, newspapers and other mass media, research institutes, public administration and also the traditional "liberal" professions have opened their doors to an increasing number of women, both married and unmarried.

For married women, of course, the requirements of domestic and working roles can be, and frequently are, conflicting. The need to readjust and redefine their proper roles and the roles of other family members (grandparents, husband, children) poses rather difficult problems and in many cases causes psychic uneasiness and intra-familial tensions. But these aspects are a common feature of all those situations in which women have successfully started on the perilous path of emancipation from a condition exclusively defined in terms of family duties.

Happy or unhappy as they may be, these women have become the symbol of the successful and modern woman. Given the high "visibility" of their occupational positions (e.g., through the implicit publicity they get in the media), they are a crucial factor in shaping a new image and in changing the culture's definition of the role of women. What is appropriate for a woman, therefore, is less and less dictated by tradition and more and more defined by this stratum of highly educated women who have successfully managed to establish an autonomous position in the economic, political, social, and cultural structure of society. It is a small stratum indeed, but a highly innovative one.

We come now to the final point of our analysis. It is our opinion that what has been changing in women's roles is largely, if not exclusively, due to the increase in the level of education. Education is a sector which, in Italy, has grown far beyond the needs of economic growth. The quest for more equality between the sexes as well as between social classes, has found in education a softer structure than the economy or the body-politic and this has set in motion a process of origination of new aspirations which is probably irreversible.

A recent attitude survey (Cazora-Russo, 1975) has shown that in almost any aspect of women's roles, innovative attitudes are more highly correlated with the level of education than with any other descriptive variable (age, region of residence, occupational status, etc.). The figures in Table 4 give one example of the influence of education on the change of attitudes.

Table 4

Percentage of people who agree with the sentence: "A woman should not work outside the home if the husband is against it"

Males		Females	
High Education	Low Education	High Education	Low Education
50.2 (N=737)	71.4 (N=543)	41.9 (N=1147)	67.0 (N=1615)

Educated women communicate more freely with their husbands, more often assume an active role in sexual relations, are less willing to monopolize housework and think their husbands should take a larger share of it, feel more uncomfortable if the husband seeks to use sole authority in decision-making without discussing matters with them, try to be less discriminatory in rearing and educating girls and boys, etc. Moreover, the distance between educated and noneducated women in these attitudes grows even greater as one moves from the advanced regions of the North to the backward ones of the South. In many instances educated women in the South show attitudes which are more emancipated and modern than educated women of the North. For example, the number of educated women willing to work outside of the family is higher in the South, where work opportunities are fewer, than in the North, where opportunities are more plentiful.

There is ample evidence, therefore, that the process of change in women's roles is powered by education, but it is also clear that it proceeds within severe structural constraints, for instance, the rigidity of the labour market on the one side, and the rigidity of the tasks needed to assure the adequate functioning of the family organization on the other.

A growing gap is thus developing between aspirations and opportunities—a gap responsible for the high level of incongruities, inconsistencies and contradictions disclosed by attitude surveys (for example, women declaring complete satisfaction with their husbands and children and, at the same time, claiming they can no longer stand family life), and for the frequency of psychic disorders in women which, in

Italy as in other countries, are on the increase. But this gap also makes room for the development of social movements and, in fact, women's liberation groups have spread, in recent years, all over the country. When the conditions for change are set, then struggle can advance it. But, to be sure, it will neither be a short nor an easy road.

REFERENCES

Balbo, Laura
    1976   *Stato di famiglia*. Milano: Etas Libri.
Banfield, C. Edward
    1958   *The Moral Basis of a Backward Society*. Glencoe: The Free Press.
Cazora-Russo, Gaetana
    1975   *Status sociale della donna*. 2 vols. Roma: U.F.I.S.A.S.

Changing Sex Roles in the Greek Family and Society

CONSTANTINA SAFILIOS-ROTHSCHILD

*The Pennsylvania State University
University Park, USA*

and

MARCELLINUS DIJKERS

Wayne State University

Detroit, USA

THE EXTENT to which sex roles are changing in a society may be measured by various indicators tapping different dimensions and life sectors. Since sex roles are multidimensional, the different dimensions are not necessarily interrelated and an indication of change in one dimension does not necessarily imply change in another. Research evidence from American studies indicates that ongoing changes in women's and men's sex role attitudes and beliefs are uneven and that some traditional sex role attitudes persist even in active feminists (Frieze, 1974; Mason, 1973 and 1975; Parelius, 1974). Furthermore, an earlier analysis of the present Greek data showed that some dimensions of sex roles are changing without the benefit of a Greek Women's Liberation Movement or an awareness of the Women's Liberation Ideology.[1] Thus, while Greek women can now enter almost any occupation and while their education is considered by many to be of equal importance with the education of men, the employment of married women is acceptable primarily in the case of college educated women and women's roles within the family have not changed significantly. Many familial behaviors and options open to men are not equally open to women (Safilios-Rothschild, 1972). In this way, the lack of correlation between the different changing dimensions of sex roles can create potentially anomic, alienating situations for Greek women whose expectations in different domains are not congruent.

In one domain, education, they are allowed and encouraged to have high and sex-differentiated expectations. But the realization of these expectations does not necessarily and proportionately imply similar kinds of expectations in other domains. Hence, at least some urban Greek women at present may be finding themselves in a

[1] At the present time the Athenian upper and upper-middle-class women are aware of and have read the American and French literature. But the study was conducted in 1970—71.

more alienating position than in the earlier, clearly traditional phase. This may be more accentuated in the case of lower-middle- and middle-class Greek women who move in circles and marry men with traditional sex role stereotypic values. These women may not be able to work because their husbands do not allow them to (especially after a child is born) and may still have to play traditional family roles only moderately modified by the influence of "modern" values.

There are many ways of assessing the extent to which sex roles are changing. The method followed in this study represents the operationalization of a cross-cultural theory of individual modernity based on options (Safilios-Rothschild, 1970). According to this theory an individual is modern to the extent that he (she) is aware of available options and can choose from among them the one which is best suited to his (her) abilities, talents, skills, interests and preferences rather than being limited to the one appropriate to his (her) gender or other categorical memberships. Guided by this theoretical framework, a number of educational, occupational, marital and familial options were formulated which, within the context of the traditional Greek culture, have been known to be open to men only—options such as marriage to a much younger spouse and initiating sexual relations; or options which, although occasionally taken by women, have traditionally been stigmatized as "deviant" such as divorce, extra-marital relations, or occasionally refusing to have sexual relations with their husbands. According to this modernity theory, a respondent is "modern" when he (she) considers that an option, traditionally precluded or viewed as "deviant" for women, is open to women. In the case of options for men, only options incompatible with masculinity have been traditionally denied men—options such as refusing to have sexual relations or not entirely shouldering the breadwinning responsibility. Because women's options represent a sensitive indicator of changing sex roles —since women have traditionally been deprived of these options—most of the options included relate to women.

Furthermore, it is important to note that when options relating to sexual behavior (such as occasionally refusing to have sex with spouse or having extramarital sex) become open to women, they are only *conditionally open*. Because under the traditional sex role pattern these same sexual options were *unconditionally open* to men, equality in behavioral options for men and women (and, hence, modernity) implies a certain degree of curtailment of men's sexual options. Modernity, then, in the case of men's sexual options, implies the transformation of unconditional availability of options into conditional availability. The same could be hypothesized about men's option to marry women much younger than themselves. Modernity can imply less acceptance of wide age discrepancies in which the wife is twenty or more years younger than the man.

This tendency for men's sexual options, as well as the option to marry much younger women, to become conditional with increasing social modernity, is the result of the fact that the traditional rights and perogatives of men are likely to be restrained and questioned. It seems, therefore, that on the way to gender equality men "lose" some of their unquestioned freedom while women gain some conditional freedom of behavior.

Methodology

The data for this article are taken from a larger study entitled "Family Modernization and Family Dynamics" and carried out in Athens, Greece from January, 1970—April, 1971 under the auspices of the Greek National Center for Social Research. The data were collected on the basis of questionnaires, containing mostly unstructured questions, administered separately to husbands and wives during interviews lasting, on the average, a total of five hours.

The population consists of 100 couples, 41 of which are upper-middle or middle class and 59 of which are lower-middle, working or lower class. About half of the couples in each class group were especially selected from those who have migrated to Athens within five years while the other half were either born Athenians or residents of Athens for over 20 years. The sample of migrants was provided by the National Statistical Service of Greece and represents all recent migrants included in the 1969 pre-census random sample drawn in Athens. The sample of nonmigrants was randomly chosen in middle- and working-class neighborhoods as a cluster sample described in detail elsewhere (Safilios-Rothschild, 1972).

Findings

The first step in the data analysis was an attempt to factor analyze the responses to the women's options. These women's options were the following:

1. Who should decide on the number of children a couple will have? (wife or both)[2]

2. Who must decide when the couple will engage in sexual intercourse? (wife or both)

3. Is it right for a woman to have sexual relations with another man, besides her husband? (yes, under some circumstances)

4. Is it acceptable for the wife to sometimes refuse to engage in sexual intercourse with her husband? (yes, under some circumstances)

5. What is your opinion about a family without children, in which the wife works outside the house, even if this is not necessary, and the husband helps with the housekeeping? (positive opinion)

---

2 The indications in parentheses refer to the type of response(s) that was coded as "modern"

6. Is it right for a woman to divorce her husband? (yes, under some circumstances)

7. Do you think education is equally important for a boy and a girl? (more or equally important for a girl)

8. If your financial means were only sufficient for the education of one of your children, which would you choose to educate? (both or the most able one)

9. Is it right for a woman to marry a man who is younger than herself? (yes)

10. With what matters or decisions should women not interfere? (no matters or decisions mentioned)

Table 1 shows that in general the correlations between these options are quite weak even when statistically significant; and only 17 out of 45 correlations (38 percent) are statistically significant. The ensuing factor analysis (principal factoring with iteration) was unsatisfactory in that the total percentage of variance explained

Table 1

*Intercorrelations between 13 Questions Referring to Sex Role Attitudes**

	1	2	3	4	5	6	7	8	9	10	11	12	13
1	—	.22	.15	.23	.06	.03	.02	.08	−.10	.05	.19	.20	.07
2	.22	—	−.06	.19	.05	.07	.18	.14	−.06	.13	.01	.15	.23
3	.15	—	—	−.15	.13	.07	.02	−.02	−.02	−.12	.43	−.11	.01
4	.23	.19	−.15	—	−.02	.06	.09	.01	.03	.20	.03	.84	.13
5	—	—	.13	—	—	.10	.16	.14	.00	.13	.07	−.01	−.14
6	—	—	—	—	—	—	.07	.16	.00	−.09	.08	.02	−.04
7	—	.18	—	—	—	—	—	.23	.10	−.10	−.03	.13	−.02
8	—	.14	—	.14	.16	.23	—	—	.07	.16	−.03	−.08	.03
9	—	—	—	—	—	—	—	—	—	−.01	−.06	.07	−.06
10	—	.13	−.12	.20	.13	—	—	.16	—	—	−.03	.08	−.04
11	.19	—	.43	—	—	—	—	—	—	—	—	.04	.10
12	.20	.15	−.11	.84	—	—	—	—	—	—	—	—	.13
13	—	.23	—	.13	−.14	—	—	—	—	—	—	.13	—

* Under the diagonal significant correlations (±.11 or better) at *.05* level.

was low and no clear-cut factors were isolated. Some of the options did not load on the first four factors extracted (e.g. options #5, 6 and 9) and almost none of the factors had more than one high loading option. The effort to isolate clusters of interrelated options for women was abandoned and the analysis proceeded on the basis of individual options.

The men's options examined were:

11. Is it acceptable for a man to have sexual relations with another woman besides his wife? (yes, in some circumstances).

12. Is it acceptable for the husband to sometimes refuse to engage in sexual intercourse with his wife? (yes, under some circumstances).

13. Is it right for a man to marry a woman who is younger than himself? (yes)

It is interesting to note here that the two highest correlations found are those between "parallel" options for men and women: a wife's right to extramarital relations (under circumstances) correlates .43 with a husband's right to do the same; and a wife's right to occasionally refuse sexual intercourse with her husband correlates .84 with the corresponding right for a husband (see Table 1). This is an indication that, as suggested above, modernization does not necessarily mean an unlimited acceptance of expanded behavior alternatives. At least in some areas of behavior modernization, to our Athenian respondents, is an increased equality between the sexes, even if in the case of men that means a limitation on behaviors that traditionally were their prerogative.

Individual Options

In pursuing the analysis of individual options, we concentrated on six of the women's options, namely, # 2, 4, 6, 7, 8, and 9 and all three of the men's options. The reasons for this selectivity are both theoretical relevance and importance as well as the nature of the obtained frequency distributions.

1. *Sex.* Table 2 shows that women in general tend—more often than men—to give "modern" answers, that is, tend to consider the different options as being open to men and women. This tendency is accentuated in the case of the options

Table 2

Frequency of no Information and of Modern and Traditional Answers, Wives and husbands

Item	Wives						Husbands					
	No answer		Modern		Traditional		No answer		Modern		Traditional	
	abs.	%	abs.	%	abs.	%	abs.	%	abs.	%	abs.	%
I_2	6	6	52	55	42	45	12	12	40	45	48	55
I_4	4	4	69	72	27	28	10	10	57	63	33	37
I_6	0	0	86	86	14	14	0	0	90	90	10	10
I_7	1	1	83	84	16	16	1	1	80	81	19	19
I_8	18	18	34	41	48	59	22	22	28	36	50	64
I_9	1	1	15	15	84	85	1	1	10	10	89	90
I_{11}	2	2	24	24	74	76	1	1	28	28	71	72
I_{12}	4	4	65	68	31	32	10	10	51	57	39	43
I_{13}	2	2	76	78	22	22	1	1	78	79	21	21

relating to women's sexual behavior in marriage (namely, her option to decide the timing of sexual relations and her right to occasionally refuse to have sexual relations with her husband) as well as with regard to the husband's right to occasionally refuse to have sexual relations with his wife. But even in the case of these options, the differences between men and women are not statistically significant.

Despite the lack of statistical significance, women's tendency to be more "modern" with regard to both men's and women's sexual roles and rights in marriage represents an important ongoing change in sex roles. Because of the importance of the respondents' sex, it has been used as a control variable in all subsequent analyses.

2. *Age*. The usual expectation is that younger people tend to be more modern in their attitudes toward men's and women's roles than older people. This overall expectation is not supported by the Greek data. The emerging patterns are much more complicated. The most modern group with regard to some options tend to be youngest women and men as in the case of the wife's option to occasionally refuse to have sex with her husband. And only the oldest group tends to be traditional as shown by their responses with regard to the choice of a child to educate in the case of limited financial means. Very few of these diverse trends are, however, statistically significant. The only significant trends are that: (a) the youngest and oldest men and women more often than those in between consider that women have at least as much right as men to decide about the timing of sexual relations in marriage; and (b) women over 45 years of age more often than younger women think that women can marry younger men.

The latter finding is of considerable importance since it suggests that as the option to marry a younger man becomes increasingly relevant with age, Greek women become more accepting of it. It must be interjected at this point that Greek women 35–40 years old often experience being seriously pursued by men and occasionally asked to marry them, a fact that renders this option more real, feasible, and plausible.

The overall lack of consistency in the direction of increased modernity across generations is probably due to other more powerful variables such as social class, rural-urban origin, level of education, and women's employment status.

3. *Education*. Previous research concerning familial values and behaviors (Safilios-Rothschild, 1972) has consistently indicated that education is a very powerful variable in determining the degree of modernity. In general, the present data tend to support these earlier reported patterns for both men and women respondents and most of these trends are statistically significant. Overall, however, education seems to play a more crucial role in determining the degree of modernity of women even more than of men. Thus, while the less educated women are significantly more often traditional with regard to the decision about the timing of sexual relations[3] ($X^2 = 10.63$ $P < .01$), the same trend for men is not significant. The same holds true for the extent to which education has equal importance to boys and girls. While 100 percent of college educated women think that education has equal importance and only the least educated (about one-third of them) disagree, the trend is less pronounced for men. Also, less well educated women significantly more often than

---

[3] That is, they think that only husbands must make this decision.

college educated women think that husbands cannot have extra-marital relations under any circumstances ($X^2=6.05$, $p<.05$), while the same trend in the responses of men is not statistically significant.[4] In the case, however, of the wife's or the husband's right to occasionally refuse to have sexual relations, and a man's marrying a older woman, significantly more often the well-educated men and women than the less-educated respondents give modern answers. Thus, in general, well-educated respondents tend to perceive that men and women have many options, although restrained by qualifications.

4. *Place of birth and migrant status.* The expectation that rural respondents would tend to be less modern than those born in large cities was largely supported by our data although the trend was statistically significant, in the majority of cases, only for women. Changing sex roles among urban born Greek women seem to be more clear-cut than among urban born Greek men. In the case, however, of the wife's right to occasionally refuse to have sexual relations, both urban men and women (from large cities and small towns) significantly more often than rural men and women mention a number of circumstances in which the wife has such a right ($X^2=9.83$, $p<.01$ and $X^2=4.68$, $p<.05$ respectively). When we come to the husband's right to occasionally refuse sex to his wife, the trend for urban respondents to grant this right is more pronounced and statistically significant among men respondents ($X^2=3.84$, $p<.05$).

The place of birth proved to be a more powerful variable than migrant status.[5] Only in the option regarding the timing of sex in marriage and the husband's right under certain conditions to extra-marital relations, do recent women migrants have more traditional attitudes than either those born in Athens or long-term Athens residents ($X^2=8.32$, $p<.01$ and $X^2=5.43$, $p<.05$ respectively).

5. *Social Class.* Since our social class measure was based on the husband's education and occupation, the trends are consistent with those followed by education although these trends are more pronounced and clear-cut in the case of social class. Lower-class Greek men and women are clearly those with the most traditional sex roles, a fact due to the composite effect of low or zero education, rural origin, recent migration to Athens, and a socialization into the core traditional ideology. Upper, upper-middle, and middle-class Greek men and especially women are the ones whose sex roles are changing most with regard to both men's and women's options and roles. These changes are evident not only in their views about the importance of education for girls (although the trend is statistically significant only in the case of women respondents) but also regarding women's sexual role and rights in marriage

---

4 In an earlier article, we have found that only very few (10 percent) upper-middle and middle-class women and men (and therefore the better educated) granted, under any condition, the same right to women (Safilios-Rothschild, 1972).

5 At least this is true for women, since we have data only about the wives' and not the husbands' migrant status.

and the husband's right to occasionally refuse sex. Although some trends are even more clear-cut in the wives' responses, it seems that well-educated, upper-middle and middle-class Greeks are changing from the traditional sex stratified values and beliefs toward a more egalitarian ideology which grants corresponding rights and privileges to men and women.

6. *Wife's working status.* Working women can be viewed as having taken one of the options which has been restricted for women, that of employment after marriage and especially after motherhood. In general, we can consider such employment as a behavioral indicator of modernity. Since, however, working and low-income Greek women sometimes work because they have to as a marital duty following the wishes (or orders) of the husband, only in the case of working women in the middle and upper-middle class can employment be clearly viewed as a behavioral indicator of a more modern sex role ideology. Our data show that while, in general, working women tend to have more modern attitudes, working status seems to be a particularly powerful factor with regard to men's and women's sexual rights and behaviors in marriage. Working women significantly more often than nonworking women find that women or equally both spouses can decide about the timing of sexual relations; and that wives and husbands can occasionally refuse to have sexual relations. It is interesting to note that these statistically significant trends are not only true for working wives but also for their husbands. In the case of many husbands who are married to working wives, at least in the upper-middle and middle classes, the fact that they allow their wives to work can be viewed as a behavioral indicator of their more modern sex role ideology.

Summary of findings. Summarizing the findings up to now we can say that:

(a) Sex role expectations concerning sexual roles and behaviors of men and women in marriage tend to change independently of other sex role expectations such as those referring to the education of women or the option to marry younger partners.

(b) A high level of education, high social class and urban origin (or lengthy stay in Athens, if migrants) increase the possibility that the respondents have changed toward an egalitarian definition of the sexual roles and rights of men and women in marriage.

(c) In general women tend to espouse more egalitarian values than men.

(d) While all the respondents' characteristics mentioned in (b) also tend to affect the respondents' egalitarian attitudes toward women's education, the respondents' education (especially in the case of women) and social class play the most crucial role.

Husband-Wife Sex Role Congruence and Family Dynamics

While it is important to examine what sex role characteristics among what groups of the population are changing, it is even more important to investigate the behavioral consequences of these changes. Because the present study also included an intensive interview on family dynamics and the interviewed men and women were married to each other, it is possible to examine the degree of sex role congruence among couples and its effects on familial behaviors as well as on the subjective assessment of marital satisfaction.

As we have already seen, education, social class, rural-urban origin, and to a lesser extent age are the important background characteristics that affect men's and women's sex roles. While there is a tendency for homogamy among Greek couples along exactly these background characteristics, it is interesting to find that as shown in Table 3 there is a high degree of homogamy in terms of sex role values and attitudes. On all sex role items (except the one referring to women's option to divorce on which 78 percent of the couples reflected modern attitudes) the husbands' and wives' attitudes are significantly related. The extent of the prevalent direction of sex role congruence varies, however. Most sex role homogamous couples are modern with respect to wives' and husbands' right to occasionally refuse to engage in sexual relations; women's right to divorce; the equal value of education for men and women; and women's right to marry younger men. Most sex role congruent couples are, on the contrary, traditional with respect to the timing of sexual relations, an option only open to men; the education of boys regardless of scholastic competence when family finances are restricted; the lack of acceptability for women to marry younger men; and the husband's almost unconditional right to extra-marital relations.

But the crucial question is to what extent and how sex role congruence between spouses affects their interactions in and feelings about their marriage.

1. *Marital Satisfaction.* Since subjective assessments such as marital satisfaction often vary considerably between husbands and wives (in this study only in 46 percent of the cases are spouses equally satisfied with their marriage[6]), both sets of responses are separately examined. Because of relatively small frequencies, the spouses were dichotomized into satisfied and dissatisfied ones. Before examining the effects of sex role congruence on marital satisfaction, it is important to examine how and to what extent modern or traditional sex role attitudes affect each spouse's marital satisfaction.

Wives' marital satisfaction is associated (but this does not reach statistical significance) with the nature of their sex role attitudes in that a greater degree of marital satisfaction is related to modern attitudes. (Attitudes, however, regarding women's

---

6 The degree of association between husbands' and wives' satisfaction assessments is high, however, since $X^2 = 91.81$, $p < .001$, gamma $= 0.79$. Still the very purpose of our analysis would be defeated, if we did not separately examine each spouse's answers.

Table 3

Sex Role Congruence and Incongruence in Husbands and Wives Responses to the 9 Individual Options*

	Item 2				Item 4				Item 6			
	Husband				Husband				Husband			
Wife	Modern	Traditional	Total		Modern	Traditional	Total		Modern	Traditional	Total	
Modern	28 (33%)	18 (21%)	46 (54%)		48 (55%)	14 (16%)	62 (71%)		8 (78%)	8 (8%)	86 (86%)	
Traditional	12 (14%)	27 (32%)	39 (46%)		8 (9%)	17 (20%)	25 (29%)		12 (12%)	2 (2%)	14 (14%)	
Total	40 (47%)	45 (53%)	85 (100%)		56 (64%)	31 (36%)	87 (100%)		90 (90%)	10 (10%)	100 (100%)	

$X^2 = 7.68$ $p < 0.01$ phi = .30 $X^2 = 16.02$ $p < 0.001$ phi = .43 $X^2 = .33$ NS phi = .06

	Item 7				Item 8				Item 13			
	Husband				Husband				Husband			
Wife	Modern	Traditional	Total		Modern	Traditional	Total		Modern	Traditional	Total	
Modern	71 (72%)	11 (11%)	82 (84%)		13 (20%)	13 (20%)	26 (40%)		4 (4%)	11 (11%)	15 (15%)	
Traditional	8 (8%)	8 (8%)	16 (16%)		9 (14%)	30 (46%)	39 (60%)		6 (6%)	77 (79%)	83 (85%)	
Total	79 (81%)	19 (19%)	98 (100%)		22 (34%)	43 (66%)	65 (100%)		10 (10%)	88 (90%)	98 (100%)	

$X^2 = 11.47$ $p < 0.001$ phi = .34 $X^2 = 5.05$ $p < 0.05$ phi = .28 $X^2 = 5.24$ $p < 0.05$ phi = .23

	Item 11				Item 12				Item 13			
	Husband				Husband				Husband			
Wife	Modern	Traditional	Total		Modern	Traditional	Total		Modern	Traditional	Total	
Modern	13 (13%)	11 (11%)	24 (24%)		40 (46%)	18 (21%)	58 (67%)		64 (65%)	12 (12%)	76 (78%)	
Traditional	15 (15%)	59 (60%)	74 (76%)		10 (11%)	19 (22%)	29 (33%)		14 (14%)	8 (8%)	22 (22%)	
Total	28 (29%)	70 (71%)	98 (100%)		50 (57%)	37 (43%)	87 (100%)		78 (80%)	20 (20%)	98 (100%)	

$X^2 = 10.20$ $p < 0.01$ phi = .32 $X^2 = 9.41$ $p < 0.01$ phi = .33 $X^2 = 4.45$ $p < 0.05$ phi = .21

* The numbers in the parentheses are the percentages calculated on the total N for each individual option.

option of marrying a younger man and men's option of extramarital relations represent the exceptions to this trend.) Furthermore, wives' marital satisfaction is also positively related to the husbands' sex role modernity,[7] but the only statistically significant associations are those referring to the equal importance of education for boys and girls and women's option to marry younger men.

Husband's marital satisfaction follows the same trends; the more modern they are, the more satisfied (except with respect to women's option to divorce and marry younger men and men's option to extramarital relations). As a matter of fact, the only statistically significant association is a negative one between the option of men to have extramarital relations and marital satisfaction. This pronounced trend as well as the direction of trends concerning this option in relation to both husbands' and wives' marital satisfaction raises a serious question as to the appropriateness of considering the affirmative response to this option as the "modern" one. Probably the curtailment of this option, traditionally open to men, indicates a more egalitarian attitude toward men and women.

Husband's marital satisfaction is also positively associated with the wife's modern sex role attitudes but none of the correlations reaches statistical significance. Again, exceptions to this positive association are men's sexual options and women's option to marry younger men.

Since there is a considerable degree of sex role congruence between spouses, an association of marital satisfaction with the other spouse's sex role attitudes could be explained on the basis of this congruence. Even after we have controlled, however, for respondent's own sex role attitudes, the relationship between marital satisfaction and spouse's sex role attitudes is maintained. The partial correlations between husband's marital satisfaction and wife's sex role attitudes (except for the option regarding the timing of sex and women's ability to marry younger men) are positive, but too low to reach statistical significance (around 0.10). The same is true for the partial correlations between wife's marital satisfaction and husband's sex role attitudes (except for women's option to divorce their husbands and men's option to extramarital sex), but these correlations reach statistical significance with regard to husband's attitude toward the value of education for women and men's option to marry younger women.

Coming now to the possible joint, interactive effects of sex role attitudes upon marital satisfaction, we could predict that:

(a) On the basis of role theory, sex role congruence (regardless as to the direction of this congruence) is positively related to marital satisfaction.

(b) On the basis of the earlier findings regarding the effect of modern sex role attitudes of either spouse on their degree of satisfaction with marriage, spouses'

---

[7] Women's option to divorce and men's to extramarital relations are again exceptions to this positive relationship.

sex role congruence toward the modern direction is positively associated to a higher degree of marital satisfaction for both spouses than sex role congruence toward the traditional direction.

Our data clearly confirm both hypotheses. Sex role incongruence results indeed in a low marital satisfaction, especially for husbands. Furthermore, traditional sex role congruent couples are less satisfied with their marriages than modern sex role congruent couples. This trend is particularly true for wives' marital satisfaction and when both spouses have traditional sex role attitudes concerning the sexual roles and behaviors of men and women. As Table 4 indicates, traditional sex role congruent couples (especially when congruent with respect to women's sexual options and behaviors and the value of education for women) tend to be relatively more often satisfied with their marriage than sex role incongruent couples. Finally, it seems that the wife's marital satisfaction tends to be somewhat lower when she has modern and her husband traditional sex role attitudes than when the reverse is true.

As an additional test of the importance of sex role congruency (regardless of direction) for marital satisfaction, couples were classified on the basis of the number

Table 4

Percentage of Wives and Husbands Reporting High Marital Satisfaction by Type of Sex Role Congruence

	Sex Role Items									Mean Percentage
	2	4	6	7	8	9	11	12	13	
A. *Wives*										
Both Modern	64	58	51	58	54	*	39	58	56	55
Both Traditional	52	35	*	*	47	52	54	37	*	46
Wife Modern, Husband Traditional	39	43	*	18	46	27	55	44	25	37
Wife Traditional, Husband Modern	33	*	33	*	*	*	40	60	50	43
B. *Husbands*										
Both Modern	75	65	56	61	54	*	31	63	61	58
Both Traditional	56	53	*	*	53	56	61	58	*	56
Wife Modern, Husband Traditional	33	43	*	18	54	35	73	44	25	41
Wife Traditional, Husband Modern	50	*	53	*	*	*	33	50	43	46

* Very few couples had this type of sex role combination and, therefore, the percentages were not calculated.

of sex role attitudes on which they agreed (Table 5). The data presented in Table 5 show that there is a positive relationship between the number of sex role attitudes on which the spouses agree and their degree of marital satisfaction. This relationship is, however, significant only in the case of husbands.

Table 5

Marital Satisfaction by Number of Attitudinal Items on Which Husband and Wife Have Similar Attitudes

	Husbands						Wives					
	Similar attitudes on						Similar attitudes on					
	8 or 9 items		7 or less items		Total		8 or 9 items		7 or less items		Total	
High marital satisfaction	32	64%	13	35%	45	52%	28	56%	14	38%	42	48%
Low marital satisfaction	18	36%	24	65%	42	48%	22	44%	23	62%	45	52%
Total	50	100%	37	100%	87	100%	50	100%	37	100%	87	100%

$X^2 = 7.10$ $p < 0.01$ phi $= .29$ $X^2 = 2.81$ NS phi $= .18$

2. *Companionship*. In this study companionship was measured by the frequency with which spouses went out together. The degree of agreement between husbands' and wives' reported frequency of going out together was .77; and it became .87 when the answers were dichotomized into two categories: those who go out once a week or more and those who go out twice a month or less often.

Husbands with modern sex role attitudes tend to more often indicate that they frequently go out with their wives than husbands with traditional sex role attitudes. Similarly, husbands married to wives with modern attitudes more often indicate that they frequently go out with their wives than men married to wives with traditional sex role attitudes. The same trends also hold true for wives, although very few of these tendencies reach statistical significance.[8] When the respondent's own sex role attitudes are held constant, the frequency of going out with the spouse is still positively associated with the spouse's modern sex role attitudes. Thus, a couple tends to go out more often when the husband or the wife has modern sex role attitudes.

Turning now to the joint effects of sex role congruence on companionship, Table 6 shows that modern sex role congruent couples report going out together "infrequently or never" less often than any other group of couples. Traditional sex role congruent couples report a low degree of companionship more often than modern sex role congruent couples but less often than sex role incongruent couples, especially those in which it is the wife who has traditional sex role attitudes.[9] When the wife

---

8 The relationship between sex role modernity and higher frequency of going out may be partly explained on the basis of the respondents' characteristics such as class which is highly related with both variables. Upper-middle and middle-class respondents have more often modern sex role attitudes and go out with their spouses more often than working and lower-class respondents.

9 As was true for marital satisfaction, these trends are particularly clearcut with regard to attitudes about men's and women's sexual behavior and options as well as the criteria for educating a child in the case of limited finances.

Table 6

Percentage of Wives and Husbands Reporting Going Out Never or Very Infrequently by Type of Sex Role Congruence

	Sex Role Items									Mean Percentage
	2	4	6	7	8	9	11	12	13	
A. *Wives*										
Both Modern	27	30	41	41	77	*	46	26	37	41
Both Traditional	44	59	*	*	50	42	47	63	*	51
Wife Modern, Husband Traditional	28	57	*	64	31	70	27	56	67	50
Wife Traditional, Husband Modern	83	*	67	*	*	*	47	40	43	56
B. *Husbands*										
Both Modern	19	28	38	40	54	*	38	26	37	35
Both Traditional	44	47	*	*	57	40	41	53	*	47
Wife Modern, Husband Traditional	28	50	*	53	31	50	27	44	50	42
Wife Traditional, Husband Modern	83	*	50	*	*	*	47	40	36	51

* Very few couples had this type of sex role combination and, therefore, the percentages were not calculated.

has traditional sex role attitudes and the husband modern, companionship seems to be stifled and inhibited. Thus, sex role incongruency is associated to a lower degree of companionship than sex role congruency, the highest degree of companionship being found when both spouses are modern.

3. *Decision-making.* The measurement of decision-making in this study represents the operationalization of methodological and theoretical concerns formulated elsewhere in detail by Safilios-Rothschild (1970a; and 1976). The important and distinctive features of this measurement are that:

(a) the decisions asked represent the universe of decisions reported by respondents in an extensive pretesting as being made frequently and (b) the respondents were asked to report the frequency with which each of these decisions is made as well as to rank the decisions according to the degree of importance they attach to each one of them. These additions made it possible to calculate a decision-making score based on important and infrequent decisions and corresponding to the "orchestration" type of power, that is, the core power in the family (Safilios-Rothschild, 1976). The spouse who has orchestration power can in fact delegate to the other spouse implementation mostly including unimportant and frequent decisions as well as the actual implementation (but not the actual decision) of time-consuming but important decisions.

Similar patterns were found for power as were found for marital satisfaction and companionship. Husbands more often report husband-dominance in orchestration power (that is, in the important and infrequently made decisions) when they themselves or their wives are traditional. And the same trend holds true for wives. Furthermore, after controlling for the respondent's own sex role attitudes, the spouse's sex role attitudes continue to be related to the type of orchestration power reported and discussed above.

Table 7

Percentage of Wives and Husbands Reporting Husband Dominance in Important, Infrequently Made Decisions by Type of Sex Role Congruence

	Sex Role Items									Mean Percentage
	2	4	6	7	8	9	11	12	13	
A. *Wives*										
Both Modern	27	37	41	37	18	*	38	32	42	34
Both Traditional	68	53	*	*	53	46	46	56	*	54
Wife Modern, Husband Traditional	29	61	*	64	50	90	30	62	45	54
Wife Traditional, Husband Modern	58	*	67	*	*	*	77	60	58	64
B. *Husbands*										
Both Modern	14	32	39	36	27	*	33	32	32	31
Both Traditional	65	61	*	*	50	41	41	37	*	46
Wife Modern, Husband Traditional	37	67	*	40	54	64	40	60	33	49
Wife Traditional, Husband Modern	60	*	50	*	*	*	57	*	62	57

* Very few couples had this type of sex role combination and, therefore, the percentages were not calculated.

Table 7 further indicates that modern sex role congruence is negatively associated with a husband-dominated orchestration type power. When, on the other hand, both spouses' sex role attitudes are traditional, orchestration power tends to be husband-dominated but less so than when the wife is traditional and the husband modern. The sex role attitude incongruence in which the wife is modern and the husband traditional seems to be associated with a less husband-dominated orchestration power than the reverse type of incongruence. It seems, therefore, that in couples in which the wife is traditional and the husband modern, there is a tendency toward traditional family patterns with regard both to companionship and decision-making. This tendency of sex role congruence probably arises because in the case of sex role incongruence the wife's sex role attitudes play a more determining role in setting the tone and style of familial behaviors.

Conclusion and Discussion

The Greek data on sex role attitudes suggest that there are three important sectors of sex role behavior included: those pertaining to the sexual options of men and women; those pertaining to women's equal access to education; and those referring to the curtailment of absolute masculine prerogatives such as extramarital relations and marrying younger women. The last sector is of considerable theoretical interest since it implies that men who traditionally had unilateral rights and options have to give up these prerogatives when sex roles are changing.

Modernity in terms of gender equality in behavioral options cannot take place without affecting the traditional unconditional freedom of men. This type of modernity and gender equality implies conditional availability of the same options for both men and women.

The data also indicate that the changing sex role attitudes in Greece affect family dynamics both in terms of behaviors as well as in terms of marital satisfaction. The direction is clear that the more modern the husband or the wife, the more egalitarian and companionate is the marital relationship and the more both spouses are satisfied with it. This trend becomes even more consolidated when both spouses are modern and is much weaker when the spouses' sex role orientation is different. Since, however, sex role attitudes are mostly changing in the upper-middle and middle classes, we cannot say that the majority of Athenians are touched by egalitarian ideologies and values. Greek men and women still have a long way to go.

REFERENCES

Frieze, Irene Hanson
    1974 "Changing Self-Images and Sex Role Stereotypes in College Women," paper presented at the American Psychological Association meetings, Orleans, September.
Mason, Karen Oppenheim
    1973 "Studying Change in Sex-Role Definitions Via Attitude Data," *Proceedings of the American Statistical Association,* Social Statistics Society, 138–141.
Mason, Karen Oppenheim and Larry L. Bumpass
    1975 "U.S. Women's Sex-Role Ideology, 1970," *American Journal of Sociology,* 80: 1212–1219.
Parelius, Ann P.
    1974 "Emerging Sex-Role Attitudes, Expectations, and Strains Among College Women," paper presented at the Society for the Study of Social Problems, New York, August.
Safilios-Rothschild, Constantina
    1967 "A Comparison of Power Structure and Marital Satisfaction in Urban Greek and French Families," *Journal of Marriage and the Family,* (May): 345–352.
    1969 "Sociopsychological Factors Affecting Fertility in Urban Greece: A Preliminary Report *Journal of Marriage and the Family* (August): 595–606.
    1970 "Toward a Cross-Cultural Conceptualization of Family Modernity," *Journal of Comparative Family Studies,* (Autumn): 17–25.

1970a "The Study of Family Power Structure: A Review Paper 1960 1969." *Journal of Marriage and the Family,* 32 (November).
1972 "The Options of Greek Men and Women," *Sociological Focus,* (Winter): 71–83.
1976 "The Dimensions of Power Structure in the Family," in: Jacob Christ and Henry Grunebaum (Eds.), *Contemporary Marriage: Structure, Dynamics, and Therapy,* Boston: Little, Brown and Co., 275–292.

C. ASIA

The Changing Status and Role of Women in Japan

YORIKO MEGURO

Sophia University, Tokyo, Japan

and

KIYOMI MORIOKA

Seijo University, Tokyo, Japan

Introduction

THIS ARTICLE is an effort to provide an overview of the changing status and role of women in Japan. It is intended to identify variables which have empirically influenced the social definition of women's role in Japan and then to evaluate the nature of their influences. In the first section, historical backgrounds and cultural constraints regarding women's role and status are discussed briefly. The second section deals with variables which, we consider, have contributed to promoting changes in the role and status of women in Japan since World War II. In the final section we present our evaluation of those variables in relation to the present situation.

As a basis for understanding the changing status and role of women, let us present a description of the general changes Japan has experienced in the post-World War II period. Industrialization and democratization are the themes underlying all aspects of change. In relation to the change in the family and kinship systems, the disorganization of the corporate kin group (Dozoku) and the shrinkage of the family size have been the major issues. Drastic changes in the mean household size—from 4.97 to 3.69—occurred between 1955 and 1970. This picture coincides with the ideological change toward nuclearization of the family taking place in the 1960's.

In his attempt to study social change in Japan, Dore (1967: 3–24) found more evidence of a move toward greater equality than toward greater individuation and rationality. Aspects that indicate a move toward greater equality are: less emphasis on birth and seniority and more on merit; and specificity of authority which tends to diminish in amount. Let us examine whether or not a move toward equality is enjoyed by women in Japan.

Historical Backgrounds and Cultural Constraints—Pre-1945 Japan

Women's status in the family is influenced by the family pattern. Under the old civil code in pre-war times the stem family system called the *Ie* was considered ideal. The *Ie* system was a family institution based on the Confucian ethic which was prevalent in the Samurai ruling class in the pre-modern (Tokugawa) period. This institution became the basis for controlling the Japanese people and was legalized by the Meiji government. To state it simply, the *Ie* was a patriarchal and patrilineal system under which the rule of primogeniture operated. The family head was ideally the male and he was the official representative of the family unit before he was a husband or a father. The most important task of the household head was related to the lineal continuity of the family and expansion of the family property. Under this system, women were submissive to the male head.

The diversity in the family pattern and the related women's status under the Meiji Civil Code, which Goode analyzed so insightfully (1963: 321–365), must be pointed out. However, the single norm regarding the family pattern and sex roles of the Samurai class was legitimized by the code and remained effective until the law was replaced by the new code. When the family system operates under a uni-standard norm, women's roles are concretely specified and the role conflicts women experience are solved on the basis of a conformity-deviance scale. The social definition of women's family roles was harmonious with the practices in family life. Under this condition, the number of options women had were considerably limited.

What roles did women play in the *Ie*? Since the major task for the household head was family continuity, his spouse was to be the procreator and socializer of the family successor. Marriage was institutionalized to support the ideology of family continuity. For farming families, the bride was a useful and often essential laborer for the farm. Thus, she was both labor force and child-bearer. Socialization of her children was often left to her mother-in-law. Though women were expected to carry out all domestic tasks, there were, theoretically, at least two adult females in a family to handle them. For the bride, marriage meant her entrance into the existing household comprising the groom's family of orientation and a subsequent assumption of the lowest position in the household. To compensate for her non-affective relation to her husband, she developed an intimate relationship with her children. They were the objects of her love and possession, and the irreplaceable mother-child relation persisted.

Where a uni-standard norm defines the role of women in the family, and when the norm emphasizes family continuity, then the position of the wife is valued primarily as the procreator and socializer of the family heir. Socialization toward family continuity legitimizes discrimination against female children and thus women as the primary socializer contribute to the continuation of non-equality between the male family heir and his female siblings.

Change-Promoting Variables

There are several variables which seem to have contributed to a move toward equality in the post-1945 period. In relation to women's rights, we consider the following three groups of variables to be of particular relevance. They are "demographic", "resources", and "cultural-normative" variables.

A. Demographic Variables

The most significant demographic changes we find in relation to women's family roles in the post-war period are in the pattern of women's life cycle and the move toward the nuclear family household.

1. Women's Life Cycle

We have evidence to suggest that role relations in the family change according to the stages of the family life cycle. Among variables related to the family life cycle stages, the family budget and the family composition seem to be of particular importance in an analysis of women's family status.

Studies on the "financial squeeze" for Japanese families indicate that the peak is experienced by families today several years later and for a longer period than for families in the 1940's (Morioka, 1973: 162–174). This means that the parents are in their 40's when the family is under the heaviest financial burden.

Table 1

Wife's Age at Pointer Events in Family History

	Wife's Age		Duration of Interval (in number of years)	
	1930	1950	1930	1950
A Marriage	22.2	23.0		
B Birth of 1st Child	23.4	24.9	1.2	1.9
C Birth of Last Child	36.9	28.0	13.5	3.1
D Marriage of Female 1st Child	47.4	48.9	12.0	22.4
Male	50.4	51.9		
E Marriage of Female Last Child	60.9	52.0	13.5	3.1
Male	63.9	55.0	1.6	14.5
F Death of Husband	64.0	68.0	7.0	7.0
G Death of Wife	71.0	75.0		

Source: K. Morioka, *Kazoku Shukiron* (Family Life Cycle), 1973: 121.

Cohort studies have provided us with a clear indication that the patterns of the family life cycle in two age groups are considerably different (Morioka, 1973: 119–123). The 1930 group (Table 1) consists of those who married in 1930 and the 1950 group of those who married in that year. Historically, the former represents the pre-war period and the latter represents the post-war period. We find the outstanding difference between the two is in the "post-parental" stage. The prolongation of that stage is caused by the shrinkage in the number of children in the family and by the longer life expectancy. Another significant difference is found in the wife's age at the birth of her last child, which produces the difference in the wife's age at her last child's marriage. The women in the 1950 cohort will have become relatively free from child-rearing in their mid-thirties and by their early fifties they will cease to hold the mother role.

These trends are closely related to the pattern of women's participation in the job market. These women were in their thirties when Japan experienced a high rate of economic growth which demanded cheap women's labor on a temporary and part-time basis, as will be described in the following section.

2. *Nuclearization of Households*

Egalitarian ideology was introduced and supported by the postwar constitution and was gradually accepted by the younger generations. The household head's power of censorship over other members of his family was no longer legitimate. Marriage became a personal matter instead of a matching between families. Based on this ideology, the conjugal family emerged as the favoured one. The proportion of the families taking the nuclear family form has increased about 14% in the past 50 years (Table 2), and it continues to increase steadily. The significance of the move toward

Table 2

Changing Proportions of the Conjugal Family (%)

Year	1920	1955	1960	1965	1970
Proportion (%)	57.5	62.0	63.4	68.2	71.3

Source: K. Morioka, ed., *Shin Kazoku Kankeigaku* (A New Approach to Family Relations), 1974: 3.

the conjugal type family in relation to the implementation of human rights is well discussed by Goode (1969: 605–614). We must now evaluate how the shift in the family type has affected women's roles and status in Japan.

B. *Resources Variables*

The changes in women's role and status in Japan have been influenced by factors which may be conceptualized as "resources" (Blood and Wolfe, 1960) contributing to women's relative increase of power in the family and society. The selection of resources variables is within the confinement of the Japanese cultural context.

1. *Legalization of Equality between Sexes*

One of the most drastic changes, if not the most drastic, in the past 30 years was in the legal sector of Japanese society. The nature of the new constitution introduced after World War II is radically different from the old and for this reason social scientists, as well as laymen, often dichotomize our experiences of modern history into the "before" and the "after" the war stages. Japan precisely witnessed a drastic change in the nature of the civil code, particularly in regard to the rights of women, when the new code of 1948 renounced women's subordination to the three categories of men in their family life, namely the father, the husband, and the son (the family heir). Women were finally guaranteed their equal rights with men; they finally became social individuals. The new law promises basic human rights and denies discrimination based on sex, geneology, faith and other individual attributes. It supports marriage based on the consent of both sexes, while under the old law the consent of the household head was the decisive factor in arranging a new marriage.

2. *Rising Level of Formal Education for Women*

In 1975, 93% of girls graduating from junior high school entered senior high school, and the percentage of female students in senior high school was roughly 50%; 32% of over 2 million students in junior and 4-year colleges and universities were female, an increase of 12% in 15 years. The majority of girls are in junior colleges. In 1975, about 32% of girls in the applicable age group entered the higher educational institutions in comparison with 44% for boys. In 1960, the proportion was less than 6% for females and 15% for males. The big leap came in the period between 1960 and 1970. The pace of growing advancement in education has been slower but steady since then (Ministry of Education, 1975).

Educational institutions for girls were the formal agent for producing the "goodwife, wise-mother" combination. In the higher educational institutions women were trained to become teachers for the girls of the coming generations. The new educational policy after World War II provided equal opportunity for both sexes for higher levels of education, and coeducation was finally realized.

Democratization of the educational system enjoyed its heyday for only a few years. Soon there were strong pressures to revise the coeducational system and the equal opportunity policy. Furthermore, the government's revised guideline for high school education emphasized a sex-based curriculum: for example, "home economics" became a requirement for girls and girls only (Fujii *et al.*, 1973: 22–38). These revisions were indicative of the turning point in the educational policy of the government. The emphasis on the personal abilities and attributes meant that girls' roles were socially defined now as home-bound and as the poor-quality members of the labor force. Educational opportunities for girls were thus mapped out. (See, for example, Okada *et al.*, 1975: 14–15; Fujii *et al.*, 1973: 17–28).

3. *Increasing Number of Gainfully Employed Women*

A large number of women have always worked as an important part of the labor force in farming and in small family businesses. But it is only in the past few decades that we have seen an increasing number of employed women. Today, close to 20 million women are working (Women's and Minors' Bureau, 1975: 34), of whom 12 million are officially employed and they constitute about one-third of the total labor force (Table 3). Let us now point out several factors which have influenced women's participation in the employed work sector in a society where women are socially defined as belonging to the family. They are:

1) the high rate of economic growth, particularly since 1960, demanded a growing labor supply;
2) the rise in the level of education and the drop in the birth rate influenced a shrinkage of the young labor force, which necessitated a policy change regarding the type of labor supply;
3) mechanization and automation in the production system allowed expansion of untrained and semi-trained work market;
4) the rise in the level of education encouraged women to pursue their interests in social participation;
5) women began to have more time free from housework due to the shorter period of child-rearing and mechanization of household appliances;
6) the rise in the cost of living, particularly in the cost of education, and the uncertainty about life in the future, both of which made additional income a necessity.

Table 3

Number of Employed Workers and the Proportion of Women

Year	Total Number of Employed Workers (10 thousand)	Female Number of Employed Workers	Female % of Women in the Total Employed Force	Male Number of Employed Workers
1955	1,778	531	29.9	1,247
1960	2,370	738	31.1	1,632
1965	2,876	913	31.7	1,963
1970	3,306	1,096	33.2	2,210
1971	3,406	1,116	32.8	2,290
1972	3,452	1,120	32.4	2,332
1973	3,595	1,186	33.0	2,408
1974	3,610	1,171	32.4	2,440

Source: Women's and Minors' Bureau, Ministry of Labor, *Fujin Rodo no Jitsujo* (Present Status of Working Women), 1975: 41.

The questions we must ask next deal with the way in which women have entered the work world and how they have been evaluated in comparison with men.

Ever since Japanese girls were recruited as factory workers at the dawn of industrialization in Japan in the late 19th century, female workers were divided into specific job categories. The jobs which are occupied predominantly by the female are either those labelled as appropriate for them or those which men abandoned as being undesirable. The largest proportion of all employed women, in 1974, fell into the clerical category (32%), followed by factory workers (27%) and service workers (13%). Statistical figures show a considerable increase in the proportion of clerical (office) workers in the past fifteen years (25% in 1960). Though small in number, sales workers and professional-technical workers (each about 11% of the total women employed) showed a slight increase in the same period (9% in 1960). Taking each occupational category, the proportion of women was the highest among clerical workers (48% in 1970, an increase of 12% since 1960), followed by professional-technical and sales workers (38% and 35% respectively). The high proportion of women in the professions and technical areas was caused by the women's predominance in nursery school and kindergarten teaching and nursing (98% and 95%, respectively) as well as among elementary school teachers and pharmaceutists (about 50% each) (Women's and Minors' Bureau, 1975).

The sex-typing of occupational categories is still prevalent though women are now taking jobs which were previously occupied predominantly by men—mainly because of a manpower shortage. According to a survey conducted by the Women's and Minors' Bureau in 1969, 22% of factories began using women in jobs where previously they had used only men. The reasons given for this change included "made special arrangement so that women could work," "mechanization made it possible," "discovery of new women's aptitude," "to replace men's labor which is becoming short in supply," and "women supply cheap labor" (Women's and Minors' Bureau, 1975: 8–9).

Usually employed women have been young and single, but more married and older women are working today than ever before. In 1955, 69% of employed women were less than 30 years of age and 65% were single while in 1974, 56% were 30 years old or over and 39% were single (Women's and Minors' Bureau, 1975: 9). The average age of working women has gone up from 25.4 in 1954 to 32.5 in 1974 (p. 60).

Table 4

Employed Women by Marital Status (%)

Year	Single	Married	Separated/Divorced	Total
1962	456(59.4)	225(29.3)	87(11.3)	769(100)
1965	466(54.2)	300(34.9)	94(10.9)	860(100)
1970	524(48.3)	450(41.4)	112(10.3)	1,086(100)
1971	514(46.3)	479(43.2)	116(10.5)	1,109(100)
1972	483(43.4)	513(46.1)	116(10.4)	1,113(100)
1973	482(40.9)	570(48.3)	126(10.7)	1,179(100)
1974	456(39.2)	582(50.0)	124(10.7)	1,163(100)

Source: Women's and Minors' Bureau, Ministry of Labor, *Fujin Rodo no Jitsujo* 1975: 58.

As part of the above trend, women engaged in piece-work increased drastically in the past ten years. The number of those in piece-work was 1.7 million in 1973 which was 2.5 times that of 1965 (Women's Organizations Federation, 1975: 94). The number of part-time workers began to increase around 1963 in conjunction with the government's manpower policy to draw housewives out of their homes to meet the market demands for cheap labor, on the one hand, and the rising cost of living, on the other. In 1969, the number of part-time workers was 1.2 million while it was 1.7 million in 1973 (Women's Organizations Federation, 1975: 92). The government's policy is commonly called the woman-power policy (1969) which was carried through under such slogans as "development of women's capacities" and the "expansion of women's job areas." What was meant in reality was the mass recruitment of housewives to part-time and temporary jobs and a revision of the labor law regarding the protection of motherhood (Kaji, 1975: 28).

C. *Cultural-Normative Variables*

Rodman's (1972) "theory of resources in cultural context" stresses the important role norms play between resources and the conjugal relation. Though women's status in the family is not confined to conjugal relations, Rodman's conception can be extended to a broader framework which includes other relations within the family. We find that the conjugal family ideology and the sex role ideology are the major normative variables relevant to women's status in Japan.

1. *The Conjugal Role Ideology*

The importance of the role that the ideology of the family plays has been noted in relation to the effective functioning of an emergent family type (Goode, 1963: 370). The legal change in the family system in Japan was introduced in 1948 but it took some time for the Japanese to accept the new principle as a new ideal. Morioka (1973) assumes that the predominance of the conjugal type family means nuclearization of the family supported by the conjugal family system. On the basis of statistical figures on the proportion of conjugal type families (Table 2), he calculated—using the life expectancy as a key variable—that the increase of 14% in the 50-year period would indicate a fair acceptance of the conjugal family system in Japan today (Morioka, 1973: 212–213). Education and mass communication media contributed to the permeation of the conjugal family ideology. If we assume a "fit" between the conjugal family system and industrialization, and if we assume, as well, the Parsonian model of the role structure in the nuclear family, then a logical conclusion is that the new family system functions as a reinforcing factor for the stable division of labor by sex, even though it liberated wives from the institutionalized position of submission to husbands. In this sense, the move toward nuclearization of the family in Japan supports Goode's claim that the ideology of the conjugal family promotes new rights for women (Goode, 1969: 609) only with a strict cultural confinement of the "division of labor by sex."

2. *The Sex Role Ideology*

When a baby is born in Japan, it is identified by its sex. A baby boy is often more welcome than a baby girl even where the ideology of family continuity through the male line no longer has legitimacy. A boy is socialized into the male role (lifetime occupational career) while a girl is socialized into the female role (marriage as a career). Up until today, work for women has been considered marginal or secondary in the role-complex of a woman.

The pattern of socialization into sex roles is one indicator of the sex role ideology. When sex roles are defined clearly and specifically and when socialization into sex roles is uniformly carried out, the ideology regarding sex roles is stable. Japanese boys and girls begin to identify their sex when they are three to four years old; they establish different sets of sex role behaviours by the time they are ten. Following their parents as models, girls are more severely disciplined than boys; boys' sex role perceptions are clear-cut while girls tend to resist acceptance of socially-defined female roles; sex-identity of boys is in accordance with the general stereotype of sex roles while girls perceive sex-identity much later than boys (Aoi, 1974: 123 and 124). The check points in home disciplines differ according to the sex of the children. Parents emphasize discipline for domestic and personal behavior for girls and on public behavior for boys (Prime Minister's Office, 1973). Parents favor the idea of disciplining children on the basis of the child's sex (94% of parents were in favor of and 4% against the idea of stressing the "maleness" and "femaleness" in Masuda's study, 1970: 78).

Another indicator of the sex role ideology is evident in the motives for getting married. According to a report by the Research Committee on Women, Japanese have the notion of an appropriate time for marriage and as a result about 60% of wives were married somewhere between 20 and 24 years of age, followed by about 27% at a slightly older age. About 97% of women over 25 years of age were or had been married in 1973. The most popular motive for marriage for women was "marriage promises woman's happiness" (34%), followed by "it's natural to get married" (25%), "psychological stability" (22%); while for men, "a man becomes socially stable" (38%), "psychological stability" (33%), "it's natural to get married" (29%). Together with other motives given, the majority of women take marriage as a natural role for adult women. The major difference by age is found in their opinions on divorce and "free sex," the younger women being more in favor (Research Committee, 1974: 29—37).

The prescription of women's achievement and autonomy within the framework of marriage and family is vividly described by Lebra and others (1976: 303) in their studies of Japanese women in all occupations. They conclude that whether Japanese women will return to their nation's own "mythic feminine cosmogenesis" remains a very hypothetical prospect and that it is difficult to project a paradigm for change in the Japanese feminine role.

Present situations

We have assumed from the beginning that the general direction of change was toward equality and we have identified several change-promoting variables in the post-war period. Each of the demographic and resource variables seems to encourage a move toward greater freedom and equality while cultural-normative variables may well have functioned as justifications of increasing freedom and equality. Let us, however, examine whether our cultural context can be characterized by "modernity" (Rodman, 1967: 324), which contributes to the functioning of resources toward greater equality.

Theoretically there is only one adult female who is responsible for all household tasks in the nuclear family. The division of labor by sex continues to be predominant in family role relations. Empirical research findings suggest that the division of labor by sex clearly exists in modern Japanese families. Koyama and his group (1967: 13) found that all domestic tasks, including child-rearing and educational tasks, were carried out predominantly by the wife. Masuda (1965: 49—66), using the typology developed by Blood and Wolfe (1960), found that the majority of both nuclear and stem families in Japan were the "autonomous" type. Vogel (1963: Ch. IX) observed the persistence of a strict division of labor among suburban families. He explains that the persistence is not entirely a result of "traditional" attitudes, and that it is, in part, a method of keeping the husband-wife equilibrium. He interprets that to mean the Japanese wife enjoys her autonomy in the family and in consequence tries to avoid the husband's interference in household tasks (1963: 183–184).

Underlying the above studies is an attempt to analyze the shift from the traditional familial division of labor to the contemporary pattern. Nojiri (1974a: 296–322) attempts to incorporate another way of relating the conjugal role responsibility pattern to the pattern of family social network, so as to provide a fuller picture of the Japanese pattern in flux. She found that there was fairly clear-cut task-labelling by sex—"to earn money" being the sole predominantly male-oriented task. The general area of child socialization and the tasks involving extra-familial units were slightly more male-oriented than the domestic, housekeeping tasks which were entirely managed by the wife. Social class had no influence on the couple's task-sharing pattern but the wife's employment showed a significant effect. The relation between the conjugal role responsibility pattern and family network was found to be not significant. These findings apparently indicate that the division of labor by sex is a consistent feature, independent of other variables, of Japanese families.

Family tasks include those related to family transactions with other social units. In the process of post-war industrialization and democratization, the disorganization of traditional aspects of kinship system has been recognized, and a move from patriarchy toward egalitarianism in the family and kinship groups has been identified. These trends, however, did not necessarily mean the diminishing of the functions of kin groups. Transactions between the family and kin groups continued to be important though the pattern of transactions changed. It is in this area that we find a change in the roles wives play. At least among the urban families, the categories of kin they interact with are on the wife's side more than on the husband's, and on the sisters' more than on the brothers' (Nojiri, 1974b: 61 and 67); the trend is in accordance with findings by Koyama (1970): 318–337) and Morioka (1968). A common factor underlying several studies suggests that kin linkages are selective rather than ascribed today (Nojiri, 1974b: 117), and the selection is made by the wife who is in charge of household management. Under the principle of the patrilineal *Ie* system, the emphasis used to be placed on the husband's kin. Though the change is within the framework of a clear-cut division of labor by sex, the lack of discriminatory emphasis of kin lineage by sex in the area of family transaction is an indicator of changing women's status in the family. As well it must be noted that an increasing number of husbands actually participate in household activities, and this may eventually encourage men to accept domestic roles as a part of their "decent" role construct.

Family life cycle studies demonstrate a prolonged post-parental stage for present-day parents. Implications of the change in the post-parental period are serious. After having been devoted to husbands and children, women, in their forties, face a situation in which they must now find their aims in life. They have always been with and lived for someone without questioning such a way of life. Suddenly, they must make their own decisions about themselves. This is a new experience for most Japanese women.

Opinion surveys all indicate the accepted notion of the changing women's career in accordance with the present-day family life cycle: that is, women should work before marriage; quit working at marriage or at the birth of the first child; return to the marketplace after child-rearing (e.g., Research Committee, 1974).

The high level of education is often correlated with a modern norm (e.g., Rodman, 1967: 324). As we have indicated, the majority of girls in higher educational institutions in Japan are in junior colleges which aim to produce either the "good-wife, wise-mother" with training in all-round liberal arts and home economics or the semi-professionals in the occupations labelled as "suitable for females." Four-year girls' colleges offer such specialties as home economics, literature, and some sciences. In co-educational universities, we find a high degree of girls concentrated in the Faculties of Letters and Education. Thus, the programs in higher educational institutions are not intended to train girls to become intelligent citizens (Fujii *et al.*, 1973; Okada *et al.*, 1975).

Since the cost of education has been rising, the girls who are able to obtain a college education, particularly in private women's colleges, are from relatively well-to-do families. Thus they feel little need for work after graduation as a source of income, and the high level of education is not necessarily related to a high degree of participation in work of any kind. (National Institute of Occupations, 1976: 44 and 46).

College education for girls is often considered an extension of preparatory training for a good marriage. Sex-typing of academic opportunities is quite clear-cut as in the case of domestic tasks (Ministry of Education, 1975: 228–229). Educational programs tend to function in the direction of the reinforcement of sexism.

Participation in gainful work is a promise of some degree of economic independence which is a basis for individual autonomy. For this reason, as we have seen, an increasing number of Japanese women are participating in the world of work.

Table 5

Monthly Salary for Employed Women

Year	Total Monthly Pay in Cash	Ratio to Male Worker
1955	9,479	44.4
1960	12,414	42.8
1965	22,275	47.8
1970	45,810	50.9
1973	76,324	53.1
1974	97,392	53.9

Source: Women's and Minors' Bureau, Ministry of Labor, *Fujin Rodo no Jitsujo*, 1975: 63.

Now, how are these women treated in the labor force? We will highlight the income and the retirement systems to characterize the problem in the Japanese cultural context. The gap between the average salary for men and women narrowed between 1960 and 1974, from 100: 43 to 100: 54. The low pay for women's work is partly due to the employment system in Japan—life-time employment based on the seniority principle. The longer one works for an employer, the higher the pay, and women usually stay on the job for fewer years than men. Another factor which causes the low average income for women is that the majority of employed women work in occupations with low pay.

The beginning salary differs by sex, and the level of education shows differential gap-patterns. The largest gap between the sexes in the beginning salary exists among the university graduates. These figures (Table 6) mean that men's salaries go up in relation to the rise in the level of education under the Japanese employment system, but the same is not true for women. Female university graduates are not placed in positions in which they can utilise their educational backgrounds. The majority of the females are doing the type of work that junior college or even high-school graduates are doing. Businesses have very little demand for female university graduates.

Table 6

Ratio of Female Graduates' Beginning Salary to Male (Male=100)

Year	1960	1965	1970	1971	1972	1973	1974
Junior High School Graduate	94.6	101.6	97.1	95.1	97.5	96.3	93.9
Senior High School Graduate	89.5	95.4	93.0	92.4	93.4	93.8	91.8
Junior College Graduate	89.8	97.0	93.6	92.2	95.4	96.4	92.1
University Graduate	95.7	94.6	83.7	84.0	85.0	86.0	89.8

Source: Women's and Minors' Bureau, Ministry of Labor, *Fujin Rodo no Jitsujo,* 1975: 64.

Women in public services and teaching receive equal pay with men, but the limited advancement opportunities for women result in a widening of the income gap in the later stages of their careers.

According to the Survey on Employment Management by the Ministry of Labor (1974), 67% of the business corporations in the sample of 13,238 had policies on retirement and 30% had sex-based differential retirement policies. The male retirement age was set at 55 years while the majority of corporations set the female retirement age lower than that for the male. Two and a half percent had a policy of not keeping women who were 35 years old or over (Women's and Minors' Bureau, 1975: 74).

The low pay and the early retirement system for female employees are the effects of deliberate discriminatory policies by the business leaders. This deliberate discrimination seems to be rooted in the notion that female labor is less productive than the male's, which is strongly related to the notion that "women's place is in the home."

When roles of women are not specifically defined by society, women have to make choices in defining their roles and thus there is a variation in their role patterns. If women are not trained to make choices, there is bound to be confusion. Choice accompanies responsibility which is a necessary condition for independence.

In the role patterns of Japanese women, there is one called the "single-role" pattern, and another called "dual-role." When a wife holds the role of a full-time housewife, she has the single-role pattern. When a wife holds a role related to gainful activities as well as the role of a housewife, she has the dual-role pattern. We cannot assume that either one provides a higher status for the wife because of the many different motives for taking the single- or dual-role. The dual-role pattern is often related to a lower status for the wife because of the conditions working women must face. Participation in work activities does not ease the burden of domestic responsibilities.

When women are expected to pursue their goals within the framework of the family, achievement outside of the family does not necessarily contribute to the elevation of their status. A high regard is the reward for women who play family roles as well as their roles related to external achievements successfully. However, choosing to separate from her husband rather than leave her job, when she receives a transfer order from her employer, is still beyond a career wife's conception. Regardless of the contributions women make in the economic sector of the society, their performances have not eased the burdens they have to cope with at home.

Conclusion

We conclude that all the demographic and resources variables can theoretically operate as promoters of change toward equality only when the sex role ideology is flexible. In the case of Japan, the sex role ideology is rigid and is the underlying factor in determining the nature of the conjugal family ideology as well as other change-promoting variables. The most fundamental ascription—sex by birth—is the aspect which operates as a factor sustaining a caste-like principle in Japanese society.

REFERENCES

Aoi, K.
    1974 "Seimondai Saiko (A Reconsideration on Sex Issues)," in Kazoku Mondai Kenkyuka (ed.), *Gendai Nihon no Kazoku* (The Modern Japanese Family), 117–138.

Blood, R. O. and Wolfe, D. M.
    1960 *Husbands and Wives: The Dynamics of Married Living.* The Free Press.

Dore, R. P. (ed.)
    1967 *Aspects of Social Change in Modern Japan.* Princeton University Press.

Fujii, et al.
    1973 *Nihon no Joshi Kyoiku* (Education of Women in Japan). Domesu.

Goode, W. J.
    1963 *World Revolution and Family Pattersn.* The Free Press.
    1969 "Family Patterns and Human Rights," in Hadden and Borgatta (eds.), *Marriage and the Family,* 605–614. Peacock Publishers. (Originally in International Social Science Journal, 23 (1966), 41–54.

Institute of Population Problems
    1960 *Selected Statistics Concerning Woman Workers in Japan.* Research Series No. 193. Ministry of Health and Welfare.

Kaji, E.
    1975 "The Invisible Proletariat: Working Women in Japan," in White Paper on Sexism-Task Force (ed.), *Japanese Women Speak Out.* WPSTF, 26–39.

Koyama, T.
    1967 *Gendai Kazoku no Yakuwari Kozo* (Role Structure of the Modern Family). Baihukan.
    1970 "A Rural Urban Comparison of Kinship Relations in Japan," in Hill and König (eds.), *Families in East and West: Socialization Process and Kinship Ties.* Mouton, 318–337.

Lebra, J., et al.
    1976 *Women in Changing Japan.* Westview Press.

Masuda, K.
    1965 "Gendai Toshikazoku niokeru Fufu oyobi Shutome no Seiryoku Kozo (Conjugal and

Mother-in-law Power Structure of Modern Urban Family)." *Konan Daigaku Bungaku Ronshu* (Konan University Periodical) 27: 49–66.
    1970 "Kateiishiki Chosa no Kaisetsu (An Intespretation of a Family Consciousness Study)," *Kobe-shi Chosa* 14: 77–78.

Ministry of Education
    1975 *Kyoiku Hakusho* (White Paper on Education).

Ministry of Labor
    1974 *Koyo Kanri Chosa* (Survey on Employment Management).

Morioka, K.
    1968 "Tokyo Kinko Danchi Kazoku no Seikatsu-shi to Shakai-sanka (Life History and Social Participation of Tokyo Suburban Family)." *International Christian University Social Sciences Journal* 7: 199–277.
    1973 *Kazoki Shukiron* (Family Life Cycle). Baihukan.

Morioka, K. (ed.)
    1974 *Shin Kozoku Kankeigaku* (A New Approach to Family Relations). Churkyo Shuppan.

National Institute of Occupations
    1976 *Fujin no Shokugyo to Raifu Saikuru* (Women's Occupations and Life Cycle).

Nojiri, Y.
    1974a "The Pattern of Conjugal Role Responsibility in Japan," in M.B. Sussman (ed.), *Cross-National Family Research:* Report on Conceptual Development: Pilot Testing; Field and Administrative Issues. Submitted to Institute of Child Health and Human Development, Washington D.C., 296–322.
    1974b *Family and Social Network in Modern Japan: A Study of an Urban Sample.* Unpublished doctoral dissertation, Case Western Reserve University.

Okada, M., et al.
    1975 *Senmonshoku no Joseitachi* (Women in Professions). Aki.

Prime Minister's Office
    1973 *Fujin ni kansuru Ishiki Chosa* (Survey on Women).

Research Committee on Women
    1974 *Gendai Nihon Josei no Ishiki to Kodo* (Opinions and Behaviors of Modern Japanese Women).

Rodman, H.
    1967 "Marital Power in France, Greece, Yugoslavia, and the United States: A Cross-National Discussion," *Journal of Marriage and the Family,* 29: 320–324.
    1972 "Marital power and the theory of resources in cultural context," in: Eugen Lupri and Günter Lüschen (eds.), Special Issue of *Journal of Comparative Family Studies* 3 (Spring): 51–69.

Vogel, E.
    1963 *Japan's New Middle Class.* University of California Press.

Women's Organizations Federation
    1975 *Fujin Hakusho* (White Paper on Women). Nihon Fujin Dantai Rengokai.

Women's and Minors' Bureau
    1975 *Fujin Rodo no Jitsujo* (Present Status of Working Women). Ministry of Labor.

PART THREE
WOMEN IN SCANDINAVIAN AND SOCIALIST COUNTRIES

A. SCANDINAVIA

The Changing Role of Swedish Women in Family and Society

JAN TROST
Uppsala University, Uppsala, Sweden

Introduction

THE TITLE implies that there have been changes in the roles of the Swedish woman. There is no doubt that this is the case. The degree to which and the speed with which changes have occurred, however, are somewhat more difficult to evaluate. At the same time, if women's roles change, men's roles should change too, especially if women's new roles begin to invade areas previously held by the men. Those of us who know something about roles, know that changes in one role in society have effects upon other roles — changes in one role bring about changes in other roles. Not only are changes in women's and men's roles of importance but also changes in girls' and boys' roles. According to observation and experience, attempts to change adult roles have often been premised on changes in the roles of children and adolescents.

This paper will present some data related to gender-roles in the family, both children's gender-roles and the gender-roles of the adult members of a family. As well, it will give some examples of child socialization and child rearing, of division of labour between the spouses and of gender-roles in relation to divorce. We will also present some aggregate data from the national level. This will provide evidence as to changes in female employment rates, fertility rates, abortion rates, the use of contraceptives as well as pertinent information on governmental policies in Sweden.

The author concludes that the changes have been very small and really of little genuine importance and relevance. Many of the changes are changes that are easy to accept in a traditional society such as Sweden's. In many parts of the world Sweden is looked upon as a radical society and as a society with a high degree of equality between the genders. However, the reality from the inside is somewhat different and it is evident that many of the radical ideas and many of the equalities are given no more than lipservice and thus are only working on the surface.

It would be comforting to be able to interpret this somewhat depressing view as an indicator of the well-known fact that the more one has the more one wants. In other words, when one's expectations are fulfilled, one always finds new expectations to be fulfilled. It is doubtful, however, if so many of the past expectations have been fulfilled that the new expectations are irrelevant or some kind of expendable or luxury extra.

Child socialization

Brun-Gulbrandsen (1958) studied the degree of gender-role socialization among eight and eleven-year-old boys and girls in Oslo, Norway. He collected data through an interview, where, among other things, he told the children a story about Per (male name) and Kari (female name) "being of the same age as you." These two children were twins and the story told what the twins did, beginning when they got up in the morning and ending when they went to bed in the evening. Quite purposely, the story regularly said that one of them did something but did not tell the listener which one did it. Every time one of these points was reached, the interviewer asked the listener, "Which one did it, Per or Kari? For example, the story began by saying "One of the twins made the bed in the morning." The question was, "Which one did so?". The respondent answered either Per or Kari.

In 1968 data were collected with the same technique as the one used by Brun-Gulbrandsen in Uppsala, Sweden by Dahl (1968). Her respondents were not only eight and eleven-year-olds but six and fifteen-year-olds, too. The main aim of the Dahl study was to compare the situation in 1968 with the situation in 1958 as reflected by the Brun-Gulbrandsen data and as well, to compare not only two age classes but four age classes as regards the degree of gender-role socialization. When the Dahl study was planned in 1968 we (i.e., Dahl and the author in the role of supervisor) assumed that the older the children were, the "better" they would have learned the traditional gender-roles. Another assumption was that the Swedish data, for two reasons, would show a lesser degree of emphasis on traditional gender-roles than would the Norwegian data: (1) Since there had been a gender-role discussion during the decade between the two studies, this discussion should have had some impact. (2) Since Norway is somewhat more "conservative" than Sweden, the gender-role distinction should be less marked in the second study. The Swedish data showed that those in the youngest category were the least conservative with 77 percent conformist answers. Next came the eight-year-olds with 83 percent conformist answers, then the eleven-year-olds with 92 percent. Those in the oldest category are not conparable with the three younger ones because the three younger age categories had only two alternatives when answering while the oldest category had three. However, our interpretation is that if the data had been comparable, the oldest group would not have been less gender-role bound than the eleven-year-olds. (The expression "conformist answer" may need an explanation. An answer is "conformist" if it has been given by a majority of the respondents. This means with two alternative answers the percentage of "conformist" answers must exceed 50 percent and with three alternative answers it must be at least 34 percent.)

It would seem that the assumption about the increasing gender-role socialization is confirmed by the Swedish data and that the Norwegian data show the same trend. The second assumption, that the Swedish data would show a lesser degree of emphasis on traditional gender-roles than the Norwegian data, is not confirmed by our study. In the Norwegian data 80 percent of the eight-year-olds give conformist answers while ten years later 83 percent of the Swedish eight-year-olds give conformist answers. In Norway, 89 percent of the eleven-year-olds gave conformist answers while 92 percent of the Swedish children did the same. Thus, there is no important difference between the Swedish and the Norwegian data in spite of the ten years between the two studies. If there are any differences between them they are in the opposite direction, as was assumed.

To our knowledge no study of this type has been done later than 1968. However, it is our hope to do one in a couple of years in order to have fresh figures for comparison. Of course the assumption will be that the past decade will have implanted ideas in the minds of children and young people that will make them less gender-role conservative. As other data in this chapter show, remarkable changes have occurred during the latest decade and the debate during the sixties must have had an influence upon parents, teachers, and the children, either directly or indirectly.

Child rearing

As mentioned above, the studies by Brun-Gulbrandsen (1958) and Dahl (1968) both showed the same tendency toward a strong gender-role differentiation in the minds of the youngsters. A couple of years ago Nordlund and Trost (1976) collected data from a Swedish sample of mothers with small children. They asked the respondents three questions about how serious it is if a child, aged 5–6 years, pilfers at home or pilfers in stores and three questions about how important it is that a child aged 5–6 years thank, greet, bow, and have good table manners. Nordlund and Trost did not want to specify the sex of the child but did so in an indirect way that does not overestimate the differences between the gender-role expectations of the mothers.

The results of this study by Nordlund and Trost are summarized in Table 1. Although the number of individuals upon which the table is calculated is low there is a clear tendency on the part of mothers of boys to count the activities as less serious and more normal than the mothers of girls do. The differences about the importance of three types of behaviour are not that clear but the tendency is in the same expected direction, i.e., that boys can be allowed to behave more "negatively" than girls can.

Table 1

Mothers whose oldest child is 4–5 years old

	How serious is it according to your opinion if a child aged 5–6 years lies?					
	Very serious	Fairly serious	Not very serious	It is normal	Σ	n
Boy	3.0	9.1	30.3	57.6	100.0	33
Girl	0	26.1	34.8	39.1	100.0	23

	How serious is it according to your opinion if a child aged 5–6 years pilfers at home?					
	Very serious	Fairly serious	Not very serious	It is normal	Σ	n
Boy	9.1	24.2	45.5	21.2	100.0	33
Girl	13.0	34.8	30.4	21.7	100.0	23

	How serious is it according to your opinion if a child aged 5–6 years pilfers in stores?					
	Very serious	Fairly serious	Not very serious	It is normal	Σ	n
Boy	21.2	51.5	21.2	6.1	100.0	33
Girl	45.5	46.4	18.2	0	100.0	22

	How important is it according to your opinion that a child aged 5–6 years thanks?					
	Very important	Fairly important	Not very important	Not important at all	Σ	n
Boy	9.1	45.5	42.4	3.0	100.0	33
Girl	0	69.6	30.4	0	100.0	23

	How important is it according to your opinion that a child aged 5–6 years greets?					
	Very important	Fairly important	Not very important	Not important at all	Σ	n
Boy	6.1	42.4	45.5	6.1	100.0	33
Girl	0	52.2	47.8	0	100.0	23

	How important is it according to your opinion that a child aged 5–6 years has good table manners?					
	Very important	Fairly important	Not very important	Σ	n	
Boy	3.0	63.6	33.3	100.0	33	
Girl	0	69.6	30.4	100.0	23	

Source: Nordlund & Trost, 1976.

Division of labour between the spouses

According to traditional gender-roles the mother is the spouse who takes care of, and has the responsibility for, the child or the children, in most respects. In the study by Nordlund and Trost (1976) the respondents fulfilling four criteria were asked which one of the two parents *most often* took care of the children in seven respects. The four criteria were: being a woman; being a mother to at least one child younger than 10 years; living together with a man who was gainfully employed; and being herself gainfully employed. The result shows that 97 percent of the mothers claimed that the responsibility for the children's clothes was mostly with the mother; that the mother in 80 percent of the cases had the responsibility for the children's food; that the mother in 74 percent of the cases mostly stayed at home when the children were ill or went with the children to the physician or dentist; that the mother in 53 percent of the cases took care of the children at night.

Table 2

Mothers with at least one child ten-years-old or younger, living together with the father of the child, in families where both spouses are gainfully employed, differentiating between part-time and full-time employment among the mothers

	The mother's employment	Mostly the father	Mostly the mother	Both	n
Who takes care of the children in the night?	Full-time	12.5	51.6	35.9	64
	Part-time	3.2	54.8	41.9	62
Who stays at home when the children are ill?	Full-time	5.1	61.0	33.9	59
	Part-time	3.4	86.4	10.2	59
Who consoles the children?	Full-time	0.0	28.1	71.9	64
	Part-time	4.8	41.9	53.2	62
Who plays with the children?	Full-time	15.6	14.1	70.1	64
	Part-time	11.3	29.9	59.7	62
Who has the responsibility for the children's food?	Full-time	0.0	65.8	34.4	64
	Part-time	1.6	93.5	4.8	62
Who has the responsibility for the children's clothes?	Full-time	0	93.8	6.3	64
	Part-time	0	100	0	62
Who goes to the physician/dentist with the children?	Full-time	4.8	68.3	27.0	63
	Part-time	4.9	78.7	16.4	61

Source: Nordlund & Trost, 1976.

The only two instances where the answer "mostly the mother" was less frequent were to the question, "who consoles the children" — only 35 percent of the mothers said that it was mostly the mother — and the question, "who plays with the children" where only 21 percent of the mothers said it was mostly the mother. To further emphasize the traditional gender-roles the mothers answered "mostly the father" only in 0 to 14 percent of the cases, while in the remaining cases the answer was "both parents equally often."

Nordlund and Trost did not ask the fathers the same questions for the simple reason that their sample consisted of subscribers to a monthly magazine called *We Parents* and 93 percent of the subscribers were women. If the fathers had been given a chance to respond, their answers would probably have been less traditional since many more of the fathers than of the mothers would be likely to claim that the responsibilities in these specific cases rested with "both parents equally often."

Since about half of the gainfully employed women with small children are employed only part-time, Nordlund and Trost assumed that part-time working mothers would, more often than full-time working mothers, answer according to the traditional stereotype. There are two reasons for this assumption. One of them is that if one of the parents is working part-time and the other one full-time it seems reasonable that the one working part-time should take more responsibility for the home and the children than the one working full-time. The other reason is that it seems probable that if the woman is working only part-time, this is because she does not want to work full-time, which again is an indicator of traditional gender-roles. The data in Table 2 show, however, that there are very small differences (according to the women's perceptions and responses in the questionnaire) between families where the wife/mother is working full-time and the families where the wife/mother is working only part-time.

Divorce

The divorce rate can be used as an indicator of change or lack of change in gender-roles in a society. An increase in the divorce rate may be an effect of changes in the law; for instance, in Italy where divorce had not existed because of the law forbidding it. As soon as the law was changed, an "enormous" increase in the divorce rate took place. With no changes in the divorce law but as a result of gender-role liberalization, a divorce rate can easily reflect an increase in the economic and social independence between married couples. In a society where, as in Sweden, the male gender by tradition has been the dominant one the divorce rate can be seen as an indicator of change in the degree of dependence of women. As is illustrated in Table 3 the divorce rate steadily increased during the first half of this century, i.e., during the period of industrialization, was stable during the fifties and until the middle of the sixties, and then started to increase enormously. During the nine year period from 1965–1973 the divorce rate increased by 67 percent, i.e., from 5.1 to 8.5 per one thousand married women.

When the divorce rate is calculated for men aged 20–54 (which is the age span when divorce is most frequent) the increase during the last decade has been 78 percent and it is spread almost equally in all age-classes: the lowest increase is in the oldest age-bracket, 50–54, where it is only 50 percent and the highest in the age-bracket 35–39, where the increase is 82 percent. A similar comparison for women shows that the total divorce rate has increased by 78 percent and in the various age-brackets the data for women show about the same tendency as for men: the lowest increase was in the highest age bracket 50–54 years with 36 percent; in the ages 45–49 the increase was 47 percent; and the highest increase was in the age class 30–34 with 98 percent. It is hard to prove that a change in the divorce rate is an indicator of gender-role equalization. However, if we look upon divorce as something not "unnatural," the paradigm can be used to explain why people do *not* divorce. If we look at it this way, then we look at the bonds keeping the marriage working as a unit in spite of all the problems that are bound to arise. This means that an increase in the divorce rate can be seen as the effect of reduced bonds and these bonds are of different types. They may have to do with social control, with economic matters, practical matters, etc.

In Sweden today it is easier for a man to divorce than it was some decades ago. The reason for this is the change in the law covering alimony. Earlier the practice in court was to grant the ex-wife a generous alimony, while today this is very uncom-

Table 3

Number of divorces per one thousand married women in Sweden

Year	Rate	Year	Rate
1901/1910	0.5	1964	5.0
1911/1915	0.8	1965	5.1
1916/1920	1.1	1966	5.5
1921/1925	1.5	1967	5.6
1926/1930	1.9	1968	5.8
1931/1935	2.2	1969	6.4
1936/1940	2.6	1970	6.8
1941/1945	3.5	1971	7.1
1946/1950	4.6	1972	8.0
1951/1955	5.1	1973	8.5
1956/1960	5.0	1974	14.3*
1961	4.9	1975	13.6
1962	4.9		
1963	4.7		

* The enormous increase from 1973 to 1974 is to a very high extent due to the radical changes in the divorce law. Thus the increase is a technical increase and not a "real" increase.
Source: Trost, 1976.

mon. A study of cases in the Swedish courts (Trost, 1975) shows that the ex-husband had to pay alimony in only about 10 percent of the cases and in most cases the alimony payments extended over only a very few years.

The traditional gender-role differentiation still exists in Sweden as regards the custody of the children. According to the law the only consideration to be taken when deciding about the custody of the children in case of a divorce should be what is best for the children. This means that the idea of who is at fault has no relevance at all. It means that the wishes of the parents need not be taken into consideration. According to a recent study (Trost, 1975) the mother receives custody of the children in 86–90 percent of the cases, while the father is granted custody 10–14 percent of the time. Trost (1975: 117) shows furthermore that the younger the child, the less the probability for the father to have custody of the child after a divorce. The father gets custody in only four to seven percent of the cases when the child is younger than three years while in cases where the child is 16 years old or older, the father is granted custody 21–24 percent of the time.

While the court decides formally who shall have custody of the child, in reality in most cases the parents themselves decide and the court merely confirms what the parents have decided. In only about six percent of the cases involving children are the parents unable to agree and in these cases the court has to decide. In cases where the court decides, more of the children are placed in the custody of the father than in the cases where the parents decide: 20 percent of the children in the cases where the court decides are placed in care of the father and 80 percent are placed in care of the mother. From this one might conclude that the courts are less conservative than the people. This is, however, too hasty a conclusion. In almost all cases the courts do not decide without a special investigation which is made by the local authorities caring for children. Normally, the court agrees with what these authorities suggest. This implies that any trend toward a nontraditional treatment of the children is in the hands of the local authorities doing the investigation and not the courts.

Furthermore, when the parents decide themselves, they only seem to make the decision. What happens in most cases is that the parents discuss, perhaps quarrel, about the custody of the children yet both "know" that there is only a very small chance for the father to get custody. Therefore, their decision is a decision very much influenced by their perception of the courts' conservatism and traditionalism. If the parents find that they really cannot agree, they seek the advice of a lawyer and in most cases he will confirm that the father has only a very small chance of gaining custody since the lawyer will be well aware of the courts' traditionalism. Which proves again that the Thomas and Thomas (1928) theorem about the definition of the situation is valid: people do not act on what they want themselves but act on their "false" perceptions of the courts.

Employment

As can be seen in Table 4, the relative number of women in the labour force is lower than the relative number of men in all age groups except in the youngest where the figures are identical for both sexes. The difference between men and women as regards the relative number in the labour force is higher among the married than in the total population. This statement, however, is true only for ages below 35 years. As we see in Table 4 the difference between men and women in this respect

Table 4

Per cent of the population in the labour force during the first quarter of 1976 in Sweden

Age	Men	Women	Married men	Married women	Not married men	Not married women	With children younger than 7 years	
							men	women
16–19	53	53	72	62	53	53	95	40
20–24	81	73	91	64	80	76	97	58
25–34	95	72	98	67	92	82	98	63
35–44	97	78	99	76	90	76	99	61
45–54	95	76	97	75	86	78	97	49
55–64	82	50	85	49	70	53	86	37
65–74	16	7	17	6	13	7	0	0
16–74	79	59	83	60	73	59	98	61

Source: Table 1a in Arbetskraftsundersökningen första kvartalet, 1976.

Table 5

Relative number of women, with at least one child younger than 17 years, in the labour force, 1970

	Not in labour force	1–19 hours per week	20–34 hours per week	35–hours per week	Total
Married women					
Youngest child					
less than 3 years	58	12	13	17	100
3–6 years	47	16	17	19	99
7–16 years	34	16	24	27	101
At least one child younger than 17 years	44	15	19	22	100
Not married women					
Youngest child					
less than 3 years	45	7	14	35	101
3–6 years	22	8	16	54	100
7–16 years	18	7	16	59	100
At least one child younger than 17 years	27	7	15	51	100

Source: AKU arsmedeltal 1970.

is very small if we consider only unmarried men and women. When looking at the first part of the table we see that if the men or women have at least one child younger than seven years, the difference between the sexes becomes very important. It should be noted here that all women with a child are considered as "having a child" here but not all men are. This is due to the fact that if an unmarried cohabiting couple have children together only the mother is considered as "having children" since the father does not have the custody of the children in an unmarried cohabiting situation. The rate of couples living together with children is very high in Sweden (Trost, 1980). Of the men and women with at least one child younger than seven years old, only 43 percent of the women are employed full-time, while 93 percent of the men are. Among all men and women the corresponding figures show that 95 percent of those men are working full-time while only 57 percent of the women are working full-time.

The biased distribution of the occupations is still remarkable. Of all those women gainfully employed 22 percent are doing office work while only five percent of the men are; 11 percent of the women are employed in the manufacturing industry and others while as many as 43 percent of the men are; 24 percent of the women are engaged in service occupations while only five percent of the men are; 40 percent of the women are engaged in educational and health care occupations while only eight percent of the men are (AKU första kvartalet, 1976).

The data for 1970 as regards the relative number of women in the labour market in relation to the age of the youngest child show that for both married and unmarried women the relative number of women gainfully employed increases with the age of the youngest child. For married women there is almost no change in the relative number of women employed less than half-time no matter the age of the child but more women work half-time or more the higher the age of the youngest child. For unmarried women, however, there is an increase in the number of women working full-time according to the age of the youngest child, while about the same proportion of women irrespective of the age of the youngest child work less than full-time.

We find the same tendency in 1975 for both married and unmarried women. The relative number of women with children younger than 17 years in the labour market is higher in 1975 than in 1970. This is true for all three categories of working women as shown in Tables 5 and 6. As regards unmarried women, however, about the same relative number of women with children younger than 17 years are gainfully employed, but more are working part-time rather than full-time.

It should be noted, however, that many of the women classified here as unmarried are only formally unmarried. In reality many of them are cohabiting under marriage-like conditions with the father of the child. The reason why the rate of unmarried women gainfully employed is higher than the rate for married women results from many factors. One of the factors is that it is easier for unmarried women (not cohabiting) to keep a job outside the home than for those who are married because of the

Table 6

Relative number of women, with at least one child younger than 17 years, in the labour force, 1975

	Not in labour force	1–19 hours per week	20–34 hours per week	35–hours per week	Total
Married women					
Youngest child					
less than 3 years	44	14	24	18	100
3–6 years	39	17	23	21	100
7–16 years	23	15	31	31	100
At least one child younger					
than 17 years	32	16	27	26	101
Not married women					
Youngest child					
less than 3 years	39	10	23	28	100
3–6 years	23	10	24	42	99
7–16 years	14	9	22	55	100
At least one child younger					
than 17 years	25	10	23	43	101

Source: AKU arsmedeltal 1975.

fact that in almost all municipalities in Sweden it is very hard for married/cohabiting parents to get a place in the day-care system for the child. First in line for space in the day-care system are single parents. Another reason is that married women who divorce go from either unemployment to full-time employment for economic reasons. On the other hand, technically unmarried (noncohabiting) women with small children who marry, either have to quit their jobs because of the lack of space in the day-care system or have to find a family where the child or children can stay at least part-time.

The lack of data in Sweden showing the degree of employment of fathers of small children is an indicator of the lack of change for men while the data presented here shows the change, in a male-directed way, for women.

Fertility, contraceptives, and abortions

During the eighteenth and nineteenth century the crude fertility rate in Sweden was about 35 (35 births per one thousand of the mean population). At the end of the nineteenth century, however, the crude fertility rate started to decrease. The low rate of 13–14 caused politicians to react because of the alarm raised by the Myrdals (Myrdal & Myrdal, 1934). The result was, among other things, a law giving the woman the right to a leave of absence because of pregnancy and the birth of a child. It was not only a law giving the right to a leave of absence; it provided too for the state employee to receive the same salary as in a case of illness. (This family political reform work as a benefit to the family was started during the thirties.)

Other means besides the one mentioned were activities aimed at helping children and pregnant women and women with small children. These activities initiated by the government and parliament did not, however, increase the fertility rate. There was an increase in the fertility during the first part of the forties which led to the baby boom, a phenomenon in many countries all over the world. Since most of these countries had not introduced any specific family political program, we know that the baby boom was not an effect of governmental family policy. Since the peak in 1946 the fertility rate has declined with a small rise in the middle of the sixties, but since then there has been a steady decrease. Thus, the crude rate in 1975 was about 12 or stated in another way the net reproduction rate in 1975 was about .8.

Until 1964 the most common birth control practices in Sweden were coitus interruptus, the condom, the diaphragm and abstinence. From 1965 on, however, the birth control pill was available on the Swedish market. The reason for the late introduction of the pill was because it was forbidden until then because of the presumed risks. However, the pill was accepted with alacrity very soon after the introduction. Thus, as Larsson-Cohn and Trost (1970) have shown more than 20 percent of all fertile women were on the pill four years after the introduction. Even today, more than ten years after the introduction, about 27 percent of the women use the pill. About five years ago the IUD's were introduced in Sweden and the present estimate is that about 11 percent of the women use an IUD of some kind (Sundström, 1976).

Sterilization of men and women has not been looked upon as an acceptable contraceptive in Sweden. Some women (but very few men) have been sterilized. Starting January 1, 1976, however, sterilization was available free for both men and women aged 25 and older. Sterilization is free in two ways: everyone over 25 years of age has the right to be sterilized and it is free of charge.

We do not know yet what the practical use of the new sterilization law will be. The figures for the first six months of 1976 show that not more than about 2000 persons have been sterilized, almost half of them men. This means about one sterilization per 1000 men and women aged 25–50 years. If this rate continues into the future it will mean that in the long run five percent of the men and women 25–50 years old will be sterilized.

Official policy

It is possible to present here only some of the data about the legal acts and other policies in Sweden that relate to gender-roles. Until 1921, for example, when a new marriage act came into effect, married women remained the wards of their husbands. In 1921 women obtained the right to vote and in 1925 an act was passed giving women equal rights with men to hold posts in the government service. In the midthirties many social reforms regarding gender equality were introduced. A national pensions act was passed in 1935 giving equal pensions to men and women. In 1936 an act was passed concerning pregnancy and confinement leave. This right was valid for *both* married and unmarried women. In 1939 a law was introduced stating that an employee should not be dismissed from employment on grounds of betrothal (engagement), marriage, pregnancy, or confinement.

As noted earlier the decrease in the birth rate stimulated a program of family policy reforms. Public assistance to families with children took the form of collective measures of various kinds and of grants tied to certain types of consumption. In the middle of the forties these grants were supplemented by a cash allowance for each child, irrespective of the income of the parents. The new family policy dealt not only with economic matters but also with the health of mothers and their children. Preventive medical care for mothers and children with free maternity nursing was introduced by a law of 1937. Mother and child clinics were started in which medical examinations were conducted by physicians and midwives. (It should be noted that in Sweden the normal birth of a child takes place in a hospital ward with the help of midwives; only in serious cases is the help of a physician provided.) From 1937 on free medicines were give to pregnant women.

During the thirties and the forties the education system was reformed in many respects as well. For instance, from 1946 all textbooks and other school materials were free for all elementary school children. The state encouraged the local authorities to provide meals for children attending the compulsory schools. This was to help the housewife and to give her a better chance to take part in the labour market, as well to provide a good technical and physical environment for the children. Today free school-lunches are served in all compulsory schools and in many noncompulsory schools (high schools).

Abortion was touched on earlier but mention must be made here of the first law passed in 1938 which permitted abortion on some grounds: medical, socialmedical, rape and eugenic grounds.

During the forties Sweden started to build day-nurseries, leisure-time homes and nursery schools. State subsidies were given to municipalities for building and running these institutions to which parents contributed in proportion to their income. This means that families with low incomes pay nothing or almost nothing for having their children in this kind of a system. It should, however, be noted that in Sweden today only a small minority of the children under school-age have the chance to be in daynurseries, leisure-time homes, etc. because of the shortage of these institutions. This shortage is partly due to the very high standards set by these institutions. They have as an average very high technical/hygenic standards and the teacher-pupil ratio is about one to three. With the high costs of salaries and social insurance in Sweden this means that space for each child is very expensive. There are long lines of children waiting for a space in these systems. The selection of children is made on social and economic grounds, thus children of one-parent families come first as do children in families with a very low income and children of immigrant parents.

Many other decisions have been taken concerning family policy but only some of them have a direct bearing on the changing roles of women. An equal pay principle in state service was established in 1947. This means equal pay for men and women for the same job and today all positions in the state hierarchy are available to both men and women. The only exception is the military service; women cannot obtain military posts either in fighting or nonfighting positions. (In 1958 women were allowed to become priests.)

In 1960 the largest trade union in Sweden and the Swedish employers confederation agreed on equal pay for men and women doing the same job.

Swedish legislation makes no distinction between men and women as regards rights and obligations except for a few fairly unimportant conditions for the majority of the population. One of the exceptions is military service.

The three biggest employees' organizations in Sweden (Swedish Confederation of Trade Unions, The Central Organization of Salaried Employees, and the Swedish Confederation of Professional Associations) have permanent committees and working groups aimed at striving for an equalization of gender-roles, especially in the labour force. The Swedish Employers' Confederation together with the employees' organizations have a special joint committee dealing with the question of gender-equality at work.

What is mentioned above would seem to show that, on the formal level, men and women are almost one-hundred-percent equal. This does not mean, however, that this equality exists in reality. Everyone knows that there is still much to be done in order to achieve a society where the gender-roles are completely equal. Even while this is being written a discussion is going on over whether Sweden should have a law giving the individual—being a woman or a man—the opportunity to go to court in order to fight for ones' right as regards equality in employment. The opponents claim that such a law will just preserve the differences between well-educated, upper-middle-class women and those who do not have the knowledge and courage to fight for their rights. The defendants of the idea claim that such a law is *one* of the ways of working toward an equality of the sexes and, furthermore, that the effects and the importance of a law lie in its usefulness as a guideline for everyday life and not only in its provision for a battle in court.

All political parties in Sweden and all organizations of different kinds strive for equalization but in different ways and with different intensity, some of them only paying lip-service, and some initiating successful action.

Conclusions

As this paper indicates the roles of women in society and in the family have changed considerably. As one indicator of these changes we have considered the employment rate of women. We have found that the relative number of women being gainfully employed has increased. Not only has the rate increased for women with teenagers or older children but also to a very great extent for women with small children. Although about half of the women are employed part-time and half full-time, we interpret this change as a liberalization of the female role. Today the woman, even a woman with small children, has improved identity, not only as a mother but also as a human being. The high employment rate is, in our view, not only a reflection of financial needs or the need for luxury consumption but the need for self-realization, self-identity and liberalization. In spite of the formal and responsible day-care system in Sweden there is an enormous shortage of places. Because the first chance is given to one-parent families or families with a low income, families with two parents and a reasonable income cannot find a space for their child or children. Therefore these two-parent families and families with higher income have to make arrangements for someone to take care of the children if both parents are gainfully employed. There are various solutions to this problem, but most of them are fairly expensive and questionable. The point to be made is that the economy *per se* is not the basic reason for the high employment rate of women. If it were, women would not put up with the extra burdens that employment brings.

The fertility rate has, as we have shown, decreased and the fewer number of children born are born later in a woman's life and during a shorter timespan. This means that many women in the twenties will finish their education and occupational training and find a job with a "tenure position" before they give birth to their first child. In order to keep their position in the labour market they take a leave of absence after the birth of the child, a leave of between seven and twelve months (which is the time during which they will receive almost full payment) after which they return to work. They may then give birth to another child, take the same amount of leave of absence and then re-enter the labour force again. This is a common phenomenon for all types of female workers; blue-collar workers as well as white-collar workers. The low fertility rate, the shorter timespan and the "delayed" birth of a child may properly be taken as indicators of changes in the female roles.

We have remarked on changes in the use of contraceptives and the use of legal abortions. Some twelve years ago women did not have the pill or the IUD, and the diaphragm was not very commonly used. Therefore, the use of a contraceptive was mostly the man's responsibility, i.e., the condom and coitus interruptus. The non-contraceptive solution was the woman's responsibility, i.e., abortion. The sexually negative contraceptives were in the hands of women—abstinence and use of rhythm. The number of legal abortions was quite low but the number of illegal abortions was probably quite high. Estimates of about twenty years ago suggest that Sweden had between 10,000 and 100,000 illegal abortions every year compared to about 100,000 live births. The number of legal abortions was 2000–3000 (Table 7).

Today illegal abortions are probably virtually nil and the legal abortions seem to be settled at the level of slightly more than 30,000 per annum. The relative decrease in the abortion rate—the total of illegal and legal abortions—is almost certainly due to the more effective and female-controlled contraceptives: the pill and the IUD.

Table 7

Number of legal abortions in Sweden

Year	Number	Year	Number
1939	439	1960	2792
40	506	61	2909
41	496	62	3205
42	568	63	3528
43	703	64	4671
44	1088		
		65	6208
45	1623	66	7254
46	2378	67	9703
47	3534	68	10940
48	4585	69	13735
49	5303		
50	5889	70	16100
		71	19250
51	6328	72	24170
52	5322	73	25990
53	4915	74	30000
54	5089		
55	4562	75	32000
56	3851		
57	3386		
58	2823		
59	3071		

Source: Hälso-och sjukvård, various years.

The fact that contraceptives have become more and more a woman's responsibility has been discussed extensively and many debaters argue that this means too high a burden for women and too little responsibility for men. On the other hand, some maintain that this means a liberalization and equalization of women in the sense that women have the right to decide if they want to become pregnant or not—they are, after all, the ones who have most of the problems with an unwanted pregnancy. According to the latter point of view a society that allows the female full control over the use of contraceptives means a society that gives a very high degree of power to women and thus changes the whole gender-role balance.

We have shown that the frequency of divorce has increased. An increase in the divorce rate is *per se* no indicator of changed gender-roles but the evidence suggests that the increase in Swedish society during the last ten years can be seen as an indicator of changed gender-roles. To a much greater extent today than earlier both the man and the woman are supposed to take care of themselves independently of the ex-spouse. However, the law has changed to some extent in this respect. Couples who want a divorce do not have to show any type of evidence to the court to indicate why a divorce should be allowed. The simple fact that one of the spouses claims for a divorce is sufficient for the court to decide (though in some cases with a six months' delay).

In practice and in law it is quite rare for the ex-husband to have to pay alimony to the ex-wife. It seems, too, as if the public opinion has moved in this same direction. No hard evidence is, however, available in this respect. The discussion among experts deals more with the problem of men having to pay alimony and child-support rather than with women's problems.

After divorce the woman will either find a job or live on social subsidies—which certainly is nothing to be ashamed of in Sweden today. The man, however, with alimony and child-support payments very often finds himself in an extremely serious economic situation when he has to pay large amounts of money every month and perhaps, at the same time support a new family or start a new household. As Eriksson (1976) has shown, it is a difficult economic and social situation for a large number of divorced men. Many argue that it is not reasonable for a woman to be dependent on a man after divorce, and that it is the man who has to pay for the marriage many years after its dissolution. The alimony thus is to some extent equivalent to paying a fine for annulling a civil contract.

We have shown that the society as a whole has over the last several decades made many attempts to equalize the gender-roles for men and women and even to change their content in various respects. So, our conclusion from the facts is that female gender-roles have changed considerably during the last few years in Sweden. This is not equivalent to saying that the change has been as rapid as some have wanted.

On the other hand, however, our data on division of labour in the household and on child socialization do not give evidence of familial changes to the same degree. Thus the division of labour, according to all studies available to us, has changed very little during the last decades. Our data show that the child socialization, too, follows the old traditional lines of thought: socializing the girls to be feminine and the boys to be masculine in all respects. Many of us who follow this pattern as parents defend ourselves by claiming that it is not right to force a child to be different from his/her playmates and so come to look upon himself/herself and his/her family as different and even deviant from other children and other children's situation.

On the verbal level most Swedes who are active in child socialization activities seem to be very radical and argue for changes in the gender-roles towards equalization, but in reality they act differently. This means that the children will grow up to be more and more tied to the traditional gender-roles. Evidence of this can be found in many instances, e.g., when children choose topics at school; when they choose occasional training and occupation; etc. At the same time society claims and demands equality, which is bound to produce some kind of a norm conflict and a risk of anomie for teenagers and even young adults.

The picture, perhaps slightly exaggerated, seems to be this. The child is socialized into the traditional gender-roles and not until the child has become a "full" member in society can he/she start changing his/her own gender-role. Thus when a young man or a young woman has got a job with a "tenure" position he/she can start the changing process. Before that time, however, the young adult or the child cannot follow the changes in gender-role because of the risk of being "deviant"—deviant from the playmates and the norms of the adult society. This somewhat pessimistic view may not be held by all but in our opinion it reflects what has been happening and what is still going on. However, it does not mean any prophecy that the process of change will continue to move in the same direction. A more optimistic point of view would be to believe that the children will *not* have a feeling of anomie or see a conflict in norms but will realize that there are usually different norms and that in a process of change there are always opposite norms. Knowing that norms may be in opposition to one another does not have to mean a state of anomie; it may mean simply taking a stand for one norm or the other.

REFERENCES

Brun-Gulbrandsen, Sverre
    1958   *Kjønsrolle og Assoialitet.* Oslo (mimeo).
Dahl, Gunvor
    1968   *Könsrollsinlärning.* Uppsala (mimeo)
Eriksson, Margareta
    1976   *Den ekonomiska situationen för föräldrar med bidragsskyldighet mot barn.* Uppsala (mimeo).
Larsson-Cohn, Ulf & Jan Trost
    1970   "Förbrukning av preventivtabletter i Sverige 1969." *Läkartidningen 67:* 85–90.
Myrdal, Alva & Gunnar Myrdal
    1934   *Kris i befolkningsfrågan.* Stocklholm: Albert Bonniers Förlag.
Nordlund, Agnethe & Jan Trost
    1976   "Some Data on Sex Role Socialization in Sweden" *International Journal of Sociology of the Family.* In press.
Sundström-Feigenberg, Kajsa
    1976   "Den fria steriliseringen." *Läkartidningen 73:* 3911–3912.
Thomas, William I & Dorothy Swaine Thomas
    1928   *The Child in America.* New York.
Trost, Jan
    1976   *A Renewed Social Institution: Cohabitation Without Marriage.* Paper presented at the Fourth World Congress for Rural Sociology, Poland, August 9–13.
    1975   "Vårdnad och underhåll; en undersökning vid ringsrätter och allmänna advokatbyräer hösten 1973" pp 33–120 in *Tre Sociologiska Rapporter SOU 1975 : 24.* Stockholm: Liber Förlag
    1980   *Unmarried Cohabitation.* International Library, Vàsterås

Economic and Family Roles of Men and Women in Northern Europe

A Historical and Cross-National Comparison

ELINA HAAVIO-MANNILA

University of Helsinki, Helsinki, Finland

IN "Women in the Modern World," edited by Raphael Patai (1967) the position of women in various countries is compared. According to this reference India and Pakistan take a fully traditional position on the status and freedom of women, followed by the muslim Middle East and the Mediterranean areas. France, West-Germany, Israel and Japan accept both traditional and modern elements in the two sex roles. Sub-Saharan African, Burmese and Southeast Asian, and Indonesian women have historically had a degree of freedom not attained by women in some Western countries until recently. In the Soviet Union and mainland China, economic, political and social equality between the sexes has been enforced by governmental measures. Finally, Scandinavia, Great Britain and the United States are generally considered the "Western spearhead" of women's rights.

Since Patai published his book the picture of the status of women in the world has been clarified and modified by numerous studies. However, all probably still agree that women in the Scandinavian and in the socialist countries are more independent and socially active than in most other countries of the world.

In this article I intend to examine sex roles in the economy and family in Norway, Sweden, Finland, Poland and the Soviet Union. In this way the position of Finnish women and men will be compared with the position of the two sexes in two Scandinavian and two socialist countries. Restricting the comparison of sex roles in Finland to these geographically and culturally adjacent countries gives better opportunities for a close examination of the special features of these roles than does a worldwide comparison in which large economic and cultural differences must necessarily be taken into consideration.

The first and major part of my analysis concerns changes in the participation of men and women in economic life. I hope to show how women and men shifted over from agriculture to industrial and service occupations. In so doing they had to accept employment outside and beyond the home, or restrict themselves to the role of housebound wives or husbands.

After a survey of the participation of men and women in economic life, some special conditions for women's employment will be investigated. Traditionally, the position of women is, more than that of men, influenced by their role in the family. Thus, there follows an analysis of the proportion of married persons in the population, and also of the birth rates. The approach throughout is comparative: women and men are compared at different points of time beginning with the late 19th century, and in five countries.

The material of this study consists of published statistics. The most useful source has been B.R. Mitchell's "European Historical Statistics 1750–1970" (1975). In addition the Year Books of Labour Statistics by the International Labour Organization, the United Nations' Demographic Yearbooks and Unesco's Statistical Yearbooks, as well as census and other statistical material from the respective countries, have been helpful.

Industrialization among men

In the five countries studied, Norway, Sweden, Finland, Poland and the Soviet Union, the transition from the primary sector of the economy (agriculture, forestry, and fishing) to the secondary (extractive and manufacturing industry, and construction) and tertiary (commerce, finance, transport and communications and services) sectors took place in a relatively linear fashion among the men as Figure 1 shows.

In Norway and Sweden men began to work in the secondary and tertiary sectors of the economy (in industry and services) before they did in Finland, Poland and the Soviet Union. In all five countries the proportion of men working in nonagricultural industries has continuously increased. Only in Sweden was there some decrease in 1970 when the proportion of the inactive male population aged 15 years or more increased because more and more men were either getting an education or becoming pensioned.

The development in Finland closely resembles that in Poland. Data from the Soviet Union are available only from years 1926, 1959 and 1970, but according to these figures the transition of men from primary to secondary and tertiary industries proceeded even more abruptly than in Poland and Finland.

Industrialization among women

Participation in economic activity outside agriculture has not developed in nearly so linear a fashion among women as it did among men. Figure 2 presents the proportion of women engaged in industrial and service occupations (secondary and tertiary sectors) out of all women aged 15 years or more. One can see the upward trend to-

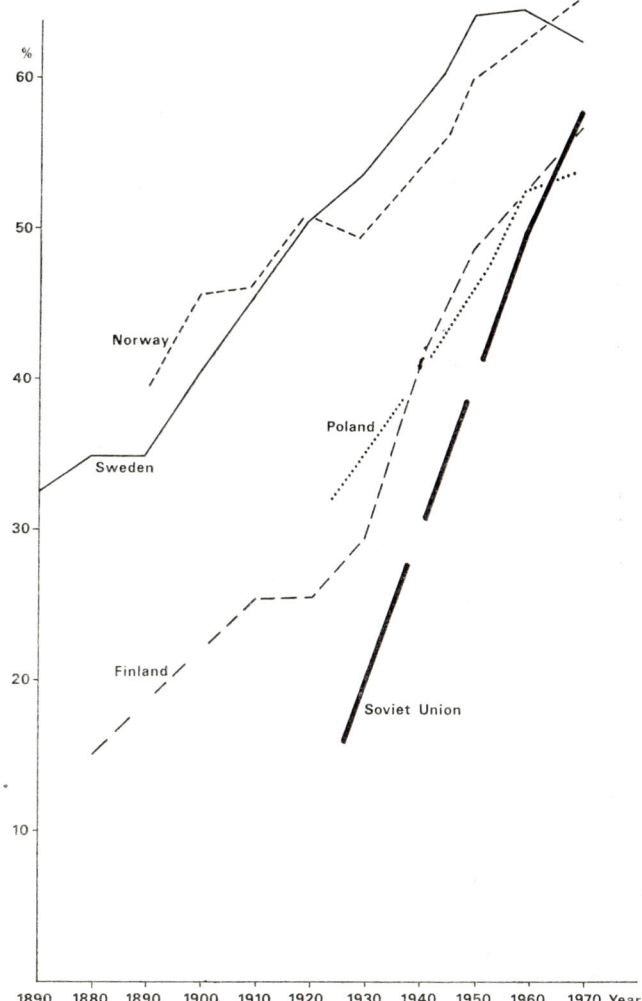

Figure 1. Percentage of men aged 15 and older who belong to the nonagricultural labour force.

wards increasing participation of women in the nonagricultural labor force in all other countries under study.

In Sweden the proportion of women working outside the home in industry and services was about 15 percent around the junction of the 19th and 20th centuries. By 1920 it had reached almost 25 percent, and it had risen to 28 percent in 1930. But by 1940 the proportion of women working in these occupations had diminished. Not until 1960 did it reach a higher level than it had before. Since 1960 the upward trend has continued. A partial explanation of why women stayed at home in Sweden in the 1930's and 1940's is found in the opinion of the trade unions which pointed

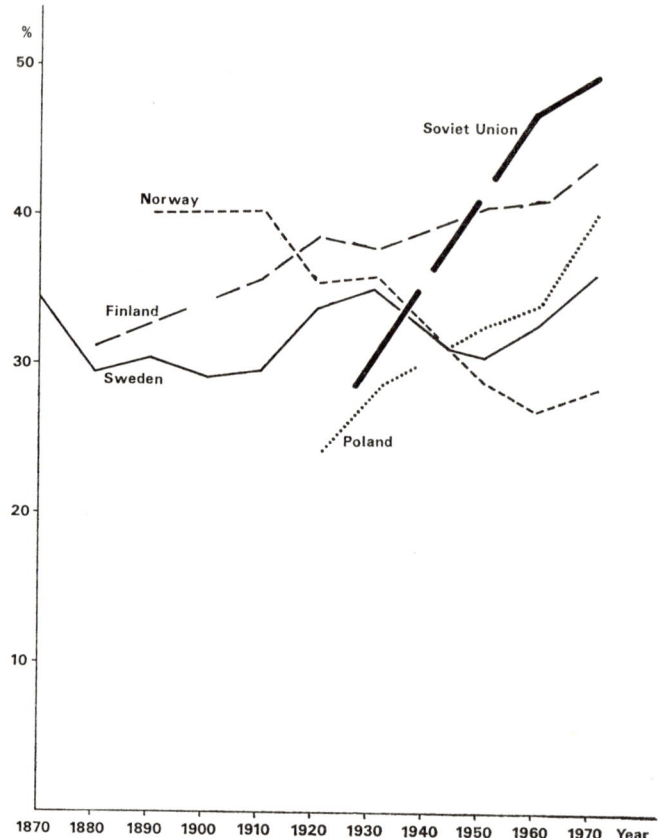

Figure 2. Percentage of women aged 15 and older who belong to the nonagricultural labour force.

out that in each family there should be at least one wage-earner. During the depression, the employment of women endangered the employment of men, and it was sometimes forbidden to employ a wife if her husband had work.

Looking at the proportion of women among those economically active in industry and services in Figure 3 reveals that the percentage has remained relatively stable in Sweden throughout the whole period investigated, from 1860–1970. Peak periods were the years 1870, 1920–1930 and 1970 when the proportion of women in secondary and tertiary sectors was about 35 percent. In the other census years it was about 30 percent of the nonagricultural labor force.

Before exploring reasons for this fluctuation in Sweden it is useful to take a look at the peculiar development in Norway. As Figure 2 shows, Norwegian women, at the beginning of the 20th century, more often engaged in nonagricultural economic activity than is the case from the 1920's to the present day. Men, on the other hand, have steadily and rapidly increased their participation in the industrial and service

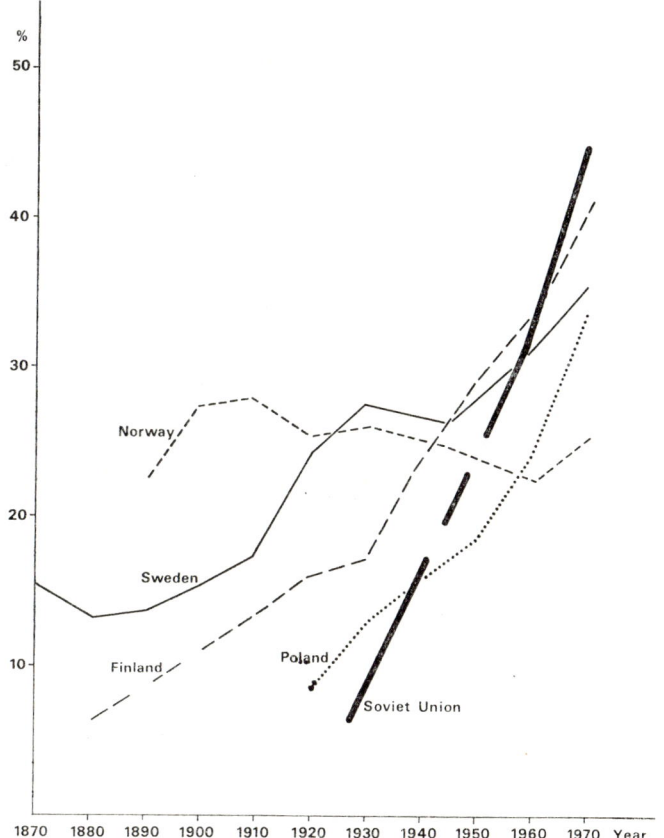

Figure 3. Percentage of women of the nonagricultural labour force.

occupations in Norway. This means that the proportion of women in the nonagricultural labor force has considerably diminished (see Figure 3). During 1890–1910 the proportion was about 40 percent but by 1960 it had declined to 27 percent. In 1970 it did not yet reach more than 29 percent, even though an upward turn had already taken place.

At the beginning of the 20th century a larger part of the Norwegian than of the Swedish women were economically active outside agriculture, but since 1930 the situation has been reversed. In Norway the "return home" movement among women has been even more pronounced than in Sweden.

In order to understand this evolution one has to study the specific branches of industry and services in which women in Sweden and Norway have been active. In Norway, at the beginning of the century, about 20 percent of women 15 years or more were employed in the tertiary sector. Earlier, even before industrialization, a majority of women in service occupations were personal servants, maids and the like.

Work in a private home was typical among young girls, as it was in the Middle and Southern European countries in the 19th century, as historians Scott and Tilly have shown (1975). But one has to be aware that around the turn of the century a larger part of the Norwegian women than ever before or later were active in the secondary sector—about eight percent were employed in industry and construction. An explanation of this may lie in the relatively important position the manufacture of textiles and food and beverages held. In 1900 the proportion of textile and food and beverage production workers of all industrial workers was 26 percent in Norway, 24 percent in Finland and 23 percent in Sweden (Jörberg, 1973: 476). In these fields of industry women were generously represented.

In Sweden there were many more women than men in the service occupations in 1920 and 1930—about 75 percent of the service workers (excluding commerce and transport) were women. The position of personal servant flourished in Sweden between the two world wars (Carlson, 1966: 722). From the 1940's on the number of people in public and community services has increased while the number in personal services has decreased. As a result of this, the proportion of women in the service occupations has declined to about 60 percent.

The peak period of women's participation in the nonagricultural labor force in Sweden in 1920 and 1930 can to a certain extent be explained by the large number of maids. But one must also pay attention to the fact that the proportion of women working in manufacture, trade, transport and communications was higher in 1920 and 1930 than in 1945. The relatively high proportion of women working in the nonagricultural sectors in 1970 is not due to an increasing number of women in the secondary sector, but in the tertiary sector. The growing participation of Swedish women in economic life outside the home is related to the recent expansion of the tertiary sector in which there is a continuing demand for female labor. Women's increasing economic activity has been made possible by several public policies which are meant to help women to solve, to take one example, their child care problems. The establishment of children's day care centers has been much more efficient in Sweden than in Norway. Both the state and the employers have agreed on the usefulness of increasing the proportion of employed women, because of the lack of an adequate labor force in the 1960's in the rapidly-developing Swedish economy.

In Finland the economic activity of women outside the home has increased more steadily than in Sweden and Norway. The proportion of women 15 years or older employed in industry and services grew from six percent in 1880 to 41 percent 1970. Among men the corresponding increase was from 15 to 56 percent. The proportion of women among persons active in the secondary and tertiary sectors rose from 31 to 44 percent; this proportion has, since 1940, been considerably higher in Finland than in Sweden and Norway. However, it has only been since the 1950's that women in Finland have been engaged in industry to a greater extent than women in Sweden and Norway. (This reflects the later industrialization of Finland.) In commerce, transport and communications Finnish women have since 1960 been represented in greater numbers than Swedish and Norwegian women have. In the services proper, women in Finland were not employed to a great extent before 1950—the home servant institution was not as widespread as in Sweden and Norway—and even in 1970 a larger proportion of Swedish than of Finnish women were engaged in service occupations. In the Finnish cities there were many maids in the 19th century, the proportion of urban population was at that time very small. Thus these homehelpers were not visible in the statistics covering the whole country.

The "return home" of Swedish women in the 1930's can also be seen from the following figures. These show the proportion of economically nonactive women out of all women aged 15 years or more in Sweden and Finland in 1920-1970 excluding farm wives.

Proportion of economically nonactive women out of all women aged 15 years or more

	1920	1930	1940	1950	1960	1970
Sweden	26	27	31	37	32	33 percent
Finland	27	27	23	28	25	28 percent

Source: Census data.

From the year 1940 on, the proportion of homestaying wives has been considerably larger in Sweden than in Finland. The percentages above also include students and pensioners because statistics of the earlier years did not differentiate them from homeworking persons. The difference between Sweden and Finland was greatest in 1950. It had diminished by 1960 and 1970 when the Swedish labor policy had begun to succeed in persuading housewives to reenter the labor market. In the beginning of the 20th century there was almost no difference in the proportion of homestaying wives between Finland and Sweden. The "return home" movement of the Swedish women, which began in the 1930's during the depression, increased the proportion of housewives in Sweden but not in Finland, where women's employment outside of home steadily increased. Perhaps the depression had less influence in less industrialized Finland (at least less industrialized when measured by the participation of men in nonagricultural production) than in Sweden. In 1940 Finland was at war, which increased the need for a female labor force.

In any study of the employment of women from a historical perspective, attention should be paid to the different age groups and to the marital structure of the female labor force at different historical periods. The employment of women in the earlier period meant to a large extent only the employment of young girls. But at present a large proportion of employed women are relatively old and often married with children. This is one of the reasons why women's employment is felt nowadays to be such a social problem due to the lack of child care facilities.

The transition from agriculture to industry and services in the case of Finnish women took place somewhat earlier than in the case of Polish and Soviet women. Polish women are still engaged in agricultural production to a large extent: 28.5 percent of the women aged 15 years or more were economically active in agriculture in 1970, and the proportion of women in the agricultural labor force has been about 55 percent since the Second World War. In the Soviet Union, women composed as much as 62 percent of the agricultural labor force in 1959, but by 1970 this proportion had declined to 52 percent.

As was previously mentioned, the timing of industrialization was very similar in Finland, Poland and the Soviet Union. However, women in Finland became engaged in industry earlier than women in the two socialist countries studied. In 1970, the Soviets, for the first time, had a greater proportion of women (and men) engaged in secondary and tertiary sectors than did Finland, as Figures 1 and 2 show. The difference is due to the different economic structure of socialist and capitalist countries. (In Poland and the Soviet Union the service sector is not as well developed as in Finland.) The high proportion of women in industry and construction in the Soviet Union does not compensate for the high proportion of women in the large service sector in Finland.

Transition from agriculture to industry and services has taken place earlier among women than among men in Finland, when one looks at the development from a cross-national perspective. While Finnish men entered industry at about the same time as men in the socialist countries included in this comparison, they clearly lagged behind men in the other Scandinavian countries. Women in Finland were, until 1960, ahead of women in the two socialist countries. From the year 1960 on, the socialist Soviet Union has, however, succeeded in mobilizing its women into secondary and tertiary occupations, and presently women's employment outside agriculture is more common in the USSR than in Finland.

Present economic roles of the sexes in Scandinavia

From the point of view of the family, it is important to know how many married persons are employed outside the home. Women's labor force participation, according to marital status and age, in the four Scandinavian countries, Denmark included, is presented in Table 1.

Even though the national definitions of economic activity differ somewhat, it is obvious that all women, but especially the married ones, are employed to a higher degree in Finland and to a lower degree in Norway than they are in Denmark and Sweden. However, young single Norwegian women are economically active more often than single women in the other Scandinavian countries. (Students are not separated in Norwegian statistics from the nonactive population.) The high employ-

Table 1

Economic activity of women in the Scandinavian countries by age and marital status in 1970

Denmark

Activity age	Single				Married				Formerly married				Together			
	14–24	25–59	60–	All	14–24	25–59	60–	All	14–24	25–59	60–	All	14–24	25–59	60–	All
Full-time empl.	34	66	18	38	41	28	7	26	65	54	6	25	37	34	8	28
Part-time empl.	17	16	3	15	16	20	4	17	14	16	3	8	17	19	3	15
Student	46	3	—	31	4	0	—	1	6	1	—	0	34	1	—	8
Not active	3	15	79	16	39	51	89	57	16	29	91	67	13	46	89	49
Total	100	100	100	100	100	99	100	101	101	100	100	100	101	100	100	100
Total (thousands)	299	89	63	451	111	856	211	1179	6	120	207	334	417	481	1066	1965

Finland

Activity age	Single				Married				Formerly married				Together			
	15–24	25–59	60–	All	15–24	25–59	60–	All	15–24	25–59	60–	All	15–24	25–59	60–	All
Econ. active	44	81	15	50	59	59	15	53	84	73	9	32	49	64	12	49
Student	39	3	0	24	6	1	0	1	4	0	0	0	30	1	0	7
Not active	17	16	85	26	36	41	85	46	12	27	91	68	21	36	88	44
Total	100	100	100	100	101	101	100	100	100	100	100	100	100	101	100	100
Total (thousands)	307	142	71	520	113	759	143	1015	2	105	188	296	422	1007	401	1830

Table 1 (continued)
Norway

Activity age	Single			Married				Formerly married				Together			
	16-24	25-59	60-	All	16-24	25-59	60-	All	16-24	25-59	60-	All	16-24	25-59	60-	All
At least 1000h/year empl.	41	71	20	44	30	24	9	22	39	47	7	19	38	31	10	26
Less than 1000h/year emp.	18	6	6	13	14	17	9	16	15	12	4	7	17	16	6	14
Not active	41	23	74	44	55	58	83	62	47	41	89	75	45	53	83	60
Total	100	100	100	101	99	99	101	100	101	100	100	101	100	100	99	100
(thousands)	182	78	73	332	84	663	174	921	2	58	147	208	268	798	394	1461

Sweden

Activity age	Single				Married				Formerly married				Together			
	15-24	25-59	60-	All	15-24	25-59	60-	All	15-24	25-59	60-	All	15-24	25-59	60-	All
At least 1000h/year emp.	42	71	14	44	44	45	10	38	60	64	7	26	42	49	10	37
Less than 1000h/year emp.	1	2	2	1	4	9	3	7	2	4	1	2	2	7	2	5
Student	49	5	0	29	5	9	0	1	99	2	0	1	39	1	0	8
Not active	9	2	84	26	47	46	87	54	29	30	91	71	17	42	88	50
Total	101	100	100	100	100	99	100	100	100	100	99	100	100	99	100	100
(thousands)	462	203	147	812	126	1413	390	1929	3	158	331	492	590	1774	868	3232

Source: Pöntinen, 1976: 6.

ment rate of young single women may be related to the limited educational participation of women in Norway; in 1970 only 30 percent of the students at the third level of education were women whereas 37 percent of the Danish, 42 percent of the Swedish, and 48 percent of the Finnish students were female (Unesco, 1973).

In the Scandinavian countries, about every second married woman is working at least part of the time except in Norway where the proportion is 38 percent. (In Finland the definition of economic activity includes all persons who report that they are working at least half of the "normal" working time for their occupation.) In Denmark and Norway the proportion of working wives is declining with increasing age but in Sweden and Finland there is no decrease for the age categories of 15–24 and 25–59 years. In all countries very few of the married women aged 60 or more are economically active.

In Norway more than 40 percent of the formerly married women under 60 years of age are not employed, whereas in the other countries these divorced and widowed women are generally economically active. The role of women in Norway really seems to differ from their role in the other Scandinavian countries—women are economically supported even after marriage, not only while it lasts.

A comparison of the economic activity rates of men and women, according to Erik Allardt's Scandinavian survey (1972, published in 1975), on welfare and need-satisfaction reveals (Table 2) that while Finnish women are economically active more often than women in other Scandinavian countries, Finnish men, on the contrary

Table 2

Employment of men and women aged 15 to 64 in the Scandinavian countries in 1971 per cent

	Denmark Men	Denmark Women	Finland Men	Finland Women	Norway Men	Norway Women	Sweden Men	Sweden Women
Not able to be employed	4	9	8	9	6	5	3	4
Sporadically employed	2	2	6	4	3	2	6	6
Studying or housewife	9	41	12	29	13	64	12	42
Almost full-time employed	6	15	9	8	4	9	10	22
Full-time employed	79	33	64	51	75	20	70	26
	100	100	99	101	101	100	101	100
N	497	498	477	517	496	509	497	508

Source: Allardt, 1975: 90.

belong to the labor force less often than men in the countries being compared. Thus the sex difference in the participation in economic life is smallest in Finland. In certain other life sectors such as education, organizational activity, politics, and health, Finnish women closely resemble women in other Scandinavian countries. However,

Finnish men are less active than men in Norway, Sweden and Denmark. Again in these "other-life" areas, as well as in the economic one, the sex difference in Finland in exceptionally small, not because of a particular activity on the part of Finnish women but because of the nonactivity of Finnish men.

Participation in marriage and family life among men and women

In a few prosperous countries and in certain periods of history, upper- and middle-class women have been able to "earn" their living through the marriage institution, without directly participating in outside economic activity. This was the case, for example, in Sweden and Norway in the middle of the twentieth century. In Finland and Eastern Europe women have more often participated in economic activity, and the homestaying housewife institution has been less developed than in the Western European countries.

The relatively high level of economic activity of Finnish women, even outside the agricultural sector, may partly be explained by the relatively low proportion of married women, compared with the other countries examined (except the Soviet Union where women's employment is even higher than in Finland). In the Soviet Union there are fewer married women in the older age classes, but more in the younger ones as Table 3 shows.

In Sweden the sharp decline of the marriage rate in the latter part of the 1960's can be seen in the young (15–29 years) age categories, in which there are fewer married women than in the other countries included in this study.

The low proportion of married women in Finland—as in the Soviet Union—can be explained by referring to war losses and to the large sex difference in life expectation (in the Soviet Union in 1968–69, 9 years; in Finland in 1966–70, 7.7 years; in Poland 1970–72, 6.9 years; in Norway in 1966–70, 5.7 years; and in Sweden in 1972, only 5.4 years). The very high proportion of married men in the Soviet Union in the older age classes (in the ages 40–59 around 95 percent) indicates that there are practically no men available for the nonmarried women in these age groups. In Finland, however, the rates of nonmarried men are not as high as the rates in Norway and Sweden, even though there are relatively more women in the Finnish than in the Norwegian and Swedish populations. The proportion of unmarried men is especially high among young and even middle-aged rural men in Finland—the latter cannot find a wife to share the responsibilities of a small farm. Thus, the proportion of the married population is low in Finland among both sexes. (In Europe only Ireland has a higher proportion of people who have never married.)

In Poland, which unfortunately could not be included in Table 3 due to the lack of data in the UN Demographic Yearbook, the proportion of married women in the population was higher (44.5 percent in 1970) than in Finland and the Soviet Union even though this country also suffered from war losses.

Table 3

Proportion of presently married women and men according to age group in Norway, Sweden, Finland and the Soviet Union in 1970

Age group	Norway	Sweden	Finland	Soviet Union
	\multicolumn{4}{c}{Percentage of married women}			
15–19	5.5	2.3	5.3	10.5
20–24	52.4	39.1	46.2	55.9
25–29	80.6	73.5	74.6	82.7
30–34	87.7	83.2	81.3	85.3
35–39	87.7	85.0	81.6	83.9
40–44	87.4	84.3	79.5	79.0
45–49	84.1	82.0	75.6	71.9
50–54	79.7	79.0	69.7	60.3
55–59	72.9	73.2	61.2	50.1
60–64	63.5	64.6	51.1	37.1
65–69	51.8	52.8	39.7	
70–74	39.7	39.7	27.4	19.6
75–	21.6	20.2	12.9	
All ages (children included)	47.2	47.7	42.3	41.6
	\multicolumn{4}{c}{Percentage of married men}			
15–19	0.8	0.2	1.1	2.1
20–24	27.6	16.7	27.8	28.9
25–29	66.5	57.3	66.2	77.2
30–34	79.7	75.5	77.5	88.7
35–39	82.8	79.8	80.5	93.3
40–44	83.4	80.0	81.2	94.6
45–49	83.2	79.8	82.9	95.2
50–54	83.4	80.4	84.7	95.2
55–59	82.4	79.0	83.5	94.8
60–64	80.6	77.5	81.0	92.0
65–69	77.1	74.4	76.7	
70–74	71.1	69.2	70.1	77.8
75–	54.0	51.8	51.3	
All ages (children included)	47.7	47.8	45.1	47.5

Source: Calculated on the basis of United Nations Demographic Yearbook 1971, Table 26.

It is obvious that Finland and the Soviet Union are the countries in this study which are characterized by an exceptionally high proportion of nonmarried women who, in consequence, cannot rely on the marriage institution for economic support. In these two countries the proportion of employed women is high, perhaps because of the lack of possibilities for a marital role, or perhaps, as Safilios-Rothschild (1971) has suggested, women have more options for not marrying because there are more occupational opportunities.

In Sweden and Finland participation of women in the marriage institution over a considerable period can be studied thanks to data collected by Gunnar Qvist and

Table 4

Proportion of "ever-married" women of all women aged 35–39 years
in urban and rural areas in Finland and Sweden in 1870(90)–1970

Year	Urban areas		Rural areas	
	Sweden	Finland	Sweden	Finland
	Proportion of "ever-married" women aged 35–39 years per cent			
1870	62.8		79.8	
1880	64.1		79.5	
1890	65.7	63.3	78.1	82.5
1900	63.1	64.3	77.3	82.6
1910	64.5	63.1	76.2	79.8
1920	67.2	57.2	75.1	74.3
1930	68.9	60.5	75.5	70.7
1940	72.2	65.0	77.6	73.2
1950	84.4	78.3	87.0	83.9
1960	89.3	83.5	90.9	86.8
1970	91.7	87.1	91.2	89.0

Source: Calculated from census data by Gunnar Qvist for Sweden and Anja-Riitta Lahikainen for Finland.

Anja-Riitta Lahikainen from the censuses since 1870 and 1890. These figures are presented in Table 4, which shows as well the proportion of "ever-married" women in the age class 35 to 39 years, separately for urban and rural areas.

Until 1910 there were more "ever-married" women (widows and divorced women included) in Finland than in Sweden, particularly in the countryside, but since 1920 Sweden has had higher percentages, especially in urban areas. This shows that Finnish women in towns and cities have not been able to rely on marriage as a "provider" institution. In 1920 and 1930 only about 60 percent of middle-aged women had ever been married. However, differences between the countries have grown less, and in 1970 the proportion of "ever-married" women exceeded 80 percent in all age classes below 65 years even in urban areas of Finland.

In general, industrialization and a declining birth rate belong together. The birth rate in the two socialist countries, Poland and the Soviet Union, has been considerably higher than in Scandinavia except for a few years in the late 1960's when the Norwegian birth rate was higher. In Finland the birth rate was higher than in Norway until 1963 and higher than in Sweden until 1970, but since the early years of the 1970's it has been the lowest of the countries studied. Rapid changes in the economic structure in the 1960's and a large emigration to Sweden in 1967–72, combined with the high participation of women in economic life outside the home may be some of the reasons for the exceptionally low birth rate (12–13%) in 1971–73 in Finland. At present the trend is, however, towards an increasing birth rate.

There seems to be no direct relationship between birth rates and women's participation in the labor force. Some kind of connection might be observable however, in Norway, where the proportion of employed women is very low. In that country the birth rate did not decrease after the Second World War as soon and as much as in the other countries studied. But since 1970 there has been a decline in the birth rate even in Norway—perhaps partly connected with the emergence of a lively feminist movement and a rapid increase in women's employment.

Discussion

As an appropriate conclusion an attempt will be made to tie up this study on sex roles in economic activity in three Scandinavian and two socialist countries with some general statements about the international variation of women's occupational opportunities. In a few studies (for example, Safilios-Rothschild, 1971 and Krauss, 1974) it has been indicated that women's options are curvilinearily related to gross national product, with the middle-range GNP countries offering the most opportunities. Thus, there are many women in "masculine" professions, such as architecture, dentistry and medicine in Greece, Costa Rica, India, Pakistan, Turkey, Scandinavia and Eastern Europe. Wilma Krauss interprets this by saying: "Rapidly developing economies provide employment opportunities for 'mixed game' gender occupational patterns; post-industrial economies with small percentage GNP increase and greater unemployment resemble 'zero-sum games', with men's mobility into the professions tending to vary inversely with women's." (Krauss, 1974: 1708).

The curvilinearity hypothesis does not get unanimous support from the data presented above. However, in the two countries with the highest GNP, Sweden and Norway (GNP per capita $ 4,040 and $ 2,860 in 1970), women are least often economically active, and in the middle-range countries, Finland and the Soviet Union ($ 2,390 and $ 1,790), they participate most. Poland with the lowest GNP ($ 1,400) falls between these extremes.

The curvilinearity hypothesis as regards women's employment outside the home can be interpreted by referring to two facts: a) rich countries can afford a homestaying housewife institution and b) poor countries are usually not well developed beyond the primary sector, and thus have few employment opportunities in the secondary and tertiary sectors.

However, the large difference in women's economic activity between Norway and Finland cannot be explained by referring to any remarkable differences in GNP. There must be deeply-rooted cultural values, in addition to economic factors, which are operating as determinants of the sex roles. According to Allardt's study, sex roles in all areas of life are more traditional in Norway and less traditional in Finland than in the other Scandinavian countries, that is, in Sweden and Denmark. There seems to be an East-West difference in this respect in Scandinavia, the Eastern part showing less and the Western part more patriarchal tendencies. According to my earlier studies (Haavio-Mannila, 1970) women in Eastern Finland are more emancipated in political life than women in Western Finland. Furthermore, the sex role attitudes in Eastern Finland are more liberal than in the Western part of the country. This East-West difference in Finland seems to have a long tradition; for example, even in the 19th century women were more often represented on school boards in the Eastern than in the Western provinces.

The economically-based curvilinearity hypothesis cannot explain but a part of the differences in women's economic activity. The social division of labor between the sexes is based on more complex factors. Some variables suggested by the results presented in this article and that may influence sex roles in economic life follow.

Variables influencing sex roles in economic life

A. *Economic variables*

— the pre-industrial social and economic structure (In this article sex roles in the economy have been examined only during the industrialization period. Further studies are needed to illuminate the preindustrial situation.)
— structure and labor intensity of industry (For example, the proportion of textile, food and beverage workers out of all industrial workers.)
— expansion of the service sector (Women in general are more often employed in services than in industry. In the socialist countries the tertiary sector is less developed than in the capitalist countries. However, the proportion of women in economic life is higher in the former than in the latter. This indicates that in the socialist countries other variables than the structure of the economy count for sex roles in employment.)
— employment situation (Lack of labor force in Sweden forced employers and the State to persuade women to work which increased children's day care needs outside the home.)

B. *Cultural variables*

— formal political ideology (In the socialist countries the economic activity of all citizens is considered a precondition for equality of the sexes.)
— informal cultural values and norms, the "everyday ethic" (Stolte-Heiskanen and Haavio-Mannila; 1967). Cultural values and norms, however, often serve and legitimize the labor market situation.
— historical traditions (Women in Finland got the vote first in Europe and second

in the world in 1906, and women's participation in political and economic life since then has been, in comparison with that of men, exceptionally active, at least from a cross-national perspective.)

C. *Demographic variables*

— proportion of married persons in the population (The more married in a society, the more possibilities there are for women to 'earn' their living through their husband's work.)
— size and composition of the family (In this article only the birth rate was studied, and no direct connection was found between it and sex roles in economic life. However, with the transition from agrarian to industrial and post-industrial society, the birth rate has declined everywhere, and the proportion of women employed outside the home has increased.)

Conclusion

In the most economically developed of the societies studied, Sweden, an interesting convergence of male and female roles in the nonagricultural labor force could be seen by 1970: the proportion of men had begun to decline and the proportion of women kept increasing. This suggests that in the future a growing number of the men will be relieved from the sole provider role in the family. This role will more and more often be shared or even taken over by the wife.

In the less-developed countries investigated, except in Norway, women have for a longer time been engaged in employment outside the home, either due to economic necessity or political ideology. Even in these countries, Finland, Poland and the Soviet Union, no trend towards "returning home" among women can be seen, even though informal values and norms may be relatively traditional in regard to the roles of the sexes. It remains to be seen what the trend in the socialist countries will be in the future. There is a strong policy in favor of larger families in order to avoid a decline in the number of people. Thus, the traditional sex roles are valued, not fought against, as is the case in many capitalist countries, at least in the case of the feminist movement. However, women are so important for the socialist economy that there is no possibility to survive without their participation in the labor force.

Finland has a special position between Eastern and Western Europe. The levelling off of sex differences in the amount (but not type and rewards) of participation in the labor force is continuing without any explicit formal ideology, public policy, or even a particularly strong feminist movement—perhaps as a result of a strong historical tradition of equality of the sexes.

REFERENCES

Allardt, Erik
    1975   *Att ha att älska att vara—om välfärd i Norden.* Lund: Argos.

Carlson, Sten
    1966   "Den sociala omgrupperingen i Sverige efter 1866." In Samhälle och riksdag. *Historisk och statsvetenskaplig framställning utgiven i anledning av tvåkammariksdagens 100-åriga tillvaro.* Stockholm: Almqvist & Wiksell.

Haavio-Mannila, Elina
    1970   "Sex Roles in politics." *Scandinavian Political Studies* 5: 209–239.
    1971   "Convergences between East and West: Tradition and modernity in sex roles in Sweden, Finland and the Soviet Union." *Acta Sociologica* 14: 114–125.

International Labour Office
    1975   *Year Book of Labour Statistics* 1974. Geneva.

Jörberg, Lennart
    1973   "The industrial revolution in the Nordic countries." In Carlo M. Cipolla (ed.), *The Fontana Economic History of Europe.* London and Glasgow: Collin.

Kon, Igor
    1975   "Women at work: equality with a difference?" *International Social Science Journal* 27 (4): 655–665.

Krauss, Wilma R.
    1974   "Political implications of gender roles: A review of the literature." *The American Political Science Review* 68 (December): 1706–1723.

Mitchell, B. R.
    1975   *European Historical Statistics 1750–1970.* London: Macmillan.

Mogey, John, and Jerzy Piotrowski
    1976   "Husband and wife in Poland." Paper prepared for the World Congress of Rural Sociology. Torun, Poland (August).

Patai, Raphael
    1967   *Women in the modern world.* New York: Free Press.

Pöntinen, Seppo
    1976   "On the social mobility of women in the Scandinavian countries." Paper presented in the Jerusalem seminar on Mobility and Social Stratification. Jerusalem, Israel (April).

Safilios-Rothschild, Constantina
    1971   "A cross-cultural examination of women's marital, educational and occupational options." *Acta Sociologiea* 14 (1–2): 96–113.

Scott, Joan W. and Louise A. Tilly
    1975   "Women's work and the family in nineteenth-century Europe." *Comparative Studies in Society and History* 17 (January): 36–64.

Stolte-Heiskanen, Veronica and Elina Haavio-Mannila
    1967   "The position of women in society—formal ideology vs. everyday ethic." *Social Science Information* 6 (6): 169–188.

Unesco
    1973   *Statistical Yearbook.* Paris: The Unesco Press.

United Nations
    1972   *Demographic Yearbook* 1971. New York: United Nations.

B. EASTERN AND SOUTHERN EUROPE

Soviet Women in Family and Society

G. A. SLESAREV and Z. A. YANKOVA
The University of Moscow, Moscow, U.S.S.R.

Introduction

THE SUPREME AIM of socialist society is to ensure freedom, happiness and well-being for the individual and the all-round, harmonious development of his personality. Needless to say, this aim cannot be achieved without, at the same time, achieving the complete social equality of women. The handling of the question of women in the Soviet Union has gained extensive international recognition. According to the noted American economist and sociologist Norton Dodge, Soviet women have come to occupy their present position of importance in social life due to the profound transformations carried out in the economic, political and social areas of society (1966: 1).

By asserting public ownership of the means of production, thus making impossible the exploitation of man by man, the Great October Socialist Revolution, quite dispassionately, provided the opportunity for a woman to work on an equal footing with man in many areas of the national economy. She was enabled to create material and spiritual values and help manage the affairs of society while remaining wife, mother and mistress of the house.

When Soviet sociologists consider the question of the social equality of women with men, they distinguish two aspects: 1) a general social aspect which reflects the position of women as part of the population and as members of definite classes and social groups and 2) a specific aspect, which reflects the woman's particular role as mother and nurturer of the rising generation. The Marxists–Leninists proceed from the assumption that procreation, alongside the production of the means of sustenance and other material values, represents a key element in the evolution of society. These are the two aides of the single and cohesive process of reproduction of social relations.

Article 35 of the Constitution of the USSR states:

"Women and men have equal rights in the USSR. Exercise of these rights is ensured by according women equal rights with men to education and vocational and professional training, equal opportunities in employment, remuneration, and promotion, and in social and political, and cultural activity, and by special labour and health protection measures for women; by providing conditions enabling mothers to work; by legal protection, and material and moral support for mothers and children, including paid leaves and other benefits for expectant mothers and mothers, and gradual reduction of working time for mothers with small children."[1]

As well as ensuring legal protection of the family and guaranteeing the complete equality of husband and wife in family relations, the Soviet state renders all-round aid to the family by setting up and developing an extensive network of child care institutions, by organizing and perfecting catering and other everyday services, by offering payments and benefits to large families, etc. These guarantees and other forms of constant aid by the state and society in support of the family represent the dominant feature of the handling of the women's question in the Soviet Union.

The ensuring of actual man-woman equality in the family and society is a prolonged and complex process; as socialist society develops, the degree of actual equality constantly increases. This does not rule out the emergence of specific problems and contradictions in the handling of the women's question and these require new social measures at each stage of the development of the communist pattern. This is paralleled by the overcoming of these contraditions left over from the past as well as new ones and including those arising from the social implications of the present scientific and technological revolutions.

An example of a contradiction which now impedes the all-round development of the woman's personality is the contrast between relative slowness in the development of the sphere of cultural and everyday service and the rate with which women are drawn into social production. Within the family there is a definite contradiction between the new family functions of a woman (as an educator of her children, as organizer of her home, etc.) and the traditional everyday functions harking back to the old intrafamily division of labour. The persistence of these and other contradictions in a number of instances slows the improvement in the overall cultural, vocational and professional level of women causing a drop in birth rate, family strife, etc.

A developed socialist society demonstrates only stray vestiges of the previous inequality of women, remnants which result from the survival of distinctions between the social classes, between intellectual and physical labour and between town and country. As these old distinctions fade, objective conditions develop which provide for complete social equality of the sexes.

Concern for the position of women in the family and society has gained ground in the Soviet Union. Studies are being conducted, by both social and natural scientists. Their findings and their practical proposals are being employed by state and public organizations to perfect the system of mother-and-child health protection and to

---

1 Constitution (Fundamental Law) of the Union of the Soviet Socialist Republics, Moscow, 1977, p. 38.

ensure optimum conditions for combining labour in the sphere of social production with the careful upbringing of the new generation.

The purpose of this article is to show how the change in the woman's position in the family and society influences the shaping of her personality. Special attention will be paid to the motives behind women's labour activity; vocational, professional and social orientation; attitudes and preferences in the leisure sphere; and the character of interpersonal relations in the family. Material for the analysis has come from the sociological research conducted by the present authors at different times, the findings of other Soviet sociologists who work on identical problems, as well as state and departmental statistics.

Women in the System of Social Production

In pre-revolutionary Russia, women accounted for only 19 percent of the population which had a special and individual occupation. Fifty-five percent of the hired female workers were servants and 25 percent farm labourers, while only 13 percent were employed in industrial enterprises and construction projects and 4 percent in institutions of public education and in the health services.

At present the Soviet Union leads the world with its high level of women's vocational and professional activity. Evidence of this can be found in the key social indices, i.e., the proportion of employed women in the labour force; the diversity of trades and professions mastered by women; the character and content of their labour; the high level of specialized knowledge; their vocational orientation and motives. According to the all-Union population census of 1970, 80 percent of the women of working-age were employed in different branches of the national economy and 7.5 percent attended educational establishments. According to the estimates of Soviet economists (Kotlyar and Turchaninova, 1975), the average seniority of each able-bodied Soviet woman (factory, office worker or collective farmer) in the public sector of the national economy equalled 28.7 years in the 1960's and 33.5 years in 1970. At present the level of vocational and professional employment of women is equal to 93.6 percent of that of men (Korchagin, 1974).

The changes in the social class composition of the female part of the population, compared to 1939, are reflected in Table I.

The changes in the women's social class composition correspond with the changes in the social structure of developed social society as a whole. The table reveals the rapid numerical growth in the number of women as factory and office workers, engineers and technicians; the drop in the number of women as collective farmers; and the complete disappearance of women peasants and individual (not part of a co-operative) craftswomen. The profound socio-economic changes in the Soviet Union substantially change the ratio between the women doing physical and mental work. The present scientific and technological revolution moves the content and character of labour in the direction of continued intellectualization thus making work in the sphere of social production increasingly attractive for women.

An exceptionally vital incentive to women's vocational, professional and social activity has been the growth in the area of general and specialized education. Now they are *on a par* with men in this area.

Table 1

Women's Division into Social Groups (in per cent)*

	1939	1959	1970	1975
All women** including:				
factory and office workers	48.2	67.1	77.9	82.3
collective farmers	49.2	32.6	22.0	17.7
individual peasants and uncooperated craftswomen	2.7	0.3	0.1	0.0

* Zhenshchiny v SSSR. Statiticheskiy sbornik (Women in the USSR. Statistical Collection), Moscow, 1975, p. 25.
** In dividing women into social groups dependents are classed with the groups of their supporters, pensioners and recipients of allowances and those to which they had belonged before they joined their present categories.

To this it should be added that in growth rates of education, women are ahead of men. For instance, in 1975 compared with 1939 the number of men with higher education rose 5.5-fold (from 16 to 88 per 1,000) and that of women 8.9-fold (from 9 to 80 per 1,000) and of those with secondary education 5.5-fold (from 120 to 662) and 7.1-fold (from 95 to 672), respectively.

The proportion of women in the total number of employed individuals with higher and specialized secondary education equalled 59 percent in 1950 as against 36 percent in 1940 and 29 percent in 1928. According to the data of one-occasion registration in 1970 the total of women with higher and specialized secondary education, employed in the national economy, was 9.9 million—11.5 times larger than in 1940 and 66 times larger than in 1928.

The high growth rates of the proportion of women in the trades and professions are also stimulated by a number of incentives at work—incentives such as an increase in the minimum pay for their work (compared to 1960, this has risen to date by an average of 15–20 percent); a regular reduction of taxes; and an increase in pensions. (Evidence that the growing level of the vocational and professional employment of women is an objective requirement of society and is protected by law.) Proof of the fact that the level of women's professional and vocational employment satisfies their subjective requirements is furnished by an analysis of the motives of women who join the labour force.

Table 2
Level of Education of Women and Men in the USSR
*(Employed Population)**

Year	Per 1,000 individuals of either sex there are			
	with higher education		with secondary (complete and incomplete) education	
	men	women	men	women
1939	16	9	120	95
1959	34	32	400	399
1970	68	62	586	589
1975	88	80	662	672

* Source: Same as Table 1.

The most typical hierarchy of the motives for the vocational activity of women with low and medium skills employed in industrial enterprises is the one identified by the present authors in the course of sociological surveys conducted in Moscow, Leningrad and Penza. According to the data obtained, 53 percent of the women said they had to work because their families needed extra earnings; 24 percent desired to stay with a team of fellow-workers; 9 percent wanted to use their vocational and other knowledge for the benefit of society; and 8.3 percent assumed that work in an industrial enterprise corresponded with their urge to be self-supporting (Slesarev and Yankova, 1969: 422).

A slightly different structure was discovered when the authors studied the motives, for doing professional and vocational work, of highly-skilled female workers, engineers and technicians. First place here was indicated to be a desire to share in socially useful labour (58 percent); second place, a desire to stay with a team of fellow-workers (21 percent); and the last two places by a desire for material reward.

The motivational differences are apparently due to the distinctions in the character and content of work in the surveyed categories of female workers, in particular, the saturation of highly-skilled work with creative and other thought-stimulating and organization functions — functions which raise the self-value of the labour process. The majority of women view professional or vocational activity as the key factor determining their equal independent position in society, their prestige in their families and the respect their husbands accord them i.e., as a factor of personal self-expression as well as of social self-assertion.

Due to a number of objective and subjective factors the model of "labour in social production during the whole working age" has been gaining significant recognition. According to N. G. Yurkevich, for instance, about 95 percent of the women confirmed their readiness to work even if their husbands could provide income the equal of what they could earn jointly.

Thus, the high level of employment of Soviet women in socialist-type enterprises is due, in addition to the planned development of the socialist economy; the laying of the material and technical foundation of communism; and the constant national economic requirements in labour force, to a continued rise in their self-conciousness. This alone, given a free choice, ensures the high level of women's employment.

At present the proportion of women in professional and vocational jobs is highest in the central regions of the country and the periphery of both town and country. In the Soviet Union as a whole, the share of women in the overall number of factory and office workers equals 51 percent. In the Russian Federation, Byelorussia, Georgia and Estonia it is slightly higher (52–53 percent) but slightly lower in the other republics (50–41 percent). The proportion of women in the overall number of rural workers, has increased since 1969 and is now 51 percent.

As the population census of 1970 revealed, out of the 290 large professional and vocational groups which include all types of relevant activity in the national economy, there are rarely any without some women workers. In 156 of them the proportion of women among those employed equalled or exceeded 50 percent (Lagutin and Sergeyeva, 1975: 8).

At present women comprise 81 percent of the workers employed in the health services, physical culture and social security; 80 percent in crediting and social insurance; 73 percent in public education and culture; 76 percent in trade, public catering and bodies of supply and sales of procured items; 68 percent in communications; 64 percent in management, cooperative and social organizations.

These statistics reveal that women have mastered those creative, organizational and managerial functions which require independent solutions to various production, social and other problems and, therefore, maximally contribute to the disclosure of relevant abilities. Possibly, says Dodge (1966), the most indicative feature of the Soviet Union is not so much the high proportion of women workers as the substantial proportion of women in the privileged trades and professions. This is a distinctive feature of the use of women's labour in the Soviet Union.

In the Soviet Union, there is indeed a rise in the proportion of women engaged predominantly in intellectual work. Evidence of this stems from a comparison of the data obtained by the population censuses taken in 1969 and 1970. According to these data, the percentage of women in the overall number of persons doing predominantly physical work has remained unchanged at 46 percent, while the proportion of women in the overall number of mental workers, in contrast, has grown 27 percent (from 32 percent in 1959 to 59 percent in 1970) (Lagutin and Sergeyeva, 1975: 11).

On the whole, the number of women doing expert work has jumped 15-fold compared to 1928. This change is evident in all regions and all populated centres of the country. For the first time in history, socialism has made professions which require maximum creative effort mass women's professions: medical doctor (74 percent); teacher and college instructor (72 percent); stage and film director, composer and conductor (39 percent); scientific and scholarly researcher (40 percent); judge

(33 percent), etc. In 1974 the number of women with Master's Degrees was 83,600; women with Doctoral Degrees 4,000 and women professors, corresponding and full members of the academies of sciences, almost 17,000.

The improved opportunities for women is also noticeable in the industrial trades. According to A. E. Kotlyar and S. I. Turchaninova (1975), in 1965-1972, the proportion of women workers who hold mechanical jobs grew by 22 percent, that of repairwomen by 60 percent and that of women who performed automated operations by 67 percent. The number of women setters of automats more than trebled, that of women who handled automatically controlled apparatuses rose 2.8-fold (Kotlyar and Turchaninova, 1975: 5). There has also been a substantial rise in the proportion of highly skilled women workers in a wide variety of trades.

The intrabranch division of male and female labour depends entirely on the conditions, character and content of work in each branch. Such branches of the national economy as the mining industry, transport, construction, forest management, in which the labour conditions are still comparatively primitive are dominated by males. (The proportion of women does not exceed 30 percent). Engineering, light and food industries, on the contrary, are dominated by women (about 70 percent). One of the leaders in the number of places held by working women is the machine-building industry. In its new branches such as the instrument-making and electronics industries women account for 45-47 percent of the total work force.

The number of women workers has grown too, in what is known as the nonproductive sphere. At present this is about 40 percent. Thus the increase in the proportion of females in professional and vocational categories is paralleled by its redistribution in branches of the national economy and its spheres of application as well as by a change in its character and content. This ensures equality of social position and explodes the myth about "new forms of economic exploitation" of the Soviet woman. Lenin repeatedly emphasized that it is inadmissible to equalize women's and men's labour productivity, volume, duration and conditions (Lenin, Collected Works, Vol. 30, Moscow, Progress Publishers, 1974, p. 43) and Marx had deemed a number of jobs to be "unhealthy for the female body or ...objectionable morally for the female sex" (Karl Marx and Frederick Engels, Selected Works in Two Volumes, Vol. II, Moscow, Foreign Literature Publishing House, 1958, p. 36).

Evidence of the profound social and personal interest of Soviet women in professional and vocational jobs is a key objective indicator in the growth of the already large number of rationalizers, inventors, heroes of socialist labour, winners of socialist emulation, and youth counsellors, whose activity bears the character of self-realization and free choice. At present the membership of the All-Union Society of Rationalizers and Inventors includes 1.5 million women. On average, one-third of the awards for meritorious labour and one-quarter of the titles of Hero of Socialist Labour go to women. More than 4 million women take part in socialist emulation and thousands upon thousands of advanced women workers share in competitions to earn the titles of "best rationalizer of the enterprise" and "best creative women's team". In other words, women's labour activity is gradually becoming a form of realization of professional and vocational knowledge and experience as well as a form of satisfaction of the need for creation and extensive social communication.

In developed socialist society the women normally exhibits high vocational and professional activity, since the social indicators of such society are not only, and not so much, the high proportion of women engaged in social production as a change in the character, content, motives and orientation of their labour. This should not be taken to mean that all problems in the field of women's work are already resolved. The position of women as a specific socio-demographic group requires constant considerararation of questions concerning their labour, the possibilities for their vocational and professional advances, etc.

On the other hand, socialism, even at the stage of complete maturity, is the first stage of communism. Public ownership of the means of production still has two forms; the material and technical base of communism is still in information and the process of change in the character and content of labour is still far from completion. This is evidenced by the presence of creative and uncreative; predominantly mental and predominantly physical; skilled and unskilled; mechanized automated and unmechanized, manual work. Different forms of labour are performed by definite groups of workers in a rigid, definite form although the attachment of work to worker is not inflexible and lifelong. (The law of occupational turnover intensifies its action.) Many of the physically easier jobs performed by women workers are not very complex or mind-stimulating. For instance, in the women-dominated branches of production which turn out consumer items, "the level of mechanization and automation of production... is high but the level of mechanization of labour is still low, the creative elements of labour are insubstantial and the skill requirements are not high" (N. M. Shishkan, 1976: 36). As a result, the women in these areas of production work at less creative tasks than do men, who dominate the fields which turn out implements of production. Moreover, in the process of automation of socialist production awaiting completion, two trends are in existence: (1) the creation of a potential for a many-sided manifestation of the creative ability of the woman and (2) a rise in partial specialization, which confines her labour activity to relatively simple operations and perpetuates her subordination to the technical system. So far, women account for the greater proportion of the workers who perform subsidiary operations where the level of mechanization is much lower than that of the principal ones (25–30 percent and 60–70 percent, respectively). For example, women comprise 80 percent of the ancillary industrial workers, 86 percent of the sorters and graders and 80 percent of the packers (Ekonomicheskaya Gazeta, 1969, No. 3, p. 3).

A key problem which still awaits a complete solution is the problem of the rational employment of women. The relevant concept hypothesizes a balance between the number of able-bodied women, their vocational and professional requirements, and the existence of job vacancies. It assumes the continued improvement of the conditions, character and content of women's work, which, on the whole, create objective prerequisites for the development of the woman's personality. A more rational employment of women presupposes an optimum labour regime, which responds to the specific psychophysiological distinctions of the female body and enables the woman to harmonize her professional and vocational activity with her family and other everyday responsibilities.

At present, the inadequate solution of this problem inhibits, to a certain extent, the removal of the leftovers of actual inequality. For instance, due to the historically developed specialization of women's work and the level of technical equipment of a number of branches of production, the share of women in individual spheres of the national economy varies between 17 and 83 percent (Kotlyar and Yankova, 1976: 88). This results in gross disparity in the rates of employment of men and women in territorial units as well as distinctions in the conditions, routine and content of, and payment for, their labour even within the limits of one enterprise. As has been pointed out, all of this, quite naturally, affects the size of women's earnings especially since the productivity of men's and women's labour in a number of enterprises and work places differs substantially. Even though they surpass men in level of education, women frequently lag behind them in industrial skill categories to say nothing of the lag in the many vocations that require the physical strength and endurance that men possess.

Sociological surveys of recent years indicate that in a number of instances women lag somewhat behind men in the level of skills. According to the data of a survey conducted in Byelorussian engineering enterprises (the Gomel Agricultural Machinery Plant, the Minsk Motor-Vehicle Works, tractor and instrument-making plants), while men and women have equal general educational levels their skill levels were found to be slightly different. For example, the proportion of men with 8–11 forms of schooling in the overall number of male workers equaled 43.2 percent, while the corresponding proportion of women workers equalled 41.9 percent. The difference is small but workers of the 1st and 2nd skill-categories accounted for 42.9 percent among the men and for 78 percent among the women, while workers of the 4th skill-category account for 19.2 percent among the men and for 1.9 percent among the women (Proizvodstvennaya deyatelnost zhenshchin i semya/Productive Activity of Women and the Family/, 1972: 41). Obviously, this, in one way or another, also affects the wages of a fair proportion of woman workers.

One of the root causes of the lag exhibited at the skill level by some of the woman workers, according to a joint Soviet-Polish survey conducted in 1966–1968, is shortage of free time—a factor which is at work to this day.

Another source of the lag stems from the forced breaches in the continuity of work life due to the need to look after babies. The persisting contradictions between the vocational/professional roles, on the one hand, and the family roles, on the other, frequently diminish the chances of professional and vocational promotion for married women, especially mothers. This is also the root cause of the lower percentage of women among the rationalizers, inventors and managers.

The gradual withdrawal of women from the sphere of arduous and unhealthy work constitutes another problem. The Soviet state, as has been its custom, takes vigorous measures to protect the women in the labour force. The Soviet Union has special laws banning the assignment of arduous and unhealthy jobs to women. There is constant improvement in the labour conditions in industrial enterprises. This ensures the good state of health of women workers and the normal development of their children. There is a constant drop in the frequency of premature childbirths, still births, etc.

At the same time many health surveys (G. A. Slesarev, 1965: 120) reveal that on some occasions mechanization of production processes and transportation facilities and the introduction of new technical equipment fail to reduce physical tension in the performance of some jobs if other adverse conditions such as industrial fumes, dust, noise, high temperature, etc. are allowed to persist. Medical experts have come to the conclusion that the influence of such factors affects the health of mothers (Slesarev, 1965: 120–130). Thus, women's work in the production sphere requires the solution of sanitation and hygienic as well as social problems.

The social development plans of labour teams incorporate various measures designed to release women from the sphere of arduous physical work (with an eye to the doctors' recommendations) and to provide them with more skilled and easier jobs.

At present efforts are being made to set differential work quotas in agriculture and some are already having a major social effect. Development of such quotas for a number of trades in the transport, the construction and other industries has been launched. The continued improvement in the fixing of women's labour rates will give a major impetus to the growth of their work activity as a whole and ultimately will affect the growth rate of the number of women seeking independence and self-determination.

Socio-Political Activity of Women

The social portrait of the modern Soviet woman would be incomplete if the characteristic of her direct social roles was confined to her vocational and professional ones.

The development of woman into a harmonious, creative and socially active personality proceeds against the background of her direct socio-political activity. As major social indicators of the latter the authors consider the proportion of the women engaged in some concrete type of social activity as well as its content and motivation. Only then is it possible to measure the significance of this activity in the process of personality formation.

One of the key indicators of this activity is the constant growth of the share of women deputies to the Supreme Soviets–the women who take direct part in the making of socially significant decisions. While women accounted for 16.5 percent of the overall number of deputies in 1937, the proportion rose to 27 percent in 1962 and to 31.3 percent in 1974. At present the USSR Supreme Soviet has 2.5 times more women deputies than the Supreme Soviet of the first convocation. This can be viewed as the crucial result of the 60-year activity of the Soviet state, as a result of the development of relations of equality. The number of women deputies is growing centrally as well as in all non-Russian republics and in both town and country, demonstrating that the socio-political activity of women has gained a universal character.

In the Supreme Soviets of the non-Russian republics, women deputies account for 35 percent of the total membership. Their proportion is 39 percent in the Supreme Soviets of the autonomous republics and is close to 50 percent in the local Soviets of Working People's Deputies. The key indicator of the mounting social activity of women is the high level of their membership in social organizations. At present women account for 28.8 percent of the membership of the Soviet Communist Party, 52 percent of the membership of the Komsomol and 37–50 percent of the leaders of various trade union organizations. Women are elected delegates to the largest forums and congresses—added evidence of their high social prestige. Suffice it to note that women accounted for 24.3 percent of the delegates to the 24th CPSU Congress and for 26 percent of the delegates to the 25th CPSU Congress.

There is hardly any all-male type or form of social thrust. According to the data collected by Kharchev and Golod (1971: 66) the proportion of women workers who contribute to social schemes in the industrial enterprises of Leningrad and Kostroma (which they surveyed at the close of the 1960's) was 43 and 45.8 percent, respectively. According to the data collected by the present authors in Moscow in the mid-1970's, 52—68 percent of the woman respondents were engaged in social work. This proportion would rise to 90 percent in the former survey and to 98 percent in the latter, if one were to include the performance of temporary assignments in addition to permanent ones. At the same time, Kharchev and Golod (1971) note that the social functions of women in the enterprises they surveyed, were, as a rule, more than modest. Nevertheless, if one were to view the matter on a countrywide scale, the significance of the socio-political activity of women for the benefit of society as a whole and for woman herself, including the development of her world outlook, defies overestimation. No matter how modest the woman's social work may be it marks a new phenomenon, primarily an identification of the woman with all of society. Evidence of this is the stable growth in the proportion of female social workers as a whole and the growth of the proportion of women who take part in the making of socially significant decisions, in the handling of the affairs of the community, region and country and, finally, in the motivational structure of this activity.

According to the data of the Kharchev–Golod survey, the most common motives for the social work performed by female workers were "the need to be with people," "Party, Komsomol duty," and "performance of the assignment received". On average, in the Kharchev–Golod sample the proportion of these motives had the following distribution: first motive—32.9 percent; second—23.7 percent; third—43.4 percent (1971: 66).

According to the data of the Moscow survey by the present authors, about 78 percent of the women included in the sample said that the most important motives for their social work were "an urge to do good to people", "to perfect the conditions of life", "to make Moscow a communist city", and "to make our district a model one"—an indication of the direct social orientation of their personal desires.

It is safe to say that the growth of the socio-political activity of many Soviet women is becoming the underlying feature of their way of life and an equally important characteristic of their personality. It is based on free choice, is performed in free time and conceived of as a way to perfect social relations.

Women in the Family

Because the woman's family and other domestic roles are different in character and content, they exercise a different influence on the formation of her individual qualities and on the growth of her vocational and professional as well as her socio-political activity. Some of these roles blend into a harmonious unity with her vocational, professional and socio-political roles because they presuppose productive, creative or organizational activity; others conflict with them. Some create conditions for relaxation and raising the level of knowledge and development; others, on the contrary, create overloads and obstruct the satisfaction of higher requirements. According to the results of the Moscow survey of 1975–1977, which covered 500 families with small children, the women themselves distinguish and estimate their everyday functions in different ways. Ninety-four percent of the women think such family-domestic functions as the rearing of children, the exercise of organizational functions and the adoption of vital family decisions are most important for themselves and stress their relationship with their vocational, professional and socio-political functions in terms of both their orientation and their content and social significance.

As regards family-domestic roles such as service to the family, the majority of the women, although they deem them to be essential for the family good, say they would like to reduce them, mechanize them as much as possible and partially turn them over to everyday service institutions or share them with other family members thereby gaining time and energy for the rearing of children and other higher forms of activity in the family.

These attitudes do not find complete realization in life due to drawbacks in the organization of everyday services and due sometimes to the stand taken by the husband. It is precisely the sphere of domestic chores as a whole in which the woman remains unequal. This is confirmed very conclusively by an analysis of the time expenditures of men and women on different types of domestic chores.

For instance, cooking takes wives 10–12 hours a week, husbands about 1.5–2 hours. Buying food takes wives about 6 hours and husbands about 3 hours; washing about 6 hours vs. about 20–30 minutes a week. These uninteresting functions thus take the lion's share the woman's time, and physical and nervous energy. They reduce her creative potential and her satisfaction with the marriage.

The time expenditures on the rearing of children (14–20 hours per week), the organization of leisure, and other organizational activity in the family (5–7 hours) are more justly divided between the husband and wife. Asked what role they think is the most significant one for themselves, vocational (professional) or the rearing of children, 90 percent of the women of different socio-vocational or socio-professional groups and educational levels said: "Either, because they are complementary". Moreover, they stressed that the woman who does vocational (professional) work commands greater respect of her husband and children, a factor which enables her to perform crucial intrafamily functions. In the families in which the woman performs responsible vocational (professional) roles she also takes a more active part in family decision-making and in supervisory, educational and organizational functions. By contrast, in the families in which the wife is not employed (3.7 percent of the families included in the sample) her responsibilities are predominantly confined to family service. Thus, in developed socialist society, woman's orientation to vocational (professional) activity, far from ruling out, complements and makes more significant her specific nature-conditioned family functions.

A major interest for the analysis of the modern family is presented by a special study of the problems of family authority, "leadership", "supremacy", etc. According to the data of a survey conducted by Pimenova (1970: 31–41), supremacy now evolves from previous veneration of the head of the family—whatever his personal qualities and the degree to which he shared in the family-life activity—and his unlimited family authority based on recognition of the actual functions and personal merits of his leadership. However, in many families included in the sample the concept of "head of the family" had lost its validity, and had become totally meaningless. For instance, the presence of supremacy was recognized by 43 percent of the overall number of families and denied by 57 percent. In more than 8 percent of the families women were deemed to be the heads. Actually, the proportion of women's supremacy in the family is much higher. According to the data of the 1970 census, based on answers to a point-blank question, "Who is the head of your family?", 50 percent of the families are headed by women.

The change in the concept of "head of the family" and the loss of its previous connotation are parallelled by the emergence in many families of two "heads" or, more exactly, of two organizers working in different spheres of intrafamily activity; husband and wife both exercise their supervising functions on the basis of their knowledge, experience and specific skills. This process characterizes the presence of new family roles for women and the growth of their prestige in the family.

Simultaneously, there is a change in the requirements which are made on the head of the family. The present authors' survey, for instance, included this question: To what extent does the head of your family share in the performance of the following functions: a) service of the family, b) the storing of food, c) the buying of industrial, cultural and everyday goods, d) the rearing of children, e) the organization of the family's leisure, f) the planning of family expenditures, g) the making of decisions on vital plans of the children and other family members? This was parallelled by a self-estimate of the individuals covered by the sample according to a five-point system (5—takes complete part, 4—takes a substantial part, 3—partially contributes, 2—insubstantially contributes, 1—negligibly contributes).

An analysis of the findings indicated that at present the spouse who takes part in all or the majority of the above forms of family activity rather than in only some of them, as in earlier times, and who exhibits a maximum of responsibility for the family as a whole, is usually regarded as head of the family. The head of the family, as a rule, is the key contributor to the rearing of children, the organization of the family's free time and the planning and making of vital decisions. This conclusion is supported by data from self-reported participation in concrete forms of domestic activity. For instance, about 80 percent of the respondents gave their child-rearing and decision-making efforts 5 points and their efforts in the organization of leisure and the planning of expenditures, 4 points. The highest estimate, according to this 5-point system, was recorded for such personal qualities of the head of the family as having extensive knowledge, intellect, intuition, energy, experience, the ability to make family decisions and to bring-up children.

The results permit us to speak of the formation of a new structure for family relations based on actual equality and co-operative effort, which are the general principles of the socialist way of life.

Nevertheless, there remain the underlying contradictions which call for immediate solution — the contradictions between the creative-productive functions of wife and mother and the unproductive mechanical functions such as washing, cleaning, etc. Furthermore, there are persisting substantial distinctions in the amount and structure of the free time for men and women.

The removal of these and a number of other contradictions, including those of growth, is the aim of the complex system of measures of aid to the family developed by the state and by social organizations. The standing commissions on the labour and everyday life of women and the protection of mother and child, which were set up under the USSR Supreme Soviet and the Supreme Soviets of the Union republics in 1976, are encouraged to carry out the continued improvement of this system so as to bring about the elimination of the elements of domestic inequality and of the conflicts between the two main roles played by women.

REFERENCES

Dodge, N.
    1966   *Women in the Soviet Economy*. Zhenshchiny v SSSR. Statisticheskii sbornik. 1972, 1975.
Kharchev, A. G. and S. I. Golod
    1971   *Professionalnaia rabota zhenshchin i semja*.
Korchagin, V. P.
    1974   *Trudovye resursy v usloviiakh NTR*.
    1960   *Narodnoe khoziaistvo SSSR v 1975 g. Statisticheskii sbornik*.
Kotlyar, A. E. and Turchaninova, S. I.
    1975   *Zaniatost zhenshchin v proizvodstve*.
Kotlyar, A. E. and Z. A. Yankova
    1975   *Sotsialno-ekonomicheskie problemy truda i byta zhenshchin v usloviakh sotsialisticheskogo obshchestva*.
Lagutin, N. S. and Sergeeva, G. P.
    1975   *Sotsialno-ekenomicheskoe polozhenie zhenshchiny v SSSR*.
Pimenova, A. Z.
    1970   Novyi byt i stanovlenie vnutrisemeinogo ravenstva. "Sotsialnye issledovaniia", N. 4.
    1972   *Proizvodstvennaia deiatelnost zhenschin i semja*.
Shishkan, N. M.
    1976   *Trud zhenshchiny v usloviiakh razvitogo sotsializma*.
Slesarev, G. A.
    1965   *Metodologiia sotsiologicheskogo issledovaniaproblem narodonaseleniia SSSR*.
Slesarev, G. A. and Z. A. Yankova
    1969   Zhenshchina na promyshlennom predpriatii i v semje. "Sotsialnye problemy truda i proizvodstva". Moskva–Warshava.

Women and the Family in Poland

RENATA SIEMIEŃSKA

The University of Warsaw, Warsaw, Poland

IN POLAND—as in other socialist countries—equality of men and women is a political and ideological question. Basic documents such as the Constitution (1952) emphasize equality of men and women as citizens: "Women in the Polish People's Republic enjoy the same rights as men in all spheres of life: state, political, economic, and culture." Equal rights for women are guaranteed by:

> equality with men in the right to work and remuneration according to the principle "equal pay for equal work", in the rights to rest and recreation, to social security, to education, to recognition and awards, to public office; mother and child-care, aid and protection of pregnant women, vacations with full pay during and after childbirth, expansion of the network of maternity wards, lying-in hospitals, creches, kindergartens, development of the services and catering establishments (Salva, 1970).

However, when we analyze the amount and kind of actual participation of women in different spheres of life, it is quite apparent that women's status in society differs from men's. In addition to the strictly biological interpretation of gender role differentiation—which everyone accepts—it is possible to indicate several factors which determine the kind of participation of women in the social life in socialist countries. These factors are determined in the main by government policy and by the cultural heritage. The following are part of government policy as we understand it:

a) opportunities are to be made available for men and women: opportunities for education; the opportunity to find jobs and different types of jobs; necessary services; education for children and for home help, etc., and

b) images of women are to be propagated by the mass media, in speeches of politicians, etc.

In contrast to this the cultural heritage refers to the status and roles of women as accepted by particular social groups in earlier times.

The influence of government policy in socialist countries is greater than in most others because of the specificity of a centralized economic and political system.

The distinction between the two basic groups of factors above as determinants

of women's status is particularly important in Poland, where, after World War II, a change in the socioeconomic and political system was associated with rapid industrialization. This interplay created a completely new situation for women. The old patterns of women's behaviour were considered passé and the state propaganda stressed new expectations. It is of interest, therefore, to look for answers to the following questions:
   a) What governmental policy for women's social participation has been established in Poland since World War II?
   b) What expectations with respect to the status of women have been and are now shared by society?
Answers to these questions and comparisons between the answers give us important interesting clues as to how government planning and spontaneous social processes interact in these spheres of activity.

Women's Roles and Family Patterns Propagated by the Mass Media

Government policy as regards the development of the country and the expectations concerning women's roles in society are accurately reflected by propaganda in the mass media. On this account, the images of women they disseminate have been changing over a period of time. These transformations parallel the changing images of a new personality that reflects the basic changes of a society adjusting to a new economic and social system (Jasińska, and Siemieńska, 1975a). The main disseminated personality patterns, linked to historical periods after World War II are these:

1. Personality patterns associated with a period of crystallization and stabilization of a new political system (1944–1949). During this time and in this new political situation, all members of the society are engaged in a fight with internal class enemies and in a process of reconstructing the national economy for the entire country—especially in northern and western regions. Women's and men's roles propagated by the mass media are similar since they are equally engaged in these processes.

2. Personality patterns associated with people who took part in the construction of the economic basis of the new socio-economic system within a "Six Year Plan Industrialization". Women's active participation in this process is strongly emphasized. For example, a content analysis of Przyjaciółka, a journal with a large circulation and addressed to women, revealed, at that time, a focus mainly on workers' and peasants' families. The vocational activity of women was a characteristic feature of the articles, and women's status in the family was determined by their occupational roles. In this sense the wives' positions inside the family are equal to their husband's positions as wage-earners and as decision-makers. The main reason for women's new prominence is their occupational success. The role of the family is, in one sense, limited to few functions which leads to a point of view that many traditional func-

tions of the family can be performed by specialized institutions, for example, kindergartens, youth centres, cafeterias at work and at school, etc. (Kłoskowska, 1959).

3. The re-evaluation of model personality patterns propagated in the late 1950's also brought about a changed image of women. The journal, mentioned above, noted that in 1956-1957 only 22% of the persons presented were from workers' and peasants' families as compared with 60% in previous years (Kłoskowska, 1959). In this period the families of the intelligentsia were often described, yet the most characteristic feature of family patterns propagated at that time reflected a lack of description of any professional roles. Women mostly played the roles of wives, mothers, fiancees, and not occupational ones. Love and emotional relationships among members of the family were very often emphasized. As in novels written in that time, tensions inside the family were often shown (Paszkiewicz, 1975); conflicts caused by relationships of husband and/or wife with other partners and also between parents and children were also described frequently. The source of the latter conflicts were mainly differences in life conditions of the older and younger generation which produced different ideological and moral approaches to life.

4. The next period of what might be called "small stabilization" began in the early 1960's and was labelled in this fashion because of a new concept in the economic development of the country. The transformation of Poland from a mainly agricultural to an industrial-agricultural country during the previous period, and the appearance during this time of an imbalance between the development of heavy industry and production of goods, resulted in a new concept of further development, one that included mass consumption. Personality patterns promoted by the mass media at the time of "small stabilization" included professional roles, qualified workers, technicians, engineers, etc., and also, in harmony with these, aspects of private life and some limited consumptive aspirations. The role of the family in personal life was enhanced. As compared to the late 1950's, women's professional roles were more often described but, simultaneously, women as presented in Przyjaciółka, in 1965-66 were very often limited to the roles of wives and mothers (Adamski, 1970).

5. By the end of 1970 growing tensions were in evidence and new social and economic policies resulted in some modification of model personality patterns in the mass media. A content analysis of some TV and radio programs shows that the professional work of women—whether they are or are not competent to do it—is no longer a problem for discussion. In the mid 1970's the question of whether it is better or not for mothers to interrupt their professional work for some period and to return later to outside work does appear as an issue for discussion. In other words, the accent has shifted from professional work as the best answer to womens' personal careers to another possibility in which women combine professional work with family duties during those periods of time when family responsibilities are clearly considered most important. Some students of society have pointed out that in the

mass media (TV, radio) a majority of families portrayed are one-parent families (usually a woman raising children) along with families experiencing different conflicts among their members (Wilska-Duszyńska, 1975), and that, generally, with the exception of some programs like "Family Matysiakowie" and some others, there is a lack of positive family patterns in the mass media.

This short resume of the content analysis of the changed images of Polish women and family as portrayed in the mass media after World War II shows clear linkages with the periods of economic, social and political development of Poland and the disseminated images of this development. The changing role of women in the labour force along with the cultural transformations of society make futile any discussion of the possibility that women's roles should be limited to the family.

Women's Occupational Activity

Women's occupational activity has a long tradition in Poland, although the extent of that activity and the structure of women's employment have both been changing over the years. Since World War I and after the restoration of Poland as an independent state, the number of women participating in the labour force has been growing rapidly. In 1921 women constituted 45% of the total number of employed people (Statystyka Polska 30) in handicrafts, agriculture and independent professions. In 1931 the percentage of women among all workers was 33.6%, and over 50% in the textile and garment industries. Many were working as domestic servants (Mały Rocznik Statystyczny, 1938). At the same time women constituted one-third of the white-collar workers. Despite this large number of occupationally active women, their wages were on the average 20–40% lower than men's. This wage difference resulted from the assumption that women did not have very high material expectations at the beginning of their occupational activity; that men's work is more intensive; that women have fewer needs and therefore can be satisfied with lower pay; and that women working was still not yet accepted at that time (Dziesieciolecie Polski Odrodzonej, 1928: 876).

In the 1930's the number of women studying in colleges began increasing. They constituted 40% of postgraduates studying in different faculties and were especially visible in dentistry (69% in 1931) and pharmacology (above 50% in 1938) (Mały Rocznik Statystyczny, 1938: 325).

As was mentioned earlier, rapid industrialization after World War II and new political conditions resulted in a great migration from rural areas to the fast-growing cities. From 1950 to 1970 the number of inhabitants of cities increased by 91%, while the number of inhabitants of rural areas remained almost unchanged. Men migrated to cities more often than women. As a result, women now managed 42%

of all farms by themselves. During this time the number of women employed in forestry grew faster than the number of men (in the period 1955–1974 the rate of growth for women was 480% while that for men was 145%). Generally, the female participation rate in forestry increased from 6% in 1955 to 18% in 1974. Nonetheless, the overall employment in agriculture and forestry decreased during this time, but the number of men employed decreased more rapidly than that of women (Knychała, 1978: 40).

At the beginning of the 1950's, when the Six-Year Plan of Economic Development went into effect, industry and construction were growing rapidly and both men and women found jobs there—but the latter usually as unqualified labourers. A scarcity of workers stimulated some governmental decisions in 1952 to guarantee an increase of participation of female workers in the nationalized economy. As a result, the number of employed women grew faster than that of employed men. The proportion of women in the total labour force rose from 31% in 1950 to 33% in 1954. Because of a stagnation of real income during this time an improvement in living conditions was only possible by increasing the number of employed family members. Governmental policy in relation to women's occupational activity was strongly linked with the economic situation of the country (Przedpelski, 1975; Rajkiewicz, 1965; Wieruszewski, 1977: 111). The year 1954 marked the beginning of a new governmental policy with respect to women's employment; diminishing investments associated with a diminished growth of employment opportunities caused difficulties in employment for women. Therefore, between 1954 and 1960 the proportion of women in the labour force remained at around 33%.

In 1975, 4,850,100 women were engaged in the national economy, out of a total number of 11,513,000 workers (Mały Rocznik Statystyczny, 1977: 45). The highest relative number of occupationally active women in this year was in the age group 35–39. Women's participation in the labour force varies by sector (Table 1). It is possible to describe three types of participation patterns:
1. with women's proportion above 50% of the total number of workers;
2. with women's proportion about 40%—which is approximately the proportion of women presently active in the labour force; and
3. with a lower proportion of employed women (Wrochno, 1971: 46). In 1974 women constituted the majority of workers in health and social care services (81%), in finance and insurance institutions (80%), in trade (73%), in education, scientific establishments and culture (64%) and in public administration and institutions of justice (56%). Women constituted the lowest percentage among the total number of those employed in construction (18%), in agriculture (25%), in forestry (19%) and in public transportation (24%) (Wieruszewski, 1975: 119). During the last twenty years the proportion of women to total numbers employed in particular sectors has remained almost unchanged, except in public administration and institutions of justice which

Table 1

*Women in the Labour Force as a Percentage of Total Employment in Each Branch of the National Economy and in Percent of all Employed Women for 1955 and 1974, Poland**

Branches of national economy	In % of the total number of employees in particular branches		Difference 1974–1955	In % of the total number of employed women	
	1955	1974		1955	1974
Industry	30.2	40.0	+9.8	39.9	38.2
Building	12.4	17.6	+5.2	4.3	4.6
Agriculture	20.5	25.2	+4.7	4.7	4.1
Forestry	6.4	18.7	+12.3	0.3	0.6
Transportation and Communication	15.2	24.4	+9.6	4.2	5.2
Trade	51.4	73.1	+21.7	16.5	15.1
Municipal economics	31.1	36.5	+5.4	2.1	3.3
Education, science, culture	56.6	64.3	+7.7	11.0	13.5
Medical care, social care services and sport	76.7	81.2	+4.5	8.6	9.1
Public administration and institutions of justice	38.8	56.2	+17.4	5.9	2.4
Finance and insurance institutions	57.0	79.7	+29.7	1.4	1.5

* Source: "Rocznik Statystyczny", 1975: 53,55.

moved from the middle sector to the category with the highest proportion of women.

The level of education of women and men varies by sector. Women with completed university education concentrate in professions traditionally more "female", while the distribution of men with higher education shows clusters in different types of work. In 1973 the distribution of workers with university education was as follows (Wieruszewski, 1975: 121):

	Women	Men
Branches with the highest proportion of women	74.2%	46.5%
Branches with a medium proportion of women	13.5%	28.3%
"Male" branches	11.7%	27.4%

The above proportions show not only women's preferences in the choice of particular professions, but also preferences for certain kinds of employment. More exact analyses show women's expansion into professions which were considered "male" professions before World War II, for example, engineering (Wrochno, 1971: 51). The number of employed women with higher education is growing faster than is the number of men.

Women's wages are lower than men's even if they are better educated and even if they hold the same position as men. Women's positions within organizations are usually lower.

Taking into consideration the structure of women's and men's employment it is quite apparent that:

1. in reality occupational segregation by sex exists;
2. "feminization" of traditionally female professions is increasing;
3. women are beginning, fairly easily and rather quickly, to enter new professions;
4. the number of women in traditionally male professions is increasing rather slowly;
5. women with higher education are concentrating mainly in humanistic studies, and they are less interested in technical professions;
6. "feminization" of professions tends to occur in those that require prolonged studies but do not have high social prestige or wages;
7. "feminization" of positions in the national economy reduce women's chances to achieve higher salaries (Waluk, 1965; Dziecielska–Machnikowska, 1968; Sobczak, 1971); and
8. changes in the occupational situation of women and their desire to continue working are strongly related to level of education.

In 1960 a study showed that 57% of the women polled would like to stop working if their husband's wage were higher. The answer, however, is strongly related to level of education: only 19% of the women with higher education wanted to stop working, as compared with 58% of the white-collar workers and 66% of the skilled workers. In particular women with higher education expressed their desire to work for nonmaterial motives; in the other occupational categories these intrinsic motives were rarely mentioned (Preiss–Zajdowa, 1967: 56, Górska, 1977).

Employers usually prefer men over women workers (Siemieńska and Bijak–Żochowski, 1975: 230). This is one of the reasons why women have more difficulty than men in finding jobs. In 1974, for example, women constituted 91% of those looking for jobs, while only 36% of free positions were available for women (Rocznik Statystyczny, 1975: 62). But not only employers' preferences cause this situation: women, on the whole, are less well educated in modern technology than men and more often seek positions as skilled workers in a constantly modernizing national economy that requires more and more highly skilled workers (Rajkiewicz, 1965; Jakubowicz, 1971).

The sex segregation within the Polish labour force is not dissimilar to women's situations in other socialist countries.

Education as a Factor of Women's Work Participation Rates

The relatively lower level of women's education has caused many difficulties in their labour force participation. Therefore, after World War II an increase in the level of women's education has been considered one of the important changes which needed to be effected.

In 1973–74, as a consequence of governmental policy and of cultural changes, the relative number of girls and women in different types of schools, was in general, higher than in earlier periods.

In 1973 there was no difference between the percentages of girls and boys in primary schools. In high schools some differences appeared because of different preferences of both sexes, with girls found more often in general orientated high schools, while boys were more likely to be found in vocational ones. (This tendency appears to have stabilized during the last ten years.) But in some of the vocationa

Table 2

Percent Women in Universities, Academies and Higher Schools For Selected Years, Poland*

School years	Total	Universities	Academies		Higher schools					
			Medical	Theological	Technical	Agricultural	Economic	Pedagogical	Sport	Artistic
1950/1951	34.5	39.9	55.5	—	8.0	65.4	35.1	44.3	34.8	51.1
1955/1956	32.2	44.1	58.4	9.3	14.5	30.8	37.8	49.9	28.4	44.5
1960/1961	34.7	49.2	62.2	8.8	13.4	29.3	27.2	52.7	28.4	44.9
1965/1966	37.5	53.2	63.5	13.0	15.6	32.8	38.4	59.1	39.2	48.5
1970/1971	42.2	58.4	66.0	41.8	19.9	38.8	58.7	67.4	39.3	48.0
1973/1974	47.0	61.9	63.9	41.4	22.8	43.3	64.0	68.9	38.3	48.5
Difference: 1950/1951 1973/1974	+12.5	+22	+8.4	—	+14.8	−22.1	+28.9	+24.6	+3.5	−2.6

* Source: Wieruszewski, 1975: 89.

schools which prepare students to work in health services, garment and textile industries, and restaurants, for example, girls constituted about 90% of those enrolled. In other vocational schools where students are prepared to work as electricians, mechanics or transportation workers, for instance, the number of girls is very low. Similar distributions appear in some other countries, for example, in the Soviet Union (Zenszczyny, 1969: 56). This situation, created spontaneously, is considered unsatisfactory from the point of view of the structure of labour force demands. Therefore, in 1967 the Ministry of Education started a program for the students just finishing primary schools to provide information about opportunities for further education in different types of high school and also established quotas on percentages to say how many girls should be educated in particular kinds of schools.

In higher schools where a similar situation exists, the proportion of males to females is controlled by quotas which specify how many candidates of each sex are to be allowed admission. (This is necessary because it has been recognized that graduates, especially women, have congregated mainly in the big cities.) The quota plan is a source of a feeling of discrimination, especially in some types of schools where female candidates want to begin studies in higher schools. For example in medical schools a ratio of 1–1 between women and men is assumed and similar ratios exist in some other professional schools and universities. But in 1970 women constituted 70% of the total number of candidates in medical schools, while in agricultural colleges they were only 42%. Moreover the numbers of women who are not accepted as students were very high, and in medical schools women constituted 73% of the total number of unaccepted candidates, and in agricultural colleges 68%, while men with poorer examination results were admitted as students. (Women usually pass candidate examinations with similar or only slightly lower results than men.)

In recent years the absolute numbers of women desiring advanced study are higher than that of men, but, considering relative numbers, men more often plan to continue education than women. In 1969 every fourth female high school graduate wanted to continue education while every third male high school graduate wanted to do so. This means that women more often than men considered high school their appropriate level for termination of education (Wyniki, 1971).

Women were 38% of the graduates (numbering 262,902) from universities for the period 1945–1973, but in 1973 the percentage of women among graduates was double what it had been in 1945. Understandably women are mainly graduates of regular universities rather than evening studies for working people, as women have many more household duties than men. Most of the women are graduates of universities, economic academies and higher schools for teachers. This means that even now women choose traditionally female professions—although in the last few years they are beginning to appear also in the new professions.

Generally, we can speak of a great increase in women's professional aspirations, (especially among younger women) and a rising level of education, but simultaneously it is necessary to point out the tendency for them to choose, in contrast to men, professions which are less attractive financially than those chosen by men.

Women as Managers and Politicians

Despite the considerable number of women graduates of universities and similar schools who work in different branches of the national economy, women occupy a disproportionately small number of higher positions. For example, in 1968 (as in 1964) women constituted one and one-half percent of the total number of directors in industry; and less than five percent of certain types of economic and technical vice-directors were female (Wrochno, 1971: 102). (The proportions are about the same today.)

In other branches of the economy the disparities are equally glaring. For example, in education, where in 1971 women constituted 80% of the total number of those employed, and in health services, were 78% of the total, they hold relatively few managerial posts.

Men predominate among highly educated persons. Women were only 28% of the total number with Ph.D. degrees and 16% with the title of Dr. *habil.*, which is the highest academic degree offered.[1] In addition, only slightly more than five percent of full professors were female (Wieruszewski, 1975: 170).

Women are very seldom high state officials. In 1974 one woman became a member of the State Council and Vice-Speaker of the Polish Parliament; a second woman was a Minister and two others were Vice-Ministers. The number of women among members of the Polish Parliament (the Sejm) has always been low. In the years 1952–1974 women constituted as little as 4% and never more than 17% of the membership (Rocznik Statystyczny, 1974: 56). However, of the lower levels of government, women's participation in officialdom is greater. In 1974 women constituted 23% (135,459 persons) of the total number of members of provincial, district, city and village councils. Usually they were rank-and-file members of these councils, and only a few women were council presidents.

Polish women's participation in high social offices is lower than in other socialistic countries such as the Soviet Union, Czechoslovakia, and the German Democratic Republic. Women are also very seldom members of either the highest bodies of political parties or of the youth organizations. For example, in 1973 only seven women (less than six percent) were members of the Central Commitee of the Polish United Workers Party (PZPR), while women constituted 23% of the total membership of the PZPR (Wieruszewski, 1975: 163). In 1975 women made up 4% of the total number of members of the Party from different bodies at lower echelons in factories, towns and cities. More women are in central bodies of youth organizations and trade unions, especially at lower levels. Yet, while the number of women in the above-mentioned organizations and in political parties is systematically increasing, the proportion does not increase in the central committees of these organizations.

The analysis of women's activities in different decision-making roles clearly indicates that women's participation is insufficient, although one can observe a small increase in the proportion of women among the total membership. Women's access to power is changing much more slowly than is their proportionate number as members of the various organizations.

---

1 Dr. *habil.* is one who has obtained a license to teach at the university; it is based on an independent piece of research and usually comes several years after one has obtained a doctorate degree; it is senior to a Ph.D.

Women's Roles as Perceived by Society

Beliefs about differences in the personalities and capacities of women and men are common in many societies. One belief about marked differences between women and men holds that women have predispositions to play *only certain roles* in society. Moreover, if they wish to participate in work activities outside the home they are suited to perform in only certain kinds (Sokołowska, 1963). Given their present high labour force participation, it is interesting to observe the kind of image of women that exists in the conciousness of members of Polish society and to learn if men and women have similar stereotypes.

Tables 3 and 4 present some results of a 1977 study carried out in six medium-sized towns (32–63 thousand inhabitants) situated in different regions of Poland, each with a different history and tradition. The towns are industrialized to different degrees and their factories belong to different parts of the economy (e.g. heavy industry, textile industry, etc.). They have one common feature: all of them have previously been administrative centers of counties. After an administrative reform made a few years ago, two of them are administrative centers of new provinces while the others have lost their status as administrative centers.

In each of the towns, a random sample of 300 respondents was interviewed about certain aspects of women's role stereotypes in society. Several statements dealing with a traditional image of women were included, namely, (1) "A woman is by nature more ready to obey than a man is", (2) "It is not good when a woman is too intelligent", (3) "Women are created to suffer", (4) "Boys and girls have different tasks in life and should therefore be brought up differently", and (5) "Politics is the business of men rather than of women."

In all towns the same trends appear although the differences in some of the respondent's opinions is small. In brief, a larger proportion of respondents disagree with the statements (2), (3) and (4), especially with (3) and (4); from 47% to 68% persons interviewed "totally disagreed" with them, and in addition between 10% to 20% of the respondents "disagreed somewhat." A reverse tendency appears when we analyze the distributions of answers to statements (1) and (5); statement (5) in particular was very often accepted "totally" or "partially", with about 80% of respondents agreeing in each town. This means that even now some traditional beliefs persist about different predispositions of men and women, and also that some kinds of social activities, such as interest in politics, are linked to sex. Of course, reactions to both of the last cited statements, and especially (5) can be considered to result from observations of social life and the ways men and women participate in it.

Results of the interviews broken down by sex of respondents are presented in Table 3 which summarizes the answers to statements (4) and (5) concerning the participation of men and women in social life in a more direct way.

The differences in opinions between men and women are very small, and for some items more men disagree; for others, more women. Statement (5) which generally was accepted by a larger share of respondents was more often accepted by women than men if we take into consideration the most extreme of the answer categories, "totally agree".

If politics is considered as mainly men's business, we tend to find that Poles are willing to accept similar roles for men and women in society. For example, when they were asked whether education is more important for a man or for a woman almost all respondents answered "equally important for both". Usually no more than 10–14% respondents in each town said that education is more important for men than for women, and there were no significant differences between male and female respondents in this respect. But at the same time women stressed, rather more often than men, the equal importance of education for men and women.

Table 3

Perception of Women's and Men's Roles in Society, in Six Different Towns of 32,000 to 63,000 Inhabitants, Poland, 1977*

	Number of town	Sex	Totally agree	Rather agree	Rather disagree	Totally disagree	I don't know	N
Boys and girls have different tasks in life and should therefore be brought up differently	1	F	19.3	13.7	23.1	40.6	3.3	160
	1	M	15.1	18.7	28.1	35.2	2.9	139
	2	F	23.0	14.5	21.2	38.2	3.1	165
	2	M	22.4	12.7	24.6	37.3	3.0	134
	3	F	14.5	11.2	31.3	39.7	3.3	179
	3	M	16.6	19.7	21.7	40.0	2.0	120
	4	F	16.7	22.5	20.8	36.3	3.7	168
	4	M	15.6	15.6	16.4	44.5	7.9	128
	5	F	14.7	18.6	25.0	32.7	9.0	156
	5	M	14.6	24.3	22.9	36.1	2.1	144
	6	F	21.2	15.8	23.6	38.8	0.6	165
	6	M	15.9	9.8	32.6	40.9	0.8	132
Politics is the business of men rather than of women	1	F	59.3	26.2	8.1	4.3	2.1	160
	1	M	51.8	32.3	9.4	4.3	2.2	139
	2	F	59.4	24.2	5.5	6.7	4.2	165
	2	M	45.5	26.9	13.4	9.0	5.2	134
	3	F	59.2	25.7	7.8	5.0	2.3	179
	3	M	51.7	30.0	11.7	5.8	0.8	120
	4	F	54.2	31.0	4.2	4.2	6.4	168
	4	M	47.7	24.2	12.5	10.9	4.7	128
	5	F	42.9	37.8	7.7	2.6	9.0	156
	5	M	47.9	31.3	6.9	9.0	4.9	144
	6	F	53.3	27.9	10.9	6.1	1.8	165
	6	M	39.4	34.1	11.4	11.4	3.7	132

* Unpublished data.

Family Patterns Accepted by Polish Society

The proportion of employed women in Poland raises the same question that is posed in other countries in similar circumstances, i.e. what is the role of the family in society? A study (Jasińska and Siemieńska, 1975b) carried out in 1972 on a national sample of respondents aged 16–60 and over showed that Poles, both men and women, put in first place among preferred life goals and desires "a good, happy family life" (60%) in contrast to "interesting work" (55%), "clear conscience" (50%), "material security" (48%), "awareness that the person is useful to other people" (38%) and other items. Small differences exist in the hierarchies of accepted life goals between women and men (Spearman's coefficient of rank-order correlation=0.97). Men somewhat less often than women preferred "good family life", "material security", "respect of others", and "mutual love"; while men more often than women preferred "wealth", "interesting work", "professional promotion and achievements", "the opportunity to influence the life of the nation", and "a life with risks". This research showed that women are slightly more oriented to small groups and personal relationships than men. An analysis of a distribution of answers in relation to age, as independent variable, showed that in all age categories "a good, happy family life" was in first position—except for the youngest (16–24) and oldest (over 60 years) respondents whose answer was in the second position.

This high priority for "a good family life" among life goals and desires is suprising when we examine it in the context of the high proportion of employed women in Poland, and if we take seriously the opinions of some people that family life becomes less attractive for women as they become occupationally active.

It is interesting that in situations in which married women are working, elements of a "traditional" model of the family are more often accepted than elements of a "modern" one (Jasińska and Siemieńska: 1975b). In the previously-mentioned study respondents chose between "traditional" and "modern" pairs of opposite behaviours and relationships inside the family. It was assumed that the following is characteristic of a model of the modern family: companionship between wife and husband with equal prominence given to their respective jobs; a way of sharing housework; freedom for each family member to express different opinions; and acceptance of individual decisions regarding how to spend part of his/her earnings and how to use part of his/her leisure time. The model of the traditional family assumed in the research included such characteristics as patriarchal relationships in the family, a clear and stable division of roles between the employed husband and the housewife taking care of home and children, and the priority given to the family as a whole over the individual interests of its members.

The "most unacceptable" features of the modern family model for respondents were independence in spending part of one's income (25%) and freedom in using one's leisure time (19%). The most acceptable attribute of the modern family was the relationship between parents and children in which parents' authority is limited and children enjoy some autonomy in having their own opinions (52%). The highest level of readiness to accept the model of the modern family was among the youngest respondents (age 16–24 years), among unmarrieds, inhabitants of the largest (above 100,000 population) and the medium-sized cities (20–100,000 population), and among the higher educated. It is interesting that "a start from zero" and "achievement of all things together" by husband and wife were less accepted by the young people (42%); instead, these were more often accepted by the oldest respondents (age 60 and over at 52%), although this feature is inconsistent with other characteristics of the traditional family model accepted by this age category.

This preference for traditional relationships in the family by respondents is congruent with results of different studies about the real time budgets of women and men in the family, division of household duties, etc.

Determinants of Actual Family Patterns

Observations of the actual division of household duties among members of the family allow us to identify three types of families:
1. families where the woman performs most of the housework and organizes it, and where the husband helps from time to time with some of the heavier work;
2. families where the wife does much housework, but all heavy and dirty work is always done by the husband;

Table 4

Perception of Need of Education for Women and Men in Six Different Towns of 32,000 to 63,000 Inhabitants, Poland, 1977*

	Number of town	Sex	For a man	For a woman	Equally important for both	I don't know	N
	1	F	14.9	1.2	83.9	—	100.0
		M	14.3	4.3	81.4	—	100.0
	2	F	10.3	1.2	87.3	1.2	100.0
		M	13.4	3.7	82.9	—	100.0
Do you think that education is more important for a man or for a woman?	3	F	11.7	2.2	85.5	0.6	100.0
		M	19.1	1.6	75.7	1.6	100.0
	4	F	10.1	4.2	85.1	0.6	100.0
		M	10.2	2.3	87.5	—	100.0
	5	F	10.9	3.2	85.6	1.3	100.0
		M	10.4	1.4	87.6	0.7	100.0
	6	F	5.5	1.8	92.1	0.6	100,0
		M	8.3	0.8	90.9	—	100.0

* Unpublished data.

3. families, where all home-making duties and work are treated by both wife and husband as common duties which should be performed together, with tasks divided between them in different ways depending on specific individual capacities, time opportunities, etc.

Studies carried on in different populations, demonstrated that the second type of family was dominant (Kłoskowska, 1965; Siemieńska, 1969). The third type in which equal division of duties was observed is rare; it appears most often in families where husband and wife have higher education. Moreover, in this group of families the amount of leisure time for men and women is similar and the division of household duties by sex does not or almost does not exist.

Research has shown that women blue-collar workers at the beginning of the 1960's needed five hours and 38 minutes for housework, while white-collar women needed only three hours and 43 minutes for the same tasks (Strzeminska, 1966: 216; Strzemińska, 1970). Generally, women had less (60–70%) leisure time than men and more housework was performed by them. Therefore students of the situation in Poland talk about women's "two occupations"—paid work and housework.

About eight million families live in Poland differentiated by type and by place of residence. Rural families constitute about 47% of the total number and the rest are urban. Among rural families we can distinguish modern rural families (27% of the total number of families in Poland), part-time farm families (11–13%), and rural nonfarm worker families in which the heads of families are employed in nonagricultural occupations but live in the villages. Urban families are divided into three main groups: worker families (32–34% of the total number of families in the country), white-collar and small bourgeois families (11%), and the intelligentsia families (7–8%).

Family type depends on the social stratum to which the head of the family belongs, the type of region, type of local community (e.g., size of city or village) and the degree of acceptance of the patterns of the family propagated by the different ideological institutions of the society.

One of the common elements running through the various theories of change in the family is the assumption that industrialization has caused a transformation of the family so that it has become a nuclear family with reduced traditional functions. These traditional functions are mainly performed, in industrialized society, by specialized institutions instead of by the family and local community.

Polish studies show an intensification of some functions of the family, although the functions themselves have changed. (Turowski, 1975: 246; Hodoly, 1971). An analysis of 5,000 diaries written in 1959–60 by youths living in rural areas demonstrates the intensification of the integrative-expressive function of the family. Actually, members of families, especially youths, aspire and also strive in life practice to deepen emotional relationships between husbands and wives, to use leisure time together, etc. This intensification is a result of the consciously oriented activity of family members to gather resources, to save time, etc.

At the same time the educational function of the family is more intensive than previously. Despite the activity of many specialized state institutions, the full reward of education is not realized without material help from parents such as help in preparation of assignments required by the school etc. This process of intensification of educational effort is related to the isolation of education in terms of both time and special place. This phenomenon is very apparent in peasant families where, previously different kinds of activities could be combined (Markowska 1964; Dobrowolski 1966; Siemieńska 1964). A similar process is going on in urban families due to the employment of women (Łobodzinska 1970). Thus the thesis assuming the reduction of historical and basic family functions is not applicable to Polish society although it must be agreed that the economic function is now less important than it was in the traditional family.

The traditional form of the family in Poland, both in urban and rural areas, was the extended family consisting of three generations. This doesn't mean there was no such thing as a nuclear family. As a matter of fact it appeared fairly often in the lower strata in villages and in small towns. However, three generational families are the mode (Piotrowski, 1970), and 67% of old people (over 65 years) are living with their children (86% of old people have children). This number is much higher than in other developed countries; for example, in England it is 41%, in the U.S.A. 18%, and in Denmark 20% of old people live with families of their children. This form of family is more frequent in rural areas than in cities.

It seems useful to point out that the existence of a three-generational family is only somewhat the result of the influence of tradition; more important are economic conditions. Occupationally active women need help in performing household duties (Piotrowski 1963; 1969), and very often grandmothers or grandfathers take care of children. A study carried out in Warsaw of engineers' families had demonstrated that it is possible to distinguish two periods in the life cycle of a family. In the first, young couples try to be independent, and in the next, they live more often with parents who help them to educate their children. This second form of family persists because young couples want to take care of their old parents. Some students of family problems assume that the existence of the three-generation family is the consequence of influences from rural traditions brought by peasant immigrants to the cities. However, the explanation that describes how economic conditions can make it necessary for a woman to work when she has small children seems to be more tenable. In some cases it may be no more than a matter of the unwillingness of a young, highly-educated mother to interrupt a professional career (Graniewska, 1971).

Relationships within the modern three-generation family are different than before. It is no longer a patriarchal family with power concentrated in the hands of old parents, especially the male(s). Now the woman's position in the family depends on her employment activity. Moreover in rural families her position is now being raised because many women manage farms alone while men work in other occupations (Tryfan, 1968).

The degree of children's independence is high, and they usually decide alone about their choice of occupation, marriage partner, etc. Sometimes the independence of children, especially in families of the intelligentsia turns into alienation of the young generation from the family, but this latter phenomenon is fairly rare.

Despite conflicts and tensions within young couples and a higher divorce rate than previously (0.5 per 1000 people in 1960, 1.1 in 1976; Rocznik Statystyczny 1977: 35), the family plays a very important role in the life of Polish society. Although the emotional relationships between members of the family have become more intense than was true earlier, it is well to remember that the adaptation of the family to new conditions such as sharing household duties is going on very slowly. As a result, women have, in total, many more duties than they had before. The patterns of family accepted by society and the ones existing in reality are highly incongruent.

Conclusion

In summary, the structure of women's employment described in this article is a result of (1) biological differences between men and women which present some limitations to opportunities for paid work; (2) stereotypes and traditional beliefs of both women and men to the effect that women can perform only certain kinds of work; (3) family duties of women which means that they mostly take care of children and the household; (4) belief that women are worse workers than men, which results in their poorer chances for more attractive jobs from a financial standpoint; (5) type and level of women's education; and (6) the lower geographical mobility of women.

Some of these reasons for the structural differences in women's and men's employment also place special demands on the labour market. Thus women's situation may to some degree be conflict-ridden, full of tensions and inconsistencies. Fairly often, for example, women are over-educated when matched with their real employment opportunities. Theoretically it is possible to interpret this phenomenon in terms of status inconsistency. But the inconsistency, of which some women are aware, does not seem to produce any special tensions because women who entered the labour force more recently are in reality fairly often traditionally oriented. Their occupational aspirations are not too high and quite frequently they are ready to give up their own careers for the sake of the careers of their husbands.

Polish law which, in general, gives equal rights to men and women, places strong economic and ideological pressures on women to begin work outside of the home. This has caused them to perceive their situation as a difficult one with too many duties and this despite the development of different institutions which help in performing child care and some housework. But at present, even if they are in good financial circumstances, many women find the proposal that they return home and limit their activity to the roles of wife and mother, unacceptable. The image of women's role has changed. However, as is usual in times of rapid social and cultural changes many discrepancies and inconsistencies appear both on the level of social consciousness and in the behaviour of society's members.

REFERENCES

Adamski, Franciszek
   1970 *Modele małżeństwa i rodziny a kultura masowa* (Models of Marriage, and Family and Mass Culture). Warsaw: Państwowe Wydawnictwo Naukowe.

Dobrowolski, Kazimierz
   1966 "Tradycyjna rodzina chłopska w południowej Polsce na przełomie XIX i XX wieku" (Traditional Peasant Family in Southern Poland on Turn of XIX and XX centuries), pp. 198–242. In *"Studia nad życiem społecznym i kultura"*. Wrocław: Ossolineum.

Dziecielska-Machnikowska, Stefania
   1968 "Problemy feminizacji zatrudnienia, zawodów i stanowisk" (Problems of Feminization of Employment, Professions, and Occupations in Poland). *Studia Socjologiczne* 1: 149–161.

Dziesieciolecie Polski Odrodzonej – Ksiega Pamiatkowa
   1928 (Ten Years of the Restored Poland – Memorial Book).

Graniewska, D.
   1971 "Możliwości i potrzeba okresowej dezaktywizacji kobiet majacych małe dzieci" (Opportunities and Need for a Temporary Deactivization of Women with Small Children). *Praca i Zabezpieczenie Społeczne 6*.

Górska, Maria
   1977 "Praca, pracownik, przełożony w świadomości robotników" (Work, Worker, and Supervisor in Workers' Perception), pp. 125–139. In M. Michalik (ed.) *Socjalistyczny wzór osobowy pracownika* (Socialist Personality Pattern of Worker). Warsaw: Instytut Wydawniczy CRZZ.

Hodoly, A.
   1971 *Gospodarstwo domowe i jego rola społeczno-ekonomiczna* (The Household and Its Socio-economic Role). Warsaw: Książka i Wiedza.

Jasińska, Aleksandra and Siemieńska, Renata
   1975a *Wzory osobowe socjalizmu* (Personality Patterns of Socialism). Warsaw: Wiedza Powszechna.
   1975b *Wzory osobowe a powieść radiowa* (Personality Patterns and Radio Serial). Warsaw: Ośrodek Badania Opinii Publicznej i Studiów Programowych.

Jakubowicz, M.
   1971 "Racjonalne zatrudnienie a praca kobiet" (Rational Economy and Women's Work). *Praca i Zabezpieczenie Społeczne* 4: 14–26.

Kłoskowska, Antonina
   1959 "Modele społeczne i kultura masowa" (Social Models and Mass Culture). *Przeglad Socjologiczny* XIII/2: 36–71.
   1965 "Rodzina w Polsce Ludowej" (The Family in the Polish People's Republic), pp. 505–531, In A. Sarapata (ed.) *Przemiany społeczne w Polsce Ludowej* (Social Changes in Poland). Warsaw: Państwowe Wydawnictwo Naukowe.

Knychała, Krystyna
    1978   *Zatrudnienie kobiet w Polsce Ludowej w latach 1955–1974* (Women's Employment in Poland in 1955-1974). Warsaw Poznań: Państwowe Wydawnictwo Naukowe.

Łobodzińska, Barbara
    1970   *Małżeństwo w mieście* (Urban Marriage). Warsaw: Państwowe Wydawnictwo Naukowe.

Markowska, Danuta
    1964   "Kierunki przeobrażeń współczesnej rodziny wiejskiej" (Trends of Changes of Present Rural Family). *Roczniki Socjologii Wsi* 2: 57–81.

Mały Rocznik Statsytyczny (Small Statistical Yearbook) Warsaw:
    1938   Główny Urzad Statystyczny.
    1977   Główny Urzad Statystyczny.

Paszkiewicz, Joanna
    1975   "Problematyka rodzinna w literaturze powojennej" (Family Problems in Post–War Literature), pp. 97–116. In J. Komorowska (ed.) *Przemiany rodziny polskiej* (Transformations of Polish Family) Warsaw: Instytut Wydawniczy CRZZ.

Piotrowski, Jerzy
    1963   *Praca zawodowa kobiety a rodzina* (Woman's Work and Family). Warsaw: Ksiażka i Wiedza.
    1969   *Aktywność zawodowa kobiet zameznych i wynikajace z niej potrzeby rodziny* (Family Needs Resulting from the Increased Employment of Married Women). Warsaw: Report of research carried out by the chair of Sociology of Work of the Institute of Social Economy.
    1970   "Rodzina wielopokoleniowa w Polsce" (The Multigeneration Family in Poland). *Problemy Rodziny* 5: 1–9.

Preiss-Zajdowa, Anna
    1967   "Sytuacja zawodowa kobiet z wyższymi kwalifikacjami" (Professional Situation of Higher Educated Women). In *Kobieta Praca–Dom* (Materials ot the conference "Women–Work–Household"). Warsaw: Wydawnictwo Zwiazkowe.

Przedpelski, Mieczysław
    1975   *Struktura zatrudnienia kobiet w Polsce Ludowej* (Structure of Women's Employment in Poland). Warsaw: Państwowe Wydawnictwo Naukowe.

Rakiewicz, Antoni
    1965   *Zatrudnienie w Polsce Ludowej w latach 1950–1970* (Employment in the Polish People's Republic). Warsaw: Ksiażka i Wiedza.

Rocznik Statystyczny (Statistical Yearbook). Warsaw:
    1974   Główny Urzad Statystyczny.
    1975   Główny Urzad Statystyczny.

Salva, Z.
    1970   *Uprawnienia pracujacych kobiet* (Rights of Working Women). Warsaw: Wydawnictwo Zwiazkowe.

Siemieńska, Renata
    1964   "Tradycyjna rodzina spiska i jej powojenne przemiany" (Traditional Family from the Spisz Region and Its Postwar Transformations). *Roczniki Socjologii Wsi* 2: 151–160.
    1969   *Nowe życie w nowym mieście* (The New Life in the New Town). Warsaw: Wiedza Powszechna.

Siemieńska, Renata and Marek Bijak-Żochowski
    1975   *Od studiów do zawodu i pracy* (Studies, Profession, Work). Warsaw: Państwowe Wydawnictwo Naukowe.

Sobczak, L.
    1971   *Rynek pracy w Polsce Ludowej* (Labour Market in the Polish People's Republic). Warsaw: Państwowe Wydawnictwo Naukowe.

Sokołowska, Magdalena
    1963   *Kobieta pracujaca—socjomedyczna charakterystyka kobiet* (Working Woman—The Socio-medical Characteristics of Woman's Work). Warsaw: Wiedza Powszechna.

Statystyka Polska (Polish Statistics) 30, Warsaw:
   1927   Główny Urzad Statystyczny.
Strzemińska, Halina
   1966   "Budżet czasu robotnic, urzedniczek i ekspedientek" (Time-Budget of Women: Workers, White-Collars, Saleswomen). In M. Sokołowska, (ed.), *Kobieta współczesna* (Modern Woman). Warsaw: Ksiażka i Wiedza.
   1970   *Praca zawodowa kobiet a ich budżet czasu* (Women's Professional Work and Their Time-Budget). Warsaw: Państwowe Wydawnictwo Ekonomiczne.
Szczepański, Jan
   1970   *The Polish Society*. New York: Random House.
Tryfan, Barbara
   1968   *Pozycja społeczna kobiety wiejskiej* (Social Status of Rural Woman). Warsaw: Ksiażka i Wiedza.
Turowski, Jan
   1975   "Struktura i funkcje rodziny a teoria rodziny nuklearnej" (Structure and Functions of Family and Theory of Nuclear Family), pp. 242–259. In J. Komorowska (ed.), *Przemiany rodziny polskiej* (Transformations of Polish Family). Warsaw: Instytut Wydawnicy CRZZ.
Waluk, J.
   1965   *Płaca i praca kobiet w Polsce* (Women's Wages and Work in Poland). Warsaw: Ksiażka i Wiedza.
Wieruszewski, Roman
   1975   *Równość kobiet i mężczyzn w Polsce Ludowej* (Equality of Women and Men in Poland). Poznań: Wydawnictwo Poznańskie.
Wilska-Duszyńska, Barbara
   1975   "Modele rodziny w środkach masowego przekazu" (Family Models in Mass Media), pp. 150–163. In J. Komorowska (ed.), *Przemiany rodziny polskiej* (Transformations of Polish Family). Warsaw: Instytut Wydawniczy CRZZ.
Wrochno, Krystyna
   1971   *Problemy pracy kobiet* (Problems of Women's Work). Warsaw: Wydawnictwo Zwiazkowe CRZZ.
Wyniki doboru kandydatów na I rok studiów wyższych w latach 1969/1970 i 1970/1971. (Results of
   1971   Candidates Selection on First Year of Study in Higher Schools in 1969/1970 and 1970/1971. Warsaw: Ministerstwo Oświaty i Szkolnictwa Wyższego.

Women in Czechoslovakia

ALENA K. WAGNEROVÁ

Saarbrücken, West Germany

THOUGH THE FUNDAMENTAL CHANGE in women's position in society is common to all industrial nations, independent of their political systems, the many similarities between women's position in the socialist countries and in the bourgeois democracies must not lead us to overlook the distinct preconditions that influence this change under different political systems. A consideration of these different preconditions is not only necessary in order to understand the whole problem, it will also be helpful in establishing a theory. Hidden and poorly understood aspects of the question of women's rights, touched on in empirical studies, will be much clearer as a result. Thus, it seems proper to begin our analysis with a brief discussion of the most important and of the specific preconditions for women's emancipation in the socialist countries.

Historical Preconditions Favouring Changes in Women's Position

Theory, as well as political practice, in the socialist countries ascribes a greater significance to the solution of the question of women's rights, than is the case in the pluralist bourgeois democracies. The latter consider woman's equality rather as a kind of group interest, whereas the socialist countries regard it as a problem relevant to the whole of society. Accordingly, women's emancipation is an integral part of the political program of socialism. The connection of the issue of women's rights to that of workers' rights in the Marxist theory of women's emancipation, which need not be considered in detail here, makes women's emancipation a prominent political question. Thus, women, along with the workers, are an important target group for social change.

Moreover, women, along with the rural population, were the principal resource for the labour group that was essential to the economic organization in Czechoslovakia. This situation in the labour market made it obvious that the "theoretical" demand to fully integrate women into the production process could be met and could be made one precondition for women's emancipation. (From 1948 to 1964, women represented 90.47% of the total increase in the labour force [D. Fukalová 1967: 67]). The linking of ideological motives and economic requirements accelerated, in practice, the change in women's social position.

Within a few years an abrupt and basic change in women's previous position had been achieved through pressure and propaganda. A relatively high level of equality was reached characterized by legal equality for the two; the opening up to women of the "male-concentrated" professions (especially the technical); the augmentation of women's political participation; the reduction of the educational differences between men and women; and by the accelerated process leading to woman "becoming an independent subject".

In Western societies change was not so abrupt and took longer to achieve. In fact, in some instances, important changes have not yet been achieved. The contrast in the two modes of development can be clearly seen in the area of law. Whereas in Czechoslovakia the package of laws covering the equality of rights, the abolition of unequal pay for men and women and the upgrading of illegitimate children, was passed in the period 1945 to 1950, this action began much later in the Federal Republic of Germany, for example, and is not yet completed. Because of this radical development, the emancipation process in Czechoslovakia assumed quite a different quality than is the case in other countries and when women *as single individuals* attempt to enter the extrafamilial and traditionally male-dominated areas. In the latter case woman are compelled to adapt to male behaviour patterns in order to succeed. However, the mass penetration of women into a society dominated by men made it possible not only to rapidly overcome the adaptation phase and to create new female models, it brought about a significant change in the extrafamilial area itself—a fact of utmost importance and an issue that will be dealt with later.

This unusual development was effected through the high degree of vertical mobility possible in the beginning stages of socialism. At a time when social advancement and decline were an everyday occurrence, the social outsider—the woman—was more likely to climb to positions that had previously been unattainable for her. What must not be overlooked, however—and this has frequently been done—is the fact that the changes in the economic system, i.e., the workers' control of the means of production, had an immediate and direct effect on women's emancipation The workers' control of the means of production signified, in its consequences, a lessening of the economic power of the patriarchy and thus an improvement in the situation of the "weaker" sex—at least in an economic sense.

As a contrast to the bourgeois legislation, beginning with the Code Napoleon that intended by a series of rules to keep women in economic dependence, the importance of this change is obvious. Although socialization measures did not concern every member of society, nor did they concern only men, they affected those classes important for the formation of social models. Private property, specifically ownership of the means of production, constituted not only the economic basis for the predominant status of the male, but was also one important element in the traditional ideal of manliness. Thus, the destruction of this economic basis of male dominance reduced the importance of male qualities as a norm and as a model for all human beings. At the same time, it now became possible to elevate, in the social scale of values, behaviour patterns that are considered as female. The two processes—reduction in male and increase in female ideals—are equally important for both the familial and extrafamilial areas. If the weakening of the male ideal (in its normative sense) contributes to democratic patterns within the family (Fišerová, 1969: 465–467), the integration of women into extrafamilial areas is hardly possible without an upgrading of female behavior patterns in the social scale of values. This destruction of the economic power of the patriarchy does not imply that *all* patriarchal structures are abolished and can no longer be pursued. They persist, in part, in some areas of public life, especially in politics. (We shall return to this point later.)

Czechoslovakia not only provided favourable conditions for a rapid change in women's position, it also presented no great obstacles to women's emancipation within the family. The Czech family has little of those hierarchical and authoritarian structures and traditions characteristic, for example, of German families almost until the present—structures and traditions which have proved to be an impediment to change in the position of German women. This fact can be traced back to the historical development of the Czech society. The opposition against Austrian foreign rule, which was shared by the influential members of the Czech people after its rebirth at the beginning of the 19th century and until it obtained its own existence as a state (1918), inhibited the formation of authoritarian and hierarchical structures in the family. In other words, criticism of the emperor's authority led easily to the question of the unlimited authority of a father or some father-figure.

From all of the above, it is proper to conclude that in Czechoslovakia favourable conditions existed for a change in women's social position. These conditions were especially effective in making it possible to surmount, though not completely eliminate, those barriers that stem from traditional notions about women's nature and destiny—notions that have proved to be a hindrance to them when they attempted to penetrate into public life. *However this is not to be taken to mean that the socialist economic and social system contains no factors that might prove to restrain the emancipation process.* Such factors exist and will be discussed later.

Women in the Work Force

With a female labour force participation rate of 48% in 1975,[1] Czechoslovakia ranks with those countries with the highest proportion of women in the work force in the world. One characteristic, shared by all industrial countries, is that married women (73% in 1972) constitute the largest group of female workers (Köhler—Wagnerová, 1974: 36). Another characteristic is the high number of working women aged 20 to 35. In 1961, for instance, 61% of all working women belonged to this group.[2] A third characteristic and one of the most important in view of the changed social position of women in Czechoslovakia since World War II is the rapid educational upgrading of the female population. The dynamic nature of this process is shown in Table I. Though, on the average, men's educational level is still higher than that of women, it is nearly equal in the age group below 40. In the age group below 35, more women than men have a higher formal education or training. Women's educational level corresponds to the high number of female trained workers in some professional fields. As Table 2 suggests, in 1970 one-third of graduates and one-half of trained workers with higher formal training were women.

Commensurate with the high proportion of women in secondary schools and universities, the number of female apprentices appears relatively low. Whereas in 1975/1976 women represented 63.6% of all high school pupils, 59.9% of pupils in colleges, 62.6% of university students, 17.5% of students in technical universities, 53.6% of students in economics, 29.1% in agricultural science, and 38.1% in arts, women only constituted 36.4% of all apprentices.[3] Girls are still more likely than boys to take up a job immediately after finishing elementary school. In 1975, 8,599 out of 10,090 young people leaving elementary school were girls; that is, 78.2%.[4]

In a certain sense there is a sex-related choice of formal education. Boys most often choose apprenticeship to obtain the requirements for a job and choose higher education specifically as preparation for university (76,000 male apprentices versus 27,000 high school pupils in 1975). Girls, on the other hand, prefer school to apprenticeship even if they do not intend to go to university (43,000 female apprentices versus 46,000 female high school pupils in 1975). Reasons for these different orientations may be the result of traditional notions about male and female jobs; the greater interest on the part of industry in male apprentices; the efforts of parents to protect girls from the sometimes rude atmosphere in industry; and the financially low rewards of higher education in Czechoslovakia. The consequences of this trend will be an inevitable overrepresentation of women in intellectual professions in the

1 Statistická ročenka ČSSR 1976.
2 Quoted after: J. Žižkova, K. otázkám dlouhodobého vyvoje zaměstnanosti žen, p. 213 (No newer references).
3 All references: Statistická ročenka ČSSR 1976.
4 Statistická ročenka ČSSR 1976.

Table 1

Proportion of women in different educational levels in relation to the whole working population in the corresponding age-classes

Age-class	Graduates	Special Training	High School Examination	Apprenticeship
50–54	16.8	43.1	33.0	24.2
45–49	15.9	30.0	42.9	25.4
40–44	17.7	30.1	39.2	24.0
35–39	24.9	40.4	48.9	21.8
30–34	32.1	46.3	56.2	20.5
25–29	47.2	51.7	60.1	21.3
20–24	(57.8)	60.3	72.4	28.9
15–19	—	(63.6)	(83.2)	(39.5)
Total	29.5	45.7	56.2	24.8

Source: Mikrocensus 1970, quoted after Ivo Možny Vyrovnávání vzdělanostní úrovně mužu a žen v ČSSR (The adjustment of the educational levels of men and women in Czechoslovakia).

future, and an apparent education deficit of men with an effect on the family that cannot yet be wholly foreseen.

It is interesting that a qualification adjustment between men and women at the lower levels of qualification usually proceeds more slowly than at the higher levels. The educational boom for women was not accompanied by a boom in qualifications. For instance, in 1963 in the category of workers, only 25% of women were skilled workers, yet the percentage of female professionals with high school examination standing was 44% (Köhler–Wagnerová, 1974: 47). A similar inequality is characteristic of the distribution of the female labour force in some professional fields (Table 2). Although within the last 30 years women have penetrated into a number of new professions where they were barely represented previously, and are still only sparsely represented in Western countries (mechanical engineering, electrical engineering), this process of penetration was much slower than the proportional increase of women into the traditional female professions (education, health services and communication).

The educational structure of the female labour force still possesses the characteristics of traditional job orientation in Czechoslovakia. Compared with the high percentage of women in the total working population, the proportion of women in the professions, especially in technical professions, is still low although it may appear rather high in comparison with some Western countries. In technical subjects women did best in chemistry: in 1970 there were 58.5% apprentices, 36.7% professionals with a high school diploma, and 21.9% graduated professionals. The high proportion of women in some professional fields implies a specific danger for women's emancipation. The accumulation of loss of working hours, closely connected with women's biological function (maternity leaves, illness of children) may rouse anti-

Table 2

Proportion of female professionals in single special fields (1970)

	Professionals with high-school examination*			Graduated professionals		
	Total	Proportion of women	Percentage of women	Total	Proportion of women	Percentage of women
Natural sciences	—	—	—	9,679	2,939	30.4
Geology and mining	13,002	767	5.9	4,116	213	5.2
Metallurgical engineering	12,326	1,387	11.3	3,656	321	8.8
Mechanical engineering	184,188	19,047	10.4	23,661	1,028	4.3
Electrical engineering	50,907	5,380	10.6	13,265	813	6.1
Chemistry	25,352	9,366	36.9	10,046	2,204	21.9
Food industry	8,737	3,475	39.8	1,512	622	41.1
Consuming ind.	34,820	14,317	41.1	1,400	291	20.8
Construction and ordinancesurvey	69,004	15,699	22.8	24,790	3,599	14.5
Transport and communication	22,614	4,206	18.6	3,398	399	11.7
Agriculture and forestry	62,025	14,838	23.6	24,525	3,794	15.5
Economy and administration	318,701	229,580	72.0	18,580	4,304	23.2
Health service	110,159	105,837	96.0	38,574	16,854	43.7
Science, education, culture	125,193	96,667	77.2	95,305	48,110	50.5
Total	1,037,028	520,507	50.2	272,507	85,491	31.3

Quoted from: Statistická ročenka ČSSR 1971.
* professional with high-school examination means a four-year special training, or a two-year special training.

feminist feelings in certain industries with the result that barriers will be erected to prevent the further integration of women into the world of production.

Even if Czechoslovakia today provides equivalent educational facilities for boys and girls, the actual job opportunities for women and the opportunities to make use of their qualifications in practice are still more restricted than are those for men. Qualified women often find themselves in inferior and middle-range positions while men are more often in middle-range and higher positions (Jungmann, 1969: 189). Women in Czechoslovakia hold only 4.8% of the key positions in industry (Bauerová 1970: 450). Furthermore, the proportion of women in higher and key positions does not correspond to the level of qualification of all working women. (This difference is confirmed by the results of an investigation of 1,000 graduates of the technical university in Pilsen (Čech & Jukl, 1976: 77). In this sample, 78% of graduated male engineers had subordinate assistants, but only 47% of the female engineers did. Of the women, 90% were rated independent trained professionals, but only 10% as managerial professionals. The proportion for men was 1:1.)

Women's Position in the Family

When evaluating women's underrepresentation in higher and key positions, the *novelty* of qualified or graduated women in the world of production has to be taken into account. The main reason why women, less than men, take advantage of their qualifications is that women "see their job position under the aspect of further duties in the family and very often deliberately renounce too demanding jobs and a rise in the hierarchy of the enterprise" (Čech & Jukl, 1976: 79). Woman's greater burden of housework and her family duties show up in the little free time she has, although there is a trend toward greater equality in this area. In 1967 workers had, for example, 32.5 hours of free time per week; female workers, on the other hand, only 20 hours. Male employees had at their disposal 35 hours, female employees only 22.5 hours (Bauerová, 1974: 145). The fact that women had at their disposal only about 62% of the free time available for men is considered a social injustice in Czechoslovakia.

The higher demand on a woman's time is due to the consequences of an economic model based on a system of heavy industry; on an underdeveloped infrastructure; and insufficient child care facilities. These deficiencies are seen as an impediment to women's emancipation in socialist countries.

Recent studies corroborate the opinion that a woman's profession is one of the most important factors giving impetus to a change in her position within the family. But even if female labour force participation has become a matter of course, as in socialist countries, its negative consequences are experienced again when women marry. Though problems related to women's work are not yet resolved, demands for equality and partnership in the family increase from one generation to the other. Women's changing position in the family thus represents a highly dynamic process in which two variables, the generation to which one belongs and the level of education one attains, play an important differentiating role.

No study has been made in Czechoslovakia to investigate separately the distribution of power in the family. Family organization and structure have always been studied in terms of the division of labour; the greater participation of the husband in household duties and in child rearing were evaluated as effects of democratic tendencies.

The investigation of this problem in 1961[5] showed that the husband's participation in child-rearing increases with the wife's professional activity. Whereas in families in which the wife worked outside the home 69% of the husbands and wives shared in the tasks of child-rearing, only 43% did so in families in which the wife did not work for pay. Again, 56% of all full-time housewives reared their children alone, while only 27% of working mothers did. As for the help of other family members, in 1970 only 15% of husbands did not help at all in the household; 33% helped daily or on

---

5 J. Prokopec, Vdaná žena v rodině ..., p. 117.

certain days, and 41% irregularly.⁶ Farmers help least in household duties (19% did not help at all), employers help a little more (40% daily or regularly; 11.1% not at all) than workers (35% daily; 18% not at all). An increase in the educational level of men and women also increases men's support in household duties and this is higher in younger than in older age-groups.

Though these data express certain trends concerning the division of labour in Czech families, conclusions about the power distribution have to be drawn cautiously. A husband's help is usually limited to several different and specific tasks, while the wife still retains control and organization of the "family business". Coupled with her economic independence, this means a strengthening of the woman's position in the family. The women often appear to be conscious of the ambivalence of their double role. Men's aid in the household and above all in child-rearing, sometimes described as man's return to the family, has an opposite kind of effect. Man's position has not been strengthened and he seems to be in search of a new expression of his role in the family after the loss of his dominance. It is of interest to note that less than 1% of women and less than 2% of men in Czechoslovakia consider a man's task to be head of the family (Köhler-Wagnerová, 1974: 88).⁷ Results of an investigation in 1966 (Wynnyczuk, 1967) give insight into the new selfconception and behaviour of the younger female generation (born in 1945). Younger women (85%) are convinced that they will share household duties with their future husbands. They consider their professional activity equal in importance to that of their future husbands. Only 18.5% of women were ready to subordinate their own urgent professional work to the equally important work of their future spouses, and to assume housekeeping tasks alone; 82.5% wanted to complete the household tasks together before each would pursue his/her own work.

These answers were highly dependent on the woman's formal education. Whereas 75% of women with elementary education argued in favour of sharing household duties with their husband, the same stand was true for 88% of women with higher education. A similar but reverse relationship was found with other answers: 21% of women with elementary education were inclined to assign priority to their husband's work, but only 11.3% of women with higher education did so. The attitudes of women in rural and urban areas did not differ considerably. According to other results of this study, women's desires for self-reliance and independence increase with education, and equally their ability to act more flexibly. Women with less education are more dependent in their attitudes, tend, at the same time, to behave less flexibly, and rather orientate their behaviours according to definite and established principles.

The importance of woman's work lies not only in her economic independence and her participation in other than family group relations, it also portends a new

---

6 Minění žen o zaměstnání domácnosti a rodině, part II, p. 13.
7 Quoted after: A. Köhler-Wagnerová, Die Frau im Sozialismus, p. 88.

dimension in the relationship between man and woman. Women's presence in the world of production implies a considerable enlargement of contacts between both sexes who now meet not only, or predominantly, in their sex roles (family, marriage), but also as colleagues, collaborators and partners on the job. Thus, in contrast to the abolition of the sex taboo in Western Nations, there is the abolition of the taboo of "the opposite" sex in the socialist countries.

Women in the Political Power System

Compared to most Western bourgeois democracies, Czechoslovakia is marked by a higher participation of women in different institutions of political power. Nonetheless, in relation to the proportion of women in the economic field and, in terms of their levels of qualification and education, this percentage of participation is insufficient. The proportion of women in various political institutions does not exceed 30%, and this decreases at higher levels of political power. As was the case with key economic positions, women are underrepresented at the political top. (An optimal proportion of women would be a proportion that corresponds to the female proportion in the population in company with participation at all levels of political power.) Thus, the increased participation of women in politics in the socialist countries continues to be a problem. Though the proportion of women in central organs and political institutions shows a gradual increase over the years, this is due to a centralized push rather than a spontaneous development. Left to self-regulation, the proportion of women in political institutions would decrease over time. Women had a representation of 25.5% in the National Assembly during the legislation period 1971 to 1975, and roughly 20% during the two previous periods. After the last election in 1975, their percentage amounted to 30% (Bártová, 1976: 44). Women held the office of the vice-president of the National Assembly several times, and since 1948 they have frequently held ministries in the government.

A heartening tendency towards improvement can be seen in the number of female deputies in different National Councils. From 1964 to 1973, the proportion of women rose from 19.6% to 23.7%. During the legislation period from 1971 to 1975, there were 29.7% women (1964—25%) in National Local Councils, 33.7% (1964—23.9%) in National District Councils, 28% (1964—22.9%) in Municipal Councils and 22.5% (1964—18.9%) in communities (Bártová, 1976: 45).

Among the important political institutions, the trade unions have the highest female percentage in their organs. (Membership in the trade union is obligatory for the working population.) Women represent 44% in work councils and 36% in the central council which is the top organization of the trade associations of the trade union. Six of a total of 17 trade associations are presided over by women (Bártová, 1976).

On the other hand, women are especially underrepresented in the decisive organs of the Czech Communist Party, though their level of participation considerably increased from the XIVth to the XVth Party Convention. This relates, however, to the fulfillment of a political task rather than to a natural development of women's political influence. Women's proportion in the Central Committee grew to 11.6% from 7% (of 121 members of the Central Committee, 14 were women); the percentage of female candidates for the Central Committee increased from 13 to 24% (of 52 candidates, 12 were women), and in the Revision Commission from 17 to 28%. In the Executive Committee and the Secretariat, women had a 5% representation (1 woman among 20 members).[8]

The same obstacles that impede the rise of women in the professions also hinder their greater participation in the political power system. It is, admittedly, the simultaneous demand on women's physical and psychic forces in profession and family, her double role, that hardly leaves sufficient time and energy for additional involvements in politics. Yet despite the high female labour force participation rate, Czech society hardly knows that type of politically active housewife who frequently becomes a professional politician in Western countries. Moreover, during those years favourable for career development and which coincide with heavy time demands in the family, Czech women simply cannot get involved in the political arena. (It is not appropriate to consider here the question of power exertion in the socialist countries and its effects on civil and political activities.)

These well-known reasons for women's lower participation in the political power structure do not, however, suffice to explain the obvious low participation rate of women at the top echelon of the Czech Communist Party, a phenomenon common to all socialist countries. The authoritarian and patriarchal structures within the organization of the Communist Party seem to create conditions, especially in the party machine, a make political career in the Czech Communist Party nearly impossible.

A successful career in the party machine requires, and generally promotes (not only in the socialist countries), a specific kind of alienation that is brought about by the strong tension between the demands of the ideology and social reality. (In Western countries, this tension develops from the attempt to resolve the conflict between party interests and political power and the interests and needs of the people.) This tension is usually eased by a strong formalism of behaviour and patterns of action which find expression in an abundance of symbolic actions and a specific, mostly redundant jargon. A man, drilled by tradition in abstract and instrumental reasoning, is more likely than a woman to accept this alienated existence between ideology and reality. A woman, however, usually cannot escape from everyday life as a man is able to do, and she is continuously confronted with this discrepancy in thousands

---

[8] Svobodné slovo (daily paper), 6 April 1976.

of details. Perhaps, one could say that a woman has greater difficulty in attaining the degree of alienation which it takes to enter a successful political career. Some points seem to indicate that a career thus attained does not seem very attractive to the majority of women, the more so as a certain discrepancy exists between the power and the prestige of a professional politician. This may be one of the reasons for women's greater political engagement at the lower level (trade-unions), where political work is at least closer to life, more concrete and less formal than at the top. And, finally, the observation that women have a different relationship to their work than men (a point to be discussed below) might confirm this supposition.

If a woman's professional activity directly influences her position in the family, as shown above, it appears that it has an indirect influence on her participation in the political power structure. (This may be different for Western countries where women's political engagement often serves as a substitute for professional activity; whereas in Czechoslovakia it is generally considered an additional activity.) The importance of women's political participation is to be seen in the formulation of their individual needs and interests, in their assertion of responsibility for public welfare and in their mitigation of authoritarian and patriarchal structures in political institutions. Furthermore, women active in public life are important as proponents of causes and leaders in the search for new female ideals and life patterns. It is rather biased, though, to do no more than question the influence of women's position in extrafamilial areas versus her position in the family, and not ask the obvious question: What does the presence of women in the world of work mean for the work world itself and how will their presence change this work world? This question, which has never been raised, is significant because it gives priority to extrafamilial activities and because it recognizes and accepts the work place as a basically unchangeable factor to which the individual must adjust.

In socialist countries, where for the last 20 years women have represented an important factor in the process of production—not only as to quantity but above all as to quality—this problem is more obvious and acute than in Western countries where women's integration into the world of work has not made the same progress. Yet, in these socialist countries, the problem has hardly been studied empirically. The data available are confined to personal observations, comparisons, statements, and a number of impressions. We are forced, therefore, to restrict ourselves to only a few comments concerning this problem.

Certainly, women bring behaviour, experience and values into the world of production that differ from those of men. Woman's age-old destiny to fulfill her duties in the family and the nature of the work she does have formed and shaped her. It is correct, therefore, to speak of a female subculture, one that is characterized by a greater emphasis on personal relationships i.e., person-oriented, compared to the more object-oriented male culture. This female culture changes much more slowly than do the economic and social conditions that have produced it. It is still transmitted, "inherited" in its basic traits, through the process of socialization, Moreover, women's life conditions, contrary to those of men, are marked by greater reference to family matters because of the still existing division of labour by sex and of the effects of traditional ideologies. Women's range of experience and biography are thus influenced, and the prolongation of the female culture is fostered. Since most working women are married, their familial relationships are especially important in the professional sphere. The greater emphasis on personal relations in the female culture is not only evident in the sphere of production but is expressed by a clearly visible inclination on the part of women to behave less formally than men in the same profession. The inclination is supported by empirical studies on work motivations which show that social contacts *per se* constitute an important motive for women to seek work.[9] Of 343 job-oriented[10] women, 39% mentioned social contacts as a reason for working, 33% mentioned work itself, and 19% gave material motives. These results are in accordance with well-known findings that good relations at work are more important for women's job satisfaction than they are for men. In a recent Czech study (not yet published) a further interesting difference between men and women seems to appear. Whereas women found satisfaction in the work itself, men needed more outside appreciation of their work.[11]

These differences above may, perhaps, be explained as a mere transfer of behaviour from the primary group to the production sphere and may be caused by the insufficient professionalization of women. The explanation while not unimportant is less interesting than the question: How do these man-woman differences shape different work attitudes and professional outlooks? And what will become of the professionalization of women? Will it vanish, diminish, or continue to exist—and what influence does it exert on the production sphere, especially on working conditions? Woman's greater involvement with household tasks, which in part, but only in part, is due to her biological make-up, causes her to consider her family situation as one of responsibility, experience, burden, but also as a value orientation, a reference point at work. The transfer from her family role to a professional one, which means the presence in the worker role of a more complex human being, almost automatically results in a greater visibility of both professional and household cognitions. This presence of a complex human being in the world of work is bound, provided that women are sufficiently represented in the world of work, to have a significant influence on man's situation. However, the mitigation of the severe norms of professional behaviour which the presence of women produces helps the men to accept their family role in the professional area. Furthermore, wives' work gives greater impetus to husbands' increased participation in household duties and ultimately

9 Mínění žen ... Part II, p. 28.
10 The term "job oriented" refers here to those women who wanted to continue working even if their husbands' wages would completely suffice to maintain the family.
11 Personal communication Dr. I. Možný.

will make possible a new formulation of sex roles. From this viewpoint, women's work is an important precondition for the abolition, or at least mitigation, of the separation of people's private and professional existence. That means that women in professional positions, the abolition of the traditional division of labour, and the separation of the private and professional areas are closely linked. It is obvious that the abolition of the separation that has existed between the personal and the professional is an important step towards making the world of production more humane.

A visible linkage between these two areas can be found in the socialist countries. The respect shown for a man's family role by his colleagues in his professional area is especially important. Its effect can be seen in a number of details, some of which appear to be insignificant, but whose overall importance becomes clearly visible by comparison. It is, for example, a common experience in Czechoslovakia for a man to leave a meeting before it ends because it is his turn to pick up his child at the nursery (nurseries in Czechoslovakia usually close at 16: 00 hours). (This can hardly be imagined in Western countries.) The same trend is seen in the greater participation of husbands of working wives in child-rearing tasks, as described earlier.

The extent to which the transfer of family roles to the world of work will take place is largely dependent on women's success in the area of production, and on the importance of female work in economic life. From a human viewpoint it may seem worthwhile to have the more complex human presence of women at work and it may seem wrong and perverse to restrict her to simple female labour. From the position, however, that places great stress on the usefulness and the singlemindedness and "pure" labour power of men in industrial production, it may seem undesirable. The impossibility of restricting women to female labour can easily be classed as a deficiency disturbance, and as a reduction in proper performances. The fact that a woman does not sell just her labour power but sells it in combination with potential family implications, makes her less able to compete with a man at work. Women, therefore, succeed especially well in fields in which there are few male competitors, fields that offer little attractive pay for men and fields in which labour is supplied at a low cost. Earlier and traditional efforts had the same goal, i.e., to reduce the number of female workers lost to the labour force through marriage, prohibition and celibacy. (These same factors are still present in the form of self-restrictiveness.) It must be asked, however, if the lower performance often mentioned in connection with female workers—without considering, of course, the loss of working hours due to pregnancy and childbirth—is an objective fact, or simply a point of view. Is it possible that only male standards and notions concerning professional performance are being followed and that the new impulses that women bring, or may bring, into the job situation are underestimated or completely neglected?

Women's situation at work in the socialist countries, which are not achievement-oriented societies in the capitalist sense, is not as much a problem as in Western bourgeois democracies. Discriminatory tendencies, however, do exist. It is interesting to note that in the discussion in Czechoslovakia of a more market-oriented economic model (1966—1968), hard attacks were made against female labourers and against too high a proportion of women in the economy. A similar tendency was observable in certain enterprises that reduced the number of female apprentices after the business was obliged to pay a training fee. However, it must be realized that the social measures necessary to assure biological reproduction of society, and taking into account the high rate of female labour force participation as it exists in most socialist countries, make high demands on the organization and flexibility of the process of production, irrespective of costs. Nevertheless, society must assume the cost for its biological reproduction. Czechoslovakia provides a completely-paid protection period of motherhood of 26 weeks and after that a further maternity leave is possible until the child's second year of life, with the previous job being guaranteed. In 1975, for example, a total of 4.5% of the more than 7,000,000 Czech workers claimed protection of motherhood; 9.5% of all working women.[12] In companies with many female workers as many as 20% of the women may be on maternity leave at one time. Protection of motherhood might well be more flexible so that not only the mother, but also the father could claim it. Equalization would surely be supported but the problems of organization would not be reduced.

In summary, the tendency to make the world of production more humane can be regarded as one of the most important consequences of the female presence in the working process. Our discussion should have made clear that such a process of making work more humane has nothing to do with "flowers in the office", nor does it suggest that women's influence is due to any mysterious characteristic, i.e., the "Eternal Woman". Rather, when considering the female culture a kind of professional "deformation" of women becomes visible, caused by age-old effects in the primary group. If, however, the female presence in the working process fosters the process of making work more humane, then this process and its results are a *conditio sine qua non* of woman's integration into the world of production, without which a total emancipation of women is not possible. The development of women's integration into the working process could thus, in a certain sense, serve as a measure for the progress of making the world of production more humane. A somewhat disturbing question cannot be wholly overlooked: Did women in the socialist countries succeed on the job because socialist countries are not "achieving societies" in a narrower meaning, or can socialist countries not be as highly achievement-oriented because women have succeeded at work?

It remains open to question what is going to happen with the female culture in the course of women's integration into the labour force. It will be the task of further studies to find an answer to this question for which some clues are already developing in the case of Czechoslovakia.

---

12 Statistická ročenka 1976.

REFERENCES

Bánhegyi, F.
    1967   *Sociológia súčasnej rodiny* (Sociology of the family today). Bratislava.

Bártová, E.
    1976   "Historický vývoj politické participace žen" (The historical development of women's political participation). *Sociologický časopis* 1, p. 36–48.

Bauerová, J.
    1970   "Rodinná problematika vedoucích pracovnic" (Family problems of female executives.) *Soc. čas.*, p. 449–461.

Bauerová, J.
    1974   *Zaměstnaná žena a rodina* (Working woman and family). Praha.

Čech, V. Jukl, E.
    1976   "Nevyužitý zdroj studia ženské otázky" (The little used source for studying women's rights). *Soc. čas.* 1, p. 75–84.

Fišerová, V.
    1969   "Rodina v sociální struktuře společnosti" (The family in the social structure of society), in: P. Machonin et al, *Československá spolecnost* (The Czech society). Bratislava.

Fukalová, D.
    1967   *Ekonomická aktivita žen v ČSSR* (Job situation of women in Czechoslovakia). (Dissertation).

Jungmann, B.
    1969   "Složitost práce jako rozměr vertikální diferenciace spolecnosti a jako individuálni šance" (Work complexity as a measure of vertical differentiation of society and as individual chance), in: P. Machonin et al, *Československá společnost*. Bratislava.

Köhler-Wagnerová, A.
    1974   *Die Frau im Sozialismus, Beispiel ČSSR* (Woman in socialism. The example of Czechoslovakia). Hamburg.

Lehr, U.
    1969   *Die Frau im Beruf* (The working woman). Frankfurt/Main—Bonn
    1972   *Míněni žen o zamestnání, domácnosti a rodině* (Women's opinion about profession, household and family).
    Ústav pro výzkum veřejného mínění Praha, part I (Text), Part II (Tables).

Možny, I.
    1973   *Proces vyrovnávání vzdělanostní úrovně mužu a žen v ekonomicky aktivní populaci ČSSR* (The process of educational adjustment between men and women in the working population of Czechoslovakia), in: Sborník prací Filosofické fakulty brněnské university (Studia minora Facultatis philosophiae universitas brunensis, G 17, p. 33–42.

Musil, J.
    1965   "Příspevek k teorii sociální organizace součastné rodiny" (Contribution to a theory of social organization of present-day family). *Soc. čas.*, p. 524–535.

Prokopec, J.
    1963   "Vdaná žena v rodině a zaměstnání" (The married woman in family and profession). *Demografie*, p. 17–29.

Slejška, D.
    1965   "Problémy aktivity žen při účasti na řízení v prúmyslovém závodě" (Problems of women's commitment in managing an industrial establishment) *Soc čas.*, p. 509–523.
    Statistická ročenka ČSSR 1948–1976 (Statistical annual of Czechoslovakia).

Wynnyczuk, Vl.
    1967   "Žena současnosti" (Contemporary woman). *Populační zprávy* 2.

Wynnyczuk, Vl.
    1967   "Venkovská žena současnosti" (The contemporary woman in villages). *Populační zprávy* 2.

Žižková, J.
    1972   "K otázkám dlouhodobého vývoje zaměstnanosti žen" (On the question of the long development of women's profession). *Demografie* 3, p. 213.

Change in the System of Social Power

Conditions for the Social Equality of Women

OLIVERA BURIĆ

Institute of Social Policy, Beograd, Yugoslavia

Introduction

THE STRUGGLE OF WOMEN for social emancipation and equality can be divided into several characteristic phases. The most common feature of the several phases is that each one starts with new demands which later give place to dissatisfaction with what has been achieved. The successive alternation of demands and dissatisfaction with achievement eventually brings matters to a point of crisis. Despite all of the improvements made in the various countries that have tried to better women's position in society, it sometimes seems that her genuine emancipation will never be achieved. It is as if the roots of inequality between the sexes are lastingly implanted in the very essence of the natural order of things. However, social practice is constantly discovering new evidence to prove that there is no good reason for such pessimism and that the source of the problem resides, not in woman's "inferiority" but rather in the social organization which she herself did not create but into which she must now become integrated and in which she must find a position of equality.

A consideration of the customary phases in the development of the process of the social emancipation of women, as well as attention to some of the contradictions, will make it possible to consider ways by which the present situation can be improved and what the further prospects are.

The first phase started with the emergence of progressive movements for women's liberation. It seemed quite clear, somehow, that all that was necessary was for the woman to leave home, get a job, and by this simple means end her position of inequality in society and family in accordance with the forces of social necessity.

There is, of course, mass *female employment* and rare are the countries in which the female labour force does not account for one-third or one-half of the total number employed, even in some cases reaching the level of employment of the male labour force. Table 1 lists some of these countries. It is a historical fact that women have joined the general work army and it seems a historical inevitability that they will remain in it.

The second phase started soon after Phase One when it was recognized that the employment of women did not in itself mean their genuine emancipation. From the start the earnings of women were considerably lower than those of men and the female labour force component was less appreciated than was that of the male. Realising that the roots keeping women in a position of inferiority lay in the economic sphere of social life, the progressive movements for women's liberation developed the slogan: "Equal pay for equal work." This requirement has become one of today's fundamental human rights set forth in the UN Declaration on Human Rights also.

Despite the accepted international value-orientation, statistical and scientific analyses have revealed that all round the world women are paid considerably less than men so that they do not benefit from their employment in the same way as men do. Early studies show that the lower earnings were mainly due to the fact that

Table 1

Percentage of employed women in the total labour force[1]

	1960[2]	1970[3]
USSR	49–(1964)	—
Finland	39	40
Hungary	39	40
Poland	40	40
Sweden	40	40–(1965)
USA	25	39
England	33	37–(1971)
Yugoslavia	27	33–(1973)

[1] Figures for agriculture, forestry, hunting, fishing and the armed forces have been left out as these are not comparable.

[2] U.N. Year Book of Labor Statistics, 1971, pp. 9–43, except for data on the USSR which applies to 1964 and is taken from "Vaprosi naradno-naselenja i demografskoj statistiki, Statistika, Moscow, 1966, p. 157.

[3] U.N. Demographic Year Book, 1972, pp. 338–351, except data on Yugoslavia which applies to 1972 and is taken from the Statistical Yearbook of Yugoslavia, 1974, p. 119.

women had a lower level of education and lesser qualifications than the men. In other words, women made up the illiterate and unskilled part of the labour force everywhere.

The third phase is marked by the demand that girls be given the same opportunities for education as boys and this demand is common to all of the progressive movements in the world. Many countries have embodied this right in their national constitutions. As a result a wave of mass education of women ensued, and some countries have, in a comparatively short space of time, achieved much higher levels of education and others are on the way towards matching them. Table 2 indicates how this change is reflected in some regions of the world. The percentages are particularly high as compared with the situation ten years earlier and in view of this it might seem as if the problem of the inequality of sexes had been eliminated from the pages of world history, and that the major conditions were ripe for the emancipation of the female portion of the population.

The fourth phase demonstrated that although women became employed, educated on an improved scale and, in many countries, received equal pay for equal work, they were concentrated in branches of the economy where profits are low and were employed in menial jobs with the lowest earnings. Even in the so-called purely female occupations, the better-paid jobs were taken, as a rule, by men even though they were in a considerable minority in the total structure of such employment.

Research has shown that it is extremely difficult for women to advance in a professional career. The employment and education of women are not a continuous process and must be flexible enough to accommodate certain stages in their lives. These interruptions seriously affect the conditions which make for a successful work and professional career. Even though women are mastering new occupations, so that

Table 2

Percentage of girls to total enrolment by level of education

	Total	First level	Second level	Third level
World Total	43	43	34	38
Western Europe	47	49	48	32
Southern Europe	46	48	42	35
Eastern Europe	48	48	50	41
Northern Europe	48	49	48	38
North America	48	49	49	40
Latin America	48	49	48	33
Western Africa	37	38	30	15
Northern Africa	35	36	23	7
Asia	38	39	35	28

Source: UNESCO—Statistical Yearbook, 1970, p. 68.

there are virtually no jobs inaccessible to them, they still tend to seek employment largely in those occupations and work places where the demands can most easily be integrated in harmony with their roles and functions in the family.

When this unfortunate social situation is examined, the reason for the dilemma is apparent. Women are so burdened by multiple roles that they find it extremely difficult to compete with the men. Woman's liberation has often meant that, concurrent with some gains, her burdens have increased considerably and this has prevented her from achieving greater equality in her personal, professional and family life.

The fifth phase is characterized by the recognition that while the mother's role in raising and socializing children and the wife's role in maintaining marriage and the family are not easily taken care of by any other means still they shouldn't be just the private responsibility of the family, and an obstacle to the improved social involvement of women. The progressive social movements have in their various programmes stressed the obligation of society to protect children, women, and the family and to seek means for the removal of the basic obstacles to the final liberation of women. In this sense the socialization of family functions reached a high level of development in some countries and has become one of the objectives of social development in others.

The sixth phase starts when it is recognized that these solutions are not proving to be entirely satisfactory. While society can aid and intervene to a large extent, the question of the liberation and equality of women can continue to remain unresolved. Fairly accurate investigation techniques have proved that despite child care institutions, household services, electrical and technically perfected household appliances, women are still burdened and must put up with excessive demands on their time. As a result they find themselves in a less favourable position than men as far as social obligations are concerned. Women are not yet sufficiently relieved of their burdens so as to be able to acquire the same conditions for promotion in their professional careers as are men. Demands continue to be made for a redistribution of tasks within the family and a redefinition of family roles so as to put an end to women's subordination and exploitation in the home.

Many progressive programmes of upbringing and education provide the new generation with preparation for marriage and the family, for humane relations between the sexes and for responsible parenthood. In many advanced societies, young people enter marriage today aware that part of the burden of housekeeping and raising children will have to be borne by both man and woman. In addition to this, the hard reality of providing the necessities of life often, beyond the will and awareness of people, dictates radical changes in the traditional pattern of family life. At a time when the woman is forced to leave the home for a part of the day to earn a salary, the man finds himself in a position where he must take up the household duties. And so, sometimes against both his and his wife's will, he breaks away from traditional taboos in order to ensure his own survival and that of his family.

The process of breaking down the traditional patterns of inequality and of subordination of women within the family is the most difficult and slowest one of all the emancipating processes whether it develops from the impulse of enlightenment and education, or from the impact of objective necessity, i.e., the modernization of social life as a whole. Family life, as an intimate sphere of man's life, is the most resistant to every change and the most persistent in maintaining traditional concepts and behaviour patterns.

The seventh phase which takes something from each of the previous ones, is woman's struggle for political emancipation—a struggle which still arouses stubborn opposition from those who believe that a woman should not be allowed to become "Homo politicus."

Women's right to vote and to be elected to public office was, for quite a long time, the fundamental aim of the many various progressive women's movements in the world. The history of these movements for the political rights of women and their victories in this respect are well-known. Today, it is difficult to find a country in which there are no women members in parliament. The same can be said for the participation of women at the executive levels of political power, as well as in a variety of leadership positions in the administration, social services, economy, etc.

A close examination of this phenomenon over the past thirty years is, however, disappointing because the expected results have not been obtained. Only a small number of women are involved in political systems and in key positions in the social structure and even this minimum amount of participation has recently suffered a reversal.

In seeking the causes for this poor and already declining involvement of women in the political, business and social structures, a number of factors which prevent women from being equal partners with men were revealed. Some of these have already been mentioned above in company with the measures toward reform taken by various social movements and systems. It has been noted that all of these measures proved to be insufficient and that they needed to be intensified. To these factors must now be added one of special significance—one that has been lately in evidence in the literature and in contemporary movements for women's emancipation: historically speaking, women acted outside hierarchical structures. They developed techniques which lay outside the social power structure. We agree with those who claim that there is a mixture of desires, fantasy and truth in such a reasoning, and that, if women wish to contribute to decentralized innovations in society, this must be achieved on the basis of realistic possibilities and facts.

However, despite the shortcomings in the experiments undertaken by various women's organizations all over the world, there have been some positive results and others will follow. It is quite clear that the solution to a genuine emancipation for women should not be sought only in different forms of social intervention and in educational measures. *Instead one must probe into the very manner in which society is organized and structured, and in which women must become fully integrated in order to find equal status with men.* It is true that throughout history women have mainly acted outside the hierarchical structures of social institutions which have been over thousands of years developed by men, creating thus a masculine civilization. It is also true that women today, having materialized many conditions for their social emancipation, cannot successfully become integrated in such a social organization without the help of men. Thus, it is not true that this question can only be settled by women themselves or that a reformed type of social organization affects only women. It is instead a question of total social development—a question which compels the whole of mankind to reexamine its cultural heritage and *to redefine the foundations of social institutions with a view to reorganizing them in a way which will be more in keeping with the needs, wishes and aspirations of all men and women today.*

There is no doubt that the hierarchical organization of society as the predominant model of social organization has been, generally speaking, theoretically superseded. But this is far from being realized in practice. In this respect, some experiences from the Yugoslav praxis may serve as an indication of the road women in this society will follow as they struggle for their full social emancipation.

The Yugoslav Example

The Yugoslav example is characterized, on the one hand, by the development of all the customary indicators of women's emancipation: an extremely advanced legislation which provides for the full equality of women with men in the legal sphere; mass female employment; education; penetration into new occupations; and social assistance with family care. On the other hand, there was a decline in women's participation in positions of leadership until a self-management style of democracy began to replace the traditional hierarchical organization of society. At that point a considerable growth in women's participation can be noted.

In order to illustrate this it is necessary to review the statistical data regarding the changes in the social position of women: their place in the major social structures, on the one hand, and their place in the management and social decision-making system, on the other.

Position of Women in the Social Structure

1. The *Female Labour Force Participation* is shown by the percentage of women employed as compared to the total number of persons employed in the period 1940–1975.*

1940	1953	1960	1970	1973	1975
18.0	22.8	27.4	31.4	33.4	33.8

* Compiled from various Yugoslav "Statistical Bulletins" and "Yearbooks."

The growth trend of female labour force participation exceeds that of the male, even at a time when economic and social reforms were at their height, and when employment was reduced to match what the economy could absorb and to be consistent with the existing work productivity.

*Index of employment growth from 1960 to 1972**

Men				Women			
1960	1966	1970	1972	1960	1966	1970	1972
100	122	123	134	100	139	149	169

* "Statistical Bulletin", SZS, 1973, No. 788, p. 22.

2. *Female employment according to branches of activities.* Above average employment of females in Yugoslavia is mainly to be found in the so-called "female" occupations. Evidence of this can be seen first in the textile, leather, tobacco industries, and then in catering, tourism, trade and transports. As far as social services are concerned women rank high in participation, in social welfare, health, finance and insurance and culture and education (Table 3).

Table 3

Ranks of female participation in the total employment expressed in percentages according to branches of activity, 1973

Rank	Activity in the socially-owned sector	% Women
1.	Social welfare	72.6
2.	Health work	69.9
3.	Textile industry	68.7
4.	Finances and insurance	63.8
5.	Social insurance	62.3
6.	Leatherwear industry	58.2
7.	Catering and tourism	57.0
8.	School activity	53.8
9.	Culture and education	52.8
10.	Tobacco industry	48.5
11.	Foreign trade	47.0
12.	Graphics industry	45.3
13.	Business associations	43.9
14.	Scientific activity	43.0
15.	Wholesale and retail trade	42.8
16.	Social organization	42.6
17.	Economic Chamber	41.3
18.	Electrical industry	39.8
19.	Management bodies	38.9
20.	Trade services	36.3
21.	Air transportation	35.7
22.	Art and Entertainment	35.3
23.	Food processing industry	34.7
24.	Construction designing	33.3
25.	Rubber industry	32.7
26.	Communications	31.3
27.	Film industry	30.0

Rank	Activity in the socially-owned sector	% Women
28.	Paper industry	29.4
29.	Crafts	25.3
30.	Physical culture	23.9
31.	Non-metallic industry	22.7
32.	Timber industry	22.5
33.	Agriculture and fishing	20.3
34.	Metal industry	20.1
35.	Housing and public works	18.2
36.	Public transportation	17.4
37.	Petrol industry	16.8
38.	Mining research	13.7
39.	Electric energy	13.2
40.	Industry of building material	12.7
41.	Shipbuilding	11.5
42.	Iron and steel industry	11,3
43.	Non-ferrous metal industry	11.2
44.	Building trade etc.	11.6
45.	Trans-shipment etc.	9.7
46.	Rail-transport	9.6
47.	River and lake transport	8.8
48.	Coal industry and forestry	7.6
49.	Construction engineering	7.4
50.	Sea transport	6.7
	Average of female employment in 1973	33.4

Source: Statistical Yearbook of Yugoslavia, 1974, p. 119.

Of the some 50 activities presented in the above classification there are 9 in which female employment is greater than that of males. In social welfare, men account for about one-fourth, and in health and the textile industry about one-third of the total work force. (We shall subsequently see that the employment structure according to sex does not correspond to the management structure.)

3. *Conquest of new activities.* If we consider the employment rate of women by basic activity groups, we observe that, besides the traditional female occupations which still tend to attract most females, women are entering new vocations which, until recently, were inaccessible to them (Table 4).

In these various activities, the growth of female employment is greater than that of male employment as, for example, in trade and catering which shows the greatest growth. It is, however, significant to note that industry, mining, transport and communications occupy third place, immediately followed by construction. If we consider that these groups of economic activities employ a female work force which is numerically lower than the Yugoslav average, then we can assume that these occupations will be increasingly "conquered" by women. It is interesting to observe that the most pronounced rate of female employment in industry and mining lies

Table 4

Rank list of the average annual growth rate of employment according to basic social activities, 1960–1972

Rank list for women	Basic activities	Average growth rate	
		Women	Men
1.	Trade and catering	8.0	5.1
2.	Health and social welfare	5.7	4.0
3.	Industry and mining	4.5	3.1
4.	Transport and communication	4.5	3.2
5.	Culture and education	3.1	—
6.	Construction	3.0	1.6
7.	Social and State services	2.8	−1.6
8.	Crafts	2'8	1.1
9.	Forestry	1.9	1.8
10.	Housing and public works	1.6	−5.7
11.	Agriculture and fishing	0.2	−1.0

Source: Yugoslav "Statistical Bulletin" SZS, 1973, No. 788, p. 119; Yugoslav Statistical Yearbook, 1961, p. 87. and 1974, p. 119.

in the sphere of the electrical equipment industry, in metal processing, ferrous metallurgy, production and processing of petrol. It is also significant that agriculture seems least likely to attract females.

4. *Occupational position and trends in education.* The position held in the occupational structure is one of the key elements that decide social position. The important questions concern how much professional training and education are required.

The rate of change in the past ten years and the comparison between the male and female employed population, allow us to identify some of the basic trends in the evolution of the social position of women (Table 5).

It is evident that over the past ten years both males and females have improved their positions within the labour force. There are, however, differences between men and women in this respect. Both in manual and nonmanual occupations, the female work force has increased more significantly than has the male force, omitting the unskilled male manual workers and the elementary educated, who leave such posts more quickly than the unskilled female worker. It is significant, however, that women workers are quicker in leaving semi-skilled jobs and in acquiring higher training than men. It is also important to note that women gain secondary, college and university education at a faster rate than men. Generally speaking, it can be concluded that the vertical mobility of the female work force has been considerable in the past ten years.

This same trend applies to the dynamics of women's education. As shown in Table 6, a continuous upward trend is to be noted at all levels of education for all pupils and for female students, particularly at the higher levels.

Table 5

Changes in the position of employed men and women, 1961–1971

	% Men			% Women		
Occupational Position	1961	1971	Index 1961= 100%	1961	1971	Index 1961= 100%
Total	100	100		100	100	
Qualification of manual workers						
Highly skilled	6.1	9.2	165.0	0.6	0.9	213.1
Skilled	29.1	31.0	116.0	9.5	13.9	203.7
Semi-skilled	11.4	10.0	95.6	14.0	11.4	112 7
Unskilled	27.3	22.0	87.8	33.3	28.7	119.5
Education of nonmanual workers						
University	3,7	6,3	184.4	3.3	4.8	203.6
College	2.2	4.3	218.5	1.5	4.5	402.4
Secondary	8.7	12.0	150.0	15.8	22.5	196.7
Elementary	11.2	4.7	45.1	21.5	12.8	82.4

Source: "1961 Population Census" SZS book IV, 1966, p. 77, and the "Statistical Bulletin" SZS, 1971, No. 700.

Table 6

Percent of girls having completed education by total numer of pupils, 1939–1971*

Level of education completed	1938/39	53/54	61/62	70/71	1975
Elementary	42.6	45.4	44.8	46.1	46.3
Secondary	—	—	33.0	42.8	43.4
High school	34.7	44.8	48.0	55.4	53.6
College	—	—	27.3	44.9	49.0
Faculties	21.1	—	27.4	36.3	39.2
M.A.	—	—	23.5	23.9	22.4
Ph.D.	5.1	14.0	19.1	22.9	21.6

Source: Compiled from various years and issues of the Yugoslav "Statistical Bulletin" and the "Statistical Yearbook".

The Position of Women in the System of Social Decision-Making

Women's place in the system of social decision-making is of a particular significance since it is in this way that they come to know about social and political power. Statistical data will illustrate some of the tendencies which are manifested with respect to:

a. the highest managerial positions, i.e. women as directors and managers of enterprises and institutions; and

b. women's participation in the self-managing system: in bodies and delegations.

Table 7

Percent of women directors in economic enterprises, 1962–1972

Enterprises	Women directors	
	1962	1972
Large enterprises (elected by workers council and management board)	1.2	0.9
Small enterprises (elected only by management board)	2.9	2.2
Agricultural cooperative	—	0.8

Source: "Statistical Bulletin" SZS, 1973, No. 788, p. 66.

1. *Women in Management.* Table 7 presents revealing trend data on the declining proportion of women directors in economic enterprises for the years of 1962 and 1972. If we bear in mind that, in 1972, of the total number of those employed in this sector 28% were women, then we can see that the extent of their participation in management is indeed minimal. As a matter of fact, in 1972 women directors made up less than 1% of the boards of large enterprises and agricultural cooperatives and slightly more than 2% of those of small enterprises. More important, the figures for the years of 1962 and 1972 reflect a decrease in women's participation in management, and this against the background of rapidly rising female employment, especially among those with the highest level of education.

Data summarized in Table 8 confirm this.

All institutions, with the exception of education and science, where there is a

Table 8

Percent of women managers and percent of women employed in various institutions, 1970–1972

Institutions	Women managers of institutions		Women employed to the total number
	1970	1972	1972
Elementary & secondary schools	8.3	8.4	52.9
University	0.8	3.5	
Scientific institutions	3.9	5.5	41.9
Cultural-educational & artistic-entertainment	14.4	13.6	34.8
Health	12.6	10.3	67.9
Social institutions	50.3	40.7	69.7
Social insurance	1.0	1.0	58.7

Source: "Statistical Bulletin", SZS, No. 684, p. 7; "Statistical Bulletin", SzS, No. 788, p. 68; "Statistical Yearbook of Yugoslavia", 1973, p. 365.

modest increase, show a decrease in the participation of women in leadership positions. It is strange that this decrease appears in social and health institutions where there is a high concentration of females. This disproportion is even greater, if we consider for example, that in 1961 35.9% women graduated from the faculty of medicine, 43.6% from the faculty of stomatology and 77.2% from the faculty of pharmaceutics. This population, we should expect, could have gained, besides professional achievement, considerably greater general advancement as well. Other institutions that comprise a great number of female workers show the same trend when in competition with the male work force of the same qualifications. Women do not nearly attain the same vertical upward mobility in the hierarchy of leadership posts and data may even, in some instances, show a downward tendency.

2. *Women in self-management.* Self-management as a basic feature of the Yugoslav socialist system offers women a special chance in their struggle for equality and emancipation. The mechanisms built into this system of social ownership of the means of production, enable all citizens, including women, to plan, control and implement policies of production and distribution of income in all work organizations such as factories, social institutions, local communities, the republics as well as the federation. It gives all citizens the chance and right to decide on all questions concerning their own life and work and those of the social community as a whole, without having to depend on higher qualifications, education and management positions. In short, these mechanisms enable women to be an important factor in a system of decentralized social power, even though they do not actually belong to the so-called social elite.

Unfortunately, we have no studies which show the extent to which women participate in this system of direct economic and political democracy. Our analysis and our conclusions, therefore, are based on a limited range of information. It is impossible, on the basis of the number of women elected to the self-management bodies, to obtain a precise and realistic picture of their actual participation in these bodies and in self-managing democracy. However, by comparing the number of employed women with those in managerial positions and those elected to self-management obdies, we can obtain some measure of the success self-management had for women in 1972 (Table 9).

Comparison of the three important elements of the social position of women indicate that women's participation in management positions, factories and institutions is least satisfactory, but has been considerably improved by higher participation rates in self-managing bodies; however, it is still below a satisfactory percent when the rate of women's employment is considered. The ratio of gross number employed to management and self-management positions held, is most favorable in social welfare institutions with health-care institutions second. Rates of participation are surprisingly low in educational and scientific institutions, although the number of women employed there is very high which is difficult to explain. The least favorable

Table 9

Women in employment, management and self-management, 1972

Enterprises and institutions	% Women Participating in		
	Employment	Director posts	Self-management
I. Economic			
1. Large enterprises	27.3	0.9	
Members of the Workers' Council			16.8
Members of the Management Board			11.7
Presidents of the Workers' Council			5.5
Presidents of the Management Board			6.5
2. Small enterprises	27.3	2.2	
Members of the Management Board			17.4
Presidents of the Management Board			11.7
II. Non-economic (Social Services)			
3. Elementary and secondary schools	52.9	8.4	
Members of the Workers' Council			38.9
Members of the Management Board			37.7
Presidents of the Workers' Council			18.7
Presidents of the Management Board			26.2
4. Colleges and Universities	62.9	3.5	
Members of the Workers' Council			22.3
Members of the Management Board			18.3
Presidents of the Workers' Council			5.2
Presidents of the Management Board			6.2
5. Scientific institutions	41.9	5.5	
Members of the Workers' Council			29.2
Members of the Management Board			21.2
Presidents of the Workers' Council			17.8
Presidents of the Management Board			13.7
6. Cultural-Educational, Arts, Recreation	34.9	13.6	
Members of the Workers' Council			35.5
Members of the Management Board			30.2
Presidents of the Workers' Council			26.7
Presidents of the Management Board			29.6
7. Health Care Institutions	67.9	10.3	
Members of the Workers' Council			43.0
Members of the Management Board			37.5
Presidents of the Workers' Council			28.1
Presidents of the Management Board			23.2
8. Social Welfare Institutions	69.7	40.7	
Members of the Workers' Council			68.1
Members of the Management Board			58.8
Presidents of the Workers' Council			54.4
Presidents of the Management Board			60.5

Source: Statistical Bulletin, SZS, No. 788, 1973, pp. 66, 67 and Yugoslav Statistical Yearbook, 1973, pp. 364–365.

ratios appear in economic enterprises, where one would expect women to be better represented, if only in self-management bodies.

However, taken as a whole, one may conclude that women are starting to take advantage of the opportunities which self-management provides for their social improvement.

3. *Women in assembly deputy and delegate systems.* Because self-management has nowhere been completely developed in all its detail as a unique social system of direct democracy, we have no ready-made models for imitation. Self-management as a social system is in a permanent process of development. It has passed through two main phases in Yugoslavia, the one more representative and the other evolving more toward direct democracy. The new Constitution of 1974 legalized the implementation of important innovations in the social political system by introducing new mechanisms of direct self-managing democracy. The delegate system has been introduced, with the aim of bringing decision-making closer to the individual so that it is possible for him to participate directly in the decision-making process. It is still too early to say to what degree the women will take advantage of these new opportunities, but some facts indicate that the working mother has never been so much involved in decision-making as she is in our society today. A comparison of the number of women delegates elected now as compared with the number elected under the earlier assembly deputy system, makes it possible to see what the latest trends show about the development of women's social position.

With the introduction of the delegate principle in the election system, the negative trend in the election of women representatives to the assemblies on all levels has been stopped. The reason for this change may reside in the essential difference between the deputy and the delegate systems. In the representative system, electors transfer their decision-making right to their deputy and thus eliminate themselves from the direct decision-making process. This is not the case with the delegate system. Under this system, citizens organized in local bodies, at work, where they live, in their "community of interest" decide jointly how they will manage the problems associated with health, social, educational, scientific, cultural, consumer and other matters. They do not lose their right as they once did to participate in the direct decision-making. Instead they instruct their delegates to the communal, provincial and federation assemblies, where the delegate may not go beyond the limits of his authorization, to transmit their decision. If necessary, the delegate returns to his constituency for further instruction so that he may have the authority to enter into negotiations with other delegates in the assembly. Delegates are under obligation to inform their electors about the achieved results, and to check on their implementation. Thus the function of a delegate is limited to very specific and concrete actions—those actions which have been directly initiated and determined by the organized citizens.

The election data in Table 10 show that this system of direct democracy is better suited to women than was the parliamentary one. Because of it, they show a new interest and engagement in social, political and professional life. Since further investigation is required the following topic might be considered: *To the extent to which their contribution is concrete and direct women will show greater readiness*

Table 10

Women deputies and delegates in the Federal, Republican, Provincial and Communal Assemblies, 1963–1974

Assembly	% Women deputies			% Women delegates
	1963	1967	1969	1974
Federal	19.6	13.3	8.1	13.6
Republican	16.1	11.4	7.5	16.8
Provincial	15.8	16.4	12.7	20.5
Communal	16.4	9.4	6.9	15.2

Source: Statistical Bulletin, SZS, No. 788, 1973, pp. 62, 63 and 888, 1974, pp. 21, 49, 65, 7.

for engagement in social, professional and political life. (It will be necessary to start with the assumption that leading positions in self-management and in the performance called for in the delegate mechanism do not provide for the exercise of power over other people, but only allow for a greater degree of involvement in the process.)

Of all the organizations, the most important ones for the delegate system are the work organizations. An examination of women's social position in the delegate systems will therefore be particularly revealing. In Table 11 we have compared the employment of women in the major occupational categories with the number of women elected as delegates within these categories.

It would appear that the introduction of the delegate system has to some extent changed the picture of women's social position in the system of decision-making.

Table 11

Percent of Women delegates by main activities and employment, 1974

Women delegates elected from the	Women delegates elected 1974 for the assemblies				Employed women 1973
	Federal	Repub.	Prov.	Commun.	
Economy enterprises	15.4	18.7	25.3	16.8	28.6
Institutions of education, science, culture	50.4	43.2	36.8	34.1	53.8
Institutions of health and social welfare	66.6	29.5	50.0	38.2	71.1

Source: Statistical Bulletin, SZS, No. 888, 1974, pp. 36–45; 51–63; 70–71; Yugoslav Statistical Yearbook, 1973, p. 119.

The data are not sufficiently detailed to provide wholly valid conclusions, but the available evidence suggests that the delegate system has put women in a more favorable position in all occupational categories, particularly in those economic enterprises where their position heretofore was considerably less favorable when measured by their participation in management and in the self-management bodies.

Research projects are being organized to look into the degree to which the basic principles of the delegate system are being realized, and these will enable us to measure more accurately the extent and quality of women's participation in this system of direct decision-making. At present, in 1975, roughly a year since the delegate system was introduced, we must be satisfied with the present statistical data as the only available validation of the theoretical assumption about the future development of the struggle for women's social equality.

Conclusions

Women's social position is commonly described by the extent to which women are represented in the labour force, by their education and qualifications, and by their entrance into new occupations and professions. On the basis of male-female comparisons conclusions usually have been drawn with regard to the extent of women's emancipation in a given society as compared with other societies.

By now, however, it has become evident that these classical indicators for measuring the extent of women's emancipation are not exhaustive. One essential indicator of social position was neglected, namely, "social power." When speaking of women, the concept of "social power" was tacitly omitted in the explanation of the early phases of women's emancipation. Indeed, women had to struggle long and hard to penetrate some of the basic structures before they were able to overcome obstacles to gaining positions of social power, i.e. leadership roles in the economic, political, educational, cultural, scientific and other sectors of society. Facts indicate that in taking responsibility in these sectors and becoming truly equal with men, women have only entered the initial stage. The reason for this is to be found not only in the traditional mistrust of women's abilities, but also in their lack of interest in authoritarian positions. Certain investigators explain this phenomenon by pointing to the multiple roles that women have to play and no doubt this contributes to the fact that women are far from being in a socially powerful position. Yet, certain other facts reveal deeper and more substantial reasons. Namely, women are not interested in the conventional system of social power. In fact, they are against it, even though they are frequently unaware of it.

Data collected in Yugoslavia show that the more the classical system of hierarchical power in decision-making is overcome and is replaced by the decentralized self-managing and self-governing system of decision-making, the more women become socially active and involved.

Comparisons of these two systems of management, one of which is resisting destruction, while the other is still in the process of growth, indicate that the latter is much better suited to women. In contrast with the very few women in the classical system, recent facts indicate that more and more women are becoming involved in the growing self-managing system, and that they are becoming more and more interested in direct democracy. Oriented toward constructive policies and the actual improvement of the conditions of life for their children and family and for society as a whole, with no interest in social power over people, self-managing democracy appeals to women and more of them are taking a part in it. There are more of them in the new self-managing organs and bodies than there ever were before in the classical system with its hierarchical structures and its class distinctions. Decentralized budgets are the responsibility of self-managing organs, and it is the right of all citizens to decide directly how the funds will be distributed and spent. Furthermore, it is the right of all working people to control the working out of their decisions as well as be responsible for their correctness and the risk they entail. In short, the self-managing society sets out to realize Lenin's vision of "managing things and not people."

Such an orientation is based on the assumption that *women more than any other social group will be interested in abolishing the hierarchical organization of social power, decentralizing such power and returning it to those from whom it was taken. Therefore, the answer to the final emancipation of women is not to be found in competition with men over powerful positions in society. Instead it lies in the support of the decentralization and the breaking down of the power structure—in brief, in an antipower position.*

Contemporary societies, independently of their political systems, reveal an increasing number of examples which seem to confirm this point of view and which offer a more appropriate picture of the ways the future process of women's emancipation is likely to develop.

PART FOUR

WOMEN IN AFRICA

Women's Roles and Conjugal Family Systems in Ghana*

CHRISTINE OPPONG

University of Ghana, Legon, Accra

Introduction

OVER THE PAST SEVERAL YEARS, numerous conferences, seminars and publications have followed up the investigations carried out in 1975 in Mexico regarding the impact of economic development on women's roles and the family as an institution and the impact of domestic constraints upon women's changing roles.[1]

A basic paradigm of the concept of development and its implications for women was spelled out in a paper written for the Mexican conference, in which development was defined broadly as referring to the process whereby a society "increases the flow of goods and services over time and the distribution thereof among the population"; a process implying "deep and durable changes in social structure, in the functioning of institutions and the cultural values of great masses of people".[2] These changes entail primarily the modification of the agricultural system, in which the farming household usually constitutes the basic economic unit, and in which women often play an active role in production (whether or not census takers record this) as well as in food processing and marketing.

However, when this situation changes, and there is spatial separation of home and workplace and, through migration, people move away from their kin, then women may suddenly be in a position in which they find it difficult, if not impossible, to combine productive labour with domestic work and child care. Homemaking becomes an activity considered quite separate from the economic system and is undervalued by the dominant male cultural pattern which emphasizes the money value of time and products.

This process has been documented over time for Britain by A. Oakley in *Wo-*

---

* An earlier version of this paper was presented to a conference on Nigerian Women and Development and Changing Family Structure, University of Ibadan, April, 1977.
1 See for instance *Women and World Development* an Annotated Bibliography O D C. 1976. Such Conferences include the Nigerian one referred to above and the meeting held on the theme of Women & Development at Wellesley College Boston in June 1976 and a subsequent seminar on the same theme held at the Johnson Foundation Centre Racine Wisconsin.
2 The integration of women in the development process as equal partners with men. U. N. June 1975 Mexico E/CONF/66/4.

men's work: *The Housewife Past and Present,* 1976. E. Boserup (1970), using data from developing countries, has indicated that the breakdown of the traditional division of labour between men and women is inevitable given the changing structure of the employment situation and urbanization etc. as the modernization process goes on. Whether it is welcomed or not "a new sex pattern of productive work must emerge". There are dangers, however, in the change process as Boserup points out. One is that women will lose their productive (economic) functions and become mere housewives and the other, looking at the matter from a social view, is that the state will lose the personpower and training and talents of at least fifty percent of its population.

The first danger is one which most Ghanaian (if not the majority of African) women have rightly feared and sought to avoid, since they realize full well the economic dependence that would follow and the increased potential for husband-dominance and domestic suffering.[3] Both of these dangers can be avoided however. The outcome from the woman's personal point of view and that of the state depends upon the structure of the situation—what Boserup (1970:) refers to as the "widely varying customs and other preconditions in different parts of the world". It is the purpose of this paper to look briefly at some of these varying customs and preconditions, on the assumption that a broad framework will indicate how West African situations compare with other regions of the world and will provide object lessons as to the potential consequences for women of their economic participation in different types of change in family systems. This paper, accordingly, concentrates on the definition of women's role in the family—a role which has rightly been singled out as the most important determinant of the extent to which women are free to participate in economic development. As has been already stressed and as is illustrated here, "It is not so much the particular form of the family as the imperatives demanded of the women in this context and the *presence or absence of supporting figures or institutions to carry out the tasks defined as familial functions*" (Nash, 1975: 5). In other words what is crucial is the extent to which individual women, in their capacities as wives and mothers, are alone responsible for the fulfillment of domestic responsibilities or conversely the extent to which sharing and delegation of conjugal and maternal duties are institutionalized.

There is considerable evidence to suggest that with the increasing spatial mobility of populations and with economic development, *"openness",* in terms of sharing and delegation of tasks and duties, gives way to relative *"closure"* of the conjugal family;

---

3 "in (Ghanaian) society women themselves believe that only two types of their species suffer — the sterile ... and the foolish. And by the foolish they refer to the type of woman who depends solely on her husband for subsistence" Christina Amma Atta Aidoo, Introduction to *The Beautiful Ones are not yet born,* a novel by Ayi Kwei Armah; Collier Books, quoted in *Womanpower Retrograde steps in Ghana* by C. Oppong, C. Okali & B. Houghton *African Studies Review* 1975.

kin are simply not available to give help with child-care and chores (Oppong, 1971; 1974). *"Openness"* may be maintained in a certain way over space and time, for instance, by sending children to be reared by kin; by importing poorer country cousins to work in the household; and, in the case of financial need, by sending money to family members elsewhere. This kind of *"openness"* may, in fact, persist longer in certain strata of a population—among the elite who can buy services (Oppong, 1974), and among the rural or urban immobile poor, who have kin around and available (Stack, 1974).[4]

Another alternative to the strategies above is societal or community assumption of conjugal, parental and filial obligations. Such institutional supports for women's (and men's) familial functions may be piecemeal, *ad hoc* or highly organized. They may affect all or only a small section of a community. The last thirty years has seen a massive expansion of such facilities in certain countries. At present there is increasing pressure, expecially from women in states where such institutional supports do not exist or are scarce, to have some of these facilities made available to all, expecially those which take over child care and rearing responsibilities.

With regard to *"jointness"*—the sharing of domestic tasks and responsibilities between husbands and wives—recent detailed and meticulous data collection and analysis using cross-cultural survey materials and time-budgets have provided important and revealing insights into the sexual division of labour (Szalai, 1975). One such insight is the fallacy of assuming that tasks needing great physical exertion are always performed by men, since water carrying, laundering, burden-bearing, are generally performed by women. The only crucial difference between the sexes of course is that women give birth and, where breast-feeding is the rule, also suckle the infants. This difference alone cannot account for all the prejudice, discrimination and barriers which women face. As more than one observer has pointed out "what really counts is not so much the physiological fact of child-bearing, but rather the culturally determined structure of motherhood and child care" (Szalai, 1975: 6). Women are not constitutionally better fitted to housework and child-care than men. That, in fact, they do most of these tasks, whether they are at home most of the day or in full-time employment, is adequately demonstrated by the time budget data from twelve countries (Szalai *et al.*, 1972). The result is that employed men have much more free time, rest and leisure than employed women. According to one writer *"joint"* egalitarian conjugal role relationships in the United States are so few and scattered that it is virtually impossible to obtain systematic survey data on them (Scanzoni, 1972).

4 A study of Ghanaian University students revealed that only one out of over thirty prescribed norms was intensely held by men and women, sharing high measures for intensity and consensus and no significant difference between the views of the sexes. That was the statement, "A married woman has the duty of helping her husband to earn a living for the family". This was the only issue of those examined on which educated young men and women agree with equal degrees of enthusiasm. (Oppong 1975e).

Changing Domestic Roles of Educated Ghanaian Women

Findings from several recent studies (Oppong, 1974: 1975; 1976) in Ghana have confirmed—with detailed documentation both from surveys and cases—some of these general findings regarding family type *("openness")* and the conjugal division of labour *("jointness")*. By using these two dimensions of classification simultaneously, four kinds of conjugal family role systems may be distinguished (or more depending upon the degree of precision with which the variables are measured and with regard to the areas of domestic behaviour or norms specified). Figure 1 depicts the possible alternatives when simple dichotomies of the two variables are used.

Figure 1

Conjugal Family Role Systems:
Chores and Child care

Sharing of activities by wife and husband

		Yes	No
By spouse and kin	Yes	I Open/Joint (1)	II Open/Segregated (6)
	No	III Closed/Joint (2)	IV Closed/Segregated (3)

⎯→ directions of change desired by wives
( ) number of couples in elite Akan panel study

In category I labelled *Open/Joint* husband and wife share household tasks and child care equally. There are also other individuals and institutions to whom tasks are delegated, including kin, servants, crèches, laundries, etc. In a panel study of elite Akan couples (Senior Civil Servants and their wives) in Accra, described in detail by Oppong (1982), only one couple fell into the relatively Open/Joint category with husband and wife and kin all participating in domestic duties and acting as substitutes for each other. The wife in this household was well satisfied with this position and content for arrangements to stay as they were. She had both her own relatives and husband willing to assume almost any kind of task or responsibility, so that she rarely showed signs of worry or strain despite looking after her children and house and working full-time.

In category II labelled *Open/Segregated,* husbands do not share tasks with wives but there are other sources of help available to them. Half of the couples in the study referred to fell into this category. In these households the wife and kin and domestics did most of the housework while the husband did only such jobs as shopping and seeing to repairs.

In category III *Closed/Joint,* the only source of help for the wife is her husband. Two couples in the elite Akan study fell into the *Closed/Joint* category since the husbands were willing to care for the children and cook and wash whenever it was necessary. But there were no other dependable figures who could completely take over major areas of responsibility, although there was some help from maids and stewards. The wives in this category were quick to praise their husbands for their participation, which they realised was unusually generous. They were, however, disturbed by the fact that they could not find any of their own relatives to come and give full-time, reliable assistance, especially at the times when they had small babies in the house. Both of their husbands were concerned that their wives should find such help and had also tried to persuade them to stop work and stay at home.

In category IV *Closed/Segregated,* the wife is in the most hardpressed and vulnerable position. She is expected to do all the chores and the child care herself. Neither her husband nor anyone else is prepared to share these tasks with her. In the elite study, the three wives in this kind of position were all trying to shift some of their burdens, either by persuading their husbands to do more or by finding other substitutes such as junior female relatives. (They did have minimal help from young maids.)

The arrows in the figure indicate the directions in which dissatisfied wives wanted change. They wanted both more participation by their husbands—a shift to a more *Joint* pattern—and more assumption of tasks by kin and others—a more *Open* arrangement. Simultaneously, they were pressing for the traditional pattern of domestic cooperation from kin to continue and for innovation, in their attempt to persuade husbands to participate more.

There is evidence to show that it is the wives whose resources in experience, education, income and assumption of responsibilities are more nearly equal to those of their husbands, who are most frequently successful in the latter aim (Oppong, 1971). These are also the wives who tend to have a more egalitarian relationship.

Data from subsequent studies collected from female nurses and teachers have shown the growing difficulty educated women face in trying to combine chores, child care and a profession (Oppong, 1975a; 1975b; 1976). Mothers who are nurses complain of exhaustion, anxiety about their children, lack of time to rest and problems in finding adequate forms of child-care arrangements. Teachers, too, complain. A major preoccupation for some married women is how to get a maidservant to look after their children. As universal attendance at primary school, especially for girls, becomes increasingly commonplace, it will be more and more difficult to procure inexpensive baby care and household help. Meanwhile, the traditional norm remains generally unchanged, viz. housework and children are woman's work, in spite of the fact that wives are expected to earn an income and provide for at least part of their own and their children's financial needs.

A Global Perspective

It is instructive to take a number of well-known conjugal family role systems and place them into the general categories in the property space. Admittedly these are only rough approximations and relate to ideology rather than practice (the gap between these differs in varying degrees). First of all both *openness* and *segregation* characterize the traditional African conjugal family role systems. Most tasks both inside and outside the home are divided according to sex, but males and females tend to have sets of kin, affines, neighbours with whom responsibilities may be shared. Sexual segregation persists in ideology. Although women do farm work, trade and produce crafts, the husband is reputedly the "breadwinner" and the wife remains responsible for nearly all household tasks and infant care. *Openness* is, however, vulnerable to change as societies reach higher levels of economic development and as migration, wage-labour etc. reduce the availability of kin and domestics, even for those who are willing to pay the formerly acceptable low wages.[5]

In the *Closed/Segregated* category are the societies in which woman's place is believed to be in the home with the small children and the housework and in which no attempt is made to find a proper substitute for maternal care. An example of such a system is described by Gavron in *The Captive Wife, Conflicts of Housebound Mothers* (1966). The title of the book sums up the dilemma of the British housewife in the isolated conjugal family of the fifties and sixties.

An example of the ideology and behaviour supporting this type of system is provided by Baxandall's essay (1975) where she discusses day-care or the lack of it in the United States. Negative attitudes towards day-care among policymakers and decision-takers arise from the *closed*, self-sufficient nuclear family ideology and the concept of the nurturant mother (absolutely vital to her child's development) and the 'bread-winning father' who supports them. Thus, it is felt to be the mother's individual duty to provide for the early care of her own children in her home. Formerly, when kin lived nearby, such child-rearing could be shared with grandparents and aunts, but today few households have kin beyond the nuclear family and relatives tend, for the most part, to be scattered. Meanwhile, the need for day-care grows as more and more mothers, either through necessity (for want of an adequate "breadwinner") or choice, work outside the home. In actual fact Baxandall's analysis of the situation shows that the gap between the need for and the provision of facilities

---

5 As Boserup (1970: 103) points out, it is a characteristic feature of countries at an intermediate stage of economic development for a large number of women to be engaged in paid housework. At an earlier stage cooking, washing etc. are carried out within the family, usually by the women. In the intermediate stage of commercialization, such services may be performed for wages by male or female domestic servants. At higher levels of economic development, there is commercialization of such services — cafeterias, launderies, cleaning services, etc.

in the U.S. has become worse rather than better in the past thirty years. Only 20 percent of the children of working mothers are in group care. The rest have various arrangements—some looking after themselves (even when under six years of age). Even families who can afford to pay often cannot find facilities.

It is women in this kind of family and social context who are described by Betty Friedan (1965) in the *Feminine Mystique*. She writes of their problem to which she gives no name, their terrible sense of dissatisfaction at the restricted nature of their lives, the endless humdrum of domesticity.

A few *Joint/Closed* examples from the Euro-American context (Bernard, 1964; Rapoport and Rapoport; 1971) have been mentioned above. Other examples of isolated couples come to mind, such as factory couples working shifts, who pass the baby from one to the other at the change of the shift.

A number of interesting societal examples fit the *Open/Joint* category, including examples from socialist and communist countries and from communes in larger social contexts.

The Israeli Kibbutzim, which involve about 100,000 people of three generations, provide an ideal example of a well-documented test case, in which the ideology of the conjugal family role system with regard to chores and child care is virtually completely *open* and *joint* (Talmon, 1972). Absolute equality between men and women in all spheres is stressed. Both spouses (ideally) take on any form of occupation as community needs dictate. The physical care and rearing of children are the responsibility of the community crèches and nurseries rather than of individual parents. The system of socialization in which the main agencies are the peer group, nurses, instructors and teachers enables mothers, as well as fathers, to continue community work. However, even here we see that ideals are not completely achieved. A gradual polarization of sex roles has been documented with women increasingly assuming the traditional women's work roles (Tiger & Shepher 1975: 227).

A further example of the *Open/Joint* arrangement is Sweden where at the end of the 19th century the debate shifted from the problem of women's two roles to a consideration of men's roles in the family and at work (Myrdal, 1971). What is even more important, the question has not remained in the realm of theory and ideology, nor has action been confined to a few experimental communes. Instead the practical details of day-to-day living have been considered, details such as the time-budget of the married couple and how fairly the hours of work in the home and with the family can be shared. Furthermore, fathers as well as mothers have opportunities for parental leave after the birth of a child and part-time jobs for both mothers and fathers are a real possibility in some cases. In spite of all this, however, there is evidence that the married woman is still responsible for the larger share of the housework (Dahlström, 1971: 30). Moreover, the education of young women and their career plans are often cut short by marriage and child-bearing and rearing. In spite of ideological equality, the mothers who try to continue to work and to take only short leaves of absence during their children's infancy are faced by almost insuperable obstacles (Dahlström, 1971: 52).

In all parts of the communist world, revolutionary changes have taken place in sex and family role ideology and practice in the past thirty to fifty or more years. These changes are in the *Joint/Open* direction, that is, towards sharing of domestic rights, tasks and responsibilities by spouses and toward the setting up of institutional frameworks including crèches, boarding schools, canteens, etc. to which many tasks, usually looked after by women, can be delegated (Bronfenbrenner, 1970; Croll, 1974; Curtin, 1975; Wrochno, 1969; Mandel, 1975).

Socialist Solutions

It is not fortuitous that the political regimes of all the states in the *Open/Joint* category with dual emphasis, i.e., emphasis upon the equality of persons and emphasis on women's involvement in the development process should be socialist, welfare states (though "capitalist" e.g., Sweden) or communist.

Kolmer (1975) provided a succinct analysis of the underlying connections in a background paper for the Mexican Conference. As she pointed out, in the socialist countries the dual approach necessary for their social structure is being pursued. On the one hand, women are being offered equal rights in the economy and, on the other hand, the problems associated with parental and other domestic responsibilities are being dealt with.

Since the full integration of women into the development of society as a whole is only possible if women's work outside the home and their contributions to society can be coordinated with their family roles, basic changes in family life-style are recognized as prerequisite. Women are increasingly being freed from household drudgery and housekeeping demands by the large-scale production of and easy availability of consumer goods and services, i.e., community laundries, ready-to-serve foods, take-out restaurants, etc.

In the meantime, old images of sex role stereotypes are being legislated out of existence as a definite government policy. The successes achieved in the past thirty years are an example to the developing countries of what can be done in a relatively short space of time.

West Africa, the Coming Crisis: Closure/Segregation

It now remains to consider the West African case and, in particular, the question of whether women in Nigeria or Ghana or elsewhere in West Africa have any need of "liberation". Before trying to answer this question, it will be useful to consider who the women are who are currently organizing a "liberation movement". In which kind of conjugal family role system, of those already described, are they located? From Figure 2 it appears that they are in category IV *Closed/Segregated,* that is women who are alone individually shouldering all the domestic burdens, without the help of husbands, kin or other agencies. They are situated in communities where nurseries

Figure 2

Examples of Conjugal Family Role Ideologies

I. Open/Joint Swedish Israeli Kibbutzim Communist, etc.	II. Open/Segregated African, etc.
III. Closed/Joint	IV. Closed/Segregated North American British, etc.

and kindergartens are minimal or nonexistent. They are in cultures in which sociologists, psychologists and politicians perpetuate myths about maternal deprivation, the wife's expressive role, the feminine personality, etc. These women suffer from the constraints of domestic burdens and institutional disregard to such an extent that it is only the needy or persevering or highly career-motivated who work, at least when their children are small, and those who do work earn salaries much smaller than do their male age-mates.

Such social contexts of female oppression are the seedbeds of rebellion in women's current fight for liberation, her fight for equality, for a shifting of part of the domestic burden onto unwilling husbands and for welfare services currently nonexistent or inadequate. And certainly not of less importance than the foregoing, is her fight against the all-pervasive sexist mores and myths regarding her strength, her brainpower, her character. What women are fighting for with regard to the conjugal family role system is greater *openness,* greater *jointness.* They want an institutional framework which will alleviate the present isolation of each mother and her children, trapped, as they now are, in a separate dwelling. They want the promotion of greater symmetry in marriage. Such changes will enable women to take their rightful place in the labour market, to contribute to the national development and to earn wages equivalent to those of men of similar age, talents and training.

What has all this got to do with West African women who are trading, farming, nursing, teaching in cultures which have become world-renowned for the independence, achievements and energy of their womenfolk? Are the problems of these housewives relevant? What is the evidence? First, there is a strong case for arguing that the positions of many women in West Africa are deteriorating in comparison with the positions of their menfolk. For example, in a recent paper about women in Ghana, entitled *Womanpower: retrograde steps in Ghana,* (Oppong, Okali & Houghton, 1975), it was pointed out that certain categories of women, through increasing *closure* of the conjugal family or from the strain of single parenthood, are under growing stress as they try to cope with their manifold tasks inside and outside the home; and that because of differential access to strategic resources, such as higher education and land, women are increasingly at a disadvantage *vis à vis* men in general and their husbands in particular, both in the economy and in the home. Indeed some women are becoming dependent upon their husbands, not only for money but also for their time to share with them the work load in the house. Yet without some kind of help, even highly educated professional women may have great difficulty in combining motherhood with a career. In terms of domestic tasks and child care, there are fewer and fewer substitutes available for mobile mothers. As has been pointed out, with increasing economic development even domestic service becomes more unattainable for the well-to-do unless through the importation of girls and youths from less economically developed neighbouring regions. These two circumstances are already in existence as indicated by comments recently recorded during visits with a number of working mothers.

Segregation of tasks along sex lines continues and women are expected to play a full-time role in the economy, as well as being held responsible for virtually all chores and child care. Several studies are currently underway devoted to an examination of these issues. One in Lagos (Fapohunda and Fapohunda, 1975) is examining how urban working mothers combine family building and child-rearing with income-earning. Few Lagos women, like their Ghanaian counterparts in Accra, see temporarily dropping out of the labour market as a viable solution to the duties of motherhood. Meanwhile, husbands contribute little if anything to household work and child care. It is not surprising to find that women's main difficulty is finding dependable household help, and that, like the Accra nurses referred to above, the great problem for nearly half of them is the lack of time to attend to family affairs or to rest. Many are exhausted and as Szalai (1975) found they have little time for leisure pursuits,

If, as seems evident, it is generally true that women's individual domestic burdens are increasing, and that many of them are doing three jobs while their menfolk do one, can it really be argued that pressure for change is irrelevant? That the so-called women's liberation movement has nothing to offer? That women do not need to take concerted action to improve their lot?

Sexual Politics

To revert finally to our global comparative framework, it should not be forgotten as one observes the positions of societies and individuals in Figure 2 that there are hard economic, political and demographic factors underlying the several domestic ideologies. For instance the *open/joint* category, towards which many women are striving, did not arise simply out of altruism on the part of the male power holders.

It came about in Sweden because of a demographic problem. The population was not replacing itself, hence welfare measures supportive of parental roles were declared vital for the encouragement of higher fertility (A. & G. Myrdal, 1934). Again, in the case of the Kibbutzim, all available personpower was needed in the early days for development and defence. Flexibility was required, hence the necessity for egalitarian sex roles and for women's participation in all spheres of economic life. At a later stage, as human replacement became a problem, well-organized and well-equipped crèches and nurseries took the burden from parents and released mothers, as well as fathers, for continued economically productive activity.

In the communist societies, these changes in family roles have only come as the aftermath of political and economic revolution in which the intention was to mobilize all available personpower for national reconstruction and development.

It is a domestic revolution of similar dimensions which the Women's Liberation Movement in the United States and Europe is trying to bring about. Significantly, this is an age in which large numbers of adult women have education and vocational and professional skills on an unprecendented scale, many of which are going unused. And often when there is opportunity to use them, it is in lower level positions than those held by their former male schoolmates.

Pressure for *jointness* (equal assumption of domestic burdens by husband and wife) can be exerted privately within the home as it is presently structured (Oppong 1982). Evidence has already been cited to indicate that, as in any political struggle, it is likely to be protagonists with strategic resources at their command who are more likely to be successful (i.e., wives with weapons of education, jobs, etc.). Retention of the advantages of openness, however, when the "extended family" or kin network has withered away and domestic labour sources have disappeared (all incidental outcomes of economic development), is a matter for neighbourhood, community, regional and state action. Women can only exert influence by banding together to form either community action groups or political pressure groups dedicated to change. Women thus need to work for change, if they want it, on two fronts, the domestic and the national. Both pressures concern power and are therefore political.

Evidence from Ghana as, for example, the micro-studies of domestic power struggles (Oppong 1982) and the activities and programmes of the National Council on Women and Development indicate the awareness of Ghanaian women to these issues and describe some of the ways in which they are confronting them.

REFERENCES

Baxandall, R. F.
    1975   "Who Shall Care for Our Children? The History and Development of Day-care in the United States." in: *Women: a Feminist Perspective.* ed. Freeman J. Mayfield Publishing Corporation.

Bernard J.
    1964   *Academic Women.* Penn. State University Press.

Boserup, E.
    1970   *Women's Role in Economic Development.* London: Allen and Unwin.

Bronfenbrenner, U.
    1970   *The Two Worlds of Childhood, U.S. & U.S.S.R.* Russel-Sage Foundation.

Croll, E.
    1974   *The Woman's Movement in China.* Anglo-Chinese Educational Institute Modern China Series, No. 6.

Curtin, K.
    1975   *Women in China.* Pathfinder Press.

Dahlström, E. ed.
    1971   *The Changing Roles of Men and Women* (first published 1962,) Beacon Press.

Fapohunda, E. R. & O. J.
    1975   *The Working Mothers in Lagos: A preliminary assessment of their problems and responses.* University of Lagos (mimeo).

Friedan, B.
    1965   *The Feminine Mystique.* Gollancz.

Gavron, H.
    1966   *The Captive Wife, Conflicts of Housebound Mothers.* London: Routledge and Kegan Paul.

Gornick, V. & B. K. Moran (eds.)
    1971   *Woman in Sexist Society: Studies in Power and Powerlessness.* A Mentor Book.

Kolmer, K.
    1975   *Report on the Implication of Scientific and Technological Developments for the Situation of Women and their Integration in Development: A point of View.* U.N. World Conference on I.W.Y. Mexico.

Leijon, A. G.
    1968   *Swedish Women, Swedish Men.* The Swedish Institute for Cultural Relations with Foreign Countries.

Mandel, W. M.
    1975   *Soviet Women.* Anchor Books.

Morgan, D. H. J.
    1975   *Social Theory and the Family.* London: Routledge and Kegan Paul.

Myrdal, A. & G.
    1934   *The Population Crisis.*

Myrdal, A.
    1971   Foreword in Dahlström E. (ed.) *The Changing Roles of Men and Women.* Beacon Press.

Nash, J.
    1975   *The integration of women in the development process as equal partners with men.* U.N. June Mexico E/CONF/66/4.

Oakley, A.
    1976   *Woman's Work: The Housewife Past and Present.* Vintage Books.

Oppong, C.
    1970   "Conjugal Power and Resources: An Urban African Example." *Journal of Marriage and the Family,* Vol. 32, No. 4. 676–680.
    1971   "Joint Conjugal Roles and Extended Families." *Journal of Comparative Family Studies,* 2, 2. 178–187.

1974 *Marriage Among a Matrilineal Elite. A family study of Ghanaian Senior Civil Servants,* Cambridge University Press.
1975a *Nursing Mothers: Aspects of Conjugal and Maternal Roles of Nurses in Accra.* I.A.S. Research Review Special issue on women. Legon.
1975b *Parenthood in a Changing Context.* Ghana Sociological Association, Kumasi, March.
1975c "Womanpower: Retrograde Steps in Ghana," with C. Okali and B. Houghton. *African Studies Review,* December. Special issue on women.
1975d "Norms and Variations: a study of Ghanaian students attitudes to marriage and family living." Legon. *Family Research Papers* No. 3 Changing Family Studies (ed.) C. Oppong.
1976 *Norms Reality and Stress. Aspects of Conjugal Family Solidarity among Ghanaian Women Teachers.* Paper presented at a conference in Women and Development held at Wellesley College, Mass. U.S.A. June.
1982 *Middle Class African Marriage.* Allen and Unwin: reprint of 1974.

Rapoport, R. and R. Rapoport
1971 *Dual-Career Families.* Harmondsworth: Penguin.

Scanzoni, J.
1972 *Sexual Bargaining: Power Politics in American Marriage.* Prentice-Hall Inc.

Stack, C.
1974 *All our Kin. Strategies for Survival in a Black Community.* Harper.

Sudarkasa, N.
1973 "Where women work: a study of Yoruba women in the market place and in the home." *Anthropological papers* No. 53. Ann Arbor. University of Michigan.

Szalai, A.
1975 *The Situation of Women, in the Light of contemporary time budget research,* U.N. Mexico.

Talmon, Y.
1972 *Family and Community in the Kibbutz.* Harvard University Press.

Tiger, L. & J. Shepher
1975 *Women in the Kibbutz.* Harcourt Brace.

Wrochno, Krvstvna
1969 *Woman in Poland.* Warsaw Interpress.

Young, M. & P. Wilmot
1973 *The Symmetrical Family: a study of work and leisure in the London Region.* Routledge and Kegan Paul.

The Changing Position of Black Women in South Africa

ANNA F. STEYN and J. M. UYS

Rand Afrikaans University, Johannesburg, South Africa

THE MATERIAL presented in this study was not originally collected in one empirical survey, but is a synopsis of the research findings of several empirical studies which were conducted by different researchers during the past 25 years on the position of Black women in the Republic of South Africa.

As these studies, considered separately, do not give an overall picture of the changes taking place with regard to the position of Black women, and as a need was felt for such a comprehensive picture, an attempt is made in this study to deduce and construct a broad and general pattern of change by combining and comparing the findings of these individual studies.

As these several studies were done at different times in different places, there were at first some misgivings as to the comparability of the material and the possibility of deducing any sort of general pattern. In studying these various reports, it became clear, however, that the main trends apparent in each of them were to a great extent similar and that the possibility of constructing such a general pattern of change was realistic.

One problem, however, which was a serious obstacle in constructing the pattern was the fact that these studies were mostly of a qualitative and descriptive nature. Consequently the trends and patterns of change could only be stated in very broad and general terms, while no inference could be made as to the statistical incidence of these trends among the Black population as a whole.

Before an analysis could be made of the apparent pattern of change in the Black woman's position, it will be necessary for the purpose of orientation to give a brief description of the Blacks in South Africa and of the factors which contributed to their changing pattern of life in general and the changing position of the Black woman in particular. It will also be necessary to outline briefly the position of the Black woman in traditional society before these changes took place.

The Blacks of South Africa and Factors which contributed to their changing Pattern of Life

The Blacks of South Africa belong to the southern Bantu and can be divided into four main groups, each consisting of several tribes:

(1) The Nguni, consisting of the Swazi, the Zulu, the Ndebele, and the Xhosa complex;
(2) The Sotho, consisting of the southern Sotho, the northern Sotho, and the western Sotho;
(3) The Venda, and
(4) The Shangana Tsonga.

The Bantu of South Africa are thus, in reality, a great diversity of ethnic groups and tribes, each with its own territory. They form distinctive and separate units, which exist independently of each other, each having its own characteristic way of life.

Confronted with such a variety of different groups and subgroups, it becomes difficult to make generalizations as to the common characteristics of the place of women in traditional Black society. It stands to reason that it will only be possible, to a limited extent, to give very broad generalizations of her position, while at the same time guarding against oversimplification. This deduction of a general broadly-outlined pattern of the position of the Black woman in traditional society is, however, possible as the social structure of these various sub-groups bears a resemblance to each other and these groups show a marked degree of cultural cohesion, despite the diversity of cultural patterns.

As far as the changing pattern of living is concerned, it can be pointed out that, during the past two centuries, the South African Blacks have increasingly been exposed to influences wich have had disintegrating effects on their traditional way of life in general, and on the position of the women, in particular.

Two sets of factors played an important role in this connection: first, the contact with Western society, and secondly, the process of urbanization which they have undergone.

The Blacks of South Africa came into contact with the Whites during the first half of the eighteenth century. Initially these contacts were sporadic and only the southern Nguni tribes were involved. These contacts increased progressively, and most of the tribes were eventually exposed to the western way of life in one way or another.

Among the important factors in the western way of life which had an influence on the Blacks in the contact situation were religion, the economy and legislation.

Since their earliest contact with the Blacks, White missionaries have tried to convert them to Christianity. The Christian religious values had implications for the position of the Black woman, since many of their family habits and customs were the direct opposite of Christian dogma. Polygamous marriages as well as levirate and sororate customs were denounced by the missionaries, which affected the position of the Black woman over a period of time.

The schools established by the Whites also had a westernizing influence on the children, as here they came into contact with western values which prepared them for integration into the differentiated economic system of the Whites. As well, boys and girls were also treated as equals, which contributed much to the relative increase in the status of women.

Contacts with Whites ultimately led to a gradual integration with the highly-diversified economic structure of the Whites, which contributed to a change in the traditional division of labour and in this way to a change in the position of the Black woman.

The formal legislation of the Whites influenced Black society strongly. Holleman (1960: 92) points out that, as far as Bantu law is concerned, it is subsidiary to the common law of the country, or, turned the other way—the common law is primary and valid for indigenous groups unless explicitly specified differently. It is, therefore, wholly understandable that the laws of the Whites would influence the Bantu society in general, and that laws concerning Bantu marriage would considerably influence the Bantu family as well as the place of the Bantu woman in society.

The contact of the Bantu with the western way of life has been intensified, and the tempo of westernization has been increased by the process of urbanization of the Blacks. Besides this intensification of the contact situation, the process of urbanization as such and the adaptation to a dynamic urban way of life also contributed to a change in the position of the Black woman.

In company with the general influences of city life, one of the most important factors contributing to the changing Black society has been the disintegration of the traditional social groups (and group control) as well as the high degree of detribalization which took place within the urban areas. Social groups, which in tribal life had played an important role in the creation and maintenance of organized community life, have either disappeared completely or else lost their functions to such an extent that they no longer have any influence.

The structure of blood lineages and groups has virtually disappeared in the urban environment, and the important control measures which are characteristic of such groups and on which an organized tribal society is based have also disappeared. Not only the consanguinal groups but also other important primary groups such as the tribal initiation schools and age groups, in which strict control has been exercised, are disappearing as a result of this shift to urban areas (Pauw, 1969: 88).

New groupings such as political groups for men, voluntary associations and women's associations, and youth gangs have been formed in the Black urban communities, but these groupings are very individualistic and not cohesive enough to serve as a foundation for a new stable social order.

Other groups within the Black urban community which exert an important influence are derived from the dominant social structure of the Whites. These are the church, the legal, administrative and labour institutions and the school. They have, however, not yet been completely integrated into the Black community life.

In summary, the problem could be stated this way: the disintegration of primary groups in Black society has resulted in the collapse of social control and codes of behaviour, but the new groups which have been formed have not as yet been able to fill this vacuum in the social structure. The result of this state of affairs is that the social structure of the Blacks—especially the urban Blacks—is in a state of flux, which could deeply affect the relevant social positions within that structure, including the position of the Black woman.

The Position of the Black Woman in Traditional Tribal Society

(a) *The general status of the woman*

In traditional tribal society the woman has an ascribed status subordinate to that of the man. Before marriage she is under the control and protection of her male relatives. When she is married these functions pass on to the husband and his kin. The woman thus remains in the position of a minor (Radcliffe–Browne, 1950: 48–49). In spite of this inferior position, the woman is not wholly unprotected.

In the case of ill-treatment by the man, she can appeal to her own family and return to them, in which case the husband may forfeit his *lobola* (marriage goods).

Within traditional society, it is taken as a matter of course that every woman should be married. A woman only attains full adult status and becomes a member of her community when she is married and has children (Van Rensburg, 1973: 28–29; Schapera, 1939 : 106).

The status of the woman is tied in with the status of the family and is characterized by its highly prescribed nature. It is, therefore, important that the various aspects of family life concerning the woman should be understood.

(b) *Marriage and the family*

Premarital relationships: The distinctly normatively prescribed nature of the woman's role is already noticeable in premarital relationships. Although there are differences of opinion among the various tribes, all tribes value virginity highly as it affects the lobola paid for each woman.

In most cases, external sexual intercourse is practised where penetration is not effected. In the Xhosa and Venda tribes the girls are regularly examined to determine whether they are still virgins (Stayt, 1968: 108; Marwick, 1966: 87; Van Rensburg, 1973: 41–49).

Rigid control in this respect is also exercised by a girl's age group as it is a reflection on the whole group if one girl contravenes the rule (Schapera, 1939: 255–259; Van Rensburg, 1973: 49–54). Premarital pregnancy is completely disapproved of, and if an unmarried girl should become pregnant, the parents try to conceal it as much as they are able. If the fact becomes known, the girl is subjected to public ridicule and humiliation and she is kept away from other girls lest she contaminate them. (Marwick, 1966: 92; Van Rensburg, 1973: 42–45).

Choice of a marriage partner: In this matter the woman has little say. The choice usually rests with the parents, although in certain cases the young people are consulted as to their preference. Mutual attraction is not regarded as an essential prerequisite (Van Rensburg, 1973: 101). In the case of the girl, her capacity to work, her disposition and to a lesser extent her looks are considered. She must also be a virgin.

The economic and social positions of the parents of the couple are also taken into consideration (Jonas, 1972: 29).

Transfer of marriage goods (lobola): After a decision has been reached with regard to the marriage partner, negotiations begin for the transfer of marriage goods, generally known as *lobola,* which form an important part of the traditional marriage. This transfer, however, is not a form of barter or purchase of the bride as is often erroneously believed, and the man receives no ownership rights over the woman (Marwick, 1966: 125).

Apart from the fact that *lobola* serves as a form of gratitude to the bride's parents for rearing their daughter, as well as compensation to them for the loss of a source of labour, it is mainly an exchange for the woman's fecundity potential and it stands in connection with the father's right to the children. When the husband has paid the *lobola* the children belong to him and he retains guardianship over them even if the woman leaves him no matter what the circumstances (Marwick, 1966: 125). *Lobola* generally consists of cattle, and the number is decided by negotiation depending on the affluence of the man and the status of the woman. The man and his relatives are responsible for the *lobola,* so that various people in a kinship group have a direct interest in the provision of as well as the division of the *lobola.*

Lobola has a stabilizing influence on the marriage relationship. If the man ill-treats the woman, she can leave him and he forfeits his *lobola.* If the woman is the guilty party, and leaves her husband, her relatives must return all or part of the *lobola.* Both sides thus have an interest in the success of the marriage, and will usually do everything in their power to make it last (Van Rensburg, 1973 : 78).

The wedding: The wedding consists of a series of rites which differ from tribe to tribe. Requirements for a valid marriage include the handing overof the bride, consent of the bridegroom and his relatives and the *implicit consent* of the bride as well as agreement to hand over the *lobola* (Jonas, 1972: 41). In exchange for the *lobola*, the exclusive sexual rights of the woman and her ability to work are transferred to the man's group.

The transfer of marriage goods endows the woman with security and a measure of status. She can demand certain rights and has social status as wife and later as mother.

Internal family relationships: The normatively prescribed and submissive nature of the woman's role is strongly emphasized in her internal family relationships, as in the case of her relationship with her in-laws, her husband and her children. The woman, as a result of patrilocal residence, has closer contact with her in-laws than the man with his. Her behaviour towards her in-laws is, therefore, more strictly prescribed than that of her husband to his. Thus, there are the so-called avoidance rules for the woman with respect to her in-laws, and especially her father-in-law, and she must obey the instructions of her mother-in-law.

Regarding her relationship with her husband, there exists within the traditional Black society a clearly defined role division between husband and wife, and their behaviour towards one another is exactly prescribed. The woman must treat her husband with respect and be subordinate to him. The man is the undisputed head of the house and has authority over his wife and children. This authority, however, is not unlimited, and the woman can seek protection from her own family in case of ill-treatment (Jonas, 1972: 122). Apart from this, the woman's contribution in terms of household goods and services is also important, and her husband is as dependent on her as she is on him. Although the relationship between man and wife may vary according to their personalities, the relationship between them is not very close. Polygamy and the division of the sexes, where the man spends most of his time with other men, lessens the prospect of much intimacy developing between husband and wife. In spite of this subordinate relationship, the woman has great security within the marriage relationship as the husband has to protect her and provide for her materially (Van Rensburg, 1973: 165–170).

Unfaithfulness on the part of the woman is strongly condemned since this is a violation of the man's rights. Unfaithfulness on the part of the man is not considered such a serious matter, unless he neglects his wife and she lays a complaint with her family.

The relationship between the woman and her children is a closer and more affectionate one than between the mother and the father. The closest attachment known to the Blacks is that between mother and child. The mother demands obedience and respect from the children, but her attitude towards them is characterized by pure, unselfish love.

In early childhood, the care of the child is in the hands of the mother, but she is not solely responsible for his/her upbringing. The numerous adults and older children within the household assist her in raising and disciplining him/her (Van Rensburg, 1973: 201–206; Steyn, 1966: 8).

Divorce: Although divorce was not unknown to the Black man, a lasting marriage was preferred. When serious differences arose pressure was applied on the married couple by the kin groups to settle their differences in order to keep the marriage intact. Grounds for divorce were mutual rejection, refusal of conjugal rights, neglect of domestic duties, theft by the woman, misconduct of the woman and desertion or ill-treatment by the man (Jonas, 1972: 124). When the man ill-treated the woman and she returned to her own people, he and his group lost the *lobola*. When the woman was the guilty party, her family lost the *lobola* or part of it. Both groups therefore did their utmost to prevent a divorce, but if it occurred, the woman returned to her own people and again came under the jurisdiction of her father and her brothers. Thus it was clear that, at all times and under all circumstances, the woman belonged to a group and on this account enjoyed a large measure of protection. This principle applied to widowhood as well.

Widowhood: When the man dies his widow remains in his kinship group and as a rule cannot remarry. His family is under an obligation to support her and her children.

In some tribes the levirate applies, in which case one of her husband's relations, usually a brother, begets children by her, who are then regarded as the dead husband's offspring.

This is in accordance with the belief that the man's kinship group is entitled to the woman's procreative faculty by virtue of the *lobola*.

From the discussion thus far it is quite clear that the woman's role is to a great extent normatively prescribed. This prescribed behaviour is learned and internalized during the process of socialization and education which takes place within the framework of the family.

(c) *Education*

In Black tribal society there is a complete lack of a formal system of schooling and education, and the training of young people to play their part in tribal life, takes place mainly within the family. The young girl is taught to help her mother in the home, and in this way she learns to perform household duties. She also learns the necessary technical skills for tilling the land by helping her mother in this respect. Further training is given in the initiation schools, where the code of conduct, customs and way of life of the tribe are conveyed to her.

(d) *Labour and the Black woman*

The most important traditional duties of the Black woman are her household chores and looking after her children. But she also has an important role in the economic sector, which is basically that of a rural subsistence economy.

In this area, there is a strict division of labour between the man and the woman. The woman cultivates the land while the man tends the cattle and hunts. In certain cases, the woman is allowed to practise a more specialized vocation such as witch doctor or potter (Van Rensburg, 1973: 120).

(e) *The legal status of the Black woman:* The legal status of the woman is traditionally that of a minor. Her father or some other male member of her family is regarded as her guardian until she is married. After marriage her husband becomes her guardian (Marwick, 1966: 103-104).

The woman is legally dependent on her husband. She cannot institute legal proceedings in the tribal court unless her husband acts as her representative. She cannot enter into a contract without his consent and must obey all his instructions (Schapera, 1939: 103-104).

Women are not allowed to own property. When cattle are allocated to them, they cannot sell them without the man's consent. This condition applies, as well, to property produced by their own labour, such as hand-made mats (Marwick, 1966: 67). It is, however, wrong to assume that this becomes the property of the husband. It remains a family possession and the man, by virtue of his position as head of the house, has control over it (Simons, 1968: 188).

In cases of assault or slander, the woman's father or husband can demand damages. Damages can also be claimed in cases of seduction and the birth of an illegitimate child. Damages then serve as compensation for the potential loss of *lobola* as a result of the daughter's seduction. The man is not expected to support his illegitimate child. This responsibility rests with the mother's relations (Simons, 1968: 229).

According to Bantu customary law, the man is the guardian of children born out of the marriage. Even in the case of divorce, where the woman is the innocent party, she is seldom granted guardianship over the children.

When the position of the Black woman in traditional society is summarized, the outstanding feature is her ascribed status which makes her perennially subordinate to the man's authority. Her role is also characterized by its normatively prescribed nature.

Her position on the one hand entails very little freedom. On the other hand it is characterized by a very high degree of security and protection. Although she has no authority, and she is continually dependent on others, she is certain that there will always be somebody to care for her and see to her interests.

The Changing Position of the Black Woman

The processes of westernization and urbanization have had and continue to have a far-reaching influence on the position of the Black woman. While it is proposed to describe these changes, it should be kept in mind that not necessarily all Black women have undergone them. Most of the women in rural areas continue to retain traditional patterns, whereas most women in large urban complexes have been influenced by westernizing and urbanizing factors, although even amongst urban women, there are those who adhere to the traditional customs.

(a) *The changing status of the Black woman*

As a result of the decline of the traditional patrilineal family groups, the status of the man has drastically been reduced. He no longer has undisputed authority in family matters, nor is he always the spokesman for his family in religious and legal affairs. In proportion to the decline of the man's authority, the status of the woman has increased. In addition, because the Black woman in the city has the opportunity to participate in a differentiated money economy, she is for the first time in a position to achieve a social and economic status, independent of her relationship to men. Through hard work and her own capabilities, she can independently achieve a high status, so that her traditional status becomes unimportant.

Brandel-Syrier (1971: 83–84) has established that the Black elite, in defining status, regard learning as the most important factor. Elite men prefer their women not only to be educated, but to follow professional careers such as nursing. The woman is able to raise the status of her husband in cases where his training or vocation has failed to give him high status. However, the woman cannot degrade the man's status. Thus women are encouraged by their menfolk to improve their qualifications and earning power.

Although the woman's status is no longer so strongly related to her childbearing potential (Van Rensburg, 1973: 33), it remains important for her to marry and bear children. A childless woman is looked down upon and has to have a strong personality to withstand the consequent contempt. An unmarried woman is still regarded as inferior (Van Rensburg, 1973: 36).

While the woman's improved social and economic status provides more freedom, there are attendant problems. These stem from the transitional situation in which the woman finds herself. She is torn between tradition (without its protection) on the one hand, and new values and norms about which she is still uncertain on the other (Longmore, 1959: 115). Often she is still treated in terms of her traditional role, while she has to contend with a series of new demands which heighten the transitional problems (Hellman, 1967: 27). This situation brings with it attendant insecurity, which renders her position in the urban community vulnerable to a high degree, as will become clear in the following sections.

(b) *Marriage and the Family*

The changing position of the woman has brought problems related to her sexual, marriage and family life. The strict control with regard to sexual conduct which characterized traditional society, has in large measure declined but has not been replaced by other norms. The result is a totally inadequate sexual code.

Premarital Sexual Relations: In contrast to the sexual code in traditional society, the majority of young people regard complete sexual intercourse as normal practice (Pauw, 1969: 111). (Nevertheless, the urban Black man still considers the ideal to be a young girl who has not become pregnant before marriage). A person who practises external sexual intercourse or total abstinence may well be treated with derision or isolation. The majority of city girls commence full sexual intercourse at the age of 15 or 16.

Girls, as well as men, often have an affair with more than one person, although generally there is only one recognized lover. Such behaviour is indicative of a lack of security, as the girl does not want to be left without a man friend, should one desert her for another girl (Pauw, 1969: 116–117). In spite of this state of affairs, prostitution is not the rule among young women. Relationships are entered into from considerations of inclination rather than economic necessity. If prostitution occurs, it is likely to be in a brothel, known as a "shebeen". Beer, brewed illegally, is sold, while waitresses encourage drinking by conferring small sexual favours on their clients (Little, 1973: 95).

One of the most important reasons for the disruption of the traditional code for sexual behaviour is the lack of sexual instruction and social control in this regard. The reason may be sought in the disruption of the initiation schools, where sexual instruction was given, and of the age groups where strict control over sexual conduct was exercised. In addition, parents have not yet taken on themselves the task of sexual instruction and the supervision of the relationships of their children with the opposite sex (Van Rensburg, 1973: 60–61; Jonas, 1972: 113).

The disruption of the sexual code has given rise to a very high percentage of illegitimate births although illegitimate births are still frowned upon. Pauw (1969: 118) established that as many as 60% of the unmarried women in his project had had one illegitimate child, and more than half the women had had two illegitimate children. In spite of the frequent occurrence of premarital pregnancies, most of the girls become very upset on discovering they are pregnant. Some have intense guilt feelings, while others are worried about their parents' anger or the termination of their school careers (Pauw, 1969: 119; Moneo, 1969: 86). Although the parents initially are dismayed, disappointed or very angry, they soon recover. They often try to excuse their daughter's conduct on the pretext that she has been seduced and the steps they take are not of such a nature as to deter other young people from premarital relations. The frequent occurrence of illegitimacy in urban areas renders sanctions by the community extremely difficult. The mother is not condemned and the child is taken into the mother's family of origin, where he/she enjoys the same social status and rights as legitimate children. It is generally accepted that illegitimacy reflects the spirit of the times and nothing can be done about it (Steyn, 1966: 31).

Although a very high percentage of women have illegitimate children, this does not mean that they have lost confidence in marriage. Moeno (1969:83) points out that 50 percent of the women with illegitimate children plan to marry the father of the child while 97 percent of these women plan to marry eventually. It is clear that marriage and family life continue to be considered as important.

The Choice of Marriage Partners: In contrast to the traditional community, choice of the marriage partner in urban areas has gained a strongly individual character, remains mostly in the hands of the individual concerned and is based on romantic love as in Western civilization (Pauw, 1969 : 125). Besides romantic love, various other factors play a role. One of these, and probably the most important one, concerns the personal attributes of the marriage partner. These include physical appearance, clothes and level of civilization (Longmore, 1959 : 23 and 33; Jonas, 1972: 35). According to Longmore (1959: 34), an added factor is the material assets of the man; even a professional woman would be prepared to marry an ordinary labourer if he were well-off. Jonas (1972 : 36) points out that women prefer men with lucrative vocations such as teachers and clerks. Another factor taken into account is the level of education of the marriage partner. Men with a high level of education are inclined to choose women who will provide intellectual companionship (Jonas, 1972 : 35).

The general procedure is that the man asks the girl of his choice for her hand in marriage. If his proposal is accepted, he refers the matter to his parents who commence negotiations with the girl's parents via a suitable representative. The relatives and friends concerned are, however, not capable of opposing the couple's choice (Pauw, 1969 : 126). Thus the woman has obtained a large measure of freedom in the choice of a marriage partner.

Transfer of lobola: In the majority of urban marriages, the tradition of *lobola* paid to the bride's parents has not disappeared. However, the character and function of *lobola* have undergone so complete a change that it has lost its traditional function of stabilizing the marriage. If anything, it exerts a negative influence on the marriage as well as on the position of the woman.

In the city, *lobola* is usually paid in money, and the man alone saves up for it, thus bringing into the marriage a commercial element. In most cases the father of the bride retains the whole sum of money for himself, or it is spent on a trousseau for the bride or on the wedding feast. This presents difficulties for the husband, should he decide to demand the money back in case of his wife's misconduct (Steyn, 1966: 23; Hellman, 1967 : 29; Pauw, 1969 : 129).

Neither the kinship group of the husband nor that of the wife has any financial interest in the *lobola*. The result is that neither group is as concerned about the success of the marriage as was the case in traditional society. As a result *lobola* has lost its function as a guarantee of the stability of the marriage and in consequence the measure of protection which the wife could expect from her relatives has disappeared.

The fact that the bridegroom has to find the *lobola* on his own, without any assistance from his relatives, has resulted in the increase of the age at marriage (Longmore, 1959 : 35; Pauw, 1969 : 109; Jonas, 1973 : 35). Often the woman has to wait for years before the man has amassed sufficient money for the *lobola* (Longmore, 1959 : 35; Steyn, 1966 : 22). This situation renders the woman particularly vulnerable. The fact that the marriage is postponed for such a length of time results in increased premarital sexual intercourse and the couple end up cohabiting (Van Rensburg, 1973 : 84). This situation weakens the position of the woman, as living with the man precludes any legal rights. The relationship is also very unstable and usually does not result in marriage (Mayer, 1963 : 265). When the arrangement breaks up, it is, in most cases, the man who deserts the woman and the woman who has to assume responsibility for the care of the children. Moeno (1969: 101) points out that there is a definite relationship between the *lobola* and the number of illegitimate children. Black women often prefer an illegitimate child to a marriage without *lobola*. A marriage without *lobola* indicates a loss of status for the wife. While illegitimacy is frowned upon, it is endured because the *lobola* still has to be paid. Often a young man exploits this situation by promising a girl that he will marry her, postponing the marriage due to a lack of funds and then deserting the girl after a child has been conceived.

In spite of the vulnerability of the woman in this situation, the majority of women evaluate *lobola* positively, as their status depends on it (Pauw, 1969: 129; Van Rensburg, 1973: 96), and most women prefer *lobola* to be paid.

The Wedding: As has been indicated earlier there is a fairly high incidence of cohabitation, which has no legal basis and which renders the position of the woman highly vulnerable. Apart from cohabitation there are three forms of legally-recognized marriage open to the Blacks viz. the traditional marriage, religious marriage and civil marriage (Longmore, 1959 : 62). This state of affairs also renders the women vulnerable, as civil and religious marriages enjoy precedence over the traditional marriage. In other words, if a Black man is married according to traditional custom and he subsequently enters into a civil marriage, the traditional marriage becomes null and void. However, if a Black man has been married according to civil rites he cannot enter into a traditional marriage, since in this case he would be committing adultery and his children would be illegitimate (Longmore, 1959: 62–63). This ruling by the Bantu Administration Law of 1927 places the woman in a most uncertain and unhappy position as the man can annul his traditional marriage simply by a civil marriage to another woman.

In most cases in the contraction of the marriage, the traditional form *(lobola)* is linked up with the religious or the civil ceremony or both, and consequently the percentage of women in urban areas who are exposed to this insecurity is low. However, the problem arises quite frequently in the rural areas.

Internal Family Relationships: The position of the woman with regard to her internal family relationships, i.e., with her in-laws, her husband and her children has also been changing extensively.

As far as the relationships with in-laws are concerned, the tradition of patrilocal residence has lapsed and with it the prescribed rules of avoidance and taboos. This is especially to the woman's advantage. Although she is still respectful towards her in-laws, she is no longer subordinate to them as was the case in tribal life (Steyn, 1966: 25–26).

The personal relationships of kin and friendship towards the in-laws continues to exist and obligations, although attenuated, are still carried out, but each woman now enjoys a greater measure of freedom and independence (Longmore, 1959: 110).

In spite of these advantages, the woman suffered a loss of protection with the disintegration of the extended family. Where previously she could depend on the aid of a number of relatives in case of a crisis, economic or otherwise, she now has to fend for herself in most cases.

The woman's relationship towards her husband has also undergone a change. In contradiction to the traditional marriage, childbearing is no longer such an important function of the family and the woman's economic services are now of secondary importance (Mokoatle, 1967: 53). In marriages in urban areas, the emotional aspect and personal satisfaction have become of primary importance. A relationship in which comradeship, friendship, mutual respect and understanding occur is considered of great importance (Van Rensburg, 1973: 190). According to Mokoatle (1967: 53) the traditional separation of the sexes has to a great extent disappeared allowing a greater measure of intimacy in the marriage (Van Rensburg, 1973: 17), and the relationship between the couple becomes more free and informal than was possible in tribal life. Although men and women still attend social functions, meetings, etc. separately, they go out visiting together more often and receive guests together, enjoy each other's company and converse together in a way which was unknown in tribal life.

Although the man is considered the breadwinner of the home and his wife is responsible for performing the household duties, the woman has more say with regard to the economic aspects of the family, as she is the one who decides how the income is to be spent (Steyn, 1966: 26). Apart from this, an increasing and significant percentage of married women are economically active outside the home, earning their own income—a fact which gives them a greater measure of economic security and increases their authority within the family. Where the woman is economically independent and earns as much or more then her husband, conflict may develop between the couple because she, in some cases, does not accept his advice any longer and does not hand over her money to him. This will weaken the marriage bonds and the woman may lose interest in keeping the marriage intact (Van Rensburg, 1973: 179—181). She may even develop the feeling that the man plays a marginal role and is dispensable (Pauw, 1969: 158).

Concerning the authority relations within the family the woman in most cases still regards the husband as head of the house (Jonas, 1972: 126; Pauw, 1969: 146; Van Rensburg, 1973: 177) although his authority has diminished compared with what it was in tribal life. The woman no longer accepts his authority unconditionally. He is expected to prove that he is worthy of this position of authority before she will treat him with the necessary respect (Van Rensburg, 1973: 174).

The Black man very often cannot accept that his authority with regard to his wife is diminishing, a fact which can cause great discord between man and wife (Mokoatle, 1967: 53).

In the settlement of differences, the woman can no longer so readily turn to her father and brother. As a result, the tendency is to regard these differences as between the man and wife only, and the woman usually tries to settle the matter herself before calling on her family for aid (Jonas, 1972: 132; Pauw, 1969: 159).

Thus, the woman has come of age in her relationship with her husband, and he has to accept her new position and treat her accordingly even though sometimes against his will. Seen as a whole the woman has exchanged her protected position in traditional society for a new independence in relation to her husband.

So far as the upbringing of children is concerned, the responsibility still rests with the wife as in traditional society. There is, however, one significant change: in the city, where the kinship groups are disintegrating, the wife no longer has the support of a number of relatives in raising the children. The child's own parents, and especially the mother, carry the responsibility in this respect, although in many cases they do not succeed in handling this responsibility successfully (Steyn, 1966: 28).

The woman's part in the upbringing of the child is further increased by the fact that the man is away at work for long periods during the day. To this is added the fact that many men desert their families in which case the total responsibility for tending the children rests with the woman (Longmore, 1959: 170). And the increase in the number of illegitimate births places a further burden on her, as in most cases she has to shoulder the responsibility for caring for the illegitimate child herself (Pauw, 1969: 138).

In his research work Pauw (1969: 145), points out that a great percentage (40.9%) of families have female heads. This, together with the changing authority relationship between the husband and the wife, and the acceptance of the illegitimate children in the family structure of the woman, indicates that the urban Black family is moving in the direction of the matrifocal family type.

If the woman, for economic reasons, has to work away from home and if she has no husband, she will find it difficult to control and discipline the children. In this predicament, the woman has lost a measure of help and security. Although she can find herself a job and attain some degree of fulfillment in this way, she has to do without the assistance and support of the kinship structure and she is continuously worried about the fact that her children may be neglected.

Divorce: Because of the nature of *lobola* in the city, the kinship groups of the husband and wife are not so deeply involved in the success of the marriage and no pressure is exerted on the couple in this respect. Notwithstanding, there are few formal divorces among the urban Blacks. What happens is that the man or woman deserts the family without seeking a divorce. According to Jonas (1972: 65), a woman who is married according to Western civil rites attains majority and she retains this majority even if she is divorced. After the divorce she loses any claim to support by the husband except where he is compelled to do so by court order. Her independence after divorce manifests itself in the fact that she does not return to her parental home or expect maintenance from her relatives as was the custom in traditional society. In her new independence, on the other hand, she has to fend for herself and this often places her in a very insecure position.

Widowhood: As a result of the disintegration of the kinship system, it is unlikely that there will be relatives willing to care for a widow and her children. This is an additional financial burden and urban Blacks try to avoid it.

The levirate system has to a great extent fallen into disuse mainly due to opposition from the church as well as the woman's aversion against being forced to live with a man to whom she is not attracted (Longmore, 1959: 288). Again while the woman has gained independence on the one hand, she has lost protection and security on the other.

The fact that the urban Black woman has lost her security and protection and is now highly vulnerable has motivated her to find ways of improving her situation. These ways are through education, through the demands of an occupation and through participation in voluntary associations.

(c) *Education*

Contrary to traditional society, where socialization and the upbringing of the children mainly take place within the family and the initiation school, formal schooling is becoming increasingly important in the raising of the child in changing Black society.

Attitude to education: According to Pauw (1969: 37), it is universally accepted that attending school is part of the life of the urban child. Originally the aim was merely to become literate, but later it became important to be educated so that

Table 1

Number of Black Schoolchildren according to sex and school standard: Republic of South Africa, 1968–1975

	Sub St A	Sub St B	Standard 1	Standard 2	Standard 3	Standard 4	Standard 5	Standard 6	Form I	Form II	Form III	Form IV	Form V	Total
Boys														
1968	265,035	190,629	162,447	115,487	88,290	63,052	48,766	41,918	15,156	11,786	8,121	2,519	1,480	1,014,686
1969	272,605	202,939	171,078	125,154	96,737	68,705	53,381	47,355	16,344	13,291	9,421	2,703	1,677	1,081,390
1970	283,669	215,767	187,098	135,561	108,216	77,340	60,284	53,667	19,495	14,291	10,545	3,378	1,752	1,171,063
1971	353,656	264,003	231,450	170,021	137,378	97,595	75,240	66,944	24,428	19,281	13,891	5,048	2,691	1,461,626
1972	360,818	277,746	243,219	178,529	146,812	105,232	82,705	72,978	29,120	21,580	15,106	6,277	3,160	1,653,282
1973	381,200	286,818	256,940	190,454	156,728	114,630	90,514	82,292	32,531	25,815	17,334	7,135	3,633	1,646,024
1974	396,752	299,529	266,470	200,984	167,914	122,971	98,354	90,502	38,103	28,987	20,387	8,752	4,272	1,743,977
1975	421,024	309,342	276,058	208,293	178,542	131,912	102,466	68,088	66,068	40,384	23,063	11,005	5,616	1,842,661
Girls														
1968	242,644	180,512	155,985	116,658	90,727	67,645	53,530	48,231	19,449	13,390	7,775	1,006	557	998,109
1969	249,058	191,420	164,813	126,461	98,632	73,373	58,238	54,620	18,764	15,337	9,477	1,118	614	1,061,925
1970	259,698	202,032	179,337	137,727	110,316	81,177	65,003	62,395	22,322	16,237	11,178	1,659	689	1,091,267
1971	322,661	247,221	220,234	172,615	145,664	107,519	85,076	81,430	29,177	23,228	15,909	2,785	1,374	1,454,893
1972	327,172	259,072	232,629	180,810	154,420	117,681	93,404	88,494	34,613	25,676	16,968	3,632	1,654	1,536,225
1973	347,572	264,277	246,456	192,572	163,878	127,870	104,071	99,163	38,180	30,283	19,841	4,209	2,103	1,640,475
1974	364,083	277,744	253,077	203,727	175,387	136,973	112,350	109,925	44,248	34,455	22,201	5,654	2,460	1,742,284
1975	387,227	288,993	263,968	210,919	187,392	148,552	118,553	77,574	83,183	50,881	26,909	7,266	3,393	1,854,780

Source: The educational data presented in Tables 1 through 4 were taken from the Annual Reports 1968–1975 by the Department of Bantu Education.

the child could enhance the status of the family as well as improve his own position, eventually. At first education for girls was frowned upon. The general attitude was that the girl would end up getting married and the effort would be wasted. Then it was realized that a girl's educational qualifications would increase her *lobola* since she could earn more if she were better qualified (Brandel-Syrier, 1971: 119-120; Van Rensburg, 1973: 89).

In order to ascertain to what extent women are educated in comparison with men, it is necessary to determine to what extent their numbers at schools and institutions of higher education differ.

School enrolment: For the purpose of this analysis, figures for the number of children at school from 1968 to 1975 were used. Earlier data broken down according to sex were not available.

According to Table 1 it is clear that the number of girls at school during the period 1968 to 1975 has gradually but definitely increased in every school standard. In order to determine to what extent the number of girls at school compares with the number of boys and whether there has been an improvement in this respect the ratio of boys to girls has been calculated for each of the school standards in 1968 and 1975.

Table 2

Ratios of boys per girl in each school standard, 1968 and 1975

Standard	1968	1975
Sub St. A	1.09	1.09
Sub St. B	1.06	1.07
Stand. 1	1.04	1.05
Stand. 2	0.99	0.99
Stand. 3	0.97	0.95
Stand. 4.	0.93	0.89
Stand. 5	0.91	0.86
Stand. 6	0.87	0.88
Form I	0.78	0.79
Form II	0.88	0.79
Form III	1.04	0.89
Form IV	2.50	1.51
Form V	2.66	1.66

Source: Same as Table 1.

As can be seen from the ratios in Table 2 there were slightly more boys than girls in Substandard A, and a boy: girl ratio of 1.09:1 was obtained during both years. The ratio however decreases for subsequent school standards and as from standard 2, the girls start outnumbering the boys giving a ratio of 0.99:1, for both years, sinking even further to 0.78:1 in 1968 and 0.79:1 in 1975 for Form I. From Form IV the boys again start to outnumber the girls, so that eventually there are far more boys than girls in the higher standards, giving a ratio of 2.66:1 in Form V for 1968 and

1.66:1 in Form V for 1975. Although the boy:girl ratio is quite high in Form V for both years, it shows an improvement from 1968 to 1975, making the number of boys and girls qualifying in the higher school standards more equal. This improvement is clearly illustrated by Graph 1.

Graph 1. Number of boys per girl for 1968 and 1975

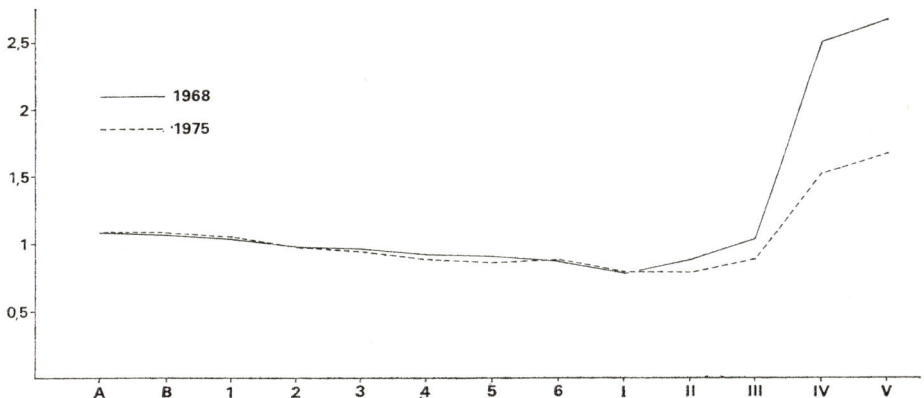

Apart from the fact that fewer girls than boys reach the highest school standards, one is struck by the fact, when studying Table 1, that the number of pupils in each consecutive school standard, decreases considerably (especially in Form I and Form IV), leaving comparatively few boys and even fewer girls in the higher standards. If the number of children in Form V of a specific year is calculated as a percentage of the number of children who entered school thirteen years earlier, one can get an idea of the high dropout rate for that specific class over the years. Because of a lack of data these percentages could not be calculated for the boys and girls separately. But it was possible to calculate it for the total number of school children. Thus the number of children who reached Form V in 1968 was only 0.4% of the number of Sub A children in 1956. In 1975 this percentage improved to 0.8% but in spite of this improvement the percentage of children reaching the highest school standard remained extremely low (Steyn, 1976: 26). It must also be taken into account that only a third of this percentage are girls, which shows that proportionally only a very small number of girls obtain the highest school qualifications, which would enable them to obtain better-paid jobs.

This tendency for a smaller percentage of girls than boys to carry on with higher education is also reflected in the university statistics.

From Table 3 it can be clearly seen that although there is an improvement from 1968 to 1975 with regard to the proportion of female students, the women are still proportionally fewer than the men, and in 1975 were only 30.9 percent of the total number of Black university students.

Table 3

Enrolment at Black Universities according to sex, 1968–1975

Year	Male	%	Female	%	Total	%
1968	1,099	76.85	331	23.15	1,430	100
1969	1,243	78.37	343	21.63	1,586	100
1970	1,577	77.99	445	22.01	2,022	100
1971	1,841	77.39	538	22.61	2,379	100
1972	2,190	74.87	735	25.13	2,925	100
1973	2,381	72.02	925	27.98	3,306	100
1974	2,444	68.03	1,101	31.06	3,545	100
1975	2,853	69.03	1,280	30.97	4,133	100

Source: Same as Table 1.

Although a far lower percentage of women compared with men continue with their studies at university level, this is not the case at the teacher's training colleges. (The position at the teacher's training colleges is just the reverse of that at the universities.)

Table 4

Enrolment at Teachers' Training Colleges according to sex, 1968–1975

Year	Males	%	Females	%	Total	%
1968	1,896	38.03	3,090	61.97	4,986	100
1969	2,361	40.96	3,403	59.04	5,764	100
1970	2,543	41.70	3,556	58.30	6,099	100
1971	2,887	35.49	5,247	64.51	8,134	100
1972	3,447	36.21	6,073	63.79	9,520	100
1973	4,252	38.23	6,869	61.77	11,121	100
1974	4,924	38.54	7,853	61.46	12,777	100
1975	5,806	37.35	9,740	62.65	15,546	100

Source: Same as Table 1.

As can be seen from Table 4 the girls, in 1975, comprised 62.7% of the total number of college students—a percentage that has remained fairly stable since 1968. It can thus be expected that since these colleges mainly provide for a Primary Teacher's Certificate, there will be more women than men employed as teachers at the primary school level.

When the data on education are considered as a whole, changes in the economic activities of women can be expected.

(d) *Labour and the Black woman*

When the data concerning the occupational participation of the woman are studied, it becomes clear that although she is to a very great extent still employed in the agricultural sector, which is traditionally ascribed to her, she is nevertheless moving away from this role and entering the structurally differentiated labour market.

Her participation in this broader labour market is considerably less than that of men, but there has been a gradual improvement in this respect, so that with the last census in 1970 women comprised 33.7% of the total Black labour force, compared with only 19.1% in 1946 (Table 5).

Table 5

Black labour market according to sex, 1946-1970

Year	Males	%	Females	%	Total	%
1946	2,350,729	80.9	554,334	19.1	2,905,063	100
1951	2,542,647	81.8	567,367	18.2	3,110,014	100
1960	3,070,338	78.9	819,408	21.1	3,889,746	100
1970	3,716,540	66.3	1,888,600	33.7	5,605,140	100

Source: Data presented in Tables 5 and 6 were taken from: Bevolkingsensus 1936; Bevolkingsensus 1946; Bevolkingsensus 1960; Bevolkingsensus 1970; Buro vir Statistiek 1960; Buro vir Statistiek 1965; Buro vir Statistiek 1974.

When the occupations of women are analyzed it can be seen that she is also, to an increasing extent, entering occupational groups with higher status (Table 6).

As can be seen from Table 6 the majority of women are still employed in the lowest income occupational categories, i.e., domestic service (37.95%) and agriculture and forestry (34.65%). But even so there was a surprising increase in the number of women in the professions—from 2,312 in 1921 to 56,000 in 1970, a percentage increase from 1.25% in 1921 to 2.97% in 1970 of the total labour force of Black women. When an analysis is made of the specific occupation of most of the professional women, it is clear that by far the greatest percentage of them are nurses (28.9% in 1970), and teachers (47.2% in 1970).

The reason for the Black woman's participation in the labour force is basically to obtain social and economic security (Van Rensburg, 1973: 125-138). Although the majority of women insist that their occupation is not meant as a substitute for marriage, they realize that an occupation provides more security than marriage, especially as marriage has become very unstable in modern Black society.

The greatest satisfaction the woman obtains from her work, seen against the background of marriage instability, is her economic independence from her husband. Apart from this economic security, her occupation also provides social security, especially if she is in a profession, as this gives her a higher social status.

Table 6

Occupational Groups of economically active Black women: Republic of South Africa, 1921–1970

Occupational Group	1921	%	1936	%	1946	%	1951	%	1960	%	1970	%**
Total Professional	2,312	1.25	4,253	1.64	10,082	1.81	13,138	2.32	25,349	3.09	56,100	(2.97)
Nursing and midwifery	—	—	612	14.4	3,050	(30.3)	—	—	12,789	(50.5)	16,186	(28.9)
Doctors and dentists	—	—	38*	(0.9)	59*	(0.6)	—	—	26	(0.1)	30	(0.1)
Medical auxiliary services	—	—	0	(0.0)	0	(0.0)	—	—	16	(0.1)	20	(0.03)
Teachers	—	—	3,442	(80.9)	6,465	(64.1)	—	—	11,587	(45.7)	26,491	(47.2)
Total Administrative	...	...	16	0.01	184	0.03	262	0.05	281	0.03	100	0.01
Total Clerical and related worker	44	0.02	162	0.06	255	0.05	294	0.05	926	0.11	7,380	0.39
Total Sales worker	425	0.23	210	0.08	475	0.09	803	0.14	3,282	0.40	18,080	0.96
Total Service worker	163,009	88.26	243,859	93.80	410,353	74.03	442,552	78.00	506,340	61.79	716,700	37.95
Domestic servants	—	—	241,230	—	437,358	—	—	—	474,400	—	641,180	—
Total Agriculture & Forestry	...	...	...	...	85,631	15.45	93,333	16.45	150,349	18.35	654,320	34.65
Total Production and Transport worker	16,345	8.85	3,372	3.10	8,897	1.60	11,384	2.01	22,606	2.76	80,120	4.24
Total not classifiable	2,553	1.38	8,098	3.11	38,457	6.94	5,601	0.99	110,275	13.46	355,800	18.84
Total	184,688	100	259,970	100	554,334	100	567,367	100	819,408	100	1,888,600	100

— No data published
... Data could not be determined
* Native doctors
** The percentages are only calculated for the total in the occupational group on the basis of the grand total. The percentages in brackets were calculated for the subgroups under "professional" on the total number of professional women.

Source: Same as Table 5.

Participating in an occupation, especially in the urban areas, has thus provided the Black woman with a means for improving her uncertain position. A further means to this same end is her participation in voluntary associations.

(e) *Voluntary associations*

The voluntary associations—especially those in the cities—constitute an important instrument whereby the Black woman attempts to re-establish the security and protection that she has lost by the changes in her position. The development of these voluntary associations must be seen against the background of the weakening and disruption of the tribal customs and the traditional grouping of the Black people, without new structures developing to take their place. The Black man (and woman) are, as it were, in a social vacuum where all their needs, of which economic security is an important one, are not provided for. The voluntary associations develop more or less spontaneously to provide for these needs.

A great variety of these voluntary associations have already developed among Black women. Three types described by Brandel–Syrier (1962 : 18) have developed under the supervision of White women. Although Black women are playing an increasingly important role in these, they do not concern us as much here as those which have developed spontaneously and have been initiated solely by Black women.

An example of this latter type of association is the so-called *Stokfel* or *Manodisana* which is solely in the hands of Black women, and the purpose of which is chiefly to render mutual aid. It consists of a certain group of women who make a regular financial contribution at regular fixed times, which is then distributed to each member in rotation. In this way, every woman, at regular intervals, has a fixed sum of money at her disposal, large enough for the purchase of an expensive item or for use in any expensive undertaking. Usually records are kept, but basically this arrangement depends on the honesty of the members, since no legal procedures are possible.

A variation of *Stokfel* is seen in the burial societies, known in East London as *masazane*. These organizations render financial and other aid in case of death or during any other crisis. When a death occurs in the family or when one of the members dies, the other members are informed. They visit the ones in mourning and give a contribution to cover the cost of the funeral and provide for the needs of the family.

Another voluntary association which plays a substantial part in the adaptation of Black women to urban circumstances is the *manyano*, a type of church organization for Black women. Almost every religious denomination with Black members has a *manyano*, mainly run by the older Black women. The organization has a definite hierarchical character with strict rules for admission and a moral code which must be obeyed (Brandel-Syrier, 1962). The *manyano* basically has three facets, viz.the purely religious, the financial and the legal. The religious activities may be attended by outsiders. In regard to financial achievements, which consist mainly of fundraising and small gifts to families in need, members are too proud to keep them secret. But their legal function is strictly kept secret so that the activities are not known.

Although the voluntary associations satisfy mainly the need for economic security, they also provide for a variety of other needs. For example they provide to a great extent for the need for sociability, especially where the woman may be faced with social isolation as a result of the disruption of the broader kinship groupings (Preston–Whyte, 1968: 16; Longmore, 1959: 111–112). Since all these voluntary associations have relatively strict rules of conduct for their members, and see to it that they are obeyed, they also provide some of the social control which has disappeared with the disintegration of the traditional groupings (Longmore, 1959: 111–112; Steyn, 1968: 2).

(f) *The Legal Position of the Black Woman*

The Roman-Dutch Common Law is the basic legal system in the Republic of South Africa but parallel to it is the Bantu Customary Law, which comes into force in certain statutory cases, such as the laws concerning marriage and succession, and in cases where the person's activities cause him to fall under Bantu Customary Law. The result is that the legal position of the Black woman is confused and uncertain. The application of common law is decidedly to the advantage of the Black woman, since the Bantu customary law treats the woman as if she were still part of the traditional society.

According to the laws dealing with the legal position of the woman under common law, all unmarried women over 21, widows and divorced women, possess full legal capability and the married woman is regarded as a major, (since she is married) except in relation to the marital rights of the husband. When she is married according to Bantu cutomary law, she is regarded as a major only if she and her husband do not live together (Simons, 1968: 190). Concerning property, unmarried women over 21, widows and divorced women, have full property rights with the exception of Natal, where the Bantu Legal Code continues to regard the Black woman as a permanent minor (Simons, 1968: 192). In the case of personal damage, such as assault or libel, the woman has the right to claim compensation. Compensation can also be paid on the grounds of seduction, if the woman had been a virgin. Where seduction results in pregnancy (even if she was not a virgin), the woman can claim compensation for the cost of the confinement and the support of the child (Simons, 1968: 230).

Common law also improves the position of the woman with regard to authority over children. Both legal systems define the father as the natural guardian of his legitimate minor children. He has the sole right to administer and control their property. However, a woman who is married according to civil law shares the authority over the child's person with the husband. Thus both parents are obliged to give their permission before a minor child may enter matrimony (Simons, 1968: 218).

However, the two legal systems differ substantially where children are affected by divorce, and the bias in favour of the father in the case of Bantu customary law is deleted in common law. A widow who is married according to civil rights is the guardian of her minor children. In the case of a divorce, the father forfeits his authority over the child as soon as he and the mother no longer live together. In this case, preference is accorded the woman, as it is accepted that, under normal circumstances, she is the best person to care for young children (Simons, 1968: 215–216). It is clear that where common law is applicable, the woman is in a much more favourable position than where she is under the jurisdiction of Bantu customary law. Except in Natal, where the Bantu Legal Code, based on Bantu customary law, is still in force, common law accords the woman the opportunity of escaping from the position of permanent minority in which Bantu customary law places her (Simons, 1968: 192).

Although the woman, under common law, has attained freedom and independence as well as acknowledgment as an independent major adult, she has also forfeited the protection which she had enjoyed under Bantu customary law. She now has to fend for herself where formerly, in the traditional society, her affairs were managed by her relatives. Often her ignorance results in her being the loser, so that the improvement of her position under common law is sometimes to her disadvantage. This situation would be eliminated if the common law ruling as regards legal competence for all women were applied unconditionally. This would also assist in decreasing the large measure of confusion which exists at the present time.

Conclusion

In reviewing the situation of the urban Black woman, it is clear that she has gained considerably greater status and independence than her traditional sister. However, she has completely forfeited the security and protection which the traditional woman enjoys as a result of traditional usage and custom. The urban Black woman is free, but at the same time largely unprotected, economically as well as socially. She is no longer a member of a group that regulated her life through group interests and group traditions, but stands alone as an individual, inexperienced in a highly organized, competitive world (Longmore, 1959: 115). She enjoys greater independence in that she may possess property and may plead her own case in a court of law, but less protection in that she is no longer free to call upon the male members of her own family for redress in the case of abuse (Steyn, 1966: 26). Owing to its instability, even marriage does not accord its former care and, more often than not, in addition to her domestic duties, she is obliged to undertake the economic provision for her family.

Particularly with regard to marriage, the woman finds herself in conflict between old and new norms and Van Rensburg (1973: 184) presents the case succinctly when he describes the Black wife as being part of two worlds, viz. the old one of docile subordination, obedience, fear of and respect for her husband on the one hand, and on the other, her inner resistance to the obstacles which impede her freedom of movement and action, as well as resistance to male domination, irresponsibility, neglect and often, violence. One may properly question the premise that she has gained more than she has lost.

Fortunately the Black woman is beginning to succeed to a considerable degree in bringing about her own security, in part through participation in voluntary associations, but especially through higher education which ensures her entry into the professional world and a chance to earn her own economic as well as social security.

REFERENCES

Anonymous
    1961 "Education for the Bantu of South Africa."
        Lantern (September: 65–96.)
Ashton, M.
    1967 *The Basuto.* London: Oxford University Press.
Bevolkingsensus. (R.S.A.)
    1936 *Deel IX: Naturelle (Bantoes) en ander Nie-Blanke Rasse.* U.G. 12/42. Pretoria: Staatsdrukker.
    1946 *Deel V: Beroepe en Bedrywe.* U. G. 41–54. Pretoria: Staatsdrukker.
    1960 *Deel VI: Nywerheid.* Pretoria: Staatsdrukker.
    1970 *Sample Tabulation: Bantu-Age, Occupation, Industry, School Standard, Birthplace.* Report no. 02–02–02. Pretoria: Staatsdrukker.
Brandel, M.
    1958 "Urban lobola attitudes." *African Studies 17:* 34–50.
Brandel-Syrier, M.
    1962 *Black Women in search of God.* London: Butterworth Press.
    1971 *Reeftown Elite.* London: Routledge en Kegan.
Buro vir Statistiek
    1960 *Unie Statistieke oor 50 jaar: Jubileum Uitgawe 1910–1960.* Pretoria: Staatsdrukker.
    1965 *Statistiese Jaarboek.* Pretoria: Staatsdrukker.
    1974 *Suid-Afrikaanse Statistieke.* Pretoria: Staatsdrukker.
Department of Bantu Education
    1970 *Annual Report for the Calendar Year, 1968* R. P. 32/1970. Pretoria: Staatsdrukker.
    1971 *Annual Report for the Calendar Year 1969.* R. P. 18/1971. Pretoria: Staatsdrukker.
    1971 *Annual Report for the Calendar Year 1970.* R. P. 94/1971. Pretoria: Staatsdrukker.
    1973 *Annual Report 1971.* R. P. 31/1973 Pretoria: Staatsdrukker.
    1973 *Annual Report 1972.* R. P. 93/1973 Pretoria: Staatsdrukker.
    1974 *Annual Report 1973.* R. P. 75/1974 Pretoria: Staatsdrukker.
    1975 *Annual Report 1974.* R. P. 45/1975 Pretoria: Staatsdrukker.
    1976 *Annual Report 1975* R. P. 36/1976 Pretoria: Staatsdrukker.
Durand, J. J. F.
    1970 *Swartman, stad en toekoms.* Kaapstad: Tafelberguitgewers.
Gutkind, P. G. W.
    1963 *African urban family life.* Den Haag: Mouton and Co.
Hellman, E.
    1956 "The development of social groupings among urban Africans in the Union of South Africa" pp. 724–743 in *Social implications of industrialization in Africa South of the Sahara.* Unesco.

1967 "The African family today" pp. 16–34 in *African Family Life*. Johannesburg: South African Institute of Race Relations.
Hellman, M.
    1967 "Legal aspects of marriage in the townships" pp. 35–48 in *African Family Life*. Johannesburg: South African Institute of Race Relations.
Holleman, J. F.
    1960 "Die Bantoe huwelik op die kruispad" in *Tydskrif vir Rasse-aangeleenthede*, Vol. II: 82–117.
Jonas, P. J.
    1972 *Die veranderende posisie van die vrou in die huwelik en gesin by die stedelike Xhosa van Oos-Londen, met besondere verwysing na die dorp Mdantsane*. M. A.-verhandeling, Pretoria: Universiteit van Suid-Afrika.
Kuper, H.
    1950 "Kinship among the Swazi" pp. 86–110 in A. R. Radcliffe-Brown (red.) *African Systems of Kinship and Marriage*. London: Oxford University Press.
Lewin, J. et al.
    1959 "The Legal Status of African Women." *Race Relations Journal 26* (no. 4): 152–159.
Little, K.
    1973 *African Women in Towns*. London: Cambridge University Press.
Longmore, L.
    1959 *The dispossessed*. London: Jonathan Cape.
Mabiletsa, D.
    1967 "The Working Mother" pp. 83–88 in *African Family Life*. Johannesburg: South African Institute of Race Relations.
Marwick, B. A.
    1966 *The Swazi*. London: Cass & company.
Mayer, P.
    1963 *Townsmen or tribesmen*. Kaapstad: Oxford University Press.
Moeno, S. N.
    1969 *The Urban African family disorganization with special reference to the problem of illegitimacy*. M. A.-verhandeling. Pretoria: Universiteit van Suid-Afrika.
Mokoatle, B. N.
    1967 "Personal relationships in married life" pp. 49–56 in *African family life*. Johannesburg: South African Institute of Race Relations.
Pauw, B. A.
    1969 *The second generation*. Kaapstad: Oxford University Press.
Phatudi, C. N.
    1967 "Education and family life" pp. 75–82 in *African family life*. Johannesburg: South African Institute of Race Relations.
Philips, J.
    1967 "Bringing up children in the home" pp. 89–95 in *African family life*. Johannesburg: South African Institute of Race Relations.
Preston-Whyte, E.
    1968 *"The adaptation of domestic servants to town life."* Paper read at "Focus on cities conference" (July) Durban.
Radcliffe-Brown, A. R.
    1950 *African systems of kinship and marriage*. London: Oxford University Press.
Schapera, I.
    1950 "Kinship and marriage among the Tswana" pp. 140–165 in A. R. Radcliffe-Brown (ed.) *African Systems of Kinship and Marriage*. London: Oxford University Press.
    1939 *Married life in an African tribe*. London: Faber.
Simons, H. J.
    1968 *African Women: Their legal status in South* Africa. London: C. Hurst.

Stayt, H. A.
   1968   *The Bavenda*. London: Cass

Steyn, Anna F.
   1966   *Die Bantoe in die stad: Die Bantoegesin*. Pretoria: SABRA.
   1968   *Die Bantoe in die stedelike lewe*. Inleidende bespreking by "Focus on cities conference" (Julie) Durban.
   1970   *Changing role of Bantu Women*. Unpublished paper.
   1976   "Die Probleme van onderwys in ontwikkeling." *Die Suid-Afrikaanse Tydskrif vir Sosiologie 13:* 7–32.

Tau, J.
   1967   "Child-rearing and parent-child relationships" pp. 63–74 in *African family life*. Johannesburg: South African Institute of Race Relations.

Van Rensburg, H. G. M. J.
   1973   *Bantoevroue se houding met betrekking tot die huwelik en gesin*. M. A.-verhandeling. Potchefstroom: Potchefstroomse Universiteit.

Vilikazi, A.
   1959   "Urban lobola attitudes." *African Studies 18:* 80–84.

PART FIVE

EMPIRICAL STUDIES OF SEX ROLE BEHAVIOUR

Economic Recession and Swiss Women's Attitudes towards Marital Role Segregation

THOMAS HELD and RENÉ LEVY
University of Zurich, Zurich, Switzerland

IN THE LITERATURE dealing with the change of sex roles or of sex role attitudes one often finds the implicit or explicit assumption of a more or less monotonous process of modernization, in the sense of decreasing sex-typing or sex-based ascription of roles, identities and related attitudes. In addition, attitudes concerning sex roles are sometimes seen to have the function of pacemakers in the process of role modernization, which is tantamount to postulating a causal link between norms and the reality of family relations. In this analysis we intend to examine the question of whether such norms are irreversible or whether they depend on the factual individual or collective situation. More precisely, we will explore the thesis that the recent halt in economic expansion has a measurable influence on the acceptance rate of norms of sex-typed role segregation. We have at hand data about such norms from two surveys that have been conducted in 1970/71 and 1976, respectively, however, with quite different purposes. A secondary analysis of the information they convey constitutes the data base of this paper.

The impact of the economic recession on the situation of women

The 1974–75 recession has had a severe impact on the economies of most of the highly developed Western countries. Unemployment, reduced working hours, lower wage increases, decreases in real incomes, and the respective manpower and income maintenance policies of governments have affected the situation of women (and families) in different ways.

First of all, the increase in unemployment has narrowed the range of options for women in the labor market. This is especially true for contexts and/or sectors where unemployment has become a long-term, structural problem rather than a short-run phenomenon. According to the OECD-report on recession and the employment of women, the women were insulated from the harshest effects of the recession because of their disproportionate concentration in the service sector. However, those women who did hold industrial jobs experienced greater employment losses than men. To the extent that jobs in these industries represent the areas of employment which women have entered only recently, the recession has restricted their opportunities. The recognition of this fact is likely to have discouraged many women from entering the industrial sector (OECD, 1976: 30–13).

Second, the situation of women may have been affected by the changing labor market conditions faced by their husbands. Given the relatively low labor force participation of married women in most West European countries (with the exception of Scandinavia), these indirect effects may influence the situation of more women than the direct effects (e.g., loss of own job). Resource theory can help to highlight these influences. According to this theory, unemployment or a reduced income of the husband entails an increase in the intra-familial status of the wife (Komarovsky, 1940). Furthermore, the scarcity in income (real or anticipated) may lead to a shift in the exchange relation of goods specific to the roles traditionally ascribed to husband and wife since household management, and the "nurturing" of children and the husband become more important. (This is also in agreement with several studies [e.g., Jahoda et al., 1971] showing that in times of crises family and kinship become the most relevant frames of reference and people tend to insulate these sectors, both on an interactional as well as on a symbolic level, from societal sectors such as the economy or politics.)

A further impact of the recession on the situation of women may stem from the effects the new economic situation has on the tax and social policy of the state. Deficits in the state budgets tend to rise due to reduced tax earnings, on the one hand, and increasing expenditures on investment programs and unemployment insurance, on the other. In Switzerland, these deficits have led to an austerity policy designed to freeze the expenditures for social welfare and to increase consumer rather than income taxes. One might hypothesize that these measures affect women more than men since women are heavily underrepresented in the decision-making bodies where the social allocation of cost and gains of a changed redistribution policy is negotiated.

Finally, on the societal level, the economic recession means that the beginning process of saturation of income as the central institutionalized value of the system is being discontinued. It has been argued that this saturation of income in the most developed countries has caused the rise and incorporation into institutionalized culture of new values such as 'quality of life' and 'self-fulfillment'. These values have been a central issue of the youth rebellion and subcultures of the 60's. A reversal of this process of saturation, then, implies that income and the other "old" values associated with industrial and/or bourgeois society become relevant again (Heintz & Heintz, 1973).

As far as the situation of women is concerned, this implies that, on a societal level, values that have been traditionally associated with men become more dominant again whereas 'feminine' traits are being returned to the family (intra-familial).

Thus, a certain advantage that the rise of 'post bourgeois' values has brought to women in extra-familial activities is again being eliminated.

Sex role attitudes and the new situation of women

Most theories of the changing roles of women assume that the massive integration of women into the labor force, especially after World War II, created new attitudes that imply a decreased acceptance of sex role segregation and a change in the relative importance of various frames of reference such as the home vs. work or politics (Ogburn and Nimkoff, 1955). Consequently, the limitation of job options for women and their partial exclusion from certain sectors of the labor market should have the opposite effect, i.e., a renewed increase of traditionalism in sex role attitudes, especially with regard to the husband-provider vs. wife-homemaker specialization. This hypothesis implies a mechanism of protection: those status and role elements are emphasized that allow for an advantageous evaluation of the actor.

Traditional sex role stereotypes will be stabilized or reinforced not only by the limited opportunities in the economy (or the extrafamilial world in general) but also by the increased chances to get gratifications through the wife's intra-familial roles and to come to a better balance of exchange with the husband, whose external status is threatened or actually reduced. The secular trend towards a change in the functions of the family is likely to be reduced by the recession (Ogburn and Nimkoff, 1955; Vincent, 1966).

We are, accordingly, confronted with two factors both of which influence the sex role attitudes of married women. By way of a defensive reaction, the reduction of options in the extra-familial world leads to lower aspirations for education and jobs and, consequently, to a re-evaluation of the traditional roles of the wife. By way of a socially creative reaction, the increased possibilities to elaborate this role (the role as wife) and to get gratification from a relatively high intra-familial status, traditional sex role attitudes represent an attitudinal adaptation to increased structural changes within the family.

These mechanisms are not quite consistent with modernization theory that assumes a more or less autonomous process of modernizing attitudes through an ever on-going process of increased societal differentiation (Inkeles, 1969). In this study we will examine the question of which one of the two theoretical images comes closer to reality. Before turning to our data, it is necessary to look briefly at some pecularities of the context of our study.

Peculiarities of the Swiss Case

Our general hypothesis, then, states that economic recession—following a period of generalized and increasing material well-being and broadening of occupational opportunities for women—leads to a backlash in women's consciousness, entailing a reinforcement of traditional sex-stereotypes, especially as regards the gender-based breadwinner vs. homemaker division of labor.

Application of this hypothesis to recent development in Switzerland needs comment, mainly concerning the postulated effect of recession itself. At first sight, one may wonder what justification there is for speaking of a recession in Switzerland, since this country is among those with the best economic indicators during the recent world-wide crisis. Not only has inflation decreased to a level close to zero (yearly index increase of 1.1 percent by June 1976), but the socially more important rate, the rate of unemployment, has not even reached a high of 1 percent (0.8% for 1976) for Swiss residents.[1]

Not only has unemployment hardly become a visible and widely threatening phenomenon in Switzerland (despite some spectacular but singular cases of factory shutdowns and forced shorttime work), its effects on women are likely to be rather limited, especially its effects on married women. Even before the recession, the rate of employment of married (Swiss) women was low (29.2% (1970), working age), which means that only a small proportion of women are faced with threatened or real unemployment. Moreover, female employment is more concentrated in those economic sectors that are not among those most significantly affected (with some exceptions, for example, the watch industry.)

Although this argument weakens the case for the impact which recession had on women's sex role attitudes in Switzerland, there is an important counterargument that tends to neutralize the first one. Recession and an increase in unemployment came after a prolonged period of extreme shortage of labor, during which the Swiss economy tended to recruit foreign laborers rather than to change its productive structure; hence the labor market was a seller's market. The majority of wage earners were not insured against unemployment and the rate of union membership was low and

---

1 This does not, of course, mean that the Swiss economy has not been touched by the recession. The rate of Swiss unemployment is artificially low, due to the fact that of the some 340,000 jobs that have been lost between 1973 and 1976, about 230,000 were occupied by foreign workers who left Switzerland, partly forced to do so by unemployment, partly on their own as a result of the meager prospects if they stayed on the job (figures estimated by the Federal Labor Administration). Although no exact figures exist, estimates have been advanced claiming that the rate of unemployment in Switzerland would match well with the percentages of other European countries (5–7%), were it not for the exportation of Swiss unemployment to the foreign workers' countries of origin (mainly Italy, Spain, Portugal and Yugoslavia), premature retirements, and the elimination of figures for women married to employed men. (Most of these women do not claim unemployment insurance and therefore do not enter the official unemployment statistics.)

decreasing. In this sociopolitical climate, the emergence of unemployment, even though numbers were small, had a high impact at the symbolic level, an impact that has been indirectly observed by such side effects as a sudden increase in unemployment insurance membership, increases in union membership and "left" votes, and reported increases in job conformity as indicated by decreasing absenteeism and lessening incidence of minor illnesses. On the whole, then, it seems possible to postulate that although the objective indicators of economic recession in Switzerland are rather modest by international comparison, the subjective impact was nevertheless notable (as highlighted, among others, by the high percentage increases of the rate of unemployment shown in the media: an increase from 0.4 (1975) to 0.8 (1976) yields, in fact, a difference of 100 percent).

The public sex role debate in Switzerland in the early 1970's is yet another element that has to be taken into account, in connection with possible changes in sex role attitudes. The acceptance of women's political rights in 1971 cannot be considered to be the result of this debate or of actual political struggles but was rather an end-product of tedious political work done during decades by the traditional women's organizations. Nonetheless it has contributed to stirring the more general sex role debate in this country, with a leading role taken by the Swiss women's liberation movement. Public discussions about the social position of women in various institutions of Swiss society have also been enhanced by events such as the publication of a large-scale sociological study sponsored by the National Swiss Commission for UNESCO, published in 1974 and widely discussed, and the National Women's Congress held in the course of International Women's Year 1975. These events led to the creation of a Federal Commission on the Status of Women, appointed by the Ministry of the Interior. All of these developments have been widely echoed in the mass media, and insofar as they have had an impact on attitudes, they will counteract the postulated tendency towards more traditional sex role attitudes in the wake of the recession.

While it seems obvious to expect increased organization of modern, if not feminist, attitudes as a result of such a public debate (Mason *et al.*, 1976: 575), the opposite tendency should also be considered, i.e., the crystallization of traditional, if not antifeminist attitudes, as a reaction to the discussion mentioned above. In addition to this consideration, still another line of thought may be developed, which is, of course, entirely speculative. As participant observers, we feel that the public discussion about women's rights, especially its wide publicity during the International Women's Year, has made adverse declarations rather difficult. However, such less-than-feminist attitudes have been socially discouraged rather than completely eliminated. There might even exist a reactionary ideological undercurrent that has been restrained by the public sex role debates and that now suddenly receives unexpected legitimacy by the recession. This speculation holds not only for men, but also for women. A tendency towards a renewed traditionalism in sex role attitudes may often appear with people and in social contexts where the discrepancy between publicized opinion and private attitudes and practices is large (for an early discussion of such discrepancies see Stolte-Heiskanen & Haavio-Mannila, 1967).

To summarize, although economic recession was comparatively restricted on the objective level, we hypothesize that Swiss women have become more traditional in their sex role attitudes as a result of the subjectively perceived importance of the recession. Another factor contributing to a stronger formation of traditional attitudes may be a counterproductive side effect of the sex role debate between 1970 and 1976.

Data and Method

Comparison of two subsequent surveys

The following analysis is based on a comparison of two surveys conducted independently and for very different purposes. The first survey, conducted in the winter of 1970/71, was part of the above-mentioned study sponsored by the National Swiss Commission for UNESCO (Held and Levy, 1974); the second, conducted in June 1976, was part of a study done for a Federal Commission on Traffic Planning. It was possible to repeat in the second survey five items from the first one to measure traditional sex role attitudes. The two surveys have one important feature in common: they were both designed according to a scheme of contextual stratification, socio-economic context being operationally defined by information on the level of the province or state (Canton) and on the level of the local communities involved. In the first survey, married men and their wives, and unmarried women were interviewed; in the second, married men and women. In the following analysis, only married women will be compared across the two surveys since in the second survey the attitude questions were only asked of women.

Selection of subsamples for time-lagged comparison

In order to avoid an unnecessary complication of results, the comparison between the 1970/71 and the 1976 survey will be made for an urban and a rural context, respectively. The two urban and the two rural contexts are comparable according to available statistical data that refer to such criteria as socio-economic development of the Canton, level or urbanization, structural completeness and cultural features of the local community.[2]

2   The following indicators were available to match contexts of the two surveys for comparison: Sectorial distribution of economically active population, proportion of self-employed, number of jobs per capita, age distribution of population, employment rate of women, proportion of Protestants (vs. Catholics, other denominations being numerically irrelevant in Switzerland), percentage ot foreign residents, percentage of unmarried, percentage of small households (not more than 3 persons).

The two urban contexts matched with the help of these criteria are Zurich with its agglomeration for 1970/71, and St. Gallen for 1976. The two rural contexts are a group of structurally similar communities in mountainous regions, mainly from the Cantons of Bern and the Grisons for 1970/71, and Laax (Grisons) for 1976.

The data used in our analysis are beset with a number of problems[3] that cannot be detailed in this paper for lack of space, but we should like to stress this fact at this juncture: The data are the best available for studying possible changes in sex role stereotypes of Swiss women, and they are worth being examined for this reason. However, their quality is less than satisfactory. Their most important drawback is the impossibility of analytically separating real change effects from structural differences between the samples that escape measurement by the indicators we are able to use. This kind of problem is, of course, quite frequent in situations where genuine longitudinal studies are lacking and data that were not collected for the purpose of change analysis must be used.

Sex role attitudes: Five items are used to measure traditionalism or nontraditionalism of sex role attitudes in the manner of an additive Likert-type scale. The items pertain to a special form of sex role attitudes, i.e., to norms of sex-specific attribution of social roles. Women who subscribed to three or more of the five items are considered as holding traditional norms of sex-specific role segregation. The following statements

---

3 There are three main problems involved in a comparison based on these two pairs of contexts: (1) In the 1970/71 sample, the resulting figures refer to an analytically defined type of sociocultural context. Technically, they correspond to averages since the sample consists of proportionately pooled local subsamples. In the 1976 survey, the two samples correspond to territorial communities. So the figures for 1970/71 are aggregated over a greater variation than those for 1976. Whether this has a blurring or an exaggerating effect on differences and relations must remain open to question.
(2) Zurich and St. Gallen, although comparable according to the set of variables used to match communities, have nevertheless some important dissimilarities that must be kept in mind when interpreting results. Zurich is a richer context, more highly developed in many respects, more tertiarized, and one of the major economic centers of Switzerland. St. Gallen has a less central position and a predominantly Catholic culture which is only partially measured by such variables as population percentage of Protestants or Catholics (St. Gallen also being the centre of a diocese). Even Protestants will generally be more traditional if they have been socialized into and are living in a Catholic context. This means that probably there is a cultural difference between the two urban contexts that cannot be eliminated by controlling for individual confessional adherence.
(3) Between the two rural contexts there are also some differences that may influence the results already influenced by the time lag. Laax has become a center of tourism and has thus added to its agricultural sector an increasingly important sector of services of a special kind, which has not been the case for the communities that constitute the 1970/71 sample. It seems that tourism can have urbanization effects that go far beyond what may be indicated by mere population figures. It has been shown, for instance, that the usual rural-urban differences in intellectual growth disappear, if rural communities with a strong touristic sector are compared to cities (Meili and Steiner, 1965.) Keeping these differences in mind, we will refer to the four subsamples simply as "rural" vs. "urban" contexts and the year of the study.

were evaluated by the interviewees on a five-point scale (abbreviations and acceptance rates for the entire Swiss sample 1970/71 in brackets): "Childrearing is mainly the wife's concern." REAR (38%)—"Tasks in the family must be arranged in such a way that the wife takes care of the household and the husband of the family's living." ROLES (66%)—"Women are good at other things than politics, therefore they should be active where they can contribute something and leave politics to men." POLIT (51%)—"A married woman should not work, the breadwinner is the man." WORK (27%)—"Boys and girls have to be prepared for different tasks in their lives, so they must be formed and educated in different ways." GOALS (46%).—The index for the Acceptance of Role Segregation will be referred to by ARS.

These items have been selected with reference to the theoretical concept of status and role configuration. They cover some of the main aspects of an adult's complete status-role configuration: occupation, housework, childrearing (on the level of task allocation and on the level of content), politics (important for two specific reasons: political participation on the level of simple active citizenship implies more than elections, and political rights for women are relatively recent in Switzerland). The five items are only in part similar to those used in other studies.[4]

Six independent variables were present in both studies, operationalized in a sufficiently similar way to allow their inclusion in the analysis: education, employment, age, farmer/nonfarmer, and religion. For reasons of sample size and minor dissimilarities in operational definitions, all variables are introduced in dichotomous form.

Education: low = the basic, compulsory level of education which is slightly more than primary according to the definitions of UNESCO; high = education that goes beyond the compulsory minimum, ranging from additional vocational formation to a university degree.

Employment: low = no gainful employment, or part-time work that is done only on occasions (less than 20 hours per week); high = full-time work or part-time work on a basis of 20 hours per week or more.

Age: low = 20–39 years; high = 40–70 years.

Religion: only Protestants and Catholics where identified since all other categories together accounted for 3 percent or less in the various subsamples.

---

4 Mason *et al.* (1976), whose study parallels ours in many respects, cite 13 items, among which only four tap the dimension of role segregation, four the dimension of acceptance of open male superiority, while the other items are less clear and rather heterogenous concerning their dimensional location. Among the four role segregation items, two overlap between their study and ours, allowing for some variation: BETTER—"It is much better for everyone involved, if the man is the achiever outside the home and family." INDEP—"Parents should encourage just as much independence in their daughters as in their sons." Thus comparability on the level of items is rather low for the Swiss and the American study.

We have already referred to the somewhat precarious quality of our data with respect to the purpose of this secondary analysis. We have drawn two consequences from this fact. First, although most variables measured are at least on an ordinal level, they will be used only in dichotomous form in order to account for minor differences in categorization between the two surveys. Second, no statistical methods will be used for the analysis in order not to pretend a degree of precision that is not warranted by the data.

Findings

Attitude, consistency and change

In order to determine possible changes in sex role attitudes, let us first look at the differences we can observe in the simple distribution of our five items. We will then analyze their interrelationship and combine them in an additive index of sex-norm traditionalism.

Table 1

Acceptance rate (percent "high") of five sex role attitude items and summary index ARS

Item	Urban context			Rural context		
	1970/71	1976	Diff.	1970/71	1976	Diff.
REAR	38.9%	66.7%	+27.8	46.0%	57.1%	+11.1
ROLES	64.3%	75.4%	+11.1	82.8%	65.3%	−17.5
POLIT	48.4%	64.3%	+15.9	69.0%	65.3%	− 3.7
WORK	23.0%	35.1%	+12.1	47.1%	18.4%	−28.7
GOALS	40.5%	49.1%	+ 8.6	69.4%	45.8%	−23.6
ARS	27.8%	46.4%	+18.6	47.1%	33.3%	−13.8
(N)	(126)	(56)		(85)	(48)	

Table 1 shows two general trends: the acceptance rates of traditional sex role attitude items increase in the urban context and decrease in the rural context. The differences vary considerably, and their size orders, taken absolutely, do not coincide in the two types of context. There is only one item, REAR, that shows a positive difference in the rural context. It is interesting to note this exception, since it represents most clearly the one element in the wife's traditional role set that is generally most positively evaluated: childrearing as a mother's speciality.

The existence of two opposite trends is quite unexpected. The urban trend corresponds to our hypothesis of an increasing attitude of traditionalism as a consequence of decreasing extra-familial options for the wives, while the rural trend contradicts it clearly, with the one exception of the childrearing item. The two opposing trends cannot be said to converge: in the 1970/71 sample, acceptance rates for all items were higher in the rural than in the urban context, while in the 1976 sample, acceptance rates (with the exception of POLIT) are lower in the rural context than in the urban one. Before interpreting these results, let us look at the interrelationships of the items.

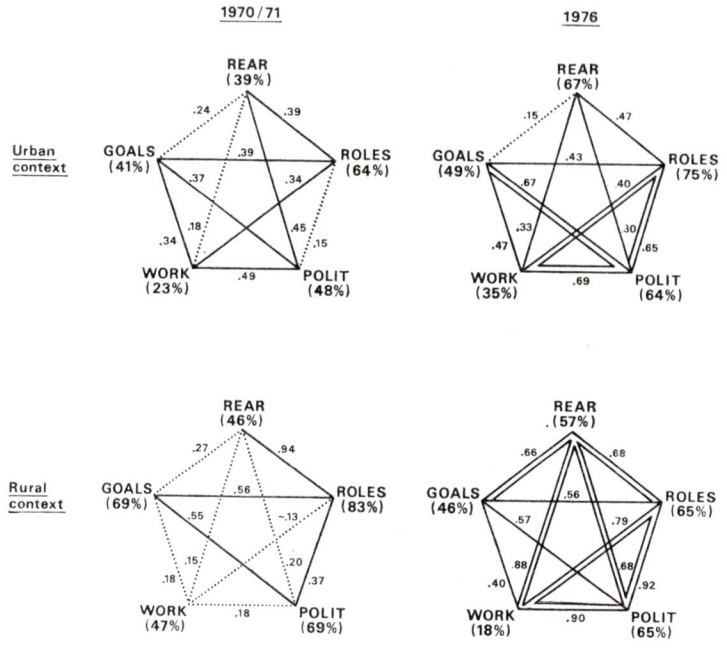

Figure 1. Intercorrelations of five items of role segregation.

Legend: .... $0.00 \leq \gamma \leq 0.29$
——— $0.30 \leq \gamma \leq 0.59$
=== $0.60 \leq \gamma \leq 0.00$

Figure 1 shows, first of all, a remarkable increase of interrelations between the two surveys for both the urban and the rural contexts. Second, there are certain differences in details, which we will discuss only in part since we are interested above all in the process of cognitive integration or consistency formation in general. For the 1970/71 survey, there are some differences between the intercorrelation patterns of the rural and the urban context, especially concerning the item WORK. Given the relatively few occupational possibilities for women in this particularly traditional context (which has the lowest employment rate of married women), this one item seems to be irrelevant for most women and it is, therefore, likely to be evaluated on a general ideological level, without a direct connection to the other role stereotypes that have a more concrete meaning in this context than in the other contexts. In the urban context, the items HOME, WORK and POLIT, which all stress the differentiation between the intra- and the extra-familial sphere, form an especially integrated cluster. On the whole, however, there are only minor differences in the intercorrelation patterns between the two surveys for both rural and urban contexts.

Referring to the main finding, one should recall our general hypothesis which stated that attitude consistency is increased by the increasing frequency and intensity of interactions concerning the matter in question. The idea that sex role attitudes need not necessarily be integrated and consistent has been stated in family sociology for some time (Motz, 1952), and the above hypothesis has been formulated in the realm of sex-stereotypes by Kammeyer (1964) with reference to the model of cognitive dissonance. The increase in attitude consistency in our samples parallels a similar finding reported by Mason et al. (1976).

The strong tendency for both contexts towards consistency can be summarized by the percentages of persons who give entirely consistent answers to all of the five items (i.e., accept each, reject each, or express neutrality towards each). They are as follows, in the order of contexts shown in Table 1: 9.5%—19.6%—17.6%—20.8%. According to the very strict criterion on consistency used for these figures, in the urban context the proportion of consistent answers has doubled while it has only slightly increased in the rural context. However, in the rural context the level of consistency in 1970/71 is only slightly lower than the one reached in the urban one 1976. We interpret this trend to be a consequence of the widespread public sex role debate and the trend towards women's emancipation that has set in with the creation of the women's liberation movement beginning in the late 60's and the early 70's. However, it seems that this public discussion did not bring about a generalized and stable 'modernization' of attitudes, but rather led to a polarization between a traditional and more modern attitude pattern, each more integrated in the 1976 survey than in the 1970/71 one. Closer scrutiny of the consistent reactions reveals another interesting fact that corresponds to the two trends present in Table 1: in the urban context, the *traditional* answers among the consistent ones become more frequent in 1976, while in the rural context, the *nontraditional* answers become more frequent.

While the findings for the rural contexts would be consistent with the hypothesis of a general modernization process, the urban findings point to more complex dynamics that correspond to our earlier speculation. Disregarding for a moment the possibility of artificial results, we may ask whether these findings are the result of a lag in consistency formation in sex role related attitudes. In the earlier survey, consistency was more pronounced on the nontraditional side of the scale while in the later survey consistency appears strengthened on its traditional side. This reminds us of another finding from the women's study in 1970/71: Refined analysis of the interrelationships of three items expressing protest attitudes against the social position of women showed higher frequency of consistent statements on the 'feminist' pole than on the 'traditionalist' pole, especially so for less developed and rural contexts

(Held and Levy, 1974: 227—229). The finding was then interpreted as pointing to a stronger process of ideology-based interaction and hence formation and integration of consciousness with those sympathetic to the renewed feminist movement than with those potentially opposed to it. In accordance with this interpretation and several processes of countermobilization linked with the publication of the women's study and the later public vote on abortion in Switzerland (1977), one may feel that there has been a reaction on the side of traditionalists. This reaction may have led to intensified discussions and consistency formation in opposition to "women's lib" and some political measures of liberalization, showing up in the urban difference in attitude consistency that we have interpreted in terms of a lag. Recently, Duncan (1979) came to similar findings.

We can summarize these findings by stating that there are, first, two opposing trends towards more traditionalism in urban contexts and towards less traditionalism in rural contexts. Second, there is a general tendency towards more attitudinal consistency or ideological integration. Third, in correspondence with the two trends, the trend towards consistency represents a reinforcement of the more traditional stand in urban contexts, while it is made up by a consolidation of nontraditional views in rural contexts. The distribution of the additive index ARS summarizes the main trends and will be used for the rest of the analysis.

In describing our findings so far, we have used a "change rhetoric", in speaking of trends and changes. In fact, two rather different interpretations of the differences found between our four subsamples are possible: the change interpretation which is the one that interests us here, and the artifact interpretation. As we have already mentioned, we cannot eliminate entirely the latter and are forced to discuss it as a competing possibility. The higher traditionalism we find in the urban context of the 1976 survey may be due to the more traditional and Catholic character of the sampling site, and the less traditional answers we obtained in the rural context of the 1976 survey may be due to the less traditional, more open and heterogeneous sampling site in this survey.

The change interpretation leads to a further question: Our hypothesis about recession-dependent attitude changes seems to hold for the urban, but not for the rural context. Does this mean that recession did not appear as a real threat in rural contexts, and that a general process of modernization goes on in these contexts uninterrupted by fluctuations of the business cycle? In fact, it seems that some processes of structural differentiation that reinforce modernization have continued to exist in these contexts, such as an expansion of the educational system, increasing geographical mobility and commuting. Moreover, agriculture as well as tourism have suffered less from the recession than some branches of industry.

Although there is no possibility of arriving at a final decision between the two interpretations, there are some hints that point to the adequacy of the change rather than the artifact interpretation. The latter could not explain the exception of REAR, a case where the acceptance rates increase also in the rural context, while in the perspective of the change hypothesis such an exception, while not expected, is not excluded either. A better indication is the fact that according to Levy (1977: 64–67), the acceptance of role segregation between husbands and wives is not a stable set of attitudes that is closely related to deep-seated personality traits, but depends considerably on situational factors (in addition to socialization variables such as education and psychic rigidity). ARS is clearly increased when marriage is anticipated, independent of age.

The best way to arrive at a judgment between the two interpretations is to control the independent variables in a comparable way. The distributions of these variables give further information about the presumed differences between the contexts, differences that may exist beyond the similarities that are at the basis of our comparison. Six variables in the two surveys can be used for an additional comparison: religion, age, education, income, working status, and farmer/nonfarmer. We summarize the differences of our contexts only verbally. *Religion:* The percentage of Catholics is markedly higher in the 1976 urban context (St. Gallen) than in the 1970/71 urban context (Zurich); it is even higher in the two rural contexts. *Age:* St. Gallen has a particularly high percentage of respondents 40 or older, while the 1976 rural context is "younger" than its 1970/71 counterpart. *Education:* The 1970/71 rural context has many more poorly educated respondents than the other three contexts. *Income:* Again, the 1970/71 rural context has a particularly high proportion of low income respondents. *Farmer/nonfarmer:* This same context is the only one with a relatively high proportion of farmers (27.9%). *Wife's working status:* The proportion of wives *not* working outside their household is especially high in the 1970/71 rural context.

Two conclusions can be drawn from these differences:

1. In the comparison of the two urban contexts, there are structural factors that point to the higher traditionalism of the 1976 context independent of the time lag (more Catholics; older; lower income), but others that point rather to the opposite (higher female rate of employment; higher education). The structural differences between the two urban contexts of comparison, in consequence, do not uniformly operate in the same direction. This fact gives more plausibility to the change rather than the artifact interpretation in the case of the urban contexts.

2. In the case of the rural contexts, the situation is different. All the differences in the six variables considered point to a higher traditionalism in the 1970/71 context due to structural rather than temporal differences: the 1976 context is younger, better educated, earns more, has less farmers, and more married women are gainfully employed. The only inverse difference is weak: there are somewhat more Catholics in the 1976 than in the 1970/71 rural context. So in the case of the rural contexts, the difference in norm traditionalism may be due entirely to structural differences. Con-

trolling for these variables will show whether the artifact or the change interpretation has more credibility.

Attitude change or structural difference?

In this section we will successively control the independent variables that were equally measured in the two studies in order to check whether the differences we observed in the frequency of traditional sex role attitudes are the result of a temporal change or instead the corollary of structural differences between the contexts. All these variables have been shown in various studies to be correlated with norm traditionalism (Held and Levy, 1974, chapter 5). In order of their correlation, they are: education, employment, age, and religion.

The correlations of these variables seem to belong to different, partly opposite processes of influence. Education (as well as income which cannot be included in the multivariate analysis due to differences in measurement between the two surveys) points to less norm traditionalism in the middle class as compared to the lower class, while the wife's employment hints at a different—more experiential—source of influence, since it is concentrated in the otherwise more traditional lower class. On the whole, there seem to be at least three different sources of influence upon the wife's norm traditionalism: age, class, and employment. In addition to these variables, we will also partially control religion since it constitutes an important compositional difference between the two urban contexts, and the farmer/nonfarmer distinction.

In urban as well as in rural contexts, nonemployed wives are more traditional than employed wives. This difference can be interpreted as the result of a process of normative adaptation to the real situation, a mechanism somewhat similar to the

Table 2

Acceptance rates (percent "high") of role segregation, controlling for wife's working status (N in brackets)

	Wife employed			Wife not employed		
	1970/71	1976	Diff.	1970/71	1976	Diff.
Urban context	23.3% (30)	33.3% (27)	+10.0	29.8% (94)	58.6% (29)	+28.8
Rural context	11.1% (9)	25.0% (20)	+13.9	48.1% (52)	40.0% (25)	−8.1

anticipatory increase of norm traditionalism with women who have a boyfriend they plan to marry. In the urban context, norm traditionalism increases markedly, and even more so among unemployed than among employed wives. We know from the 1976 survey that among the unemployed wives the percentage of those who have lost their jobs is negligible. So the difference cannot be the result of a direct reaction to a personal experience, linked to the recession.[5] Moreover, the general level of wive's employment is even higher in 1976. A more adequate interpretation suggests a reaction to the general economic situation with less options for women outside the family. The higher traditionalism, especially in women who are not employed, seems thus to be due to a normative adaptation that re-emphasizes traditional values and intra-familial activities as a result of the perception of decreased extra-familial opportunities.

Table 3

Acceptance rate (percent "high") of role segregation, controlling for wife's education (N in brackets)

	Wife's education high			Wife's education low		
	1970/71	1976	Diff.	1970/71	1976	Diff.
Urban context	12.9% (62)	36.7% (30)	+23.8	42.2% (64)	56.0% (25)	+13.8
Rural context	12.5% (16)	8.7% (23)	−3.8	55.1% (69)	56.0% (25)	+0.9

Education is also consistently correlated with ARS, higher education 'leading' to less traditionalism. In the urban context, differences in the sense of higher traditionalism in 1976 are maintained at both levels of education, and remain in both cases sizable, being stronger for the higher education group. This means, first, that the slight difference in education between the two urban contexts do not explain the difference in ARS between these contexts. Second, it sheds some critical light on the often-stated 'enlightening' function of education. The higher shift towards norm traditionalism on a higher level of education may, in fact, be interpreted as being the result of a reversal of this enlightening effect of higher education on norms due to structural situation. High education creates occupational and consumptional aspirations that are suddenly frustrated by the recession, be it in reality or in anticipation (e.g., for women who planned to re-enter the workforce at the launching stage in family life). If this interpretation holds true, the correlation between education and ARS should be considerably lower in 1976. In fact, the gamma coefficient is —.43 for 1970/71 and only —.15 for 1976. These findings may also be seen in connection with the distinction between consciousness expansion through diffusion of values and norms, i.e., by way of a purely cultural process, from consciousness formation as provoked by real experiences (such as experience of structural barriers in professional or political life). We postulate that attitudes linked to the latter are more stable than attitudes merely implanted by socialization processes, especially

---

5 At any rate, in the case of unemployment, we would not hypothesize a reactivation of traditional role-attitudes as a main reaction, but rather anomic types of behavior (cfr. Jahoda et al., 1971).

secondary socialization. Thus, here again, the results point to the situational dependence of sex role norms.

In the rural context, quite a different picture emerges: controlling education makes differences in norm traditionalism practically disappear. So it seems that the large difference in the educational level between the two rural contexts almost entirely accounts for the difference in ARS found between these contexts. Put differently, the variation between the rural contexts is structural or compositional rather than temporal. This is especially interesting because it corroborates our initial thesis, and accounts for the unexpected finding of less traditional norms in the rural context of 1976.

Table 4

Acceptance rate (percent 'high') of role segregation, controlling for wife's age (N in brackets)

	Wife 40–70 years old 1970/71	1976	Diff.	Wife 20–39 years old 1970/71	1976	Diff.
Urban context	36.4% (66)	51.4% (37)	+15.0	18.6% (59)	(25.0%) (16)	(+6.4)
Rural context	57.1% (42)	40.0% (20)	−17.1	34.1% (41)	26.9% (26)	−7.2

In the case of age as well as with the other independent variables there is a clear correlation with ARS, older women being consistently more traditional than younger women. However, age differences between contexts do not account for ARS differences. For older and for younger wives, the general differences between the contexts remain: more traditionalism in the urban context, less traditionalism in the rural context. The interesting facts are the higher differences in both directions for the older women. Again, a situational interpretation can account for this difference. For women in the 40+ age group, the "mothering phase" of the family life cycle is over or its end can be immediately anticipated. This means that a major factor of emphasis and relevance of intra-familial activities disappears, which in turn increases the relative relevance of extra-familial events and structures (Heintz et al., 1975; Levy, 1977: 43–73). The higher relevance of the extra-familial domain explains the stronger reaction of the wives to either the impact of recession, which seems to dominate in the urban contexts, or the differences in structural differentiation, which seem to be the main factor in rural contexts.

So far we have controlled for the wife's working status, her education and age. There are two other variables at hand that can, however, only be partially controlled due to extreme distributions: religion and farmer/nonfarmer. As they are not highly correlated with ARS, this does not seem to be a major drawback. We summarize the results verbally. In the case of religion, comparison is only possible for the Catholics throughout all contexts since the proportion of Protestants in the less-developed contexts is very low. Comparison is, however, more important for the urban contexts since religion constitutes another of their main compositional differences. In these contexts, for Protestants as well as for Catholics, the ARS difference found in all the tables, pointing to a process of increased traditionalism, is corroborated, with percentage differences of +27.5 and +21.3, respectively. This shows that the differrences found between the two urban contexts cannot be explained by the compositional effect of religion.

In the case of the farmer/nonfarmer distinction, distributions are even more extreme. In the two urban contexts, there are simply no farmers, while in the 1976 rural context there are only 6% farmers, and only in the 1970/71 rural context does their proportion rise to roughly 28%. This restricts multivariate analysis to purifying the subsamples and comparing ARS distributions for the nonfarming respondents with the overall results. This comparison shows that even in the one context with a substantial proportion of farmers, the overall distribution is practically identical with the nonfarmer one. The maximal difference can be found in the 1970/71 rural context, where the acceptance rate is 47% overall and 43% for the nonfarmers. This shows, even more clearly than in the case of religion, that compositional effects due to this variable are negligible, i.e., rural-urban differences cannot be explained in terms of differences between the farmers and the nonfarmers.

The results and interpretations of this section may now be summarized as follows:

1. *Urban contexts:*
— There is a consistent difference between the urban contexts in the sense of more norm traditionalism in 1976 than in 1970/71.

— This difference is maintained through all controls made, especially so for religion, age and education, where compositional effects could be expected on the basis of differential distributions and correlations of these variables with ARS.

— These results support the plausibility of the change rather than the artifact interpretation in the case of the urban contexts. If one adopts this view, our initial hypothesis is corroborated for these contexts.

2. *Rural contexts:*
— There is a consistent difference between the rural contexts in the sense of less norm traditionalism in 1976 than in 1970/71.

— This difference is maintained through some of the controls made, but it disappears when controlling for education, which is also one of the major compositional differences between these contexts.

— Since this difference is consistent with all the other compositional differences between the rural contexts (with the minor exception of religion, where the difference is weak), we conclude that in these contexts, the ARS difference found in our analysis is due to compositional or structural rather than temporal differences. This means in particular that on the one hand, the initial hypothesis could not be proven for rural contexts, but also that there is no basis for assuming that the reverse difference found here is the result of a reverse trend, leading towards structurally induced modernization.

Discussion

Our analysis had as its starting point the thesis that under the impression of a generalized decrease in accessibility of extra-familial options, married women tend to adapt themselves by re-emphasizing their traditional, intra-familial sex roles as expressed in our measure of sex-specific role segregation. Our analysis has shown that differences in acceptance rates of the role segregation attitude index in fact hold. These differences are in agreement with our hypothesis for urban contexts while they contradict it for rural contexts. The data do not allow us to decide definitely between a change interpretation and an artifact interpretation: the attitude differences may be due to changes independent of compositional effects, changes that may be attributed to the symbolic experience of the recession; but they may also be due to structural or compositional differences between the contexts we compare that are not linked to the change in the overall economic situation.

Closer scrutiny of the data, especially with the help of multivariate analysis, has given support to different interpretations of the variations found in urban and those found in rural contexts. It seems that in the urban contexts, it was possible to measure the kind of change that is formulated in terms of the basic hypothesis, whereas in the rural contexts, the difference found can be almost fully explained by compositional differences. These differences concern mainly the differential diffusion of education in the two rural contexts.

The situational dependence of norm traditionalism in wives is an important fact because of some rather strategic functions the complex of ARS seems to have in the formation of women's consciousness.[6] Our own earlier study has shown that ARS seems to partly determine the readiness and/or capacity of a woman to get politicized, i.e., to develop attitudes of protest against women's social situation, as well

---

6 Our stress on the priority of situational, i.e., 'objective' factors rather than attitudinal or 'subjective' cultural factors is in agreement with materialist conceptions of social structure and change. In this specific area of application Mason et al.'s observation will serve as an example: "until the mid-1950's, changes in women's and men's attitudes towards the propriety of married women's labor force participation lagged well behind increases in married women's employment rates." (1976: 575, footnote 3). A similar observation is made concerning historical changes in female occupations by Sullerot (1971).

as her readiness to accept male dominance.[7] According to this study (Held and Levy 1974: 209–213 and 239–243), the presence of ARS is a necessary but not sufficient condition for the emergence of norms expressing acceptance of male superiority and dominance; women with strong acceptance of role segregation (ARS) in part accept also male dominance, whereas women who do not accept role segregation also do not accept male dominance. In the same vein, women who accept role segregation do not protest against women's social situation, while women who do not accept role segregation in part develop attitudes of protest. The relation between ARS and protest is particularly strong in the case of married women who live in families with a traditional *de facto* role structure (sex-typed segregation as postulated by ARS). Protest is especially frequent with those whose segregation norms are moderate and especially rare with those whose segregation norms are high and thus coincide with their real situation. We interpret ARS to constitute the perceptional frame of reference for the domain of roles considered by the wife (and the husband) to be legitimate fields of personal action and satisfaction seeking. If this frame is narrow—or narrowed down by way of a normative adaptation to exogenous changes—aspirations for other sectors of activity disappear and so does protest in cases where the real situation does not allow a realization of these aspirations. If this frame is enlarged by increasing options and parallel processes of norm liberalization or real experiences, protest develops if the wife remains in a traditional role restricting her to the domestic sphere.

An interesting additional finding is the strong increase in attitude consistency between the two surveys, an increase that holds for both the rural and the urban context. We have interpreted this increase as being the result of a process of attitudinal integration stimulated by increased communication about the topic of sex roles and women's emancipation and by a developing polarization of outlooks in this field. Some data have pointed to a lag in the sense that in a first phase of this overall process, feminist attitudes have started to crystallize, and in a second phase, partly in reaction to the manifestation of the feminist pole, a traditionalist attitude formation has taken place as well. Two public campaigns may be cited that are cases in point: a fierce and widely publicized press campaign by the conservative Catholic party against the UNESCO study, and the equally determined campaign against abortion by the Catholic church and various affiliated organizations. A similar increase in sex role attitude consistency has recently been found by Mason *et al.* (1976) in a study that is comparable to ours. In their analysis of more recent surveys, the evaluation of extra-familial roles coincides more distinctly with the evaluation

---

[7] See also the finding cited earlier that ARS is being increased in young unmarried women who concretely *anticipate* getting married. In the next step of a woman's institutionalized life course, really getting married, acceptance of male dominance "follows suit", being in turn increased, a process that is probably facilitated by the anticipatory increase in acceptance of role segregation (Levy, 1977: 65—66).

of intra-familial roles than in the former surveys. Their other finding, however, does not coincide with ours; while, in Switzerland, the overall trend is in the direction of more norm traditionalism, Mason *et al.* find a trend towards more modern, i.e., less sex-stereotyped attitudes. This difference may be due to two factors, either of which may be in effect. First, the period covered by their surveys just ends with the recession (1974), well in the middle of the interval between the two Swiss surveys. Second, there is no doubt that the new women's movement was much stronger in the USA than in Switzerland and that it has succeeded in obtaining institutional and legal strongholds that are not as easily swept away by the recession as are individual attitudes. This, in turn, will also help to reinforce individual attitudes, and therefore we would expect that even a follow-up in the USA with the same interval will show a weaker impact of recession than in Switzerland, where objective structural changes in favor of female equality have remained somewhat scarce. A third, partial similarity between the two studies also fits into this interpretation: in the US as in the Swiss study, education and employment are among the variables strongly related to norm-traditionalism, but it seems that this relation is more stable in the USA than in Switzerland, where we have seen a marked decrease in the correlation between education and norm traditionalism. Probably, the difference is due to the differential possibility to realize occupational aspirations created by education which seems to be higher in the USA than in Switzerland, making the education/norm traditionalism relation more stable, i.e. less reversible. Here again, then, we find a hint of the importance of structural rather than merely cultural factors (as education without occupation would be).

Attitude change, recession, and modernization theory

Our findings should be placed within the larger framework of change in the realm of women's position in family and society at large. It is one of the well-established beliefs of much of family sociology that the increasing participation of women in the labor force since World War II has been one of the most important determinants of change in sex role and in the corresponding attitudes. According to Holter (1971), most sociological and psychological theories of sex role change use incentives or pressures emanating from the economic system as independent variables in the explanation of the change. Industrialization and increased demands for labor (Goode, 1963), technological change and the emergence of new jobs for women (Ogburn, 1955) as well as political or economic crises that force women to take over posts formerly held by men (Holter cites Boulding, 1966, as an example for what she terms crisis theories) are some of the factors invoked to explain modernizing changes in sex role attitudes. On a general level, all these concepts are based on the assumption of a steadily increasing enlargement of options for women outside the family and home. Parallel to this development, the intra-familial options of women seem to be reduced as a consequence of decreasing fertility rates observable in all highly developed countries, together with a loss of instrumentality of biological reproduction to the family of procreation. These inverse trends, manifested by the decreasing number of children per mother, an increasing number of single women and an increase in divorce rates, and paralleled by a secular increase in relative wages for women (decrease in wage discrimination and better promotional opportunities), mean that the opportunity costs for the traditional female role may become very high (the argument of opportunity costs has been advanced, for instance, by Mason et al., 1976).

This argument is an extension of modernization theory, and it shares with it the basic belief in continuous economic growth. However, in the face of the youth unrest in many developed European countries, the ecological crisis and the increased consciousness thereof, and last but not least, the world-wide economic recession of 1973–1974, the consequences of which are still the major political concern for most West European governments, the assumption of growth and continuous expansion and hence continuously growing opportunities can no longer be maintained. In this context, the question arises whether the process of change towards such 'new' attitudes has become autonomous and irreversible, i.e., independent from its structural determinants (as implicitly assumed by some modernization theories). We hold that actual and historical evidence shows that the integration of women into the economy (but also into the political system), and their exclusion from these domains, depends heavily on business cycles and changes in the economic structure, quite in accord with the thesis of their function as a reserve army (Ferber and Nowry, 1976). Disintegration of the economy in a situation of decreased functions and satisfaction potential of the family must lead to a loss of meaning of the intra-familial roles for women. One of the strategies they have at hand in order to cope with such a development (anomie and resulting psychosocial tensions) is to re-emphasize traditional, sex-linked values. This seems to be the dominant development in Switzerland in the wake of the recession.

This interpretation has direct implications for modernization theory. If the assumption of a concomitant change in sex role norms with economic change is correct, modernization of values can no longer be considered to be an independent process of cultural change, as some versions of modernization theory would have it. Individual mentality as a prime motor of economic change and modernization— e.g., Lerner's empathy (1964) or McClelland's (1961) need for achievement—cannot be isolated from its sociostructural background. This does not mean, however, that cultural factors can be discarded in the field of women's emancipation. While structural conditions are of great importance, there are also strong arguments for the importance of socialization and consciousness formation. Holter (1971) on a general level, Stolte-Heiskanen and Haavio-Mannila (1967) on a more concrete level, show that changes in macrostructures may be a necessary, but not sufficient condition for an overall change in women's situation and that cultural factors have their important role to play. It seems that besides structural opportunities, a form of "cultural revolution" is needed that still has to be brought about.

We would like to close this analysis with some further pertinent comments. As previously stated, conclusions from our comparison of a "boom-time" with a post-recession-time sample cannot be carried too far since structural or compositional differences between the contexts may account for at least part of the hypothesized shift towards more traditionalism in sex role attitudes. Nevertheless, the results for the urban contexts point to a relationship between the economic situation and attitudes in the sense of our hypothesis. Such a dependency—it may be the result of a very complex set of mechanisms—has a number of implications for social and labor policy. If women (and foreign workers who are still important in Switzerland) are considered to be a labor reserve that is only used to satisfy short-run demands of the economy, a continuous change of sex role attitudes and a real role redistribution in the families appears to be impossible. Concerning the emancipation of women and the liberation of men and women from traditional sex role ascription, labor policy should strive for full employment as a priority goal. Given the structural shortage of work opportunities this can only be achieved by a new distribution of work, which is to be considered a social "good" like education, income, or other elements of the "good life". Redistribution of this "good" necessitates part-time work at acceptable conditions for both men and women. Only in this case will men have the chance to participate more fully in the family and thereby contribute to eliminating the husband-provider vs. wife-homemaker model.

REFERENCES

Boulding, Elise
    1966 "The Road to Parliament for Women." *International Seminar on the Participation of Women in Public Life.* Rome.
Duncan, Otis D.
    1979 "Indicators of Sex Typing: Traditional and Egalitarian, Situational and Ideological Responses." *American Journal of Sociology* 85: 251–260.
Ferber, Marianne A. and Helen M. Nowry
    1976 "Women: the New Reserve Army of the Unemployed." Martha Blaxall and Barbara B. Reagan (eds.), *Women and the Work place.* Chicago: Chicago University Press.
Goode, William J.
    1963 *World Revolution and Family Patterns.* Glencoe: Free Press.
Heintz, Peter et al.
    1975 "Family Structure and Society." *Journal of Marriage and the Family,* 37: 861–870.
Heintz, Peter and Suzanne Heintz
    1973 *The Future of Development.* Bern: Huber.
Held, Thomas and René Levy
    1974 *Die Stellung der Frau in Familie und Gesellschaft.* Frauenfeld: Huber.
Holter, Harriet
    1971 "Sex Roles and Social Change." *Acta Sociologica* 14: 2–12.
Inkeles, Alex
    1969 "Making Men Modern." *American Journal of Sociology* 75: 208–225.

Jahoda, Marie et al.
    1971 *Marienthal: The Sociography of an Unemployed Community.* Chicago: Aldine.
Kammeyer, Kenneth
    1964 "The Feminine Role: An Analysis of Attitude Consistency." *Journal of Marriage and the Family* 26: 295–305.
Komavrosky, Mirra
    1940 *The Unemployed Man and His Family.* New York: Dryden Press.
Lerner, Daniel
    1964 *The Passing of Traditional Society: Modernizing the Middle East.* New York: Free Press.
Levy, René
    1977 *Der Lebenslauf als Statusbiographie.* Stuttgart: Enke.
Mason, Karen Oppenheim et al.
    1976 "Change in U. S. Women's Sex-Role Attitudes, 1964–1974." *American Sociological Review* 41: 573–596.
McClelland, David C.
    1961 *The Achieving Society.* Princeton: Van Nostrand.
Meili, Richard and Heinrich Steiner
    1965 "Eine Untersuchung zum Intelligenzniveau Elfjähriger der deutschen Schweiz." *Schweizerische Zeitschrift für Psychologie und ihre Anwendung* 24: 23–32.
Motz, Annabelle Bender
    1952 "The Role Conception Inventory: A Tool of Research in Social Psychology." *American Sociological Review* 17: 465–471.
OECD (Organization for Economic Co-operation and Development)
    1976 *The 1974–75 recession and the employment of women.* Paris: OECD.
Ogburn, William F. and Meyer Nimkoff
    1955 *Technology and the Changing Family.* Cambridge, Mass.: Houghton Mifflin.
Pross, Helge
    1973 *Gleichberechtigung im Beruf?* Frankfurt/M: Athenäum.
Stolte-Heiskanen, Veronika and Elina Haavio-Mannila
    1967 "The Position of Women in Society: Formal Ideology vs. Everyday Ethics." *Social Science Information* 6: 169–188.
Sullerot, Evelyne
    1971 *Woman, Society and Change.* New York: World University Library.
Vincent, Clark E.
    1966 "Familia Spongia: the Adaptive Function." *Journal of Marriage and the Family* 28: 29–36.

Egalitarianism in Marriage?
Graduate Education and the Sexual Division of Labour in the Canadian Family*

GLADYS L. SYMONS

The University of Calgary, Calgary, Canada

Introduction

A) *Women in Graduate Education in Canada*

THE STRUGGLE FOR EQUALITY of educational opportunity for women in Canada has been long and arduously fought. Admission of women to Canadian universities came in the 19th century, but development of equality of access has been a slow process. Moreover, views of women's education differed by province, for in Canada, education is a provincial concern. New Brunswick was the first province to admit women students to university, followed in 1858 by Mount Allison University (MacLellan, 1972: 6). In 1870, Queen's University in Ontario instituted a "few classes for ladies" (Queen's University, 1974: 2). The first woman graduated with a university degree from Mount Allison in 1875. Other universities granted degrees to women in 1879 (University of King's College, Halifax), 1884 (Queen's and Acadia Universities), 1885 (Dalhousie University, University of Toronto), and 1888 (McGill University) (MacLellan, 1972: 6, 7).

After admission to the university, the next step for women was to attain graduate education. In the early 20th century, women began entering graduate schools, and the proportion of women in both master's and doctoral programmes peaked in 1929–30, with 28% of the graduate enrolment made up of women.[1] The proportions declined to a low of 16% in 1955–56 and rose to 19% in 1968–69 (Black, 1974). Interpreting these statistics, Black notes that "neither the modest expansion of graduate work in the '50s nor the enormous expansion in the '60s has been to the advantage of women."

Table 1 presents the number and proportion of Ph.D.'s awarded to women in Canada from 1930 to 1975. The numbers of women obtaining this degree rose substan-

---
* I would like to thank Eugen Lupri, Jarmila Horna and Walter Zwirner from The University of Calgary, and Hugh Lautard from the University of New Brunswick for their most valuable comments on an earlier draft of this paper. Revised version of a paper presented at the Western Association of Sociology and Anthropology Annual Meetings, Calgary, December, 1978.

1 The relatively high percentage of women in graduate school in the late 1920s probably reflects the emancipation of women brought about by World War I and their participation in the war effort.

Table 1

Doctorates Earned in Canada, Selected Years, 1930-31 to 1974-75

Academic Year	Total Number PhD's Awarded	Number PhD's Awarded to Women	Women PhD's as % of Total
1930-31	46	7	15.0%
1940-41	75	5	7.0
1945-46	104	12	11.5
1950-51	202	11	5.0
1955-56	266	17	6.0
1960-61	305	26	8.5
1963-64	481	38	8.0
1964-65	569	54	9.5
1966-67	788	60	8.0
1969-70	1,248	128	9.0
1970-71	1,625	151	9.3
1971-72	1,724	160	9.3
1972-73	1,929	217	11.2
1973-74	1,896	234	12.3
1974-75	1,840	296	16.1

Source: For 1930-31 to 1969-70, Vickers and Adam (1977: 113). For 1970-71 to 1974-75, Statistics Canada, Catalogue 81-211, (1977a: 18, 19).

tially over this forty-five year period, from 7 in 1930-31 to 296 in 1974-75. However, until as late as 1973-74, the proportions of women in this category actually dropped, and only surpassed the 1930-31 figure in 1974-75. Although recent trends indicate an increasing participation of women in graduate education, today, as in the past, women are still a sizeable minority in the university.

The organization of academic professions in Canada is essentially a masculine one. There is some variation by departments, of course, such as Nursing Science and Rehabilitation Therapy, which are predominantly feminine occupations, but on the whole, university teaching is still a male preserve. In the university, male professors and male graduate students far outnumber their female colleagues. Furthermore, female academics are found more often at the lower echelons (Adam, 1971; Eichler et al., 1973; Hitchman, 1974; Ambert and Hitchman, 1976) and female students are more numerous in the lower degree programmes (Bowen, 1973; Hitchman, 1974). In Canadian universities, both the proportion and numbers of women students and faculty members drop drastically as one proceeds up the educational ladder. Table 2 presents the diminishing flow of women throughout the ranks in Canadian universities for the academic year 1974-75. Women made up 41.4% of all full-time undergraduate students, 29.7% of master's candidates and 22.8% of doctoral students. The diminishing flow can also be seen in terms of women faculty. Women comprised 29.7% of all faculty in the rank below assistant professor, 14.7% of assistant professors, 8.8% of associates, and 3.8% of full professors.

Table 2

Percent Women in Various Status Categories in Canadian Universities 1974-75

Status Category	Percent Women	Total Number
Full-time women students		
Undergraduate students	41.4	309,541
Masters students	29.7	20,959[1]
Ph. D. students	22.8	9,290[1]
TOTAL STUDENTS	40.3	329,635[1]
Full-time women faculty		
Rank below Assistant Professor	29.7	2,932
Assistant Professors	14.7	9,740
Associate Professors	8.8	8,046
Full Professors	3.8	5,827
TOTAL FACULTY[2]	12.8	27,731

1 Based on cases where gender was reported.
2 Includes 'Other' category.
Source: Calculated from Statistics Canada. Catalogues: 81-243 (1977c: 32, 33); 81-204 (1977b: 27, 29).

Given these statistics, and employing Merton's definition of sex-typed professions as those in which "a very large majority are of one sex and ... there is an associated normative expectation that this is as it should be" (quoted in Epstein, 1971: 68), university teaching can be classified as a masculine profession, and the training environment as a male milieu. Many of the attitudes, perspectives and role postures that are part of the university culture are typified in our society as masculine ones, acquired by males through primary socialization and retained through cultural expectations. For example, traits such as aggressiveness and competition, achievement-orientation, drive, etc., that are found in the academic role, are considered by Canadian society to be masculine, and are fostered in male children and discouraged in the majority of female children, at least after puberty. It is the institutional sphere of graduate school that provides one part of the focus of this study; the other is marriage and the family.

B) *Graduate Education and the Family*

In this paper we shall examine the condition of women and men graduate students with respect to the intersection of two institutional spheres, namely, graduate education and the family.

In the literature on the sociology of the family, two main indicators have been used to measure egalitarianism or democratic marital relations, namely, decision-making between husband and wife, and the sexual division of labour in the domestic sphere. The former indicator of decision-making has been examined at great length and in cross-cultural perspective (Blood and Wolfe, 1960; Rodman, 1967, 1972; Lupri, 1969, 1976; Safilios-Rothschild, 1970). A number of variables have been isolated which affect the degree of egalitarianism in marriage, such as industrialization, urbanization, social status of the husband, employment status of the wife, education, income, social participation and so on. Moreover, some Canadian researchers (Davids, 1976; Hobart, 1973) have speculated that Canadian marriages of the future will be more egalitarian.

The methodology of this vast body of research has come under some recent criticism by Brinkerhoff and Lupri (1978). Essentially, they argue, with supporting empirical evidence from Canada, that the indicator of egalitarianism used is inadequate for the tasks. Wives may indeed report decision-making, but the areas in which those decisions are made tend to be of lesser importance than those controlled by the husband. They (Brinkerhoff and Lupri, 1978: 20) state,

> In sum, according to decision-making scales wives may appear to be equal to, or even more powerful than, their husbands. But, in reality, wives only make decisions in areas in which they are expected to—areas of lesser importance.

The second indicator which has been used to measure egalitarianism in marriage concerns the sexual division of labour in the home. The rise of capitalism heralded the division of the work world into public and private spheres of activity (Smith, 1973). The labour of men is performed in the public realm and women's work is relegated to the private sphere of the home.[2] Hence, the traditional sexual division of labour in the family is such that the husband is responsible for labour outside the home, while the woman bears the major responsibility for tasks of housekeeping and child-bearing—tasks performed in the private sphere. Although there are variations in this pattern among certain individual families, at the societal level, the Canadian norm of the sexual division of labour in the family appears, by and large, to follow this pattern (Eichler, 1975; Elkin, 1964).

Studies have been done, again some in cross-cultural perspective (Blood and Wolfe, 1960; Gendell, 1963; Michel, 1970; Young and Willmott, 1973; Lupri, 1976), demonstrating the relationship between certain variables and egalitarianism in marriage as measured by the sexual division of labour. The results suggest a positive correlation between wife's employment status and egalitarianism. In recent years, this correlation has been examined more closely in the Canadian context. Meissner *et al.* (1975) undertook 24-hour time-budget studies of 350 married couples of varying

---

2 Benston (1969) uses a Marxist analysis to elaborate on the effects of women's status on this basic sexual division of labour. Because women as a group work outside the money economy, the work they do is not considered "real work," and hence their status is secondary to that group (men) which works for wages. Women's status in capitalist societies is linked to the specific economic relationship they hold to the means of production. The term "public sphere" is used to refer to the world outside the home, while the "private sphere" refers to the domestic realm.

socio-economic and parental statuses in eight areas of Greater Vancouver. The researchers delineate a typology of the sexual division of household labour: an adaptive partnership theory, and a dependent labour theory. The former case describes the situation where female employment is a resource which makes for more sharing in the domestic labour on the part of the husband. The dependent labour theory postulates that, given the different relationship of men and women with respect to the structure of work in Canadian society, relations of dominance and dependence are articulated. Hence, woman's paid employment has few consequences for the sexual division of labour in the home and tends to increase her hours of labour, while having little or no effect on the work hours of the husband. In other words, the adaptive partnership theory suggests egalitarianism within marriage with respect to the sexual division of labour in the home, while the dependent labour theory postulates that the traditional division more closely approximates the norm.

The extent to which particular marital arrangements in Canada may be classified as one or the other of these typologies is open to empirical investigation. Meissner *et al.* (1975) demonstrate that for their sample, the latter theory appears to be more applicable.

This paper further explores this question by focusing on a particular type of marriage in Canada. The intersection of two institutional spheres in Canadian society, that of education and the family, is examined. An analysis is made of the inter-relationship between the position of women within the educational system and their position within the family. The case chosen for analysis is that of married full-time doctoral candidates in two Canadian universities, located in one of Canada's largest metropolitan centres. Given the criticisms of the decision-making method for measuring marital power, only the indicator of the sexual division of labour in the private sphere of the home will be used here.

Such a study is important for several reasons. First of all, Canada, as a post-industrial society, has need of professionals, and women are beginning to enter these fields in increasing numbers. As has been shown, the number of women receiving earned doctorates has increased steadily in Canada since 1940. A second important reason for studying the intersection of the educational and marital institutions is that these women who are preparing for advanced degrees also tend to get married, albeit at a later age than women in the general population. Hence, if Canada is to utilize her person-power to the fullest, the relationship of these two institutional spheres must be understood, and efforts made to coordinate them as efficiently as possible. Hence, the role of the educated, married, professional woman in training deserves careful attention. Thirdly, to this author's knowledge, no research has been done on the impact of graduate education on the family in Canada. Does the intersection of these two institutional spheres lead to changes in the face of the modern Canadian marriage? Are such marriages actually among the most emancipated ones? Do these marriages represent the prototypes of egalitarianism? Another important feature of this study involves an analysis of the situation of professional men in training in relation to their marital and familial roles. The majority of the research concerning the intersection of the occupational and marital worlds, the public and private spheres, has dealt with that of the wife. A few notable exceptions are Poloma and Garland (1971), Garland (1972), Bailyn (1971). Without analyzing the masculine case, the impact of graduate education on marriage and the family cannot be fully understood.

Methodology

A) *The Sample*

The sample consists of 167 married doctoral candidates in two Canadian graduate schools.[3] At the time of data collection (1974-75), all of the respondents were living with their spouses. Ninety-five (57%) of the respondents are men, and 72 (43%) are women. The women in the sample are, on average, older than men: the former average 29.5 years, the latter 27.4. Correspondingly, the spouses of the women are usually older than those of the men. The average age of wives of graduate student respondents is 26.2; the average age of husbands is 31.8.

The respondents tend to come from middle-class homes, with 51% of both men and women having fathers with professional or managerial occupations, and 48% of the men and 50% of the women having fathers with at least some university education. These data are not surprising, since graduate students in Canada tend to come from the higher socio-economic classes. For example, in the academic year of 1968-69, 39.2% of graduate students in Canadian universities came from a family where the parental income was $ 10,000 or more, compared to 18.0% from families whose

---

[3] The sample used in the present analysis comprises the married student contingent of the total sample of 359 graduate students enrolled in two Canadian metropolitan universities in Toronto, Ontario. Included in the total sample were all women Ph.D. candidates enrolled full-time and in residence during the 1974-75 academic session, and enrolled in a Ph.D. programme offered by both universities. A corresponding sample of male Ph.D. students, matched in terms of discipline, university and year of study was drawn. The academic disciplines chosen for study were categorized as natural science, including biology, zoology, chemistry and physics; social sciences including political science, psychology, history, sociology, social and political thought; and humanities consisting of English and philosophy. Questionnaires were mailed to Ph. D. candidates in the period between November 1974 and February 1975. Three hundred and fifty-nine (63%) usable questionnaires were returned, the final sample consisting of 176 women and 183 men. One hundred and twenty-two or 34% of the sample is comprised of York University students and 237 or 66% of the respondents are from the University of Toronto. In the spring of 1975, 21 intensive interviews were conducted with a sub-sample of both male and female respondents.

income was $4,999 or less (Hiller, 1976: 54).[4]

The spouses of the women are much better educated than those of the men. This is not unexpected, since men tend to marry women with less education than themselves. Fifty-eight percent of the women have husbands with at least one graduate degree, whereas only 24% of the men have wives with at least one graduate degree; 45% of the wives have a bachelor's degree and 35% of the husbands have such a degree; 17% of the wives and 5% of the husbands have no university training. (The operation of this mating gradient means, incidentally, that women with high educational attainment have a smaller pool of potential mates.)

B) *Data Limitations*

The data on which this analysis is based were compiled from questionnaires and tape-recorded interviews. The data are part of a larger study of doctoral students which focused on the professional socialization process of graduate education in Canada (Hitchman, 1976). Since the data were collected from two graduate schools in one province in Canada, the analysis is essentially a case study, and one should be cautious about generalizing to the total population of Canadian graduate students. However, the study provides a first step in analyzing the intersection of the two institutional spheres of education and the family in Canada.

The data collection was limited to responses given by the graduate students themselves, and no information was elicited from spouses. Hence, a perceptual bias may exist in our sample. The only information on the respective spouses is given by the respondents, and relates to the amount of responsibility taken for house management and child care. We have no data on the actual time spent on different tasks by the respective spouses of the respondents, and therefore, the nature of the marital

---

4 The corresponding data for graduate students from other income groups as well as for university undergraduates and community college students are as follows:

Distribution of Post-Secondary Students by Parents' Income, Academic Year 1968–69

Family Income Group	% University Graduate	% University Undergraduate	% Community College
Less than $ 2,000	1.4	1.0	0.9
2,000–2,999	5.1	4.1	4.3
3,000–3,999	6.7	4.9	6.3
4,000–4,999	4.8	6.2	8.8
5,000–6,999	21.1	20.7	29.7
7,000–7,999	21.7	24.6	27.0
10,000 and over	39.2	38.5	23.0
	100.0	100.0	100.0

Source: Hiller 1976: 54.

division of labour is seen through the eyes of the respondents. Another shortcoming of the data arises from the fact that the men and women in the sample are members of different marital pairs.[5] Hence, we have no data on actual couples. Moreover, time-use refers to average hours spent per week, with no breakdown by workday or weekend day. Hence, estimates tend to be rather crude.

However, in spite of these limitations, our data are superior to some in that we have not only the responses of wives, but also those of husbands, albeit of different marital pairs. Hence, a comparison is possible between husbands' opinions and the perspectives of wives engaged in the same educational pursuits. Commenting on the merits of this method of data collection, Safilios-Rothschild points out (1969: 249)

> Although such a sampling does not permit the matching of answers of husbands and wives married to each other, it permits the comparison of husbands' opinions, judgements, and evaluations with those of (unrelated) wives so that the derived family patterns (descriptive or dynamic) are not based solely upon wives' perceptions.

C) *The Variables*

This paper considers the effects of graduate education on the institution of the family, specifically on the sexual division of labour. Studies of graduate students are rare in Canada, and those considering the variable of marital status are even less frequent. Moreover, the case of women as graduate students has seldom been explored. American data (Feldman, 1973, 1974) suggest that marriage may have differential effects on graduate education for women. Similar results have been found in Canada (Hitchman, 1976). However, in this paper we wish to reverse the dependent and independent variables and consider, not the effects of marriage on graduate education, but rather the effects of graduate education on marriage. Thus, education is the independent variable and marriage type (i. e. egalitarian or non-egalitarian) is the dependent variable.

For the purpose of this analysis, indicators of egalitarianism in marriage include the sharing of household tasks, and if children are present, the sharing of child care. Four indicators are considered, two relating to the partitioning of houschold tasks, and two relating to child care. These are presented below.

1) "Who takes the *major* responsibility for managing the household?: I do; my partner/spouse does; shared equally; outside help."
2) "Approximately how many hours *per week* do you spend on house management/work?"
3) "Who takes the *major* responsibility for the care of your children?" I do; my partner/spouse does; shared equally; outside help."
4) "Approximately how many hours *per week* do you spend on child care?"

5 It should be noted, however, that this is not a problem for the statistical analysis undertaken in the paper. Indeed, independent samples are necessary for the use of the chi-squared tests shown in Tables 4 and 6.

Two phenomena are being considered here. One refers to *perceptions* of egalitarianism in the division of labour in the home. The other concerns the *actual time spent* on this labour. Hence, by using these two types of indicators, we can compare perceptions of egalitarianism with actual behaviour.

Results

In order to obtain a clearer picture of the processes at work in the intersection of the educational and marital spheres, the analysis is broken down by the occupational status of the spouses. Three possible marital arrangements are isolated: i) spouse employed in paid labour in the public sphere; ii) spouse not employed in the public sphere—either a housewife, househusband or unemployed; iii) spouse also a student. Table 3 shows the distribution of respondents in each category. Approximately three-quarters of the spouses of male graduate students (74%) and four-fifths of the spouses of female graduate students (81%) are employed in wage labour in the public sphere.

Table 3

Spouse's Occupation by Sex of Respondent

Occupation of Spouse	Males %	Females %
Employed in Paid Labour	74	81
Not Employed Outside the Home	9	1
Student	17	18
Total %	100	100
Total N*	88	68

* Ns vary due to varying response rates.

Nine percent of the wives and 1% of the husbands of graduate students are not employed outside the home, and 17% of the spouses of male graduate students and 18% of the spouses of female graduate students are themselves students. Hence 18% of the sample consists of dual-student marriages. The very few numbers of families with one spouse not gainfully employed nor engaged in educational pursuits are not surprising. Since graduate students are generally poorly funded in Canada, it is usually necessary for at least one spouse to be earning an income.[6] Indeed, many

---

6 The approximate income of graduate students before taxes in 1973 was minimal, indeed. Almost one-half of the sample (49%; 45% of men and 54% of women) reported annual incomes of $ 3,999.00 or less. Over four-fifths (85%) of the sample (84% men; 87% women) reported annual incomes of less than $ 6, 999.00 for themselves alone. It is little wonder that most of the respondents have spouses bringing in a wage of some sort.

graduate students live below the poverty line.[7] In the case of the female graduate student, and generally in the case of most wives, it is the norm for the husband to be employed. In the case of the male graduate student, many women are engaged in supporting their husbands economically if they do not have independent careers of their own.

For the purposes of this paper we shall consider those families where the spouse of the graduate student respondent is employed in paid labour outside the home, or where he/she is a student. This choice reflects expediency, since there are too few cases in the group where the spouse is not employed to make accurate comparisons.

A) *The Sexual Division of Labour and Household Tasks*

Table 4 presents two sets of data, placed together for easy comparison. The first set of data, listed in the two columns on the left, concerns the degree of perceived egalitarianism in the marriage. This is measured by the degree of sharing of the household management. The second set of data, appearing under the columns "Hours Spent per Week" refers to the reported number of hours spent per week by men and women on household tasks. The table presents this information for the sample as a whole, and also controls for the occupation of the spouse.

For the sample as a whole, there is a statistically significant difference between men and women in the degree of perceived egalitarianism in their respective marriages. More men than women report egalitarian marriages, that is, marriages where the responsibility for managing the household is shared equally. Two-thirds of the men but only 46% of the women make this claim. Moreover, many more women graduate students than men take the major responsibility for housework; 53% of women as compared to 15% of men. Similarly, 19% of men but only 1% of women state that their spouse is the major caretaker of the household. It is enlightening to compare the perceptions of egalitarianism with actual hours spent on household labour. In general, graduate student women average 17.9 hours per week, as compared to 9.3 hours for men ($p<.001$) (not shown in table). Moreover, regardless of the occupation of the spouse, and excepting those cases where the respondents suggest that the spouse takes the major responsibility for this labour, women report spending more time on housework than do men. For example, when the spouse is employed, and the respondent states that he/she is the major housekeeper, women report spending 22.9 hours per week on these tasks, as compared to 11.1 hours for men ($p<.01$). When the respondent states that the labour is shared equally, women spend 16.3 hours and men 10.1 hours per week on domestic labour ($p<.05$). Similar differences are

---

7 The Canadian Senate Special Committee on Poverty estimated that in 1969, the poverty line income for a family of two was $ 3,570. It was estimated at $ 4,290 for a family of three, $ 5,000 for a family of four and $ 6,570 for a family of 5 or more (Marchak, 1975: 19).

Table 4

Male and Female Perceptions of Egalitarianism, and the Total Hours Spent on Housework by Respondent Controlling for Spouse's Occupation

Perceived Egalitarianism Major Responsibility for Managing the Household Taken by:	Males %	Females %	Hours Spent per Week		
			Males %	Females %	Mann-Whitney U.
Total Sample					
Respondent	15	53	10.4	19.9	.01
Spouse	19	1	7.1	5.0	N.S.
Shared equally	66	46	9.8	16.3	.01
Total, percent	100	100			
Total, number	94	70			
	$\chi^2 = 31.9$ p<.001				
Spouse a Student					
Respondent	7	75	10.0	12.6	N.S.
Spouse	7	0	5.0	—	
Shared equally	86	25	10.4	16.7	.06
Total, percent	100	100			
Total, number	15**	12			
Spouse Employed					
Respondent	14	48	11.1	22.9	.01
Spouse	20	2	7.3	5.0	N.S.
Shared equally	66	50	10.1	16.3	.05
Total, percent	100	100			
Total, number	64	54			
	$\chi^2 = 21.0$ p<.001				
Spouse Not Employed					
Respondent	3	0	10.0	—	
Spouse	49	0	6.8	—	
Shared equally	48	100	7.8	7.0	N.S.
Total, percent	100	100			
Total, number*	8**	1			

* Ns vary due to varying response rates.
** Cell size too small for χ^2 test.

found for dual-student marriages, although the differences are smaller in the case where the respondent states that he/she is the major housekeeper.

By way of comparison, female faculty stand in a similar relation to their male counterparts as do female to male graduate students. In a study done on the status of women at one Canadian university (York University, 1975) it was found that the average number of hours spent on household chores was greater for female academics (9.93) than for their male counterparts (6.61). Moreover, the number of hours reported by males for their spouses (16.13) was approximately four times that of the spouses of female respondents (4.37).

A comparison of different marital arrangements according to the occupation of the spouses suggests some interesting findings. As Table 4 shows, regardless of the employment status of the spouse, more men than women report egalitarian marriages. Let us look more closely at these marital arrangements.

i) *Dual-Student Families:* Little research has been done on dual-career families, among which we might classify dual-student families. Notable exceptions are the works of Rapoport and Rapoport (1971), Holmstrom (1972), and Poloma and Garland (1971). Examination of the sexual division of labour in these families reveals changes in the traditional pattern of man the breadwinner and woman the child-rearer. However, even though more men are sharing in tasks traditionally assigned to the women and performed in the private sphere of the home, husbands still consider the performance of this work as "helping" their wives. In short, the main responsibility for labour in the private sphere still rests with the wife.

In our study, although we have only 27 cases in the category of dual-student families (families where both partners are students), it is instructive to compare the situations of women and men graduate students. Among this group, 86% of the men and 25% of the women report egalitarian marriages. Less than one man out of ten takes the major responsibility for the household tasks, whereas three-quarters of the women do so. However, regardless of the stated egalitarianism in the household, women still report spending more time on housework than their male counterparts. This is particularly evident in the case of perceived egalitarian marriages, where men devote 10.4 hours per week to this labour and women devote 16.7 hours ($p<.06$).

ii) *Spouse Employed:* For this subgroup, statistically significant differences appear between men and women with respect to perceptions of egalitarianism within marriage. When the spouse of the graduate student is employed in paid labour, two-thirds of the men and one-half of the women state that their marriages are egalitarian. However, these women spend 16.3 hours per week on housework while the men spend 10.1 hours ($p<.05$). Graduate student women still do the bulk of the household chores with 48% of them taking the major responsibility for this work. Only 14% of the men in this status do so. Moreover, even when the respondents state that they do the majority of the housework, women spend twice as many hours per week as men (22.9 for women as compared to 11.1 for men ($p<.01$)) on this labour.

Another way to address the question of the effects of graduate education on the sexual division of labour in marriage is to focus on the husband's position, and the possible constraints it may put on egalitarianism in marriage. In order to do this, the data are regrouped to create a marriage typology consisting of three types, namely, husband-employed/wife student (HE/WS), dual-student marriage (HS/WS) and ihusband-student/wife employed (HS/WE). Student marriages in which the spouse is not employed are omitted due to the small number of cases in this category. In the HS/WS category, both male-respondent-student/spouse-student and female-espondent-student/spouse-student groups are included.

Considering the probable contribution of the husband to the performance of household tasks, one would expect the husband to make the greatest contribution in the HS/WE category, and the least in the HE/WS category. The dual student situation (HS/WS) would probably occupy an intermediary position. Hence, ranking the potential contribution of the husband to household management from most to least, the pattern would be as follows: HS/WE, HS/WS, HE/WS. Such a ranking is suggested, taking into consideration time scheduling constraints of both graduate study and employment in the paid labour force. This analysis allows us to consider the effect of marriage type, and hence the husband's position (whether employed in the paid labour force, or a student) on the reported division of household tasks.

Table 5 presents the data regrouped by marriage type. It may be seen that the proportion of husbands assuming major responsibility for household management is about nine times greater when the husband is a student and the wife is employed than when the husband is employed and the wife is a student, or when both spouses are students.

Table 5

Major Responsibility for Managing Household by Marriage Type

Marriage Type	Major Responsibility for Managing Household Taken By:			
	Husband %	Wife %	Shared Equally %	Total %
HE/WS	9	54	31	37
HS/WS	9	19	20	19
HS/WE	82	27	49	44
TOTAL %	100	100	100	100
TOTAL N	11	48	86	145

Legend: HE/WS Husband employed, wife a student
HS/WS Dual-student marriages
HS/WE Husband a student, wife employed

In the case of the household management as the primary responsibility of the wife, this occurs more often in the HE/WS group than in either the HS/WS group or the HS/WE group. Moreover, the household labour is shared equally more often when the wife is employed and the husband is a student, than when the reverse is the case.

Comparing the percentages given in Table 5, more egalitarianism in marriage, that is, more husband-sharing in the labour in the home, occurs among those graduate student marriages where conditions are most favourable, that is, where the husband is a student, and the wife employed in the paid labour force. In this case, the husband's schedule is more flexible, and he may in fact spend more time in the home. One might also suggest, using the resource theory (Blood and Wolfe, 1960), that the employment status of the wife gives her more power, resulting in more sharing of household labour between spouses.

B) *The presence of Children and the Sharing of Child Care*

One of the guiding principles of the Royal Commission on the Status of Women in Canada states that "the care of children is a responsibility to be shared by the mother, the father and society" (Report of the Royal Commission on the Status of Women in Canada, 1973: xii). However, in spite of this policy statement, the Report goes on to acknowledge that in Canadian society, the major responsibility for child care continues to rest with the mother. Fathers may "help" with child care, but mothers are still expected to be the primary caretakers. When children are sick, for example, if both parents work outside the home, it is the mother who is expected to tend the child. Moreover, as Eichler (1975: 224) points out, this sexual division of labour is manifested in Canadian welfare legislation, where child allowances are usually paid to the mother rather than to the father.

The maternal responsibility for child care is also seen in the data presented by Meissner *et al.* (1975: 432). In their time-budget study, wives reported spending 43% of their time in child care, as compared to 21% spent by the husband. Wives estimated 3.3 weekly hours[8] spent on child care, while men estimated 0.9 hours engaged in this labour.

It is a well-known fact that in Canadian society, the nature and organization of the family unit is radically altered with the arrival of children. In the case where one or more of the parents is a graduate student, the presence of children can be a heavy burden. It is therefore not surprising to find that most of the respondents (69%) are childless. It is interesting, nonetheless, that slightly more women (36%) than men (27%) have children. Other studies (Bernard, 1964; Patterson, 1971; Rossi, 1965) have shown that female university professors are less often married and have fewer children than their male counterparts. Trends appear to be changing, and although a small difference is still found in terms of marital status, with more women being single, the married women in our sample have slightly more children than married men. These data suggest a modification in the role of women. In the past, women were forced to choose between the career role and the wife-mother role. This no longer appears to be the case, and young women are combining both roles to a greater extent than before.

This changing trend is also evident in the general Canadian population, where the increase in female participation in the labour force is primarily due to the influx of married women, and those with children. In 1964, 14.5% of the total labour force was made up of married women. This figure increased to 17.8% in 1969 and to 19.7% in 1974. In 1964, 24.1% of married women were in the labour force, and the figure increased to 31.2% in 1969 and 36.7% in 1974 (Information Canada, 1975: 29). Moreover, for those same years, married women comprised 51.1%, 55.8% and

---

8 Estimated weekly hours were computed as the sum of five times the average workday hours and two times the average weekend-day hours.

57.1% of the female labour force (Information Canada, 1975: 31). The proportion of women with children in the labour force in Canada has also been on the increase. In 1967, for example, 20% of all mothers were in the labour force (Royal Commission on the Status of Women, 1973: 263), while by 1973 this figure had risen to 35.1% (Information Canada, 1975: 269).

Respondents in this sample average 0.5 children (men average 0.4; women 0.6). The number of children among the graduate students sampled is considerably lower than that of the general population, which was 1.7 children per family in 1971 (Perspective Canada, 1974: 23). Sixty-nine percent of the respondents (73% of the men and 64% of the women) are childless, as compared to only 30.5% of the Canadian population (Wakil and Wakil, 1976: 392). Seventeen percent of the sample (18% of men; 15% of women) have one child, while the statistic for the general population is 20.6. Ten percent of the respondents and 21.2% of the general population have two children, 3% of respondents and 13.4% of the general population have three children, 1% of the sample and 7.2% of the population have four children, while none of the sample, but 7.1% of the general population has five or more children.

In the subsample of 52 respondents with children, 92% of the men (N=24) and 65% of the women (N=17) have children under five years of age. Twenty-three percent of men (N=6) and 35% of women (N=9) have children between five and fourteen years of age, and 15% of the women (N=4) but none of the men, have children fifteen years of age or older. It appears that more women than men wait until their children are older before embarking on graduate education. This is consistent with the prevailing ideology in Canada that the place of the mother is with her children when they are small (Gibbins, Ponting, and Symons, 1978). The care of pre-school children is still the prime responsibility of the woman.

Table 6 presents the degree of perceived egalitarianism with respect to child care and the total hours spent per week on this task, for men and women, controlling for the spouse's occupation. All reports of hours spent refer to work done by the respondent. As was the case with the household work, among the sample as a whole, female graduate students are much more likely than their male counterparts to take the major responsibility for the care of the children. This is consistent with the statement of Perrucci and Targ (1974) that regardless of the degree of egalitarianism in marriage before children, a more traditional sexual division of labour appears when children arrive. Sixty-five percent of the women and only 12% of the men state that they are the major caretakers of children. Forty-five percent of the men and 31% of the women state that their marriages are egalitarian in this regard. Moreover, 39% of the men, but none of the women state that their spouse is the major caretaker of children. Four percent of both men and women have outside help taking the major responsibility for the care of the children. This low proportion is of course not surprising, given the high cost of paid domestic labour in Canada. Female graduate students average 21.4 hours per week on child care, and their male counterparts

Table 6

Male and Female Perceptions of Egalitarianism, and The Total Hours Spent on Child Care by Respondent Controlling for Spouse's Occupation

Perceived Egalitarianism Major Responsibility for Child Care Taken By:	Male %	Females %	Hours Males %	Spent per Females %	Week Mann-Whitney U.
Total Sample					
Respondent	12	65	20.0	22.1	N.S.
Spouse	39	0	8.4	—	
Shared equally	45	31	16.6	23.4	.05
Outside help	4	4	11.0	20.0	N.S.
Total, percent	100	100			
Total, number	26**	26			
Spouse a Student					
Respondent	0	0	—	—	
Spouse	0	0	—	—	
Shared equally	100	0	9.0	—	
Outside help	0	0	—	—	
Total, percent	100	0			
Total, number	2**	0			
Spouse Employed					
Respondent	19	67	20.0	23.1	N.S.
Spouse	21	0	8.5	—	
Shared Equally	54	29	18.0	22.7	N.S.
Outside help	6	4	11.0	20.0	N.S.
Total, percent	100	100			
Total, number	16**	24			
Spouse Not Employed					
Respondent	0	0	—	—	
Spouse	83	0	8.3	—	
Shared equally	17	100	20.0	28.0	N.S.
Outside help	0	0	—	—	
Total, percent	100	100			
Total, number*	7**	1			

* Ns vary due to varying response rates.
** Cell size too small for χ^2 test.

average 11.4 (0<.01) (not shown in table). Moreover, it is interesting to note that even when both male and female respondents state that child care is shared equally, women spend significantly more time on these tasks than do men (23.4 hours for women as compared to 16.6 hours for men ($p<.05$)).

Similar results have been found for female academics (York University, 1975). Among those sampled, women faculty report spending 19.45 hours per week on child care, as compared to 10.36 hours reported by male faculty. Women faculty spend almost twice as much time in this activity as do men. Moreover, male respondents reported that their spouses spend 29.33 hours per week on child care, as compared to 9.96 hours for the spouses of female faculty—about one-third the time of spouses of male faculty.

In this sample of graduate students, controlling for the employment status of the spouse, all but 10 of the respondents with children have spouses who are working. The situation becomes complicated by the occupation of the spouse. If the spouse is not employed outside the home, one would expect that more time is spent on housework and child care than if the spouse is working, or is a student. Do we see any sex differences here? It is worthy of note that only two of the respondents, both males, have student spouses, and have children. Both say that they and their wives share child care equally. Moreover, they average 9 hours per week in child care. It would appear that their wives are carrying a much heavier load, since child care is surely more than an eighteen hour a week job. Moreover, it is not surprising that this category is devoid of full-time doctoral candidates and contains only two males. The financial burden of such a situation is most likely too much for the majority of graduate students to shoulder, not to mention the time burden of child care coupled with graduate study, as well as the uncertainty of the future. Since there are so few respondents in the categories of spouse not employed and spouse a student, a comparison of the three categories is not undertaken.

Conclusion

This analysis has demonstrated that the intersection of the two institutional spheres of education and the family does not necessarily produce egalitarianism in marriage, nor freedom and change from traditional sex roles for women. The articulation of the sexual division of labour in the public and private spheres is very much in evidence. In terms of the adaptive partnership/dependent labour typology set out by Meissner *et al* (1975), the dependent labour theory most closely approximates the norm among graduate students in this Canadian sample.

Hence, we are presented with a paradox. According to Eichler (1975: 225, 226), one should expect to find more egalitarian (that is, more adaptive partnership) marriages in dual-career families, i.e., families in which both spouses work, have some form of independent income, and have a high degree of education. Except for 9 cases in our sample, the respondents possess these characteristics.[9] Yet, we have found that not an adaptive partnership, but rather a dependent labour model applies. Even in a particularly highly educated population such as this one, women still do the majority of the household and child care tasks. Moreover, women spend more hours per week engaged in this type of labour than do their male counterparts. Hence, the husband's position may be seen as a barrier for the development of egalitarian marriages.

---

9 Here we are loosely defining "work" to include graduate study, and "income" to include graduate student stipends.

However, comparing marriage types, we do see degrees of egalitarianism, with greater sharing of household labour being found in those marriages where the husband is a student and the wife is employed in the paid labour force. The least amount of sharing exists when the reverse is the case, that is, when the wife is a student and the husband is employed. Dual-student marriages fall somewhere in between these two poles.

It is interesting to note the responses of the graduate students themselves, both men and women, with respect to the effects of the intersection of the educational and marital spheres in their lives. One male student, atypical, as our data show, makes the following statement.

> Marriage affects my academic career ... Being married, I want to give some of my time to my wife ... As an undergraduate I would spend a lot of time working at night, late at night and 24 hours a day type of thing. I find I can't do this quite as easily since I'm married. There are responsibilities, plus household responsibilities and this kind of thing which do take some time, a fair amount of time ... My wife works and she often works evenings. ... Plus she has a lot of paper work so she usually ends up working at least two nights a week plus she takes courses and I feel since I'm at home, that well, since I'm at home much of the household responsibility ends up on me. I've always done the cooking, ... I always do the laundry and groceries and housecleaning. It gets left often times. Much of this type of household stuff I end up doing simply because I'm there. And I've got a little more flexible schedule. She may be working up until 9 or 10 at night and it's no fun to end up having to come home and do the dishes. If I've got time I'll do them. It's easier for me to fix a meal and have it ready when she gets home than to have her get home and do it. Besides, I think I'm a better cook, so does she. So I end up doing more of the household stuff really, which I feel is in some sense fair. I've got more time, in one sense, since I'm home most of the time. And she's doing a good part of the supporting right now.

As a conclusion, here is a quote from an interview with a woman graduate student, who sums up rather pointedly the condition of graduate student women in Canada and the sexual division of labour in the family. This comment provides a radical critique of the intersection of the educational and marital sectors in Canada today.

> I think that careers as we know them are set up for male heads of families. The reason I say this is because the things that are demanded of people to succeed, either at the university, or out in business are so awful and arduous that they can hardly be done by anybody who doesn't have a back-up group in the form of a wife and children to give him emotional support for one thing, and secondly to do all the shit-work that he needs to keep going, the housework and other things which he otherwise would have to do himself. So when a woman tries to play the same game, she runs into a lot of problems because she doesn't have this back-up.
> My criticism of this whole set-up is very radical ... As a feminist and a socialist I think that productive work should be balanced off with what you might call reproductive work. Individuals should only be required to do what they are able to do on their own behalf, and they should demand the services of other people. Occupations will have to be completely redefined or restructured. The way I apply it to myself is that I share the housework and the child care with the man. I also plan out my academic work, in what I consider a sensible manner. I think it's a phony ideal for people to be wholly immersed in some job to the exclusion of their personal life. I think it's important to recognize the value of all areas of life.

REFERENCES

Acker, Sandra
    1974   "A comparison of ambition of men and women graduate students at an American university." Paper presented at the VIIIth World Congress of Sociology, Toronto.

Adam, June
    1971   "A profile of women in Canadian universities." A paper prepared for the A.U.C.C. 1971 Annual Meeting.

Ambert, A. M. and G. Symons Hitchman
    1976   "A case study of status differential: women in academia" pp. 113-146 in A. M. Ambert, *Sex Structure*. Don Mills: Longman, 2nd edition.

Astin, Helen S.
    1969   *The Woman Doctorate in America*. New York: Russell Sage Foundation.

Bailyn, Lotte
    1971   "Career and family orientations of husbands and wives in relation to marital happiness" pp. 545-567 in A. Theodore (ed.), *The Professional Woman*. Cambridge, Mass.: A. Schenkman.

Benston, M.
    1969   "The political economy of women's liberation." *Monthly Review* 21 (4) (September): 13-27.

Bernard, Jessie
    1964   *Academic Women*. University Park, Pennsylvania: Pennsylvania State University Press.
    1971   *Women and the Public Interest*. Chicago: Aldine-Atherton.

Black, N.
    1974   "Women and post-secondary education in Ontario." Paper prepared for the Ontario Status of Women Council.

Blood, R. O. and D. M. Wolfe
    1960   *Husbands and Wives*. Glencoe, Ill.: Free Press.

Bowen, N.
    1973   "The academic woman and the Canadian university." *University Affairs* (July): 2-3.

Brinkerhoff, M. and E. Lupri
    1978   "Theoretical and methodological issues in the use of decision-making as an indicator of conjugal power: some Canadian observations." *The Canadian Journal of Sociology* 3 (1): 1-20.

Davids, Leo
    1976   "North American marriage: 1990" pp. 426-436 in L. E. Larson (ed.), *The Canadian Family in Comparative Perspective*. Scarborough: Prentice-Hall.

Davis, J. A.
    1962   *Stipends and Spouses*. Chicago: Aldine.

Dominion Bureau of Statistics
    1944   *Higher Education in Canada 1940-42*. Ottawa.
    1946   *Higher Education in Canada 1942-44*. Ottawa.
    1956   *Survey of Higher Education 1952-54*. Ottawa.

Eichler, M.
    1975   "The egalitarian family in Canada?" pp. 223-235 in S. Parvez Wakil (ed.), *Marriage, Family and Society: Canadian Perspectives*. Toronto: Butterworth.

Eichler, M. et al.
    1973   *The Report of the President's Advisory Committee on Equal Rights for Women and Men*. Supplement to *The University of Waterloo Gazette*. Wednesday, November 21.

Elkin, F.
    1964   *The Family in Canada*. Ottawa: Canadian Conference on the Family.

Epstein, C. F.
    1971   "Encountering the male establishment: sex-status limits on women's careers in the professions" pp. 52-73 in A. Theodore (ed.), *The Professional Woman*. Cambridge, Mass.: Schenkman.

Farley, J.
   1970 "Graduate women: career aspirations and desired family size." *American Psychologist* 25 (12) (December): 1099–1100.
Feldman, S. D.
   1973 "Impediment or stimulant? marital status and graduate education" pp. 220–232 in J. Huber (ed.), *Changing Women in a Changing Society*. Chicago: University of Chicago Press.
   1974 *Escape from the Doll's House. Women in Graduate and Professional School Education*. New York: McGraw-Hill.
Garland, T. N.
   1972 "The better half? the male in the dual profession family" pp. 199–215 in C. Safilios-Rothschild (ed.), *Toward a Sociology of Women*. Lexington, Mass.: Xerox.
Gendell, Murray
   1963 *Swedish Working Wives*. Ottawa: Bediminster.
Gibbins, R., J. R. Ponting and G. L. Symons
   1978 "Attitudes and ideology: correlates of liberal attitudes towards the role women." *Journal of Comparative Family Studies* 9 (1) (Spring): 19–40.
Hiller, Harry H.
   1976 *Canadian Society: A Sociological Analysis*. Scarborough, Ontario: Prentice-Hall of Canada.
Hitchman, G. Symons
   1974 "A report on the reports: the status of women in Canadian universities." *Canadian Sociology and Anthropology Association Bulletin* (October): 11–13.
   1976 "The professional socialization of women and men in two Canadian graduate schools." Unpublished doctoral dissertation. Toronto: York University.
Hobart, Charles W.
   1973 "Egalitarianism after marriage" pp. 168–156 in Marylee Stephenson (ed.), *Women in Canada*. Toronto: New Press.
Holmstrom, L. L.
   1972 *The Two-Career Family*. Cambridge, Mass.: Schenkman.
Husbands, S. A.
   1972 "Women's place in higher education." *School Review* 80: 261–274.
Information Canada
   1975 *Women in the Labour Force: Facts and Figures*. Ottawa: Information Canada.
Lupri, Eugen
   1969 "Contemporary authority patterns in the West German family. A study in cross-national validation." *Journal of Marriage and the Family*. (February): 134–144.
   1976 "Gesellschaftliche Differenzierung und familiale Autorität", pp. 323–352 in Eugen Lupri and Günther Lüschen (eds.), Soziologie der Familie. Zweite Auflage. Köln: Westdeutscher Verlag.
Marchak, Patricia M.
   1975 *Ideological Perspectives on Canada*. Toronto: McGraw-Hill Ryerson.
MacLellan, M. E.
   1972 "History of women's rights in Canada." *Study #8* of the *Report of the Royal Commission on the Status of Women in Canada*. Ottawa: Queen's Printer.
Meissner, Martin, E. W. Humphrey, S. M. Meis, and W. J. Scheu
   1975 "No exit for wives: sexual division of labour and the cumulation of household demands." *The Canadian Review of Sociology and Anthropology* 12 (4): 424–439.
Michel, Andrée
   1970 "Statut professionnel féminin et interaction dans le couple en France et aux Etats-Unis" pp. 281–91 in A. Michel (ed.), *La Sociologie de la Famille; Recueil de Textes Présentés et Commentés*. Paris: Mouton.
Parsons, T. and R. F. Bales (eds.)
   1955 *Family Socialization and Interaction Process*. Glencoe, Ill.: Free Press.

Patterson, M.
   1971 "Alice in wonderland: a study of women faculty in graduate departments of sociology." *American Sociologist* 6 (August): 226–234.

Perrucci, Carolyn C. and Dena B. Targ (eds.)
   1974 *Marriage and the Family – A Critical Analysis and Proposals for Change.* New York: David McKay.

Perspective Canada
   1974 Ottawa: Information Canada.

Poloma, M. M. and T. N. Garland
   1971 "The myth of the egalitarian family: family roles and the professionally employed wife", pp. 741–761 in A. Theodore (ed.), *The Professional Woman.* Cambridge, Mass.: Schenkman.

Price-Bonham, Sharon
   1973 "Student husbands versus student couples." *Journal of Marriage and the Family* (February): 33–37.

Queen's University
   1974 *Report of the Principal's Committee on the Status of Women at Queen's University.* A supplement to Volume VI, Number 9, Thursday, February 28.

Rapoport, R. and R. Rapoport
   1971 *Dual-Career Families.* Harmondsworth, England: Penguin.

Report of the Royal Commission on the Status of Women in Canada
   1973 Ottawa: Information Canada.

Rodman, Hyman
   1967 "Marital power in France, Greece, Yugoslavia, and the United States: a cross-national discussion." *Journal of Marriage and the Family,* 29: 2 (May): 320–324.
   1972 "Marital power and the theory of resources in cultural context." *Journal of Comparative Family Studies* 3 (1): 50–69.

Rossi, Alice
   1965 "Barriers to the career choice of engineering, medicine or science among American women". pp. 51-127 in J. A. Mattfeld and C. G. Van Aken (eds.), *Women and the Scientific Professions.* Cambridge, Mass.: MIT Press.

Safilios-Rothschild, C.
   1969 "Family sociology or wives' family sociology? A cross-cultural examination of decision-making." *Journal of Marriage and the Family* 31 (May): 290–301.
   1970 "The study of family power structure: a review 1960–1969." *Journal of Marriage and the Family* 32 (November): 539–552.

Smith, Dorothy
   1973 "Women, the family and corporate capitalism" pp. 2–35 in Marylee Stephenson (ed.), *Women in Canada.* Toronto: New Press.

Statistics Canada
   1977a *Degrees, Diplomas and Certificates Awarded by Universities, 1975.* Catalogue 81-211. Ottawa (November).
   1977b *Fall Enrolment in Universities 1974–75.* Catalogue 81-204. (February).
   1977c *Teachers in Universities. Part III. Qualifications and Age, 1972–73 and 1974–75.* Catalogue 81-243. Ottawa (April).

Vickers, Jill and June Adam
   1977 *But Can You Type? Canadian Universities and the Status of Women.* Buffalo and London: Clarke, Irwin & Company.

Wakil, S. P. and E. A. Wakil
   1976 "Marriage and family in Canada: a demographic-cultural profile", pp. 380–407 in K. Ishwaran (ed.), *The Canadian Family* Revised. Toronto: Holt, Rinehart and Winston.

York University
    1975 *Report of the Senate Task Force on the Status of Women at York University.* Toronto.
Young, M. and P. Willmott
    1973 *The Symmetrical Family: A Study of Work and Leisure in the London Region.* London: Routledge.

Wife and/or Worker

*Sex Role Concepts of Canadian Female Students**

ANN B. DENIS

University of Ottawa, Ottawa, Canada

IN THIS PAPER, female role concepts of Canadian women post-secondary students are examined, together with the ethnic differences in their prevalence. Since the major thrust of the study to which this paper pertains is students' educational and occupational aspirations, the roles of primary concern here are those of wife-mother and participant in the paid labour force. The extent to which these are conceived of as contradictory, complementary or unrelated roles is also considered, with comparisons being made among the ethnic categories. Finally, the implications of these preferences for the nature of the family and female participation in the labour force will also be examined.

One variable affecting aspirations for adult life is the nature of behaviour deemed appropriate for one's sex. A person's concept of appropriate sex role behaviour will be influenced both by the socialization experiences undergone from childhood through to adulthood and by structural features of the society which may facilitate or impede the playing of certain roles. The primary agents of socialization in contemporary Canadian society are the family and the school. A body of research on sex role socialization in the schools is beginning to develop (Rowbotham, no date; Pyke, 1975; Jean, 1974) but the work on current sex role socialization in the Canadian family is less developed.

Sex Role Socialization in the Schools

Sex role socialization can occur in a number of direct and indirect ways in the schools. Perhaps the most pervasive are through the images conveyed by school textbooks and through the differential expectations made of male and female students. Analyses of school tests (Rowbotham, no date; Pyke, 1975) document that male

---

* The research on which this chapter is based has been supported by Canada Council Research Grants Nos. 573-0462 and 575-0243, and by the Humanities Research Fund, University of Ottawa. These supports are gratefully acknowledged.

characters are more numerous than female ones and play more varied and active roles. Adult females are typically housewives with secondary roles as far as the stories are concerned, while girls tend to be followers or observers. It has been suggested that these materials would encourage girls to envisage a relatively limited number of roles as being open to them other than that of housewife. Similarly vocational guidance material has tended to reinforce the sex stereotyping of possible occupations, with females either not in evidence at all or else in subordinate positions: the nurse for a male doctor; the technician for a male scientist; the secretary for a male business man or administrator. One might suspect that to the extent that this vocational material continues to be used, guidance counsellors do not find its contents unduly objectionable and in fact may themselves be reinforcing the stereotypes. That girls have been successfully encouraged to select relatively short-term programmes of study preparing them directly for the labour market is reflected in the sex ratios at the end of secondary school in contrast with those for universities. These effects of the school system will be experienced by all girls educated in Canada, regardless of ethnic origin.

Structural Variables

Some of the structural variables which might affect the social roles played by women are also common to all, while some will be differentially experienced by subcategories of the population.[1] Since we are dealing in very large part with students who have attended English language schools and have just completed their secondary studies, the differential availability of university preparatory programmes for francophone girls is not of significance here. Of general applicability are features of the social structure which inhibit the participation in the paid labour force of women with children. (Allingham and Spencer, 1968; Canadian Review of Sociology and Anthropology, 1975; Cook, 1976). Such features include the relatively rigid working hours; the difficulty of obtaining part-time, yet career-line, responsible jobs; the societal expectation that it is the mother who has primary responsibility for early socialization of children; the difficulty of arranging adequate alternatives to the mother's full-time presence in the home, particularly for young children; and the societal expectations that the wife adapt to and complement her husband's career rather than the reverse or some more equitable sharing of adaptation.

Sex Role Socialization in the Family

The family contributes to sex role socialization in two important ways: through the expectations communicated to the children by their relatives, notably their

---

[1] See the contribution of Eugen Lupri and Donald L. Mills in this volume.

parents, and through the role models and their evaluation which the children can observe within the family. Until the 1960's the emphasis in the socialization of women in North America was on the preparation for the roles of homemaker and mother. Except in cases of economic necessity, participation in the paid labour force was conceived of primarily as a prelude to child rearing, rather than as an accompaniment or alternative to it (Zay, 1974; Stephenson, 1973). This attitude was reflected in behaviour: there were low levels of participation in the paid labour force by married women, and most of these women were in low skill and low paying jobs; only rarely were they in highly skilled ones. In the past decade, labour force participation by married women has risen (Labour Canada, 1973; Cook, 1976), suggesting a shift from the wife-mother to member-of-the-paid-labour-force role by women, or a greater tendency to combine the two. Participation by married women in the labour force is most prevalent among younger women. It is, however, unclear whether the more extensive paid labour force participation is the result of perceived economic necessity, of a desire for economic independence from one's spouse, or because of the intrinsic attractions of working. In view of the structural difficulties experienced by married women who work, labour force participation motivated primarily by economic necessity is less likely to be positively evaluated than that due to other reasons. The fact of female participation in the paid labour force, then, is not necessarily associated with a positive evaluation of it.

The presence of a role model may make it easier for an individual to conceive of the particular role as a possible one for self. This is most likely to occur if the behaviour in question is positively evaluated by the person providing the role model and if this individual is one of the self's significant others. Where the person providing the role model negatively evaluates the behaviour in question, it is likely that self's evaluation of it will be even more negative than if no role model had existed. In the present case the mother is considered an important female role model for the female respondents with regard to paid labour force participation. It is argued that the presence of a role model (i.e., a mother who works) will be associated with either lower or higher degree of favourableness towards combining family and labour force roles than will the absence of a role model. Lower favourableness indicates the combination of behaviour with a negative evaluation of it, while higher favourableness indicates positive evaluation of the role model's behaviour.

Insofar as ethnic differences in sex role expectations and behaviour are concerned, we can consider both census and more qualitative data. Unfortunately, most labour force data on women do not distinguish concurrently by marital status and ethnic origin. We can, however, discover for selected ethnic origin categories the proportion of women aged 15–64 who are working, together with the percentage of these women who are in managerial and professional, clerical and sales, and manual occupations. We can also ascertain for the ethnic categories what proportion of men are in each of these occupational groupings. If high proportions of women are associated with high proportions of men and women in manual occupations, it is argued that economic necessity is probably a prime motivation for working, and that female labour force participation is not necessarily associated with a positive evaluation of this behaviour. Similarly, low rates of female participation in conjunction with male and female concentration in low status occupations are an indicator of a negative evaluation of female labour force participation. On the other hand, high female labour force participation in conjunction with higher percentages of males and/or females in high status occupations is more likely to be associated with a positive evaluation of women working, although this is probably less true with the inflation of the 1970's than it was previously. The comparison of the incidence of these variables among ethnic categories gives an indication of the more general prevalence of female labour force role models within each ethnic category and the evaluation of this role.

Table 1

Labour Force Participation by Ethnic Group, Quebec and Ontario, 1971

	British %	French %	German %	Italian %	Jewish %	Ukrainian %	Others %
Ontario 1971							
% Women aged 15–64 in labour force	50.6	42.9	49.6	45.8	50.5	52.7	45.5
% Women in labour force in:							
Managerial & Professional occupations	20.4	18.2	18.7	6.4	22.0	15.3	16.0
Clerical and Sales occupations	47.2	39.9	38.3	27.1	58.7	39.3	30.3
Manual occupations	32.4	41.9	43.0	66.6	19.4	45.4	53.7
Quebec 1971							
% Women aged 15–64 in labour force	42.9	35.7	42.9	44.5	46.2	43.1	41.4
% Women in labour force in:							
Managerial & Professional occupations	22.4	21.2	23.8	6.0	22.3	17.1	16.3
Clerical and Sales occupations	49.1	34.7	42.0	24.7	53.1	40.5	27.1
Manual occupations	28.6	44.1	34.2	69.3	24.6	42.4	46.7

From Table 1 we find that there is greater female labour force participation in Ontario than in Quebec, with the differences being most noticeable for those of French and Ukrainian origins. The only notable variation in participation among ethnic groups within a province is the low participation of the French. Apart from the

French then, there is little variation among ethnic categories in terms of the general prevalence of female labour force role models. In the previous two decades the amount of variation between participation rates was even lower, with less interprovincial variation. The French and especially the Jews had somewhat lower participation rates than the other ethnic groups. There is, however, as Table 1 shows, greater variation when one considers the occupational distribution of those who are working. Italian men and women are underrepresented in professional and managerial occupations, as are French men. The same phenomenon obtains for the Italians in clerical and sales occupations. The data suggest that economic necessity is a prime motivating factor in the case of the Italians; that those of French ethnic background tend to evaluate female labour force participation more negatively than do Canadians of other origins; and that the Jews, and perhaps also the British, tend to evaluate it more positively. Within the French category, however, it seems that the negative evaluation of work is less strong among the higher status French women.

Turning to qualitative evidence about female roles in the various ethnic groups, Rocher (1964) has suggested that the ideology which conceives of female labour force participation as a prelude to child rearing except in cases of economic necessity was stronger among the French than the English in Canada. In support of this he noted that "economic necessity" has seemed to imply a greater level of need before French women work than is the case for the British. On the other hand, Hobart's (1973) analysis of young people's attitudes suggests that regardless of the presence of role models young francophone women may be more positive than their anglophone counterparts to the idea of working. In the case of Italians, Danziger (1971) argues that female labour force participation is evidence of economic necessity, not of the internalization of new norms valuing women's working. This conclusion is supported by Grygier's (1975) data of fairly recent Italian immigrants. Jansen (1971) also notes the relatively high rate of labour force participation of Italian women, but does not draw conclusions about the dissonance between behaviour and values. If Danziger is correct, we could expect to find a combination of the existence of the role model and a negative evaluation of the combination of work and family for the Italians in the current study.

Grygier (1975) also noted a greater tendency on the part of British wives in his sample to work in Canada than had been the case in Britain, though no reasons for this were advanced. In contrast, fewer German women worked in Canada and Grygier suggested this might be due to less economic necessity to do so in Canada together with the higher status of women here. Similarly Ishwaran has observed (1971a; 1971b) that the norms for Dutch Canadians favour labour force participation by women only until marriage. Although it was the more educated Hungarian women who were likely to work in Canada, Grygier (1975) felt that economic constraints were still the main reason for Hungarian women working outside the home.

On the other hand, in an analysis of traditional and contemporary Jewish culture,

Latowsky (1971) noted that traditionally, performance of the wife-mother role has entailed the assumption of some economic responsibilities by the women. Although being a wife and mother takes precedence, this is not deemed to be necessarily inimical to activity in the paid labour force. Structural difficulties in doing so rather than value conflict would seem to be why more Jewish women do not combine the two.

Hypotheses

In the current analysis six ethnic categories are distinguished: British, French, Jewish, northern European (German and other northern European), southern European (Italian and other southern European), and Eastern European (Ukrainian and other eastern European). In terms of these broad groupings it is predicted from the above that there will be no differences among ethnic categories with regard to the favouring of the wife-mother role, and that southern Europeans will be significantly less and Jews significantly more in favour of women playing a professional role. Furthermore, it is hypothesised that Jews and eastern Europeans will be significantly more likely than other categories to favour combining the work and domestic roles, while southern Europeans and possibly the French will be less likely to, regardless of the role model provided by their mothers. For all ethnic categories except the southern European, it is hypothesized that regardless of ethnic origin, having a mother who is part of the labour force will be associated with a more favourable attitude toward combining work and a domestic role.

Data

The analysis is based on data from questionnaires completed by a random sample of 666 female students in their first year at Toronto and anglophone Montreal post-secondary institutions. Those in both university and technology programmes are included. The student's ethnic origin was determined using the Canadian census notion of the cultural or ethnic origin of the first male ancestor on the father's side to come to North America or the respondent's cultural origin if she had migrated to North America. This question has some conceptual limitations, which are explored elsewhere, but it does have the advantage of permitting comparisons between the sample and those of the same origin category in the total population. About 75% of the respondents were Canadian born, as were about half of their parents.

Analysis

In considering married women's roles, three scales relating to different aspects of women's role definition have been developed here and are used as the dependent variables. The first scale measures the degree of preference expressed by the respondent for playing the role of wife and mother. The second scale is based on the degree of preference by the respondent for holding a job outside the home (both being qualified to and actually doing so). For each scale there is a range of values from 0 (very negative) to 1 (highly positive). The third scale relates explicitly to the combining of work and family life, asking the respondent whether as a married woman she would prefer to work full-time, part-time, or have no outside job at three stages in her life: when she had no children, preschool children, and school-aged children. Responses are scored to reflect the type of effort or commitment to working implied in each combination, from 0 for no job with no children to 8 for a full-time job with preschool children. Summing the individual's scores for their preferences at these three stages of their life cycle produces a range of scores from 3 to 20. Low scores (3 to 12) indicate low commitment to combining work and family life, with part-time work being all that is preferred, even when the respondent is childless. Scores of 19 and 20 indicate high commitment, with full-time work being preferred either throughout or except while there are preschool children. Even with young children, at least part-time work is desired. Medium commitment, typically in the form of wanting to work full-time while childless, part-time with school age children and not all with preschoolers was the most frequent preference, indicating that the interrupted pattern of labour force participation remains popular with young women. Tables 2 to 4 summarize the distribution of respondents on the three scales by ethnicity.

Table 2

Ethnicity by Favouring the Wife-Mother Role, for Women

	British	French	Northern European	Southern European	Jewish	Eastern European	Total
Mean score	.82	.83	.76	.81	.83	.78	.81
s.d.	.27	.28	.32	.26	.22	.28	.27
$F=.77$. N.S.							

Table 3

Ethnicity by Preference for having an Outside Job, for Women

	British	French	Northern European	Southern European	Jewish	Eastern European	Total
Mean score	.87	.75	.88	.92	.92	.92	.88
s.d.	.28	.36	.26	.22	.20	.21	.27
$F=4.13$. Sig. $>.001$							

Table 4

Ethnicity by Combining Work and Family, for Women

	British	French	Northern European	Southern European	Jewish	Eastern European	Total
Degree of interest in doing so	%	%	%	%	%	%	%
Low (3–12)	10.0	22.2	11.4	17.1	14.5	7.3	10.7
Medium (13–18)	73.4	65.1	61.4	58.6	58.1	60.0	59.2
High (19–20)	16.6	12.7	27.3	24.6	27.4	32.7	18.3
Mean score	13.9	13.4	14.6	14.2	15.0	15.0	14.2
$F = 2.94$. Sig. $= .05$							

As predicted, women of all ethnic origins were quite uniformly in favour of playing the wife-mother role. They were, with the exception of the French, even more in favour of being able to work outside the home and here the ethnic differences were statistically significant. There is a mild negative correlation between the two scales (Tau $= .08$, $p = .02$), which in fact reflects the preponderance of the British in the sample, since the correlation is not even marginally significant for any other origin category, nor always negative. The roles are not, then, perceived as necessarily contradictory. The standard deviations indicate most homogeneity of attitude among the southern Europeans and eastern Europeans with regard to working and among the Jews on both scales. There are wider divergences in opinion about outside work among the French than for any other group on either scale.

Although the mean scores of the different ethnic categories do not differ significantly, on the scale for combining work with children, the distributions of responses do. The French are the least enthusiastic, while more of the noncharter groups are highly committed to the idea of combining work and children than either the French or the British are. The scale is positively correlated with being able to work outside the home (Tau $= .20$, $p > .001$) and negatively with playing the wife-mother role (Tau $= .22$, $p > .001$) for the whole sample. The direction of the correlations is the same for each of the ethnic groups individually, but at lower levels of significance, notably with the wife-mother scale, where the correlation is only significant at the .01 level for the British.

For the sample as a whole, there are no significant differences in wanting to be a wife and mother by any of the other independent variables—parents' occupations, parents' education and whether or not the mother works. On the other hand, those whose fathers have a lower status occupation are significantly more likely to favour the concept of the woman working ($.05 < p < .01$), as are those whose mothers work ($.01 < p < .001$). The remaining independent variables did not result in significant variations. Students whose mothers work are also significantly more likely to want to combine working and child-rearing, with no other variable resulting in significant variations for the whole sample.

For particular ethnic categories there were differing effects by the independent variables. None resulted in significant variations for particular ethnic categories in favouring the idea that women work. Southern European students of lower socio-economic background were significantly more likely to favour the wife-mother role than were those of higher socioeconomic background ($.01 < p < .001$ for each parent's occupation and $.05 < p < .01$ for mother's education). The reverse obtained for the British ($.05 < p < .01$ for father's occupation). British ($p > .001$) and Northern European ($.01 < p < .001$) students were significantly more likely to favour combining work and child-rearing if their mothers had done so. British students whose fathers' occupations were lower status were also more likely to favour doing so, as were students of southern European origins whose mothers had higher status occupations ($.05 < p < .01$ in both cases).

Discussion

Overall, then, this sample of well-educated young women strongly favours working, without at the same time rejecting the role of being a wife and mother. The perception of incompatibility between the roles is only significant for the British; some of the other groups do not even perceive the relation between the roles as negative. The favourable attitude towards working indicates some departure from the sex role norms portrayed in school texts. The variations in preference for these roles among those of different socio-economic status and ethnicity are not great, nor do they necessarily go in the same directions. As hypothesised, Jews were the most favourable to the notion of combining child-rearing and labour force participation, but the Eastern Europeans were equally favourable and the Northern Europeans not far behind. The prediction that women of Southern European origin would be least favourable to the idea of working or combining work and child-rearing was not supported. Rather it was the French (as predicted) and the British who were the least enthusiastic, and much less likely to indicate high interest in combining the two roles than any other ethnic category. On the other hand the British were not averse to the idea of women being able to work, though the French took a relatively dim view of that as well. These are, however, a particular subgroup of French origin: the minority Franco-Ontarians and Quebecers of French origin who are attending English educational institutions. Most of the latter are partially assimilated, as measured by parental intermarriage or use of English in the home. Hopefully data from an ongoing A.S.O.P.E. study in Quebec will eventually allow for comparisons with French origin students who are attending francophone institutions.

Labour force participation seemed to be favoured for economic reasons by most (those of low socio-economic status were more likely to favour it), although the Southern Europeans present an interesting subdivision. Those of low socio-economic status are significantly more likely to favour mother's playing the wife-mother role, while those of high socio-economic status are unusual in favouring the combination of work and child-rearing more than their lower status counterparts do. This suggests that they do so for intrinsic rather than for economic reasons.

That those women whose mothers work are significantly more likely than the others to favour combining work with child-rearing suggests the importance of having a role model in this case. It is notable that even for the ethnic categories where the difference is not statistically significant its direction is always the same. The only other cases where such consistency exists are for the relationships between mother working and favouring the idea of working and between the father's occupation being of low status and favouring the idea of working. In neither case, however, are the differences statistically significant for any individual ethnic group.

On the whole, the women prefer to envisage a career that is interrupted during the period when they have preschool children. Parenthetically, we can note that the male students in the sample were rather less enthusiastic than the women about the idea of a wife eventually combining child-rearing and an outside job, perhaps because they are unwilling to accept the additional domestic responsibility that is likely to fall on them under such conditions. It is likely that this sex difference in the concept of appropriate roles for women will be a source of strain within families. In the current research it is not possible to ascertain the reasons for the preferences stated by either the men or the women. It is possible that they reflect a strongly-held belief in the importance of having a parent present during the early years of socialization. They may also reflect an awareness of the structural and economic difficulties of achieving an alternative child care arrangement which is satisfactory.

What the results do suggest is that there is likely to be an increasing incidence of women combining outside work and domestic responsibilities in one way or another. There is therefore likely to be increasing pressure to institutionalize more flexible career patterns. In this way women choosing an interrupted career pattern or part-time work will be less constrained to play a marginal role in the labour force. Some flexibility is currently evident in selected occupations where there is a predominance of women, such as nursing or sales clerking, but the pattern of its availability unfortunately reinforces sex-typed occupational choices (Armstrong and Armstrong, 1975). If the expressed preference for not working while one has preschool children is due to the difficulties posed by alternative child care arrangements, continuing pressure for more adequate solutions can be anticipated.

Overall, there seems to be less tendency than in the past to see the roles of homemaker and member of the labour force as alternatives, at least among the well-educated. That perception seems to have been strongest in the two charter groups, but their labour force participation rates, like those of other ethnic categories, have been increasing. Whether from preference or necessity there is a shift to playing the two roles simultaneously. This change is likely to be accompanied by modifications of the expectations associated with each role. Otherwise the burden on women who do not make an either/or choice between these two roles will continue to be inordinate (Meissner *et al.*, 1975).

REFERENCES

Allingham, John D. & Byron Spencer
    1968 *Women Who Work;* Part 2. *Married Women in the Labour Force; The Influence of Age, Education, Child-Bearing Status and Residence.* (Statistics Canada Cat 71-517). Ottawa: Queen's Printer.

Armstrong, Hugh & Pat Armstrong
    1975 "Women in the Canadian labour force, 1941-1971," *Canadian Review of Sociology and Anthropology,* 12 (4) part 1. pp. 370-384.

Canadian Review of Sociology & Anthropology
    1975 *Women in the Canadian Social Structure.* C.R.S.A., Special Issue. 12: 4 part. 1.

Cook, Gail, ed.
    1976 *Opportunity for Choice:* Ottawa: Statistics Canada.

Danziger, Kurt
    1971 *The Socialization of Immigrant Children,* Part 1. Toronto: Ethnic Research Programme, Institute of Behavioural Research.
    1976 "The Acculturation of Italian Immigrant Girls." K. Ishwaran. *The Canadian Family.* (Revised) Toronto: Holt, Rinehart & Winston. pp. 200-212.

Grygier, T.
    1975 "Integration of Four Ethnic Groups in Canadian Society: English, German, Hungarian, Italian," P. Migus ed. *Sounds Canadian.* Toronto: Peter Martin Associates. Pp. 158-186.

Hobart, C. W.
    1973 "Egalitarianism after marriage," M. Stephenson, ed. *Women in Canada.* Toronto: New Press. pp. 138-156.

Ishwaran, K.
    1971a "Calvinism and Social Behaviour in a Dutch Canadian Community," K. Ishwaran ed. *The Canadian Family.* Toronto: Holt, Rinehart & Winston. pp. 225-247.
    1971b "Family and Community Among the Dutch Canadians," K. Ishwaran, ed. *The Canadian Family.* Toronto: Holt, Rinehart & Winston. pp. 297-314.

Jansen, Clifford
    1971 "The Italian Community in Toronto," Jean Elliott ed. *Immigrant Groups.* Scarborough: Prentice-Hall, pp. 207-215.

Jean, M. ed.
    1974 *Québecoises du 20e siècle.* Montréal: Editions du Jour.

Labour Canada
    1973 *Women in the Labour Force. Facts and Figures 1973.* Ottawa: Labour Canada, Womens' Bureau.

Latowsky, Evelyn
    1971 "Family Life Styles and Jewish Culture," K. Ishwaran. *The Canadian Family.* Toronto: Holt, Rinehart & Winston. pp. 94-110.

Meissner, Martin, Elizabeth Humphreys, Scott Meiss and William Scheu
    1975 "No exit for wives: sexual division of labour," *Canadian Review of Sociology and Anthropology.* 12: 4, part 1, pp. 424-439.

Pyke, S. W.
    1975 "Children's Literature: Conceptions of Sex Roles," R. Pike & E. Zureik ed. *Socializtion and Values in Canada* Vol. 2. Toronto: McClelland & Stewart. pp. 51-74.

Rocher, Guy
   1964   "Les modèles et le statut de la femme canadienne-française," P. H. Chombart de Lauwe (ed.). *Images de la femme dans la société*. Paris: Editions ouvrières. pp. 194–204.

Rowbotham, Beverly
   no date *Teaching Sexism: An Analysis of Ontario Elementary School Readers*. Mimeo.

Stephenson, Marylee, ed.
   1973   *Women in Canada*. Toronto: New Press.

Zay, H.
   1974   "Analyse statistique de la femme mariée dans la province de Québec," M. Jean, ed. *Québecoises du 20e siècle*. Montréal: Editions du Jour. pp. 124–40.

The Industrialization of Housework*

MARGRIT EICHLER

Ontario Institute for Studies in Education, Toronto, Ontario, Canada

UNDERSTANDING the nature and functions of housework is central to an understanding of the position of all women and all men in our society—not just housewives. The basic social distinction between women and men in highly industrialized societies is that men do mostly paid work, and women do mostly unpaid work which coincides largely with the popular distinction of so-called "work" from so-called "housework". An example of the importance of housework as an explanatory factor for social sex differences is very evident in the wage differential between male and female workers. Rather than explain the wage differential in terms of psychic or biological differences between the sexes, or by simply outright discrimination, we can, at least partially, explain it by a combination of two factors: occupational sex segregation and the presence of a large number of housewives who, at some point in their lives, are willing to accept low-paying jobs. By so doing, these housewives create competition to women in the labor force and depress female wages (or, seen in reverse, help to inflate male wages).

Given the importance of housework for an understanding of the relative position of the sexes, one would expect a great deal of attention focussed on housework and those people who are primarily responsible for housework: housewives. However, this is not the case; social scientists have almost completely ignored housework (and housewives). This is understandable from a sociology of knowledge perspective: most researchers are either men, or women trained by men — and, as a rule, men tend not to do housework. When one is not responsible for housework, it is easy to consider it a matter of little importance. Perhaps, too, there may be a reluctance on the part of publishers to publish whatever research has been done on such a mundane topic.

---

* I would like to thank Tsilia Romm Ben-Dor, Audrey Cohn, Eugen Lupri and Alison Prentice for suggestions on improving an earlier version of this paper. I would also like to thank Milada Disman for some assistance in the preparation of this paper. This is a revised version of a presentation made at the National Council of Family Relations Meeting held in New York City, October, 1976.

In addition to the few individual researchers who have concerned themselves with housework and/or housewives (e.g., Gavron, 1966; Lopata, 1971; Oakley, 1974; Glazer, 1976; Eichler, 1976) the only group of people who have occasionally discussed housework are the neo-marxists. According to their point of view, women can only be liberated if and when they become reintegrated into the public sector, and when, as a precondition, housework will be industrialized. This notion, which derives from Engels, has hardly—if ever—been challenged. Yet, when applied unaltered from Engels' time to our own, it reveals a profound misunderstanding of the nature of the industrialization of housework. This is due on the one hand, to a lack of clarity in our conceptualization of housework and, on the other, to the fact that although housework *has* been industrialized by now, women are *not* liberated. (The lack of the predicted effect has led to a denial that the phenomenon itself has occurred.)

Let us, first, consider the meaning of the terms "housework" and "housewife".

All women and some men do housework (referring to the labour involved in maintaining a household, i.e., housekeeping). No men and not all women are housewives so that housework cannot simply refer to the work that is done by housewives —in other words, housework and housewives do not mean the same thing. All housewives are (or at least, have been) married, i.e., they are wives—but not all wives are housewives. If a woman is married and in the labour force, she is a "working woman"—meaning she receives some legal minimum pay for the labour she performs. All housewives are housekeepers (they perform all the functions associated with maintaining a household and servicing family members) but "housekeepers" as an occupational category are not necessarily housewives (unless their employer marries them in which case they become housewives without any necessary change in their functions). Most, but not all, housewives are mothers; but not all mothers are housewives. If a woman has children and is in the labour force, she is apt to be categorized as a "working mother". If she is unmarried and has children, she is an "unwed mother". If a nonmarried mother stays at home looking after her children, she is *not* a housewife unless she falls into the rare category of a divorced wife who receives alimony. If she receives public assistance, she is a "welfare mother", not a housewife.

Empirically, being a housewife and being a mother are closely tied, and it is the resulting interrelationship which is crucial for an understanding of the changes that have occurred during the past few decades. Women in Canada are more likely to have more children if they are housewives than if they are "working mothers"; (Boyd *et al.*, 1976: 41–43) and they are more likely to be housewives if they are mothers. A change in their active mothering status (when children grow up) may result in a change in occupational status (they may become "working women" again).

The term housewife, to attempt a definition, refers to a member of one sex only (female); a marital status (married); an economic relationship (economic dependence of the wife on the husband, and the receipt of goods such as shelter, food and clothes in exchange for services—essentially a feudal type of relationship in a basically money-oriented society); a type of task performed (housekeeping); often, but not always, parental status (mother); and the tasks associated with that parental status (mothering). Housework, in turn, refers to all work performed by a housewife as well as to those activities related to household maintenance performed by non-housewives. Obviously, neither "housework" nor "housewife" are clearly delimited concepts.

The basic conceptual problem lies in the attempt to blend housekeeping tasks with childrearing tasks under the label of "housework". Obviously, the two often take place simultaneously—one may watch a child while stirring the soup, or go shopping with a child—but the conceptual overlap has blinded us to the fact that the tasks associated with housekeeping and with child care have changed dramatically over the past few decades, and in different directions. Housework has become industrialized, while child care has become professionalized. Both processes are a direct consequence of the increasing level of technology in our society. The changes that have taken place are so drastic that one might call them social revolutions.

Let us consider the first revolution, the industrialization of housework, and then the second revolution, the professionalization of child care and then, lastly, let us examine the interaction of these two revolutions and their joint effect on women, men, children, and the family unit.

The Industrialization of Housework

Industrialization, in the strict sense of the term, refers to "the extensive use of inanimate sources of power in the production of economic goods and services" (Moore, 1968: 263). The main thesis of this paper is that housework has, on a worldwide level, become progressively more industrialized. The process has taken place (and is still taking place) at varying speeds (and with variations in its implementation) in all industrialized nations. The speed with which housework becomes industrialized varies not only according to society, but also according to regions within a country, according to rural-urban distinctions, and according to class. (The upper classes in urban areas in comparatively well-to-do regions experience it more quickly than do other areas and other people.)

The three examples that follow are meant, by providing contrasts, to help make vivid the degree to which housework has become industrialized today. They are drawn from three different societies: a sixteenth century German household; a nineteenth century British household; and a contemporary Canadian household. The examples are not meant to imply that all features discussed in each type of household form part of a linear development. The only developmental sequence that is implied conceives of a world-wide process of industrialization of housework in all highly industrialized societies.

1. *Katherina von Bora's (Martin Luther's Wife's) Household*

Katherina von Bora ran a large establishment for her family which consisted routinely of about forty people. The Luthers resided in a former cloister (in which Luther had previously lived as a monk) which was turned over to the couple by the Elector. In it lived Luther, his wife, their six children, some relatives, some students, and some Protestant fugitives from foreign countries. "So large an establishment was more than one person could handle alone. Katie herself herded, milked, and slaughtered the cattle, made butter and cheese, brewed, planted, and reaped, but help was indispensable. There were maid servants and men servants, sometimes faithful, sometimes unreliable" (Bainton, 1971: 32). Luther was a professor and had a salary, but it was not adequate to maintain such an establishment.

"Katie resolved to make the household self-sustaining. She did some remodelling in the Black Cloister, making three cellars with an extra stairway. A bath was installed, which served presumably also as a laundry, and there was a brewery. The Black Cloister carried with it a small garden yielding peas, beans, turnips, cabbage, lettuce, cucumbers, and melons. An orchard was developed which supplied cherries, pears, apples, peaches, nuts, grapes, mulberries, and figs. Katie, having extracted her husband's consent by eloquence and tears, acquired another garden through which ran a brook. To Luther's delight she hooked from it pike, trout, perch, and carp. Her livestock included various horses. A precise count in 1542 listed eight pigs, five cows, nine calves, besides chickens, pigeons, geese, and of course the immortal dog Tölpel, whom Luther fully expected to meet in heaven" (Bainton, 1971: 33).

This, it must be remembered, is admittedly an example of an unusually large and complex, *urban* household of the sixteenth century the equivalent of which would probably be identified today as an upper-middle-class household. Everything that was needed could be supplied from within the household, and only on special occassions, such as when the Luthers' held a festive banquet to celebrate the completion of a doctoral thesis of one of his students or a wedding, did they purchase special dainties, such as birds, rabbits, etc. In a situation such as this, the housewife carries a large responsibility. Without her good management, the household will not prosper. Her work is essential for the well-being of her husband and the other household members, since there are no easy alternatives for any private citizen to being attached in one way or another to the family household.

The situation in frontier America was quite similar to Katherine von Bora's household. Most of the foods were grown and processed within the home as well as other necessities, such as soap, candles and clothes. Sometimes, even the shelter was constructed by hand. In other words, each household went through the same or similar work processes and activities to produce the means for survival and for functioning, without drawing heavily on purchased industrialized goods.

2. *A Working Class Household in Britain at the End of the Nineteenth Century*

While in Britain by the end of the nineteenth century a fair number of products previously produced within the household were already available for purchase (for instance, many people would send to the baker, or to the butcher for finished, ready-to-eat or cooked products), a large number of functions still needed to be performed within the household. One of these was the care of clothes which meant washing by hand and constant repair in the form of mending and darning the expensive, hard-to-care-for materials. Preserving of fruits and vegetables was another time-consuming and necessary process to insure vitamin rich food during the winter season.

All in all, by the end of the 19th century in Britain, housework was, to a greater degree than in previous centuries, supplemented by non-kin centrally-operated production processes such as butcheries, bakeries, weaving factories, etc. for the production of necessary household supplies. However, essential services such as the maintenance of clothing and the provision of food were still primarily located within the framework of the family or pseudo-family (for instance, by a housewife for a lodger).

The family organization of British working-class households at the turn of the century has some interesting aspects which are important for an understanding of the relative position of a housewife in this type of household. In working-class households, the husband traditionally handed over a portion of his income to his wife for her to use for housekeeping needs. As a child started to earn money, whether boy or girl, he or she usually handed over, at the beginning, all of his or her earnings, out of which the mother would give him or her a few pennies to be spent at lunchtime, or for transportation fares, or for pocket-money. When the earnings of the child had risen to such a point that the mother would make a profit by retaining the full wages, a different arrangement was usually entered into. The child now paid his or her mother for board and lodging and kept the rest of the money for himself or herself. There was a standard range of charges which were customarily allowed for board and lodging, and if dissent within the family arose, a child had the option to find board and lodging elsewhere for similar rates of pay (Booth, 1970a, 2nd series, vol. 5: 319–321). This arrangement meant that the mother earned some money for her labours, that the adolescents could leave home if they felt dissatisfied, and, most importantly, that housework was treated as a purchasable commodity that might be bought from one's mother (or other relative) or from some non-kin person, at prices which were generally known and similar. Women could substitute lodgers for children of their own if they wanted to earn more money for their housework.

It is interesting to note that along with the comparative economic equality that came to women who either took in lodgers or who had adolescent or adult children who paid for their board and lodging, many lived in common law marriages. Booth notes that legal marriage was the general rule at the outset of life, "but later, among those who come together in maturer years, nonlegalized cohabitation is far from uncommon, and this irregular relationship is commented upon not always to its disadvantage. It is even said of rough labourers that they behave best if not married to the women with whom they live. 'The difficulty' (said one of the clergy) 'is that these people manage to live together fairly peaceably so long as they are not married, but if they marry it always seems to lead to blows and rows'. They do not trust each other sufficiently to marry. A missionary mentioned the case of an old couple, whose real relationship transpired when the man was ill, who had lived together unmarried for forty years. 'He would have married me again and again' (said the woman) 'but I never could see the good of it.' On the other side it is remarked that 'marriage lines' are valued by some of the less independent poor, for the sake of the charitable relief which the respectability thus vouched for helps them to secure" (Booth, 1970b, final vol.: 41–42).

A most interesting change in family relations occurred when the male earnings rose from the subsistence level to one of comparative affluence (i.e., from under 20 to 40 shillings a week). The increase in male earnings resulted in a decided worsening of the position of the proletarian wife since the husband kept the larger share of the increase for himself. "What seemed to be happening was that as wages advanced men took the bulk of the gain for themselves and abandoned the traditional pattern of turning most of their income over to their wives for family use" (Stearns, 1971: 166). The re-allocation of resources was reflected in a more rapid increase in male consumption items, particularly food items such as meat and recreation, whereas female consumption interests, primarily clothing and housing, lagged behind. The common pattern among workers with earnings above subsistence was to give a fixed allowance to their wife which did not proportionately increase with their increased earnings. Wives no longer knew how much their husbands earned and the importance of their economic role in the family declined (Stearns, 1971: 117).

This is an important example because it illustrates both how economic changes can affect family relations and why we cannot automatically identify the benefits which accrue to one family member with the overall well-being of the family. Yet the latter is precisely what modern family sociology tends to do—the breadwinning function of the husband-father is equated with his parental and spousal role and it is assumed that he fulfills these roles better if he improves his performance as a wage earner. However, in practice this equation does not necessarily hold after the basic necessities have been met. We therefore need to carefully re-examine our understanding of the father/husband roles in the modern family. The same applies, of course, to the mother/wife roles.

We call women who spend major portions of their lives in unremunerated housework and child care "traditional", implying that this pattern is one which has been around for a long time and is well-established. In fact, the circumstances under which housework and child care are performed nowadays have changed so drastically, compared with earlier times, that the "traditional housewife" is, in reality, a brand-new creature.

3. Contemporary Canadian Households

In Canada, the industrialization of housework which became prominent in the fifties has been virtually completed. Of course, the speed with which the process occurred (and is still occurring in some areas) varies with respect to regional, urban-rural and class differences; nevertheless, it is only a difference in speed of implementation, not in the substance of the process. What happened was that technology invaded the household on a large scale. Table 1 summarizes items over time that indicate the technologizing of Canadian households.

Table 1

Percentages of Canadian Households surveyed that had Certain Household Equipment, 1948–1975*

Item	1948	1953	1958	1963	1968	1975
Hot and cold running water	—	62.57	73.50	84.86	90.97	96.73
Gas or electric stove**	48.49	62.73	76.66	87.24	94.03	98.33
Mechanical refrigerator	29.26***	66.33***	86.24***	94.20	97.44	99.25
Home freezer	—	2.22	8.17	17.66	29.16	41.83
Electric washing machine	59.21	76.68	84.28	86.81	83.57	76.86
Vacuum cleaner	32.02	48.01	60.94	72.45	—	86.54
Electric Sewing Machine	—	23.43	36.30	49.03	—	65.43
Gas or electric clothes dryer	—	—	—	21.60	36.79	51.62
Automatic dishwasher	—	—	—	2.08	5.08	15.20

* Does not include households in the Yukon, Northwest Territories or on Indian reservations.
** Includes piped and bottled gas and oil or kerosene.
*** Includes both gas and electric refrigerators. The number of gas refrigerators, however, dwindled rapidly so that their exclusion from the statistics after 1958 probably makes little difference.
— No statistics available.
Source for 1948–1968 figures, adapted from Report of the Royal Commission, 1970: 34 (table 3). For 1975 data, see Statistics Canada, Ottawa: Information Canada, 1975, Tables 16, 21, 22, 23, 37, 38, 39.

The implications of these household appliances for housework are staggering. Automatic washing machines, for example, have completely changed one of the most arduous, physically strenuous and time-consuming work processes. On this account, it is somewhat puzzling to see from the table that they are the only household appliance which shows a relative retrogressive trend. Since it seems unlikely that this indicates less use of washing machines, it must reflect the higher proportion of people living in apartment buildings which have washing machines in common laundry rooms. It may, as well, indicate the increased utilization of automatic washing machines in laundromats.

At the same time as the care of clothes was lightened to such a degree that if we compare it to the type of laundry performed in earlier times we cannot recognize it as the same type of work, food processing, distribution and storage were being revolutionized. Virtually all Canadian households now have a refrigerator which makes it possible to shop for an entire family's food needs with one weekly, rather than a daily, shopping trip. Frozen and ready-to-serve foods have reduced the necessary labour for the preparation of foods to a minimum. Prepared baby foods are accepted staples in households with babies. Breads are available everywhere, as are preserves of all types. Fresh vegetables are available year-round due to massive importation from southern areas (which is only possible with a highly-developed transportation system) and large-scale out-of-season production. The result is that the preparation of vegetables and fruits in the summer for use in the winter has become superfluous. If canning and preserving are still done, they are done through personal preference and must be considered a luxury rather than a necessity.

The introduction of new materials has made the acquisition and care of clothes much easier. Comparatively cheap ready-made clothes have made mending and darning a negligible occupation, and special fabrics make some ironing entirely unnecessary.

Cleaning the living space has also become vastly different, due to modern floor coverings and modern cleaning agents and cleaning machines which have turned a physically demanding and tiring job into a physically nonstrenous job.

In other words, all of the important functions necessary for the maintenance of a household have been transformed, through the utilization of machines into (comparatively speaking) physically nonstrenuous tasks. These same machines are used on a large scale in industry which produces all the goods that in earlier times were prepared within a household—especially food and clothes—on a mass basis and offers them for purchase at prices which are within the reach of most people. Full-time housekeeping is no longer a necessity for maintaining a one- or multi-person household.

Basically, then, the industrialization of housework refers, first, to a very high level of technology within individual households, and, second, to the availability for purchase in the general market place of every product that was once produced within the household—specifically clothes (production as well as cleaning), food (production as well as preparation), and shelter (production as well as minimization of maintenance due to industrial products). Naturally, availability for purchase does not mean that all people actually buy all these products at all times. There are many reasons why they might not: individual preference may lead to the home-production of goods (many women still bake cakes; the point is that in urban industrialized centers they could just as well buy them). Some production activities may be experienced as enjoyable. And price is an important consideration. If goods are available for purchase but are so expensive that many people cannot buy them, then for those people who cannot afford them, housework has only been partially industrialized.

Whether or not household goods are home-produced or purchased, their consumption and maintenance take time and effort. Pots still have to be washed (even a dishwasher needs to be loaded and unloaded). However, consumption and maintenance of other industrial goods, such as cars, also take time and effort. Indeed, if a person is a hobbyist, he or she may spend an enormous amount of time tinkering with cars. Yet nobody would dispute that cars are industrial products of highly technologized societies. The same argument applies to goods which were previously produced within individual households.

With all these changes, one might reasonably expect that the housewife role has, dwindled to the point where it takes only a marginal amount of time each day. This however, is not the case. While time budget studies are difficult to interpret with respect to the sorting out of different types of activities performed, they demonstrate unambiguously that the average amount of time spent on housework and child care has not decreased over the past few decades (Vanek, 1973: Meissner et al., 1975).

If the foregoing analysis is correct, we need to explain why there is no appreciable difference in the amount of time spent on housework. Two different types of reasons come to mind: For one, housekeeping standards seem to have gone up. In some frontier households, for instance, laundry was done only four times a year! For housewives who are mothers, however, it appears likely that the nonreduction in time spent on household tasks is primarily due to dramatic changes in child care practices—changes made necessary by the same technological forces which produced the changes in housekeeping functions. (These changes led ultimately to the professionalization of childcare.)

The Professionalization of Child care

The same forces which have brought about the technologization of housekeeping have also created a physical environment which is increasingly hostile to little children. In most urban areas it is impossible nowadays to leave small children unsupervised in unenclosed areas because of heavy traffic and other urban hazards. Furthermore, the same technology which has reduced the physical burden of housekeeping has also contributed to the increasing social isolation of the housewife: if most of the major functions of housekeeping can be performed within one's own home, institutionalized contacts with other adults will dwindle. An unprecedented loneliness for adult com pany is likely to confront women, all of whom perform their daily chores in daily parallel action, each action of which is increasingly less crucial for the well-being of the adult members of the family, since foods and services are so easily available (e.g., food in a restaurant, laundry services for cleaning clothes, a new ready-made shirt for one that is torn, etc.).

The comparative leisure that was created through the industrialization of housework has made possible an increased attention to the child care role of the mother. At the societal level, we see the emergence of child care experts, such as child-development psychologists, a vast toy industry which caters exclusively to children of specific age groups, etc. At the individual level, Slater (1970: 62) has noted that mothers have accepted "the Spockian challenge"—but Slater neither asks nor answers the question: Why? The answer lies, I believe, in the demographic change that has taken place since the Second World War. Women have fewer children today than they used to have in earlier times, and those children that they bear are likely to live due to drastically reduced infant mortality. Not only has the number of children born decreased dramatically (in Canada, for example, the total fertility rate of women in 1956 was 3,858; in 1973 it was 1,931) but the span in which women bear children has been sharply compressed. In other words, women bear fewer children in a shorter period of time. What is the effect of this on child care?

In earlier times, adolescents learned how to care for children within their own family, either by watching smaller siblings being raised or, when they were the youngest, by watching the children of an older sister or brother being raised by their respective parents. If, however, the average number of children born is two for each family and if those two are born only two years apart the age span is not great enough to allow for either a meaningful learning experience (with respect to child care) by watching one's younger siblings being raised, or for the opportunity of watching an older sibling raising his or her children. Therefore, today's mothers may lack experience in child care and so be poorly equipped for mothering. The same applies to fathers, of course.

The lack of family experience has created a need for other sources of instruction, predominantly child care books written by child care experts, since public schools seem not to have perceived the challenge of filling the gap as yet. This, in turn, has resulted in a professionalization of child care with increased expectations concerning the product of the educational process, the child.

Childrearing has thus become a reflective rather than traditional activity: Particular techniques utilized are subject to potential improvement—if you use the right techniques you'll be able to raise a brighter and better child. For examples, a best-selling book by Joan Beck is entitled "How to Raise a Brighter Child: The Case for Early Learning" (New York: Trident, 1967). This book makes a convincing case that: "You can help your child to become brighter, more intelligent, happier. There is no doubt about it. And in the process, your off-spring will have a more satisfying childhood, and you will enjoy him more" (Beck, 1967: 16). The basic theoretical reasoning—probably correct—is the thesis that "Your child does not have a fixed intelligence, or a predetermined rate of intellectual growth, contrary to such widespread opinion in the past. His level of intelligence can be changed—for better or worse—by his environment and especially during the earliest years of his life" (Beck, 1967: 19). In other words, while you can supposedly raise a "mini" genius, you can also fail your child by not educating yourself sufficiently or by utilizing the wrong techniques. The child is seen as a product through which the success of the educational techniques of the mother is gauged. If the child turns out well, it means that the mother did not spoil the naturally good substance. If the child turns out badly, she did. Either way, she cannot win. The easing of the housekeeping functions provides housewives with comparative leisure which allows mothers to make mothering their main function—and which therefore allows time for a reflection on failure; the existence of a measure of success implying the existence of a measure of failure.

Another significant change has occurred in family life. Older children and adolescents are increasingly dependent on their parents. Previously, most young adults of working class background were in the labour force as early as age fourteen, and usually for certain by sixteen. This meant that they could contribute to household expenses and had some independence and maturity. Today, the age level at which this occurs has been pushed higher and higher, resulting in prolonged emotional, legal, and financial dependence of adolescents on their parents. Denying adolescents their independence and treating them as legal and economic minors makes them that much more difficult to handle, and makes family life much more complex.

The Effects of the Industrialization of Housework and the Professionalization of Child care

Overall, lower fertility and the fewer years given to childbearing have resulted in the professionalization of childrearing with attendant insecurity on the part of mothers which is sharpened in its effects by increased interaction between mothers and young children due to an increasingly child-hostile urban environment. Housework has been technologized to such a degree that we must regard housekeeping as having already gone through the process of industrialization. This seems to have escaped notice thus far because we did not conceptually separate housework into housekeeping tasks and child care. The two developments went in opposite directions: while housekeeping has been industrialized, childrearing has *not* been communalized, on the contrary, it has become more individualized in the child's early years, and has been burdened with higher expectations on the mother's performance. The effects of these simultaneous but opposing changes on women, men, chlidren, and the family are major.

The role of women as housekeepers has been dramatically devalued since every function that is performed by a housewife in the course of her housekeeping tasks is also available for purchase on the market, due to the technological changes that have occurred. No longer is an adult dependent on a housewife for meals, clean clothes, clean living quarters, etc. While it may be considered vastly preferable by most people to have such services performed by a family member, an adult not attached to a family can quite easily survive in our society. This was not the case in earlier times. Housekeepers, are, in short, replaceable. This is not true for mothers.

The role of women as mothers has been greatly upgraded in importance while at the same time it has become a much more difficult role to fulfill. Consequently, when the last child enters public school, the change in the nature of the work performed by the housewife and in the evaluation of this work is greater than in previous decades.

From the point of view of men the changes are much less dramatic. The husband does not profit *directly* from the increased effort that mothers put into their children. He profits only indirectly and to the extent to which he identifies himself with the well-being of the child and agrees with the mothers' educational methods. (And, of course, he, too, may blame the mother if the child(ren) do(es) not fulfill all expectations.) The husband may find that he pays more for lesser services to himself personally. Overall, the wife has become more dependent on the husband while the man as husband, not as father, has become less dependent on his wife. The asymmetrical spousal dependence has shifted the balance of spousal power in favour of the husband rather than in favour of the wife (Eichler, 1981).

There is some evidence that nonemployed housewives experience more strain than "working women", e.g., their suicide rates are higher (Cumming et al., 1975). It seems that the internal contradictions inherent in the housewife/mother roles have become such that they provide a sufficient explanation for the emergence of the women's liberation movement in the sixties. Previous explanations for the emergence of this major social movement have focussed on ideological changes or specific political events. None of them, however, can explain why women's groups started in all highly industrialized countries in the middle sixties. To explain their emergence by changes in the specific female roles of housewife and mother, changes which were occasioned through an interplay of demographic and technologic forces means to ground the movements in *structural* rather than *ideological* changes. If the relationship just traced is correct, then we can expect still further changes and a further rejection of the nontraditional "traditional" role of women.

With respect to child care, the family has been put into the impossible situation of being expected to provide professional standard services without professional training and with very little help from the community—indeed, against the concerted efforts of the mass media to convert children into mass consumers of socially undesirable and even harmful products.

A possible side effect of the raising of educational objectives with respect to children may be that the cultural gap between children may be widening rather than narrowing by the time they enter the public school system. With the availability of reading materials such as the "How-to-raise-a-child" books, concerned parents may, indeed, be increasing the intelligence, or at least the school "readiness", of their children. Since the majority of children will not have had the advantage of intensive pre-school training, the talent differential of children at the onset of public schooling may therefore become increasingly more marked.

We may not be able to lower the educational expectations for children (and probably we should not even try to do so), but we can certainly recognize the process that has started and provide present and future parents with some of the training that they are supposed to hand on to their children without ever having previously been fitted for the task.

REFERENCES

Bainton, Roland H.
    1971 *Women of the Reformation in Germany and Italy*. Boston: Beacon Press.
Beck, Joan
    1967 *How to Raise a Brighter Child. The Case for Early Learning*. New York: Trident Press.
Booth, Charles
    1970a *Life and Labour of the People in London*. 2nd Series: Industry. Vol. 5, Comparisons, Surveys and Conclusions. New York: AMS Press, (1902–1904).
    1970b *Life and Labour of the People in London*. Final Vol. Notes on Social Influences and Conclusion. New York: AMS Press, (1902–1904).
Boyd, Monica, Margrit Eichler and John Hofley
    1976 "Family: Functions, Formation and Fertility," in Gail C. A. Cook (ed.) *Opportunity for Choice*. Ottawa: Statistics Canada in association with the C. D. Howe Research Institute, 13–52.
Cumming, Elaine, Charles Lazer, and Lynne Chisholm
    1975 "Suicide as an index of role strain among employed and not employed married women in British Columbia," *Canadian Review of Sociology and Anthropology*, Vol. 12, No. 4 (Part I): 462–470.
Eichler, Margrit
    1981 "Power, Dependency, Love and the Sexual Division of Labour. A Critique of the Decision-making Approach. With an Appendix: On Washing My Dirty Linen in Public." *Women's Studies International Quarterly*, Vol. 4, No. 2, 201–220.
Eichler, Margrit, with the assistance of Neil Guppy and Janet Siltanen
    1977 "The Prestige of the Occupation Housewife." Pp. 151–175 in Patricia Marshak (ed.). *The Working Sexes*. Vancouver: University of British Columbia Institute of Industrial Relations.
Gavron, Hannah
    1966 *The Captive Wife*. London: Routledge and Kegan Paul.
Glazer-Malbin, Nona
    1976 "Housework," *Signs*, Vol. I, No. 4, p. 905–922.
Lopata, Helen Znaniecki
    1971 *Occupation Housewife*. New York: Oxford University Press.
Meissner, Martin et al.
    1975 "No exit for wives: sexual division of labour and the cumulation of household demands." *Canadian Review of Sociology and Anthropology*, Vol. 12, no. 4 (Part I): 424–439.

Moore, Wilbert
   1968 "Industrialization" *International Encyclopedia of the Social Sciences,* Vol. 7.
Oakley, Ann
   1974 *The Sociology of Housework.* New York: Random House.
Report of the Royal Commission on the Status of Women
   1970 Ottawa: Information Canada.
Slater, Philip
   1970 *The Pursuit of Loneliness. American Culture at the Breaking Point.* Boston: Beacon Press.
Stearns, Peter N.
   1971 "Working-Class Women in Britain, 1890–1914," in Martha Vicinus (ed.) *Suffer and Be Still. Women in the Victorian Age.* Bloomington and London: Indiana University Press 100–120.
Vanek, Joan
   1973 *Keeping Busy: Time Spent in Housework, United States, 1920–1970.* Unpublished Ph.D. Dissertation, University of Michigan.

CONTRIBUTORS

Dr. Olivera Burić is a Senior Scientific Research Associate at the Institute of Social Policy in Beograd, Yugoslavia. She is the author of a book entitled *Impact of Maternal Employment on Family* Life (1975), the article "Re-definition of the structure of social power for the social equality of women," *Sociologija*, Vol. XIV, No. 2, as well as monographs and many other articles in the areas of family life, gender relations and social policy. Dr. Burić has presented many papers at international conferences and meetings in an effort to inform the international social scientific community on socialist experiments in Yugoslavia. She was among the first group of European scholars to replicate Blood and Wolfe's resource theory of marital power which resulted in her (with Andjelka Zećevic) "Family authority, marital satisfaction, and the social network in Yugoslavia," *Journal of Marriage and the Family*, Vol. 29, No. 2, 1967.

Alessandro Cavalli is Professor and Director of the Institute of Sociology at the University of Pavia, Milano, Italy. His research interests include the study of the family, social change and rural sociology. For many years Dr. Cavalli has been an Associate Editor in the International Department of the *Journal of Marriage and the Family*.

Dr. Ann B. Denis studied in Canada and England and received her Ph. D. from the London School of Economics in 1969. She is Associate Professor of Sociology and presently chairperson of the Department of Sociology at the University of Ottawa, Ottawa, Canada. Dr. Denis teaches courses in the areas of gender relations, sociology of education and ethnic relations. Her current research projects include studies on the relationship of ethnicity, social class and sex with education and work plans of post-secondary students in Montreal, and a textbook on the sociology of education in Canada (with Raymond Murphy). She is the author of several articles published in Canadian journals of education and sociology.

Marcellinus Dijkers is a graduate student in the Department of Sociology and a research assistant in the Family Research Center, Wayne State University, Detroit, Michigan.

Margrit Eichler was educated in West Germany (Berlin, Göttingen) and the United States, where she received her Ph. D. in Sociology from Duke University in 1972. She is Associate Professor in the Department of Sociology in Education at the Ontario Institute for Studies in Education, Toronto, Ontario, Canada, where she teaches courses in the sociology of education, social change and the sociology of women. Dr. Eichler has published articles on women and the family in the *Canadian Review of Sociology and Anthropology, Journal for the Scientific Study of Religion, Journal of Marriage and the Family, The Historian, Sociological Inquiry*, as well as other learned journals, and has contributed several chapters to anthologies. One of her most recent articles is entitled "Towards a sociology of feminist research in Canada" which appeared in *Signs: Journal of Women in Culture and Society*, Vol. 3, No. 2, 1978.

Elina Haavio-Mannila is Associate Professor of Sociology in the Department of Sociology, University of Helsinki, Helsinki, Finland. She teaches in the areas of family sociology, demography and gender relations. She has published widely in her own country and is also known for her articles

"Some consequences of women's emancipation," in *Journal of Marriage and the Family*, Vol. 31, No. 1, 1969; "The position of Finnish women, regional and cross-national comparisons," *ibid.*, No. 2, 1969; "Sex roles in politics," in C. Safilios-Rothschild (ed.), *Toward a Sociology of Women*, 1972, and "The position of women in society: formal ideology vs. everyday ethic" (with Veronica Stolte-Heiskanen), *Social Science Information*, Vol. 6, No. 6, 1967. Dr. Haavio-Mannila is presently International Editor of the International Department, *Journal of Marriage and the Family*.

Dr. Thomas Held is research associate at the Soziologisches Institut, University of Zürich, Zürich, Switzerland. He is the author of *Die Stellung der Frau in Familie und Gessellschaft: Eine soziologische Analyse am Beispiel der Schweiz*, 1974 (with René Levy), and co-author of "Family structure and society," *Journal of Marriage and the Family*, Vol. 37, No. 4, 1975. He has also published in Swiss and German social science journals.

H. M. in't Veld-Langeveld, once a Professor of Sociology, is now a member of the Scientific Council for Government Policy in the Netherlands, The Hague, The Netherlands. Her research interests include family sociology and social and cultural change. As a member of the Council she is engaged in a number of projects that require long-term planning and have policy implications. Dr. in't Veld-Langeveld is the author of "Woman, profession, society: analysis of a retarded emancipation," and of "Values affecting women's position in society," *Planning and Development in the Netherlands*, Vol. III, No. 1, 1976.

Eva Köckeis-Stangl is *Universitäts-Dozent* at the University of Innsbruck, Innsbruck, Austria. Dr. Köckeis-Stangl's special interests are adolescent psychology, social psychology, aging, family relations and youth. She has published widely on the sociology of both aging and the family. She is co-author (with Leopold Rosenmayr) of a major study of the family in old age, *Umwelt und Familie alter Menschen*, 1965, *Kulturelle Interessen von Jugendlichen*, 1966 (with L. Rosenmayr and H. Kreutz), and a contributor to several anthologies. One of Dr. Köckeis-Stangl's recent publications appeared in the *Osterreichische Zeitschrift für Soziologie* (1976) under the title "Bildungsforschung in Südtirol" (Educational Research in South-Tyrol).

Dr. René Levy is research associate at the Soziologisches Institut, University of Zürich, Zürich, Switzerland. In 1977 he was a Visiting Professor of Sociology at the University of Ottawa. He is co-author of *Die Stellung der Frau in Familie und Gesellschaft: Eine soziologische Analyse am Beispiel der Schweiz*, 1974, and also co-author of "Family structure and society," *Journal of Marriage and the Family*, Vol. 37, No. 4, 1975. Dr. Levy is author of a forthcoming monograph on biographical analyses.

Eugen Lupri was educated in Germany and the United States. He is Professor of Sociology at the University of Calgary, Calgary, Alberta, Canada. Dr. Lupri joined the Calgary Department after having taught in Germany and the United States. His main fields of interest are in family sociology, comparative methodology, family theory, aging and political sociology. Dr. Lupri is author of a forthcoming monograph on *Family and Marriage in Contemporary West Germany: A Sociological Interpretation*, *Soziologie der Familie*, 2. Auflage, 1976, (with Günther Lüschen) and editor of *Marriage and the Family in Comparative Perspective*, 1972 (with Günther Lüschen). He has published articles in the areas of family power, aging, right-wing extremism in West Germany, comparative methodology and husband-wife relations in journals such as the *Kölner Zeitschrift für Soziologie und Sozialpsychologie, European Journal of Sociology, Journal of Marriage and the Family, Zeitschrift für Soziologie, Current Sociology*, and the *Canadian Journal of Sociology*. His recently published article on "Theoretical and methodological issues in the use of decision-making as an indicator of conjugal power: some Canadian observations" (with M. B. Brinkerhoff) appeared in the *Canadian Journal of Sociology*, Vol. 3, No. 1, 1978. Dr. Lupri has been an Associate Editor of the International Department of the *Journal of Marriage and the Family* since its inception in 1967.

Yoriko Meguro is Associate Professor of Sociology at Sophia University, Tokyo, Japan. She was educated in Japan and the United States and received her Ph. D. from Case Western Reserve University, Cleveland, Ohio, in 1974. Her doctoral dissertation is entitled, "Family and social network in modern Japan: a study of an urban sample," 1974. Dr. Meguro teaches courses in gender relations, family sociology and social network theory.

Andrée Michel is Research Director at the Centre National de la Recherche Scientifique, Paris, France. Her special interests are in the study of sex roles, sociology of the family and human development. Dr. Michel is the author of many books and monographs, including *Famille, Industrialisation, Logement*, 1959, *Sociologie de la Famille et du Mariage*, 1972, *Travail Professional de la femme et Vie Conjugale*, 1974, and editor of *Family Issues of Employed Women in Europe and America*, 1971. She has published widely in French, European and American professional journals articles such as "Kinship relations of proximity in French working class household" in Norman Bell and Erza Vogel (eds.), *A Modern Introduction to the Family*, 1960; "The French woman's role in urban married life," *International Journal of Social Sciences* XVI, No. 1, 1964; "Fonctions et structures de la famille," *Cashiers Internationaux de Sociologie*, Vol. 29, déc., 1960; "Comparative data concerning the interaction in French and American families," *Journal of Marriage and the Family*, Vol. 31, No. 2, 1967; "Wife's satisfaction with husband's understanding in Parisian urban families," *ibid.*, Vol. 30, No. 3, 1970; "Interaction and family planning in the French urban family," *Demography*, Vol. 4, No. 2, 1969; and "Some differentials of the marital satisfaction of French working wives in the Paris area," *International Journal of Family Sociology*, Vol. 1 (March), 1971. Dr. Michel has lectured at French, American and Canadian universities.

Donald L. Mills is Professor of Sociology at the University of Calgary, Calgary, Alberta, Canada. Previously he taught briefly at the Universities of Oregon and Washington, and at Stanford University; he was also a Research Sociologist at the Stanford Research Institute in California. His main fields of interest are the sociology of work, comparative sociology, and occupational and industrial sociology, especially the changing occupational roles of women and men in the labour force. Dr. Mills is co-editor (with Howard M. Vollmer) of *Professionalization*, 1966, and the author of *Chiropractors, Naturopaths and Osteopaths in Canada*, 1964. He has published widely on the sociology of work in American and Canadian professional journals and contributed chapters to several volumes. Dr. Mills' most recent contribution (with Donald E. Larsen) is entitled "The professionalization of Canadian chiropractic" and will appear in D. Coburn, *et al.*, *Health and Canadian Society: A Sociological Prespective*. Professor Mills is a Fellow of the American Sociological Association and has been a member of The Royal Commission on Health Services.

Kiyomi Morioka is Professor of Sociology and Senator at Tokyo University, Tokyo, Japan. Dr. Morioka has studied and taught in the United States and various European countries, and has served as a consultant for many international organizations. He teaches in the areas of family sociology, human development and life cycles. He is the author of many books and monographs, among them *Kazoku Shukiron* (Family Life Cycles), 1973, and *Shin Kozoku Kankeigaku* (A New Approach to Family Relations), 1974, as well as of several articles in Japanese, English and American social science journals. For many years Professor Morioka has been an Associate Editor of the International Department of the *Journal of Marriage and the Family*.

Christine Oppong teaches at the University of Ghana and is a Senior Research Fellow at the Institute of African Studies, Legon, Accra, Ghana, Africa. Professor Oppong has also taught in England and the United States. Her areas of research interest include the sociology of the family, sex roles and the study of social change. She is the author of the book *Marriage Among a Matrilineal Elite*, and the co-author of "Womanpower: retrograde steps in Ghana" (with C. Okali and B. Houghton), published in a special issue of *African Studies Reviews*, 1975. Dr. Oppong has published not only in her own country but also in the *Journal of Marriage and the Family*, Vol. 32, No. 4, 1970 ("Conjugal power and resources: an urban African example"), and in the *Journal of Comparative Family Studies*, Vol. 2, No. 2, 1972 ("Joint conjugal roles and extended families"). Dr. Oppong has presented many papers dealing with the status of women in Ghana at several international conferences at home and abroad. She is also an Associate Editor of the International Department of the *Journal of Marriage and the Family*, and Fellow of the Royal Anthropological Institute.

Constantina Safilios-Rothschild was educated in Greece and the United States. She is Professor of Sociology and Director of the Family Research Center, Wayne State University, Detroit,

Michigan, USA. Her main research activities have focused on the sociology of women, sociology of the family, comparative family theory and methodology, and social change. She is the author of *The Sociology and Social Psychology of Dissability and Rehabilitation,* 1970, *Women and Social Policy,* 1974, editor of *Toward a Sociology of Women,* 1972, and a highly sought after contributor to many anthologies. She was one of the few European scholars to critically assess and replicate Blood and Wolfe's resource theory of marital power, the results of which were first reported in "A comparison of power structure and marital satisfaction in urban Greek and French families," published in the *Journal of Marriage and the Family,* Vol. 29, No. 2, 1967. Additional critiques of the resource theory and its methodology are found in Dr. Safilios-Rothschild's "Family sociology of wives' family sociology: a cross-national examination of decision-making," *ibid.,* Vol. 31, No. 3, 1969; "The study of family power: a review, 1960–1969," *ibid.,* Vol. 32, No. 3, 1970; and many others in the *Comparative Journal of Family Studies, Acta Sociologica, The American Sociologist* and *Sexual Behavior.* She has been an Associate Editor of the International Department of the *Journal of Marriage and the Family* since its founding in 1967.

I. J. Schoonenboom is a sociologist presently working on the staff of the Scientific Council for Government Policy in the Netherlands, The Hague, The Netherlands. Dr. Schoonenboom's research activites are related to a long-term study of the normative orientation of the Dutch political parties. He is co-author of "Values affecting women's position in society," *Planning and Development in the Netherlands,* Vol. VIII, No. 1, 1976.

Renata Siemieńska is Associate Professor of Sociology and a staff member of the Institute of Sociology at the University of Warsaw, Warsaw, Poland. She has been a Visiting Scholar (1973/74) at the Institute for Social Research and Political Studies at the University of Michigan, Ann Arbor, Michigan, USA. Dr. Siemieńska has been involved in research concerned with comparative studies on the value of political participation of leaders in Polish society, youth's values and attitudes as well as women's participation in decision-making processes. She is author of four books, two of which are *New Life in a New Town,* 1969, and *Personality Patterns of Socialism,* 1975. She has published more than two dozen articles and papers in the areas of higher education, rural and urban sociology, personality patterns, social change, family and sex roles, ethnic relations and socialist models.

G. A. Slesarev is a member of the Institute for Sociological Research at the Academy of Sciences, Moscow, U.S.S.R. He has co-authored a book (with Z. A. Yankova), the English title of which is *Woman in the Industrial Enterprise and the Family: A Soviet-Polish Comparative Study.*

Anna F. Steyn is Professor and Head of the Department of Sociology, Rand Afrikaans University, Johannesburg, South Africa. Dr. Steyn is author of the book *Die Bantoe in die stad: Die Bantoegesin* (The Bantu in the City), 1966, and several other articles dealing with the changing position of Bantu women. Her article, "The Bantu family in South Africa," *Journal of Marriage and the Family,* Vol. 30, No. 3, 1968, is considered a classic in the field.

Gladys L. Symons is Associate Professor of Sociology at the University of Calgary, Calgary, Alberta, Canada. She has studied in Canada and in France. Dr. Symons teaches courses in the areas of gender relations, social stratification, Canadian society and French-Canadian society. Her research interests include the comparative study of women in the professions, family relations among students and the status of women in Canadian universities. She has contributed chapters to several anthologies and published, among other articles, "A report on the reports: the status of women in Canadian universities," *Canadian Sociology and Anthropology Association Bulletin,* October, 1974, and more recently, "Attitudes and ideology: correlates of liberal attitudes towards the role of women," *Journal of Comparative Family Studies,* Vol. IC, No. 2, 1978.

Aida K. Tomeh studied at the American University of Beirut, Lebanon and at the University of Michigan, Ann Arbor, Michigan, USA. Dr. Tomeh is Professor of Sociology at Bowling Green State University, Bowling Green, Ohio, USA. Her teaching areas include social psychology, social organization, urban sociology and gender relations. Dr. Tomeh is author of the book *The Family and Sex Roles,* 1975, and of numerous articles that have appeared in the *Journal of Marriage and the Family, Journal of Comparative Family Studies, International Journal of the Sociology of the Family,* and the *Journal of Social Psychology*. One of her recent articles is entitled "Birth order and alienation among college women in Lebanon" and appeared in the *Journal of Comparative Family Studies*, Special Issue: Women in the Family and Employment: A Cross-cultural View, Vol. IX, No. 1, 1978.

Jan Trost is Associate Professor of Sociology, Uppsala University, Uppsala, Sweden, He has both studied and taught in Sweden and the United States. His main research interests include the study of family relations, cohabitation, mate selection and divorce patterns. Dr. Trost is author of *To Cohabit and Marry, The Family in Society* and *Diffusion of Innovation to and among Physicians*. He has contributed several chapters to books and written numerous articles and papers for social science journal in Sweden and North America such as the *Journal of Marriage and the Family, Family Process*, and the *Journal of Sociology of the Family*. Most recently, Dr. Trost has published "Attitudes towards and occurrence of cohabitation without marriage," *Journal of Marriage and the Family*, Vol. 40, No. 2, 1978. He is past president of the Swedish Sociological Society and vice-president of the International Sociological Association. For many years Dr. Trost served as an Associate Editor of the International Department of the *Journal of Marriage and the Family*.

J. M. Uys is a senior student in the Department of Sociology, Rand Afrikaans University, Johannesburg, South Africa.

Alena K. Wagnerová did her doctoral studies in biology at the University of Masaryk, Brünn (Brno), Moravia, Czechoslovakia. After receiving her doctorate she was for several years a free-lance writer in Prague reporting on current social issues for newspapers, magazines and the radio. Dr. Wagnerová is author of the book *Die Frau im Sozialismus – Beispiel CSSR* (The Woman in Socialism: The Case of Czechoslovakia), 1974. She lives now in Saarbrücken, West Germany.

Z. A. Yankova is a member of the Institute for Sociological Research at the Academy of Sciences, Moscow, U.S.S.R. She has coauthored (with G. A. Slesarev) the book, entitled (in English) *Woman in the Industrial Enterprise and the Family: A Soviet-Polish Comparative Study*.

INDEX OF NAMES

Abbott, Edith, 3, 34
Acker, Joan, 8, 34
Acker, Sandra, 414
Adam, June, 397, 414, 416
Adamski, Franciszek, 278, 293
Allardt, Erik, 251, 257, 260
Allingham, John D., 53, 73, 419, 428
Amann, A., 178
Ambert, A. A., 43, 73, 397, 414
Andrews, Frank, 104, 114
Anonymous, 368
Aoi, B., 215, 220
Arber, Sara, 103, 107, 108, 109, 117
Armstrong, Hugh, 43, 58, 61, 68, 69, 73, 427, 428
Armstrong, Pat, 43, 58, 67, 68, 69, 73, 427, 428
Aronoff, Joel, 6, 34, 98, 114
Ashton, M., 368
Astin, Helen S., 414
Axelson, L., 96, 114
Azumi, Koya, 103, 106, 108, 115

Bailyn, Lotte, 401, 414
Bainton, Roland H., 433, 442
Balbo, Laura, 186, 189
Bales, R. F., 6, 17, 38, 54, 76, 133, 134, 414
Bandt, M. L. den, 128, 134
Banfield, C. Edward, 189
Bánhegyi, F., 310
Bártová, E., 304, 310
Bartunek, Ewald, 177
Bauerová, J., 301, 302, 310
Baumert, G., 25, 34
Baxandall, R. F., 336, 342
Bayer, Alan E., 101, 102, 103, 107, 108, 109, 112, 114

Beauvoir, Simone de, 34
Bebbington, A. C., 95, 96, 115
Beck, Joan, 439, 440, 442
Bell, N., 24, 39
Benston, M., 399, 414
Berger, P., 61, 73
Bergmann, Barbara R., 97, 115
Bernard, Jessie, 23, 35, 73, 107, 115, 139, 146, 337, 342, 409, 414
Bevolkingcensus (R. S. A.), 363, 364, 368
Black, N., 396, 414
Blake, Judith, 43, 73
Blood, R. O., 67, 73, 156, 167, 176, 216, 220, 399, 408, 414
Bodzenta, E., 177
Booth, Alan, 83, 115
Booth, Charles, 434, 435, 442
Boigeol, Anne, 143, 146
Boserup, Ester, 82, 115, 332, 336, 342
Boulding, Elise, 392, 394
Bowen, N., 397, 414
Boyd, Monica, 43, 51, 59, 64, 67, 73, 431, 442
Bradburn, N. M., 96, 118
Brandel, M., 368
Brandel-Syrier, M., 352, 360, 365, 368
Brandis, Walter, 168, 176
Brinkerhoff, M. B., 24, 35, 54, 59, 67, 73, 74, 399, 414
Brogan, Donna, 103, 107, 115
Bron, J. A. H., 130, 134
Bronfenbrenner, U., 338, 342
Bronzaft, Arline L., 102, 115
Bronzaft, Gilda F., 102, 115
Bronverman, Inge, 101, 115
Brown, B. W., 67, 74
Bruce, Christopher J., 51, 74
Brun-Gulbrandsen, Sverre, 226, 227, 242

Bruntz, F., 71, 74
Bumpass, Larry, 99, 103, 115
Bundesministerium für Soziale Verwaltung, 157
Burke, Ronald J., 60, 72, 74, 95, 96, 115
Burić, O., xiv, 17, 19, 21, 24, 35, 311
Burnstein, M., 62, 63, 74
Buro vir Statistiek, 363, 364, 368
Butler, P. M., 74

Calderwood, Ann, 102, 118
Calot, Gérard, 137, 146
Canada, Department of Labour, Women's Bureau, 44, 57, 74
Canadian Review of Sociology and Anthropology, 419, 428
Carlsson, Sten, 248, 260
Caroll, Eleanor E., 170, 177
Cavalli, A., xiv, 15, 16, 179
Cazora-Russo, Gaetana, 188, 189
Čech, V., 301, 302
Centers, R., 67, 74
Central Bureau of Statistics, 123, 126, 134
Chisholm, Lynne, 60, 74, 441, 442
Citizens Advisory Council on the Status of Women, 91, 115
Collins, Randal, 8, 31, 35
Commission of the European Communities, 144, 146
Connelly, P. M., 58, 74
Cook, Alice, 60, 74, 85, 87, 115
Cook, Gail, 43, 51, 419, 420, 428
Cook, R., 74
Coser, Lewis, A., 31, 35
Coser, Rose Laub, 88, 115
Crano, William D., 6, 34, 98, 114,
Croll, E., 338, 347
Cromwell, R., 24, 35
Cumming, Elaine, 60, 74, 441, 442
Curtin, K., 338, 342
Czajka, John L., 103, 107, 108, 109, 117

Danziger, Kurt, 422, 428
Daheim, Hansjürgen, 35
Dahl, Gunvor, 226, 227, 242
Dahlström, Edmund, 35, 37, 124, 134, 337, 342
Dahrendorf, Ralph, 31, 35
Danneberg, Erika, 163, 176
Darelius, Ann P., 190, 205
David, S. J., 77
Davids, Leo, 399, 414
Davis, J. A., 414
Day, Lincoln, 83, 115
DeJong, J. R., 89, 115

Decision-Marketing Research Ltd., 58, 74
Deggeler, L., 134
Department of Bantu Education, 359, 360, 362, 368
Denis, A., 418, xiv
DeVille, Jean-Claude, 137, 146
DeVries, H., 123, 127, 134
Dijkers, M., 190, xiv
Dixon, Marlene, 8, 35
Dobrowolski, Kazimierz, 291, 293
Dodge, Norton T., 35, 266, 275
Dominion Bureau of Statistics, 50
Dore, R. P., 207, 220
Duberman, Lucile, 103, 106, 108, 115
Dulury, George, 86, 115
Duncan, Otis D., 384, 394
Duncan, R. Paul, 99, 115
Durand, J. J. F., 368
Durkheim, Emile, 11, 35
Dziecielska-Machnikowska, Stefania, 293
Dziesieciolecie Polski Odrodzonej — Ksiega Pamiatkowa, 279, 282, 293

Ehrlich, C., 93, 115
Eichler Margrit, xiv, 43, 51, 74, 75, 397, 399, 409, 412, 414, 430, 431, 441, 442
Elkin, F., 399, 414
Engels, Friedrich, 4, 35, 37, 267
Epstein, Cynthia Fuchs, 35, 89, 90, 102, 115 116, 398, 414
Ericksen, E. P., 33, 35
Ericksen, J. A., 33, 35
Eriksson, Margareta, 242

Fapohunda, E. R., 340, 342
Fapohunda, O. J., 340, 342
Farley, J., 414
Farrell, Warren, 101, 116
Featherman, David L., **43**, **53**, 69, 77, 89, 116.

Feld, Sheila, 95, 96, 116
Feldman, H., 92, 96, 116
Feldman, M., 92, 96, 116
Feldman, S. D., 403, 414
Felson, Marcus, 83, 116
Ferber, Marianne A., 393, 394
Ferriss, Abbott L., 83, 116
Firestone, Shulamith, 9, 36
Firnberg, Hertha, 154, 155, 156, 176
Fischer, Marina, 171, 177
Fišervoá, V., 298, 310
Fogarty, Michael P., 36, 75
Fong, M. S., 88, 116
Frideres, J., 61, 62, 75
Frieze, Irene Manson, 190, 205

Freese, Hans-Ludwig, 171, 176
Friedan, B., 337, 342
Fau, G., 184
Fujii, et al., 211, 217, 220
Fukalová, D., 297, 310
Furnschuss, Grete, 148, 177

Garland, Neal, 96, 118
Garland, T. N., 401, 407, 414
Gaudart, Dorothea, 148, 150, 158, 172, 176
Gavron, Hanna, 336, 342, 431, 442
Gendell, Murray, 399, 414
Gianapoulous, A., 96, 116
Gibbins, R., 59, 75, 410, 414
Gilda, F., 102, 115
Gillespie, Dair, L., 94, 116
Glazer-Malbin, Nona, 431, 442
Glick, Paul, 136, 137, 140, 141, 146
Golod, S. I., 271, 272, 275
Goode, William J., 6, 36, 208, 210, 214, 215, 220, 392, 394
Gornick, V., 342
Gorska, Maria, 282, 293
Gouldner, Alvin W., 31, 36
Gover, D. O., 96, 116
Grafinger, Josef, 174, 176, 178
Graniewska, D., 291, 293
Grinseth, Erik, 36
Gross, Edward, 84, 116
Grygier, T., 422, 428
Gstettner, Peter, 177
Gunderson, M., 43, 61, 65, 66, 68, 69, 75
Guppy, Neil, 442
Gutkind, P. G. W., 368

Haavio-Mannila, Elina, xiv, 14, 17, 24, 258, 260, 378, 393, 395
Habermas, Jürgen, 36
Hacker, Helen, 8, 36
Haller, Max, 148, 159 160, 161, 175, 176, 178
Handl, J., 178
Hartman, Heidi, 36
Hausa, Horst, 148, 171, 176
Hauser, Robert, M., 89, 116
Hargens, Lowell L., 83, 118
Heintz, Peter, 374, 388, 394
Heintz, Suzanne, 374, 394
Heizer-Winter, Martha, 177
Held, Thomas xiv, 373, 378, 384, 386, 391, 394
Hellman, F., 342, 354, 368, 369
Hellman, M., 352, 354, 368, 369
Henderson, Dorothy, 168, 176
Hess, Elaine, 83, 115
Hewer, V. H., 82, 116

Hill, Christopher, 4, 36
Hill, Reuben, 24, 36
Hiller, Harry H., 401, 402, 414
Hitchman, G. Symons, 397, 403, 410, 414
Hobart, C. W., 399, 414, 422, 428
Hodoly, A., 290, 293
Hoffman, Lois W., 37, 67, 75, 88, 96, 103, 116
Hofley, John, 51, 73, 441, 442
Holl, A., 178
Holleman, A., 346
Höllinger, Sigurd, 172, 177, 178
Holmstrom, Linda L., 96, 99, 100, 116, 407, 414
Holter, Harriet, 103, 116, 392, 394
Holzinger, W., 178
Hoogerwerf, A., 128
Horkheimer, Max, 36
Horna, J., 36
Huber, Joan, 7, 36
Hudis, Paula M., 82, 83, 88, 116
Humphreys, Elizabeth, 76, 293, 400, 428, 438
Husbands, S. A., 414

Information Canada, 409, 410, 414
Inkeles, Alex, 375, 394
Insee, 136, 137, 140, 141, 146
Institute of Population Problems, 210, 220
Instituut voor psychologisch Marktonderzoek, 128, 134
International Labour Office, 15, 244, 260
Intven, C. J. H., 128, 134
Ishwaran, K., 75, 422, 428

Jacobsen, R. Brooke, 83, 90, 117
Jahoda, Marie, 374, 387, 395
Jakubowicz, M., 282, 293
James, Estille, 97, 117
Janik, Wilhelm, 177
Jansen, Clifford, 422, 428
Jasinska, Aleksandra, 272, 282, 288, 293
Jaulerry, Eliane, 141, 146
Jean, M., 418, 428
Johnson, Shirley, 97, 117
Jonas, P. J., 348, 349, 354, 355, 357, 358, 369
Jong, J. R. de, 128,
Jörberg, Lennart, 248, 260
Judek, Stanislaw, 44, 75
Jukl, E., 301, 302, 310
Jungmann, B., 301, 310

Kaji, E., 214, 220
Kammeyer, Kenneth, 79, 117, 383, 395
Kandel, D., 36
Kanter, R., 17, 36
Karl, Elfriede, 148, 149, 151, 152, 157, 158, 159, 172, 177

Kaufmann, Albert, 177, 178
Kemper, Theodore, D., 86, 117
Kharchev, A. G., 271, 272, 275
Kirkaldy, Anne, 75
Kirkpatric, Jeanne J., 91, 117
Klein, Kurt, 177
Klein, V., 10, 37
Kloskowska, Antonina, 278, 290, 293
Knoke, David, 83, 116
Knollmayer, Eva, 178
Knudsen, Dean, 36, 84, 117
Knuchala, Krystyna, 280, 294
Köckeis-Stangl, Eva xiv, 15, 24, 148, 161, 162, 168, 171, 177
Köhler-Wagnerová, A., 296, 299, 300, 303, 310
Kohn, Melvin, 168, 170, 177
Kolmer, K., 338, 342
Kamarowsky, Mirra, 96, 117, 170, 177, 374, 395
Kon, Igor, 260
Kooy, G. A. 132, 134
Korchagin, V. P., 263, 275
Kotlyar, A. E., 263, 267, 269, 275
Koyama, T., 216, 217, 220
Krauss, Wilma R., 257, 260
Kreutz, Henrik, 148, 168, 170, 173, 177
Krishnan, P., 64, 75
Kroath, Franz, 178
Kubat, D., 75
Kunzel, P., 64, 75
Kunzel, Renate, 142, 146
Kuper, H., 369
Kurian, George, 36, 75
Kutner, Nancy, 103, 107, 115

Labour Canada, 51, 419, 420, 428
Lagutin, N. S., 266, 275
Lamousé, Annette, 36
Lansing, Marjorie, 91, 117
Larson, Lyle E., 75
Larsson-Cohn, Ulf, 236, 242
Lashuk, Maureen Wilson, 36, 75
Latowsky, Evelyn, 423, 428
Lazer, Charles, 60, 74, 441, 442
Lebra, J., 215, 220
Lehr, U., 310
Leijon, A. G., 342
Lekachman, Robert, 97, 117
Lerner, Daniel, 393, 395
Lesser, G., 36
Levy, René, xiv, 373, 378, 384, 385, 386, 388, 391, 394, 395
Lewin, J., 369
Lipman-Blumen, Jean, 106, 117

Little, K., 353, 369
Lobodzinska, Barbara, 291, 294
Long, Larry H., 99, 117
Longmore, L., 352, 354, 355, 356, 357, 358, 366, 369
Lopata, Helen, 36
Lopata, Z., 431, 442
Luckmann, T., 61, 73
Lupri, Eugen, xiv, 8, 9, 14, 16, 19, 21, 24, 25, 34, 35, 37, 39, 43, 59, 62, 67, 74, 75, 163, 167, 169, 177, 178, 221, 396, 399, 414, 415, 419, 430
Lüschen, G., 37, 75, 177, 178, 221
Mabilesta, D., 369

Mackie, Marlene, 60, 75
MacIntosh, Anita, 89, 118
MacLellan, M. E., 396, 414
MacPherson, Myra, 90, 117
Maly Rocznik Statystyczny, 279, 280, 294
Mandel, W. M., 338, 342
Marchak, Patricia M., 43, 75, 405, 414, 442
Markowska, Danuta, 291, 294
Marmor, Judd, 79, 117
Marsden, L. R., 65, 70, 76
Marsh, Robert, 12, 37
Martin, Patricia Yancey, 85, 94, 117
Martin, Thomas W., 83, 90, 117
Marwick, B. A., 348, 351, 369
Marx, Karl, 37, 267
Mason, Karen Oppenheim, et al., 103, 107, 108, 109, 117, 190, 205, 377, 383, 390, 392, 393, 395
Masuda, N., 215, 220, 221
Mayer, P., 355, 369
McClelland, David C., 393, 395
McDonald, L., 58, 68, 76
McGlendon, McKee J., 89, 117
McIlveen, N., 65, 76
Mechler, Hans-Jürgen, 160, 173, 174, 178
Meguro, Y., xiv, 16, 19, 207
Meier, Harold C. 103, 117
Meili, Richard, 379, 395
Meiss, Scott, 76, 399, 400, 428, 438,
Meissner, Martin, 37, 59, 60, 61, 76, 399, 400, 409, 412, 428, 438
Michal, Marie G., 140 146
Michel, Andrée, xiv, 14, 16, 24, 37, 142, 143, 146, 399, 414
Miller, Herman, 87, 88, 89, 119
Mills, Donald L., xiv, 8, 9, 14, 16, 19, 21, 22, 24, 25, 43, 419
Ministry of Education, 211, 218, 221
Ministry of Labor, 219, 221
Mitchell, B. R., 244, 260

INDEX OF NAMES

Mitchell, H. W., 96, 116
Mitchell, Judith, 85, 118
Mitchell, Juliet, 9, 37
Mitchinsin, Wendy, 74
Mittenecker, Erich, 160, 178
Moeno, S. N., 353, 354, 355, 369
Mogey, John, 260
Mokoatle, B. N., 356, 357, 369
Moore, Wilbert, 432, 442
Morgan, D. H. J., 6, 7, 37, 342
Morgan, James, 104
Morioka, K., xiv, 16, 19, 207, 209, 210, 214 217, 221
Mostow, E., 61, 76
Motuz, C., 53, 76
Motz, Annabelle Bender, 383, 395
Možný, I., 300, 307, 310
Murdock, A. P., 98, 118
Musil, J., 310
Myrdal, Ava, 235, 242, 337, 342
Myrdal, Gunnar, 10, 37, 235, 242, 337, 341, 342

Nash, J., 332, 342
National Institute of Occupations, 218, 221
Nederlands Interuniversitair Demografisch Instituut, 129, 132, 134
Neubeck, G., 82, 116
Newberry, P., 61, 76
Newson, Elizabeth, 168, 178
Newson, John, 168, 178
New York Times, January 13, 1976, 98
Nilsen, Aileen Pace, 93, 115
Nimkoff, Meyer, 375, 395
Nimwegen, N. van, 123, 134
Nojiri, Y., 216, 217, 221
Nordlund, Agnethe, 227, 228, 229, 230, 242
Nowry, Helen M., 393, 394
Nye, F. I., 62, 75, 76, 96, 103, 118

Oakley, Ann, 331, 342, 431, 443
Ogburn, William Fielding, 375, 392, 395
Okada, M., 211, 217, 221,
Olson, D., 24, 37
O'Neill, W. L., 37, 43, 73, 76
Oppenheimer, V. K., 18, 37, 57, 76
Oppong, C., xiv, 16, 24, 37, 331, 332, 333, 334, 335, 340, 341, 342, 343
Orden, S. R., 96, 119
OECD (Organization for Economic Co-operation and Development), 374, 395
Osmond, Marie Withers, 85, 94, 118
Ostry, Sylvia, 43, 53, 69, 76

Parelius, Ann P., 101, 112, 118

Parsons, Talcott, 6, 7, 17, 30, 31, 38, 54, 76, 133, 134, 414
Paszkiewicz, Joanna, 278, 294
Patai, Raphael, 243, 260
Patterson, M., 409, 414, 416,
Paulsen, Susan B.,
Pauw, B. A., 346, 353, 354, 355, 357, 369
Perrucci, Carolyn C., 99, 115, 410, 416
Perspective Canada, 416
Peters, J. F., 63, 76
Pfeil, Elisabeth, 150 ,162, 163, 178
Phatudi, C. N., 369
Philips, J., 369
Picard, F., 143, 146
Pike, Robert, 76
Pimenova, A. Z., 273, 275
Piotrowski, Jerzy, 260, 291, 294
Pitrou, Agnes, 143, 146
Platt, Wolfgang, 23, 38
Pleck, Joseph E., 9, 10, 16, 31, 33, 34, 38
Plossnig, Franz, 178
Poloma, M. M., 96, 118, 407, 416
Pöntinen, Seppo, 253, 260
Ponting, J. R., 59, 75, 410, 414
Pol, Ian D., 67, 76
Poulsen, Susan B., 79, 119
Powell, K. S., 96, 118
Preiss-Zajdowa, Anna, 282, 294, 294
Preston-Whyte, E., 366, 369
Price-Bonham, Sharon, 416
Prime Minister's Office, 215, 221
Prokopec, J., 302, 310
Pross, Helge, 23, 38, 395
Przedpelski, Mieczyslaw, 280, 294
Pyke, S. W., 418, 428

Queen's University, 396, 416

Radcliffe-Brown, A. R., 347, 369
Rajkiewicz, Antoni, 280, 282, 294
Rapoport, Rhona,10 38, 75, 95, 118, 337, 342, 407, 416
Rapoport, Robert N., 10, 38, 75, 95, 118, 337, 343, 407, 416
Raven, B. H., 67, 74
Rechnitzer, E., 53, 77
Reitz, Gertraud, 174, 178
Report of the Royal Commission on the Status of Women in Canada, 409, 410 416, 436, 443
Research Committee on Women, 215, 217, 221
Riandey, Benoit, 145, 147
Ritter, Kathleen V., 83, 118
Robb, L. A., 69, 70, 76

Rocher, Guy, 422, 429
Rocznik Statystyczny, 281, 282, 285, 292, 294
Rodman, Hyman, 24, 38, 163, 167, 178, 214, 216, 217, 221, 399, 416
Rodrigues, A., 67, 74
Rokoff, Gerald, 88, 115
Rosenmayr, Leopold, 148, 155, 159, 171, 178
Ross, Heather L., 89, 118
Rossi, Alice S., 102, 118, 409, 416
Rossi, Peter H., 83, 118
Roussel, Louis, 137, 138, 141, 147
Rowbotham, Beverly, 418, 429
Royal Commission on the Status of Women in Canada, 43, 76
Rutschka, Ludwig, S., 154, 155, 156, 176,

Sabran, Jacques, 143, 147
Safilios-Rothschild, C., xiv, 24, 38, 61, 67, 76, 77, 190,191, 192, 195, 196, 203, 205, 206, 255, 257, 260, 399, 403, 416
Saipt, O. W., 178
Salva, Z., 276, 294
Sangster, D, 53, 77
Santos, Fredricka Pickford, 89, 118,
Scanzoni, John, 80, 94, 98, 102, 103, 106, 107, 112, 118, 333, 343
Schapera, I., 347, 348, 351, 369
Scheu, William, 76, 379, 400, 428, 438
Schmid, Carol, 43, 77
Schmidt-Relenberg, N., 31, 38
Schoonenboom, I. J., xiv, 14, 120, 135
Schreiber, E. M., 59, 77
Schulz, Wolfgang, 148, 149, 150, 172, 176, 178
Schwind, Fritz, 150, 178
Scientific Council for Government Policy, 120, 132, 134
Scott, Joan W., 248, 260
Scott, John Paul, 86, 118
Seidl, Hadwig, 177
Seidl, Peter, 177
Sergeyeva, G. P., 266, 275
Sexton, Patricia, 93, 118
Shepher, J., 337, 343
Shiskhan, N. M., 268, 275
Siemieńska, Renata, xiv, 14, 19, 21, 22, 24, 276, 277, 282, 288, 290, 291, 293, 294
Siltanen, Janet, 442
Simmel, Georg, 31, 38
Simons, H. J., 351, 366, 367, 369
Sims, H., 65, 76
Skoulas, N., 43, 53, 69, 77
Slater, Philip, 439, 443
Slejska, D., 310
Slesarev, G. A., xiv, 14, 17, 20, 21, 26, 261, 265, 270, 275

Smelser, Neil, 5, 6, 38
Smith, Dorothy E., 8, 9, 31, 38, 39, 77, 399, 416
Scobczak, L., 282, 294
Social and Cultural Planning Bureau, 129, 130, 132, 135
Sokolowska, Magdalena, 286, 294
Sonquist, John, 104, 114
Spencer, Byron, 43, 53, 69, 70, 77, 419, 428
Sprey, J., 24, 39
Stack, C., 333, 343
Statistical Bulletin, SZS, 316, 317, 319, 320, 321, 323, 325
Statistická ročenka ČSSR 1948—1976, 299
Statistisches Jahrbuch der Republik Österreich, 151
Statistics Canada, 44, 47, 48, 49, 50, 52, 55, 56, 65, 66, 68, 70, 77, 397, 398, 416, 436
Statystyka Polska, 295
Stayt, H. A., 348, 369
Stearns, Peter N., 435, 443
Steiner, Henrich, 379, 395
Stephenson, Marylee, 43, 77, 420, 429
Steyn, Anna F., xiv, 16, 344, 350, 353, 354, 355, 356, 357, 361, 366, 367, 369, 370
Stock, Franz-Michael, 148, 178
Stolte-Heiskanen, Veronika, 258, 260, 378, 393, 395
Stolzenberg, Ross M., 82, 99, 119
Stouffer, S. A., 52, 53, 77
Strolz, M., 178
Strzeminska, Halina, 290, 295
Sudarkasa, N., 343
Sullerot, Evelyne, 390, 395
Sundström-Feigenberg, Kajsa, 236, 242
Suter, Larry E., 87, 88, 89, 119
Sweet, James A., 88, 119
Symons, G. L., xiv, 53, 59, 70, 75, 77, 396, 410, 414, 415
Szalai, A., 25, 26, 27, 39, 77, 333, 340
Szinovácz, Maximiliane, 148, 159, 160, 164 165, 166, 167, 168, 170, 178
Szymanski, A., 8, 34, 39

Tabard, Nicole, 143, 144, 147
Talmon, Y., 337, 343
Targ, D. B., 410, 416
Tau, J., 370
Terrill, K., 83, 85, 98, 119
Theodore, Anthena, 39
Thomas, Dorothy Swaine, 232, 242
Thomas, William I., 232, 242
Thompson, E. P., 5, 39
Thornton, D., 75
Tienhaara, N.,

INDEX OF NAMES

Tiger, Lionel, 86, 119, 337, 343
Tilly, Louise A., 248, 260
Tomeh, Aida K., xiv, 8, 16, 21, 24, 78, 87, 93, 119
Treas, Judith, 89, 19
Treiman, Donald J., 83, 85, 89, 119
Trost, Jan, xiv, 14, 24, 225, 227, 228, 229, 230, 231, 232, 236, 242
Tryfan, Barbara, 292, 295
Turchaninova, S. I., 263, 267, 275
Turk, J., 24, 39
Turowski, Jan, 290, 295
Tyree, Andrew, 89, 119

United Nations, 22, 244, 254, 255, 260, 312
Unesco, 251, 260, 313
U'ren, Marjorie B., 93, 119
U.S. Department of Commerce, 98, 119
U.S. Department of Labor, 83, 119
U.S. Department of Labor, Bureau of Labor Statistics 82, 119
U.S. Department of Labor, Women's Bureau, 88, 119
U.S. Bureau of the Census, 83, 89, 98, 103, 119
Uys, J. M., xiv, 16, 344

Vallot, Francoise, 141, 147
Vanek, Joan, 438, 443
Van Rensburg, H.G.M.J., 347, 348, 349, 350, 351, 352, 353, 355, 356, 357, 360, 363, 367, 370
Veenhoven, R., 132, 135
Veld, L., in't, xiv, 14
Veld-Langeveld, H.M., in't, xiv, 14, 120, 135
Vickers, Jill, 397, 416
Vilikazi, A., 370
Vincent, Clark E., 395
Visser, P., 128, 134
Vogel, E., 216, 221

Wagnerová, A., xiv, 14, 19, 24, 296
Waite, Linda J., 82, 99, 119

Wakil, E. A., 410, 416
Wakil, S. P., 410, 416
Waluk, J., 282, 295
Weir, Tamara, 60, 72, 74, 95, 96, 115
Weitzman, Lenore, 93, 119
Westoff, Charles, 99, 115
Whitley, Marily Peddicard, 79, 119
Wieruszewski, Roman, 280, 281, 282, 285, 295
Wieser, Ilsedore, 171, 178
Wilkening, E. A., 39
Willmott, P., 10, 39, 343, 399, 417
Wilska-Duszynska, Barbara, 278, 295
Winston, Fern, 7, 8, 39
Winston, Henry, 7, 8, 39
Wolfe, D. M., 67, 73, 156, 176, 216, 220, 399, 408, 414
Women's and Minors' Bureau, 212, 213, 218, 219, 221
Women's Organizations Federation, 214, 221
Wrochno, Krystyna, 280, 281, 295, 338, 343
Wynnyczuk, Vi. 303, 310
Wyniki doboru kandydatow na I rok studiow wyzszyck w latach 1969/1970 i 1970/1971, 284, 295

Yancey, Wl. L., 33, 35
Yankova, Z. A., xiv, 14, 17, 20, 21, 26, 261, 265, 269, 275
York University, 406, 410, 417
Young, M., 10, 39, 343, 399, 417
Yugoslav Statistical Yearbook, 316, 317, 318, 319, 320, 321, 323, 325

Zaidi, A. M., 76
Zaretsky, Eli, 3, 4, 39
Zay, H., 420, 429
Zecević, A., 35
Zelditch, Morris, 6, 39
Zenszczyny i dieti w SSSR, 283, 295
Žižková, J., 299, 310
Zsigmond, Z. E., 53, 77

INDEX OF SUBJECTS

Abortion, 180, 235—236, 239—240
Africa, South
  Bantu, 345–352
  black women, 344–368
  Customary Law, 366–367
  changing status of women, 352–368
  choice of marriage partner
    changes in, 354
    in tribal society, 348
  divorce
    changes in, 358
    in tribal society, 350
  education
    attitudes toward, 358–360
    by sex, 358–362
    changes in, 358–360
    in tribal society, 350
  husband-wife relationship
    changes in, 356–358
    in tribal society, 349–350
  labour force participation
    changes in, 356–358
    in tribal society, 349–350
  legal status of women
    changes in, 336–367
  lobola
    changes in, 354–355
    in tribal society, 348–350
    transfer of, 348, 354
  marriage goods, 348
  marriage and the family, 347–351, 353, 358
  premarital sexual relations
    changes in, 353–354
    in tribal society, 347–348
  Roman Dutch Common Law, 366
  status of women, 348, 352
  tribal society, 345–352
  voluntary associations, 365–366
  wedding
    changes in, 355–356
    in tribal society, 348–349
  widowhood, 348, 358
Africa, West, 332, 338, 341
Austria
  age at marriage, 151
    change in, 151, 152
  anticipatory socialization for marriage, 171–174
  attitudes toward
    marriage, 171–716
    mothers' working, 157, 158, 159, 169
  changing positions of women in family, 148–177
  educational attainment, women, and attitudes, 171, 172, 173
    by sex, 171, 172
    by education and marriage, 171, 172, 173
  family decision-making
    by wife's employment status, 163, 164
    by wife's occupational status, 165, 166
    by social class. 167, 168, 169
  mate selection criteria, 171, 172, 173–175
  women's work in,
    and changes, 153–157
    and commitment, 160, 161, 162
    and family decision-making, 163, 164–166
    by age, 157, 158
Bantu, 345–349, see also, Africa, South

Bora, Katherina von, household of, 433–434; see also, Luther, Martin
Canada
  age at marriage in, 48
  attitudes towards women's work, 58
  birth rate in, 49
  child care in, 409, 410, 412
  division of labour in,
    at home, 59, 60, 405–407
    at work, 61, 66, 67, 68
  divorce in, 48, 63–64
  education of, women, 69–70, 396–398
    and marriage, 398–399
  egalitarianism in, 67, 396–417
  equality, 58
  Family composition and labour force activity in, 46–47, 50
  family size in, 49
  fertility rate in, 49, 50
  household in, 436–438
    appliances of, 436
    technology of, 436–438
  life cycle "squeeze" in, 57, 58
  role overload, women, 59, 60, 61
  sex role
    concept of, 61, 418
    by ethnicity, 424
    of female students, 418–429
    perception of, 425, 426–428
    socialization in the family, 419
    socialization in school, 418
  underemployment in, 65, 66
  unemployment in, 65, 66
  women's work in, 43–76
    and income differences, 68–69
    and occupational segregation, 67, 68
    by age, 51, 52
    by education, 53, 54, 56
    by marital status, 50, 51, 52
    by occupation, 54, 55, 56, 57
    by presence of children, 50, 51
Capitalist countries, 43–223
Changing Role Perspective, 10–11, 34
Childcare
  professionalization of, 432, 438–442
Childrearing, 438–442
Code Napoleon, 297
Comparative Perspective, xiv, 11–29
Conflict theory, 7–9, 33–34
Confucian ethic, 208
Constitution, USSR, 261
Curvilinearity thesis, 257–258

Czechoslovakia
  Code Napoleon, 297
  Communist Party, women in, 305
  division of labour
    at home, 302–303, 307
    at work, 299–301
  education
    comparison of men and women, 299–300
  employment
    by marital status, 299
    of women by level of education, 299–300
    of female professionals, 301–302
  equality, 297
  female culture, 306–307
  familial authority, 298
  free time, 302–303
  household tasks, 302–303
    by level of education, 303
  Marxist theory, 296, 298
  political power of women, 303–309
  position of women, 296–307
    history of, 296–298
    in socialism, 296–297
    in the family, 302–304
    in the political system, 304–305
    in trade unions, 304–305
    in the world of production, 309–310
  social change in, 298
  separation, private and professional spheres of, 307–309
  sex roles
    and education, 299
  women
    and equality of, 297
    and private property, 297–298
    legal status of, 297
    mobility of, 297
    work activity of, 299–301
Denmark, 251–253
Division of labour
  at home, 3–7, 22–23
  at work, 3–7, 20–21, 25–29, 332, 376
Divorce, world trend in, 23–24
Economic dependence, women of, 4–5, 431–432
Education, women of, 18–20
Equality, sexual
  barriers, xi–xiv, 18–21, 312–314
Europe, countries of and women's roles in, 120–206

Factory system, 4, 29
family economy, 4–6
Federal Commission on the Status of Women (Switzerland), 377
Feminists, xi, 8–9
Finland
  agriculture, 244, 246, 247
  birth rate, 256
  employment
    by branches, 246–250
    by sectors, 246–250
    by marital status, 250, 251–253
    men, 244, 245
    women, 245, 246, 259
      by age, 248, 249–250
  GNP, 257
  industrialization, 244–250
    among men, 244–250
    among women, 244–250
  marriage rate, 254
    by age, 255
    by residence, 256
  political participation of women, 258–259
  sex roles, 257–258
France
  age at marriage, 136–139
    and education, 138
    and occupation, 137, 139
  authority, see power
  Commission of the European Community, 144
  Divorce, 140–142
    by education, 142
    by employment status of women, 141–142
  division of labour
    at home, 142, 144
    at work, 142, 143, 144
  feminism, 141, 142
  labour force participation of women, 140–142
  marriage rate in, 136, 137
  political role of women in, 144
  power, marital, 143, 144
  sexual equality, 143, 144
  women in, 136–137
    attitudes toward, 142–144
    and equality, 142–144
    and labour force participation, 140, 184, 185
    and occupational segregation, 139
    trend towards equality of women, 142–144

Gender roles
  comparative study of, 11–29
  explanation of, 6–11
Germany, Federal Republic of, 243, 297–298
Ghana
  child-rearing in, 333–334
  domestic roles, of women, 332–333
    and change in, 334–335
  division of labour, 332–334
    by sex, 333
  economic development, 331
  family functions, women of, 332–333
  family ideology, 336–337
  household tasks, 333–340
  husband-dominance, 332
  sex role
    equality, 341
    ideology, 338–341
    politics, 341
    segregation, 336
  women
    and economic development, 331
    and housework, 333–335
    family roles of, 332
    liberation of, 338
Great Britain, see United Kingdom
Great October Socialist Revolution, 261
Greece
  congruence, husband-wife sex role, 198–204
    and companionship, 202
    and decision-making, 203, 204
    and marital satisfaction, 198–201
  egalitarianism in, 197, 205
  equality in, 191, 205
  family dynamics, 198–204
  options, sexual, individual
    and age, 195
    and education, 195
    and migrant status, 196
    and place of birth, 196
    and sex, 196
    and wife's work status, 197
  sex role
    congruence, 198
    expectations, 197
    homogamy, 205–206
    stereotypes, 191
Holland, see The Netherlands
Home, separation from workplace of, 3–7, 331

INDEX OF SUBJECTS

Household
  Britain in, 434–436
  Canada in, 436–438
  Germany in, 433–434
Housewives, 430–442
  definition of, 431–432
  in industrialization, 432–438
Housework, 430–442
  definition of, 431–432
  different from childcare of, 438–442
  industrialization of, 432–442
Ideology, 3
  changes in, 440–442
India, 243
Industrial Revolution, 3–7, 185
Industrialization, 3–7, 29–30
  Japan of, 212–214
  housework of, 430–442
Israeli Kibbutzim, 338, 339–341
Italy
  abortion in, 180
  age at marriage in, 184
  attitudes toward women's work, 188
  labour force participation of women, 183–186
    by rural classes, 186
    by social classes, 186, 187
  legal status of women in, 180
  modernization, 180
    and educational opportunity, 180, 181
    and social change, 180, 181
    and status of women, 180, 181
  position of women in, 179–189
  population
    by education, 181, 182
    by region, 182
    by sex, 181, 182
  putting-out system, 185
  rights of women, 179, 180
  rural family, 180
  women
    attitudes toward, 188, 189
    role changes in, 179, 180
Japan
  attitudes toward women's work, 216–217
  Confucian ethic, 208
  demographic factors, 209, 211
  division of labour
    at home, 216, 217
    at work, 216–219
  Dozoku, 207

  education, women, 211, 217–218
  employment, see women's work
  equality, 207, 210–211
  household, 209–210
  kin group, 212–214, 217
  legal status of women, 210–211
  life cycle, women, 209–210
  male's work in, 211–214
  Meiji Civil Code, 208
  Research Committee on Women, 215
  Samurai, ruling class, 208
  Sex role
    conjugal ideology of, 214–215
    history of, 208–209
    ideology of, 212–214, 216
    socialization of, 215–216
    typing of, 212–213, 217–218
  Socialization, sex role, 215, 216
  status of women, traditional, 208–209
    and cultural factors, 214–216
    and demographic factors, 209–211
  women's work in, 211–214
    and income, 218, 219
    by age, 212–213
    by marital status, 213–214
    by sex, 212–213
    by type of job, 216–217, 218, 220
    difference in income between men and women, 218–219

Knowledge, sociology of, xii
Labour force participation
  married women of, 13, 14–18
  men of, 15–21
  young mothers of, 16–21
  world trend in, 14–21, 312–313
Luther, Martin, household of, 433–434
Marxist theory, 3, 7–9, 296
Meiji Civil Code (Japan), 208
Mexico, 331
Modernity theory, 191
Modernization
  and educational opportunity, 180–181, 375
  and social change, 180–181, 332, 373
  theory of, 180, 332, 375, 392–394
North America, women in, 43–119
Norway
  agriculture, 244, 246, 247
  birth rate, 256
  employment
    by branches, 246–250
    by sectors, 246–250

by marital status, 250, 251–253
  men, 244, 245
  women, 245, 246, 259
GNP, 257
industrialization, 244–250
  among men, 244–250
  among women, 244–250
marriage rate, 254
  by age, 255
  by place of residence, 256
sex roles, 257–258

Nuclear family, women in, 23–29
Occupational status, women of, 20–22, 31–32
Occupational segregation by sex, 20–22, 31–32
Pakistan, 243
Poland
  agriculture, 244, 245, 247
  birth rate, 256
  division of labour
    at home, 289–292
    at work, 279–282
  divorce rate, 292
  education of women, 283, 284
  employment
    by branches, 246–250, 280–282
    by sector, 246–250, 280–282
    by marital status, 250, 251–253, 282
    men, 245, 246, 259
    women, 245, 246, 259, 279–283
      by level of education, 282
      and occupational segregation, 279–282
      in higher positions, 284, 285
  equal rights of women, 276, 292–293
  family
    conflicts in, 278
    role of in society, 288–289
    women's status in, 277
  GNP, 257
  industrialization, 244–250, 277, 288
  governmental policy, 276, 277, 280
  mass media
    and economic policy, 278
    and family conflict, 278
    and image of women, 279
    and model of personality in, 278
    and propagation of sex roles, 277
  marriage rate, 254
    by age, 255
    by place of residence, 256
  sex roles, 257–258
    as perceived by society, 286–287
  Six Year Plan Industrialization, 277
  status of women, 276, 277
    as perceived by society, 286–287

structural factors
  in women's work role, 292, 293
women's
  income, 279, 280, 282
  income difference in, 282
  image of, 278, 293
  occupational role, 277
  political participation, 285
  status of, 277
Power
  familial, 24–25, 332
  social, of women, 326–328
Putting-out system, 3, 16, 185
Scandinavia, countries of and
  women in, 225–260
Socialist countries, women in, 225–239
Societal differentiation, 12
Social institutions, changes in, 315–316
Structural-functional theory, 6–7, 30–31, 33, 132, 133
Structural changes, 315–316, 440–442
Structural differentiation, 11–12, 386
Structured inequality, women of, 29–32
Sweden
  abortion in, 235–236
  agriculture, 244, 246, 247
  birth rate, 237–256
  child rearing, 227
  child socialization, 226–227
  custody of children, 232
  division of labour, 229
    at home, 229
    at work, 233–235
  divorce, 230, 241
    and custody of children, 232
    by age, 231–232
    by sex, 231–232
  employment, 233–235
    by branches, 246–250
    by marital status, 233, 250, 251–253
    by occupation and sex, 233
    by sex, 233
    of men, 244–245
    of women, 245–246
    of women by number of children, 234–235
    of women, part-time, 235
  family policy, 236–238
  fertility rate, 235, 239, 240
  gender roles
    and children, 226–227
    and legal policy, 236, 241
    attitudes toward, 232
    change in, 230, 232, 235, 241, 242, 257–258
  GNP, 257
  governmental policy, 236–238

INDEX OF SUBJECTS 461

and abortion, 237
and gender roles, 236–237
industrialization, 244–250
    among men, 244–250
    among women, 244–250
IUD, 236, 239
marriage rate, 254
    by age, 255
    by place of residence, 256
nurseries in, 237–238
sex roles, see gender roles
socialization
    among children, 226–227, 241–242
    and gender roles, 226–227, 241–242
spouses
    and employment, part-time, 229, 235
    division of labour, 229
sterilization, 236
Switzerland
    attitude change and sex roles, 392–394
    economic recession and women, 373–375, 376, 378, 392–394
    education, women, 387
    employment, see women's work
    modernization, theory of, 375, 392–394
    National Swiss Commission for UNESCO, 377, 378, 391
    OECD, 373
    sex role
        and age, 385, 388
        and education, 383, 385
        and religion, 385
        attitudes toward, 373–376, 378, 379, 381, 382, 383, 386, 391
        feminist attitudes, 377
        ideology of, 377
        public debate of, 377, 379
        rural context in, 381, 383, 388–389
        segregation, 382, 384–391
        stereotypes, 375
        traditionalism, 384
        urban context in, 381–382, 387–391
        structural change, theory of, 375, 392–394
    structural differentiation, 386, 390
unemployment of women, 373, 376
women's work, 376, 385, 386
The Netherlands
    birth rate in, 123
    feminism in, 120–124
    labour force participation
        by age, 127–128
        by sex, 127–128
    legal position in, 128, 129
    political participation of women in, 128
    position of women in, 120–135

    and education, 125, 126
    and employment, 126, 127
    and family life, 129
    sexual equality, 130–133
    structural-functional theory, 132, 133
    women in
        attitudes toward, 129–133
        and economic change, 130–133
        and inequality, 130–133
        and political involvement, 128–129
        trend towards equality, 129–133
Tribal society, 345–351; see also Africa, South
UN Declaration on Human Rights, 312
United Kingdom, 183–185, 312, 331–332
USA
    attitudes towards women's work, 84, 100, 101
    Civil Rights Act (1968), 88
    education in, women, 92–94
        and affirmative action, 92
        and upward mobility, 92
        and sex role reinforcement, 92, 93
    family in, 94–101
        changes, 95–96, 97
        division of labour, 97, 98
        economic activity, 97, 98, 99
    family size, in 98, 99
    feminism, 80, 81
    fertility rate in, 99, 100
    legal status of women in, 88
    marriage rate in, 136, 137
    National Organization for Women, 80
    National Women's Political Caucus, 91
    political participation in, women, 90–92
        and cultural definition, 90, 91
        and demographic composition, 91
        and political power, 91, 92
    position of women in, 78–114
    sex role
        and demographic variables, 106, 107, 108
        and family variables, 109, 110
        and role conflict, 86, 87
        and structural correlates, 101–111
        changes in, 78, 79
        egalitarianism, 102
    reinforcement in education, 93
    socialization, 79
        stereotypes, 101, 102
    social status in, women, 82, 83
    women's work in, 81–90
        and commitment, 88
        and female mobility, 89
        and life cycle, 83
        and income differences, 88

and occupational segregation, 84
  and self-actualization, 81, 82
  by marital status, 81, 82
  by presence of children, 82, 83
  by social status, 82, 83
USSR
  agriculture, 244–247 270
  birth rate, 256, 262
  Constitution, 262
  division of labour
    at home, 262, 272–275
    at work, 263, 256
  education
    men, 263–265
    women, 263–265
  employment
    by branches, 246–250, 264–265
    by sectors, 246–250, 264–267
    by marital status, 250–253
    of men, 244–245, 263–266
    of women, 245–246, 259, 263–266
      by type of service, 264–268
      in professions, 264–268
  equality, 261, 262
  family roles, contradiction in, 269–270, 272–275
  family, women in, 272–275
  GNP, 257
  Great October Socialist Revolution, 261
  head, family of, 273–275
  household tasks, of women, 273–274
  industrialization, 244–250
  marriage rate, 254–256
  Marxists–Leninists, 261
  political participation, women, 270–272
  position of women, 262
  sex roles, 257–258
  Supreme Soviets, 271
  women
    and social class, 263
    inequality of, 269
    in the family, 272–275
    in pre-revolutionary Russia, 262
    motivation to work, 265–266
Working class, 4–6
Workplace separation from home of, 3–7, 331
Yugoslavia
  employment of women, 311, 312, 316, 317
    by branches of activity, 316–318, 319
    by education, 319–320
    by level of qualification, 320
    by occupational position, 319–320
    by sex, 319–320
    in assembly systems, 324–326
    in deputy systems, 324–326
    in management, 321–322
    in self-management, 322–324
  liberation of women, 311–314
  position of women, 316–326
    in decision-making systems, 320–326
    in social structure, 316–320
  social power of women, 311–328